AËRIUS REDIVIVUS

OR THE

HISTORY

OF THE

PRESBYTERIANS

Aërius Redivivus:

OR THE

HISTORY

OF THE

Presbyterians.

CONTAINING

The *BEGINNINGS, PROGRESSE,* and *SUCCESSES* of that Active Sect.

Their *Oppositions* to Monarchical and Episcopal Government.

Their *Innovations* in the Church; and their *Imbroilments* of the Kingdoms and Estates of Christendom in the pursuit of their Designs.

From the Year 1536 *to the Year* 1647.

By *PETER HEYLYN,* D. D.
And Chaplain to CHARLES I. *and* CHARLES II.
Monarchs of Great Britain.

The Second Edition.

LONDON:
Printed by *Robert Battersby* for *Christopher Wilkinson* at the Black Boy over against S. *Dunstans* Church, and *Thomas Archer* under the Dial of S. *Dunstans* Church in Fleetstreet, and *John Crosley* in *Oxford.*
M. DC. LXXII.

S.B.N. - GB. 576.78525.3

Republished in 1969 by Gregg International Publishers Limited
Westmead, Farnborough, Hants., England

Printed in offset by Anton Hain KG, Meisenheim/Glan
Western Germany

To the Right Honorable,

The LORDS SPIRITUAL & TEMPORAL, and

COMMONS in Parliament assembled.

May it pleafe Your Honors,

YOU are here moft humbly implored for the Patronage of a Poft-humous *birth of my dear and honored Fathers Laborious mind, in the Caufe of this Kingdoms profeft and fettled Religion. You may fafely believe the Title-Page reports to You the true and genuine Author of the Book, but it's moft humbly intreated that You would not: For if You rather pleafe to read it, You will be affured of the Parent, by the Lineaments remarkable upon the Child; and therewith to receive, I hope, fuch fatisfaction as may juftly flow from the perufal of an* History *which in fome meafure confirms the* Excellency *of thofe Laws You have devifed, and Sacred Majefty confirm'd, for the Protection of that* Religion *and* Government *You profefs and ftand for. The Beauty, Juftice and Prudence of the Sanctions, will not a little appear in the ill ufage of that* Party, *whofe* Rude humor *and ungoverned* Zeal *is here reprefented. It would be an*

immodeft

immodeft boldnefs in me to prefs Your belief with my Affertions. of the happy performances herein. And they being for the moft part but faithful Collections of matter of Fact, tranfacted by the Anceftors of a Sect, to this day more then enough warm in the Bowels of thefe Kingdoms, are to ftand and fall in Your Grave and Judicious opinions, according to their correfpondency with the Annals of your own and other Countreys. If I had nothing to plead for the Publication *of this* Hiftory, *but the zeal of a Son to preferve his Fathers Off-spring from treading too clofe after him to the Grave, I doubt not it would eafily prevail with fo much* Noblenefs *as the* High and Honorable Court of Parliament *doth imply : But I am moreover apt to believe, that when* Your Wifdoms *pleafe to confider, that the* Party *hereby proved peccant, are ftill fo far from* Repentance, *that they dare to boaft their* Innocency, *and vie Loyalty and peaceable mindednefs at the fame rate (at leaft they did before our late* Troubles *and prefent* Diftempers *made their* Turbulencies *and* Seditions *notorious;) I may then reafonably, I hope, beg Your favorable acceptance of this* Dedication; *or at leaft depend upon that pardon from you, which the offended* Party *will be unwilling to allow to him, who though unworthy fo great an honor, craves leave to fubfcribe himfelf,*

(Right Honorable Lords and Gentlemen)

Your moft Devoted and Obedient Servant,

Henry Heylyn.

The Pre-

THE

PREFACE.

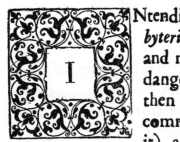Ntending a compleat History of the *Presbyterians*, in all the Principles, Practices, and moft remarkable Proceedings of that dangerous Sect; I am to take a higher aim then the time of *Calvin* (though he be commonly pretended for the Founder of it) and fetch their Pedigree from thofe whofe fteps they follow. For as our Saviour faid to fome of the Jews, that they *were of their Father the Devil, and the works of their Father they would do*: So by their works, that is to fay, by the Opinions which they hold, the Doctrines which they preach, and the Difturbances by them made in thefe parts of Chriftendom, we may beft find from what Original they derive themfelves. I know that fome out of pure zeal unto the Caufe would fain intitle them to a defcent from the Jewifh *Sanhedrim*, ordained by God himfelf in the time of *Mofes*: And that it might comply the better with their ends and purpofes, they have endeavoured to make that famous Confiftory of the

Seventy

Seventy Elders, not only a co-ordinate power with that of *Moses*, and after his decease with the Kings and Princes of that State in this Publick Government ; but a Power Paramount and Supreme, from which lay no appeal to any but to God himself : A power by which they were enabled not onely to control the actions of their Kings and Princes, but also to correct their persons. Which as I can by no means grant to be invested in the *Sanhedrim* by God himself, or otherwise usurped and practised by them in the times of that Monarchy ; though possibly they might predominate in those times and intervals in which there was no King in *Israel* (as such times there were) so neither can I yield unto the Presbyterians any such Prerogative, as to derive themselves and their pretensions, whether it be over Kings or Bishops, from the Jewish *Sanhedrim*. And yet I shall not grutch them an Antiquity as great as that which they desire, as great as that of *Moses* or the Jewish *Sanhedrim*, from which they would so willingly derive themselves.

For if we look upon them in their professed opposition, as well to all Monarchical as Episcopal Government, we cannot but give them an Extraction from that famous Triumvirate, *Korah, Dathan* and *Abiram*, combined in a Design against *Moses* and *Aaron*, against the Chief Priest and the Supreme Prince ; though otherwise of different Families, and having different Counsels amongst themselves. For *Dathan* and *Abiram* were descended from the Line of *Reuben*, the eldest Son of Father *Jacob* ; and therefore thought themselves more capable of the Soveraign Power then *Moses*, who descended from a younger house. And *Korah* thought himself as much neglected, in seeing *Elizaphan* the Son of *Uzziel* to have been made the Prince of the *Kohathites* (the principal Family of the *Levites* next to that of *Gerson*) when he himself descended of the elder Brother. Nor was he able to discern, but that if there were any such necessity of having one Priest above the rest in place and power, the Mitre might sit

as

as well upon his head as on that of *Aaron*, whose readiness in complying with the peoples humor in setting up the Golden-Calf, had rendred him uncapable of so great a trust. Having conferred their notes, and compared their grievances, they were resolved to right themselves, and to have neither any Chief Priest or Soveraign Prince to Lord it over them ; but to erect a parity both in Sacred and Civil matters, as most agreeable to the temper of a free born Nation. They had got little else by being set at liberty from the House of Bondage, if they should now become the Vassals of their Fathers Children. But first they were to form their Party; and they did it wisely, drawing no fewer then two hundred and fifty of the chief men of the Assembly to conspire with them in the Plot. And that they might allure the people to adhere unto them, they flatter them with an hope of an absolute Freedom, and such a power in Sacred matters, as should both authorize and justifie their approaches to the holy Altar, without the intervention of Priest or Prelate. Which being done, they boldly shew themselves against *Moses* and *Aaron* ; and told them plainly to their faces, that they took more upon them then belonged to either ; that all the Congregation was holy, every one of them, in regard that God appeared so visibly amongst them ; and therefore that they had done that which they could not justifie, in lifting themselves above the Congregation of the Lord. In which it is to be observed, that though some of the chief Princes of the House of *Dan*, and perhaps many also of the other Tribes did appear in the Action ; yet it is plainly called in Scripture, *The Gain-saying of Korah* ; either because the practice was of his Contrivement, or chiefly carried on by the power and credit which he and his Accomplices of the Tribe of *Levi* had gained amongst the common people, by reason of their Interests and Concernments in Sacred matters : so excellent are the opportunities which are afforded to unquiet and seditious men, when either by a seeming zeal to the Worship of God, or by some special place and interest in his Publick Service, they are become considerable in the eyes of the Vulgar.

These

These were the firſt ſeeds of thoſe dangerous Doctrines, and moſt unwarrantable practices, which afterwards brought forth ſuch ſad effects toward the latter end of the Jewiſh State, when the Phariſees began to draw unto themſelves the managing of all affairs, both Sacred and Civil. They were not ignorant of that high diſpleaſure which God had manifeſtly ſhewn againſt the principal Authors of that firſt Sedition, who under the pretence of regulating the Authority of his two Chief Miniſters, had put a baffle, as it were, upon God himſelf, whoſe Servants and Miniſters they were. The Phariſees therefore were content, that both the Chief-Prieſt and the Supreme Prince ſhould ſtill preſerve their rank and ſtation, as in former times; but ſo, that neither of them ſhould be able to act any thing of weight and moment, but as directed by their counſels, and influenced by their aſſiſtance. For the obtaining of which point, what arts they uſed, what practices they ſet on foot, and by what artifices they prevailed upon mens affections; as alſo into what calamities they plunged that Nation by the abuſe of their Authority, having once obtained it, ſhall be laid down at large in the following Hiſtory. All the particulars whereof, the Reader is deſired to obſerve diſtinctly, that he may ſee how punctually the Presbyterians of our times have played the Phariſees; as well in the getting of their power by leſſening the Authority both of Prince and Prelate, as in exaſperating the people to a dangerous War for the deſtruction of them both; the calling in of Forein Forces to abet their quarrel, the Fractions and Diviſions amongſt themſelves; and the moſt woful Deſolation which they have brought upon the happieſt and moſt flouriſhing Church which the Sun of Righteouſneſs ever ſhined on ſince the Primitive times. *Nec ovum ovo, nec lac lacti ſimilius.* *Jupiter* could not make himſelf more like *Amphitrio,* nor *Mercury* play the part of *Sociæ* with more reſemblance then the enſuing Story may be parallel'd in our late Combuſtions; Actor for Actor, Part for Part, and Line for Line; there being nothing altered (in a

man-

manner) in that fearful Tragedie, but the Stage or Theatre.

Change the Stage from *Palestine*, or the Realm of *Juda*, and we shall see the same Play acted over again in many parts and Provinces of the Christian Church. In which we find the Doctrines of the Pharisees revived by some; their Hypocrisie, or pretended purity, taken up by others; their Artifices to encrease their party in the gaining of Proselytes, embraced and followed by a third, till they grew formidable to those powers under which they lived; and finally, the same Confusions introduced in all parts of Christendom, in which their counsels have been followed   Which I shall generally reduce under these four heads; that is to say, The practices of the *Novatians* in the North; the *Arrians* in the East; the *Donatists* in *Affrick*, or the Southern parts; and the *Priscillianists* in the Western. The arts and subtilties of the Pharisees were at first suppos'd to be too Heterogeneous to be all found in any one Sect of Hereticks amongst the Christians, till they were all united in the Presbyterians; the Sects or Hereticks above mentioned, participating more or less of their dangerous counsels, as they conceived it necessary to advance their particular ends: In the pursuance of which ends, as the *Arrians* ventured upon many points which were not known to the *Novatians*, and the *Donatists* upon many more, which were never practised by the *Arrians*; so the *Priscillianists* did as much exceed the *Donatists* in the arts of mischief, as they themselves have been exceeded by the *Presbyterians* in all the lamentable consequents and effects thereof: which I desire the Reader to consider distinctly, that he may be his own *Plutarch*, in fitting them, and every one of them with a perfect parallel in reference to those men, whose History I shall draw down from the time of *Calvin* unto these our days, tracing it from *Geneva* into *France*, from *France* into the *Netherlands*, from the *Netherlands* to *Scotland*, and from thence to *England*: And in this search I shall adventure upon nothing but what is warranted by the Testimony of unquestioned Authors, from whose sence I shall never vary,

though

though I may find it sometimes neceffary not to ufe their words And by fo doing, I fhall keep my felf unto the rules of a right Hiftorian, in delivering nothing but the Truth ; without omitting any thing for fear, or fpeaking any thing in favour of the adverfe party, but as I fhall be juftified by good Authority.

THE

THE
CONTENTS.

Lib. I.

Containing

The first Institution of Presbytery in the Town of Geneva : the Arts and Practices by which it was imposed on the neck of that City, and pressed upon all the Churches of the Reformation ; together with the dangerous Principles and Positions of the chief Contrivers, in the pursuance of their project, from the year 1536 to the year 1585.

Lib. II.

Containing

Their manifold Seditions, Conspiracies, and Insurrections in the Realm of France ; their Libelling against the State, and the Wars there raised by their procurement, from the year 1559 to 1585.

Lib. III.

Containing

Their Positions and Proceedings in the Higher Germany ; their dangerous Doctrines and Seditions ; their Innovations in the Church, and alteration in the Civil Government of the Belgick Provinces, from the year 1559, to the year 1585.

Lib. IV.

Containing

Their Beginning, Progress and Positions ; their dangerous Practices, Insurrections, and Conspiracies in the Realm of Scotland, from the year 1544, to the year 1566.

Lib. V.

Containing

A further discovery of their dangerous Doctrines, their oppositions to Monarchical and Episcopal Government in the Realm of Scotland ; their secret Practices and Conspiracies to advance their Discipline ; together with their frequent Treasons and Rebellions in the pursuance of the same, from the year 1565 till the year 1585.

Lib. VI.

Containing

The beginning, progress, and proceedings of the Puritan Faction in the Realm of England, in reference to their Innovations both in Doctrines and Forms of Worship ; their Opposition to the Church, and the Rules thereof ; from the beginning of the Reign of King Edward VI. 1548, to the fifteenth year of Queen Elizabeth, Anno 1572.

THE CONTENTS.

Lib. VII.

Containing

A Relation of their secret and open Practices; the Schism and Faction by them raised for advancing the Genevian Discipline in the Church of England, from the year 1572 to the year 1584.

Lib. VIII.

Containing

The Seditious practices and positions of the said English Puritans ; their Libelling, Railing, and Reviling, in order to the setting up of the holy Discipline; from the year 1584 to the year 1589. The undutiful carriage of the French and the horrible insolencies of the Scottish Presbyters; from the year 1585 to the year 1592.

Lib. IX.

Containing

Their Disloyalties, Treasons, and Seditions in France, the Country of East-Friesland, and the Isles of Britain, but more particularly in England, together with the several Laws made against them, and the several exceptions in pursuance of them, from the year 1589 to the year 1595.

Lib. X.

Containing

A relation of their Plots and Practices in the Realm of England; their horrible Insolencies, Treasons, and Seditions in the Kingdom of Scotland, from the year 1595 to the year 1603.

Lib. XI.

Containing

Their successes either good or bad in England, Scotland, Ireland, and the Isles of Jersey, from the year 1602 to the year 1623; with somewhat touching their affairs, as well in France and Sweden, as the Belgick Provinces.

Lib. XII.

Containing

Their tumultuating in the Belgick Provinces ; their Practices and Insurrections in the Higher Germany ; the frustrating their design on the Churches of Brandenburg; the revolts of Transylvania, Hungary, Austria and Bohemia, and the Rebellions of the French; from the year 1610 to the year 1628.

Lib. XIII.

Containing

The Insurrection of the Presbyterian and Puritan Faction in the Realm of Scotland; the Rebellions raised by them in England ; their horrid Sacrileges, Murders, Spoils and Rapines in pursuit thereof; their Innovations both in Doctrine and Discipline, and the great Alteration made in the Civil Government, from the year 1536 to the year 1647, when they were stript of all Command by the Independents.

AERIUS

AERIUS REDIVIVUS:
OR THE
HISTORY
OF THE
Presbyterians.

LIB. I.

Containing

The first institution of Presbyterie in the Town of Geneva; the Arts and Practices by which it was imposed on the neck of that City, and pressed upon all the Churches of the Reformation; together with the dangerous Principles and Positions of the chief Contrivers in the pursuance of that project, from the Year 1536 to the Year 1585.

 **A**T such time as it pleased God to raise up *Martin Luther*, a Divine of *Saxonie*, to write against the errours and corruptions of the Church of *Rome*; *Ulderick Zuinglius*, a Canon of the Church of *Zurick*, endeavoured the like Reformation amongst the *Switzers*: but holding no intelligence with one another, they travelled divers ways in pursuance of it; which first produced some Animosities between themselves, not to be reconciled by a Personal Conference, which by the *Langtrave* of *Hassia* was procured between them; but afterwards occasioned far more obstinate ruptures between the followers of the Parties

1517.

B in

in their several stations. The *Zuinglian* Reformation was begun in defacing Images, decrying the established Fasts and appointed Festivals, abolishing set forms of worship, denying the old Catholick Doctrine of a Real Presence, and consequently all external reverence in the participation of the blessed Sacrament; which *Luther* seriously laboured to preserve in the same estate in which he found them at the present. They differed also in the Doctrine of Predestination, which *Luther* taught according to the current of the ancient Fathers, who lived and flourished before the writings of St. *Augustine*; so that the *Romanists* had not any thing to except against in that particular, when it was canvassed by the School-men in the Council of *Trent*. But *Zuinglius* taught, as was collected from his writings, " That God was the total cause of " all our Works, both good and evil; that the Adultery of *David*, the " cruelty of *Manlius*, and the treason of *Judas*, were the works of God, " as well as the vocation of *Saul*; that no man hath power to think " well or ill, but that all cometh of absolute necessity; that man doth " nothing towards his Predestination, or Reprobation, but all is in " the Will of God; that the Predestinate cannot be condemned, nor " the Reprobate saved; that the Elect and Predestinate are truely justi- " fied; that the justified are bound by Faith to believe they are in the " number of the Predestinated; that the justified cannot fall from " Grace, but is rather bound to believe, that if he chance to fall from " Grace, he shall receive it again; and finally, that those who are not " in the number of the Predestinate, shall never receive Grace, though " offered to them. Which difference being added unto that of the Sacrament, and eagerly pursued on both sides, occasioned such a mortal and implacable hatred between the parties, that the *Lutherans* have solemnly vowed rather to fall off roundly to the Church of *Rome*, then yeild to those *Predestinarian* and *Sacramentary pestilences*, as they commonly called them. But *Zuinglius* in the mean time carried it amongst the *Switzers*; five of those thirteen Cantons entertain his Doctrine, the like did also divers Towns and Seignories which lay nearest to them; of which *Geneva* in a short time became most considerable.

2. *Geneva* is a City of the *Alpian* Provinces belonging anciently to the *Allobroges*, and from thence called *Aurelia Allobrogum* by some Latine Writers; situated on the South-side of the Lake *Lemane*, opposite to the City of *Lozanne* in the Canton of *Berne*, from which it is distant six Dutch Miles: the River *Rhosno* (having passed through the Lake with so clear a colour, that it seemeth not at all to mingle with the waters of it) runneth the lower part thereof, over which there is a passage by two fair Bridges; one of them the more ancient, and the better Fortified, belonging heretofore to the old *Helvetians*, but broken down by *Julius Cæsar*, to hinder them from passing that way into *Gallia*. The compass of the whole City not above two Miles, the Buildings fair, and for the most part of Free-stone; the number of the Inhabitants about seventeen thousand, and the whole Territory not exceeding a Diameter of six Leagues where it is at the largest. Brought under the obedience of the *Romans* by the power of *Cæsar*, it continued a member of that Empire; till the *Burgundians*, in the time of *Honorius*, possessed themselves of all those *Gallick* Provinces which lay toward
the

the *Alpes*. In the Division of those Kingdoms by *Charles* the *Bald* it was made a part of *Burgundie*, called *Transjurana*, because it lay beyond the *Jour*; and was by him conferred on *Conrade* a *Saxon* Prince, son of Duke *Witibind* the Third, and younger Brother of *Robert* the the first Earl of *Anjou*. At the expiring of whose Line by which it had been held under several Titles of King, Earl, and Duke, it was by *Rodolph* the last Prince bestowed on the Emperour *Henry* sirnamed the *Black*, as his nearest Kinsman; and by that means united to the *German* Empire, governed by such Imperial Officers as were appointed by those Emperours to their several Provinces; till by the weakness or improvidence of the Lords in Chief those Officers made themselves Hereditary Princes in their several Territories.

3. In which division of the prey the City and Seignory of *Geneva*, which before was governed by Officiary and Titular Earls, accountable to the *German* Empire, was made a Soveraign Estate under its own Proprietary Earls, as the sole Lords of it. Betwixt these and the Bishops (Suffragans to the Archbishop of *Vienna* in *Daulphine*) grew many quarrels for the absolute command thereof. In time the Bishops did obtain of the Emperour *Frederick* the first, that they and their Successors should be the sole Princes of *Geneva*, free from all Taxes, and not accountable to any but the Emperours: which notwithstanding, the Earl continuing still to molest the Bishops, they were fain to call unto their aid the Earl of *Savoy*, who took upon him first as Protector onely, but afterwards as Lord in Chief. For when the Rights of the Earls of *Geneva*, by the Marriage of *Thomas* Earl of *Savoy* with *Beatrix* a Daughter of the Earls, fell into that House; then *Ame* or *Amade* the first of that name obtain'd of the Emperour, *Charles* the Fourth, to be *Vicar General* of the Empire in his own Countrey, and in that right Superiour to the Bishop in all Temporal matters: and *Ame* or *Amade* the first Duke got from Pope *Martin* (to the great prejudice of the Bishops) a Grant of all the Temporal Jurisdictions of it. After which time the Bishops were constrained to do homage to the Dukes of *Savoy*, and acknowledge them for their Soveraign Lords: the Authority of the Dukes being grown so great (notwithstanding that the people were immediately subject unto their Bishop onely) that the Money in *Geneva* was stamped with the Dukes Name and Figure; Capital Offenders were pardoned by him; no Sentence of Law executed, till his Officers first made acquainted; nor League contracted by the people of any validity without his Privity and Allowance; and finally, the Keys of the Town presented him as often as he should please to lodge there: as once for instance to *Charles* the Third, coming thither with *Beatrix* his Wife, Daughter of *Portugal*. But still the City was immediately subject to the Bishops only, who had as well the Civil as the Ecclesiastial Jurisdiction over it, as is confest by *Calvin* in a Letter unto Cardinal *Sadolet*, though as he (a) thought, extorted fraudulently, or by force, from the lawful Magistrate: which lash he added in defence of the *Genevians*, who had then newly wrested the Supream Authority out of the hands of the Bishop, and took it wholly upon themselves; it being no Felony (as he conceived) to rob the Thief, or to deprive him of a power, to which he could pretend no Title but an Usurpation.

(a) Habebat jus gladii & alias civilis jurisdictionis partes, sed magistratui ereptas.

4. In

1528. **4.** In this condition it continued till the year 1528, when thoſe of *Berne*, after a publick Diſputation held, had made an Alteration in Religion ; defacing Images , and innovating all things in the Church on the *Zuinglian* Principles. *Viretus* and *Farellus*, two men exceeding ſtudious of the Reformation , had gained ſome footing in *Geneva* about that time, and laboured with the Biſhop to admit of ſuch Alteretions as had been newly made in *Berne*. But when they ſaw no hopes of prevailing with him, they practiſed on the lower part of the people, with whom they had gotten moſt eſteem ; and travelled ſo effectually with them in it, that the Biſhop and his Clergie in a popular tumult are expelled the Town, never to be reſtored to their former Power. After which they proceeded to reform the Church, defacing Images, and following in all points the example of *Berne*, as by *Viretus* and *Farellus* they had been inſtructed ; whoſe doings in the ſame were afterwards countenanced and (*b*)approved by *Calvin*, as himſelf confeſſeth. Nor did they onely in that Tumult alter every thing which had diſpleaſed them in the Church, but changed the Government of the Town ; diſclaming all Allegeance either to their Biſhop or their Duke ; and ſtanding on their own liberty as a Free Eſtate, governed by a Common Council of 200 perſons, out of which four are choſen annually by the name of *Syndicks* , who ſit as Judges in the Court, the Mayors and Bayliffs (as it were) of the Corporation. And for this alſo they were moſt indebted to the active counſels of *Farellus* , whom *Calvin* therefore calls the Father of the publick liberty (*c*) ; and ſaith in an Epiſtle unto thoſe of *Zurick* , dated 26 *November* 1553, that the *Genevians* did owe themſelves (*d*) wholly to his care and counſels. And it appears by *Calvin* alſo , that the people could have been content to live under their Biſhop , if the Biſhop could have been content to reform Religion ; and more then ſo, that they had deſerved the greateſt Cenſures of the Church , if it had been otherwiſe. For thus he writes in his ſaid letter to Cardinal *Sadolet* ; *Talem nobis Hierarchiam ſi exhibeant, &c.* If (ſaith he) they could offer to us ſuch a Hierarchy, or Epiſcopal Government , wherein the Biſhops ſhall ſo rule, as that they refuſe not to ſubmit themſelves to Chriſt; that they alſo depend upon him as their onely Head, and can be content to refer themſelves to him ; in which they will ſo keep brotherly ſociety amongſt themſelves, as to be knit together by no other bond then that of Truth ; then ſurely, if there ſhall be any that will not ſubmit themſelves to that Hierarchy reverently , and with the greateſt obedience that may be , I muſt confeſs there is no kind of *Anathema* , or caſting to the Devil, which they are not worthy of. But in regard the Biſhop could not ſatisfie them in their expectations , they are reſolved to ſatisfie themſelves out of his Eſtate ; and either for his ſake , or their own, to caſt off all relation to the Duke of *Savoy*, as their Patron Paramount. And though both Lords did afterwards unite againſt them, and beſieged the Town ; yet by the help of thoſe of *Berne* (with whom they joyned themſelves in a ſtrict Confederacie) they repulſed them both. Since which time they have ſtrongly Fortified the Town on all ſides , but moſt eſpecially on that ſide which lies toward *Savoy* ; and would never ſince permit the Duke to arm any Boats or Galleys upon the Lake, for fear he might make uſe of them to their diſadvantage.

(b) *Quæ à Vireto & Farello facta ſunt, ſuffragio meo comprobavi.*

(c) *Libertatis ſuæ patrem, &c.*

(d) *Farellus, cui ſe totos debent, &c.*

5. The

5. The Power and Dominion of that City being thus put into the hands of the Common people, it could not be expected that any Discipline or good Order should be kept in the Church. The Common Council of the Town disposed of all things as they pleased; and if any Crime which anciently belonged to the Ecclesiastical Discipline did happen to be committed in it; it was punished by order from the Council. No Censures Ecclesiastical, no Sentence of Excommunication, was either thought on at *Geneva*, or at that time in any other of the Popular Churches, modelled according to the form devised by *Zuinglius*; as(e)*Beza* hath observed in the life of *Calvin.* The like affirmed by *Calvin* also in his Letter above mentioned to those of *Zurick*; who grants it to have been a received opinion, with some very grave and learned men,(f)that Excommunication was not necessary under Christian Magistrates. And so it stood till *Calvin*'s coming to the City, *Anno* 1536, who being born at *Noyon*, (*Noviodunum*) the chief Town of *Picardie*,was by his Father destined to the Civil Laws: but his own inclination carried him rather to the studie of Divinity, in the pursuit whereof he first began to phansie the Reformed Religion; and finding no assurance in the Realm of *France*, resolved to fix himself in *Strasburgh* or *Basil.* But taking *Geneva* in his way, upon the importunity of *Farellus*, he condescended to make that place the Scene of his actions and endeavours; and his assent being once made known, he was forthwith admitted to be one of their Preachers, and in the Moneth of *August* chosen their Divinity-Reader. This done, he presently negotiates with them not onely to abjure the Papacie, with all obedience to their Bishop for the time to come, but to admit some heads of Doctrine,and such a(g)form of Discipline as he and his Collegues had devised for them. And he prevailed in it at the last, though with no small difficulty; the said Discipline being generally sworn and subscribed unto, 20 *July* 1537. Which Form of Discipline what it was I have now here found; but sure I am, that it had no affinity with the practice of the Primitive Church; which (h)*Calvin* plainly doth acknowledge in his letter to *Sadolet*,who had objected it against him. But the people being proud and headstrong, and not willing to be stripped so easily of the precious Liberty which so happily they had acquired, became soon weary of the yoke, though they disguised it under colour of not giving offence to those of *Berne*, *Zurick*, and the rest of their Neighbours, whose friendship was most necessary for them in all time of trouble. But *Calvin* being peremptory not to administer the Communion unto any of those who could not quietly without contradiction submit themselves unto the Discipline which themselves had sworn to; and having *Farellus* and *Coraldus* two of his Associates in conjunction with him, together with his two Associates, is expelled the Town.

6. Three years, or thereabouts, he continued in his exile, being bountifully entertain'd at *Strasburgh*, where by his diligent Preaching; and laborious Writings he grew into a greater reputation then the rest of their Ministers; the Fame whereof being daily posted to *Geneva*, made them first sensible of the loss that they suffered in him, and afterwards procured them to sollicite the Chief Magistrates of the City of *Strasburgh* to license his return unto them: from whence at last with unresistable

(e) Si quidem Excommunicationi in aliena Ecclesia nullus locus.
(f) Quibus sub Principibus Christianis non videtur esse necessaria Excommunitatio.

(g) Quod Doctrinam & Disciplinam capitibus aliquot comprehensam admitterent. Bez. in vit. Calv.

1537.

h)Disciplinam qualem vetus habuit Ecclesia apud nos non esse (dicis) neq; nos disfitemur.

1538.

resistable importunity he was again recalled by that unconstant multitude : A desire to which by no means he would hearken , unless both they and all their Ministers would take a solemn Oath, to admit a compleat Form of Discipline, not arbitrary, nor changeable, but to remain in force for ever after. Upon assurance of their Conformity herein he returns unto them, like another *Tully* unto *Rome* ; and certainly we may say of him, as the Historian (*b*) doth of the other, that never man was banished with greater insolence, nor welcomed home again with an equal gladness. On the 13 day of *September* 1541, he is received into the Town , and on the 20 of *November* following he confirm'd his Discipline, which he had modelled in this manner : A standing Ecclesiastical Court to be established ; perpetual Judges in that Court to be the Ministers; others of the people annually chosen (twice so many in number) to be Judges together with them in the same Court: this Court to have care of all mens Manners , power of determining all kind of Ecclesiastical causes, and Authority to convent, to control, and to punish as far as with Excommunication, whensoever they should think to have deserved it, none either small or great excepted. To this device he brought the people to submit without any reluctancie : for what cause had they to suspect any yoke to bondage to be intended in that project, wherein they had a double Vote to each single Minister , and consequently a double number on their side upon all occasions. But when the first year was expired , and that the Elders of that year were to leave their places, they then perceived how much they had inthralled themselves by their own facility. And now they began to have some fear , that the filling up of the Seats in the Consistory with so great a number of Laymen was but to please the mindes of the people , to the end they might think themselves of some power therein ; that their Pastors being men of parts, and practised in affairs of that nature, would easily over-rule the rest , though the greater number ; that the Lay-elders being onely annual, and changed from one year to another, might first or last come under the severe lash of their Pastors, who were in a perpetual residencie, if they should dare at any time to act against them by their double Vote ; and that amongst the Ministers themselves, one being far in estimation above the rest, the rest of the voices are most likely to be given with reference to his will and pleasure ; which what else were it in effect , but to bring in Popery again by another name , in setting over them a Supreme Pastor, or perpetual Residence, with power to carry all before him ?

7. But nothing gave them more offence then the confidence of that vast and unlimited power , which was to be put into the hands of the *Presbytery* , in reference unto crimes and persons ; and the unhandsome manner of proceeding in it : for power was given unto them by the Rules of the Discipline, not onely to proceed to Excommunication, if the case required it, against Drunkards, Whore-masters, Blasphemers of Gods Holy Name , disturbers of the peace by Fighting, or contentious words ; but also against such as pleased themselves with modest Dancing, which was from henceforth looked on as a grievous crime : and what disturbances and disquiets did ensue upon it, we shall see anon. Nor were they onely Authorized to take notice of notorious crimes,

(b) Nec quisquam aut expulsus est invidiosius, nec receptus lætius. Paterc. Hist. lib. 2.

1541.

when

when they gave juſt ſcandal to the Church, or ſuch as paſt in that account by the voice of *Fame*; but alſo to inquire into the lives and converſations of all ſorts of perſons, even to the private ordering of their ſeveral Families. In reference to which laſt, they are required to make a diligent and ſtrict enquiry, whether men lived peaceably with their Wives, and kept their Families in good order; whether they uſe conſtantly ſome courſe of morning and evening Prayer in their ſeveral houſholds, ſit down at their Tables without ſaying Grace, or cauſe their Children or Servants diligently to frequent the Churches; with many others of that nature. And to the end they may come the better to the knowledge of all particulars, it is not onely permitted by the Rules of their Diſcipline to tamper with mens Neighbours, and corrupt their Servants; but to exact an Oath of the parties themſelves, who are thereby required to make anſwer unto all ſuch Articles as may or ſhall be tendered to them in behalf of the Conſiſtory: which odious and unneighbourly office is for the moſt part executed by thoſe of the Laity, or at the leaſt imputed wholly unto their pragmaticalneſs; though the Lay-elders poſſibly have done nothing in it, but by direction from their Paſtors. For ſo it was contrived on purpoſe by the wiſe Artificer, that the Miniſters might be thereby freed from that common hatred, which ſuch a dangerous and ſaucie inquiſition might elſe draw upon them. And yet theſe were not all the miſchiefs which their ſubmitting to that yoke had drawn upon them; by which they had enthralled themſelves to ſuch hard conditions, that if a man ſtood Excommunicate, or in contempt againſt the cenſures of the Church for the ſpace of a twelve Moneth, he was to ſuffer a whole years baniſhment by Decree of the Senate; not otherwiſe to be reſtored but upon ſubmiſſion, and that ſubmiſſion to be made upon their knees in the open Church.

8. Theſe melancholick thoughts had not long poſſeſſed them, when an occaſion was preſented to try their courage. *Perinus* Captain of the people, and of great power in that capacity amongſt the multitude, pretends the common liberty to be much endangered by that new ſubjection, and openly makes head againſt him in defence thereof. Ten years together did it ſtruggle with the oppoſition, and at laſt was almoſt ruined and oppreſſed by it. For whereas the Conſiſtory had given Sentence againſt one *Bertilier*, even in the higheſt cenſure of Excommunication; the Common-council not onely abſolved him from that cenſure under their Town-ſeal, but fooliſhly decreed that Excommunication and Abſolution did properly belong to them. Upon this he is reſolved again to quit the Town, and ſolemnly takes his leave of them at the end of one of his Sermons, which he had fitted for that purpoſe: but at the laſt the Controverſie is reduced to theſe three queſtions, *viz.* Firſt, after what manner by Gods Ordinance, according to the Scripture Excommunication was to be exerciſed. Secondly, whether it may not be exerciſed ſome other way then by ſuch a Conſiſtory. Thirdly, what the uſe of other Churches was in the like caſe. And being reduced to theſe three queſtions, it was ſubmitted to the judgement and determination of four of the *Helvetian* Churches; to whoſe Decree both parties were obliged to ſtand. But *Calvin* knew beforehand what he was to truſt to, having before prepared the Divines of *Zurick* to

pronounce

pronounce Sentence on his side; of whom he earneſtly deſired that they would ſeriouſly reſpect that cauſe, on which the whole State of the Religion of the City did ſo much depend; that God and all good men were now inevitably in danger to be trampled on, if thoſe four Churches did not declare for him and his Aſſociates, when the cauſe was to be brought before them; that in the giving of the Sentence, they ſhould paſs an abſolute approbation upon the Diſcipline of *Geneva*, as conſonant unto the Word of God, without any Cautions, Qualifications, Ifs or Ands: and finally, that they would exhort the *Genevian* Citizens from thenceforth not to innovate or change the ſame. Upon which pre-engagement they returned this Anſwer, directed to the Common-council of *Geneva*, by which their judgement was required; that is to ſay, That they had heard already of thoſe Conſiſtorial Laws, and did acknowledge them to be Godly Ordinances, *drawing towards* the Preſcript or Word of God; in which reſpect they did not think it good for the Church of *Geneva* to make any innovation in the ſame, but rather to keep them as they were. This caution being interpoſed, that Lay-elders ſhould be choſen from amongſt themſelves; that is to ſay, ten of them to be yearly out of the Council of two hundred; and the other two (for there were to be but twelve in all) to be elected out of the more powerful Council of the five and twenty.

9. Now for the quarrel which he had with Captain *Perine*, it was briefly this, as he himſelf relates the ſtory in his own Epiſtles. Dancing had been prohibited by his ſollicitation, when he firſt ſettled in that Town; and he reſolved to have his will obeyed in that, as in all things elſe. But on the contrary, this *Perine*, together with one *Corneus* (a man of like power amongſt the people) one of the *Syndicks*, or chief Magiſtrates in the Common-wealth; one of the Elders for the year, who was called *Henricus*, together with other of their Friends, being merry at an Invitation, fell to dancing: Notice hereof being given to *Calvin* by ſome falſe Brother, they were all called into the Conſiſtory, excepting *Corneus* and *Perinus*; and being interrogated thereupon, (a) They lyed (ſaid he) moſt impudently both to God and us, (*moſt Apoſtolically ſaid.*) At that (ſaid he) I grew offended, as the indignity of the thing deſerved; and they perſiſting in their contumacie, (b) I thought it fit to put them to their Oaths about it, (*by which it ſeems that the Oath* Ex Officio *may be uſed in* Geneva, *though cryed down in* England;) ſo ſaid ſo done. And they not onely did confeſs their former dancing, but alſo that upon that very day they had been dancing in the houſe of one *Balthaſal's* Widow. On which confeſſion he proceeded to the cenſure of all the parties, which certainly was ſharp enough for ſo ſmall a fault, (for a fault he was reſolved to make it) the *Syndick* being diſplaced, the Elder turned out of his Office, *Perine* and his Wife clapt up in Priſon, and all the reſt expoſed to ſome open ſhame. So he in his Epiſtle to his Friend *Farellus, Anno* 1546. Upon this ground *Perinus* always made himſelf of the oppoſite party, and thereupon ſollicited the relaxation given to *Bertilier*; but in the end was forced together with the reſt to ſubmit themſelves unto this yoke; and the final ſentence of the ſaid four Churches was impoſed upon them. And ſo we have the true begining of the *Genevian* Diſdipline, begotten in Rebellion, born in Sedition, and nurſed up by Faction.

     10. Thus

(a) *Impudenter Deo & nobis mentiti ſunt.*
(b) *Cenſui, ut jurejurando ad veri confeſſionem adigerentur. In* Epiſt. ad Farell.

10. Thus was the Discipline confirmed, and *Calvin* setled in the Jurisdiction which he had aspired to : But long he could not be content with so narrow a Diocess as the Town and Territory of *Geneva* ; and would have thought himself neglected, if all those Churches which embraced the *Zuinglian* Doctrines had not withall received the *Genevian* Discipline ; for the confirming whereof at home and the promoting it in all parts abroad, there was no passage in the Scripture, which either spake of Elders or Excommunication, but he applyed the same for justifying the Authority of his new *Presbytery*, in which the Lay-elders were considered as distinct from those which laboured in the Word and Sacraments, but joyned with them in the exercise of a Jurisdiction (even that of the Ordination also) which concerned the Church. Assuredly, we are as much in love with the children of our Brains as of our Bodies, and do as earnestly desire the preferment of them. *Calvin* had no sooner conceived and brought forth this Discipline, but he caused it first to be nourished and brought up at the charge of *Geneva* ; and when he found it strong enough to go abroad of it self he afterwards commended it to the entertainment of all other Churches, in which he had attained to any credit : proceeding finally so far, as to impose it upon the World as matter necessary, and not to be refused on pain of Gods high displeasure : by means whereof, what Jealousies, Heart-burning, Jars and Discords have been occasioned in the Protestant Reformed Churches, will be made manifest by the course of this present History : Which notwithstanding might easily have been prevented, if the Orders which he devised for the use of this City had not been first established in themselves, and then tendered unto others, as things everlastingly required by the Law of that Lord of Lords, against whose Statutes there was no exception to be taken. In which respect it could not chuse but come to pass, that his Followers might condemn all other Churches which received it not, of manifest disobedience to the Will of Christ : And being once engaged, could not find a way how to retire again with Honour. Whenas the self-same Orders having been established in a Form more wary and suspence, and to remain in force no longer then God should give the opportunity of some general Conference ; the *Genevians* either never had obtruded this Discipline on the rest of the Churches to their great disquiet, or left themselves a fair liberty of giving off, when they perceived what trouble they had thereby raised to themselves and others.

11. Now for the means by which this Discipline was made acceptable to the many Churches which had no dependance on *Geneva*, nor on *Calvin* neither ; they were chiefly these, that is to say, First, The great contentment which it gave the common People, to see themselves intrusted with the weightiest matters in Religion : and thereby an equality with, if not (by reason of their number, being two for one) superiority above their Ministers. Secondly, The great Reputation which *Calvin* had attained unto for his diligence in Writing and Preaching, whereby his Dictates came to be as authentick amongst some Divines, as ever the Popes *Ipse dixit* was in the Church of *Rome*. Thirdly, his endeavours to promote that Platform in all other Churches, which was first calculated for the Meridian of *Geneva* onely : of which we shall speak
more

more particularly in the course of this History. Fourthly, the like endeavours used by *Beza*, who not content to recommend it as convenient for the use of the Church (higher then which *Calvin* did not go) imposed it as a matter necessary upon all the Churches ; so necessary, that it was utterly as unlawful to recede from this, as from the most material Points of the Christian Faith : of which more hereafter. Fifthly, the self-ends and ambition of particular Ministers, affecting the Supremacy in their several Parishes ; that themselves might Lord it over Gods Inheritance, under pretence of setting Christ in his Throne. Upon which ground they did not only *prate* against the Bishops *with malicious words* (as *Dieotrephes* did against the Apostles) but were resolved to *cast them out of the Church, neither receiving them amongst themselves*, nor suffering those that would have done it if they might. Sixthly, the covetousness of some great persons, and Lay-Patrons ; of which the one intended to raise themselves great Fortunes by the spoil of the Bishopricks ; and the other to return those Titles to their own proper use, to which they onely were to nominate some deserving person. For compassing of which three last ends, their followers drove on so furiously, that rather then their Discipline should not be admitted, and the Episcopal Government destroyed in all the Churches, they are resolved to depose Kings, ruine Kingdoms, and subvert the Fundamental constitutions of all Civil States.

1537.

12. Thus have we seen the Discipline setled at the last, after many struglings ; but setled onely by the forestalled judgement and determination of four neighbouring Churches, which neither then did entertain it, nor could be ever since induced to receive the same. And we have took a general view of those Arts and Practices by which it hath been practised and imposed upon other Nations ; as also of those grounds and motives, on which it was so eagerly pursued by some and advanced by others. We must now therefore cast our eyes back on that Form of worship which was by him devised at first for the Church of *Geneva*, commended afterwards to all other Churches, which were not of the *Lutheran* Model ; and finally received, if not imposed upon most Churches which imbraced the Discipline. Which Form of Worship (what it was) may best be gathered from the summary or brief view thereof, which *Beza* tendereth to the use of the *French* and *Dutch* Churches, then established in the City of *London* ; and is this that followeth. The publick Meetings of the Church to be held constantly on the Lords (a) day, to be alike observed both in Towns and Villages ; but so, that in the greater Towns some other day be set apart, on which the Word is to be Preached unto the people at convenient times : Which last I take to be the grounds of those Week-day-Lectures, which afterwards were set up in most of the great Towns or Cities of the Realm of *England* ; a Prayer to usher in the Sermon, and another after it ; the frame of which two Prayers, both for Words and Matter, wholly left unto the building of the Preacher : but the whole action to be Sanctified by the Singing of Psalms. At all such Prayers the People to kneel reverently upon their knees. In the Administration of Baptism a Declaration to be made in a certain Form, not onely of the promises of the Grace of God, but also of the Mysteries of that

(a) *Congressus publici Ecclesiæ diebus Dominicis,* &c. *Bez. Epist.* 24.

Holy

Holy Sacrament; (*a*) Sureties or Witnesses to be required at the Baptizing of Infants. The Lords Supper to be Ministred on the Lords day at the Morning-Sermon; and that in sitting at the Table, (for no other gesture is allowed of;) the Men sit first, and the Women after or below them : which though it might pass well in the *Gallick* Churches, would hardly down without much chewing by the Wives of *England*. The publication of intended Marriages, (which we call *the bidding of the Bans*) to be made openly in the Church, and the said Marriages to be solemnized with Exhortation and Prayer. No Holy-days at all allowed of; nothing directed in relation unto Christian Burials, or the visiting of the Sick, or to the Thanksgiving of Women after child-birth; all which were pretermitted, as either superstitious or impertinent actions.

14. That naked Form of Worship which *Calvin* had devised for the Church of *Geneva*, not beautified with any of those outward Ornaments which make Religion estimable in the sight of the People; and by the which the mindes of men are raised to a contemplation of the glorious Majesty which they come together to adore : All ancient Forms and Ceremonies which had been recommended to the use of the Church, even from the times of the Apostles, rejected totally, as contracting some filth and rubbish in the times of Popery, without being called to answer for themselves, or defend their innocencie. And as for the habit of the Ministry, whether Sacred or Civil, as there was no course taken by the Rules of their Discipline, or by the Rubricks of the Book of their publick Offices; so did they by themselves and their Emissaries endeavour to discountenance and discredit all other Churches, in which distinct Vestures were retained. Whence came those manifold quarrels against Coaps and Surplices; as also against the Caps, Gowns, and Tippets of the lower Clergie, the Rochets and Chimeres of the Bishops, wherewith for more then twenty years they exercised the patience of the Church of *England*. But naked as it was, and utterly void of all outward Ornaments, this Form of Worship looked so lovely in the eyes of *Calvin*, that he endeavoured to obtrude it on all Churches else. Having first setled his new Discipline in the Town of *Geneva*, *Anno* 1541, and crusht *Perinus* and the rest in the Dancing business about five years after; he thought himself to be of such confidence, that no Church was to be reformed but by his advice. Upon which ground of self-opinion, he makes an offer of himself to Archbishop *Cranmer* (*b*), as soon as he had heard of the Reformation which was here intended; but *Cranmer* knew the man, and refused the offer. Which though in was enough to have kept him from venturing any further in the business and affairs of *England* : yet he resolved to be of counsel in all matters, whether called or not. And therefore having taken Order with *Martin Bucer*, on his first coming into *England*, to give him some account of the English Liturgie; he had no sooner satisfied himself in the sight thereof, but he makes presently his exceptions and demurs upon it; which afterwards became the sole ground of those many troubles, those horrible disorders and confusions, wherewith his Faction have involved the Church of *England* from that time to this.

15. For

(a) Testium se
concuratorum,
and pædo-ba-
piesmum ad-
vocat. Ib.

1547.

(b) Si quis
mei usus fo-
ret, &c.

15. For prefently on the account which he received of the English Liturgy, he writes back to *Bucer*, whom he requireth to be inftant with the Lord Protector, (b) that all fuch Rites as favoured of fuperftition might be taken away: and how far that might reach we may eafily guefs. Next he difpatched a long Letter to the Protector himfelf, in which he makes many exceptions againft the Liturgie; as namely againft *Commemoration of the dead*, which he acknowledgeth notwithftanding to be Ancient; alfo againft *Chrifme*, or Oyl in Baptifm, and the Apoftolical Rite of *Extream Unction*; though the laft be rather permitted then required by the Rules of that Book: which faid, he wifheth that all thefe Ceremonies fhould be abrogated (c); and that withall he fhould go forwards to reform the Church without fear or wit, without regard of peace at home, or correfpondencie abroad; fuch confiderations being onely to be hand Civil matters, but not in matters of the Church, (d) wherein not any thing is to be exacted, which is not warranted by the Word; and in the managing whereof (faith he) there is not any thing more diftafteful in the eyes of God then worldly Wifdom; (e) either in moderating, cutting off, or going backward, but meerly as we are directed by his will revealed. In the next place, he toucheth on the Book of *Homilies*, which very faintly he permits for a feafon onely, but not allows of; and thereby gave the hint to many others, who ever fince almoft have declaimed againft them. But finding nothing to be done by the Lord Protector, he tryes his Fortune with the King, and with the Lords of the Council, and is refolved to venture once again on Archbifhop *Cranmer*. In his Letter to the King he lets him know, that in the State of the Kingdom there were many things which required a prefent Reformation: in that to the moft Reverend *Cranmer*, that in the Service of this Church there was remaining a whole Mafs of Popery, (f) which feemed not onely to deface, but in a manner to deftroy Gods publick Worfhip: and finally, in thofe to the Lords of the Council, that they needed fome excitements to go forwards with the Work in hand, in reference to the Alteration (for that I take to be his aim) of the publick Liturgie.

16. But not content to tamper by his Letters with thofe Eminent Perfons; he had his Agents in the Court, the City, the Univerfities, the Countrey, and the Convocation; all of them practifing in their diftinct and proper Circuits, to bring the people to diflike that Form of Worfhip, which at the firft was looked on by them as an Heavenly Treafure, compofed by the efpecial aid of the Holy Ghoft. Their Actings of this kind for bringing down the Communion-Table, decrying the Reverent ufe of Kneeling at the Participation, inveighing againft the fign of the Crofs, abolifhing all diftinction of days and times into Fafts and Feftivals, with many others of that nature, I purpofely omit till I come to *England*. Let it fuffice, that by the eagernefs of their follicitations, more then for any thing which could be faulted in the Book it felf, it was brought under a review, and thereby altered to a further diftance then it had before from the Rituals of the Church of *Rome*. But though it had much lefs of *Rome* then before it had, (though nothing was meerly *Roman*, and not Primitive alfo) yet was it ftill as far off from the Rules of *Geneva*, as it was at that time; which

gave

(b) *Vt ritus illos, qui fuperftitionis aliquid redolent, tollentur è medio.*

(c) *Illa omnia abfcindi femel.*

(d) *In qua nihil non ad Dei verbum exegi fas eft.*
(e) *Vt vel moderemur, vel refcindamus,* &c.

1551.

(f) *Quæ non obfcurèt modo, fed propemodum obruat purum & genuinum Dei cultum.* Epift.

1554.

gave a new Alarm to *Calvin*, that he should take so much pains, and trouble so many of his Friends to so little purpose: And long it shall not be before he lets us know his resentment of it. The English *Protestants* being scattered in the Reign of Queen *Mary*, betake themselves to divers places in *Germany*, at *Geneva*, and amongst the *Switzers*. In *Germany* some of them procure a Church in the City of *Frankfort*; but they were such as had more mind to conform themselves to *Calvins* Models, then to the Liturgie of *England*: and such a deviation thereupon was made from the Rules of this Church, as looked little better then an open Schism. The business bad enough before, but made much worse when (*Knox* that great Incendiary of *Scotland*,) took that charge upon him; when at his coming he found many not well pleased with those alterations which had been made by others from the Church of *England*; which he resolved not to admit of, how much soever the continuance of it had been recommended by such Divines as had retired to *Strasburgh*, *Zurick*, and elsewhere. To over-ballance whose Authority, which he found much valued, he flees for succour unto *Calvin*, sends him a Summary or Abstract of the English Book (in the Latine Tongue) and earnestly desires his opinion of it; not doubting but all Opponents would submit to his final Sentence. What *Calvin's* judgement was in the present Point, and what sentence he was like to give in the case before him, *Knox* could not but have good assurance when he wrote that Letter, having lived with *Calvin* at *Geneva*, and published some Seditious Books from thence with his approbation, before his coming unto *Frankfort*: and it succeeded answerably to his expectation, as may appear by *Calvin's* answer to that Letter; which in regard it was the ground of all those troubles which afterwards were raised against the Liturgy by the Puritan Faction, I shall here subjoyn.

17. *It is no small affliction to me, and in it self no less inconvenience, that a contention should be raised between brethren professing the same Faith, and living as banished men or exiles for the same Religion; especially for such a Cause, which in this time of your dispersion, ought to have been the Bond of Peace to bind you the more firmly to one another: for what ought rather to be aimed at by you in this woful condition, then that being torn away from the bowels of your native Countrey, you should put your selves into a Church, which might receive you in her bosom, conjoyned together (like the Children of the same Parent) both in hearts and tongues? But at this time in my opinion it is very unseasonable, that troubles should be raised amongst you about Ceremonies and Forms of Prayer, (as happens commonly amongst those who live in wantonness and ease) by means whereof you have been hindered hitherto from growing into one body. I do not blame the constancy of those men, who being unwillingly drawn into it, do earnestly contend in an honest Cause; but rather the stubbornness of those, which hitherto hath hindered the Holy purpose of forming and establishing a Church amongst you. For as I use to shew my self both flexible and facile in things indifferent, as all Rites and Ceremonies are; yet I cannot always think it profitable to comply with the foolish waywardness of some few men, who are resolved to remit nothing of their Ancient Customs. (a) I cannot but observe many tolerable fooleries in the English Liturgy, such as you have described it to me. By which two words (those names of tolerable fooleries) I mean onely this, that there is not such Purity or Perfection, as*

(a) In Liturgia Anglicana, qualem mihi describitis, multas video tolerabiles ineptias.

was

was to be desired in it ; which imperfections, notwithstanding not being to be remedied at the first, were to be born with for a time, in regard that no manifest impiety was contained in them. It was therefore so far lawful to begin with such beggerly Rudiments, that the Learned, Grave and Godly Ministers of Christ might be thereby encouraged for proceeding farther in setting out somewhat which might prove more pure and perfect. (b) *If true Religion had flourished till this time in the Church of* England, *it had been necessary that many things in that Book should have been omitted, and others altered to the better. But now that all such Principles are out of force, and that you were to constitute a Church in another place, and that you were at liberty to compose such a Form of Worship which might be useful to the Church, and more conduce to Edification, then the other did, I know not what to think of those* (c) *who are so much delighted in the dregs of Popery. But commonly men love those things best, to which they have been most accustomed. Which though in the first place it may seem a vain and childish folly; yet in the next place it may be considered, that such a new Model is much different from an alteration. Howsoever, as I would not have you too stiff and peremptory, if the infirmity of some men suffer them not to come up unto your own desires ; so I must needs admonish others, not to be too much pleased with their wants and ignorances; nor to retard the course and progress of so good a work by their own perverseness ; nor finally, to be transported in the manner by such a foolish Emulation. For what other ground have they for this contention, but that they think it a disgrace to yeild unto better counsels? But possibly I may address my words in vain to those, who peradventure may not ascribe so much unto me, as to vouchsafe to hearken unto any advice which doth proceed from such a despicable Author. If any of them fear that any sinister report will be raised of them in* England, *as if they had forsaken that Religion for which they put themselves into a voluntary exile ; they are much deceived. For this ingenuous and sincere Profession will rather compel those Godly men which are left behind, seriously to consider what a deep* Abyss *they are fallen into; whose dangerous estate will more grievously wound them, when they shall see that you have travelled beyond the middle of that course, from which they have been so unhappily retracted, or brought back again. Farewel my most dear Brethren, the faithful Servants of* Jesus Christ ; *and be you still under the governance and protection of the Lord your God.*

(b) Si hactenus in Anglia viguisset sincera Religio, aliquid in melius correctum multaq; detracta esse oportet.
(c) Quæ sibi velint nescio quos tæcis Papisticæ tantopere delectant.

18. This Letter bearing date on the fifteenth of the Calends of *February*, and superscribed in general to the *English* which remained at *Frankfort*, carried so great a stroke with the *Knoxian* Party, that there was no more talk of the *English* Liturgie; the Order of *Geneva* being immediately entertained in the place thereof. And when the matter was so handled by Dr. *Cox*, first Tutor, and then Almoner to King *Edward* the Sixth, brought thither by the noise of so great a Schism, that the Liturgie of *England* was again restored ; *Knox* was so far from yeilding to the Gravity and Authority of that Learned man, that he inveighed against him in the Pulpit without fear or wit. But *Cox* not able to endure a baffle from so mean a fellow, informs against him to the Senate touching some passages in one of his Seditious Pamphlets ; in which it is affirmed, that Queen *Mary* (whom elsewhere he calls by the odious name of *Jezabel*, and a *Traytoress* to *England*) ought not to joyn her self in Marriage with the Emperours Son, because the Emperour himself *maintained Idolatry*, and *was a greater Enemy to Christ* then

ever

ever was *Nero*. *Knox* hereupon departs by Moon-light, but howsoever quits the Town, and retires to *Geneva*; leaving the Liturgie for the present in a better condition then he had found it at his first coming thither.   But *Cox* considering with himself how necessary *Calvins* favour might be to him, salutes him with a civil Letter, subscribed by himself and fourteen others; all of them being men of Note in their several places: In which they excused themselves for having set that Church in order without his advice; not without some rejoycing that they had brought the greatest part of those who withstood their doings to be of the same Opinion with them. Which how agreeable it was to *Calvin*, may be seen by his return to *Cox* and his Adherents, (*Coxo & Gregalibus suis*, as the Latine hath it) bearing date *June* 14. 1555.

19. In which Letter (having first craved pardon for not writing sooner) he lets them know that he had freely signified to Dr. *Sampson*, (a very fit man to be acquainted with his secrets) what he conceived of the Disputes which were raised at *Frankfort*; as also that he had been certified by some Friends of his who complained much of it, that they did stand so strictly on the English Ceremonies, as shewed them to be too much wedded to the Rites of their Country. And further certified, that he had heard somewhat of those Reasons which they stood on most, for not receding any thing from the Form established; but they were such as might receive an easie Answer: that he had writ to those of the opposite party, to carry themselves with moderation in the present business, though nothing was therein remitted by *Cox* and his, and howsoever was now glad to hear that the difference was at last composed. He speaks next touching their (*a*) retaining of *Crosses*, *Tapers*, and such other trifles of that nature, proceeding at the first from superstition; and thereupon infers, that they who so earnestly contended for them, when it was in their choice not to do it, did draw to neer upon the dregs.   He adds, that he could see no Reason why they should charge the Church with frivolous and impertinent Ceremonies, which he should no way wrong if he called them dangerous; when they were left at liberty to compose an Order for themselves, more pure and simple: that in his judgement it was done with little Piety, and less brotherly love; on any clancular informations to call *Knox* in question; (for so I understood him by his letter *N*.) and that they had done better to have stay'd at home, then to have kindled the coals by such a piece of unjust cruelty in a Forein Countrey, by which others also were inflamed: and finally, that he had written howsoever unto some of the adverse party, of whose intent to leave that place he had been advertised, that they should continue where they were, and not violate the League of their Friendship by their separations, with other things to that effect.   But notwithstanding this advice, many of the Schismatical party removed from *Frankfort*, and put themselves into *Geneva*; the principal of which were *Whittingham, Knox, Goodman*, and he which afterwards was able to do more then all the rest, Mr. *Francis Knollis*, allyed by Marriage to the *Caryes*, descended from a younger Sister of Queen *Anne Bullen*, and consequently neer of Kin to Queen *Elizabeth*. These men grew very great with *Calvin*, with whose good leave they
put

(a) *Certe luminaria, cruces, & ejus facinæ nugas ex superstitione manasse, nemo sani judicii negabit; unde Constituo, qui eas in liberâ optione retinent, nimis cupide & fæces haurire.*

put themselves into the form of a Congregation, chose *Knox* and *Good-man* for their Brethren, and in all points comformed themselves to the Rules of that Church; which afterwards they laboured to promore in in *England*, and actually did effect in *Scotland*, to the no small disturbance of either Kingdom. By the perswasion of these men, he is resolved to try his Fortune once again on the Church of *England*, before the resetling of the Liturgie under Queen *Elizabeth* might render the design impossible, or at least unprosperous. To which end he addresseth his desires to the Queen her self, at her first coming to the Crown. The like he doth to Mr. Secretary *Cecil*, by his letters bearing date the 17. of *January* 1558, in which he makes mention of the other; in both he spurs them on to a Reformation, complaining that they had not shewed such a forwardness in it, as all good men expected, and that cause required. But above all things he desires that a pure (a) and perfect Worship of God may be fully setled, that the Church may be throughly purged of its former filth, and that the children of God in *England* might be left at liberty to use such purity in all Acts of publick Worship as to them seemed best. And what else could he aim at by these expressions (comparing them with the Contents of his two last letters) but that the former Liturgie should be abolished, or brought unto a neerer conformity to the Rules of *Geneva*; or at the least, that liberty might be left to the Godly party, to use any other Form of Worship which they though more *pure*? But finding no such good return to either letter, as he had promised to himself, he leaves the cause to be pursued by such English Zealors, as he had trained up at *Geneva*, or otherwise had setled their abode amongst the *Switzers*, where all set Forms of Worship were as much decryed, as they were with him. And that they might not slacken in the midst of their course, he recommends the general Superintendents of the Church of *England* to the care of *Beza*, who after his decease succeeded both in his place and power; of whose pragmaticalness in pursuing this design against the Liturgie, condemning all established Orders of this Church, his interposing in behalf of such of his Followers as had been silenced, suspended, or deprived for their inconformity, we shall speak more large at when we came to *England*.

(a) *Vt vigeat purus & integer Dei cultus---Ecclesia à sordibus repurgetur, --- deinde ut filiis Dei apud vos liberum sit nomen ejus purè invecare*

20. There happened another quarrel in the Church of *England*, and he must needs make himself a party in it. Mr. *John Hooper* having well deserved by his pains in Preaching and Publishing some Books, which very much conduced to the peace of the Church, is nominated by the King to the See of *Glocester*. Willing enough he was to accept the charge; but he had lived so long at *Zurick*, in the Reign of King *Henry*, where there was no distinction of Apparel, either Sacred or Civil, that he refused to wear such Robes at his Consecration, as by the Rules of the Church were required of him. And by the Rules of the Church it was required, that for his ordinary Habit he should wear the *Rochet* and *Chimere*, with a square Cap upon his head, and not officiate at the Altar without his Coap, or perform any Ordination without his Crosier. Incouraged by his refusal, many of the inferiour Clergie take the like exceptions against Caps and Surplices, as also against Gowns and Tippets, the distinct Habits of their Order. Upon this ground

Archbishop

Archbishop *Cranmer* makes a stop of his Consecration, and would not be perswaded to dispute with him in that particular, though he much desired it. He had fastned some dependance upon *Dudley*, then Earl of *Warwick*, and afterwards created Duke of *Northumberland*; who did not onely write his own letters, but obtained the Kings, that without pressing him any further to conform himself to those Robes and Habits, the Bishop should proceed immediately to his Consecration. But *Cranmer* weighing the importance of that ill Example, held off his hand, till he had satisfied the King, and so cooled the Earl, that *Hooper* was left unto himself; and still continuing in his contumacy, was committed Prisoner. The news being brought to *Calvin*, he must needs play the Bishop in another mans Diocess, or rather the Archbishop in another mans Province. But having little hope of prevailing with *Cranmer*, who had before rejected his assistance in the Reformation, he totally applies himself to the Duke of *Sommerset*: And he writes to him to this purpose; That the Papists would grow every day more insolent then other, unless the differences about the Ceremonies were first composed. But then they were to be composed in such a manner, as rather might encourage the dissenters in their opposition, then end in the reduction of them to a due conformity. And to this end, he is unseasonably instant with him, to lend a helping hand to *Hooper*, as the head of that Faction. By which encouragement, if not also by his setting on, the like was done by *Peter Martyr*, and by *John Alasco*; the first of which was made Divinity-Reader in *Oxon*, and the other Preacher to the *Dutch* in *London*; both ingaged in stickling for the unconformable Party against the Vestments of the Church. But they both gained as little by it as *Calvin* did; who seeing how little he effected in the Church of *England*, more then the getting of the name of a *Polypragmon*, a medler in such matters as concerned him not, gave over the affairs thereof to the charge of *Beza*; who being younger then himself, and of less discretion, might live to see some good success of his Travels in it. And he accordingly bestirred himself in this very quarrel, as if the safety of the Church and the preservation of Religion had been brought in danger; writing his letters unto *Grindal*, when Bishop of *London*, not to insist so far on those matters of Ceremony, as to deprive any of his Ministery upon that account. He also signifies unto the Brethren his dislike of those Vestments, and thereby strengthned and confirmed them in their former obstinacy: And finally, left no stone unmoved, no kind of practice unattempted, by which this Church might be at last necessitated to a Reformation upon *Calvins* Principles, whose counsels he pursued to the very last.

21. But as for *Calvin*, he had some other game to fly at, and of greater nature, then to dispute the lawfulness of Caps and Surplices, and other Vestments of the Clergie; or to content himself with altering the old Forms of Government and publick Worship: The Doctrine was to be refined, and all Idolatry removed, whether it were Civil or Spiritual. In point of Doctrine he came neerest unto that of *Zuinglius*, as well in reference to the Sacrament, as Predestination; but pitched upon the last for the main concernment, which was to difference his own Followers from all other Christians. The straining of which string to so

great

great a height, hath made more difcord in the harmony of the Church of Chrift, then any other whatfoever. For not content to go the way of the Ancient Fathers, or to rely upon the judgment of St. *Auguftine*, *Fulgentius*, *Profper*, or any others which have moderated his exceffes in it, he muft needs add fo much unto thofe extravagancies which he found in *Zuinglius*, as brought him under a fufpition with fome fober men, for making God to be the Author of fin: For by his Doctrine God is made to lay on our Father *Adam* an abfolute and an unavoidable neceffity of falling into fin and mifery; that fo he might have opportunity to manifeft his Mercy in Electing fome few of his Pofterity, and his Juftice in the remedilefs rejecting of all the reft. In which as he could find no countenance from the Ancient Fathers, fo he pretendeth not to any ground for it in the Holy Scripture. For whereas fome objected in Gods behalf, *De certis verbis non extare*, that the Decree of *Adam:* Fall, and confequently the involving of his whole Pofterity in fin and mifery, was no where extant in the Word; he makes no other anfwer to it, then a *quafi vero*; As if (faith he) God had made and created Man the moft exact Piece of his Heavenly Workmanfhip, without determining of his End, either Heaven or Hell. And on this point he was fo refolutely bent, that nothing but an abfolute Decree for *Adams* Fall, feconded by the like for the involving of all his Race in the fame perdition, would either ferve his turn, or preferve his credit. If any man fhall dare to opine the contrary, as *Caftillo* did, he muft be fure to be difgraced and cenfured by him, as *Caftillo* was; and as all others fince have been, which prefumed to queftion that determination, for which himfelf can give us no better name than that of an *Horrible Decree*, as indeed it is; a cruel and *Horrible Decree*, to pre-ordain fo many Millions to deftruction, and confequently unto fin, that he might deftroy them.

22. I had not ftood fo long upon this particular, but in regard of thofe confufions and diftractions which by his Followers have been occafioned in the Church, by their adhering to this Doctrine, and labouring to obtrude it upon all mens confciences. The *Zuinglian* Gofpellers, as Bifhop *Hooper* rightly calls them, began to fcatter their Predeftinary Doctrines in the Reign of King *Edward*. But they effected little in it, till fuch of our Divines as had retired themfelves to *Bafil*, *Zurick*, and amongft the *Switzers*, or otherwife had been brought up at the Feet of *Calvin*, encouraged by his Authority, and countenanced by his name, commended them to all the people of this Realm, for found Catholick verities. The like diligence was alfo ufed by his Difciples in all places elfe. By means whereof it came to be generally received, as a truth undoubted, and one of the moft neceffary Doctrines of Mans Salvation, in all the Churches of his Platform: In which as his Doctrine in fome other points had firft prepared the way to bring in his Difcipline; fo fo was it no hard matter for the Difcipline to fupport thefe Doctrines, and crufh all them that durft oppofe them. Onely it was permitted unto *Beza* and his Difciples to be fomewhat milder then the reft, in placing the Decree of Predeftination before the Fall: which *Calvin* himfelf, though in fome paffages of his Writings he may feem to look the fame way alfo, hath placed more judicioufly in *Maffa corrupta*, in the corrupted

rupted mafs of mankind, and the more moderate *Calvinians* as rightly prefuppofe for a matter neceffary, before there could be any place for *Election* or *Reprobation* of *particular Perfons*. But being they concurred with the reft, as to the perfonal Election or Reprobation of particular men; the reftoring of the benefit of our Saviours fufferings to thofe few particulars, (whom onely they had honoured with the glorious Name of *Gods Elect*) the working on them by the irrefiftable power of Grace in the act of Converfion, and bringing them infallibly by the continual affiftance of the faid Grace unto life everlafting; there was hardly any notice taken of their Deviation; infomuch that they were fcarce beheld in the condition of erring brethren, though they differed from them in the main Foundation which they built upon; but generally paffed under the name of *Calvinifts*, as the other did. Which Doctrines, though I charge not wholly on the fcore of Presbytery, in regard that many of our Englifh Divines, who abhorred that Government, appeared in favour of the fame; yet I may truely father them on the two grand Patrons of the *Presbyterians*, by whom they have been fince expofed as their deareft Darling; and no lefs eagerly contended for, then the Holy Difcipline.

23. Another of *Calvins* great defigns was to cry down that Civil Idolatry, which he conceived had been committed unto Kings and Princes, in making them Supreme and uncontrollable in their feveral Countries. For pulling down of whofe Authority, even in Civil Matters, he attributes fuch power to fuch popular Officers as are by them appointed for the eafe of their Subjects, that by his Doctrine they may call the Supreme Magiftrate to a ftrict account, whenfoever they fhall chance to exceed thofe bounds which they had prefcribed unto themfelves; onely by which they may be circumfcribed by others: For having in the laft Chapter of his *Inftitutions*, firft publifhed in the year 1536, exceeding handfomely laid down the Doctrine of Obedience, and the unlawfulnefs of Refiftance in what cafe foever; he gives in the clofe fuch a qualification, as utterly overthrows his former Doctrine, and proved the fole ground of fuch Rebellions, Treafons and Affaffinates as have disfigured the otherwife undefiled beauty of the Church of Chrift. Which paffages I fhall here lay down in the Authors words, with a tranflation by their fide, that the Reader may perceive there is no wrong done him; and afterwards proceed to the difcovery of thofe fad effects which have enfued upon them in too many places, wherein his Difcipline hath either been received or contended for. His Doctrine in which point is this that followeth:

24. *Neque enim fi ultio Domini eft effranata, dominationis correctio ideo protinus demandatum nobis arbitremur, quibus nullum aliud quam parendi & patiendi datum eft mandatum. De privatis hominibus femper loquar. Nam fi qui nunc fint* Populares Magiftratus *ad moderandum*

24. Nor may we think: becaufe the punifhment of Licentious Princes belongs to God, that prefently this power is devolved on us, to whom no other warrant hath been given by God, but onely to *obey and fuffer*. But ftill I muft be underftood of private perfons For: Inftitut. *lib.*4. *c.*10 .8,31.

Regum libidinem conſtituti (quales olim erant qui Lacedemoniis Regibus *oppoſite erant* Ephori, *aut* Romanis Conſulibus Tribuni Plebis, *aut* Athenienſium *Senatui* Demarchi, *& qua etiam forte poteſtate, ut nunc res habent, funguntur in ſingulis Regnis,* tres Ordines, *cum primarios conventus peragunt :) adeo illos ferocienti* Regum *licentiæ pro officio intercedere non veto, ut ſi.* Regibus *impotenter graſſantibus, & humili plebeculæ inſultantibus conniverunt, eorum diſſimulationem nefaria perfidio non carere affirmem, quia populi libertatem (cujus ſe, Dei ordinatione, tutores poſitos norunt) fraudulenter produnt.*

For if there be now any *Popular Officers* ordained to moderate the licentiouſneſs of Kings (ſuch as were the *Ephori* ſet up of old againſt the Kings of *Sparta,* the *Tribunes* of the people againſt the *Roman* Conſuls, and the *Demarchy* againſt the *Athenian* Senate, and with which power perhaps, as the world goes, the *three States* are ſeiz'd in each ſeveral Kingdom, when they are ſolemnly aſſembled;) ſo far am I from hindering them to put reſtraints upon the exorbitant power of Kings, as their Office binds them; that I conceive them rather to be guilty of a perfidious diſſimulation, if they connive at Kings when they play the Tyrants, or wantonly inſult on the common People, in that they treacherouſly betray the Subjects liberties, of which they knew they were made Guardians by Gods own Ordinance.

25. Which dangerous Doctrine being thus breathed and broached by *Calvin,* hath ſince been both profeſſed and practiſed by all his Followers, as either they had opportunity to declare themſelves, or ſtrength enough to put the ſame in execution. Some of whoſe words I ſhall here adde as a taſte to the reſt, and then refer the reſt to their proper places. And firſt we will begin with *Beza,* who in his twenty fourth Epiſtle, inſcribed to the Outlandiſh Churches in *England,* doth reſolve it thus : If (a) *any man (ſaith he) contrary to the Laws and Liberties of his Native Countrey, ſhall make himſelf a Lord or Supreme Magiſtrate ove all the reſt; or being lawfully inveſted with the Supreme Magiſtracie, ſhould either unjuſtly ſpoil or deprive his Subjects of thoſe Rights and Priviledges which he hath ſworn to them to obſerve, or otherwiſe oppreſs them by open Tyranny, that then the Ordinary and inferiour Officer s are to oppoſe themſelves againſt them, who both by reaſon of their ſeveral Offices, and by Gods appointment, are bound in all ſuch caſes to protect the Subjects, not onely againſt Forein, but Domeſtick Tyrants.* Which is as much as could be poſſibly contained in ſo narrow a compaſs : And if he were the Author (as ſome ſay he was) of the Book called *Vindiciæ contra Tyrannos,* publiſhed under the name of *Stephanus Brutus;* there hath been no Rebellion raiſed ſince that Book was written, or likely to be raiſed in the times enſuing, which may not honeſtly be charged upon his account. But becauſe the Author of this Book is commonly reported to be meerly *French,* and none of the *Genevian* Doctors; we may poſſibly hear more of him in that part of our Hiſtory which relateth to the Actings of the *Presbyterians* in the Realm of

France.

(a) Si quiſquis repugnantibus legibus, & patriæ privilegiis, ſeſe Dominum aut Magiſtratum conſtituit, &c. Epiſt. 24.

France. What was taught afterwards in pursuance of *Calvins* Doctrines by *Hottaman*, and him that calls himself *Eusebius Philadelphos* amongst the French; by *Ursene* and *Parens*, in the *Palatine* Churches; by *Buchanan* and *Knox* amougst the *Scots*, and by some principal Disciplinarians amongst the English, we shall hereafter see in their proper places: And we shall then see also what was done in point of practice, first by the Princes of the House of *Bourbon*, and afterwards by some great Lords of the *Huguenot* party against *Francis* the Second, *Charles* the Ninth, *Henry* the Third, *Louis* the Thirteenth, Kings of *France*; by *William* Prince of *Orange*, and other of the *Belgick* Lords, in the final Abdication of King *Philip* the Second; by the *Hungarians* and *Bohemians*, in their revolting from the Princes of the House of *Austria*; by the Rebellious *Scots*, in deposing, imprisoning, and expelling of their rightful Queen, and finally, by the *Genevian* Faction in the Realm of *England*, in their imbroylments of the Nation under Queen *Elizabeth*, and that calamitous War (but more calamitous in the issue and conclusion of it) against *Charles* the First.　All which are built upon no other ground then this Doctrine of *Calvin*, accommodated and applyed to their several purposes, as appears plainly by the Answer of the *Scots* to Queen *Elizabeth*, who justified the deposing of their natural and lawful Queen, on those words of *Calvin*, which they relyed on for the sole ground of that horrible Treason, and their Indemnity therein; of which more hereafter.

26. In the mean time I shall content my self with the following passage, faithfully gathered out of the *Common Places* of *William Bucan*, Divinity-Reader in the small University of *Lausanna*, situate on the Lake *Lemane*, in the Canton of *Berne*, and consequently a neer Neighbour to the Town of *Geneva*; who treating in his forty one Chapter of the Duty of *Magistates*, propounds this question toward the close, *viz. What a good Christian ought to do if by a cruel Prince he be distressed by some grievous and open injury?* To which he thus returns his Answer: *That though Princes and Subjects have relation unto one another; yet Subjects in the course of nature were before their Princes, and therefore that such Princes (if they asurp not a plain Tyranny in their several Kingdoms) are not Superiour to the rest by nature, in the right of Father hood, but are settled by the suffrages and consent of the people, on such conditions as originally were agreed between them; and that it follows thereupon, (according unto* Buchanans *Doctrine) that Subjects are not born for the good of their Kings, but that all Kings were made to serve for the good of the people: that it is lawful to defend Religion by force of Arms, not onely against the assaults of such Forein Nations as have no jurisdiction over us, but also against any part of the same Common-wealth (the common consent of the Estates being first obtained) which doth endeavour to subvert it: that no violence is to be offered to the person of the Supreme Magistrate, though he play the Tyrant, by any private man whatsoever, except he be warranted thereunto by some extraordinary and express command from the Lord himself; but the oppression rather to be born with patience, than that God should be offended by such rash attempts: that the Protection of the Supreme Magistrate was to be required against the unjust oppressions of inferiour Officers: and that in a free Common-wealth the Supreme Magistrate is rather to be questioned in a course of Law, than by open Force; that Subjects may lawfully take up Arms in defence of their Wives and Children,*

if

if the Chief Magiſtrate make any violent aſſault upon them , as Lyons ard other brute Creatures fight to defend their young ones ; this laſt exemplified by that of *Trajan,* giving the Sword to the Captain of his Guard, with theſe following words : *Hoc enſe pro me juſta faciente , injuſta faciente contra me utaris :* that is to ſay, *That he ſhould uſe the Sword againſt him in defence of himſelf , and for the protection of all thoſe who in regard of his Office were ſubject to him : that therefore it was well done by the* Switzers *to free themſelves of their ſubjection to the Houſe of* Auſtria *, when the Princes of the Houſe had exerciſed more then ordinary cruelty in moſt parts of the Countrey ; that* David *might lawfully have killed* Saul *, becauſe he gave his Wife to another man, expelled him from his Native Countrey, murdered the Prieſts for doing ſome good Offices to him, and purſued him from one place to another with his flying Army, but that he did forbear to do it, leſt he ſhould give an Example to the people of* Iſrael *of killing their Kings , which other men prompted by ambition might be like enough to imitate.*

27. Such is the Commentary of *Buchanus* upon *Calvins* Text, by which all Chriſtian Kings are made accountable even in Civil Matters to the three Eſtates, or any other ordinary Officers of their own appointing. Which Doctrines being once by him delivered, and inforced by others, what elſe could follow thereupon, but firſt an undervaluing of their tranſcendent Authority, afterwards a contempt of their perſons ; and finally, a reviling of them with reproachful Language ? From hence it was that *Calvin* calls (a) *Mary* Queen of *England* by the name of *Proſerpine,* aſſuring us that all the Devils in Hell were not half ſo miſchievous ; and that *Knox* could not finde for her any better titles then that of *Jezabel,* miſchievous *Mary* of the *Spaniards* blood, the profeſſed enemy of God. From hence it was, that *Beza* calls *Mary* Queen of *Scots,* by the names of *Medea* and *Athaliah* ; of which the one was no leſs infamous in the Sacred, then the other was in the Heathen ſtory ; that the Engliſh *Puritans* compared Queen *Elizabeth* to an idle Slut, who ſwept the middle of the room, but left all the duſt and filth thereof behind the doors ; that *Didoclavius* calls King *James* (b) the greateſt and moſt deadly enemy of the holy Goſpel ; and poſitively affirms (c) of all Kings in general, they are naturally enemies to the Kingdom of Chriſt. And finally, from hence it was that the ſeditious Author of the baſe and unworthy Dialogue, entituled *Euſebius Philadelphus,* hath ſo beſpattered the great Princes of the Houſe of *France,* that he hath made them the moſt ugly Monſters in their luſts and cruelty, which ere Nature produced ; and could deviſe no fitter names for Queen *Mary* of *Scotland,* then thoſe of *Medea, Clytemneſtra, Proſerpine,* with that of *monſtrum Exitiale* in the cloſe of all : And that the late moſt mighty Monarch of Great *Britain,* was handled by his Subjects of this Faction with no leſs ſcurrility, then if he had been raiſed on high for no other purpoſe then to be made the mark againſt which they were to ſhoot their Arrows, even moſt bitter words, the object of all falſe tongues, and calumnious Pens. Thus do they deal with Kings and Princes, as *Pilate* in the Goſpel did with Chriſt our Saviour, adorned them in their Royal Robes, with their Crowns and Sceptres, and then expoſed them to the ſcorn of the common Souldiers, the inſolencies and reproaches of the Raſkal Rabble.

(a) Cancellarius Proſerpinæ illius, quæ nunc in Anglia omnes ſuperat Diabolos. Calv. in Amos, cap. 7.

(b) Infenſiſſimus Evangelii hoſtis. Ad Altar. Damaſc. Epiſt.
(c) Natura inſitum eſt in omnibus Regibus Chriſti odium. Ibid.

28. Nor

28. Nor do they deal much better with them, in reference to their power in Spiritual Matters; which they make either none at all, or such as is subservient onely to the use of the Church. *Calvin* first leads the way in this, as he did in the other, and seems exceedingly displeased with King *Henry* the Eighth, for taking to him the Title of Supreme Head on Earth of the Church of *England*. Of this he makes complaint in his Commentary on the *7th* of *Amos*; not onely telling us (a) what inconsiderate men they were who had conferred upon him any such Supremacy, but that himself was very much disquieted and offended at it. And though he be content to yield him so much Authority, as may enable him to make use of the Civil Sword to the protecting of the Church and the true Religion; yet he condemns all those of the like inconsiderateness, who make them more spiritual (that is to say, of greater power, in Sacred Matters) then indeed they are. The Supreme power according to the Rules of *Calvins* Platform, belongs unto the Consistory, Classes, or Synodical Meetings, to which he hath ascribed the designation of all such as bear publick Office in the Church, the appointing and proclaiming of all solemn Fasts, the calling of all Councils or Synodical Meetings, the censuring of all misdemeanours in the Ministers of holy Church : in which last they have made the Supreme Magistrate an incompetent Judge, and therefore his Authority and final Judgment in such cases of no force at all. *Beza* treads close upon the heels of his Master *Calvin*, and will allow no other power to the Civil Magistrate, then to protect the Church and the Ministry of it, in propagating and promoting the True Worship of God. It is, saith (b) he, the office of the Civil Magistrate to use the Sword in maintenance and defence of Gods holy Church; as it is the duty of the Ministers and Preachers of it, to implore their aid as well against all such as refuse obedience to the Decrees and Constitutions of the Church, as against Hereticks and Tyrants, which endeavoured to subvert the same. In which particulers if the Magistrate neglects to do his duty, and shall not diligently labour in suppressing Heresie, and executing the Decrees of the Church against all opponents; what can the people do, but follow the Example of the Mother-City, in taking that power upon themselves, though to the total alteration and subversion of the publick Government. For from the Principles and practice of these great Reformers, it hath ever since been taken up as a *Ruled case* amongst all their Followers, that if Kings and Princes should refuse to reform Religion, that then the inferiour Magistrates, or the common people, by the direction of their Ministers, both may and ought to proceed to a Reformation and that by force of Arms also, if need so require.

29. That by this Rule the *Scots* did generally walk in their Reformation, under the Regencie of *Mary* of *Lorraign*, Queen-Dowager to *James* the Fifth; and after her decease, in the Reign of her Daughter; we shall shew hereafter. And we shall shew hereafter also, that it was published for good *Genevian* Doctrine by our English *Puritans*, *That if Princes hinder them that travel in the search of this holy Discipline, they are Tyrants to the Church and the Ministers of it; and being so, may be deposed by their Subjects.* Which though it be somewhat more the *Calvin* taught as to that particular, yet the conclusion follows well enough on such faulty

(a) *Fuerunt certe homines inconsiderati, &c. & hoc me semper graviter vexavit. In Amos, cap.7.v.13.*

(b) *Officium magistratûs est Ecclesiam Dei gladio tueri ac conservare, &c. Bez. Epist. 24.*

faulty *Premiſes*; which makes it ſeem the greater wonder in our Engliſh *Puritans*, that following him ſo cloſely in purſuit of the Diſcipline, their diſaffection unto Kings and all Soveraign Princes, their manifeſt contempt of all publick Liturgies, and pertinaciouſly adhering to his Doctrine of Predeſtination; they ſhould ſo viſibly diſſent him in the point of the Sabbath. For whereas ſome began to teach about theſe times (a) that the keeping holy of one day in ſeven was to be reckoned for the Moral part of the fourth Commandment; he could not let it paſs without ſome reproof: for what, ſaith he, can be intended by thoſe men, but in defiance of the Jews to change the day, and then to add a greater Sanctity unto it then the Jews ever did? Firſt therefore, he declares for his own Opinion, that he made no ſuch reckoning of a ſeventh-day-Sabbath, (b) as to inthral the Church to a neceſſity of conforming to it: And ſecondly, that he eſteemed no otherwiſe of the Lords-day-Sabbath, then of an Eccleſiaſtical Conſtitution, (c) appointed by our Anceſtors in the place of the Jewiſh Sabbath; and therefore alterable from one day to another at the Churches pleaſure: Followed therein by all the Churches of his party, who thereupon permit all lawful Recreations, and many works of neceſſary labour on the day it ſelf, provided that the people be not thereby hindred from giving their attendance in the Church at the times appointed. Inſomuch, that in *Geneva* it ſelf all manlike exerciſes, as running, vaulting, leaping, ſhooting, and many others of that nature, are as indifferently indulged on the Lords day, as on any other. How far the Engliſh *Puritans* departed from their Mother-Church, both in Doctrine and Practice (with reference to this particular) we ſhall ſee hereafter, when they could finde no other way to advance *Presbytery*, and to decry the Reputation of the ancient Feſtivals, then by erecting their new Sabbath in the hearts of the people.

30. It is reported by *John Barkley*, in his book called *Pareneſis ad Scotos*, that *Calvin* once held a Conſultation at *Geneva*, for transferring the Lords day from Sunday to Thurſday. Which though perhaps it may be true (conſidering the inclination of the man to new devices;) yet I conceive, that he had greater projects in his Head, and could finde other ways to advance his Diſcipline, then by falling upon any ſuch ridiculous and odious Counſel. He had many Irons in the fire, but took more care in hammering his Diſciple then all the reſt; Firſt by entitling it to ſome expreſs Warrant from the holy Scripture, and afterwards by commending it to all the Churches of the Reformation. In reference to the firſt, he lets us know in his Epiſtle to *Farellus, Septemb.* 16. 1543. (a) that the Church could not otherwiſe ſubſiſt, then under ſuch a Form of Government, *as is preſcribed in the Word*, and obſerved in old times by the Church. And in relation to the other, he was reſolved to make his beſt uſe of that Authority, which hy his Commentaries on the Scriptures, his Book of *Inſtitutions*, and ſome occaſional Dicourſes againſt the Papiſts, he had acquired in all the Proteſtant and reformed Churches. Inſomuch that *Gaſper Ligerus*, a Divine of *Witteberge*, by his Letters bearing date *Feb.* 27. 1554, acknowledgeth the great benefit which he had received by his Writings, acquaints him with the peaceable eſtate of the Church of *Saxonie*; but ſignifies withall, (b) that *Excommunication*

Marginal notes (left column):

(a) *Moralem eſſe unius diei obſervationem in hebdomada.* Inſtitut. lib. 2. c. 8. Sect. 34.

(b) *Numerum Septenarium non ejus ſervitute Eccleſias aſtringam.* Li. Ibid.

(c) *Quem veteres in eorum ſabbatum ſubrogarunt.*

De transferenda ſolennitate dominica in feriam quintum Lib. 1. c. ult.

(a) *Non poſſe conſiſtere Eccleſiam, niſi certum Regimen conſtitueretur, quale ex verbo Dei nobis preſcriptum eſt, & in veteri Eccleſia ſuit obſervatum.* Epiſt. ad Farell.

(b) *Excommunicationem apud nos adhuc ullam eſſe.*
n

munication was not used amongst them : whereunto *Calvin* makes this Answer, That he was glad to hear that the Church of *Saxony* continued in that condition ; but sorry (c) that it was not so strenghned by the Nerves of Discipline, as might preserve the same inviolated to the times to come. He adds, that there could be no better way of correcting vice, then by the joynt consent of all the Pastors of one City ; (d) and that he never thought it meet, that the power of Excommunicating should reside in the Pastors onely, (that is to say, not in conjunction with their *Elders*;) which last he builds on these three Reasons. First, in regard it is an odious and ungrateful Office; next, because such a sole and absolute power might easily degenerate into tyranny ; and finally, because the Apostles had taught otherwise in it. By which we see, that as he builds his Discipline on the Word of God, or at the least on Apostolical tradition, which comes close unto it ; so he adventureth to commend it to the *Lutheran* Churches, in which his Reputation was not half so great, as amongst those which had embraced the *Zuinglian* Doctrines.

31. But in the *Zuinglian* Churches he was grown more absolute; his Writings being so highly valued, and his person so esteemed of in regard of his Writings, that most of the Divines thereof depended wholly upon his judgment, and were willing to submit to any thing of his Prescription. The Church of *Strasbourgh*, where he had remained in the time of his exile, received his Discipline with the first, as soon as it was finally established in *Geneva* it self. For it appeareth by the Letter which *Gasper Oberianus* sent to *Calvin*, bearing date *April* 12. 1560. (a) that the Eldership was then well settled in that Church, and the Elders of it in a full possession of their power, the exercise whereof they are desired to suspend in one particular, which is there offered to his view. This *Gasper* was chief Minister of the Church of *Tryers*, so passionately affected to the name of *Calvin*, that he accounted it for one of his greatest honours to be (b) called a *Calvinian* Preacher. Acquainting him with the condition of the Church of *Tryers*, he tells him amongst other things, that he found the people very willing to submit to Discipline ; and thereupon intreats him for a Copy of those Laws and Orders (c) which were observed in the Consistory of *Geneva*, to the end he might communicate them to such of the Senators as he knew to be zelously affected. *Calvin*, who was apt enough to hearken to his own desires, sends him a large draught of the whole Platform, as well relating to the choice of the Members, either Lay or Ministers, as to the power and juridiction which they were to exercise, with all the penalties and particularities (with reference unto crimes and persons) which depended on it. And having given him that account, he thus closeth with him : *This summary* (saith he) *I had thought sufficient, by which, or out of which* (d) *you may easily frame to your self such a form of Government, as I have no reason to prescribe. To you it appertains modestly to suggest those counsels, which you conceive to be most profitable for the use of the Church; that godly and discreet men, who seldom take it ill to be well advised, may thereupon consider what is best to be done.* Which words of his, though very cauteously couched, were so well understood by *Oberianus*, that the Discipline was first admitted in that Church, and afterwards propagated

into

(c) *Sed non simul conjuctos esse Disciplinæ nervos, docendum est,* &c.

(d) *Nunquam utile putavi jus Excommunicandi permitti singulis pastoribus : nam & res odiosa est,* &c. *Alium usum Apostoli tradiderunt.*

(a) *De hac re cuperem abs te commonefieri, Ecclesiam Argentinens.* &c. *cujus Ecclesiæ consideraturos spero & Seniores,* &c.

(b) *De me concionatore Calviniana,* &c. *Ibid.*

(c) *Leges Consistorii vestri optavi tuto ad me transmitti,* &c.

(d) *Ex quo formam aliquam conciperes, quam prescribere non debui.*

into thofe of the Neighbouring Provinces.

32. He hath another way of fcrewing himfelf into the good opinion of fuch Kings and Princes as he conceived to be inclinable to the Reformation ; fometimes congratulating with them for their good fuccefs; fometimes encouraging them to proceed in fo good a work ; of which fort were his Letters to King *Edward* the Sixth, to Queen *Elizabeth*, and Mr. Secretary *Cecil*; to the Prince Elector *Palatine*, Duke of *Wirtinburgh*, Lantgrave of *Heffe*. But he beftirred himfelf in no place more then he did in *Poland*; which though he never vifited in perfon, yet he was frequent in it by his Lines and Agents. The *Auguftane* Confeffion had been brought thither fome years before ; of which he took but little notice. But he had heard no fooner that the Doctrines of *Zuinglius* began to get fome ground upon them, under the Reign of *Sigifmund*, firnamed *Auguftus*, when prefently he pofts his Letters to the King, and moft of the great Officers which were thought to encline that way. Amongft which, he directs his Letters to Prince *Radzeville*, one of the Chief *Palatines*, and Earl Marfhal ; *Spirtetus Caftelan* of *Sunderzee*, and Lord high-Treafurer ; to *John* Count of *Tarnaco*, *Caftelan* of *Craco*, and Lord General of his Majefties Armies : befides many other *Caftelans*, and perfons of great power in the Affairs of that Kingdom. In his firft Letters to that King, dated the fourth of *December* 1554, he feems to congratulate with him for imbracing the Reformed Religion, (though in that point he was fomewhat out in his intelligence;) and thereupon exhorts him to be earneft in the propagating of the Faith and Gofpel, which in himfelf he had impreft ; and that he would proceed to reform the Church from the dregs of Popery, without regard to any of thofe dangers and inconveniences which might follow on it. But in his next addrefs (1555) he comes up more clofe, fpeaks (a) of *erecting a Tribunal or Throne to Chrift* ; fetting up fuch a perfect Form of the true Religion, as came neereft to the Ordinance of Chrift. And we know well, that in the meaning of his Party, the fettling of *Presbytery* was affirmed to be nothing elfe then fetting Chrift upon his Throne, holding the Sceptre of the Holy Difcipline in own right-hand. And fomewhat to this purpofe he had alfo written to the Count of *Tarnaco*, whom in his firft Letter he applauds for his great readinefs to receive the Gofpel : But in his fecond, bearing date the nineteenth of *November* 1558, he feems no lefs grieved that the *Count* demurred on fomething which he had recommended to him, under pretence that (b) it was not fafe to alter any thing in the State of the Kingdom, and that all innovations feemed to threaten fome great danger to it; which cauteloufnefs in that great perfon could not relate to any alteration in the State of Religion, in which an alteration had been made for fome years before ; and therefore muft refer to fome Form of Difcipline which *Calvin* had commended to him for the ufe of thofe Churches. And no man can conceive that he would recommend unto them any other Form then that which he devifed for the Church of *Geneva*.

32. But *Calvin* did not deal by Lettes onely in the prefent bufinefs, but had his Agents in that Kingdom, who bufily imployed themfelves to advance his projects. Amongft whom none more practical, or pragmatical rather, then *John Alafco*, of a Noble Family in that Country,

(a) Quanti nobis effe debeat fincera Religio, per quam Chrifto inter nos Tribunal erigitur.

(b) In ftatu Regni nil movendum, quod omnis novitas graves motus & exitiales minaretetur.

tty,

try, but a profeſſed *Calvinian*, both for Doctrine and Diſcipline; for the promoting whereof, when he had ſetled himſelf and his Church in *London, Anno* 1550, he publiſheth a Pamphlet in defence of ſitting at the Holy Sacrament, incouraged thoſe who had refuſed conformity to the Cap and Surplice, and eagerly ſolicited *M. Bucer* (a man of great parts, but of more moderation) to ſhew himſelf on their behalf. Driven out of *England*, he betakes himſelf to the Dukedom of *Saxony*, where he behaved himſelf with ſuch indiſcretion, that he was fain to quit thoſe parts and retire to *Poland*, in which the greatneſs of his kindred was his beſt protection. There he ſets up again for *Calvin*. By the Activity of this man, the diligence of *Utenhorius*, and the compliance of ſome great perſons upon Politick ends; the Elderſhip is advanced in many places of that Kingdom, as appears by the Letters of the ſaid *Utenhorius*, bearing date *Jan.* 27. 1559. In which he ſignifies unto him, that the moſt illuſtrious Prince, the *Palatine* of *Vilna* in *Lithuania*, being come to the Aſſembly of the States which was held at *Petrico*, reſolved not to depart from thence before ſome Convention of the Brethren ſhould be held there alſo; to which (*a*) as well the Elders which his Highneſs brought thither with him, as thoſe that he found there at his coming, ſhould conſult together for the eſtabliſhing of a greater purity in Rites and Ceremonies to be uſed amongſt them. For with admiſſion of the Diſcipline into *Lithania*, *Calvin* expreſſeth no ſmall joy in his Letters to a namelefs Friend in that Country, bearing date *Octob.* 9. 1561. In which he lets him know how much he did congratulate the happineſs of the Realm of *Poland*, and more particularly of the Province of *Lithuania*, that the Reformed Religion made ſo great a progreſs in thoſe Countries, by which addition Chriſts Kingdom had been much enlarged; that his joy was very much increaſed, (*b*) by hearing that together with the ſame Religion they received the Diſcipline; that it was not without very good cauſe, that he uſed to call the Diſcipline the *Nerves of the Church*, in regard of the great ſtrength which it added to it. By which laſt words we may perceive what kind of Church-Government it was which he commended to *Ligerus* before remembred, under this very title of the *Nerves of Diſcipline*, by which Religion was to be preſerved inviolable for the times to come.

33. In the Aſſembly at *Petrico*, before remembred, the *Palatines*, and other great men of the Kingdom, obtained a Priviledge, (*c*) whereby it was made lawful for them to reform all the Churches under their command, & to reform them in ſuch manner as to them ſeemed beſt. It was then alſo moved by the Count of *Tarnaco*, that the Biſhops ſhould no longer hold their place or ſuffrage in the Aſſembly of Eſtates, but keep themſelves only to ſuch matters as concerned the Church: which though it did not take effect, yet the attempt appeared ſo dreadful in the eye of thoſe Prelates then preſent, that they became more tractable and obſequious to great State-Officers, then they had been formerly. And what could follow hereupon, but that the great men being left to pleaſe themſelves in their own Religion, and the Biſhops not daring to oppoſe; not onely *Zuinglianiſm* and the *Diſcipline*, but many other Sects and Innovations ſhould get ground upon them? In reference to the Diſcipline, as it was fitted and accommodated to whole Realms and Nations, they had

not

(*a*) *Ad quem noſtri his Seniores, ac etiam ſui quidem quos ſecum adduxit,*&c.

(*b*) *Cum audio Diſciplinam Evangelii profeſſione conjungi.*

(*c*) *Ut toti nobilitati libera reformandæ ſuam Eccleſiam facultas permitti debeat,* Utenh. Calv. Jan. 27.1559.

not onely their *Presbyteries*, as in *Geneva*, *Strasbourg*, and some other Cities; but their *Classical* and *Synodical* Meetings, as in *France* and *Scotland*; wherein they took upon them to make Laws and Ordinances for the directing of their Churches after *Calvins* Model. For in the Synod held at *Tzenger*, in the year 1564, it was Decreed that they should use no other Musick in their Churches, then the singing of Psalms (after the manner of *Geneva*, understand it so) condemning that which was then used in the Church of *Rome*, partly because the Psalms and Hymns were sung in the Latine Tongue, and partly because the Priests did bellow in them (as they pleased to phrase it) like the Priests of *Baal*. Concerning which we are to know, that the device of turning *Davids* Psalms into Rhyme and Meter was first taken up by *Clement Marrot*, one of the Grooms of the Bed-chamber to King *Francis* the first; who being much addicted to Poetry, and having some acquaintance with those which were thought to wish well to the Reformation, was perswaded by the learned *Vatablus* (Professor of the Hebrew Tongue iu the University of *Paris*) to exercise his Poetical Phancy in translating some of *Davids* Psalms. For whose satisfaction and his own he translated the first fifty of them into *Gallick* Meters; and after flying to *Geneva*, grew acquainted with *Beza*, who in some tract of time translated the other hundred also, and caused them to be fitted unto several Tunes. Which thereupon began to be sung in private Houses, and by degrees to be taken up in all the Churches of the French and other Nations which followed the *Genevian* Platform. For first, in imitation of this Work of *Marrot's*, *Sternhold*, a Groom of the Privy-Chamber to King *Edward* the Sixth, translated thirty seven of them into English Meter, *Anno* 1552, the rest made up by *John Hopkins* and some others, in the time of Queen *Mary*; but most especially by such as had retired unto *Geneva* in those very times. Followed therein by some *Dutch* Zealots, who having modelled their Reformation by the Rules of *Calvin*, were willing to imbrace this Novelty amongst the rest. So as in little tract of time, the singing of these Psalms in Meter became a most especial part of their publick Worship; and was estemed as necessary to the Service of God, as were the acts of Prayer and Preaching, and whatsoever else was esteemed most Sacred. In the next place, to take away all difference in Apparel, whether Sacred or Civil, and all distinction in the choice of Meats and Drinks, he

(b)*Stultum & ridiculum est hæredes Domini & omnium creaturarum, &c. Cap. de vestitu.*   accounted it (*b*) a ridiculous and ungodly thing for those which are the Heirs of all things, (with dominion over all the Creatures) to suffer themselves to be restrained by any superstitious use of Meats, Drinks, or Vestments. The Temples built unto their hands they were contented to make use of for their publick Meetings, being first purged of Idols, Altars, the Bellowings beforementioned, and other the like dregs of Popery; though formerly they had been abused (who sees not a *Calvinian* spirit walking in all these lines?) by the Priests of *Baal*. They seem content also to allow their Ministers Meat, Drink and Wages; condemning those which grutch them such a sorry Pittance. But as for Tithes, and Glebes, and Parsonage-Houses, they kept them wholly to themselves, that being the Fish they angled for in those troubled waters, and the chief bait that tempted them to swallow down those alterations in religion, which afterwards made them a reproach and a by-word to the rest of Christendom.

34. I have some reason to believe, that sitting at the Lord's Table came first in with *Calvinism*, as being most agreeable to the Rules of the Discipline and the Doctrine of the *Zuinglian* Church. But afterwards, upon consideration of the scandal which was given thereby, as well to the *Lutherans* as the Papists; (a) it was thought fit to change that posture into standing or kneeling; and then to charge the introduction of that sawcy custom on the *Arrain* Hereticks who looking on Christ no otherwise then their Elder Brother, thought it no robbery at all to be equal with him, (b) and sit down with him at his Table. And it was well for them, though it happened very ill for the peace of Christendom, that they could finde so fair a Plaster for so foul a Soar. For so it was, that both the Heresies of *Arrius*, the impieties of *Servetus*, the extravagancies of the *Anabaptists*, and the exploded errors of the *Samosatenians*, who from the least reviver of them are now called *Socinians*, grew up together in this Kingdom with the Doctrine of *Calvin*, and might receive some good encouragement from the Rules of his Discipline, by which that slovenly gesture or posture of sitting was imposed as necessary. Nor was the Discipline of force sufficient to repress those Heresies; though *Calvin* thought it such a great preservative of the true Religion, and that it was confirmed at the Synod of *Sendomier* 1570, (c) as grounded on the Word of God, and warranted both by Christs command, and the example of his Apostles; which gives the *Presbyterian* Discipline more Divine Institution, then *Calvin* durst ascribe unto it, or any of our Sabbatarians could ever find for their Lords-day-Sabbath. Some difference there was in the choice of their Elders, between these *Polish* Churches, and the rest of that Platform; the Government of the rest being merely popular; but these retaining somewhat in them of an Aristocracy. For besides the several *Presbyteries* of particular Churches, they have a more general superintendencie in every Diocess, or any other large District, of what name so ever. For managing whereof some of the principal Ministers are chosen by consent of their Synods, whom they call by the name of *Spiritual Superintendents*, each of them being associated with two or three Elders of the Lay-Nobility; and for the most part of the ranck and degree of Knights. By means whereof, they keep the ordinary Presbyteries and Parochial Sessions within the bounds appointed for them, nor suffering them to intrench upon the priviledges of Prince or People, as they have done in other places, where they want this curb.

35. Leaving the *Polish* Churches under this establishment, we must follow *Calvin* into *Scotland*, where he imployed *John Knox* as his Vicar-General. He knew the spirit of the man by his Factious Writings, his actings in the Schism at *Frankfort*, and the long conversation which he had with him in *Geneva* it self; and having given him a Commission to return to *Scotland*, instructed and incouraged him in his following courses. And *Knox* applyed himself so well to his Instructions, that presently on his return he inflamed the people to the defacing of Images, the destroying of Altars, demolishing of Monasteries and Religious Houses, and making havock of all things which formerly were accounted Sacred. This *Calvin* calls (a) the propagation of the Gospel, and by his Letters doth congratulate with him for his good success:

So

(a) *Ut stantes & genua flectentes, corpus & sanguinem Christi sumant.* Syn. Petrico. num. 4.

(b) *Ceremonia tantum Arianicum Domino pari solio sese collocantibus, propria.* Synod. Wladisla. Num. 6.

(c) *Secundum verbum Dei, --- & mandatum Jesu Christi, & exemplum Apostolorum.* Num. 11.

(a) *Evangelium apud vos tam felices, laetos progressus facere vehementer ut par est laetor.*

So that if *Tally*'s Rule be true, and that there be little or no difference between the advising of mischief, and the rejoycing at it when the deed is done; (*b*) *Calvin* must be as guilty of those spoils and Sacrileges, as even *Knox* himself. And that he might proceed as he had begun, he lays this Rule before him for his future carriage; that is to say, that the Church was to be cleared from all filth which had issued out of errour and superstition; (*c*) and the Mysteries of God were not to be defiled with idle and impertinent mixtures. Under which general Rule, and such a general Rule as hath no exceptions, there was no Ceremony used in the Church of *Rome*, though Primitive and Apostolical in it self, which was not presently to be discharged as *impure* or *idle*, or otherwise abhominated, as some part of the filth of Popery. And because all things must be done to the honour of *Calvin*, he is consulted in all such doubts and emergent difficulties, as could not be sufficiently determined by a less Authority. It is reported in the History writ by Venerable *Bede*, that when *Augustine* the Monk was sent into *England* by Pope *Gregory* to convert the *Saxons*, he met with many difficult and intricate cases, which he was not able to resolve. In which respect he sent them all in writing to the Pope himself, requiring his judgment in the same, that he might have the better ground to proceed upon; either in ordering of such matters which concerned the Church, or determining finally such cases as were brought before him. *Knox* looks on *Calvin* with as great a Reverence, as *Augustine* did upon the Pope; accounts him for the Supreme Pastor of the Reformation, and therefore sends his doubts unto him concerning the baptizing of Bastards, as also of the Children of Idolaters, and Excommunicate persons. He makes another *Quære* also, but such as seemed to be rather a Matter of Concupiscence, then a case of Conscience; whether the Monks and Parish-Priests which remained in *Scotland*, were to receive their Tythes and Rents as in former times, considering that they did no service in the Church of Christ. To which last *Quære* he returned such answer (for in the other he was Orthodox and found enough) as served to strip the Monks and Priests of all their livelyhood; it being clearly his opinion, (*a*) that they ought not to be fed and cloathed at the publick charge, in regard they lived in idleness, and did nothing for it; but that they rather were to get their livings by the sweat of their brows, and by the labour of their hands. According to which resolution no man is sure of his Estate, but may be stript of it as an idle boy, or an unprofitable servant, when the Brethren please.

36 But *Calvins* thoughts were not confined to *Poland* or to *Scotland* onely: He now pretends to a more general or Apostolical care over all the Churches, sending abroad his Missives like the *Decretals* of some former Popes; which being made in reference to those emergent difficulties which were brought before them, served afterwards for a standing Rule to regulate the like cases for the times to come. It would be thought a matter of impertinency, or curiosity at the best, to touch upon all particulars of this nature, in which he signified his good pleasure to the rest of the Churches. The Reader may satisfie himself out of his Epistles, if he hath any list or leisure to consult the same; or otherwise may make a judgement of them by this small scantling, as the wise Mathematician

Marginal notes:

(*b*) *Nihil interest otium velim fieri, an gaudeam factum.* Cicer. in Phil. 2.

(*c*) *Vt Ecclesia sordibus purgetur, quæ ex errore & superstitione manarunt, & ne fœdentur Dei Mysteria ludicris & insipidis mixturis.* Calv. Knoxo, April. 23.1561.

(*a*) *Monachis & Sacrificulis victum ex publico non debere certum est, ut in otio inutiles degunt, &c.--- Sed potius ut justo labore sibi victum querunt.* Calv. Knoxo, Novemb.8.1559.

thematician

thematician took the just measure of the body of *Hercules*, by the impression which he made in the sand by one of his Foot. And therefore I shall look no further then upon such specialities as have relation to the Doctrine, Discipline, or Forms of Worship, which are most proper to the rest. Some of the Brethren not fully setled in a Church, had laid aside the singing of Psalms, either for fear of being discovered, or otherwise terrified and discouraged by the threats of the adversary. For this he reprehends them in a tedeous Letter, dated *July* 19. 1559. (*b*) imputes it to their fearfulness or pusillanimity, accuseth them of plain tergiversation, and shutting up all passages against the entrance of the Graces of Almighty God. The Brethren of *Mont Pelyard* (for I think the former lived in *Mettz*, the cheif City of *Lorrein*) were required by the Guardians of their Prince (that is to say, the *Palatine* of *Zuibrook*, and the Duke of *Wirtenberge*) to hold conformity in some Ceremonies with the *Lutheran* Church, as namely in the Form of their Catechising, the manner of Administring the Holy Sacrament, the Form of publick Prayers, and Solemnizing of Marriages. They were required also to imploy themselves in Preaching down the errours and corruptions of the Church of *Rome*, in some small Seigniories which were lately fallen unto their Prince, and had not formerly been instructed in the Doctrine of the Protestant Churches. But absolutely they refused the one, and would do nothing in the other without *Calvins* leave; to whose infallible judgement and determination they refer the points: whereunto he returns such answer by his Letters, bearing date *September* 25. 1562, as confirmed them in their first refusal; excepting more particularly against suffering Midwives to Baptize, and against praying for the Joyful Resurrection of a man deceased, at the time of his Burial. But in the other he adviseth them to accept the charge; as visibly conducing to the propagation of the true Religion, and the inlarging of Christs Kingdom.

(b) Vestra timiditas atque pusillanimitas vos ita constringit, &c—ut potius retro feramini, & gratiæ Dei januam clausatis.

37. So for the Discipline which seemed to be devised at first upon humane prudence, accommodated to the present condition of *Geneva* onely; the use of Excommunication had been discontinued in the Protestant Churches, and no such creatures or Lay-Elders heard of in the Primitive times, or glanced at in the holy Scriptures. So that to trust them with the power of the Church-censures, could not pretend to any ground in the Word of God, supposing that the use of Excommunication was to be every where received. *Calvin* himself confesses in his Letters unto those of *Zurick*, (*a*) that in the judgment of most Learned and Religious men, there was no need of Excommunication under Christian Princes. *Beza* acknowledgeth the like in the Life of *Calvin*; and what *Ligerus* saith for the Church of *Saxonie*, hath been shewed already. But by degrees it came to be intituled to Divine Authority; at first commended as convenient, and at last as necessary. With the opinion of the Sacred and Divine Authority of the holy Discipline, he had so far possessed *Saligniar*, a man of Eminent power in the City of *Paris*, and one that for thirty years before, had declared himself in favour of the Reformation, that he acknowledgeth it in the end to be *Apostolical*: For in his Letter written unto *Calvin* on the Ides of *December*, he lets him know how vehemently he did desire, that (*b*) they might have such a Form of Ecclesiastical *Polity*, as *Calvin* seemed to

(a) Nec me latet doctos & pios esse homines, quibus principibus Christianis non videtur esse necessaria Excommunicatio.

(b) Eam nos habere Reipub. Christianæ formam, uti tu spiras & Apostolicam fuisse legimus.

breath,

breath, and could not be denyed to be Apostolical. From hence it was that he declared so positively in his Epistle to *Poppius*, *February* 25. 1559, that the (c) Magistrates were to be sollicited for the Exercise of Excommunication by publick Authority; which if it could not be obtained, the Ministers were to make this protestation, that they durst not give the Sacrament to unworthy receivers, for fear of coming under the censure of casting that which was holy before Dogs and Swine. More fully in his answer to some questions about the Discipline; in which we finde (and that goes very high indeed) (d) that the safety of the Church cannot otherwise be provided for, then by the free use of Excommunication, for the purifying of the same from filth, the restraint of licentiousness, abolishing enormous crimes, and the correcting of ill manners; the moderate exercise whereof he that will not suffer, doth plainly shew himself to be no sheep of our Saviours Pasture.

(c)Vt publica Authoritate, Excommunicatio in Ecclesia vigeat.

(d) Quam si ad eam pergendam, &c.— vigeat Excommunicatio, &c.

38. And so far *Calvin* had proceeded, but he went no further; neither condemning the Estate of Bishops as Antichristian and unlawful, nor thinking his Lay-elders so extreamly necessary, that no Decree of Excommunication could be past without them. But *Beza*, (a) who succeeded in the Chair of *Calvin*, is resolved on both : For *Calvin* having sate eight and twenty years in the Chair of *Geneva*, ended his life in the year 1564. During which time he had attained to such an height of Reputation, that even the Churches of the *Switzers* lost the name of *Zuinglians*, and thought it no small honour to them, as well as those of *Germany, France, Pole,* or *Scotland*, to be called *Cavinian*. Onely the English held it out, and neither had imbraced his Doctrines, nor received his Discipline. And though the *Puritan* party in it took the name of *Calvinists* (our *Divines commonly called Calvinists,* say the two *Informers*) yet both *Saravia* stomached it to be so accounted, *Mountague* in answer to the two *Informers* doth protest against it, and all the true sons of the Church of *England* do as much disclaim it. *Beza* endeavoured what he could to introduce his Discipline and Forms of Worship into all the Churches which did pretend to any Reformation of their ancient Errours. In the pursuit whereof he drives on so furiously, like *Jehu* in the holy Scriptures, as if no Kings or Princes were to stand before him. Scarce was he setled in his Chair, when one of his professed Champions for Presbytery puts himself into *Heidelberg*, which had not long after admitted the *Calvinian* Doctrines, but not submitted to the Discipline, as extrinsecal to them. This Champion therefore challenges the Divines thereof to a Disputation, publickly holds forth this proposition, which he then defended; that is to say, *That to a Minister with his Elders there is power given by express warrant from Gods Word, to Excommunicate all offenders, even the greatest Prince.* From hence proceeded that dispute which afterwards *Erastus* (of whom more hereafter) maintained with *Beza*; the point being put upon this issue, *Whether all Churches ought to have their Eldership invested with a power of Excommunication; and that Lay-elders were so necessary in every Eldership, that nothing could be done without them.* In which dispute (as it is very well observed by judicious *Hooker*) they seemed to divide the whole truth between them; *Beza* most truely holding the necessity of Excommunication in a

(a)Principio sub D. Jo. Calvini Ministerio, in cujus labores successimus. Bez. Epist. 33.

Church

Church well conftituted ; *Eraftus* no lefs truly fhewing that there was no neceffity of Lay-elders to the Minifters of it.

40. But his main bufinefs was to fettle the *Calvinian* Forms in the Realms of *Britain,* in which he aimed at the acquiring of as great a name as *Calvin* had obtained in *France* or *Poland Knox* had already fo prevailed amongft the *Scots,* that though they once fubfcribed to the Rites and Ceremonies of the Church of *England,* yet he had brought them to admit fuch a Form of Worfhip, as came more neer to the Example of *Geneva.* And he had brought the Difcipline to fo good a forwardnefs, that *Beza* was rather wanting to confirm then to introduce it, as fhall appear at large when we come to *Scotland.* But *Knox* had many opportunities to effect his bufinefs, during the abfence of their Queen, the Regencie of Queen *Mary* of *Lorrain,* and the unfettlednefs of affairs in the State of that Kingdom, which the Brethren could not finde in *England,* where the Fabrick of the State was joyned together with fuch Ligaments of Power and Wifdom, that they were able to act little, and effect much lefs. Some oppofition they had made after their coming back from *Franfort* and *Geneva,* their two chief Retreats, againft the Veftments of the Church, and the diftinction of Apparel betwixt Priefts and Lay-men: In which fome of them did proceed with fo vain an obftinacie, that fome of them were for a time fufpended, and others totally deprived of their Cures and Benefices; fome of them alfo had begun to take excepion againft fome parts and Offices of the publick Liturgie, refufing thereupon to conform unto it ; and thereupon likely to incur the very fame penalties which were inflicted on the other. In both thefe cafes they confult the Oracle, refolving to adhere to his determination in them, whatfoever it was. Firft therefore he applyes himfelf to *Grindal,* then Bifhop of *London,* and very zealoufly affected to the name of *Calvin:* to whom he fignifies by his Letter of the 26 of *June* 1566, how much he was afflicted with the fad reports out of *France* and *Germany,* by which he was advertifed that many Minifters in *England* , (a) being otherwife unblameable both for Life and Doctrine, had been exauctorated or deprived by the Queens Authority, (the Bifhops giving their confent and approbation) only for not fubfcribing to fome Rites and Ceremonies; but more particularly, that divers of them were deprived, not onely for refufing to wear (b) thofe Veftments which were peculiar to *Baals* Priefts in the times of Popery, but for not conforming to fome Rites which had degenerated into moft fhameful fuperftitions, fuch as the Crofs in Baptifm, kneeling at the Communion, and the like to thefe. That Baptifm was admitted fometimes by Midwives. (c) That power was left unto the Queen to ordain other Rites and Ceremonies, as fhe faw occafion: and finally, that the Bifhops were invefted with the fole authority for ordering matters in the Church; (d) the other Minifters not advifed with, or confulted in them.

41. Such is the fubftance of his charge againft each particular point whereof he bends his forces, as if he had a minde to batter down the Bulworks of the Church of *England,* and lay it open to *Geneva.* I fhall not note how much he blames the Ancient Fathers for bringing in fo many Ceremonies into ufe and practice, which either had been borrowed from the *Jews,* or derived from the *Gentiles;* or how he magnifieth the nakednefs and fimplicity of thofe Forein Churches which abominate nothing more then fuch outward trappings. But the refult of all is this

(a) Multos illic Miniftros verbi, inculpata alioqui tum vita tum Doctrina hominess, idcirco fuiffe Regia Majeftate exauctoratos, &c.

(b) Quod veftes illas Baali facerdotum infignia, &c. ——non admittunt.

(c) Quod alicrum fuperinducendorum Rituum poteftas Regia Majeftate feeret.

(d) Quod folis Epifcopis de conftituendis rebus Ecclefiafticis omnis potentia tribuatur &c. Epift. 8.

this (e), that whatsoever Rite or Ceremony was either brought into the Church from the *Jews* or *Gentiles*, not warranted by the institution of Christ, or by any examples of the Apostles; as also all significant Ceremonies, which by no right were at first brought into the Church, ought all at once to be prohibited and suppressed, there being no hope that the Church would otherwise be restored to her native Beauty. I onely note, that he compares the Cross in Baptism to the Brazen Serpent, abused as much to Superstition and Idolatry; and therefore to be abrogated with as great a Zeal in a Church well ordered, as that Image was destroyed by King *Hezekiah*. He falls foul also on that manner of singing which was retained in the Queens Chapels, all the Cathedrals, and some Parish-Churches of this Kingdom, because perhaps it was set forth by Organs, and such Musical Instruments (a) as made it fitter (in his judgment) to be used in Dancing, then in Sacred actions; and tended more to please the ears, then to raise the affections. Nor seems he better pleased with that Authority which was enjoyed and exercised by the Archbishop of *Canterbury*, in granting Licences for Pluralities, non-Residence, contracting Marriages in the Church, and eating Flesh on days prohibited; with many other things of that nature, which he accounts not onely for so many stains and blemishes in the Face of Christendom, (b) but for a manifest defection even from Christ himself; in which respect they rather were to be commended then condemned and censured, that openly opposed themselves against such corruptions.

(a) Choreis plerumq; potius quam Sacra actione, & de mulcendis auribus potius quam commovendis animis accommodatus. Ibid.

(b) Quæ non tantum corruptela Christianismi, sed manifesta à Christo defectio. Ibid.

42. Yet notwithstanding these complaints he grants the Matters in dispute, and the Rites prescribed, to be things indifferent, not any way impious in themselves, nor such as should necessitate any man to forsake his Flock, rather then yeild obedience and conformity to them. But then he adds, that if they do offend, who rather chuse to leave their Churches, then to conform themselves to those Rites and Vestments against their Consciences, (c) a greater guilt must be contracted by those men before God and his Angels, who rather chuse to spoil these Flocks of able Pastors, then suffer those Pastors to make choice of their own Apparel; or rather chuse to rob the people of the Food of their souls, then suffer them to receive it otherwise then upon their knees. But in his Letter of the next year he adventureth further, and makes it his request unto all the Bishops, that some fit Medicine be forthwith applyed to the present mischief, which did not onely give great scandal to the weak and ignorant, but even to many Learned and Religious Persons. And this he seems to charge upon them, as they will answer for the contrary at the Judgement-Seat of Almighty God, to whom an account is to be given of the poorest Sheep which should be forced to wander upon this occasion from the rest of the Flock. Between the writing of which Letters, some of their brethren had propounded their doubts unto him, touching the calling of the Ministers, as it was then, and still is used in the Church of *England*; the wearing of the Cap and Surplice, and other Vestments of the Clergy which was then required; the Musick and melodious singing in Cathedral Churches; the interrogatories proposed to Infants at the time of their Baptism; the signing of them with the sign of the Cross, kneeling at the Communion, administring the same in unleavened Bread; though the last were

(c) Multo majore reatu coram Deo. & ipsius Angelis teneri, qui greges à pastoribus privati, &c. potius sustineant, quam Ministros hoc quam illo habitu vestitos cernent. Ibid.

were left at liberty by the Rules of the Church, and used in some few places onely. Of all which he not onely signified a plain dislike, but endeavoured to shew the errours and absurdities contained in them; for such they must contain, if he pleased to think so. And what could follow hereupon, but an open Schism (a), a separation from the Church, a resort to Conventicles; which he takes notice of in his last to *Grindal*, but imputes it unto that severity which was used by the Bishops, in pressing such a yoak of Ceremonies upon tender Consciences. The breach not lessened, but made wider by another Letter directed to the *French* and *Dutch* Churches at *London* (b); in which he sets before them the whole Form of Worship which was established at *Geneva*, insisteth upon many points, neither agreeable to the Discipline or Doctrine of the Church of *England*; and finally, so restrains the power of the Supreme Magistrate, that he is left to the correction and control of his under Officers. Of which two Letters, that which was writ for satisfaction of the English brethren bears date *Octob.* 24. 1567, the other *June* 21, in the year next following.

(a)Rem tandem in iniquum & pertinax schisma evasisse--- Nonnulli tam seorsim suos cœtus habeant,&c.Bez. Epist. 23.
(b) Ad peregrinarum in Anglia Ecclesiarum fratres. Epist. 24.

43. With great Zeal he drives on in pursuit of the Discipline, the Form and Power whereof we will first lay down out of his Epistles, and then observe to what a height he doth endeavour to advance the same; excluding the Episcopal Government, as Antichristian, if not Diabolical. First then he tells us, that to each Minister which officiates in the Country-Villages within the Signiory of *Geneva*, (c) two Over-seers are elected as Assistants to him; and that to them it appertains to keep a watchful eye over all men in their several Parishes, to convent such before them, as they finde blame-worthy, to *admonish* them of their misdeeds; and finally, if he cannot otherwise prevail upon them, to turn them over to the censure of the Eldership which resides in the City. This Eldership he compounds of the six ordinary Pastors, and twelve Lay-elders; the last continually chosen from amongst the Senators. To whose charge and office it belongs to take notice of all scandals and offences of what sort soever within the bounds assigned unto them, and every Thursday to report to the Court or Consistory what they have discovered. The parties thereupon are to be convented, fairly admonished of their faults, sometimes suspended from the Sacrament, if the case require it, and excommunicated at the last, if they prove impenitent. To this Eldership also it belongs, to judge in all cases and concernments of Matrimony, according to the Word of God, and the Laws of the City; to repel such from the Communion as do not satisfie the Ministers by a full confession of their Faith and Knowledge. And in the company of an Officer of each several Ward, to make a diligent inquiry (over them) in every Family, (a) concerning their proficiencie in the Word of God, and the ways of Godliness.

(c)In singulis pagis adjuncti sunt duo inspectores, qui una cum pastore omnes ἄτακτες, observant.Epist. 20

(a)Singulas domos & familias adeuntes, &c. Ibid.

44. We must next see to what a height he doth endeavour to advance this Discipline, which (if we take it on his word) is not to be received onely as a matter necessary, but to be had in equall Reverence with the Word of God. *Sarnixius* had acquainted him with some news from *Poland*, concerning the Divisions and Subdivisions in the Churches there; whereunto *Beza* makes his answer by his Letters of the first of *November*, 1566; (b) *That unless some Form of Ecclesiastical Discipline, according*

(b)Nisi quædam firma inter vos statuatur Disciplina Ecclesiastica, &c. Epist. 14.

cording to the Word of God, were received among them, he could not see by what means they were able to remedy their discords, or to prevent the like for the time to come; that he had many times admired, that being warned by the confusion of their Neighbours in Germany, they had not considered before this time, as well of the necessity to receive such Discipline, as for the strict observing of it when it was received; that there was onely one and the self-same Author, *(c)* both of Doctrine and Discipline; and therefore that *it must seem* strange (which I would have the Reader mark with his best attention) *to entertain one part of the Word of God, (d) and reject the other* ; that it was most ridiculous to expect or think, that either the Laws could be observed, or the Peace maintained, without Rules and Orders, in which the very life of the Law did so much consist, that for the avoiding of some new Tyranny*(e)*which seemed to lye disguised under the Mask and Vizard of the present Discipline, they should not run themselves into such Anarchy and discords as were not otherwise to be prevented ; and finally, that no severity could be feared in the use of that Discipline, as long as it was circumscribed within the bounds and limits assigned unto it by the Word of God, and moderated by the Rules of Christian charity. So that we are not to admire, if the Discipline be from henceforth made a Note of the Church, every way as essential to the nature of it, as the Word and Sacraments; which as it is the common Doctrine of the Presbyterians, so we must look on *Beza* as the Author of it ; such Doctrine being never preached in the Church before.

45. But because *Beza* seems to speak in that Epistle concerning the necessity of admitting some certain Form of Ecclesiastical Discipline, without pointing punctually and precisely unto that of *Geneva;* we must next see what Form of Discipline he means, and whether a Church-Government by Bishops were intended in it. And first he tells us in a Postscript of a Letter to *Knox,* dated the third of *July* 1569, wherein he much congratulates his good Fortune, *(f)* for joyning the Discipline in his Reformation with the truth of Doctrine, beseeching him to go forward with it as he had begun, lest it might happen to him as it did to others, either to slacken in their speed, or not be able to advance were they never so willing. And we know well what Discipline, what Form of Government and Worship had been by *Knox* established in the Kirk of *Scotland* But secondly, many of the *Scots* being still unsatisfied in the point of Episcopacy, and not well pleased with any other Government of a late invention ; it was thought fit to send to *Beza* for his judgment in it, who was now looked upon as the Supreme Pastor, Successor unto *Calvin,* both in place and power. *Beza* considers of the business, and by his Letters of the 12*th* of *April* 1572, returns this Answer, *viz.* That he beheld it as an extraordinary blessing on the Church of *Scotland,* *(a)* That together with the true Religion, they also had received the Discipline for the Bond thereof. Both which he earnestly conjures them so to hold together, as to be sure that there is no hope to keep the one, if they lose the other : *(b)* which being said in reference to the Holy Discipline, he next proceeds to spend his judgment in the point of Episcopacy. In reference to which, he first tells them this, that as the Bishops were the first means to advance the Pope, so the pretended Bishops would maintain the Reliques of the Popery. And then

(c)Scis unum & eandem esse tum Doctrinæ tum Disciplinæ Authorem. Ibid.

(d) Quorsum enim unam verbi partem, altera repudiata, recipere. Ibid.

(e)Timetur alia tyrannis, &c. Ibid.

(f) Quam recte illud quod Doctrina simul Disciplina conjungetis, &c. Ep. 674.

(a)Magnum hoc Dei munus, quo una & Religionem puram & εὐταξίαν Doctrinæ, retinendæ vinculum in Scotiam intulistis. Epist. 79.

(b)Hæc duo simul retinete, ut uno amisso, alterum diu permanere non posse memineritis. Ibid.

then he adds, that it concerns all thofe to *avoid that Plague* (c) (by which he means undoubtedly the Epifcopal Order) who pretend to any care of the Churches fafety.   And therefore fince they had fo happily difcharged that calling in the Church of *Scotland*, (d) they never fhould again admit it, though it might flatter them with fome affurance of peace and unity.

46. What followed thereupon in *Scotland*, we fhall fee hereafter. But his defires of propagating the *Genevian* Forms, was not to be reftrained to that part of the Ifland.   In his firft Letter unto *Grindal*, he doth not onely juftifie the *Genevian* Difcipline, and the whole Order of that Church in Sacred Offices, as grounded on the Word of God ; but findes great fault with the Epifcopal Government in the Church of *England*, and the great power which was afcribed unto the Queen in Spiritual Matters.   How fo ? Becaufe (faid he) he found no warrant for it in the Word of God, or any of the ancient Canons, by which it might be lawful for the Civil Magiftrate (of his own Authority) either to abrogate old Ceremonies, or eftablifh new ; or for the Bifhops onely to ordain and determine any thing, (e) without the judgment and confent of their Presbyteries being firft obtained.   And in his anfwer to the Queries of the Englifh brethren, he findes no lefs fault with the manner of proceedings in the Bifhops Courts ; in regard that Excommunications were not therein paffed by the common confent of a Presbytery, (f) but decreed onely by fome Civil Lawyers, or other Officers who fate as Judges in the fame.   But firft, the man was ignorant of the courfe of thofe Courts, in which the fentence of Excommunication is never publifhed or pronounced, but by the mouth of a Minifter ordained according to the Rules of the Church of *England*.   And fecondly, it is to be conceived in Reafon, that any Batchelor or Doctor of the Civil Law is far more fit to be imployed and trufted in the exercife of that part of Difcipline, then any Trades-man of *Geneva*, though poffibly of the number of the five and twenty.   For the redrefs of which great mifchief, and of many other, he applies himfelf unto the Queen, to whom he dedicates his *Annotations* on the *New Teftament*, publifhed in the year 1572.   In the Epiftle whereunto, though he acknowledgeth that fhe had reftored unto this Kingdom the true Worfhip of God, yet he infinuates that there was wanting a full Reformation of Ecclefiaftical Difcipline ; that our Temples were not fully purged ; that fome high places ftill remained, not yet abolifhed : and therefore wifheth that thofe blemifhes might be removed, and thofe wants fupplyed.   Finally, underftanding that a Parliament was then fhortly to be held in *England*, and that *Cartwright* had prepared an *Admonition* to prefent unto it ; he muft needs interpofe his credit with a Peer of the Realm to advance the fervice, as appears plainly by his Letter of the fame year, and the *Nones* of *July*.   In which, though he approves the Doctrine, yet he condemns the Government of the Church as moft imperfect, not onely deftitute of many things which were good and profitable, but alfo of fome others which were plainly neceffary.

47. But here it is to be obferved, that in his Letter to this great perfon, whofoever he was, he feems more cautelous and referved then in that to *Grindal* ; but far more modeft then in thofe to *Knox*, and the Englifh

(c) *Hanc peftem caveant qui falvere Ecclefiam cupiant.* Ibid.
(d) *Ne quæfo illam unquam admittas, quamvis unitatis retinendæ fpecie blanditur.* Ibid.

(e) *Vel folis Epifcopis, abfque fui Presbyterii judicio & voluntate, aliquid novi ordinare,&c.* Epift. 8.
(f) *Non ex Presbyteri fententia, fed ex quorundam juris-confultorum & aliorum ejufmodi Authoritate.* Ibid.

lish Brethren. The Government of *England* was so well setled, as not to be ventured on too rashly. And therefore he must first see what effect his counsels had produced in *Scotland*, before he openly assaults the *English Hierarchy*: But finding all things there agreeable to his hopes and wishes, he published his Tract *De Triplici Episcopatu*, calculated for the Meridian onely of the Kirk of *Scotland* (as being writ at the desire of the Lord Chancellor *Glammis*) but so that it might generally serve for all Great *Britain*: In which Book he informs his Reader of three sorts of Bishops; that is to say, the Bishop by *Divine Institution*, being no other then the Minister of a particular Church or Congregation; the Bishop by *humane appointment*, being the same onely with the President of a Convocation, or the *Moderator* (as they phrase it) in some Church-Assembly; and finally, the *Devils Bishops*, such as presume to take upon them the whole charge of a Diocess, together with a superiority and jurisdiction over other Ministers. Which Book was afterwards translated into English by *Feild* of *Wandsworth*, for the instruction and content of such of the Brethren as did not understand the Latine. To serve as a Preface to which Work the Presbyterian Brethren publish their Seditious Pamphlets in defence of the Discipline, some in the English Tongue, some in the Latine; but all of them Printed at *Geneva*: For in the year 1570 comes out *The plain and full Declaration of Ecclesiastical Discipline, according to the Word of God*, without the name of any Author, to gain credit to it. And *Traverse*, a furious Zealot amongst the English, had published at *Geneva* also in the Latine Tongue, a discourse of *Ecclesiastical Discipline*, according to the Word of God (as it was pretended) with the declining of the Church of *England* from the same, *Anno* 1574; which for the same reason must be turned into English also, and Printed at *Geneva* with *Beza*'s Book *Anno* 1580. What pains was took by some of the *Divines* of *England*, but more particularly by Dr. *John Bridges* Dean of *Sarum*, and Dr. *Adrian Saravia*, preferred upon the merit of this service in the Church of *Westminster*, shall be remembred in a place more proper for it, when we shall come to a review of those disturbances which were occasioned in this Church by the *Puritan* Faction. Most of which did proceed from no other Fountain then the pragmaticalness of *Beza*, the Doctrines of *Calvin*, and the Example of *Geneva*; which if they were so influential on the Realms of *Britain*, though lying in a colder climate, and so far remote; it is to be presumed that they were far more powerful in *France* and *Germany*, which lay nearer to them; and in the last of which the people were of a more active and *Mercurial* Spirit.

48. What influence *Calvin* had upon some of the Princes, Cities and Divines of *Germany*, hath been partly touched upon before; and how his Doctrines did prevail in the *Palatine* Churches, and his Discipline in many parts and Provinces of the *Germane* Empire, may be shown hereafter. In *France* he held intelligence with the King of *Navar*, the Brethren of *Rouen*, *Aix*, *Mont-Pelier*, and many leading men of the *Hugonot* party; none of which can be thought to have asked his counsel about purchasing Lands, the Marriages of their Children, or the payment of Debts: And when the Fortune of the Wars, and the Kings just anger necessitated many of them to forsake their Country, they

found

found no place so open to them as the Town of *Geneva*, and none more ready to befriend them then *Calvin* was, whose Letters must be sent to all the Churches of the *Switzers*, and the Neighbouring *Germany*, for raising Contributions and Collections toward their relief: which so exasperated the French King, that he threatned to make War upon the Town, as the fomenter of those discords which embroyled his Kingdom, (a) the Receptacle of his Rebels, the *Delphos* as it were of that *Sacred Oracle* which Soveraignly directed all affairs of moment. But of these things, and how *Beza* did co-operate to the common troubles which did so miserably distract the peace of *France*, shall be delivered more particularly in the following Book.

49. As for the Town and Territory of *Geneva* it self, it had so far submitted unto their Authority, that *Calvin* wanted nothing of a Bishop in it, but the Name and Title. The City of *Geneva* had been anciently an Episcopal See, consisting of many Parishes and Country-Villages; all subject by the Rules of the Discipline unto one Presbytery, of which *Calvin* for the term of his life had the constant Precedency (under the style of *Moderator*) without whom nothing could be done which concerned the Church. And sitting as chief President in the Court or Consistory, he had so great an influence on the Common-council, as if he had been made perpetual *Dictator* also, for ordering the affairs of the Common-wealth. The like Authority was exercised and enjoyed by *Beza* also, for the space of ten years or thereabouts, after his decease. At what time *Lambertus Danaus*, one of the Ministers of that City, thinking himself inferiour to him in no part of Scholarship, procured the Presidency in that Church to go by turns, that he and others might be capable of their courses in it: By which means the *Genevians* being freed from those powerful Riders, would never suffer themselves to be bridled as they had been formerly. For thereupon it was concluded by a Decree of the Senate, that the Presbytery should have no power to convent any man before them, till the Warrant was first signed by one of the *Syndics*. Besides which curb, as the *Elders* are named by the lesser Council, and confirmed by the greater, the Ministers advice being first had in the nomination; so do they take an Oath at their admission, *to keep the Ecclesiastical Ordinances of the Civil Magistrate*. In which respect their Consistory doth not challenge an exorbitant and unlimited power, as the *Commissioners of Christ* (as they did afterwards in *Scotland*) but as Commissioners of the State or Seigniory; by which they are restrained in the exercise of that Jurisdiction, which otherwise they might and would have challenged by their first institution, and seemed at first a yoke too insupportable for the necks of the people. In reference to their Neighbouring Princes, their City was so advantageously seated, that even their Popish Neighbours were more ready to support and aid them, then suffer the Town to fall into the power of the Duke of *Savoy*. And then it is not to be doubted but such States and Kingdoms as were Zealous in the Reformation, did liberally contribute their assistance to them. The confluence of so many of the *French* as had retired thither in the heat of the Civil Wars, had brought a miserable
ble

ble P ague upon them ; by which their nnmbers were ſo leſſened, and their ſtrength ſo weakned, that the Duke of *Savoy* took the opportunity to lay Siege unto it : in which diſtreſs they ſupplicate by Letters to all their Friends, or ſuch as they conceived might wiſh well unto them in the cauſe of Religion ; and amongſt others, to ſome Biſhops and Noble-men of the Church of *England*, *Anno* 1581. But *Beza* having writ to *Traverſe*, a moſt zealous *Puritan*,to negotiate in it, the buſineſs ſped the worſe for the Agents ſake ; no great ſupply being ſent unto them at that time. But afterwards when they were diſtreſſed by the *Savoyard*, *Anno* 1589, they were relieved with thirteen thouſand Crowns from *England*, twenty four thouſand Crowns from the State of *Venice* ; from *France* and *Florence*, with intelligence of the enemies purpoſes : onely the *Scots*, though otherwiſe moſt zealous in advancing the Diſcipline, approved themſelves to be true *Scots*, or falſe Brethren to them. For having raiſed great ſums of mony, under pretence of ſending ſeaſonable relief to their friends in *Geneva* ; the moſt part of it was aſſigned over to the Earl of *Bothwell*, then being in Rebellion againſt their King, and having many ways endeavoured to ſurpriſe his perſon, and in fine to take away his life. But this prank was not play'd untill ſome years after, and therefore falls beyond the time of my deſign ; which was, and is, to draw down the ſucceſſes of the *Presbyterians* in their ſeveral countries till the year 1585, and then to take them all together, as they related unto *England*, or were coincident with the Actions and Affairs thereof. But we muſt make our way by *France*, as lying neareſt to the practices of the Mother-city ; though *Scotland* at a greater diſtance firſt took fire upon it, and *England* was as ſoon attempted as the *French* themſelves.

The end of the Firſt Book.

AERIUS REDIVIVUS:

OR THE

HISTORY

OF THE

Presbyterians.

LIB. II.

Containing

The manifold Seditions, Conspiracies, and Insurrections in the Realm of France, *their Libelling against the State, and the Wars there raised by their procurement, from the year* 1559 *to* 1585.

THe Realm of *France*, having long suffered under the corruptions of the Church of *Rome*, was one of the first Western Kingdoms which openly declared against those abuses. *Beringarius* in the Neighbouring *Italy*, had formerly opposed the Gross and Carnal Doctrines of the Papists in the point of the Sacrament : Whose opinions passing into *France* from one hand to another, were at last publickly maintained by *Peter Waldo*, one of the Citizens of *Lyons*, who added thereunto many bitter invectives against the Supremacy of the Pope, the Adoration of Images, the Invocation of Saints, and the Doctrine of Purgatory.   His Followers, from the place of his habitation

bitation, were at first called in contempt, *The poor men of Lyons*; as afterwards, from the name of their Leader, they were by the Latines called *Waldenses*, by the French *Les Vaudoise*. But *Lyons* proving no safe place for them, they retired into the more desart parts of *Languedoc*, and spreading on the banks of the River *Alby*, obtained the name of *Albigenses* in the Latine Writers, and of *Les Albigeoise* in the French : supported by *Raymond* the Fourth, Earl of *Tholouse*, they became so insolent, that they murthered *Trincanel* their Viscount in the City *Beziers*, and dasht out the teeth of their Bishop, having taken Sanctuary in St. *Magdalens* Church, one of the Churches of that City. For which high outrages, and many others of like nature which ensued upon them, they were warred upon by *Lewis* the Ninth of *France*, Sirnamed the *Saint*, and many Noble Adventurers, who sacrificed many of them in the self-same Church wherein they had spilt the blood of others. After a long and bloody War, which ended in the year 1250, they were almost rooted out of the Country also; the residue or remainders of them having betook themselves into the mountainous parts of *Daulphine*, *Provence*, *Piemont*, and *Savoy*, for their greater safety. By means whereof becoming neer Neighbours to the *Switzers*, and possibly managing some traffick with the Town of *Geneva*, their Doctrines could neither be unknown to *Zuinglius* amongst the one, nor to many Inhabitants of the other of best note and quality.

2. The rest of *France* had all this while continued in the Popes obedience, and held an outward uniformity in all points with the Church of *Rome*; from which it was not much diverted by the Writings of *Zuinglius*, or the more moderate proceedings of the *Lutheran* Doctors, who after the year 1517. had filled many Provinces of *Germany* with their opinions. But in the year 1533 the *Lutherans* found an opportunity to attempt upon it. For *Francis* the First favouring Learned men and Learning (as commonly they do, whose Actions are worthy a learned Pen) resolved to erect a University at *Paris*, making great offers to the most Learned Scholars of *Italy* and *Germany* for their entertainment. *Luther* takes hold of that advantage, and sends *Bucer*, and some others of his ablest Followers; who by disputing in such a confluence of Learned men, might give a strong essay to bring in his Doctrines. Nor wanted there some which were taken with the Novelty of them, especially because such as were questioned for Religion had recourse into *Aquitaine*, to *Margaret* of *Valois*, the Kings Sister, married to *Henry* of *Albret* King of *Navar*, who perhaps out of hatred to the Bishop of *Rome*, by whom her Husbands Father was deprived of that Kingdom, might be the more favourable to the *Lutherans*; or rather moved (as she confessed before her death) with commiseration to those condemned persons that fled to her protection, she became earnest with her brother in defence of their persons; so that for ten years together she was the chief means of maintaining the Doctrines of *Luther* in the Realm of *France*. Nor was the King so bent in their Extermination, as otherwise he would have been, in regard of those many *Switz* and *Germans* that served him in his Wars against *Charles* the Fifth; till at last, being grievously offended

offended with the contumacy of the men, and their continual opposition to the Church of *Rome*, he published many Edicts and Proclamations against them, not onely threatning, but executing his penal Laws, untill he had at last almost extinguished t e name of *Luther* in his Kingdom.

3. But *Calvins* stratagem succeeded somewhat better, who immediately upon the Death of *Francis* the First (whilst King *Henry* was ingag'd in the Wars with *Charles*) attempted *France* by sending his Pamphlets from *Geneva*, writ for the most part in the *French* Tongue, for the better captivating and informing of the common people. And as he found many possessed with *Luthers* opinions, so he himself inflamed them with a Zeal to his own ; the Vulgar being very proud to be made Judges in Religion, and pass their Votes upon the abstrusest Controversies of the Christian Faith. So that in short time *Zuinglius* was no more remembred, nor the Doctrine of *Luther* so much followed as it had been formerly. The name of *Calvin* carrying it amongst the *French*. The sudden propagating of whose Opinions, both by preaching and writing, gave great offence unto the Papists ; but chiefly to *Charles* Cardinal of *Lorrain*, and his Brother *Francis* Duke of *Guise*, then being in great power and favour with King *Henry* the Second. By whose continual sollicitation, the King endeavoured by many terrible and severe executions to suppress them utterly ; and did reduce his Followers at the last to such a condition, that they durst neither meet in publick, or by open day, but secretly in Woods or Private-houses ; and for the most part in the night, to avoid discovery. And at this time it was, and on this occasion, that the name of *Hugonots* was first given them ; so called from St. *Hugo's* Gate in the City of *Towrs*, out of which they were observed to pass to their secret Meetings ; or from a night-spirit, or Hobgobling, which they called St. *Hugo* ; to which they were resembled, for their constant night-walks. But neither the disgrace which that name imported, nor the severity of the Kings Edicts so prevailed upon them, but that they multiplied more and more in most parts of the Realm ; especially in the Provinces which either were nearest to *Geneva*, or lay more open towards the Sea, to the trade of the English. And though the fear of the danger, and the Kings displeasure, deterred such as lived within the air of the Court from adhering openly unto them ; yet had they many secret favourers in the Royal Palace, and not a few of the Nobility, which gave them as much countenance as the times could suffer. The certainty whereof appeared immediately on the death of King *Henry*, who left this Life at *Paris* on the tenth of *July*, *Anno* 1559, leaving the Crown to *Francis* his Eldest Son, then being but fifteen years of Age, neither in strength of body, nor in vigour of Spirit, enabled for the managing of so great an Empire.

4. This young King in his Fathers life-time had married *Mary* Queen of *Scots*, Daughter and Heir of *James* the Fifth, by *Mary* of *Lorrain* a Daughter of the House of *Guise*, and Sister to the two great Favourites before remembred. This gave a great improvement to the power and favour which the two Brothers had before, made

greater

1546,

1559.

greater by uniting themselves to *Katherine de Medicis*, the young Kings Mother ; a Woman of a pestilent Wit, and one that studied nothing more then to maintain her own greatness against all opposers. By this confederacy the Princes of the House of *Bourbon*, Heirs in Reversion to the Crown, if the King and his three brothers should depart without Issue Male (as in fine they did) were quite excluded from all office and imployment in the Court or State. The principal of which was *Anthony* Duke of *Vendosme*, and his brother *Lewis* Prince of *Conde*, men not so near in birth, as of different humours ; the Duke being of an open nature, flexible in himself, and easily wrought upon by others: but on the other side, the Prince was observed to be of a more enterprising disposition, violent (but of a violence mixed with cunning in the carrying on of his designs) and one that would not patiently dissemble the smallest injuries. These two had drawn unto their side the two *Chastilions* ; that is to say, *Gasper de Collignie* Admiral of the Realm of *France*, and Monsieur *D'Andilot* his brother Commander of the Infantry of that Kingdom ; to which Offices they had been advanced by the Duke of *Montmorency*, into whose Family they had married, during the time of his Authority with the King deceased , for whose removal from the Court by the confederacy of the Queen Mother with the House of *Guise*, they were as much disquieted, and as apt for action, as the Princes of the House of *Bourbon* for the former Reasons. Many designs were offered to consideration in their private Meetings ; but none were more likely to effect their business, then to make themselves the Heads of the *Hugonot* Faction, which the two *Chastilions* had long favoured as far as they durst. By whose assistance they might draw all affairs to their own disposing, get the Kings person into their power, shut the Queen-mother into a Cloyster, and force the *Guises* into *Lorrain* out of which they came.

5. This counsel was the rather followed, because it seemed most agreeable to the inclinations of the Queen of *Navar* Daughter of *Henry* of *Alb. et* and the Lady *Margaret* before-mentioned, and Wife of *Anthony* Duke of *Vendosm*, who in her Right acquired the title to that Kingdom. Which Princess being naturally averse from the Popes of *Rome*, and no less powerfully transported by some flattering hopes for the recovery of her Kingdoms, conceived no expedient so effectual to revenge her self upon the one, and Inthrone her self in the other, as the prosecuting this design to the very utmost. Upon which ground she inculcated nothing more into the ears of her Husband, then that he must not suffer such an opportunity to slip out of his hands, for the recovery of the Crown which belonged unto her ; that he might make himself the Head of a mighty Faction, containing almost half the strength of *France* ; that by so doing he might expect assistance from the *German* Princes of the same Religion, from Queen *Elizabeth* of *England*, and many discontented Lords in the *Belgick* Provinces, besides such of the Catholick party, even in *France* it self, as were displeased at the *Omni*-Regency of the House of *Guise* ; that by a strong Conjunction of all these interesses he might not only get his ends upon the *Guises*, but carry his Army cross the Mountains, make himself Master of *Navar*, with all the

Rights

Rights and Royalties appertaining to it. But all this could not ſo prevail on the Duke her Husband, (whom we will henceforth call the King of *Navar*) as either openly or under-hand to promote the enterprise. which he conceived more like to hinder his affairs then to advance his hopes. For the Queen-Mother having ſome intelligence of theſe ſecret practices, ſends for him to the Court, commands unto his care her Daughter the Princeſs *Iſabella*, affianced to *Philip* the Second King of *Spain*, and puts him chief into Commiſſion for delivering her upon the Borders to ſuch *Spaniſh* Miniſters as were appointed to receive her. All which ſhe did (as ſhe aſſured him) for no other ends, but out of the great eſteem which ſhe had of his perſon, to put him into a fair way for ingratiating himſelf with the Catholick King, and to give him ſuch a hopeful opportunity for ſolliciting his own affairs with the Grandees of *Spain*, as might much tend to his advantage upon this imployment. Which device had ſo wrought upon him, and he had been ſo finely fitted by the Miniſters of the Catholick King, that he thought himſelf in a better way to regain his Kingdom, then all the *Hugonots* in *France*, together with their Friends in *Germany* and *England*, could chalk out unto him.

6. But notwithſtanding this great coldneſs in the King of *Navar*, the buſineſs was ſo hotly followed by the Prince of *Bonde*, the Admiral *Collignie*, and his Brother *D'Andelot*, that the *Hugonots* were drawn to unite together under the Princes of that Houſe. To which they were ſpurred on the faſter by the practices of *Godfrey de la Bar*, commonly called *Renaudie*, from the name of his Seigniory; a man of a moſt miſchievous Wit, and a dangerous Eloquence; who being forced to abandon his own Country for ſome miſdemeanors, betook himſelf unto *Geneva*, where he grew great with *Calvin*, *Beza*, and the reſt of the Conſiſtory; and coming back again in the change of times, was thought the fitteſt inſtrument to promote this ſervice, and draw the party to a body. Which being induſtriouſly purſued, was in fine effected; many great men, who had before conceal d themſelves in their affections, declaring openly in favour of the Reformation, when they perceived it conntenanced by ſuch Potent Princes. To each of theſe, according as they found them qualified for parts and power, they aſſigned their Provinces and Precincts, within the limits whereof they were directed to raiſe Men, Arms, Money, and all other neceſſaries, for carrying on of the deſign; but all things to be done in ſo cloſe a manner, that no diſcovery ſhould be made till the deed was done. By this it was agreed upon, that a certain number of them ſhould repair to the King at *Bloiſe*, and tender a Petition to him in all humble manner for the free exerciſe of the Religion which they then profeſſed, and for profeſſing which they had been perſecuted in the days of his Father. But theſe Petitioners were to be backed with multitudes of armed men, gathered together from all parts on the day appointed; who on the Kings denyal of ſo juſt a ſuit, ſhould violently break into the Court, ſeize on the perſon of the King, ſurpriſe the Queen, and put the *Guiſes* to the Sword: And that being done, *Liberty* was to be Proclaimed, Free exerciſe of Religion granted by publick Edict, the managery of affairs committed to the Prince of *Conde*, and all the reſt of the Confederates

federates gratified with rewards and honours. Impossible it was, that in a business which required so many hands, none should be found to give intelligence to the adverse party: which coming to the knowledge of the Queen-Mother, and the Duke of *Guise*, they removed the Court from *Bloise* a weak open Town, to the strong Castle of *Amboise*, pretending nothing but the giving of the King some recreation in the Woods adjoyning. But being once setled in the Castle, the King is made acquainted with the threatned danger, the Duke of *Guise* appointed Lieutenant-General of the Realm of *France*. And by his care the matter was so wisely handled, that without making any noise to affright the Confederates, the Petitioners were admitted into the Town; whilst in the mean time, several Troopes of Horse were sent out by him to fall on such of their Accomplices as were well Armed, and ready to have done the mischief, if not thus prevented.

1560.   7. The issue of the business was, that *Renaudie* the chief Actor in it was killed in the fight, many of the rest slain, and some taken Prisoners, the whole body of them being routed and compelled to flie: yet such was the clemency of the King, and the discreet temper of the *Guises*, in the course of this business, that a general pardon was proclaimed on the 18th of *March*, (being the third day after the Execution) to all that being moved onely with the Zeal of Religion, had entred themselves into the Conspiracy, if within twenty four hours they laid down their Arms, and retired to their own Houses. But this did little edifie with those hot spirits which had the conduct of the Cause, and had befooled themselves and others with the flattering hopes of gaining the Free exercise of their Religion. It cannot be denyed but that they were resolved so to act their parts, that Religion might not seem to have any hand in it, or at the least might not suffer by it, if the plot miscarried. To which end they procured the chief Lawyers of *France* and *Germany*, and many of the reformed Divines of the greatest eminence, to publish some Writings to this purpose; that is to say, that without violating the Majesty of the King, and the dignity of the lawful Magistrate, they might oppose with Arms the violent Domination of the House of *Guise*, who were given out for Enemies to the true Religion, hinderers of the course of Justice, and in effect no better then the Kings Jaylors, as the case then stood. But this Mask was quickly taken off, and the design appeared bare faced without any vizard. For presently upon the routing of the Forces in the Woods of *Amboise*, they caused great tumults to be raised in *Poicttou*, *Languedoc* and *Provence*. To which the Preachers of *Geneva* were forthwith called, and they came as willingly; their followers being much increased both in courage and numbers, as well by their vehemency in the Pulpit, as their private practices. In *Daulpheny*, aud some parts of *Provence*, (a) they proceeded further, seized upon divers of the Churches for the Exercise of their Religion, as if all matters had succeeded answerable to their expectation. But on the first coming of some Forces from the Duke of *Guise* they shrunk in again, and left the Country in the same condition wherein first they found it. Of this particular, *Calvin* gives notice unto *Bullenger*, by his Letters of the 27th.

of

(a) *In quibusdam Provinciæ & Delphinatus & urbibus nostri homines templa occuparent, ac si votorum jam essent compotes, &c.*

of *May*, *Anno* 1560, complaining much of the extreme rashnefs, and fool-hardinefs of fome of that party, (*b*) whom no fober counfels could reftrain from thofe ingagements which might have proved fo dangerous and deftructive to the caufe of Religion.   Which words of his relate not onely to the Action of *Daulphine* and *Provence*, but to fome of the attempts preceding, whatfoever they were, by him difcouraged and diffwaded, if we may believe him.

8. But though we may believe him, as I think we may, the Pope and Court of *France* were otherwife perfwaded of it.   *Reinadoes* going from *Geneva*, to unite the party, was as unlikely to be done without his allowance, as without his privity.   But certainly the Minifters of *Geneva* durft not leave their Flocks to Preach Sedition to the *French* of *Provence* and *Languedoc*, if he had neither connived at it, or advifed them to it ; (*c*) and fuch connivings differ but little from commands, as we find in *Salvian*.   Once it is fure that the Pope fuggefted to the *French* King by the Bifhop of *Viterbo*, whom he fent in the nature of Legate, that all the mifchief which troubled *France*, and the Poyfon which infected that Kingdom and the Neighbouring Countries, (for fo I find in my Author) came from no other Fountain then the Lake of *Geneva* ; that by digging at the very root, he might divert a great part of that nourifhment by which thofe mifchiefs were fomented ; and that by profecuting fuch a Forein War, he might evacuate thofe bad humours which diftempered his Kingdom: and therefore if the King be pleafed to engage herein, his Holinefs would not onely fend him fome convenient Aids, but move the *Scotch* King, and the Duke of *Savoy*, to affift him alfo.   But neither the Queen-Mother, nor the *Guife* (for the King acted little in his own affairs) could approve the motion, partly for fear of giving offence unto the *Switzers*, with whom *Geneva* had confederated thirty years before ; and partly becaufe none being like to engage in that War, but the Catholicks onely, the Kingdom would thereby lye open to the adverfe party.   But nothing more diverted the three Princes from concurring in it, then the impoffibility of complying with their feveral interefles in the difpofing of the Town when it fhould be taken.   The Duke of *Savoy* would not enter into the War before he was affured by the other Princes that he fhould reap the profit of it; that belonging anciently to his jurifdiction.   But it agreed neither with the intereft of *France* nor *Spain*, to make the Duke greater then he was, by fo fair an addition as would be made to his Eftate, were it yeilded to him.   The *Spaniard* knew that the *French* King would never bring him into *France*, or put into his hands fuch a fortified Pafs, by which he might enter when he pleafed.   As on the other fide, the *Spaniards* would not fuffer it to fall into the power of the *French*, by reafon of its neer Neighbour-hood unto the County of *Burgundy*, which both then was, and ever fince hath been appendant on the Crown of *Spain*. By reafon of which mutual diftrufts and jealoufies the Pope received no other anfwer to his motion in the Court of *France*, but that it was impoffible to apply themfelves to matters abroad, when they were exercifed at home with fo many concernments.

9. This anfwer pinched upon the Pope, who found as much confufion

(*b*) *Ab initio vaticinatus fum quo accidit, fed nefcio quo fafcini genere fic captæ erant multorum mentes, ut fruftra impetum illum fædare conatus fim.*

(*c*) *Quam longe quæfo eft a jubente permittente.* Salv. De Gubern. Dei, lib. 8.

fuſion in the State of *Avignion*, belonging for ſome hundreds of years to the See of *Rome*, as the *French* could reaſonably complain in the Bowels of *France*. For lying as it did within the limits of *Provence*, and being viſited with ſuch of the French Preachers as had been ſtudied at *Geneva*, the people generally became inclined unto *Calvins* Doctrines, and made profeſſion of the ſame both in private and publick ; nay, they reſolved upon the lawfulneſs of taking up of Arms againſt the Pope, though their natural Lord ; partly upon pretence that the Country was unjuſtly taken from the Earls of *Tholouſe* by the Predeceſſors of the Pope ; partly becauſe the preſent Pope could prove no true Lineal Succeſſion from the firſt Uſurper ; but chiefly in regard that perſons *Eccleſiaſtical* were diſabled by Chriſts Commandments from exerciſing any Temporal Juriſdiction over other men. Being thus reſolved to rebel, they put themſelves, by the perſwaſion of *Alexander Guilatine*, a profeſſed Civilian, into the protection of *Charles Count de Montbrun*, who had then taken Arms againſt the King, in the Country of *Daulphine*. *Montbrun* accepts of the imployment, enters the Territory of *Avignion* with three thouſand Foot, reduceth the whole Country under his command ; the Popes Vice-Legate in the City being hardly able for the preſent to make good the Caſtle. But ſo it hapned, that the Cardinal of *Tournon*, whoſe Niece the Count had married, being neer the place, prevailed with him after ſome diſcourſe to withdraw his Forces, and to retire unto *Geneva* ; aſſuring him not onely of his Majeſties pardon, and the reſtitution of his Goods which had been confiſcated, but that he ſhould have liberty of conſcience alſo, which he prized far more then both the other. By which Action the people were neceſſitated to return to their old obedience ; but with ſo many fears and jealouſies on either ſide, that many years were ſpent before the Pope could be aſſured of the love of his Subjects, or they relye upon the Clemency and good will of their Prince. Such iſſue had the firſt attempts of the *Calvinians* in the Realm of *France*.

10. In the mean time it was determined by the Cabinet Council in the Court, to ſmother the indignity of theſe inſurrections, that the hot ſpirits of the *French* might have time to cool, and afterwards to call them to a ſober reckoning, when they leaſt looked for it. In order whereunto, an Edict is publiſhed in the Kings name, and ſent to all the Parliamentary Courts of *France* (being at that time eight in all) concerning the holding of an Aſſembly at *Fountainbleau* on the 21 of *Auguſt* then next following, for compoſing the diſtractions of the Kingdom. And in that Edict he declares, that without any evident occaſion, a great number of perſons had riſen and taken Arms againſt him ; that he could not but impute the cauſe thereof to the *Hugonots* onely, who having laid aſide all belief to God, and all affections to their Country, endeavoured to diſturb the peace of the Kingdom ; that he was willing, notwithſtanding, to pardon all ſuch, as having made acknowledgement of their errours, ſhould return to their Houſes, and live conformable to the Rites of the Catholick Church, and in obedience to the Laws ; that therefore none of his Courts of Parliament ſhould proceed in matters of Religion, upon any manner of

infor-

information for offences past, but to provide by all severity for the future against their commiting of the like : and finally, that for reforming all abuses in Government, he resolved upon the calling of an Assembly, in which the Princes and most eminent Persons of the Kingdom should consult together: the said Assembly to be held at his Majesties Palace of *Fountain-bleau* on the twenty first of *August* then next following, and free leave to be therein granted to all manner of persons, not onely to propound their grievances, but to advise on some expedient for redress thereof. According unto which appointment the Assembly holds, but neither the King of *Navar* nor the Prince of *Conde* could be perswaded to be present, being both bent, as it appeared not long after. on some further projects. But it was ordered, that the Admiral *Collignie*, and his brother *D Andelot* should attend the service, to the end that nothing should be there concluded without their privity, or to the prejudice of their cause. And that they might the better strike a terrour into the Heart of the King, whom they conceived to have been frighted to the calling of the present Assembly, the Admiral tenders a Petition in behalf of those of the reformed Religion in the Dukedom of *Normandy*, which they were ready to subscribe with one hundred and fifty thousand hands, if it were required. To which the Cardinal of *Lorrain* as bravely answered, that if 150000 seditious could be found in *France* to subscribe that paper, he doubted not but that there were a million of Loyal Subjects, who would be ready to encounter them, and oppose their insolencies

11. In this Assembly it was ordered by the common consent, that for rectifying of abuses amongst the Clergy, a meeting should be held of Divines and Prelates, in which those discords might be remedied, without innovating or disputing in matters of Faith ; and that for setling the affairs of the Kingdom, an Assembly of the three Estates should be held at *Orleance*, in the beginning of *October* ; to which all persons interested were required to come. All which the *Hugonots* imputed to the consternation which they had brought upon the Court by their former risings, and the great fear which was conceived of some new insurrections, if all things were not regulated and reformed according unto their desires. Which misconceit so wrought upon the principal Leaders, that they resolved to make use of the present fears, by seizing on such Towns and places of consequence, as might enable them to defend both themselves and their parties, against all opponents. And to that end it was concluded, that the King of *Navar* should seize upon all places in his way betwixt *Bearn* and *Orleance* ; that the City of *Paris* should be seized on by the help of the Marshal of *Montmorency* the Dukes Eldest Son, who was Governour of it ; that they should assure themselves of *Picardy* by the Lords of *Tenepont* and *Bouchavanne*, and of *Britain* by the Duke of *Estampes*, who was powerful in it ; that being thus fortified, well armed, and better accompanied by the *Hugonots*, whom they might presume of, they should force the Assembly of the Estates to depose the Queen, remove the *Guises* from the Government, declare the King to be in his minority till he came to twenty two years of age, appoint the King of *Na-*

var, the Conſtable, and the Prince of *Conde*, for his Tutors and Governours: which practice as it was confeſsed by *Jaques de la Sague*, one of the Servants of the King of *Navar*, who had been intercepted in his journey to him ; ſo the confeſſion was confirmed by ſome Letters from the Viſdame of *Chartres* which he had about him. But this diſcovery being kept ſecret, the *Hugonots* having taken courage from the firſt conſpiracy at *Amboiſe*, and the open profeſſion of the Admiral, began to raiſe ſome new commotions in all parts of the Kingdom ; and laying aſide all obedience and reſpect of duty, not onely made open reſiſtance againſt the Magiſtrates, but had directly taken arms in many places, and practiſed to get into their hands ſome principal Towns, to which they might retire in all times of danger: Amongſt which none was more aimed at then the City of *Lyons*, a City of great Wealth and Trading, and where great numbers of the people were inclined to *Calvins* Doctrine, by reaſon of their neer Neighbourhood to *Geneva*, and the Proteſtant Cantons. Upon this Town the Prince of *Conde* had a plot, and was like to have carried it, though in the end it fell out contrary to his expectation ; which forced him to withdraw himſelf to *Bearn*, there to provide for the ſecurity of himſelf and his Brother.

12. But the King of *Navar*, not being ſo deeply intereſted in theſe late deſigns, in which his name had been made uſe of half againſt his will, could not ſo much diſtruſt himſelf and his perſonal ſafety, as not to put himſelf into a readineſs for his journey to *Orleance*. To which he could by no means perſwade the Prince, and was by him much laboured not to go in perſon, till they were certified that the King was ſending Forces to fetch them thence ; which could not be without the waſting of the Country, and the betraying of themſelves unto thoſe ſuſpitions which otherwiſe they might hope to clear. No ſooner were they come to *Orleance*, but the Prince was arreſted of high Treaſon, committed cloſe Priſoner with a Guard upon him, the cognizance of his cauſe appointed unto certain Delegates, his Proceſs formed, and ſentence of death pronounced againſt him ; which queſtionleſs had been executed both on him and the King of *Navar*, who was then alſo under a Guard, if the death of the young King had not intervened on the fifth of *December*, which put the Court into new Counſels, and preſerved their lives. For the Queen wiſely took into conſideration, that if theſe two Princes were deſtroyed, there could be no fit counterpoiſe for the Houſe of *Guiſe* ; which poſſibly might thereby be tempted to revive the old pretenſions of the Houſe of *Lorrain*, as the direct Heirs of *Charles* the *Great*. For which they could not have a better opportunity, then they had at the preſent ; the Eldeſt of her three Sons not exceeding ten years of age, none of them of a vigorous conſtitution, and therefore the more likely to want Friends in their greateſt need. Upon theſe apprehenſions ſhe ſends ſecretly for the King of *Navar*, and came at laſt to this agreement, *viz.* that during the Minority of her ſon King *Charles* the Ninth the Queen-mother ſhould be declared Regent, and the King of *Navar* Lord Lieutenant of *France* ; all ſupplications from the Provinces to be made to the Lord-Lieutenant ; but all Ambaſſadors and Letters

of

of Negotiation from forein Princes to be presented to the Queen; that the Prince of *Conde*, the Visdame of *Chartres*, with all other Prisoners of their party to be set at liberty, and the sentences of their condemnations to be so declared null and void ; that the Queen-Regent should make use of her power and interest with the Catholick King, for restoring to the King of *Navar* the entire possession of that Kingdom, or at the least the Kingdom of *Sardinia*, as a recompence for it. And at last it was also yielded, though long first, and published by the Edict of the 28 of *January*, *That the Magistrates should be ordered to release all Prisoners committed for matters of Religion, and to stop any manner of Inquisition appointed for that purpose against any Person whatsoever ; that they should not suffer any disputation in matters of Faith, nor permit particular Persons to revile one another with the Names of* Heretick *and* Papist ; *but that all should live together in peace, Abstaining from unlawful Assemblies, or to raise Scandals or Sedition.*

13. By this Edict the Doctrines of *Calvin* were first countenanced in the Realm of *France*, under the pretence of hindring the effusion of more Christian blood: which carryed an appearance of much Christianity, though in plain truth it was to be ascribed to the Queens Ambition, who could devise no other way to preserve her Greatness, and counterbalance the Authority of the House of *Guise*. But the *Hugonots* not being content with a bare connivance, resolved to drive it on to a Toleration ; and to drive it on in such a manner, and by such means only by which they had extorted (as they thought) these first concessions. For thinking the Queen-Regent not to be in a condition to deny them any thing, much less to call them into question for their future Actings, they presently fell upon the open exercise of their own Religion, and every where exceedingly increased both in power and numbers. In confidence whereof, by publick Assemblies, insolent Speeches, and other acts the like unpleasing, they incurred the hatred and disdain of the Catholick party ; which put all places into tumult, and filled all the Provinces of the Kingdom with seditious rumours : so that contrary to the intention of those that governed, and contrary to the common opinion, the remedy applyed to maintain the State and preserve peace and concord in the Kings Minority, fell out to be dangerous and destructive, and upon the matter occasioned all those dissentions which they hoped by so much care to have prevented. For as the Cardinal informed the Council, the *Hugonots* were grown by this connivance to so great a height, that the Priests were not suffered to celebrate their daily Sacrifices, or to make use of their own Pulpits ; that the Magistrates were no longer obeyed in their jurisdictions ; and that all places raged with discords, burnings and slaughters, through the peevishness and presumption of those, who assumed to themselves a liberty of teaching and believing whatsoever they listed. Upon which points he so enlarged himself with his wonted eloquence, that neither the King of *Navar* nor any other of that party could make any reply. And the Queen-Mother also being silent in it, it was unanimously voted by the Lords of the Council, that all the Officers of the Crown should assemble at the Parliament of *Paris* on

the

the thirteenth of *July*, there to debate in the Kings prefence of all thefe particulars, and to refolve upon fuch remedies as were neceffary for the future. At which time it was by general confent exprefly ordered, upon complaint made of the infurrection of the *Hugonots* in fo many places, that all the Minifters fhould forthwith be expelled the Kingdom; that no manner of perfon fhould from thenceforth ufe any other Rites or Ceremonies in Religion, that were not held and taught by the Church of *Rome*; and that all Affemblies of men armed or unarmed fhould be interdicted, except it were of Catholicks in Catholick Churches, for Divine performances according to the ufual Cuftom.

14. The Admiral and the Prince of *Conde* finding themfelves unable to crofs this Edict, refolved upon another courfe to advance their party, and to that end encouraged the *Calvinian* Minifters to petition for a Difputation in the Kings prefence, to be held between them and the Adverfaries of their Religion. Which Difputation being propounded, was oppofed by the Cardinal of *Tournon*, upon a juft confideration of thofe inconveniencies which might follow on it; the rather, in regard of the General Council then convened at *Trent*, where they might fafely both propofe and difpute their Opinions. But on the other fide the Cardinal of *Lorrain*, being willing to imbrace the occafion for making a general Mufter of his own Abilities, his fubtilty in Divinity, and his Art of fpeaking, prevailed fo far upon the reft, that the fuit was granted, and a Conference thereupon appointed to be held at *Poyffie*, on the tenth day of *Auguft* 1561. At which time there affembled for the Catholick party, the Cardinals of *Tournon*, *Lorrain*, *Bourbon*, *Armagnac* and *Guife*, with many Bifhops and Prelates of greateft eminency, fome Doctors of the *Sorbon*, and many great Divines from the Univerfities. The Difputants authorized for the other fide were of like efteem amongft thofe of their own party and perfwafions; as namely, *Theodore Beza*, *Peter Martyr*, *Francis de St. Paul*, *John Raimond*, and *John Vizelle*, with many other Minifters from *Geneva*, *Germany*, and others of the Neighbouring Countries. But the refult of all was this, as commonly it happeneth on the like occafions, that both parties challenged to themfelves the Victory in it, and both indeed were victors in fome refpects. For the King of *Navar* appeared much unfatisfied by noting the differences of the Minifters amongft themfelves, fome of them adhering to the *Auguftane*, and others to the *Helvetian* Confeffion, in fome points of Doctrine; which made him afterwards more cordial to the intereft of the Church of *Rome*, notwithftanding all the arguments and infinuations ufed by his Wife, a moft zealous *Hugonot*, to withdraw him from it. But the *Hugonots* gave out on the other fide, that they had made good their Doctrines, convinced the Catholick Doctors, confounded the Cardinal of *Lorrain*, and gotten Licenfe from the King to Preach. Which gave fuch courage to the reft of that Faction, that they began of their own Authority to affemble themfelves in fuch places as they thought moft convenient, and their Minifters to preach in publick, and their Preachings followed and frequented by fuch infinite multitudes, as well of the Nobility as the common People, that it was thought impoffible to

suppress, and dangerous to disturb their Meetings. For so it was, that if either the Magistrates molested them in their Congregations, or the Catholicks attempted to drive them out of their Temples, without respect to any Authority they put themselves into Arms; and in the middle of a full Peace, was made a shew of a most terrible and destructive War.

15. This being observed by those which sate at the Helme, and finding that these tempests were occasioned by the Edict of *July*, it was resolved to steer their course by another wind. For the Queen being setled in this Maxime of State, That she was not to suffer one Faction to destroy the other, for fear she should remain a prey to the Victor, not onely gave order for conventing all the Parliaments to a Common-Council, but earnestly sollicited for a Pacification; which gave beginning to the famous Edict of *January*, whereby it was granted that the *Hugonots* should have the Free exercise of their Religion; that they might assemble to hearing of Sermons in any open place without their Cities, but on condition that they went unarmed, and that the Officers of the place were there also present. Which Edict so offended the chief Heads of the Catholick party, that a strict combination and confederacy was concluded on between the King of *Navar*, the Constable, and the Duke of *Guise*, for maintenance of the Religion of the Church of *Rome*. And this reduced the Queen-Regent to the like necessity of making a strict union with the Admiral and the Prince of *Conde*, whereby she was assured of the power of the *Hugonots*, and they became as confident of her Protection. In which condition they were able to form their Churches, to cast them into Provinces, Classes, and other subdivisions of a less capacity; to settle in them their Presbyteries and Synodical Meetings, grounded according to their Rules of *Calvins* Platform, in Doctrine, Discipline and Worship. The Forms whereof being described at large in the former book, may there be found without the trouble of a repetition. In so much that it was certified to the Fathers in the Council of *Trent*, that the *French Hugonots* were at that time distributed into two thousand one hundred and fifty Churches, each of them furnished with their proper and peculiar Preachers, according to a just computation which was taken of them: which computation was then made, to satisfie the Queen-Regent in the strength of that party, for which she could not otherwise declare her self, unless she were first made acquainted with their power and numbers. But being satisfied in those points, she began to shew her self much inclined to *Calvinism*, gave ear unto the Discourses of the Ministers in her private Chamber, conferred familiarly with the Prince, the Admiral, and many others in matters which concerned their Churches; and finally, so disguised her self, that the Pope was not able to discover at what port she aimed. For sometimes she would write unto him for such a Council as by the *Calvinians* was desired, at other times for a national one to be held in *France*; sometimes desiring that the Communion might be administred under both kinds, otherwhile requiring a Dispensation for Priests to Marry; now solliciting that Divine Service might be said in the vulgar tongue, then proposing such other like things as were wished and

preach-

preached for by the *Hugonots*. By which diffimulations fhe amufed the World, but gave withal fo many notable advantages to the reformation, that next to God fhe was the principal promoter and advancer of it ; though this profperity proved the caufe of thofe many miferies which afterwards enfued upon it.

16. For by this means the Preachers having free accefs into the Court, became exceeding y refpected in the City of *Paris*, where in fhort time their followers did increafe to fo great a multitude, as put the Prince of *Conde* into fuch a confidence, that he affumed unto himfelf the managery of all great affairs : Which courfe fo vifibly tended to the diminution of the King of *Navar*, that he refolved by ftrong hand to remove him from *Paris*. And to that end, directed both his Meffages and his Letters to the Duke of *Guife*, to come in to help him. The Duke was then at *Joinville* in the Province of *Champaigne*, and happened in his way upon a Village called *Vaffey*, where the *Hugonots* were affembled in great numbers to hear a Sermon. A fcuffle unhappily is begun between fome of the Dukes Footmen, and not a few of the more unadvifed and adventurous *Hugonots* : which the Duke coming to part, was hit with a blow of a ftone upon one of his Cheeks, which forced him with the lofs of fome blood to retire again. Provoked with which indignity, his followers, being two Companies of Lances, charge in upon them with their Fire-locks, kill fixty of them in the place, and force the reft for prefervation of their lives into feveral houfes. This accident is by the *Hugonots* given out to be a matter of defign ; the execution done upon thofe fixty perfons, muft be called a Maffacre ; and in revenge thereof the Kingdom fhall be filled with Blood and Rapine, Altars and Images defaced, Monafteries ruined and pulled down, and Churches bruitifhly polluted. The Queen had fo long juggled between both parties, that now it was not fafe for her to declare for either. Upon which ground fhe removed the Court to *Fountain-bleau*, and left them to play their own Games, as the Dice fhould run : The prefence of the King was looked upon as a matter of great importance, and either party laboured to get him into their power. The City of *Orleance* more efpecially was aimed at by the Prince of *Conde*, as lying in the heart of the Kingdom, rich, large and populous, fufficiently inclined to novelty and innovations ; and therefore thought the fitteft Stage for his future Actings. Being thus refolved, he firft fends *D'Andelot* with fome Forces to poffefs the Town, and pofts himfelf towards *Fountain-Bleau* with three thoufand Horfe. But the Catholick Confederates had been there before him, and brought the King off fafely to his City of *Paris* : which being fignified to the Prince as he was on his way, he diverts towards *Orleance*, and came thither in a luckie hour to relieve his friends : which having feized upon one of the Gates, and thereby got poffeffion of that part of the City, was in apparent danger to be utterly broken by the Catholick party, if the Prince had not come fo opportunely to renew the fight : but by his coming they prevailed, made themfelves Mafters of the City, and handfelled their new Government with the fpoil of all the Churches and Religious Houfes, which either they defaced, or laid wafte and defolate. Amongft which none was ufed more courfely then the Church of

of St. *Crosse*, being the Cathedral of that City; not so much out of a dislike to all Cathedrals (though that had been sufficient to expose it unto Spoil and Rapine) as out of hatred to the name. Upon which furious piece of Zeal, they afterwards destroyed all the little Crosses which they found in the way between *Mont Martyr* and St. *Denis*, first raised in memory of *Denis* the first Bishop of *Paris*, and one that passeth in account for the chief Apostle of the *Gallick* Nations.

17. But to proceed: to put some fair colour upon this foul action, a *Manifest* is writ and published; in which the Prince and his adherents signifie to all whom it might concern, that they had taken arms for no other reason, but to restore the King and Queen to their personal liberty, kept Prisoners by the power and practice of the Catholick Lords; that obedience might be rendred in all places to his Majesties Edicts, which by the violence of some men had been infringed; and therefore that they were willing to lay down Arms, if the Constable, the Duke of *Guise*, and the Marshall of St. *Andrewes* should retire from *Paris*, leaving the King and Queen to their own disposing; and that liberty of Religion might be equally tolerated and maintained unto all alike. These false Colours were wiped off by a like Remonstrance made by the Parliament of *Paris*: In which it was declared amongst other things, that the *Hugonots* had first broke those Edicts by going armed to their Assemblies, and without an Officer: That they had no pretence to excuse themselves from the crime of Rebellion, considering they had openly seized on many Towns, raised Souldiers, assumed the Munition of the Kingdom, cast many pieces of Ordnance and Artillery, assumed unto themselves the Coyning of Mony; and in a word, that they have wasted a great part of the publick Revenues, robbed all the rich Churches within their power, and destroyed the rest, to the dishonour of God, the scandal of Religion, and the impoverishing of the Realm. The like answer was made also by the Constable and the Duke of *Guise* in their own behalf, declaring in the same, that they were willing to retire, and put themselves into voluntary exile, upon condition that the Arms taken up against the King might be quite laid down, the places kept against him delivered up, the Churches which were ruined restored again, the Catholick Religion honourably preserved, and an intire obedience rendred to the lawful King, under the Government of the King of *Navar*, and the Regency of the Queen his Mother. Nor were the King and Queen wanting to make up the breach, by publishing that they were free from all restraint, and that the Catholick Lords had but done their duty in waiting on them into *Paris*; that since the Catholick Lords were willing to retire from Court, the Prince of *Conde* had no reason to remain at that distance; that therefore he and his adherents ought to put themselves, together with the places which they had possessed, into the obedience of the King; which if they did, they should not only have their several and respective Pardons for all matters past, but be from thenceforth looked upon as his Loyal Subjects, without the least diminution of State or Honour.

18. These Paper pellets being thus spent, both sides prepare
more

more furiously to charge each other. But first the Prince of *Conde*, by the aid of the *Hugonots*, makes himself Master of the great Towns and Cities of chief importance; such as were *Rouen*, the Parliamentary City of the Dukedom of *Normandy*; the Ports of *Diepe* and *New-haven*; the Cities of *Angiers*, *Towres*, *Bloife*, *Vendofme*, *Bourges* and *Puictiers*; which laft were reckoned for the greateft of all the Kingdom, except *Rouen* and *Paris*; after which followed the rich City of *Lyons*, with that of *Valence* in the Province of *Daulphiny*, together with almoft all the ftrong places in *Gafcoigne* and *Languedock*, Provinces in a manner wholly *Hugonot*, except *Tholcufe*, *Bourdeaux*, and perhaps fome others. But becaufe neither the Contributions which came in from the *Hugonots*, though they were very large, nor the fpoil and pillage of thofe Cities which they took by force, were of themfelves fufficient to maintain the War; the Prince of *Conde* caufed all the Gold and Silver in the Churches to be brought unto him, which he coyned into Mony. They made provifion of all manner of Artillery and Ammunition which they took from moft of the Towns, and laid up in *Orleance*, turning the Covent of *Francifcans* into a Magazine, and there difpofing all their ftores with great art and induftry. The Catholicks on the other fide drew their Forces together, confifting of 4000 Horfe and fix thoufand Foot, moft of them old experienced Souldiers, and trained up in the War againft *Charles* the Fifth. The Prince had raifed an Army of an equal number, that is to fay, three thoufand Horfe, and feven thoufand Foot; but, for the moft part, raw and young Souldiers, and fuch as fcarcely knew how to ftand to their Arms: And yet with thefe weak forces he was grown fo high, that nothing would content him but the banifhment of the Conftable, the Cardinal of *Lorrain*, and the Duke of *Guife*; free liberty for the *Hugonots* to meet together for the Exercife of their Religion in walled Towns; Cities and Churches to be publickly appointed for them; the holding of the Towns which he was prefently poffeffed of as their abfolute Lord, till the King were out of his Minority, which was to laft till he came to the age of two and twenty. He required alfo that the Popes Legate fhould be prefently commanded to leave the Kingdom: that the *Hugonots* fhould be capable of all Honours and Offices: and finally, that fecurity fhould be given by the Emperour, the Catholick King, the Queen of *England*, the State of *Venice*, the Duke of *Savoy*, and the Republick of the *Switzers*, by which they were to ftand obliged, that neither the Conftable nor the Duke of *Guife* fhould return into *France*, till the King was come unto the age before remembred.

19. Thefe violent demands fo incenfed all thofe which had the Government of the State, that the Prince and his Adherents were proclaimed Traytors, and as fuch to be profecuted in a courfe of Law, if they laid not down their Arms by a day appointed. Which did as little benefit them, as the propofals of the Prince had pleafed the others. For thereupon the *Hugonots* united themfelves more ftrictly into a confederacy to deliver the King, the Queen, the Kingdom, from the violence of their oppofers, to ftand to one another in the defence of the Edicts, and altogether to fubmit to the Authority of the Prince of *Conde*,

as the head of their Union : publiſhing a tedious Declaration with their wonted confidence, touching the motives which induced them to this Combination. This more eſtranged the Queen from them then ſhe was at firſt ; and now ſhe is reſolved to break them by ſome means or other, but rather to attempt it by Wit then by Force of Arms : And to this end ſhe deals ſo dexterouſly with the Conſtable and the Duke of *Guiſe*, that ſhe prevailed with them to leave the Court, and to prefer the common ſafety of their Countrey before their own particular and perſonal greatneſs : which being ſignified by Letters to the Prince of *Conde*, he frankly offered under his hand, that whenſoever theſe great Adverſaries of his were retired from the Court (which he conceived a matter of impoſſibility to perſwade them to) he would not onely lay down Arms, but quit the Kingdom. But underſtanding that the Conſtable and the Duke had really withdrawn themſelves to their Countrey-houſes, deveſted of all power both in Court and Council, he ſtood confounded at the unadviſedneſs and precipitation of ſo raſh a promiſe as he had made unto the Queen. For it appeared diſhonourable to him not to keep his word, more dangerous to relinquiſh his command in the Army, but moſt deſtructive to himſelf and his party to diſſolve their Forces, and put himſelf into a voluntary exile, not knowing whither to retreat. At which dead lift he is refreſhed by ſome of his *Calvinian* Preachers with a cordial comfort. By which learned Caſuiſts it was reſolved for good Divinity, that the Prince having undertaken the maintenance of thoſe who had imbraced the purity of Religion, and made himſelf by Oath Protector of the Word of God, no following obligation could be of force to make him violate the firſt. In which determining of the caſe, they ſeemed to have been guided by that Note in the Engliſh Bibles, Tranſlated and Printed at *Geneva*, where in the Margine to the ſecond Chapter of Saint *Matthews* Goſpel, it is thus advertiſed : *viz. That promiſe ought not to be kept, when Gods honour and the Preaching of the Truth is hindred ; or elſe it ought not to be broken.* They added, to make ſure work of it (at the leaſt they thought ſo) that the Queen had broken a former promiſe to the Prince, in not bringing the King over to his party, as ſhe once aſſured him ; and therefore that he was not bound to keep faith with her, who had broke her own.

20. But this Divinity did not ſeem ſufficient to preſerve his honour ; another temperament was found by ſome wiſer heads, by which he might both keep his promiſe, and not leave his Army. By whoſe advice it was reſolved, that he ſhould put himſelf into the power of the Queen, who was come within ſix Miles of him with a ſmall retinue, onely of purpoſe to receive him ; that having done his duty to her, he ſhould expreſs his readineſs to forſake the Kingdom, as ſoon as ſome Accord was ſettled ; and that the Admiral *D'Andelot*, and ſome other of the principal Leaders, ſhould on the ſudden ſhew themſelves, forcibly mount him on his Horſe, and bring him back into the Army. Which Lay-device, whether it had more cunning or leſs honeſty then that of the Cabal of Divines, it is hard to ſay : But ſure it is, that it was put in execution accordingly ; the Queen thereby deluded, and all the hopes of Peace and Accommodation made void and fruſtrate.

But

But then a greater difficulty seized upon them. The King had re-inforced his Army by the accession of ten Cornets of *German* Horse, and six thousand *Switz*. The Princes Army rather diminished then increased, and which was worse, he wanted Mony to maintain those Forces which he had about him ; so that being neither able to keep the Field for want of men, nor keep his men together for want of Mony, it was resolved that he must keep his men upon free-quarter in such Towns and Cities, as followed the Fortune of his side, till he was seconded by some strength from *England*, or their Friends in *Germany*. The Queen of *England* had been dealt with ; but she resolved not to engage on their behalf, except the Port of *Havre de-grace*, together with the Town of *Diepe* were put into her hands, and that she might have leave to put a Garrison of English into *Rouen* it self. Which Proposition seemed no other to most knowing men, then in effect to put into her power the whole Dukedom of *Normandy*, by giving her possession of the principal City, and hanging at her Girdle the two Keys of her Province, by which she might enter when she pleased with all the rest of her Forces. But then the Ministers being advised with, who in all publick Consultations were of great Authority, especially when they related unto Cases of Conscience ; it was by them declared for sound Doctrine, That no consideration was to be had of worldly things, when the maintenance of Cœlestial Truths, and the propagation of the Gospel was brought in question ; and therefore that all other things were to be contemned, in reference to the establishment of true Religion, and the freedom of Conscience. According to which notable determination, the Seneschal of *Rouen*, and the young Visdame of *Chartres* are dispatched to *England* ; with whom it was accorded by the Queens Commissioners, that the Queen should presently supply the Prince and his Confederates with Monies, Arms and Ammunition ; that she should aid him with an Army of eight thousand Foot, to be maintained at her own pay, for defence of *Normandy*; and that for her security, in the way of caution, the Town of *New-haven*, (which the French call *Havre-de-grace*, as is before said) should be forthwith put into her hands, under a Governour or Commander of the *English* Nation ; that she should place a Garrison of two thousand *English* in the City of *Rouen*, and a proportionable number in the Town of *Diepe* ; but the chief Governours of each to be natural *French*. Which Covenants were accordingly performed on both sides, to the dishonour of the *French*, and the great damage and reproach of the Realm of *England*, as it after proved. For so it was, that the Prince of *Conde* being forced to disperse his Souldiers, and to dispose of them in such manner as before was noted, the King being Master of the Field, carryed the war from Town to Town, and from place to place ; and in that course he speeds so well, as to take in the Cities of *Angiers*, *Tours*, *Bloise*, *Poictiers*, and *Bourges*, with divers others of less note ; some of which were surrendred upon composition, some taken by assault, and exposed to spoil. And now all passages being cleared, and all rubs removed, they were upon the point of laying Siege to the City of *Orleance*, when at the Queens earnest sollicitation, they changed that purpose for the more profitable expedition to the King and Kingdome. *Norman-*
dy

dy was in no small danger of being wilfully betrayed into the hands of the *English*, who therefore were to be removed, or at the least to be expulsed out of *Rouen* before the Kings Army was consumed in Actions of inferiour consequence. The issue of which War was this, That though the *English* did brave service for defence of the City, and made many gallant attempts for relief thereof by their men and shipping from *New-haven*; yet in the end the Town was taken by assault, and for two days together made a prey to the Souldiers. The joy of the Royalists for the reduction of this great City to the Kings obedience, was much abated by the death of the King of *Navar*, who had unfortunately received his deaths wound in the heat of the Seige, and dyed in the forty fourth year of his age, leaving behind him a young Son called *Henry*, who afterward succeeded in the Crown of *France*. And on the contrary, the sorrow for this double loss was much diminished in the Prince of *Conde* and the rest of his party, by the seasonable coming of four thousand Horse and five thousand Foot, which *Monsieur d'Andelot* with great industry had raised in *Germany*, and with as great courage and good fortune had conducted safely to the Prince.

22. By the accession of these Forces, the *Hugonots* are incouraged to attempt the surprizing of *Paris*; from which they were disswaded by the Admiral, but eagerly inflamed to that undertaking by the continual importunity of such Preachers as they had about them. Repulsed from which with loss both of time and honour they were encountred in a set battel near the City of *Dreux*, in the neighbouring Province of *Le Beausse*. In which battel their whole Army was overthrown, and the Prince of *Conde* taken prisoner; but his captivity sweetned by the like misfortune which befel the Constable, took prisoner in the same battel by the hands of the Admiral; who having drawn together the remainder of his broken Army, retires towards *Orleance*, and leaving there his Brother *D Andelot* with the Foot to make good that City, takes with him all the *German* Horse, and so goes for *Normandy*, there to receive such Monies as were sent from *England*. But the monies not coming at the time, by reason of cross winds and tempestuous weather, the *Germans* are permitted to spoil and plunder in all the parts of the Country, not sparing places either Profane or Sacred, and reckoning no distinction either betwixt Friends or Enemies. But in short time the Seas grew passable, and the Monies came (an hundred and fifty thousand Crowns according to the French) together with fourteen pieces of Canon, and a proportionable stock of Ammunition; by which supply the *Germans* were not onely well paid for spoiling the Country, but the Admiral was thereby inabled to do some good service, from which he had been hindred for want of Canon. In the mean time the Duke of *Guise* had laid Siege to *Orleance*, and had reduced it in a manner to terms of yeilding, where he was villanously murdred by one *Poltrot*, a Gentleman of a good Family and a ready Wit; who having lived many years in *Spain*, and afterwards imbracing the *Calvinian* Doctrines, grew into great esteem with *Beza* and the rest of the Consistorians, by whom it was thought fit to execute any great Attempt. By whom commended to the Admiral, and by the Admiral excited to a

work

work of so much merit, he puts himself without much scruple on the undertaking ; entreth on the Kings service, and by degrees became well known unto the Duke. Into whose favour he so far insinuated, that he could have access to him whensoever he pleased ; and having gained a fit opportunity to effect his purpose, dispatched him by the shot of a Musket laden with no fewer then three bullets, in the way to his lodging.

23. This murder was committed on *Feb.* 24. *an.* 1562. and being put to the Rack, he on the Rack confessed upon what incentives he had done the fact. But more particularly he averred, that by the Admirall he was promised great rewards, and that he was assured by *Beza*, that by taking out of the world such a great persecutor of the Gospel, he could not but exceedingly merit at the hands of Almighty God. And though both *Beza* and the Admiral endeavoured by their Manifests and Declarations to wipe off this stain ; yet the confession of the murtherer, who could have no other ends in it then to speak his conscience, left most men better satisfied in it, then by both their writings. But as it is an ill wind which blows no body good, so the Assassinate of this great person, though very grievous to his friends, served for an Introduction to the peace ensuing. For he being taken out of the way, the Admiral engaged in *Normandy*, the Constable Prisoner in the City, and the Prince of *Conde* in the Camp: it was no hard matter for the Queen to conclude a peace upon such terms, as might be equal to all parties. By which accord it was concluded, that all that were free Barons in the Lands and Castles which they were possessed of, or held them of no other Lord then the King himself, might freely exercise the Reformed Religion in their own jurisdictions ; and that the other which had not such Dominions might doe the same in their own Houses and Families only, provided that they did not the same in Towns and Cities: that in every Province certain Cities should be assigned, in the Suburbs whereof the *Augonots* might have the free exercise of their Religion : that in the City of *Paris*, and in all other Towns and places whatsoever, where the Court resided, no other Religion should be exercised but the Roman Catholick : though in those Cities every man might privately enjoy his conscience without molestation : that those of the Reformed Religion should observe the Holy Days appointed in the Roman Kalendar, and in their Marriages the Rites and Constitutions of the Civil Law ; and finally, that a general pardon should be granted to all manner of persons, with a full restitution to their Lands and Liberties, their Honours, Offices and Estates. Which moderation or restriction of the Edict of *January*, did much displease some zealous *Hugonots*, but their Preachers most ; who as they loved to exercise their gifts in the greatest Auditories, so they abominated nothing more then those observances.

1563.   24. After this followed the reduction of *New-haven* to the Crown of *France*, and the expulsion of the *English* out of *Normandy* ; the Prince of *Conde*, and some other leading men of the *Hugonot* faction, contributing both their presence and assistance to it ; which had not been so easily done, had not God fought more against the *English*, then the whole *French* Armies : for by cross winds it did not only hinder all
supplyes

supplyes from coming to them, till the surrendry of the Town ; but haſtened the ſurrender by a grievous Peſtilence, which had extreamly waſted them in reſpect of number, and miſerably dejected them in point of courage.   And yet the anger of God did not ſtay here nei-ther, that Plague being carried into *England* at the return of the Soldi-ers, which raged extreamly both in *London* and moſt parts of the Realm, beyond the precedent and example of former ages.   It was on the 17 of *July, an.* 1563, that *New-haven* was yielded to the *French*, that be-ing the laſt day of the firſt war which was raiſed by the *Hugonots*, and raiſed by them on no other ground, but for extorting the free exerciſe of their Religion by force of Arms, according to the doctrine and example of the Mother-City.   In the purſuit whereof, they did not only with their own hands ruinate and deface the beauty of their na-tive Country, but gave it over for a prey to the luſt of Strangers. The calling in of the *Engliſh* to ſupport their faction, whom they knew well to be the antient enemies of the Crown of *France*, and putting into their hands the chief ſtrength of *Normandy*, of whoſe pre-tenſions to that Dukedom they could not be ignorant ; were two ſuch actions of a diſloyal impolitick nature, as no pretence of zeal to that which they called the Goſpel, could either qualifie or excuſe.   Nor was the bringing in of ſo many thouſand *German* Souldiers of much better condition, who though they could pretend no title to the Crown of *France*, nor to any particular Province in it, were otherwiſe more deſtructive to the peace of that Country, and created far more miſ-chief to the people of it, then all the forces of the *Engliſh* ; for being to be maintained on the pay of the *Hugonots*, and the *Hugonots* not be-ing able to ſatisfie their exorbitant Arrears, they were ſuffered to waſte the Country in all parts where they came, and to expoſe the whole Kingdom, from the very borders of it toward *Germany*, to the *Engliſh* Chanell, unto ſpoyle and rapine ; ſo that between the *Hugo-nots* themſelves on the one ſide, and theſe *German* Souldiers on the o-ther, there was nothing to be ſeen in moſt parts of the Kingdom, but the deſtruction of Churches the profanation of Altars, the defacing of Images, the demoliſhing of Monaſteries, the burning of Religious Hou-ſes, and even the digging up of the bones of the dead, deſpitefully thrown about the fields and unhallowed places.

25. But this firſt fire was only raked up in the Embers, not ſo ex-tinguiſhed by the Articles of the late agreement, but that it broke out ſhortly into open flames ; for the *Hugonots* preſſing hard for the perfor-mance of the Edict of *January*, and the *Romaniſts* as earneſtly inſiſting on ſome clauſes of the pacification ; the whole Realm was filled in a man-ner with ſuch fears and jealouſies, as carryed ſome reſemblance of a War in the midſt of Peace.   The *Hugonots* had ſome thoughts of ſur-priſing *Lyons*, but the Plot miſcarryed ; they practiſed alſo upon *Nar-bunne*, a chief City of *Languedock*, and openly attempted the Popes Town of *Avignion* ; but were prevented in the one, and ſuppreſſed in the other.   A greater diffidence was raiſed againſt them by the unſeaſonable Zeal of the Queen of *Navar*, who not content with ſetling the reformed Religion in the Country of *Berne*, when ſhe was abſolute and ſupreme, ſuffered the Catholicks to be infeſted in her own

1566.

Pro-

Provinces which she held immediately of the Crown ; insomuch that at *Pamiers* the chief City of the Earldom of *Foix*, the *Hugonots* taking offence at a solemn Procession held upon *Corpus Christi* day, betook themselves presently to Arms ; and falling upon those whom they found unarmed, not onely made a great slaughter amongst the Church-men but in the heat of the same fury burnt down their Houses. Which outrage being suffered to pass unpunished, gave both encouragement and example to some furious Zealots to commit the like in other places, as namely at *Montaban*, *Calion*, *Lodez*, *Preieux*, *Valence*, *&c.* being all scituate in those Provinces in which the *Hugonots* were predominant for power and number. But that which most alarmed the Court, was a seditious Pamphlet, published by a Native of *Orleance* ; in which it was maintained (according to the *Calvinian* Doctrines) that the people of *France* were absolved from their Allegiance to the King then Reigning, because he was turned an Idolater. In which reason it is lawfull also to kill him, as opportunity should be offered. Which Doctrine being very agreeable unto some designs which were then every where in agitation amongst the *Hugonots*, was afterward made use of for the justifying of the following Wars, when the opinion grew more general, and more openly maintained both from Press and Pulpit.

1567.

26. The Catholicks on the other side began to put themselves into a posture of Arms, without so much as taking notice of misdemeanors ; which they seemed willing to connive at, not so much out of any inclinations which they had in themselves, but because they found it not agreeable to the will of the Court, where such dissimulation, were esteemed the best arts of Government. The Catholick King had sent the Duke of *Alva* with a puissant Army, to reduce the Low Countries to obedience, where the *Calvinians* had committed as great spoils and rapines as any where in *France* or *Scotland*. This Army being to pass in a long march near the Borders of *France*, gave a just colour to the King to arm himself ; for fear lest otherwise the *Spaniards* might forget their errand, and fall with all their Forces into his Dominions. To this end he gives order for a Levy of six thousand *Switz*, which he caused to be conducted through the heart of the Kingdom, and quartered them in the Isle. of *France*, as if they were to serve to a Guard for *Paris*, far enough off from any of those parts and Provinces by which the *Spaniards* were to pass. But this gave a jealousie to the heads of the *Hugonots*, that they resorted to *Chastillion* to consult with the Admiral. By whose advice it was resolved, that they must get the King and Queen into their power, and make use of both their names, as the Catholicks had made of them in the former War. This to be done upon the sudden, before the opening of the war, by the raising of Forces, should render the surprize impossible, and defeat their purposes. The King and Queen lay then at *Manceux*, an House of pleasure within the Territory of *Brye* in *Champaigne*, not fearing any the least danger in a time of peace, and having the *Switz* near enough to secure their persons against any secret Machinations. And thereupon it was contrived, that as many Horse as they could raise in several places, and suspecting nothing less then the present danger, might very easily be routed ; and that being done, they should possess themselves of

Paris,

Paris, and from thence issue out all Mandates which concerned the Government both of Church and State. Some *Hugonots* which afterwards were took in *Gascoyne*, and by the Marshal of *Monluck* were exposed to torture; are said to have confessed upon the Rack, that it was really intended to kill the King, together with the Queen and the two yung Princes; and having so cut off the whole Royal Line, to set th Crown upon the head of the Prince of *Conde*. But Charity and Christianity bids me think the contrary, and to esteem of this report as a Popish calumny, devised of purpose to create the greater hatred against t e Authors of those Wars.

27. But whether it were true or not, certain it is, that the design was carried with such care and closeness, that the Qu en had hardly time enough to retire to *Meux*, a little Town twelve Leagues from *Paris*, before the whole Body of the *Hugonots* appeared in sight; from whence they were with no less difficulty conducted by the *Switz* (whom they had suddenly drawn together) to the Walls of *Paris*; the *Switz* being charged upon the way by no fewer then eleven hundred Horse, and *D'Andelot* in the head of one of the parties; but gallantly making good their March, and serving to the King and the Royal Family for a Tower or Fortress. No sooner were they come to *Paris*, but the *Hugonots* take a resolution to Besiege the City before the Kings Forces could assemble to relieve the same. To which end they possessed themselves of all the passes upon the River by which provisions came into it, and burned down all the Wind-mills about the Town, which otherwise might serve for the grinding of such Corn as was then within it. No better way could be devised to break this blow, then to entertain them with a Parley for an accommodation, not without giving them some hope of yeilding unto any conditions which could be reasonably required. But the *Hugonots* were so exorbitant in their demands, that nothing would content them, but the removing of the Queen from publick Government; the present disbanding of the Kings Forces, the sending of all strangers out of the Kingdom; a punctual execution of the Kings Edict of *January*; liberty for their Ministers to Preach in all places, even in *Paris* it self; and finally, that *Calice*, *Metz*, and *Havre-de-grace* might be consigned unto them for Towns of caution; but in plain truth, to serve them for the bringing in of the *English* and *Germans* when their occasi n so required. The Treaty notwithstanding was continued by the Queen with great dexterity, till the King had drawn together sixteen thousand men, with whom the Constable gives Battel to the Enemy on the 10 of *November*, compels t em to dislodge, makes himself master of the Field, but dyed the next day after, in the eightieth year of his age, having received his deaths wound from the hands of a *Switz*, who most unmanfully shot him when he was not in condition to make any resistance.

28. In the mean time the City of *Orleance* was surprised by the *Hugonots*, with many places of great importance in most parts of the Realm; which serving rather to distract then increase their Forces, they were necessitated to seek out for some Forain aid. Not having confidence enough to apply themselves to the Queen of *England*, whom in the business of *New-haven* they had so betrayed, they send their Agents to sollicite   1568.

licite the Elector *Palatine*, and prevailed with him for an army of seven thousand Horse, and four thousand foot, to which the miserable Country is again exposed. Encouraged with which great supplies, they laid Siege to *Chartres*, the principal City of *La Beaue*, the loss whereof must of necessity have subjected the *Parisians* to the last extremities. The chief Commanders in the Kings army were exceeding earnest to have given them battel, thereby to force them from the Siege. But the Queen not willing to venture the whole State of the Kingdom upon one cast of the Dice, especially against such desperate Gamesters who had nothing to lose but that which they carried in their hands, so plyed them with new Offers for occommodation, that her conditions were accepted, and the *Germans* once again disbanded, and sent back to their Country. During which broyls, the Town of *Rochel* strongly scituated on a bay of the Ocean, had declared for the *Hugonots*, and as it seems had gone so far, that they had left themselves no way to retreat. And therefore when most other places had submitted to the late Accord, the *Rochellers* were resolved to stand it out, and neither to admit a Garrison, nor to submit to any Governour of the Kings appointment; in which rebellious obstinacy they continued about sixty years, the Town being worthily esteemed for the safest sanctuary, to which the *Hugonots* retired in all times of danger, and most commodious for the letting in of a forain army, when they found any ready to befriend them in that cause and quarrel. The standing out of which Town in such obstinate manner, not only encouraged many others to doe the like, but by the fame thereof drew thither both the Admiral and the Prince of *Conde*, with many other Gentlemen of the *Hugonot* Faction, there to consult about renewing of the war which they were resolved on. To whom repaired the Queen of *Navar* with the Prince her Son, then being but fifteen years of age, whom she desired to train up in that holy war, upon an hope that he might one day come to be head of that party, as he after was. And here being met, they publish from hence two several *Manifests*; one in the name of all the *Hugonots* in general, the other in the name of that Queen alone; both tending to the same effect, that is to say, the putting of some specious colour upon their defection, and to excuse the breaking of the peace established, by the necessity of a War.

29. This rapture so incensed the King and his Council, that they resolved no longer to make use of such gentle medicines as had been formerly applyed in the like distempers; which resolution was the parent of that terrible Edict by which the King doth first revoke all the former Edicts which had been made during his minority in favour of the Reformed Religion; nullifying more particularly the last capitulations, made only in the way of *Provision* to redress those mischiefs for which no other course could be then resolved on. And that being done, it was ordained and commanded, ' That the exercise of any other Re-
' ligion then the Roman Catholick (ever observed by him and the King
' his predecessors) should be prohibited, and expresly forbidden, and
' interdicted in all places of the Kingdom; banished all the *Calvinist*
' Ministers and Preachers out of all the Towns and places under his

Domi-

' Dominion, and within fifteen days upon pain of death to avoid the
' Realm : pardoned through special grace all things past in matters of
' Religion, but requiring for the future under pain of death a gene-
' ral Conformity to the Rites of the Catholick Church : and finally
' ordained that no person should be admitted to any office, charge, dig-
' nity, or magistracy whatever, if he did not profess and live confor-
' mable in all points to the Roman Religion.   And for a Preamble
hereunto the King was pleased to make a long and distinct Narration
of the indulgence he had used to reduce the *Hugonots* to a right understanding, and of the ill requital they had made unto him, by the seditions and conspiracies which they raised against him, their bringing in of
forein forces, and amongst others the most mortal enemies of the *French*
Nation, putting into their hands the strongest places and most flourishing parts of the Kingdom, to the contempt of his authority, the despi-
sing of his grace and goodness, and the continual disquieting of his Dominions, and the destruction of his subjects.   To counter poise which
terrible Edict, the Princes and other Leaders of the *Hugonots* which
were then at *Rochel*, entred into a solemn Covenant or Association, by
which they bound themselves by Oath to persevere till death in defence
of their Religion, never to lay down arms, or condescend to any a-
greement without the general consent of all the Commanders ; and
not then neither, but upon sufficient security for the preservation of
their lives, and the enjoying of that Liberty of Conscience for which
they first began the war.

30. But the Admiral well knowing that the business was not to
be carried by Oaths and Manifests, and that they wanted mony to proceed by arms, advised the *Rochellers* to send their Navy to the sea, which
in a time when no such danger was expected, might spoyle and pillage
all they met with, and by that means provide themselves of mony, and
all other necessaries to maintain the war.   Which Counsel took such
good effect, that by this kind of Piracy they were enabled to give a
fair beginning to this new Rebellion ; for the continuance whereof, it
was thought necessary to sollicite their Friends in *Germany*, to furnish
them with fresh recruits of able men, and Queen *Elizabeth* of *England*,
for such sums of money as might maintain them in the service.   And
in the first of these designs there appears no difficulty ; the inclination
of the Prince Elector, together with the rest of the *Calvinian* Princes,
and Imperial Cities, were easily intreated to assist their Brethren of the
same Religion.   And the same spirit governed many of the people also,
but on different grounds ; they undertaking the imployment upon hope
of spoil, as Mercenaries, serving for their Pay, but more for Plunder.   In *England* their desires were entertained with less alacrity, though
eagerly sollicited by *Odet* Bishop of *Beauvais*, a younger Brother of the
Admiral ; who having formerly been raised to the degree of a Cardinal, therefore called most commonly the Cardinal of *Chastilion*, had
some years since renounced his Habit and Religion, but still kept his
Titles.   By the continual sollicitation of so great an Advocate, and
the effectual interposing of the Queen of *Navar*, *Elizabeth* was perswaded to forget their former ingratitude, and to remember how
conducible it was to her personal interest to keep the French
                                                            King

King exercifed in perpetual troubles; upon which Reafon of State fhe
is not onely drawn to accommodate the *Hugonots* with Ships, Corn,
Arms and Ammunition, but to fupply them with a hundred thoufand
Crowns of ready mony for the maintaining of their Army, confifting of
fourteen thoufand *Germans*, and almoft as many more of the natural
French. And yet it was to be believed, that in all this fhe had done
nothing contrary to the League with *France*, which fhe had fworn not
long before; becaufe, forfooth, the Forces of the *Hugonots* were raifed to no other end but the Kings mere fervice, and the affiftance of the
Crown againft the Enemies of both, and the profeffed Adverfaries of
the true Religion. But neither this great lone of mony, nor that which
they had got by robbing upon the Seas, was able to maintain a
War of fo long continuance. For maintainance whereof, they were
refolved to fell the Treafures of the Churches in all fuch Provinces as they kept under their Command; the Queen of *Navar* ingaging her Eftate for their fecurity, who fhould adventure on the pur-
chafe.

31. I fhall not touch on the particulars of this War, which ended
with the death of the Prince of *Conde* in the battel of *Jarnar*; the rigorous proceedings againft the Admiral, whom the King caufed to be
condemned for a Rebel, his Lands to be confifcated, his Houfes plundred and pulled down, and himfelf executed *in Effigie*; the lofs of the
famous battel of *Mont-Contour* by the *Hugonots* party *Anno* 1569, which
forced them to abandon all their ftrong holds, except *Rochel*, *Angou-
lefme*, and St. *Jean d'Angeli*, and finally to fhut themfelves up within
Rochel only: after which followed fuch a diffembled reconciliation between the parties, as proved more bloudy then the War: The fudden
and fufpected death of the Queen of *Navar*, the Marriage of the
Prince her Son with the Lady *Margaret* one of the Sifters of the King,
the celebrating of the wedding in the death of the Admiral on St. *Bar-*
1572. *tholomews* day 1572, and the flaughter of thirty thoufand men within
few days after; the reduction of the whole Kingdom to the Kings o-
bedience, except the Cities of *Nifmes*, *Montauban* and *Rochel* onely; the
obftinate ftanding out of *Rochel*, upon the inftigation of fuch Preachers
as fled thither for fhelter, and the reduction of it by the Duke of *Anjou* to the laft extremity; the raifing of the Siege, and the Peace enfuing, on the Election of that Duke to the Crown of *Poland*; the refolution of the *Hugonots* to renew the War, as foon as he had left the
Kingdom; and their ingaging in the fame, on the Kings laft ficknefs.
In all which traverfes of State there is nothing memorable in reference
to my prefent purpofe, but only the condition of the Pacification which
was made at the Siege of *Rochel*; by which it was accorded between
1573. the parties on the 11 of *July*, *Anno* 1573, that all offences fhould be
pardoned to the faid three Cities, on their fubmiffion to the King; and
that it fhould be lawful for them to retain the free Exercife of their
Religion, the people meeting in the fame unarmed, and but few in
number; that all the inhabitants of the faid three Cities fhould
be obliged to obferve, in all outward matters (except Baptifm and
Matrimony) the Rites and Holy-dayes of the Church; that the ufe of
the Catholick Religion fhould be reftored in the faid Cities and all
other

other places, leaving unto the Clergy and Religious persons their Houses, Profits, and Revenues ; that *Rochel* should receive a Governour of the Kings appointment, (but without Garrison) renounce all correspondencies and confederacies with Forain Princes, and not take part with any of the same Religion against the King ; and finally, that the said three Towns should deliver Hostages for the performance of the Articles of the present Agreement, to be changed at the end of every three months, if the King so pleased : It was also condescended to in favour of particular persons, that all Lords of free Mannors throughout the Kingdoms, might in their own Houses lawfully celebrate Marriage and Baptism, after their own manner, provided that the Assembly exceeded not the number of ten ; and that there should be no inquisition upon mens Consciences, Liberty being given to such as had no mind to abide in the Kingdom, that they might sell their Lands and Goods, and live where they pleased.

32. Such were the actings of the *French Calvinians*, as well by secret   1574. practices as open Arms, during the troublesome Reign of *Francis* the Second and *Charles* the Ninth, and such their variable Fortunes according to the interchanges and successes of those broken times, in which for fifteen years together, there was nothing to be heard but Warrs and rumours of Wars ; short intervals of Peace, but such as generally were so full of fears and jealousies, that they were altogether as unsafe as the Wars themselves. So that the greatest calm of Peace, seemed but a preparation to a War ensuing ; to which each party was so bent, that of a poyson it became their most constant food. In which distraction of affairs dyed King *Charles*, the Ninth, in the five and twentieth year of his age, and fourteenth of his Reign, leaving this life at *Paris* on the 30 of *May*, 1574. He had been used for some months to the spitting of bloud, which brought him first into a Feaver, and at last to his grave, not without some retaliation of the Heavenly Justice, in punishing that Prince by vomiting up the bloud of his body natural, which had with such prodigious cruelty exhausted so much of the best bloud of the body Politick. After whose death, the Crown descended upon *Henry* the new King of *Poland*, who presently upon the news thereof forsook that Kingdom, and posted with all speed to *Venice*, and from thence to *France*, where he was joyfully received by all Loyal Subjects. At his first coming to the Crown, he resolved to put an end to those combustions which had so often inflamed his Kingdom, and extinguish all those hearts which had exasperated one party against another ; that he might sit as Umpire or Supreme Moderator of the present differences, and draw unto himself an absolute Soveraignty over both alike : which to effect, he resolves to prosecute the War so coldly, that the *Hugonots* might conceive good hopes of his moderation ; but still to keep the War on foot, till he could find out such a way to bring on the peace, as might create no suspition of him in the hearts of the Catholicks. By which means hoping to indulge both parties, he was perfectly believed by none, each party shewing it self distrustful of his inclinations, and each resolving to depend on some other Heads.

33. About this time, when all men stood amazed at these proceedings

ings of the Court, the State began to swarm with Libels and Seditious Pamphlets, published by those of the *Hugonot* Faction, full of reproach, and fraught with horrible Invectives, not only against the present Government, but more particularly against the persons of the Queen and all her Children.　Against the Authors whereof, when some of the Council purposed to proceed with all severity, the Queen-mother interposed her power, and moderated by her prudence the intended rigors ; affirming, as most true it was, that such severity would only gain the greater credit to those scurrilous Pamphlets, which would otherwise vanish of themselves, or be soon forgotten.　Amongst which Pamphlets, there was none more pestilent then that which was composed in the way of a Dialogue, pretending one *Eusebius Philadelphus* for the Author of it. *Buchanan* building first upon *Calvins* Principles had published his Seditious Pamphlet *De jure Regni apud Scotos*, together with that scurrilous and infamous Libel which he called *The Detection*, repleat with nothing but reproaches of his lawful Soveraign.　But this *Eusebius Philadelphus*, or whosoever he was that masked himself under that disguise, resolved to go beyond his patern in all the acts of Malice, Slandering, and Sedition ; but be out-gone by none that should follow after him in those ways of wickedness.　Two other Tracts were published about this time also, both of them being alike mischievous, and tending to the overthrow of all publick Government ; but wanting something of the Libel in them as the other had : Of these the one was called *Vindiciæ contra Tyrannos*, or the rescuing of the people from the power of Tyrants ; published under the Name of *Stephanus Brutus*, but generally believed to be writ by *Beza*, the chief surviving Patron of the *Presbyterians*. In which he prostitutes the dignity of the Supreme Magistrate to the lusts of the people, and brings them under the command of such *popular* Magistrates, as *Calvin* makes to be the Conservators of the publick Liberty.　The other was intituled *De jure Magistratus in subditos*, built on the same grounds, and published with the same intention as the others were.　A piece so mischievous in it self, and so destructive of the peace of Humane Society, that each side was ashamed to own it ; the Papists fathering it upon *Hottoman* a *French Civilian*, the Presbyterians on *Hiclerus* a Romish Priest. But it appears plainly by the Conference at *Hampton-Court*, that it was published by some of the *Disciplinarians*, at whose doors I leave it.

34. But for *Eusebius Philadelphus*, he first defames the King and Queen in a most scandalous manner, exposes next that flourishing Kingdom for a prey to strangers ; and finally lays down such Seditious Maxims, as plainly tend to the destruction of Monarchical Government.　He tells us of the King himself, that he was trained up by his Tutors in no other qualities then drinking, whoring, swearing, and forswearing, frauds and falsehoods, and whatsoever else might argue a contempt both of God and Godliness ; that as the Court by the Example of the King, so by the Example of the Court all the rest of the Kingdom was brought into a reprobate sense, even to manifest Atheism ; and that as some of their former Kings were honoured with the Attributes of *fair, wise, debonnaire, well-beloved*, &c so should this King be known by no other name then *Charles the Treacherous*.　The Duke of *Anjou* he

sets

ſets forth in more ugly colours then he doth the King, by adding this to all the reſt of his Brothers vices, that he lived in a conſtant courſe of *Inceſt* with his Siſter the Princeſs *Magaret*, as well before as after her Eſpouſal to the King of *Navar*.　For the Queen-mother he can find no better names then thoſe of *Fredegond*, *Brunechild*, *Jezabel*, and *Meſſaline*; of which the two firſt are as infamous in the ſtories of *France*, as the two later in the Roman and Sacred Hiſtories.　And to expoſe them all together, he can give the Queen-mother and her children (though his natural Princes) no more cleanly Title then that of a *Bitch-Wolfe and her Whelps*; affirming, that in Luxury, Cruelty and Perfidiouſneſs, they had exceeded all the Tyrants of preceding times (*a*): which comes up cloſe to thoſe irreverent and lewd expreſſions which frequently occur in *Calvin*, *Beza*, *Knox*, &c. in reference to the two *Mary*s, Queens of *England* and *Scotland*, and other Princes of that age; which have been formerly recited in their proper places.

Lupa illa cum catulis ſuis part 1.p.87.
(*a*) Part 1. pag. 11.

35. The Royal Family being thus wretchedly expoſed to the publick hatred, he next applyes himſelf to ſtir up all the World againſt them both at home and abroad.　And firſt he laboureth to excite ſome deſperate Zealot to commit the like aſſaſſinate on the King then Reigning, as one *Bodillus* is reported in ſome *French* Hiſtories to have committed on the perſon of *Chilprick* one of the laſt Kings of the *Merovignians*, which he commemarates for a Noble and Heroick action, and ſets it out for an example and encouragement to ſome gallant French-men for the delivery of his Countrey from the Tyranny of the Houſe of *Valois*, (*b*) the ruine whereof he mainly drives at in his whole deſign.　And though he ſeem to make no doubt of prevailing in it, yet he reſolves to try his Fortune otherwiſe if that ſhould fail.　And firſt beginning with their next neighbour the King of *Spain*, he puts them in remembrance of thoſe many injuries which he and his Anceſtors had received from the Houſe of *Valois*; acquaints him with the preſent opportunity which was offered to him of revenging of thoſe wrongs, and making himſelf Maſter of the Realm of *France*; and chalks him out a way how he might effect it; that is to ſay, by coming to a preſent Accord with the Prince of *Orange*, (*c*) indulging liberty of conſcience to the *Belgick* Provinces, and thereby drawing all the *Hugonots* to adhere unto him: which counſel if he did not like, he might then make the ſame uſe of the Duke of *Savoy* (for whom the *Hugonots* in *France* had no ſmall affection;)* and by beſtowing on him the adjoyning Regions of *Lyonoiſe*, *Daulphine*, and *Provence*, might make himſelf Lord of all the reſt without any great trouble.　The like temptation muſt be given to the Queen of *England*, by putting her in mind of her pretences to the Crown it ſelf, and ſhewing how eaſie a thing it might be for her (*d*) to acquire thoſe Countries, whoſe Arms and Titles ſhe aſſumed.　With like diſloyalty he excites the Princes of the Empire (*e*) to husband the advantage which was offered to them, for the recovering of *Metz*, *Toule* and *Verdun*, three Imperial Cities, by this Kings Father wreſted betwixt fraud and force from *Charles* the Fifth, and ever ſince incorporated with the Realm of *France*.　If all which failed, he is reſolved to caſt himſelf on the Duke of *Guiſe*, though the moſt mortal and implacable enemy of the *Hugonot* Faction; and makes a full addreſs to him in a ſecond Epiſtle prefixt before the Book it ſelf; in

(*b*) *Qui domum* Valeſium *tunditus deleant,ſi ſemel furor exardeſcet.* p.75.
(*c*) *Non ſolum illos* Belgiam *pacatam redituros, ſed ante annum* Franciam ipſam *(hodie a regis amicitiæ alienatam) illius imperio adjuncturos*,p.68
* *Vt ulli cedant* Lugduneſis tractus, Delphinatus, & Provincia *ſinitimæ Regionis*, &c. p 69.
(*d*) *Facile poterit eas* Regiones recipere *quarum nomina & ſtemmata geſtat.* p. 71.
(*e*) *Facile recuperare poſſit* Metas, Viriodarum & Tullum, &c. p. 71.

in which he put him in remembrance of his old pretensions to the Crown of *France*, extorted by *Hugh Capet* from his Ancestors of the House of *Loraigne*; offereth him the assistance of the *Hugonot* party for the recovery of his Rights; and finally, beseeches him to take compassion of his ruined Countrey (f), cheerfully to accept the Crown, and free the Kingdom from the spoil and tyranny of Boys and Women, together with that infinite train of Strangers, Bawdes and Leachers which depend on them: which was as great a Master-piece in the art of mischief, as the wit of malice could devise.

(f) *Regnum capessere velis a Tyranno mulierculis, Italos, ganeonibus, & lenonibus dilapidatum.* Præf.

36. As for his Doctrines in reference to the common duties between Kings and Subjects, we may reduce them to these heads, that is to say; 1. That the Authority of Kings and Supreme Magistrates is circumscribed and limited by certain bounds, which if they pass, their Subjects are no longer tyed unto their obedience; that Magistrates do exceed those bounds, when either they command such things as God forbiddeth, or prohibit that which he commands; that therefore they are no longer to be obeyed, if their Commands are contrary to the Rules of Piety or Christian charity; of which the Subjects must be thought the most competent Judges. 2. That there were companies and societies of men before any Magistrates were set over them; which Magistrates were no otherwise set over them then by common consent; that every Magistrate so appointed was bound by certain Articles and Conditions agreed between them, which he was tyed by Oath to preserve inviolable; that the chief end for which the people chose a Superiour Magistrate, was, that they might remain in safety under his protection; and therefore if such Magistrates either did neglect that end, or otherwise infringe the Articles of their first Agreement, the Subjects were then discharged from the bond of obedience; and that being so discharged from the bond of obedience, it was as lawful for them to take up Arms against their King in maintenance of their Religion, Laws and Liberties, if indangered by him, as for a Traveller to defend himself by force of Arms against Thieves and Robbers. 3. That no Government can be rightly constituted, in which the Grandeur of the Prince is more consulted then the weal of the People; that to prevent all such incroachments on the common Liberty, the people did reserve a power of putting a curb upon their Prince or Supreme Magistrates, to hold them in, such as the *Tribunes* were in *Rome* to the Senate and Consuls, and the *Ephori* to the Kings of *Sparta*: that such a power as that of the *Spartan Ephori* is vested in the seven Electors of the *German* Empire, which gives them an Authority to depose the Emperour, if they see cause for it; and that the like may be affirmed of the English Parliaments, who oftentimes have condemned their Kings, but he knows not whom. 4. That by the first constitutions of the Realm of *France*, the Supreme power was not entrusted to the King; but the three Estates; so that it was not lawful for the King to proclaim a War, or to lay Taxes on the People, but by their consent; that these Estates assembled in a Common Counsel, did serve instead of eyes and ears to a prudent Prince, but to a wicked and ungoverned, for Bit or Bridle; and that according to this power they Dethroned many of their Kings for their Lusts, Luxuries, Cruelty, Slothfulness, Avarice, &c, that if they proceeded not in like manner with the

the King then Reigning, it was because they had an high esteem (with scorn and insolence enough) of his eminent Vertues, his Piety, Justice and Fidelity, and the great commendations which was given of his Mothers Chastity: and therefore finally (which was the matter to be proved by those Factious Principles) that it was altogether as lawful for the *French* to defend themselves, their Laws and Liberties, against the violent assault of a furious Tyrant (so he calls their King) as a Traveller by Thieves and Robbers. Which Aphorisms he that listeth to consult in the Author, may find them from Pag. 57. to 66. of the second Dialogue, and Part 1. Pag. 8.

37. But notwithstanding these indignities and provocations, the King resolved to proceed in his former indifferency, hoping thereby to break the *Hugonots* without blows and bloodshed, and thereby to regain the good opinion of his Popish Subjects.   To which end he was pleased to grant such Priviledges to the *Hugonot* Faction as they durst not ask, and never had aspired unto in their greatest heats; which he conceived he had more reason to do in the present pinch, then any of his Predecessors had in far less extremities: For the *Hugonots* had not onely brought in a formidable Army of *Switz* and *Germans*, under the conduct of Prince *Casimir*, one of the younger Sons of *Frederick* the Third then Elector *Palatine*, but had also made a fraction in the Court it self, by drawing *Francis* Duke of *Alanzon* his youngest Brother to be Head of their Party, who brought along with him a great number of Romish Chatholicks, who then past under the name of the *Male-contents*.   To break which blow, and free his Kingdom from the danger of so great an Army, he first capitulates to pay the *Germans* their Arrears, amounting to a Million and two hundred thousand Ducats; to gratifie Prince *Casimir* with the Signory of *Chasteau Thierry* in the Province of *Champaigne*, with a Pension of fourteen thousand Crowns, and a Command of a hundred Lances: To confer the Government of *Picardie* with the strong Town of *Perrone* on the Prince of *Conde*, and settle on his Brother the Duke of *Alanzon* the Provinces of *Berry*, *Touraine* and *Anjou*, together with one hundred thousand Crowns of yearly Pension; and made him also Duke of *Anjou* for his greater honour.   And then to pacifie and oblige the *Hugonots* (if such men could be gained or pacified by acts of favour) he grants unto them by his Edict of the 14 of *May* 1576, that they should peaceably enjoy the exercise of their Religion, together with full power for erecting Colleges and Schools, for holding Synods, of celebrating Matrimony, and administring the Sacraments, with the same freedom as was used by his Catholick Subjects: that those of the Reformed Religion should be permitted to execute any Places or Offices, and enjoy any Dignities of what sort soever, without such distinction betwixt them and the rest of that Nation, as had been of late times observed: that in each Parliament of *France* a new Court should be presently erected, consisting equally of Judges and Officers of both Religions, and they to have the cognizance of all causes which concerned the *Hugonots*: that all Sentences past against the Admiral, the Count of *Montgomery*, and the rest of that party, should be revoked and made null; and the eight cautionary Towns, being all places of great strength and consequence, should remain with the *Hugonots*, till all these Articles were confirmed, and the Peace concluded.   38. The

38. The paffing of this Edict gave great fcandal to the Catholick party, which thereupon was eafily united by the Duke of *Guife* into a common Bond or League for maintainance and defence of their Religion, apparently indangered by thofe large Indulgences; by the firft Article whereof they bound themfelves for the Eftablifhment of the Law of God in its firft Eftate; to reftore and fettle his Holy Service, according to the Form and Manner of the Catholick Apoftolick Roman Church; and to abjure and renounce all errors contrary thereunto. Then followed many other Articles, relating to the prefervation of the Kings Authority, the maintainance of the common liberties and Priviledges of their Countrey; the mutual defence of one another in defence of this League againft all perfons whatfoever; the conftancy of their obedience to any one whom they fhould chufe to be the Head of their Confederacy; and finally, the profecuting of all thofe without exception, who fhould endeavour to oppofe and infringe the fame. And for the keeping of this League, they feverally and joyntly bound themfelves by this following Oath, viz. *I fwear by God the Creator (laying my hand upon the Holy Gofpel) and under pain of Excommunication and eternal Damnation, that I enter into this Holy Catholick League according to the Form thereof now read unto me; and that I do faithfully and fincerely enter into it with a will either to command or to obey, and ferve as I fhall be appointed: And I promife upon my life and honour unto the laft drop of my blood never to depart from it, or tranfgrefs it, for any command, pretence, excufe or occafion, which by any means whatfoever can be reprefented to me.* And as the *Hugonots* had put themfelves under the Protection of the Queen of *England*, and called the *Germans* to their aid; fo they refolved according unto this example to put themfelves under the Patronage of the Catholick King, and to call in the Forces of the King, Pope, and the Princes of *Italy*, if their occafions fo required. The news of which confederacy fo amazed the King, that he proceeded not to the performance of thofe Indulgences contained in the Edict of the 14 of *May*, which feemed moft odious and offenfive in the eyes of the Catholicks; fo that both fides being thus exafperated againft one another, and each fide jealous of the King, the old confufions were revived, the diforders multiplyed, and all things brought into a worfe condition then at his firft coming to the Crown. For though the Catholick King had willingly confented to be head of the League, yet to break off all fuch dependance as was by that means to be faftned on him by the reft of the Leaguers, the *French* King finds himfelf neceffitated to affume that honour to himfelf. And thereupon, in the Affembly held at *Blois*, having in vain tryed many ways to untie this knot, he publickly declared himfelf to be the Principal Head and Protector of it, with many fpecious proteftations, that he would fpend his laft breath in a caufe fo glorious, as the reducing of his people unto one Religion: which as it raifed many jealoufies in the minds of the *Hugonots*, fo it begot no confidence of him in the hearts of their oppofites.

39. Hereupon a new War breaks out, and a new Peace followeth, by which fome Claufes in the former Edict were reftrained and moderated, though otherwife fufficiently advantageous to all thofe of the Reformation; fo as now hoping that all matters were accorded between the parties, the King pretends to betake himfelf wholly to his private

Devo-

Devotions ; falls on the Inftitution of a new Order of Knighthood, called, *The Order of the Holy Ghoft* ; commends his Brother for a Suiter to the Queen of *England*, to keep him out of harmes way for the time to come ; and finally, failing of the project, procureth his advancement to the Dukedom of *Brabant*, and to be made the General-Governour of the *Belgick* Provinces, which had withdrawn themfelves from their Obedience to the King of *Spain*.

40. But in the midft of thefe devices, the Leaders of the *Hugonots* are again in Arms, under colour that the former Edict had not been obferved ; but in plain truth upon a clear and manifeft experience, that Peace was the ruine of their Party, and that they could not otherwife preferve their power then by open War. The Prince of *Conde* feizeth on *La Fere* in *Picardy*, and the King of *Navar* makes himfelf Mafter by ftrong hand on the City of *Cahors* ; which draws the King again from his Meditations, under which muft be covered his retirement from all publick bufinefs. But *La Fere* being regained from the Prince of *Conde*, the facking of *Cahors* was connived at, and the breach made up, that fo the *Hugonots* might be tempted to confume their Forces in the Wars of *Flanders*, to which they were invited by their Brethren of the *Belgick* Provinces, who had called in the Duke of *Anjou* againft their King. And fo long *France* remained in quiet, as that War continued. But when the Duke returned after two or three years, and that there was no hopes of his reverting to fo great a charge ; the *Hugonots* wanting work abroad, were furnifhed with this occafion to break out at home. The Catholick League had now layn dormant for fome years, none feeming more Zealous then the King in the Caufe of *Rome*. But when it was confidered by the Duke of *Guife*, and the reft of the League, that the Duke of *Anjou* being dead, and the King without any hope of Iffue, the Crown muft fall at laft to the King of *Navar* ; it was refolved to try all means by which he might be totally excluded from the right of Succeffion. For what hope could they give themfelves to preferve Religion, when the Crown fhould fall upon the head of an Heretick, an Heretick relapfed, and therefore made uncapable of the Royal Dignity by the Canon-Laws ? Of thefe Difcourfes and Defignes of the *Guifian* Faction, the King of *Navar* takes fpeedy notice, and prepares accordingly, thinking it beft to be beforehand, and not to be taken unprovided when they fhould come. And to that end, having firft cleared himfelf by a Declaration from the crime of Herefie, and now particularly from being a relapfed Heretick, with many foul recriminations on the Houfe of *Guife*, he fends his Agents to follicite the *German* Princes to come in to aid him againft the oppreffions of the League, which feemed to aim at nothing but the ruine of the Realm of *France* : which fo exafperated thofe of the *Guifian* Faction, that they prevailed by their Emiffaries with Pope *Sixtus* the Fifth, to excommunicate the King of *Navar*, and the Prince of *Conde*, and to declare them both uncapable of the Royal Succeffion, as relapfed Hereticks : Which he performed in open Confiftory on the ninth of *September* 1585. and publifhed the fentence by a fpecial Bull within three days after.

41. The *French* King in the mean time findes himfelf fo intangled in the

1581.

1584.

1585.

the Snares of the League, and such a general defection from him in most parts of the Kingdom, that he was forced by his Edict of the ninth of *July*, to revoke all former grants and capitulations which had been made in favour of the *Hugonot* party. After which followed a new War; in which the *Switz* and *Germans* raise great Levies for the aid of the *Hugonots*, sollicited thereunto amongst many others by *Theodore Beza*; who by his great eloquence and extraordinary diligence, did prevail so far, that the Princes *Palatine*, the Count *Wirtemberge*, the Count of *Monthelguard*, and the Protestant Cantons of the *Switz*, agreed to give them their assistance. Amongst whom, with the helps which they received from the King of *Denmark*, and the Duke of *Saxony*, a mighty Army was advanced, consisting of thirty two thousand Horse and Foot, that is to say, twelve thousand *German* Horse, four thousand foot, and no fewer then sixteen thousand *Switz*. For whose advance, besides a general contribution made on all the Churches of *France*, the sum of sixty thousand Crowns was levyed by the Queen of *England*, and put into the hands of Prince *Casimire* before remembred, who was to have the chief command of these forein Force. These forein Forces made much greater by the accession of eight thousand *French* which joyned unto them, when they first shewed themselves upon the Borders; Of which, 200 Horse and 800 foot were raised by the Signory of *Geneva*. But before this vast Army could come up to the King of *Navar*, the Duke of *Joyeuse* gives him battel near a place called *Coutrasse*; at which time his whole Forces were reduced to four thousand Foot, and about two thousand five hundred Horse; with which small Army encountred a great power of the Duke of *Joyeuse*, and obtained a very signal Victory, there being slain upon the place no fewer then 3000 men, of which the Duke of *Joyeuse* himself was one; more then 3000 taken prisoners, together with all the Baggage, Arms and Ammunition which belonged to the Enemy. After which followed the defeat of the *Germans* by the Duke of *Guise*, and the violent proceedings of the Leaguers against the King, which brought him to a necessity of joyning with the King of *Navar*, and craving the assistance of his *Hugonot* Subjects, whose Arms are now legitimated, and made acts of duty. In which condition I shall leave them to their better Fortunes; first taking a survey of the proceedings of the *Calvinists* in the neighbouring *Germany*, passing from thence to the *Low Countries*, and after crossing over to the Isles of *Britain*.

The end of the Second Book.

AERIUS REDIVIVUS:

OR THE

HISTORY

OF THE

Presbyterians.

LIB. III.

Containing

Their Positions and Proceedings in the Higher Germany: their dangerous Doctrines and Seditions ; their Innovations in the Church and alteration of the Civil Government ; of the Belgick Provinces, from the year 1559, to the year 1585.

He Doctrine of the Reformation begun by *Luther*, and pursued by *Zuinglius*, was entertained in many Provinces of the Higher *Germany*, according as they stood affected to either party, or were transported by the ends and passions of their several Princes: But generally at the first they inclined to *Luther*, whose way of Reformation seemed less odious to the Church of *Rome*, and had the greatest approbation from the States of the Empire ; the Duke of *Saxony*, adhered unto him at his first beginning, as also did the Marquess of *Brandenbourg*, the Dukes of *Holsteine*, the two Northern Kings, and by degrees the rest of the *German* Princes of most power and value,

1.

lue,

lue, except only those of *Austria*, and the Duke of *Bavaria*, the three Elector Bishops, the Duke of *Cleve*, the Marquess of *Baden*, and generally all the Ecclesiasticks which were not under the Command of the *Lutheran* States. The Prince Elector *Palatine* came not in to the party till the year 1546. At which time *Frederick* the Second, though scarce warm in his own Estate, on which he entred *Anno* 1544, took the advantage of the time to reform his Churches ; the Emperour being then brought low by the change of Fortune, and forced not long after to abandon *Germany*. Upon the 10th. of *January* he caused Divine Offices to be celebrated in the Mother tongue, in the chief Church of *Heidelberg*, the principal City of the lower *Palatinate*, and the chief Seat of his Residence. The news whereof encouraged all the rest of the Protestant Princes to congratulate with him, and to desire him to embrace the Confession of *Ausberge* ; to which he readily accorded, and setled all things in his Countries by the *Lutheran* Model, as well for Government and Doctrine, as for Forms of Worship. In which condition it continued during the residue of his life, and the short Government of *Otho-Henry*, who succeeded him in those Estates, and was the last of the direct Line of the House of *Bavaria*. After whose death, *Anno* 1559, succeeded *Frederick* Duke of *Simmerin*, descended from *Steven Palatine* of *Zuidbrook* or *Bipont*, younger son of the Emperour *Rupert* : From whom the Princes of the other House had delivered their Pedigree. Which Prince succeeding by the name of *Frederick* the III. appeared more favourable to the *Zuinglian* then the *Lutheran* Forms, animated thereunto by some needy Courtiers, in hope to make a prey of Glebe and Tythes, and other poor remainders of the Churches Patrimony.

1546.

1556.

1559.

2. For the advancing of this Work *Gualter* a very moderate and learned man is desired from *Zurick*, and cheerfully undertakes the Service ; in which he prospered so well, that he took off most of the Princes from their former opinions, and brought them to conform their judgements in all points of Doctrine to the Confession of the *Switzer* or *Helvetian* Churches. The Discipline of which Churches differed at that time from *Calvins* Platform, as appears clearly by some passages in a Letter of *Bullingers*, bearing date *Decemb.* 13. 1553, when *Calvin* was necessitated to beg some tolerable approbation of his new Device. For there it is expresly said, that though (a) their Discipline at *Zurick*, and the rest of the Cantons, agreed not in all points with that of the Consistory which had been setled at *Geneva*, but was accommodated to the temper of their own Dominions ; yet they desired not the subversion of *Calvins* Model, which seemed so necessary at that time for the Town of *Geneva*, that they advised not to have it altered. But more particularly it appears by *Beza* in the life of *Calvin*, and by the Letter of *Ligurus* before remembred, that Excommunications were not used in any of the Reformed Churches, whether they were of *Lutheran* or *Zuinglian* judgement. But scarce had *Gualter* so setled *Zuinglianism* in the Church of *Heidelberg*, and those which did depend upon it, when a bold Challenger from *Geneva* defies them all, and undertakes to prove this Proposition in the publick Schools, *That to a Minister assisted with the help of his Eldership, doth appertain the power of Excommunication by the*

(a) *Et quamvis nostra disciplina vestra per omnia non respondeat, &c. ---- nec ideo vestram velle subversam.* Bull. Epist

the *Law of God.* Hereupon followed that famous Disputation in the Schools of *Heidelberg,* the substance whereof we find drawn up in *Ursines* Catechism, from pag. 835. to pag. 847. of the *English* Edition. By which it doth appear, that the name of the Respondent was *George Withers,* a Native of *England;* and that one *Peter Boquine* was the Moderator; and therefore *Withers* must be taken to have made the Challenge. The *Theses* then maintained by *Withers* were these two that follow, viz. *That to the sincere Preaching of the Word, and the lawful Administration of the Sacraments, is required an Office or Power of Government in the Church.* 2. *That a Minister with his Eldership ought to enjoy and exercise a Power of Convicting, Reproving, Excommunicating and Executing any part of Ecclesiastical Discipline; on any Offenders whatsoever, even on Princes themselves.*

3. The Arguments by which the Respondent was assaulted, together with the answers which were made unto them, were taken by the Pen of *Ursine,* a Divine of *Heidelberg,* who was present at the Disputation, and by his means transmitted to the use of the Church; the Title of his Abstract this, viz. *Certain Arguments assoyled, whereby some in a publick Disputation held in* Heidelberg 1568, June 10. (*Dr.* Peter Boquine *being Moderator,* and *Mr.* George Withers *English-man Respondent) endeavoured to abolish Ecclesiastical Discipline: Which Arguments and their solutions were taken word for word from the mouth of Dr.* Ursine, *at the repetition of his disputation on the next day privately made in Colleg. Sapient.* For further satisfaction, I refer the Reader to the Book it self, and shall now onely add this note, viz. that as the Arguments were not found sufficient to beat down that power which Christ had left unto his Church for excommunicating scandalous and notorious Sinners; so neither were the Answers strong enough to preserve Lay-elders in the possession of a power that belonged not them. Which was in time the issue of the disputation, which afterwards was so hotly followed, between *Theodore Beza* on the one side, and Dr. *Thomas Erastus,* (whom *Calvin* mentioneth in his Epistle to *Olerianus*) Doctor of Physick, on the other; *Beza* evincing the necessity of excommunication in the Church of Christ, and *Erastus* proving nothing to the contrary, but that Lay-elders were not necessary to the exercise of it. Which disputation lasted long, and effected little, managed on both sides in Printed Tractates; the last of which was that of *Beza,* first published at *Geneva,* reprinted afterwards at *London Anno* 1590. But in the mean time the *Genevian* Discipline was admitted in both *Palatinates,* the Countrey divided into Classes and Synodical Meetings; those Classes subdivided into their *Presbyterians,* and each *Presbytery* furnished with a power of excommunication, and exercising such Church-censures as the Fact required. But then we are to know withall, that those wise Princes being loath to leave too much Authority in the hands of the Elderships, with whose encroachments on the power of the Civil Magistrate they were well acquainted, appointed some Superiour Officers of their own nomination to sit as Chief amongst them, without whom nothing could be done; and they were sure that by them nothing would be done, which either might intrench upon their Authority, or their people's liberty. A temperament for which they were beholden to the said *Erastus,* who being a Doctor of Physick (as before was noted) devised this *Pill* to *purge Presbytery* of

some

ſome *Popiſh humours*, which ſecretly lay hid in the *body* of it.

4. The like alloy was mixed with the *Genevian* Diſcipline in the Churches of *Haſſia*, *Naſſaw*, and thoſe other petite Eſtates and Signories, which make up the Confederacie of the *Wetteravians*. Which having once received the Doctrine of *Zuinglius*, did ſhortly after entertain the *Calvinian* Elderſhips, but moderated and reſtrained in thoſe Exorbitancies which the *Presbyterians* actually committed in the Realm of *Scotland*, and in moſt places elſe ſubjected unto their Authority. But in regard the *Palatine* Churches are eſteemed as a Rule to the reſt (the reſt of *Germany* I mean) in all points of Doctrine; and that the publick Catechiſm thereof is generally reckoned for Authentick, not onely in the Churches of the Higher *Germany*, but in the *Netherland*-Churches alſo; it will not be amiſs to take notice of them in ſuch Doctrinal Points, in which they come up cloſe to *Calvin*, and the Rules of *Geneva*. Firſt therefore taking them for *Zuinglians* in the point of the Sacrament, and *Anti-Lutherans* in defacing Images, aboliſhing all diſtinction of Faſts and Feſtivals, and utterly denying all ſet-Forms of publick Worſhip; they have declared themſelves as high in maintainance of *Calvins* Doctrines touching Predeſtination, Grace, Free-will, *&c.* as any *ſub-lapſarian*, or *ſupra-l pſarian*, which had moſt cordially eſpouſed that Quarrel. For proof whereof, the Writings of *Urſine* end *Pareus*, *Alſted*, *Piſcator*, and the reſt, Profeſſors in the Schools of *Heidelberg*, *Herborne*, and *Sedan* (being all within the limits of the Higher *Germany*) might be here produced, did I think it neceſſary. But theſe not being the proper cognizances of the *Presbyterians*, and better to be taken by their actings in the Synode of *Dort*, then in ſcattered Tractates; I ſhall take notice onely of thoſe points of Doctrine which are meer *Genevian*, in reference to their oppoſition to Monarchial Government; a Doctrine not unwelcome to the *Zuinglian* Princes in either *Germany*, becauſe it gives them a fit ground for their juſtification, not onely for proceeding to reform their Churches without leave of the Emperour, whom they muſt needs acknowledge for their Supreme Lord; but alſo for departing from the Confeſſion of *Ausberg*, which onely ought to be received within the bounds of the Empire.

5. Firſt then, beginning with *Urſine*, publick Profeſſor for Divinity in the Chair of *Heidelberg*, he thus inſtructs us in his Commentary on the *Palatine Catechiſm*. *Albeit* (ſaith he) *that wicked Men ſometimes bear Rule, and therefore are unworthy of honours; yet the Office is to be diſtinguiſhed from their Perſons, and that the Man whoſe vices are to be deteſted, ought to be honoured for his Office, as Gods Spiritual Ordinance*: which is a truth ſo conſonant to the Holy Scriptures, that nothing could be ſaid more piouſly in ſo ſhort a poſition. But then he gives us ſuch a Gloſs as corrupts the Text, telling us in the words next following, That *ſince Superiours are to be honoured in reſpect of their Office, it is therefore manifeſt, that ſo far onely we muſt yeild obedience unto their commands, as they exceed not in the ſame the bound of their Offices*. Which plainly intimates, that if Princes be at any time tranſported beyond the bound of their Offices, of which the people and their popular Magiſtrates are the onely Judges, the Subjects are not bound to yeild obedience unto their commands, under pretence that they are paſt beyond their bounds, and have no influence on the

People,

People, but onely when they shine within the compass of their proper Spheres.

6. More plainly speaks *Pareus*, who succeeded him both in place and Doctrines; out of whose Commentary on the 13 Chapter of St. *Paul*s Epistle to the *Romans*, the following propositions were extracted by some Delegates and Divines of *Oxon*, when the unsoundness of his Judgement in this particular was questioned and condemned by that University. First then it was declared for a truth undoubted, *That Bishops and other Ministers or Pastors in the Church of Christ, both might and ought, with the consent of their several Churches, to Excommunicate, or give over to the power of Satan, their Superiour Magistrates, for their impiety towards God, and their injustice towards their Subjects, if they continued in those errours after admonition, till they gave some manifest signs of their repentance.* 2. *That Subjects being in the condition of meer private men, ought not without some lawful calling either to take Arms to assault a Tyrant, before their own persons be indangered; or to defend themselves though they be indangered, if by the ordinary Magistrates they may be defended from such force and violence.* 3. *That Subjects being in the conditi. of meer private men, may lawfully take Arms to defend themselves against a Tyrant, who violently shall break in upon them as a Thief or Ravisher, and exped te themselves from the present danger, as against a common Thief and Robber, when from the ordinary Magistrates there appeareth no defence or succour.* 4. *That such Subjects as are not meerly private men, but are placed in some inferiour Magistracy may lawfully by force of Arms defend themselves, the Common-wealth, the Church and the true Religion, against the pleasure and command of the Supreme Magistrate: These following conditions being observed, that is to say, if either the Supreme Magistrate become a Tyrant, practiseth to commit Idolatry, or blaspheme Gods Name; or that any great and notable injustice be offered to them, as that they cannot otherwise preserve their consciences and lives in safety: condit oned finally, that under colour of Religion, and a Zeal to Justice, they do not rather seek their private ends then the publick good.* And this last proposition being so agreeable to *Calvins* Doctrine, he flourisheth over, and inforceth with those words of *Trajan*, which before we cited out of *Buchan*, when he required the principal Captain of his Guard to use the Sword in his defence, if he governed well; but to turn the point thereof against him, if he did the contrary.

7. Building their practice on these Doctrines, we find the *Palatine* Princes very forward in aiding the French *Hugonots* against their King upon all occasions. In the first risings of that people, Monsieur *d'Andelot* was furnished with five thousand Horse, and four thousand Foot, most of them being of the Subjects of the Prince Elector, *Anno* 1562, when he had but newly entertained the thoughts of *Zuinglianism*, and had not fully settled the *Calvinian* Doctrines. But in the year 1566, when the *Hugonots* were upon the point of a second War, he joyns with others of the *German* Princes in a common Ambassie, by which the French King was to be desired, that the Preachers of the Reformed Religion might Preach both in *Paris*, and all other places of the Kingdom without control, and that the people freely might repair to hear them in what numbers they pleased. To which unseasonable demand, the King, though naturally very Cholerick, made no other answer, then that he would preserve a friendship and affection for those Princes so long as
they

1567.

they did not meddle in the Affairs of his Kingdom, as he did not meddle at all in their Estates. After which, having somewhat recollected his Spirits, he subjoyned these words, with manifest shew of his displeasure, that it concerned him to solicite their Princes to suffer the Catholicks to say Mass in all their Cities. With which nipping answer the Ambassadors being sent away, they were followed immediately at the heels by some of the *Hugonots*, who being Agents for the rest, prevailed with Prince *John Casimir* the second Son of the Elector, to raise an Army in defence of the common Cause. To which purpose they had already furnished him with a small sum of money, assuring him that when he was come unto their Borders, they would pay down one hundred thousand Crowns more towards the maintainance of his Army. Which promises perswading more then the greatest Rhetorick, excited him, with many Captains and Commanders, who for the most part lived upon spoil and plunder, to raise an Army of seven thousand Horse and four thousand Foot, with which they made foul work in *France*, wasting and spoiling all Countries wheresoever they came: for being joyned unto the rest of the *Hugonots* Army, they found them brought to such a poor and low condition, that they were not able to advance the least part of that sum which they had promised to provide against their com-

1568. ing. Somewhat was raised by way of Contribution, to keep them in some present compliance; and for the rest, they were permitted to pay themselves in the spoil of the Countrey, especially Churches, Monasteries, and Religious Houses. But the Queen offering terms of Peace, none were more forward then these *Germans* to imbrace the offer, and *Casimir* more forward in it then all the rest. The King had offered to disburse a great part of the money which belonged to the Souldiers for their pay; which to those mercenary spirits was too strong a temptation to be resisted or neglected.

8. These *Germans* were scarcely setled in their several Houses, when the *Hugonots* brake out again, and a new Army must be raised by the Duke of *Zudibruck* (whom the French call the Duke of *Deuxponts*) a **1569.** Prince of the Collateral Line to the Electoral Family; who upon hope of being as well paid as his Cozen *Casimir*, tempted with many rich promises by the Heads of the *Hugonots*, and secretly encouraged by some Ministers of the Queen of *England*, made himself Master of a great and puissant Army, consisting of eight thousand Horse and six thousand Foot. With this Army he wastes all the Countrey, from the very edge of *Burgundy* to the Banks of the *Loire*; crosseth that River, and commits the like outrages in all the Provinces which lye between that River and the *Aquitain* Ocean. In which action, either with the change of air, the tediousness of his Marches, or excessive drinking, he fell into a violent Feaver, which put a period to his travails within few days after. Nor did this Army come off better, though it held out longer: for many of them being first consumed with sickness, arising from their own intemperance, and the delicious lusts of the Strumpets of *France*; the rest were almost all cut off at the Battail of *Mont-counter*, in which they lost two Colonels, and twenty seven Captains of Foot, and all their Horse except two thousand, which saved themselves under Count *Lodowick* of *Naslaw*. But the love of money prevailed more
with

with them then the fear of death: For within few years after, *Anno* 1575, we find them entring *France* again under Prince *John Casimir*, in company with the young Prince of *Conde*, who had follicited the Cause. The Army, at that time confisting of eight thousand Horse, three thousand *French* Fire-locks, and no fewer then fourteen thousand *Switz* and *Germane* Foot, joyned with the *Hugonots*, and a new faction of Politicks or *Male-contents*, under the command of the Duke of *Alanzon*, who had revolted from his Brother ; became so terrible to the King, that he resolved to buy his Peace upon any rates. To which end, having somewhat cooled the heats of his Brother, he purchaseth the departure of the *Germane* Souldiers, by ingaging to pay them their Arrears, which came in all to twelve hundred thousand Crowns on a full computation : Besides the payment of which vast sum he was to gratifie Prince *Casimir* with the Signory of *Chasteau-Thierry* in the Province of *Champagne*, the command of one hundred *French* Lances, and an annual pension of fourteen thousand Crowns, as before was said.

9. In the mean time the flames of the like civil War consumed a great part of *Flanders*, to which the Prince Elector must bring Fewel also : For being well affected to the House of *Naffaw*, and more particularly to the Prince of *Orange*, and knowing what encouragements the *Calvinians* in the *Netherlands* had received from them ; he hearkned cheerfully to such Propositions as were made to him at the first by Count *Lodowick* his Ministers, and after by the Agents of the Prince himself. But those small Forces which he sent, at their first ingaging doing no great service, he grants them such a large supply after the first return of Prince *Casimirs* Army, *Anno* 1568, as made them up a Body of *French* and *Germans*, consisting of seven thousand Foot, and four thousand Horse ; with which he sent Prince *Christopher* a younger son, to gain experience in the War, and to purchase Honour. And though he might have been discouraged by the loss of that Army, and the death of his Son into the bargain, from medling further in that quarrel ; yet the *Calvinian* spirit so predominated in his Court and Counsels that another Army should be raised, and *Casimir* imployed as Commander of it, as soon as he could give himself the least assurance that the *French* required not his assistance. During the languishing of which Kingdom between Peace and War, the War in *Flanders* grew more violent and fierce then ever, which moved the Provinces confederated with the Prince of *Orange* to enter into a strict union with the Queen of *England*, who could not otherwise preserve her self from the plots and practices of *Don John* of *Austria*, by which he laboured to embroyl her Kingdom. By the Articles of which League or Union, she bound her self to aid them with one thousand Horse and five thousand Foot ; the greatest part whereof she raised in the Dominions of the Prince Elector, or indeed rather did contribute to the payment of so much mony for his Army which was drawn together for the service of the Prince of *Orange*, as might amount unto that number. And that they might receive the greater countenance in the eye of the World, she sends for *Casimir* into *England*, where he arrived about the latter end of *January* 1578, is Royally feasted by

the

the Queen, rewarded with an annual Pension, and in the next year made Knight of the Garter also.   By these encouragements he returns to his charge in the Army which he continued till the calling in of the Duke of *Anjou*, and then retired into *Germany* to take breath a while ; where he found such an alteration in the State of affairs, as promised him no great assurance of employment on the like occasion.

10. For *Lodowick* the fifth succeeding Prince Elector in the place of his Father, and being more inclined to the *Lutheran* Forms, did in time settle all his Churches on the same foundation on which it had been built by the Electors of the former Line ; so that it was not to be thought that either he could aid the *Hugonots*, or the *Belgick Calvinists* in any of their Insurrections against their Princes, if either of them possibly could have had the confidence to have moved him in it.   But he being dead, and *Frederick* the Fourth succeeding, the *Zuinglian* Doctrines and the *Genevean* Discipline are restored again ; and then Prince *Casimir* is again sollicited to raise a greater power then ever for the aid of the French.   The Catholicks of which Realm had joyned themselves in a common League not onely to exclude the King of *Navar* and the Prince of *Conde* from their Succession to the Crown, but wholly to extirpate the Reformed Religion.   To counterpoise which Potent Faction, the King of *Navar* and his Associates in that cause implored the assistance of their Friends in *Germany*, but more particularly the Prince Elector *Palatine*, the Duke of *Wirtemberge*, the Count of *Mombelliard*, and the Protestant Cantons ; who being much moved by the danger threatned unto their Religion, and powerfully stirred up by *Beza*, who was active in it, began to raise the greatest Army that ever had been sent from thence to the aid of the *Hugonots* : And that the action might appear with some face of Justice, it was thought fit to try what they could do towards an atonement, by sending their Ambassadors to the Court of *France* before they entred with their forces.   But the Ambassador of Prince *Casimir* carried himself in that imployment with so little reverence, and did so plainly charge the King with the infringing of the Edicts of Pacification, that the King dismist them all with no small disdain ; telling them roundly, that he would give any man the lye which should presume to tax him of the breach of his promise.   This short dispatch hastned the coming in of the Army, compounded of twelve thousand *German* Horse, four thousand *German* Foot, sixteen thousand *Switz*, and about eight thousand *French* Auxiliaries which staid their coming on the Borders.   With which vast Army they gained nothing but their own destruction ; for many of them being consumed by their own intemperance, more of them wasted by continual skirmishes with which they were kept exercised by the Duke of *Guise*, most of the rest were miserably slaughtered by him near a place called *Auneaw* (a Town of the Province of *La Beausse*) or murthered by the common people, as they came in their way.

11. Such ill success had *Frederick* the fourth in the Wars of *France*, as made him afterwards more careful in engaging in them, until he was therein sollicited on a better ground to aid that King against the Leaguers, and other the disturbers of the Common Peace.   Nor did

some

ſome other of the petty Princes ſpeed much better in the ſucceſs of this Affair ; the Country of *Monthelguard* paying dearly for the Zeal of their Count, and almoſt wholly ruined by the forces of the Duke of *Guiſe.* *Robert* the laſt Duke of *Bouillon,* of the Houſe of *Marke,* had ſpent a great part of his time in the acquaintance of *Beza,* and afterwards became a conſtant follower of the King of *Navar,* by whom he was imployed in raiſing this great Army of *Switz* and *Germans,* and deſtined to a place of great Command and Conduct in it : Eſcaping with much difficulty in the day of the ſlaughter, he came by many unfrequented ways to the Town of *Geneva* ; where, either ſpent with grief of mind, or toyl of body, he dyed ſoon after, leaving the Signory of *Sedan* to his Siſter *Charlot,* and her to the diſpoſing of the King of *Navar,* who gave her in Marriage, not long after, to the Viſcount *Turenne* ; but he had firſt eſtabliſhed *Calviniſm* both for Doctrine and Diſcipline in all the Towns of his Eſtate ; in which they were afterwards confirmed by the Marriage of *Henry Delateure* Viſcount of *Turenne,* Soveraign of *Sedan* and Duke of *Bouillon* by his former Wife, with one of the Daughters of *William* of *Naßaw* Prince of *Orange,* a profeſſed *Calvinian* ; the influence of which Houſe, by reaſon of the great Command which they had in the *Netherlands,* prevailed ſo far on many of the Neighbouring Princes, that not onely the Counties of *Naßaw* and *Hanaw,* with the reſt of the Confederacy of *Vetteravia,* but a great part of *Halſia* alſo gave entertainment to thoſe Doctrines, and received that Diſcipline, which hath given ſo much trouble to the reſt of Chriſtendom. Which ſaid, we have an eaſie paſſage to the *Belgick* Provinces, where we ſhall find more work in proſecution of the Story, then all the Signories and Eſtates of the Upper *Germany* can preſent unto us.

12. The *Belgick* Provinces, ſubject in former times to the Dukes of *Burgundy,* and by deſcent from them to the Kings of *Spain,* are on all ſides invironed with *France* and *Germany,* except toward the *Weſt,* where they are parted by the Inter-current-Ocean from the Realm of *England,* with which they have maintained an ancient and wealthy Traffick. Being originally in the hands of ſeveral Princes, they fell at laſt by many diſtinct Titles to the Houſe of *Burgundy* ; all of them, except five, united in the perſon of Duke *Philip the good* ; and thoſe five added to the reſt by *Charles* the V. From hence aroſe that difference which appears between them in their Laws and Cuſtoms, as well as in diſtinct and peculiar Priviledges ; which rendred it a matter difficult, if not impoſſible, to mould them into one eſtate, or to erect them into an abſolute and Soveraign, though it was divers times endeavoured by the Princes of it. The whole divided commonly into ſeventeen Provinces, moſt of them ſince they came into the power of the Kings of *Spain,* having their own proper and ſubordinate Governours accountable to their King, as their Lord in Chief, who had the ſole diſpoſal of them, and by them managed all Affairs both of war and peace, according to their ſeveral and diſtinct capacities : All of them priviledged ſo far, as to ſecure them all (without a manifeſt violation of their Rights and Liberties) from the fear of Bondage. But none ſo amply priviledged as the Province of *Brabant,* to which it had

been

been granted by some well-meaning, but weak Prince amongst them, that if their Prince or Duke (by which name they called him) should by strong hand attempt the violation of their ancient privileges, the Peers and People might proceed to a new Election, and put themselves under the Clyentele or Patronage of some just Governour.

13. The whole Estate thus laid together, is reckoned to contain no more in compass then twelve hundred miles; but is withall so well planted, and extremely populous, that there are numbered in that compass no fewer then three hundred and fifty Cities, and great Towns equal unto Cities; besides six thousand and three hundred Villages of name and note, (some of them equal to great Towns) not taking in the smaller Dorps and inferiour Hamlets. But amongst all the Cities and great Towns, there were but four which anciently were honoured with Episcopal Sees, that is to say, the Cities of *Utrecht*, *Cambray*, *Tournay*, and *Arras*; and of these four, they onely of *Arras* and *Tournay* were naturally subject to the Princes of the House of *Burgundy*; the Bishop of *Cambray* being anciently a Prince of the Empire, and *Utrecht* not made subject to them till the Government of *Charles* the V. Which paucity of the Episcopal Sees in so large a Territory subjected some of the Provinces to the Bishops of *Leige*, some to the jurisdiction of the Archbishops of *Rheims* and *Colen*, and others under the authority of the Bishops of *Munster*. Of which the first were in some sort under the Protection of the Dukes of *Burgundy*, the three last absolute and independent, not owing any suit or Service at all unto them. By means whereof, concernments of Religion were not looked into with so strict an eye, as where the Bishops are accomptable to the Prince for their Administration, or more united with and amongst themselves in the publick Government. The inconvenience whereof being well observed by *Charles* the Fifth, he practised with the Pope then being for increasing the number of the Bishopricks, reducing them under Archbishops of their own, and Modelling the Ecclefiastical Politie under such a Form, as might enable them to exercise all manner of spiritual jurisdiction within themselves, without recourse to any Forein Power or Prelate but the Pope himself. Which being first designed by him, was afterwards effected by King *Philip* the Second, though the event proved contrary to his expectation. For this enlargement of the number of the Sees Episcopal, being projected only for the better keeping of the Peace and Unity of the *Belgick* Churches, became unhappily the occasion of many Tumults and Disorders in the Civil State, which drew on the defection of a great part of the Country from that Kings obedience.

14. For so it was, that the Reformed Religion being entertained in *France* and *Germany*, did quickly find an entrance also into such of the Provinces as lay nearest to them; where it found people of all forts sufficiently ready to receive it. To the increase whereof the Emperor *Charls* himself gave no small advantage, by bringing in so many of the *Switz* and *Cerman* Souldiers to maintain his power, either in awing his own subjects, or against the *French*, by which last he was frequently invaded in the bordering Provinces. Nor was Queen *Mary* of *England*

wanting

wanting (though she meant it not) to the increasing of their numbers. For whereas many of the Natives of *France* and *Germany*, who were affected zealously to the Reformation, had put themselves for Sanctuary into *England* in the time of King *Edward*; they were all banished by Proclamation in the first year of her Reign. Many of which not daring to return to their several Countries dispersed themselves in most of the good Towns of the *Belgick* Provinces (especially in such as lay most neer unto the Sea) where they could best provide themselves of a poor subsistance. By means whereof the Doctrine of the Protestant and Reformed Churches began to get much ground upon them; to which the continual intercourses which they had with *England* gave every day such great and manifest advantage, that the Emperour was fain to bethink himself of some proper means for the suppressing of the inconveniences which might follow on it. And means more proper he found none in the whole course of Government, then to increase the number of the former Bishopricks, to re-inforce some former Edicts which he made against them, and to bring in the *Spanish Inquisition*, which he established and confirmed by another Edict, bearing date *April* 20. 1548. Which notwithstanding the Professors of that Doctrine, though restrained awhile, could not be totally suppressed; some Preachers out of *Germany*, and others out of *France* and *England*, promoting underhand those Tenents, and introducing those opinions, which openly they durst not own in those dangerous times. But when the Emperour *Charles* had resigned the Government, and that King *Philip* the Second, upon some urgent Reasons of State had retired to *Spain*, and left the chief command of his *Belgick* Provinces to the Dutchess of *Parma*, they then began to shew themselves with the greater confidence, and gained some great ones to their side, whom discontent by reason of the disappointment of their several aims had made inclinable to innovation both in Church and State.

15. Amongst the great ones of which time, there was none more considerable for Power and Patrimony then *William* of *Naßaw* Prince of *Orange*, invested by a long descent of Noble Ancestors in the County of *Naßaw*, a fair and goodly Territory in the Higher *Germany*; possest of many good Towns and ample Signories in *Brabant* and *Holland*, derived upon him from *Mary* Daughter and Heir of *Philip* Lord of *Breda*, &c. his great Grand-fathers Grand-mother; and finally, enriched with the Principality of *Orange* in *France*, accruing to him by the death of his Cousin *Rene*; which gave him a precedencie before all other *Belgick* Lords in the Court of *Brußel*. By which advantages, but more by his abilities both for Camp and Counsel, he became great in favour with the Emperour *Charles*; by whom he was made Governour of *Holland* and *Zealand*, Knight of the Order of the Fleece; imployed in many Embassies of weight and moment, and trusted with his dearest and most secret purposes. For Rivals in the Glory of Arms he had the Counts of *Horn* and *Egmond*, men of great Prowess in the field, and alike able at all times to command and execute. But they were men of open hearts, not practised in the Arts of Subtility and Dissimulation, and wanted much of that dexterity and cunning which the other had for working into the affections of all forts of people. Being advanced unto this

eminencie

eminencie in the Court, and knowing his own ſtrength as well amongſt the Souldiers as the common people, he promiſed to himſelf the Supreme Government of the *Belgick* Provinces on the Kings returning into *Spain.* The diſappointment of which hope, obliterated the remembrance of all former favours, and ſpurred him on to make himſelf the Head of the Proteſtant party, by whoſe aſſiſtance he conceived no ſmall poſſibility of raiſing the *Naſſovian* family to as great an height as his ambition could aſpire to.

16. The Proteſtants at that time were generally divided into two main bodies, not to ſay any thing of the *Anabaptiſts* and other Sectaries who thruſt in amongſt them. Such of the Provinces as lay toward *Germany,* and had received their Preachers thence, embraced the Forms and Doctrines of the *Lutheran* Churches, in which not onely Images had been ſtill retained, together with ſet-Forms of Prayer, kneeling at the Communion, the Croſs in Baptiſm, and many other laudable Ceremonies of the Elder times; but alſo moſt of the ancient Faſts and Feſtivals of the Catholick Church, and ſuch a Form of Eccleſiaſtical Polity, as was but little differing from that of Biſhops: which Forms and Doctrines being tolerated by the Edicts of *Pauſſaw* and *Auſberg,* made them leſs apt to work diſturbance in the Civil State, and conſequently the leſs obnoxious to the fears of the jealouſies of the Catholick party. But on the other ſide, ſuch Provinces as lay toward *France* participated of the humour of that Reformation which was there begun, modelled according unto *Calvins* Platform both in Doctrine and Diſcipline. More ſtomacked then the other, by all thoſe who adhered to the Church of *Rome,* or otherwiſe pretended to the peace and ſafety of the Commonwealth: for the *French* Preachers being more Practical and Mercurial then the other were, and not well principled in reſpect of Monarchical Government, were looked upon as men more likely to beget commotions, and alienate the peoples hearts from their natural Governour. And at the firſt the Prince of *Orange* enclined moſt to the *Lutheran* party, whoſe Forms and Doctrines had been ſetled by his Father in the County of *Naſſaw:* And for the clear manifeſtation of the good opinion which he harboured of them, he Married *Anne* the Daughter of *Maurice* Duke Elector of *Saxony,* the greateſt of the *Lutheran* Princes. At which when the Dutcheſs of *Parma* ſeemed to be diſpleaſed, he openly aſſured her of his Adheſion to the Catholick cauſe, and cauſed his eldeſt Son which he had of that Marriage to be Baptized according to the Preſcript of the Church of *Rome*; but underhand promoted for a time the *Lutheran* Intereſt, which he had ſucked in as it were with his Mothers Milk. But it was onely for a time that he ſo promoted it: For finding the *Calvinians* to be men of another Metal, more quick and ſtirring of themſelves, more eaſily exaſperated againſt their Governours, and conſequently more fit to advance his purpoſes; he made himſelf the great Protector of that faction, and ſpared not to profeſs himſelf for ſuch upon all occaſions; inſomuch, that being afterwards queſtioned about his Religion by the Duke of *Areſcot,* he diſcovered to him his bald head, and told him plainly, that there was not more *Calviſm* on his head, then there was *Calviniſm* in his heart.

17. But to make way for theſe deſigns, there were two obſtacles to be

be removed, without which nothing could be done in pursuance of them.
King *Philip* at his going for *Spain*, had left three thousand Spanish Souldiers (the onely remainder of those great Armies which had served his
Father and himself against the *French*) in Garrison upon the Borders,
under pretence of shutting up the back-door against the *French*, but generally thought to be left of purpose for a curb to the Natives, in case
of refractoriness or opposition unto his Commands. They must be first
removed, and the Countrey cleared of all such rubs as otherwise would
have made the way less passable unto private ends. For though the
King had put those Souldiers under the Command of two Lords of the
Netherlands, that is to say, the Prince of *Orange* himself, and the Count
Egmont, that they might rather seem to be the natural *Militia* of the
Countrey, then a power of strangers; yet that device did little edifie amongst them: for the two Lords, especially the Prince of *Orange*, expressed such contentment in the trust and honour which was therein conferred upon them, that they excited the whole Countrey both to move
the King before his going, and the Governess after his departure to dismiss those Souldiers which could not be imposed upon them without
breach of their Priviledges. To this request the King had given a gratious answer, and promised to remove them within four months after his
going into *Spain*; but secretly gave order to the Lady Regent to retain
them longer, till the new Bishops and the *Inquisition* were confirmed
amongst them. And she conceived her self so bound to those instructions, and their detaining there so necessary for his Majesties Service,
that she delayed time as long as possibly she could: Which being observed by those which were of greatest power and credit with the common
people, it was resolved that no more contribution should be raised on
the several Provinces toward the payment of their wages; and on the
other side, the Regent was so constant to her resolution, that she took up
money upon interest for their satisfaction. But being wearied in the end
by the importunity of all sorts of people, counselled by her Husband the
Duke of *Parma* to give way unto it, and authorized at last by the King
himself to hearken unto their desires; she gives order to have them drawn
out of their several Garrisons, and Shipt at *Flushing*; from thence to be
transported into *Spain* with the first fair wind.

18. The easie removing of this rub, incouraged those who managed
the design for innovating in the Church and State, to make the like attempt against the Cardinal *Granvel*; whose extraordinary parts and
power they were more affraid of, then of all the Spaniards in the Countrey. This man being of the *Perenots* of *Granvel* in the Countrey of
Burgundy, was trained up by a Father of such large abilities, that he
was by *Charles* the Fifth made Chancellor of the *German* Empire, and
trusted by him in Affairs of the greatest moment: And he declared himself to be such a quick proficient in the Schools of Learning, that he became the Master of no fewer then seven Languages; (in all which he
was able to express himself with a fluent eloquence) and at twenty four
years of age was made Bishop of *Arras*: commended by his Father to
the Emperour *Charles*, and by him unto King *Philip* the Second, he served them both with great fidelity and courage; and had withall such a
dexterity of dispatch in all concernments, as if he had been rather born
                                                                    then

then made a States-man. And unto these he added such a moderation in his pleasures, such abstinence both from food and sleep when the case required it, such extraordinary pains in accommodating all the difficulties which came before him, and such a diligent observance of his Princes motions, that his greatest Adversaries could not chuse but say, that he was a Jewel, fit to be owned by none but the greatest Kings. By means whereof, he so prevailed upon the King whilst he staid amongst them, that he did nothing either at home or abroad, made neither Peace nor League with Kings or Nations; concluded no Marriage, quieted no Seditions, acted nothing that related to Religion or the Church, in which the counsels of this man were not influential. The like Authority he held with the Dutchess of *Parma*, not onely out of that report which the King made of him, but her own election, who found his counsel so applyable to all occasions, that seldom any private or publick business came in agitation, in which his judgement had not been previously required, before it was openly delivered. And though his previous resolutions in matters of counsel, were carried with all imaginable care and closeness from the eyes of the Courtiers; yet no man doubted but that all Affairs were transacted by him, imputing many things unto him, as it often happeneth, which he had no hand in.

19. In the first risings of this man, he was despised for an upstart by the Prince of *Orange*, and some other great men of the Countrey; not fearing any thing from him, as an alien born, unfurnished of dependants, and who by reason of his calling could make no strong Alliance to preserve his Power. But when they found that his Authority increased, that all things bended to that point at which he aimed, and that some of the Nobility began to apply themselves unto him, and became his Creatures; they then conceived it necessary to make head against him, for fear of being brought to the like submissions. First therefore they began to clash with him at the Counsel-Table, and to dissent from many things which he appeared in, though otherwise of great advantage in themselves to the publick Service. But finding that those oppositions did rather serve to strengthen his power, then take any thing from it, they misreport him to the King in their several Letters for a turbulent spirit, a man of proud thoughts, and one that hated the Nobility. By whose depressing, he aspired to more personal greatness then was consistent either with his Majesties safety or the *Belgick* Liberties. And that being done, they generally traduce him by their Whisperers amongst the people, to be the onely man that laboured for the bringing in of the Inquisition, and for establishing the new Bishops in their several Sees, under pretence of stopping the increase of Sects and Heresies: And unto these reports of him, he gave some fair colour, by prosecuting the concernments of the Church with more zeal then caution; lying the more open to the practices of the growing party, by a seeming neglect of their intendments, and a reliance onely on his Masters favour. From hence it was, that such as did pretend to any licentiousness in Life or Doctrine, exclaimed against him as the Author of those severities wherewith the King had formerly proceeded against divers of them; as on the other side, they cryed up all the Lords which appeared against him, as the chief Patriots of the Countrey, the principal Patrons and Assertors of the publick liberty.   20. The

20. The people being thus corrupted, it was no hard matter for the Lords to advance the Project, in rendring *Granvel* as unpleasing in the eyes of the King, as they had made him odious in the sight of the people. In order whereunto, some of them shewed themselves less careful of the Cause of Religion, by smothering the publication of his Majesties Edicts which concerned the Church in the Provinces under their command. Others dealt under-hand with the common people, perswading them not to yeild submission to those new Tribunals, which only served for the exercise of superstition, and the Popes Authority. And some again connived at the growth of Heresie (by which name they called it) by suffering the maintainers of those new opinions to get ground amongst them; encouraged secretly some seditious practices, and finally omitted nothing, by which the King might understand by a sad experiment how much he had misplaced his favours, and to what imminent danger he exposed the *Netherlands*, by putting such Authority over them in the hands of a Foreiner. Of all which practices the Cardinal was too intelligent, and had too many friends abroad to be kept in ignorance; which made him carry a more vigilant eye upon their designs, to cross their Counsels, and elude their Artifices, when any thing was offered to the prejudice of the publick Peace : but in the end, the importunity of his Adversaries became so violent, and the breach had such a face of danger in the sight of the Governess, that she moved the King for his dismission; to prevent which, he first retired into *Burgundy*, and from thence to *Rome*; preferred not long after to be Vice-Roy of the Realme of *Naples*; and finally, made President of the Council for *Italy* in the Court of *Spain*.

21. In the mean time the *Calvinists* began to try their Fortunes in those Provinces which lay next to *France*, by setting up two of their Preachers on the same day in two great Cities, *Valenciennes* the chief City of *Haynalt*, and *Tournay* the chief City of *Flanders Gallicant* : In the first of which, the Preacher having finished in the Market-place where he made his Sermon, was followed in the Streets by no fewer then one hundred people; but in the other, by a train of six hundred, or thereabouts, all of them singing *Davids* Psalms of *Marots* Translation, according to the custom of the *Hugonots* amongst the *French* Some tumults hereupon ensued in either City; for the repressing the Governour of that Province, rides in post to *Tournay*, hangs up the Preacher, seizeth on all such Books as were thought Heretical, and thereby put an end to the present Sedition. But when the Marquess of *Bergen* was required to do the like at *Valenciennes*, he told the Governess in plain terms, that it was neither agreeable to his place or nature to put an Heretick to death. All that he did was the committing of two of their Preachers to the common Prison; and that being done, he made a journey unto *Leige* to decline the business: Which so incouraged the *Calvinian* party to proceed in their purposes, that they threatned mischief to the Judges, if any harm happened to the Prisoners. But sentence at the seven months end being past upon them to be burnt, and all things being made ready for the execution, the Prisoners brought unto the Stake, and the fire ready to be kindled, there presently arose a tumult so

fierce

fierce and violent, that the Officers were compelled to take back their Prisoners, and to provide for their own safety, for fear of being stoned to death by the furious multitude. But the people having once begun, would not so give over; for being inflamed by one of their company, whom they had set up in the midst of the Market-place to preach an extemporary Sermon, two thousand of them ran tumultuously to the common Goal, force open the doors, knock off the Shackles of the Prisoners, restore them to their former Liberty, and so disperse themselves to their several dwellings. The news of which Sedition being brought to *Brussels*, the Governess dispatcheth certain Companies of foot, and some Troops of Horse, with order to the Marquess of *Bergen* to appease the disorders in the Town. But they found all things there so quiet, that there was little need of any other Sword then the Sword of Justice; by which some of the chief Ring-leaders of the Tumult, and one of their Preachers (who had unhappily fallen into their hands) were sentenced to that punishment which they had deserved.

22. The *Calvinists* conceiving by this woful experiment, that it was not safe jesting with Edged-tools, and that they were not of sufficient power for so great a business, betook themselves to other courses. And finding that some of the principal Lords were much offended at the exorbitant power of *Granvel*, that others shewed no good affection to his Majesties Government, and that the rest had no desire to see the new Bishops setled in their several Sees, for fear of being over-powered by them in all publick Councils; they seriously applyed themselves to foment those discords, and make the rupture greater then at first it was. The new Bishops being fourteen in nnmber, were in themselves so eminent in point of Learning, and of a conversation so unblameable in the eyes of all men, that malice it self could make no just exception against the persons: A quarrel therefore must be picked against the Form and Manner of their indowment, which was by founding them in such wealthy Monasteries as were best able to maintain them; the Patrimony which anciently was allotted to the use of the Abbot, being to be inverted (after the death of the incumbent) to the use of the Bishop. This was presented to the Monks as a great disfranchisement, a plain devesting of them of their Native Priviledges; not only by depriving them of the choice of their Governour, but by placing over them an imperious Lord instead of an indulgent Father. The Magistrates and people of such of the Cities as were designed for the Sees of the several Bishops, were practised on to protest against their admission; by whose establishment the common people must be subject to more Masters then before they were, and the Magistrates must grow less in power and reputation then they had been formerly. They represented to the Merchants, that without liberty of Conscience it was not possible there could be liberty of Trade; the want whereof must needs bring with it their impoverishing, a sensible decay of all sorts of Manufactures; and consequently, an exposing of the common people to extremest beggery. Which consideration, as appeared soon after, was alone sufficient, not only to ingage the Merchants, but to draw after them that huge rabble of Mechanical people (which commonly make up the greatest part of

all

all populous Cities) that depended on them.   But nothing better pleased the discontented Nobility, then their Invectives against *Granvil*, a-
gainst whom, and such of the Court-Lords as adhered unto him, they
fastened their most scandalous and infamous Libels upon every post; not
sparing through his sides to wound the honour of the King, and reproach
the Government, which by this means they made distasteful to the common subjects.

23. By these devices, and some others of like dangerous nature, they
gained not only many of the common people, but divers of the greatest
Lords; some also of the principal Cities, and not a few of the *Regulars*,
or Monastick Clergy.   By means whereof, their Friends and Factors
grew so powerful, as to oppose such motions both in Court and Council, as tended to the prejudice of the Reformation; insomuch, that
when King *Philip* had given order to the Dutchess of *Parma* to send two
thousand Horse to the aid of *Charles* the *French* King against the *Hugonots*; the Prince of *Orange* and his party did openly oppose, and finally
over-rule it at the Council-Table.   This gave incouragement to the
Calvinists to try their Fortune once again, not in *Valenciennes* as before,
but in the principal Cities of *Brabant* and *Flanders*.   At *Rupelmond*, a
chief Town of *Flanders*, a Priest which had been gained unto their o-
pinions, and was imprisoned for the same, fell on a desperate design
of firing the next room unto him, wherein were kept the Monuments
and Records of the Prince; to the end that while the Guards were busied in preserving things that concerned the publick, he might find a
handsome opportunity to get out of their hands.   But the fire being
sooner quenched then he had imagined, both he and his Accomplices,
which were nine in number, were brought unto the place of Execution, and there justly suffered; the Priest himself declaiming bitterly against *Calvin* at his Execution, and charging all his sufferings upon that account.   At *Antwerp* one *Fabricius*, once a *Carmelite* Fryar,
but now a great promoter of *Calvins* Doctrines, had gained much
people to that side; for which being apprehended, he had judgement
of death.   But being brought unto the Stake, such a shower of Stones
was seen to fall upon the head of the Hang-man, that not daring to
abide the storm till the fire had done, he drew his Sword and sheathed
it in the Prisoners body, and after saved himself by seeming to make
one in the Tumult.   And the next day they caused some Verses writ
in bloud to be posted up, in which was signified, that there were some
in *Antwerp* who had vowed revenge for the death of *Fabricius*; though
afterwards they surceased, upon the execution of one of the Mutineers,
and entertained more sober and religious counsels.   But the distemper
seemed much greater in the Town of *Bruges*, where the Inquisitors Deputy had sent a man to prison, on a suspition of Heresie, with a Guard
of three Officers to attend him; at which the Senate was so moved, that
they commanded the Officers to be seized upon, to be committed close
prisoners, and to be fed with nothing but bread and water; the party in
the mean time being set at liberty.

24. Startled with Tumult after Tumult, but more with the unhandsome carriage of the Senate of *Bruges*; the King gives order to his Sister
the Lady Governess, to see his Fathers Edicts severely executed,

1564.

1565

and

and more particularly to take special care that the Decrees and Canons of the Council of *Trent* be presently received and obeyed in all the Provinces: Against which Orders of the King, though many of the great Lords opposed at the Council-Table, yet the Governess carried it at the last. And thereupon the opposite party incensed the *Brabanters* against admitting the Edicts or the *Tridentine* Council, as tending manifestly to the violation of their ancient priviledges: At which though most of them took fire, yet it burned but slowly, proceeding onely at the first in the way of Remonstrance, which for the most part carried more smoke then flame. But after the Ministers and Agents of *Lodowick* Count of *Nassaw* (one of the younger brothers of the Prince of *Orange*) were returned from *Heidelberg*, there appeared a kind of new spirit amongst the people. He had before with certain other Noble-men of his age and quality betook himself unto *Geneva*, either for curiosity or study, or for some worse purpose, where being wrought upon by the *Calvinians* which conversed with them, and finding their own people to be very inquisitive after new opinions, they were not sparing in the commendation of the Religion which they found exercised in that City, and seemed to wish for nothing more then that they might have liberty of Conscience to profess the same. But knowing that so great a business could not be carried on successfully but by force of Arms, he had his Agents in the Court of the Prince Elector for getting some assistance, if it came to blows, or under colour of his name to awe the Governess. And it fell out according unto his desire : for hereupon the party animated with new hopes, renewed their former course of libelling against the present Government with greater acrimony then before, dispersing no fewer then 5000 of those scandalous Pamphlets within the compass of a year, by which the people were exasperated and fitted for engaging in any action, which by the cunning of their Leaders, and the insinuations of their Preachers, should be offered to them.

25. But these were only the preparatives to the following Tumults ; for in the middle of these heats, nine of the Lords not being Officers of State, convened together at *Breda*, the principal Seat and most assured hold of the Prince of *Orange*, where they drew up a Form of an *Association*, which they called the *Covenant*, contrived by *Philip Marnixius* Lord of *Aldegand*, a great admirer of the person and parts of *Calvin*. In the preamble whereof they inveighed bitterly against the Inquisition, as that which being contrary to all Laws both Divine and Humane, did far exceed the cruelty of all former Tyrants : they then declared in the name of themselves and the rest of the Lords, that the care of Religion appertained to them as Councellors born, and that they entred into this *Association* for no other reason, but to prevent the wicked practices of such men, as under colour of the sentences of death and banishment, aimed at the Fortunes and destructions of the greatest persons: that therefore they had taken an holy Oath not to suffer the said Inquisition to be imposed upon their Country : praying therein, that as well God as man would utterly forsake them, if ever they forsook their Covenant, or failed to assist their Brethren which suffered any thing in that Cause ; and finally, calling God to witness, that by this Covenant and Agreement amongst themselves, they intended nothing but the Glory of God,

God, Honour of their King, and their Countries peace.   And to this
Covenant as they fubfcribed before their parting, fo by their Emiffaries
they obtained fubfcription to it over all their Provinces; and for the
credit of the bufinefs, they caufed the fame to be tranflated into feveral
Languages, and publifhed a Report that not onely the chief Leaders of
the Hugonets in *France*, but many of the Princes of *Germany* had fubfcribed it alfo: which whether it were true or not, certain it is, that the
Confederacie was fubfcribed by a confiderable number of the Nobility,
fome of the Lords of the Privy-Counfel, and not a few of the companions
of the Golden Fleece.

26. Of the nine which firft appeared in the defign, the principal were
Henry Lord of *Brederode*, defcended lineally from *Sigefride*, the fecond
Son of *Arnold*, the fourth Earl of *Holland*; Count *Lodowick* of *Naffau*
before mentioned; and *Florence* Count of *Culemberg*, a Town of *Guel-
dres*, but anciently priviledged from all fubjection to the Duke thereof.
Accompanied with two hundred of the principal Covenanters, each of
them having a cafe of Piftols at his Saddle bow, *Brederode* enters *Bruffels*
in the beginning of *April*, to which he is welcomed by Count *Horne* and
the Prince of *Orange*, which laft had openly appeared for them at the
Counfel-Table, when the unlawfulnefs of the confederacy was in agitation.   And having taken up their Lodging in *Culemberg*-houfe, they
did not only once again fubfcribe the Covenant, but bound themfelves
to ftand to one another by a folemn Oath.   The tenour of which Oath
was to this effect, That if any of them fhould be imprifoned, either for
Religion or for the Covenant, immediately the reft, all other bufinefs
laid afide, fhould take up arms for his affiftance and defence.   Marching the next day by two and two till they came to the Court, they prefented their Petition to the Lady Regent, by the hands of *Brederode*, who
defired her in fhort Speech at the tendry of it, to believe that they were
honeft men, and propounded nothing to themfelves, but obedience to
Laws, Honour to the King, and fafety to their Countrey.   The fum of
the Petition was, That the *fpanifh* Inquifition might be abolifhed, the
Emperours Edicts repealed, and new ones made by the advice of the
Eftates of the Countries.   Concerning which we are to know, that the
Emperour had paft feveral Edicts againft the *Lutherans*, the firft of which
was publifhed in the year 1521, and the fecond about five years after
Anno 1526, by means whereof many well-meaning people had been
burnt for Hereticks: but that which moft extremely gaulled them, was
the Edict for the bringing in of the *Inquifition*, publifhed upon the 29 of
April as before was faid.   Againft thefe Edicts they complained in the
faid Petition.   To which upon the morrow fhe returned fuch an anfwer
by the confent of the Counfel, as might give them good hopes that the
Inquifition fhould be taken away, and the Edicts moderated; but that
the King muft firft be made acquainted with all particulars before they
paffed into an Act.   With which anfwer they returned well fatisfied
unto *Culemberg-houfe*, which was prepared for the entertainment of the
chief Confederates.

27. To this Houfe *Brederode* invites the reft of his company, beftows
a prodigal Feaft upon them; and in the middle of their Cups it was put
to the queftion, by what name their Confederacie fhould be called.
                                                                Thofe

Thofe of their party in *France* were differenced from the reft by the name of *Hugonots*, and in *England* (much about that time) by the name of *Puritans*; nor was it to be thought but that their followers might be as capable of fome proper and peculiar appellation, as in *France* or *England*. It happened that at fuch time as they came to tender their Petition, the Governefs feemed troubled at fo great a number, and that Count *Barlamont* (a man of moft approved fidelity to his Majefties fervice) advifed her not to be difcouraged at it; telling her in the *French* Tongue betwixt jeft and earneft, that they were but *Gueux* (or *Gheufes*, as the Dutch pronounced it) that is to fay, men of diffolute lives and broken fortunes, or in plain Englifh *Rogues* and *Beggars*. Upon which ground they animated one another by the name of *Gheufes*, and calling for great Bowls of Wine, drank an health to the name; their Servants and Attendants crying out with loud acclamations, *Vive les Gueus*, long live the *Gheufes*. For the confirming of which name, *Brederode* takes a Wallet which he fpyed in the place, and laid it on one of his Shoulders as their Beggars do, and out of a Wooden difh brim-full drinks to all the Company; thanks them for following him that day with fuch unanimity, and binds himfelf upon his honour to fpend his life, if need fhould be, for the generality of the Confederates, and for every member of them in particular: Which done, he gave his Difh and Wallet to the next unto him, who in like manner paft it round, till they had bound themfelves by this ridiculous Form of initiation to ftand to one another in defence of their Covenant; the former acclamation of *Long live the Gheufes*, being doubled and redoubled at every Health. The jollity and loud acclamations which they made in the Houfe, brought thither the Prince of *Orange*, Count *Egmont*, and Count *Horn*, men of moft Power and Reputation with the common people; who feemed fo far from reprehending the debauchery which they found amongft them, that they rather countenanced the fame; the former Healths and Acclamations being renewed and followed with more heat and drunken bravery then they were at firft: on which incouragement they take upon themfelves in earneft the name of *Gheufes*, and by that name were folemnly proclaimed by that Raskal Rabble at their coming out; which name being taken thus upon them, as the mark of their Faction, was afterwards communicated to all thofe of the fame Religion.

28. Returning to their feveral dwellings, they caufed a mifchievous report to be fpread abroad, not onely that they had obtained a fufpenfion of the Emperours Edicts, and an exemption from the power of the Inquifition; but that the Companions of the Order of the Golden Fleece, being men of moft Authority both in Court and Council, had declared for them in the caufe. To gain belief to which report, a falfe and counterfeit paper is difperfed amongft them, in which it was notified to all that fhould read the fame, that the Lords and Companions of the Fleece had fworn by their Order to the Gentlemen chofen by the Eftates of the Countrey, to prefent the defires of the people to the Lady Regent, *That from thenceforth the Ecclefiaftical Inquifitors and other Magiftrates fhould punifh no man for his Religion, neither by imprifonment, exile, or death, unlefs it were joyned with a popular tumult, and the publick ruine of their Countrey; of which the Covenanters themfelves were to be the Judges.* And though

though the Governels took the wisest and most speedy course both to discover and proclaim the danger of so lewd a practice, and used all honest ways for the undeceiving of the people in that Particular; yet either she obtained no credit to her *Anti-Remonstrances*, or found the Venome too far spread for so weak an Antidote. For presently upon the scattering and dispersing of the said Declaration, as many of the Reformed parties as had fled the Countrey, returned again unto their Houses; and such as had concealed themselves, or otherwise dissembled their Religion, began more confidently to avow the profession of it. For whose incouragement and increase, there was no want of diligence in such of the Ministers as reforted to them out of *France*; first Preaching to them in the Fields, and afterwards in some of their open Towns; but every where bitterly inveighing against the Tyranny of the Pope, the pride of *Spain*, and the corruptions of the Clergy; but most especially of the Bishops, whom they chiefly aimed at. By these invectives, and their continual Preaching up of a popular liberty, their followers so exceedingly increased in a very short time, that in the Fields near the City of *Tournay*, there were seen no fewer then eight thousand persons at a Sermon; a greater multitude then that in the Fields near *Lisles*, and sometimes more then double that number in the Fields near *Antwerp*. But in such Parts and Provinces as lay nearest *France*, they took greater liberty, and fell from Preaching to the Ministration of the Sacraments and Sacramentals; Marrying some, and Baptizing others, according to the Form devised by *Calvin*; but *Sanctifying* all by a continual intermixture of *Davids* Psalms, translated into French Meter as before was said.

Together with these *French* Preachers and *Calvinian* Minister, there entred several Emissaries sent from the Admiral *Colligni*, the Prince of *Conde*, and others of the Heads of the *Hugonots* Faction, whose interest it was to imbroyl the *Netherlands*, that they themselves might fear no such danger on that side, as formerly they had received. And these men play'd their parts so well, that a confused Rabble of the common people, furnished with Staves, Hatchets, Hammers and Ropes, and armed with some few Swords and Muskets, upon the Eve of the Assumption of the Blessed Virgin, fell violently into the Towns and Villages about St. *Omers*, one of the chief Cities of *Artois*, forced open all the Doors of Churches and Religious Houses, if they found them shut; demolished all the Altars, and defaced the Shrines, and broke the Images in pieces, not sparing any thing which in the Piety of their Ancestors was accounted Sacred. Encouraged by which good success, they drive on to *Ipres*, a Town of *Flanders*, where they were sure to find a party prepared for them, by which the Gates of the City were set open to give them entrance: no sooner were they entered, but they went directly to the Cathedral, (their multitudes being much increased all the way they came) where presently they fell to work; some beating down the Images with Staves and Hammers, some pulling down the *Statues* of our Saviour with Ropes and Ladders; other defacing Pulpits, Altars, and Sacred Ornaments, burning the Books, and stealing the confecrated Plate. With the same fury they proceeded to the burning of the Bishops Library, and the destroying of all Churches and Religious Houses
within

within that City; in which they found as little oppofition from the hands of that Magiftrate, as if they had been hired and imployed in that fervice by the common Counfel. About the fame time, that is to fay, on the morrow after the Affumption, another party being of the fame affections, and taking both example and encouragement from this impunity, fall into *Menim, Commines, Vervich*, and other Towns upon the *Lys*: In all which they committed the like impious out-rages, carrying away with them Plate and Veftments, and all other confecrated things which were eafily portable; but burning or deftroying what they could not carry. The like they would have done alfo at the Town of *Seclin*, but that the people rofe in Arms, affaulted them, and drove them back, not without great flaughter of that mutinous and feditious Rabble, and fome lofs of themfelves.

30. In *Antwerp* the chief City of *Brabant* they found better fortune. They had before attained to fo great a confidence, that having affembled in the Fields to hear a Sermon according to their ufual cuftom, and finding their number to amount unto fifteen thoufand; they mounted their Preacher on a Horfe, and brought him triumphantly into the the City, attended by a ftrong Guard both of Horfe and Foot, to the great terrour and affrightment of the principal Magiftrate. For remedy of which diforders, the Governefs fent thither the Count of *Megen*, and afterwards the Prince of *Orange* with fome flender Forces; on the approaching of which laft (for the firft was prefently recalled, as a man lefs popular) infinite multitudes of the people went out to meet him; entertained him with the accuftomed acclamation of *Vive les Gueux*, and cryed him up for the great Patron and Protector of the *Belgick* Liberty. At which though he feemed outwardly to be fomewhat offended, yet it was eafie to be feen that he received a fecret contentment in it; and therefore acted nothing whilft he ftayed amongft them, by which he might become lefs gracious in the eye of that Faction then he was before. Encouraged by which remifnefs, and being privately excited by fome of his Followers, they abate little or nothing of their former infolencies, which they difcovered not long after his departure to the Court of *Bruffels*, by their violent difturbance of a folemn Proceffion made by the Clergy of that City, in honour of their fuppofed Patronefs the Bleffed Virgin; and that too on the very Feftival of her Affumption, when the like outrages were committed in other places: for not content to jeer and taunt them in the Streets as they paffed along, they follow them into the principal Church of that City; where firft they fall to words, and from words to blows, and from blows to wounds; to the great fcandal of Religion, and the unpardonable prophanation of that holy Place.

31. But this was onely an Effay of the following mifchief. For on the fame day Sennight, being not onely more numerous, but better armed, they flocked to the fame Church at the Evening Service; which being ended, they compel the people to forfake the place, and poffefs themfelves of it. Having made faft the Doors for fear that fome difturbance might break in upon them, one of them begins to fing a Pfalm in *Marots* Meter, wherein he is followed by the reft; that fuch a Holy exercife as they were refolved on, might not be undertook without

fome

fome preparation : which fit of Devotion being over, they firſt pulled down a maſſie Image of the Virgin, afterwards the Image of Chriſt, and ſuch other Saints as they found advanced there, on their ſeveral *Pedeſtals* ; ſome of them treading them under foot, ſome thruſting Swords into their ſides, and others hagling of their Heads with Bills and Axes : In which work as many were imployed in moſt parts of the Church, ſo others got upon the Altars, caſt down the ſacred Plate, defaced the Pictures, and disfigured the paintings on the Walls, whilſt ſome with Ladders climbed the Organs, which they broke in pieces ; and others with like horrible violence, deſtroyed the Images in the Windows, or rather brake the Windows in deſpight of the Images. The conſecrated Hoſt they took out of the Pixes, and trampled under their feet ; carouſe ſuch Wine as they brought with them in the ſacred Chalices, and greaſed their ſhooes with that Chryſome, or anointing Oyl, which was prepared for ſome Ceremonies to be uſed at Baptiſm, and in the viſiting of the ſick. And this they did with ſuch diſpatch, that one of the faireſt Churches in *Europe*, richly adorned with Statues and maſſie Images of Braſs and Marble, and having in it no fewer then ſeventy Altars, was in the ſpace of four hours defaced ſo miſerably, that there was nothing to be ſeen in it of the former beauties. Proud of which fortunate ſucceſs, they brake into all other Churches of that City, where they acted over the ſame ſpoils and outragious inſolencies ; and afterwards forcing open the doors of Monaſteries and Religious Houſes, they carryed away all their Conſecrated Furniture, entred their Stote-houſes, ſeized on their Meat, and drank off their Wine ; and took from them all their Mony, Plate, and Wardrobes, both Sacred and Civil, not ſparing any publick Library whereſoever they came : a ruine not to be repaired but with infinite ſums : the havock which they made in the great Church only, being valued at four hundred thouſand Ducates by indifferent rates. The like outrages they committed at the ſame time in *Gaunt* and *Oudenard*, and all the Villages about them ; the ſeveralties whereof would make up a Volume : let it ſuffice, that in the Province of *Flanders* onely, no fewer then four hundred Conſecrated places were in the ſpace of ten days thus defaced, and ſome of them burnt down to the very ground.

32. The news of theſe intolerable outrages being poſted one after another to the Court at *Bruſſels*, occaſioned the Governeſs (when it was too late) to ſee her errour in ſending back her Spaniſh Souldiers, and yeilding to the improvident diſmiſſion of the prudent Cardinal, by whoſe Authority and Counſel ſhe had ſo happily preſerved thoſe Provinces in peace and quiet ; and then ſhe found that ſhe had good reaſon to believe all the information which Count *Mansfield* gave her, touching a plot of the *Calvinian* party in *France* (from whence came moſt of theſe new Preachers) to imbroyl the *Netherlands* ; which till that time ſhe looked on as a groundleſs jealouſie. But as it is in ſome Diſeaſes, that when they are eaſie to be cured, they are hard to be known ; and when they are eaſie to be known, they are hard to be cured : ſo fared it at that time with theſe diſtempers in the *Belgick* Provinces ; which now were grown unto that height, that it was very difficult, if not almoſt impoſſible to find out a remedy. For having called

led together the great Council of State, and acquainted them with the particulars before remembred, she found the Counts of *Mansfield*, *A-remberg*, and *Barlamont*, cheerfully offering their assistance to reduce the people to obedience by force of Arms; but *Egmont*, *Horn*, and *Orange*, (whose Brother Count *Lodowick* was suspected for a chief contriver of the present mischief) of a contrary judgement, so that she could proceed no further, and indeed she durst not; for presently a secret rumour was dispersed, that if she did not so far gratifie the Covenanters and their adherents, that every man might have liberty to go to Sermons and no man be punished for Religion, she should immediately see all the Churches in *Brussels* fired, the Priests murthered, and her self imprisoned. For fear whereof, though she took all safe courses for her own security, yet she found none so safe as the granting of some of their demands to the Chief Conspirators, by which the Provinces for the present did enjoy some quiet. But this was only like an Intermission in the fit of an Ague: For presently hereupon she received advertisement that those of the Reformed party were not onely suffered to take unto themselves some Churches in *Machlin*, *Antwerp*, and *Tournay*, which till then had never been permitted; but that at *Utrecht* they had driven the Catholicks out of their Churches, and at the *Bosch* had forced the Bishop to forsake the City, as their holy Fathers in *Geneva* had done before them. And in a word, to make up the measure of her sorrows, and compleat their insolencies, she had intelligence of the like Tumult raised at *Amsterdam*, where some of the Reforming Rabble had broken into a Monastery of the *Franciscans*, defaced all Consecrated things, beat and stoned out the Religious persons, not without wounding some of the principal Senators who opposed their doings.

33. Provoked with these indignities, she resolves upon the last remedy, which was, to bring them to obedience by force of arms: and therein she had no small encouragement from the King himself, and good assurance of assistances from such Princes of *Germany* as still adhered unto the Pope. The news whereof so startles the chief of the Covenanters, that they enter into consultation of Electing a new Prince, or putting themselves under the power of some potent Monarch, by whom they might be countenanced against their King, and priviledged in the enjoyment of their Religion. It was advised also, that three thousand Books of *Calvinian* Doctrine should be sent into *Spain*, and dispersed in the chief Cities of it; to the end, that whilst the King was busied in looking to his own peace at home, he might the less regard the Tumults which were raised in the *Netherlands*: and yet for fear that Project might not take effect, it was agreed upon that a combination should be made between the heads of the Covenanters, and the principal Merchants; between whom it was finally concluded, and the conclusion ratified by a solemn taking of the Sacrament on either side, that the Covenanters should protect the Merchants against all men whatsoever, who laboured to restrain them in the freedom of Conscience; and that the Merchants should supply the Covenanters with such sums of mony as might enable them to go through with the Work begun. It also was agreed upon, that the *Calvinian* party for a time should suppresse their own, and make profession of conformity to the *Lutheran* Doctrines,

Doctrines, contained in the Cofeffion of *Ausberg*, in hope thereby of having fuccour and relief from the *Lutheran* Princes, if the King fhould feek to force them in the way of Arms : which was accordingly perfor-med. And that being done, they caft themfelves into a feparate and diftinct Republick from that of the State, erect a Supreme Confiftory in the City of *Antwerp*, and fome inferiour Judicatories in the other Cities, (but all fubordinate unto that of *Antwerp*) in which they take upon them the choice of Magiftrates, for managing and directing all Affairs which concerned the Faction.

34. Of all thefe Plots and Confultations, the King is punctually in-formed by the vigilant Governefs ; and thereupon caufed a report to be difperfed, that he intended to beftow a Royal vifit on his *Belgick Provin-ces* ; but firft to fmooth the way before him by a puiffant Army.   On this advertifement the Governefs refumes her courage, complains how much the Covenanters had abufed her favours ; and publickly declares, that fhe had onely given them leave to meet together for hearing Ser-mons of their own, but that their Minifters had took upon them to Bap-tize and Marry, and perform all other Sacred Offices in a different man-ner from that allowed of by the Church ; That they had fet up divers Confiftories and new Forms of Government, not warranted by the Laws of the feveral Provinces ; That they had opened divers Schools for training up their Children in Heretical Principles ; That they had raif-ed great fums of Money under pretence of purchafing a toleration of the King (whofe Piety was too well known to be fo corrupted) but in plain truth, to levy Souldiers for a War againft him ; That therefore fhe com-mands all Governours and Deputy-Governours in their feveral Provin-ces, not onely to diffolve Heretical Meetings (otherwife then for Ser-mons onely) in the time to come, but to put Garrifons into fuch of the Towns and Cities as were held fufpected, or were moft likely to be feized on to the Kings differvice,   By this Remonftrance, feconded with the news of the Kings intention, the leading Covenanters were fo ftartled, that they refolved on the beginning of the War, and were accordingly in Arms, before the Governefs had either raifed Horfe or Foot, more then the ordinary Train-bands, which were to be maintained in con-tinual readinefs, by the Rules of that Government.   But firft, they thought it moft agreeable to the State of Affairs, to poffefs themfelves of fuch ftrong Towns as either ftood convenient for the letting in of Forreign Succours, or otherwife for commanding the adjoyning Terri-tories.   In which defign they fpeed fo well, that many great Towns de-clare for them of their own accord ; fome were furprifed by fuch of the *Calvinian* Leaders as had friends amongft them ; and fome were willing to ftand neutral till they faw more of it.   But none fared better at the firft then *Anthony* of *Bomberg*, one of the *Calvnifts* of *Antwerp*, who ha-ving formerly ferved the *Hugonot* Prince in the Wars of *France*, had put himfelf into the *Bofch*, from whence the Faction had not long before ex-pelled their Bifhop : And there he played his game with fuch fraud and cunning, that he put the people into Arms, made himfelf Mafter of the Town, and turned the Cannon upon the Count *Meghen*, who was Com-miffionated by the Governefs, amongft other things, to plant a Garri-fon in the fame..

35. This

35. This good succefs encouraged many of the reſt to the like attempts, but few of them with ſo good Fortune. The Count of *Brederode* having Fortified his own Town of *Viana*, a ſmall Town of *Holland* ſtretcheth his Arms from thence to imbrace the reſt, and takes in *Amſtridam* it ſelf without oppoſition ; but having the like aim on *Utrecht*, he found his hopes defeated by the Count of *Meghen*, who got in before him. Worſe fared it with *Philip de Marnix*, Lord of *Tholouſe*, another of the *Antwerpian Calviniſts*, of greater power then *Bomberg*, but of leſs dexterity : holding intelligence with the Provoſt of *Middleberg*, he entertained a deſign of ſurpriſing *Vlaſhing*, and therewith the whole Iſle of *Walcherin*, and the reſt of *Zealand*. To which end he embarks his men, and ſails down the *Scheldt*, not without ſome good hope of effecting his enterpriſe before any diſcovery was made of it. But the Governeſs knew of what importance the ſaid Iſland was, and was there before him in her Forces, though not in her perſon. Repulſed from thence he marcheth back again towards *Antwerp*, takes up his Quarters in the Borough of *Oſtervill*, the *Southwark* as it were of *Antwerp*, and from thence ſo named ; where he is ſet upon by *Lanoy*, another of the Regents Captains ; the Borough fired about his ears, himſelf burned in a Barn, fifteen thouſand of his Souldiers killed in the flight, three hundred of them taken and then put to the Sword : Which execution was thought neceſſary as the caſe then ſtood, for fear the *Calviniſts* in the City might renew the fight, and put him worſe to it then before : Nor were they wanting to their Friends in that deſperate exigent, whoſe ſlaughter they beheld from the Walls of the City. But when they thought to paſs the Bridge, they found no Bridge at all to give them paſſage : the Prince of *Orange* being then at *Antwerp*, had cauſed it to be broken down the day before, not out of any deſign to prevent the *Calviniſts* from aſſiſting their Brethren, but rather to hinder the Victorious Catholicks (if it ſhould ſo happen) from making any uſe of it to poſſeſs the City. But the *Calviniſt*, not knowing of his ſecret purpoſes, tumultuouſly aſſembled to the number of fourteen thouſand men, fell foul upon him in the Streets, reviled him by the name of Traytor, and clapped a Piſtol to his Breaſt, and queſtionleſs had proceeded to ſome greater outrage, if the *Lutherans* (hating the *Calviniſts*, and as hateful to them) had not joyned with the *Papiſts*, and thereby over-powered them both in ſtrength and numbers.

36. But none fared worſe then the *Calvinians* of *Tournay* and *Valenciennes*, though they were both ſtronger and more numerous then in other places. Thoſe of *Valenciennes* had refuſed to admit a Garriſon, encouraged by their *French* Preachers to that diſobedience. But being beſieged by *Norcarmius*, Deputy Governour of *Haynalt* for the Marqueſs of *Bergen*, they were compelled in the end to ſubmit to mercy ; which was ſo intermixed with juſtice, that thirty ſix of the principal Incendiaries were beheaded, ſome of their Preachers hanged, and ſome Souldiers executed ; the Liberties of the City being ſeiſed, and declared to be forfeit till the King ſhould be pleaſed to reſtore them. Thoſe of *Valenciennes* had been animated by the Conſiſtories of ſome other Cities to make good the Town againſt *Norcarmius*, as long as they could ; aſſuring them that he muſt ſhortly raiſe the Siege, to quench the fire

fire that would be kindled in another Province. Accordingly it was contrived that ſome Foot-Companies which lay in *Armentieres* ſhould waſte the Countrey about *Liſle* in *Flanders Gallicant*; and that whilſt *Raſſinghen* the Governour of *Liſle* drew out of the City to ſuppreſs them, the *Calviniſts* of *Tournay* by the aid of their Brethren within that City ſhould poſſeſs themſelves of it. And ſo far it ſucceeded as they had projected, that the *Armenterians*, being conducted by one *Cornelius*, who of a Smith became a Preacher, and would needs make himſelf a Commander alſo, acted their part in the deſign, but eaſily were ſubdued by *Raſſinghen* at the firſt aſſault. The news whereof not onely terrified the Conſiſtorians within *Liſle* it ſelf, but ſo diſheartned thoſe of *Tournay*, who hoped to have made themſelves Maſters of it, that they thought it beſt for them to retire; but being ſet upon by *Norcarmius*, who had drawn ſome Forces from his Camp before *Valenciennes* to perform this ſervice, they were utterly routed, moſt of their men (amounting to four thouſand) either killed or taken; two Barrels of Powder, twenty Field-pieces, and nine Colours, falling into the hands of the Conquering Army: with which *Norcarmius* marching on directly to the Gates of *Tournay*, commands them in the name of the Governeſs to receive a Garriſon, entered the Town, diſarms the People, impriſoned the Incendiaries, reſtored the Biſhop and Clergy to their former power; and finally, impoſed ſuch a Governour over them, as was like to give a good account of them for the times enſuing.

37. The taking of theſe Towns to mercy, the like ſucceſs in other places, and a report that *Ferdinand* of *Toledo* Duke of *Alva*, was coming forwards with an Army to make way for the King, did ſo deject the Heads of the *Gheuſes*, and the reſt of the Covenanters, that moſt of them began to droop; whereof the Governeſs did not need to be advertiſed, and was reſolved to make ſome preſent uſe of the Conſternation. She therefore cauſes a new Oath or Proteſtation to be forthwith made, and to be taken by all Magiſtrates and Officers both of Peace and War; by which they were to bind themſelves without exception to obey any who ſhould be appointed in the Kings name for their Supreme Governour. And this ſhe was reſolved upon againſt all diſwaſions; not that ſhe meant to uſe it for a diſcrimination, by which ſhe might diſcover how they ſtood affected to his Majeſties Service; but that ſhe might with leſs envy diſplace all ſuch as willfully refuſed the Oath, or puniſh them with death and confiſcation if they brake their Faith. Being propounded to the Counſel, it was cheerfully approved and ſubſcribed by ſome, and reſolutely oppoſed by others, under pretence that they had formerly took the Oath of Allegiance to the King himſelf, and that Oaths were not to be multiplyed without juſt neceſſity. But none more pertinaciouſly refuſed it then the Prince of *Orange*, who deviſed many plauſible reaſons in his juſtification, but ſuch as were of little weight when they came to the ballance. Count *Egmont* for a while demurred, but at laſt ſubmitted, and took the Oath as others of the Counſel had done before: the falling off of which great men ſo amazed the reſt, that every one thought it now high time to provide for himſelf. The Prince of *Orange* with his Family retireth unto his County of *Naſſaw*, but leaves his Miniſters behind him to maintain his Intereſt: Count *Brederode* departs for

1567.

Germany,

Germany, where he dyed soon after : Count *William de la March* , commonly called the Baron of *Lume* , takes Sanctuary in the Realm of *England* : *Bomberg* not finding any safety to be had in the *Bosch*, abandoneth it to the Regents Empire, by whom it was not onely forced to receive a Garrison,but also to redeem their Priviledges for a sum of money. After which most of the revolted Cities came in so speedily , that there was nothing to be seen of the late Rebellion.

1568   38. And here the Countrey might have been resetled in its firm obedience, if either the King had gone in person to confirm the Provinces, or had imployed a Minister less odious then the Duke of *Alva*,the cruelty of whose nature was both known and feared ; or rather, if the Prince of *Orange*, and the rest of that Faction, had not preserved themselves for an aftergame. But the King stays behind, and the Duke comes forward. And coming forward with an Army of experienced Souldiers, entereth the Provinces, assumes the Government, imprisoneth many of the Nobility ; the Counts of *Horn* and *Egmont* amongst the rest , whom he after executed. The news whereof being brought unto Cardinal *Granvel*, he is reported to have said, That *if one Fish* (by which he meant the Prince of *Orange*) *had escaped the Net , the Duke of* Alva's *draught would be nothing worth.* And so it proved in the event ; for the Prince being strong in Kindered and Alliances in the Higher *Germany,* made use of all his interest in them for the securing of his life, and the recovery of his Lands and Honours , of which he was judicially deprived by the Duke of *Alva* , who caused the sentence of condemnation to be passed upon him, confiscates his Estate, proscribes his person, placeth a Garrison in *Breda* , entereth on all the rest of his Towns and Lands ; and finally, seizeth upon *Philip* Earl of *Buren* his eldest Son , whom he sent prisoner into *Spain.* The news whereof gave little trouble to the Prince,because it made his taking Arms the more excusable in the sight of men: for now besides the common quarrel of his Countrey, and the cause of Religion, he might pretend an unavoidable necessity of fighting for his Life, Lands, Honours and Posterity , unless he would betray them all by a willful sluggishness. Besides, he was not without hope, that if he should miscarry in the present enterprise, his Eldest Son, being brought up in the Court of *Spain*, might be restored to those Estates which himself had lost ; but if he prospered in his work, and that the King should still think fit to detain him Prisoner , he had another Son by the Daughter of *Saxonie* , who might succeed him , as he did, in his power and greatness.

39. But first, he thought it most agreeable to his present condition, to employ other hands and heads besides his own ; to which end he had so contrived it , that whilst his Brother *Lodowick* invaded *Friesland* , and Count *Hostrat* out of *Juliers* and the Lower *Palatinate* crossed over the *Mose* , an Army of the *French Hugonots* should fall into *Artois* , to give the *Spaniards* the more work by this treble invasion. But the *French* Forces being followed at the heels by some Troops of Horse , whom the King sent after them, were totally defeated neer the Town of St. *Vallery* ; their chief Commanders brought to *Paris* , and there beheaded. Count *Hostrat* with his Forces had the misfortune , first broken, and afterwards totally vanquished by *Sancho d' Avila* one of *Alva*'s Generals: Onely

Count

Count *Lodowick* had the honour of a signal Victory, but bought it with the death of his brother *Adolph* whom he lost in the Battail; though afterwards encountring with the Duke himself, he lost six thousand of his Men, besides all his Baggage, Ordnance and Ammunition, hardly escaping with his life.   And now it is high time for the Prince to enter; who having raised an Army of eight and twenty thousand Horse and Foot (increased not long after by the addition of three thousand Foot and five hundred Horse, which the *French Hugonots* out of pure Zeal unto the Cause had provided for him) takes his way toward *Brabant*, which he had marked out for his Quarters; but there he found the Dukes whole Army to be laid in his way, whom he could neither pass by, nor ingage in fight; the Duke well knowing, that such great Armies wanting pay, would disband themselves, and were more safely broken by delay then battail; onely he watched their motions, and ingaged by parties, in which he always had the better: and by these Arts so tired the Prince that in the end he was compelled to dissolve his Forces, and retire once more in *Nassaw*. But whilst the Duke was thus imployed in securing the passages of the Country which lay next to *Germany*, he left the ports and Sea Towns open to the next Invadour: Which being observed by *William de March* Baron of *Luma*, who with few Ships kept himself upon the Seas out of *Alva*'s reach, he suddenly seized upon the *Brill*, a port of *Holland*, where he defaced such Images as he found in their Churches, omitting no irreverence unto any thing which was accounted Sacred; but otherwise so fortified and intrenched the Town, that it proved impregnable. This hapned on *Palm* Sunday, *Anno* 1570; and on the Sunday following, being *Easter*-day, the *Spanish* Garrison is turned out of *Vlushing*, the chief port of *Zealand*: by gaining of which two places, it might not be unfitly said, that they carried the keys of *Holland* and *Zealand* at their Girdle, and were inabled by that means to receive succours from all parts and Nations which lay towards the Seas, as they after did.

40. The loss of these two ports drew along with it a defection of most of the strong Towns in *Holland*, which at the instigation of the Baron of *Luma*, put themselves under the command of the Prince of *Orange*, and at his motion took the Oath of fidelity to him; from him they received their Garrison, Shipping and Arms, and to him they permitted the disposing of all places of Government, making of Laws, and the distributing of the Revnues which belonged to the Clergy: To him such multitudes repaired out of *France* and *England*, (besides Auxiliary *Scots*) that within less then four months, a Navy of one hundred and fifty Sail lay rigged in *Vlushing*, and from thence spoiled and robbed all Merchants of the *Spanish* party. Nor were the Dukes affairs in much better order in the parts next *France*, in which Count *Lodowick* with the help of some *French Hugonots* had made himself Master of *Mons*, the chief City of *Huynalt*; which seemed the more considerable in the eyes of *Alva*, because the *French* King openly but for different ends, had avowed the Action.   By whose permission, *Gasper Colligny*, the great Admiral of *France*, and one of the chief Leaders of the *Hugonot* party, had raised an Army in the Borders, consisting of six or seven thousand men, which he put under the command of the Lord of *Jenlis*, who had before conducted the *French* Succours to the Prince of *Orange*. But *Jenlis* being defeated by *Don Frederick* the Dukes

Eldest

Eldest Son, and the Prince of *Orange* wanting power to relieve the Besieged, the Town was re-delivered into the hands of the *Spaniards* upon terms of honour, and *Lodowick* retires to *Dilemberg*, the chief Town of *Nassaw*.

41. The Prince of *Orange* in the mean time, animated by the general revolt of almost all the strong Towns in *Holland*, raised a new Army of no fewer then eleven thousand Foot and six thousand Horse; with which he entered into *Brabant*, possest himself of some of the principal Towns, and suffered others to redeem themselves with great sums of money, with which he satisfied his Souldiers for their pains and hazard in the obtaining of the rest. *Dendermond* and *Oudenard*, two strong Towns of *Flanders* which had made some resistance, he both stormed and plundered; the Souldiers in all places making spoil of Churches, and in some tyrannizing over the dead, whose Monuments they robbed and pillaged. But none fared worse then the poor Priests, whom out of hate to their Religion, they did not onely put to death, but put to death with tortures; and in some places which fell under the power of the *Baron* of *Luma*, hanged up their mangled Limbs or Quarters, as Butchers do their small Meats in a common Shambles: which spoils and cruelties so alienated the affections of all the people, that his power in those parts was not like to continue long; and having failed of his attempt in relieving *Mons*, crossed the Countrey into *Holland*, as his surest receptacle; on whose retreat the Duke recovers all the Towns which he had taken in *Brabant* and *Flanders*, follows him into *Holland*, and besiegeth *Harlem*; in which the Souldiers, to demonstrate of what Sect they were, made a meer Pageant of Religion: for setting up Altars on the Bulwarks, they dressed them with Images and representations of the Saints; and being attired in Copes and Vestments, they sung Hymns before them, as if they were offering Devotions. After which mockery they brought out the resemblances of Priests and Religious persons made of straw, whipt them, and stabbed them into the body; and finally, cutting off their heads, flung them into the Leaguer: Sometimes they also placed the Images of Christ, and many of the Saints, against the mouth of the Cannon, with many other Arts of the like impiety; for which they were brought to a dear reckoning when the Town was taken; at which time most of them were either put to the Sword, or Hanged, or Drowned.

42. *Frederick* the Prince Elector *Palatine* had hitherto ingaged no further in the *Belgick* troubles then the rest of his Neighbours. But now he doth more cordially espouse the quarrel, upon some hope of propagating the *Calvinian* Doctrines, which he had lately introduced into his Dominions. And being well affected to the House of *Nassaw*, and knowing what encouragements the *Calvinian* Faction in the *Netherlands* had received from them, cheerfully hearkened to such propositions as were made to him at the first by Count *Lodowick* his Ministers, and after by the Agent of the Prince himself. He had sent some aid not long before to support the *Hugonots*: But now his Souldiers being returned from *France*, and grown burdensome to him, are drawn together into a body; and with the help of some others out of *France* and *Germany*, compound an Army of seven thousand Foot and four thousand Horse, with which he sends Prince *Christopher* a younger Son,

under

under the conduct of Count *Lodowick* and his Brother *Henry*. But they had scarce entred within the Borders of *Gelderland*, where they expected an addition of fresh Forces from the Prince of *Orange*, when they were set upon by *Sanchio d Avila* before mentioned, and routed with so great a slaughter, that almost all the whole Army were either taken prisoners, remedilesly wounded, or slain outright : and as for their three Generals, *Lodowick* of *Naßaw*, *Grave Henry*, and the young Prince *Christopher*, they were either slain fighting in the battail, or trampled under the Horses Feet, or finally, stifled in the flight, as they crossed the Fens ; the last more probable, because their bodies were not to be found on the strictest search.

43. But notwithstanding this misfortune, neither the Prince Elector nor the Prince of *Orange* could be moved to desert the Cause: which by the temptation of revenge was grown dearer to them. For after this we find Prince *Casimir*, another of the *Palatine* Princes, in the Head of an Army raised for assisting the Confederates in the *Belgick* Provinces, (by which name they began to be commonly called) after the death of *Requesenes*, who had succeeded *Alva* in the publick Government ; but wanting time before his death to settle the command in some trusty hands, till some Supreme Officer might be sent unto them from the Court of *Spain* ; the Government devolved for the present on the Council of State, and was invaded afterwards by the States themselves, whose Deputies assembling in the Council-house or Court of *Brussels*, made up the body of that Council which governed all Affairs both of Peace and War. But great contentions growing betwixt them and the Souldiers, and those contentions followed on either side with great animosities, the Prince of *Orange* had a most excellent opportunity for the establishing of his new Dictatorship over *Holland* and *Zealand*, and some of the adjoyning Provinces of less name and note. But being weary at the last of their own confusions, and more impatient of the insupportable insolencies of the Spanish Souldiers, an Association is first made in the Provinces of *Brabant*, *Flanders*, *Artois* and *Haynalt*. By which it was agreed in Writing, and confirmed by Oath, that they should mutually assist each other against the *Spaniards* till they had cleared the Country of them. And with these Provinces, consisting for the most part of such as were counted Catholicks, *Holland* and *Zealand*, with the rest, though esteemed heretical, did associate also: which Union is called commonly the *Pacification of Gaunt*, because agreed on in that City, and was so much insisted on by the Heads of the Leaguers, that it was counselled by the Prince, not to admit of *Don John* for their Supreme Governour, till he had ratified and confirmed that Association.

44. But because there was no mention of maintaining the Kings Authority, or preserving the Catholick Religion in the Originals of the League ; it was found necessary to provide for both by some explication, to take away the envy and suspition of that great disloyalty which otherwise must have fallen upon them. And by that explication it was thus declared, *viz.* that they would faithfully from thenceforth maintain the League, for the conservation of their most Sacred Faith, and the Roman Catholick Religion ; for preserving the

Paci-

Pacification made at *Gaunt*; for the expulsion of the Spaniards and their adherents ; their due obedience to the Kings most excellent Majesty being always tendered.   According to which explication it was confirmed by *Don John* under the name of the *perpetual Edict*, with the Kings consent ; who thought his own Authority and the Roman Religion to be thereby sufficiently provided for, but he found the contrary.   For when the Prince of *Orange* was required to subscribe to the Pacification, with the addition of two Clauses for constancy in this Religion, and the Kings obedience, he refused it absolutely, assuring such as moved it to him, that the Provinces under his command or confederacy with him were barred in Conscience from subscribing to the preservation of the *Romish* Faith.   And at this time it was, that he merrily told the Duke of *Arescot*, who was one of the Delegates, that there was not more *Calvism* on his head, then there was *Calvinism* in his heart.   He well foresaw that the agreement betwixt *Don John* and the Estates of the Country would not long continue ; and he resolved to make some advantage of the breach, whensoever it hapned.   Nor was he any thing mistaken in the one or the other ; for discontents and jealousies encreasing mutually between the parties, *Don John* leaves *Brusels*, and betakes himself to the Castle of *Namure* for fear of an Assassinate (as it was given out) which was intended on his person : which so incensed the Estates, that by a general consent, a *Dictatorian* or Soveraign power was put into the hands of the Prince of *Orange* by the name *Ruart*, according to the priviledge and practice of the *Brabanters* in extreme necessities.   Invested with which power, he instituteth a new face of Government both in *Brusels* it self, and many of the Towns adjoyning, modelled after the Example of *Holland* and *Zealand*.   He demolished also the great Fort at *Antwerp*, which had been raised with so great Pride and Ostentation by the Duke of *Alva*: The like done also in demolishing the Castles of *Gant, Utrecht, Lisse, Valenciennes*, and some other places ; performed by such alacrity by them that did it, as if they had shaken off the Yoke of some Forein servitude.   An Oath was also framed for renouncing all obedience to *Don John* their Governour, and people of all sorts compelled to take it : for the refusal whereof by the *Jesuits* of *Antwerp*, a rabble of *Calvinian* Zealots, on the day of *Pentecost*, forced open the doors of that *Society*, plundred their houses of all things Sacred and Prophane, and set the Father on board a Ship of the *Hollanders* with great scorn and insolencie, to be landed in some other Country.

45.   The like done also to the Fathers of *Tournay, Bruges*, and *Maestricht*, banished on the same account from their several Cities ; with whom were also exiled in some places *Franciscan* Fryars, in others many secular Priests, who would not easily be perswaded to abjure their Loyalty.   By whose departure divers Churches were left destitute, and unprovided of incumbents to instruct the people : which so increased the confidence and hopes of the *Colvinians*, that they not only petitioned the Estates for liberty of Conscience, but for the publick use of Churches in their several Territories : but being refused in their desires, (though the Prince of *Orange* openly appeared for them) they were resolved no longer to expect the lazie temper of Authority, but actually

ally took poſſeſſion of ſome of the Churches in *Brabant, Gelderland*, and *Flanders*, and openly exerciſed that Religion, which till then they had profeſſed in ſecret; nor durſt the Eſtates do any thing in vindication of their own Authority, conſidering what neceſſary uſe they might have of them, in the preſent War againſt *Don John*, and from how great a perſon they received incouragement. But in the midſt of this career, they received a ſtop; for the Confederates being vanquiſhed by *Don John* at the battail of *Gemblack, Bruſſels* and all the Towns of *Brabant* ſubmitted themſelves one after another to the power of the conquerour. *Philipivil*, a ſtrong Town of *Haynalt, Limburg* and *Dalem*, with ſome others, not ſo eaſily yeilding, were either forced by long ſiege, or ſome violent ſtorming, or otherwiſe ſurrendred upon capitulations. During which Sieges and Surrendries, the Prince of *Orange*, who had eſcaped with ſafety from the battail of *Gemblack*, was buſied in eſtabliſhing his Dominion on the Coaſt of *Holland* : In which deſign he found no oppoſition but at *Amſterdam*, conſtant at that time, even to miracle, both to their old Religion and their old Obedience. But being beſieged on all ſides both by Sea and Land, they yeilded on condition of enjoying the free exerciſe of their former Faith, and of the like Freedom from all Garriſons, but of Native Citizens : But when they had yeilded up the Town, they were not onely forced to admit a Garriſon, but to behold their Churches ſpoil'd, their Prieſts ejected, and ſuch new Teachers thruſt upon them as they moſt abominated. But liberty of Religion being firſt admitted, a confuſed liberty of opinions followed ſhortly after; till in the end that Town became the common Sink of all Sects and Sectaries which hitherto have diſturbed the Church, and proved the greateſt ſcandal and diſhonor of the Reformation.

46. *Holland* had lately been too fruitful of this viperous brood, but never more unfortunate, then in producing *David George* of *Delfe*, and *Henry Nicholas* of *Leiden*, the two great Monſters of that age: but the impieties of the firſt were too groſs and horrid to find any followers; the latter was ſo ſmoothed over as to gain on many, whom the Impoſtor had ſeduced. The *Anabaptiſts* out of *Weſtphalia* had found ſhelter here in the beginning of the Tumults ; and poſſibly might contribute both their hearts and hands to the committing of thoſe ſpoils and outrages before remembred. In imitation of whoſe counterfeit piety, and pretended ſingleneſs of heart, there ſtarted up another Sect as dangerous and deſtructive to humane Society as the former were; for by inſinuating themſelves into the heart of the ignorant multitude, under a ſhew of ſingular Sanctity and Integrity, did afterwards infect their minds with damnable Hereſies, openly repugnant to the Chriſtian Faith. In ordinary Speech they uſed new and monſtrous kinds of expreſſions, to which the ears of men brought up in the Chriſtian Church had not been accuſtomed, and all men rather wondred at then underſtood. To difference themſelves from the reſt of mankind, they called their Sect by the name of the *Family of Love*, and laboured to perſwade their hearers, that thoſe only were elected unto life Eternal, which were by them adopted Children of that Holy Family; and that all others were but Reprobates and Damned perſons. One of their Paradoxes

was

was (and a safe one too) that it was lawful for them to deny upon oath whatsoever they pleased, before any Magistrate, or any other whomsoever, that was not of the same *Family* or Society with them. Some books they had, in which their dotages were contained and propagated ; first writ in *Dutch*, and afterwards translated into other Languages as tended most to their advantage ; that is to say, *The Gospel of the Kingdom* ; *The Lords Sentences* ; *The Prophesse of the Spirit of the Lord* ; *The publication of peace upon earth* : by the Author *H. N.* But who this *H. N.* was, those of the *Family* could by no fair means be induced or inforced by threatnings to reveal. But after, it was found to be this *Henry Nicholas* of *Leiden*, whom before we spake of : Who being emulous of the Glories of King *John* of *Leiden*, that most infamous Botcher, had most blasphemously preached unto all his followers, that *he was partaker of the Divinity of God, as God was of his humane nature.* How afterwards they past over into *England*, and what reception they found there, may be told hereafter.

50. By giving freedom of Conscience to all Sects and Sectaries, and amongst others, to these also, the Prince of *Orange* had provided himself of so strong a party in this Province, that he was able to maintain a defensive War against all his opposites, especially after he had gained the Ports of *Brill* and *Vlushing*, which opened a fair entrance unto all adventurers out of *England* and *Scotland*. For on the Rumour of this War, the *Scots* in hope of prey and plunder, the *English* in pursuit of Honour and the use of Arms, resorted to the aid of their *Belgick* Neighbours, whose absolute subjugation to the King of *Spain* was looked on as a thing of dangerous consequence unto either Nation. And at the first they went no otherwise then as Voluntiers of their own accord, rather connived at then permitted by their several Princes : But when the Government was taken into the hands of the States, and that the War was ready to break out betwixt them and *Don John* ; the Queen of *England* did not only furnish them with large sums of mony, but entred into a League or Confederation ; by which it was agreed, That the Queen should send unto their aid one thousand Horse and five thousand Foot ; that they should conclude nothing respecting either Peace or War, without her consent and approbation ; that they should not enter into League with any person or persons, but with her allowance, and she, if she thought good, to be comprehended in the same ; that the States should send the like aid unto the Queen, if any Prince attempted any act of Hostility against her or her Kingdoms ; and that they should furnish her with forty Ships of sufficient burthen, to serve at her pay under the Lord Admiral of *England*, whensoever she had any necessary occasion to set forth a Navy : and finally (not to insist upon the rest) that if any difference should arise amongst themselves, it was to be referred and offered unto her Arbitrament. And to this League she was the rather induced to grant her Royal assent, because she had been certainly advertised by the Prince of *Orange*, that *Don John* was then negotiating a marriage with the Queen of *Scots*, that under colour of her Title he might advance himself to the Crown of *England*. And yet she ventured neither men nor mony, but on very good terms : receiving in the way of pawn the greatest part of the rich Jewels and massie Ornaments

ments of Plate which anciently belonged unto the Princes of the House of *Burgundy*.

51. This League exceedingly increased the reputation of the new *Confederacy*, and made the *States* appear considerable in the eye of the world. And more it might have been, if either *Don John*'s improsperous Government had continued longer, or if the Prince of *Orange* had not entertained some designs apart for himself. But *Don John* dyes in the year 1578, and leaves his Forces in the power of *Alexander Farneze* Prince of *Parma*, Son to that Dutchess whom we have so often mentioned in this part of our History. A Prince he was of no less parts and Military Prowess, then any of his Predecessors; but of a better and more equal temper then the best amongst them; whereof he gave sufficient testimony in following Government, in which he was confirmed (after the Kings occasioned lingrings) with great state and honour: For having regained from the States some of the best Towns of which they had possessed themselves before the arrival of *Don John*, he forced them to a necessity of some better counsels then those by which they steered their course since they came to the Helm. And of all counsels none seemed better to the Prince of *Orange*, then that the Countrey should be so cantoned amongst several Princes, that every one being ingaged to defend his own, the whole might be preserved from the power of the *Spaniards*. To this end it had been advised that *Flanders* and *Artois* should return to the Crown of *France*, of which they were holden, and to the Kings whereof the Earls of both did homage in the times foregoing. The Queen of *England* was to have been gratified with the Isles of *Zealand*; the Dukedom of *Guelders* to divert to the next Heirs of it; *Groning* and *Deventer* to be incorporated with the *Hans*; *Holland* and *Friesland*, together with the distrisht of *Utrecht*, to be appropriated wholly to the Prince of *Orange*, as the reward of his deservings: the *Brabanters* to a new Election, according to their native rights: the rest of the Provinces to remain to the *German* Empire, of which they had anciently Eleired.

52. This distribution I confess had some cunning in it, and must have quickly brought the *Spanish* pride to a very low ebb, if he that laid the plot could have given the possession. It is reported that when the Pope offered the Realms of *Naples* and *Sicily* to King *Henry* the Third, for *Edmond* Earl of *Lancaster* his youngest Son, he offered them on such hard conditions, (and so impossible in a manner to be performed) that the Kings Embassadors merrily told him, he might as well create a Kingdom in the Moon, and bid his Master climb up to it, for it should be his. And such a Lunary conceit was that of the division and subdivision of the *Belgick* Provinces, in what *Calvinian* head soever it was forged and hammered. For being that each of the *Donees* was to conquer his part before he could receive any benefit from it, the device was not like to procure much profit, but onely to the Prince of *Orange*, who was already in possession, and could not better fortifie and assure himself in his new Dominion, then by cutting out so much work for the King of *Spain*, as probably might keep him exercised to the end of the World. But this device not being likely to succeed, it seemed better to the Prince of *Orange* to unite the Provinces under his command into a Solemn

League

League and Afsociation, to be from thenceforth called the *Perpetual Union*. Which League, Afsociation, or perpetual Union, bears date at *Utrecht* on the 23 of *January* 1578, and was then made between the Provinces of *Holland*, *Zealand*, *Guelders*, *Zutphen*, *Utrecht*, *Friefland* and *Over-Yfsel*, with their Afsociates, called ever fince that time the *United Provinces*. In the firft making of which League or perpetual Union, it **1579.** was provided in the firft place, that they fhould infeparably joyn together for defence of themfelves, their Liberty and Religion, againft the power of the *Spaniard*. But it was cautioned in the fecond, that this Afsociation fhould be made without any diminution or alteration of the particular Priviledges, Rights, Freedom, Exemptions, Statutes, Cuftoms, Ufes, Preheminencies, which any of the faid Towns, Provinces, Members, or Inhabitants at that time enjoyed. Liberty of Religion to be left to thofe of *Holland* and *Zealand*, in which they might govern themfelves as to them feemed good: and fuch a Freedom left to thofe of other Provinces, as was agreed on at the Pacification made at *Gaunt*; by which it was not lawful to moleft thofe of the Church of *Rome* in any manner whatfoever.

53. But more particularly it was provided and agreed on, that fuch Controverfies as fhould grow between the faid Provinces, Towns, or Members of this Union, touching their Priviledges, Cuftoms, Freedoms, &c. fhould be decided by the ordinary courfe of Juftice, or by fome amicable and friendly compofition amongft themfelves; and that no other Countries, Provinces, Members or Towns, whom thofe Countries did no way concern, fhall in any part meddle by way of friendly intermiffion tending to an accord. Which caution I the rather note in this place and time, becaufe we may perhaps look back upon it in the cafe of *Barnevelt*, when they had freed themfelves from the power of the *Spaniards*, and were at leifure to infringe the publick Liberties, in the purfuit of their particular Animofities againft one another. But to proceed: this Union, as it was more advantagious unto Queen *Elizabeth*, than the general League; fo was it afterwards more cordially affected by her, when their neceffities inforced them to caft themfelves and their Eftates upon her protection. But thefe proceedings fo exafperated the King of *Spain*, that he profcribed the Prince of *Orange* by his **1581.** publick Edict, bearing date *June* 18. 1581. And on the other fide, the Prince prevailed fo far upon thofe of the Union, as to declare by publick Inftrument, that the King of *Spain*, by reafon of his many violations of their Rights and Liberties, had forfeited his Eftate and Intereft in the feveral Provinces, and therefore that they did renounce all manner of fidelity and obedience to him. Which Inftrument bears date on the twenty fixth of *July* then next following. Upon the publifhing whereof, they brake in pieces all the Seals, Signets, and Counter-fignets of the King of *Spain*; appointed others to be made by the States General; for difpatch of fuch bufinefs as concerned the *Union* or Confederation; requiring all fubjects to renounce their Oaths to the faid King of *Spain*, and to take a new Oath of Fidelity to the general Eftates, againft the faid King and his Adherents: the like done alfo by all Governours, Superintendents, Chancellors, Counfellors, and other Officers, &c. They had before drawn the Sword againft him, and now they throw away the Scabberd,

berd. For to what end could this action aim at, but to make the breach irreparable between them and the King, to swell the injury so high, as not to be within the compass of future pardon? And when men once are brought unto such a condition, they must resolve to fight it out to the very last, and either carry away the Garland as a sign of Victory, or otherwise live like Slaves, or dye like Traytors. But this was done according to *Calvins* Doctrine in the Book in *Institutes*, in which he gives to the Estates of each several Countrey such a Coercive Power over Kings and Princes, as the *Ephori* had exercised over the Kings of *Sparta*, and the *Roman Tribunes* sometimes put in practice against the *Consuls*. And more then so, he doth condemn them of a betraying of the Peoples Liberty, whereof they are made *Guardians* by Gods own appointment (so he saith at least) if they restrain not Kings when they play the Tyrants, and wantonly insult upon, or oppress the Subjects. So great a Master could not but meet with some apt Scholars in the Schools of Polity, who would reduce his Rules to practice, and justifie their practice by such great Authority.

54. But notwithstanding the unseasonable publication of such an unprecedented sentence, few of the Provinces fell off from the Kings obedience; and such strong Towns as still remained in the hands of the States, were either forced unto their duty, or otherwise hard put to it by the Prince of *Parma*. To keep whom busied in such sort, that he should not be in a capacity of troubling his Affairs in *Holland*, the Prince of *Orange* put the *Brabanders* (whose priviledges would best bear it) to a new Election: And who more fit to be the man then *Francis* Duke of *Anjou*, Brother to *Henry* the Third of *France*, and then in no small possibility of attaining to the Marriage of the Queen of *England*? Assisted by the Naval power of the one, and the Land Forces of the other, What Prince was able to oppose him. and what power to withstand him. The young Duke passing over into *England*, found there an entertainment so agreeable to all expectations, that the Queen was seen to put a Ring upon one of his Fingers; which being looked on as the pledge of a future Marriage, the news thereof posted presently to the *Low Countries* by the Lord *Aldegund* who was then present at the Court, where it was welcomed both in *Antwerp* and other places with all signs of joy, and celebrated by discharging of all the Ordnance both on the Walls, and in such Ships as then lay on the River. After which triumph comes the Duke, accompanied by some great Lords of the Court of *England*, and is invested solemnly by the Estates of those Countries, in the Dukedoms of *Brabant* and *Limburg*, the Marquisate of the Holy Empire, and the Lordship of *Machlin*: which action seems to have been carryed by the power of the Consistorian *Calvinists*; for besides that it agreeth so well with their common principles, they were grown very strong in *Antwerp*, where *Philip* Lord of *Aldegund*, a profest *Calvinian*, was Deputy for the Prince of *Orange*, as they were also in most Towns of consequence in the Dukedom of *Brabant*. But on the other side, the Romish party was reduced to such a low estate, that they could not freely exercise their own Religion, but onely as it was indulged unto them by Duke *Francis*, their new-made Soveraign, upon condition of taking the Oath of Allegiance to him, and abdicating the Authority of the King of *Spain*; the grant

grant of which permiſſion had been vain and of no ſignificancy, if at that time they could have freely exerciſed the ſame without it. But whoſoever they were that concurred moſt powerfully in conferring this new honour on him, he quickly found that they had given him nothing but an airy Title, keeping all power unto themſelves: So that upon the matter he was nothing but an honourable Servant, and bound to execute the command of his mighty Maſters. In time perhaps he might have wrought himſelf to a greater power; but being young, and ill adviſed, he raſhly enterpriſed the taking of the City of *Antwerp*; of which being fruſtrated by the miſcarriage of his plot, he returned ingloriouſly in *France*, and ſoon after dyes.

55. And now the Prince of *Orange* is come to play his laſt part on the publick Theatre: his winding Wit had hitherto preſerved his Provinces in ſome temrs of peace, by keeping *Don John* exerciſed by the General States, and the Prince of *Parma* no leſs buſied by the Duke of *Anjou*; nor was there any hope of recovering *Holland* and *Zealand* to the Kings obedience, but either by open force, or ſome ſecret practice; the firſt whereof appeared not poſſible, and the laſt ignoble. But the neceſſity of removing him by what means ſoever, prevailed at laſt above all ſence and terms of Honour. And thereupon a deſperate young Fellow is ingaged to murther him; which he attempted by diſcharging a Piſtol in his Face, when he was at *Antwerp* attending on the Duke of *Anjou*; ſo that he hardly eſcaped with life. But being recovered of that blow, he was not long after ſhot with three poyſon Bullets by one *Balthaſar Gerard* a *Burgundian* born, whom he had lately taken into his ſervice: which murder was committed at *Delph* in *Holland*, on the 10 of *June* 1584, when he had lived but fifty years, and ſome Moneths over. He left behind him three Sons, by as many Wives. One *Anne* the Daughter of *Maximilian* of *Egmont* Earl of *Bucen*, he begat *Philip* Earl of *Bucen* his eldeſt Son, who ſucceeded the Prince of *Orange* after his deceaſe. By *Anne* the Daughter of *Maurice* Duke Electtor of *Saxony*, he was Father of *Grave Maurice*, who at the age of eighteen years was made Commander General of the Forces of the States United, and after the death of *Philip* his Elder Brother, ſucceeded him in all his Titles and Eſtates. And finally, by his fourth Wife *Loviſe* Daughter of *Gaſper Colligny* great Admiral of *France* (for of his third, being a Daughter to the Duke of *Montpenſier*, he had never a Son) he was the Father of Prince *Henry Frederick*, who in the year 1625 became Succeſſor unto his Brother in all his Lands, Titles. and Commands. Which *Henry* by a Daughter of the Count of *Solmes*, was Father of *William* Prince of *Orange*, who married the Princeſs *Mary*, Eldeſt Daughter of King *Charles*, the ſecond Monarch of great *Britain*: And departing this life in the flower of his youth and expectations, *Anno* 1650, he left his Wife with child of a *Poſt-humous* Son, who after was Baptized by the name of *William*, and is now the onely ſurviving hope of that famous and illuſtrious Family.

1584.   56. But to return again to the former *William*, whom we left weltring in his blood at *Delph* in *Holland*: He was a man of great poſſeſſions and Eſtates, but of a ſoul too large for ſo great a Fortune. For beſides the Principality of *Orange* in *France*, and the County of *Naſſaw* in *Germany*, he he was possessed in right of his first Wife of the Earldom of *Bucen* in *Gelderland*, as also of the Town and Territories of *Lerdame* and *Iselstine* in *Holland*; and in his own Patrimonial Right was Lord of the strong Towns and goodly *Seignories* of *Breda, Grave* and *Diest*, in the Dukedom of *Brabant*. In the right of which last Lordship he was *Burgrave* of *Antwerp*. He was also Marquess of *Vere* and *Vlusting*, with some jurisdiction over both, in the Isle of *Walcheren*; by *Charles* the Fifth made Knight of the Golden Fleece, and by King *Philip* Governour of *Holland, Zealand*, and the County of *Burgundy*. All which he might have peaceably enjoyed with content and honor, as did the Duke of *Aresehot*, and many others of the like Nobility, if he had aimed only at a personal or private greatness. But it is possible that his thoughts carryed him to a higher pitch, and that perceiving what a general hatred was born by the Low-Country-men against the *Spaniard*, he thought it no impossible thing to dispossess them at the last of all those Provinces, and to get some of them for himself. And he had put fair for it, had not death prevented him, by which his life and projects were cut off together. For compassing which projects he made use of that Religion which best served his turn: being bred a *Lutheran* by his Father, he profest himself a *Romanist* under *Charles* the Fifth; and after finding the *Calvinians* the more likely men to advance his purposes, he declared himself chiefly in their favour, though he permitted other Sects and Sectaries to grow up with them; in which respect he openly opposed all Treaties, Overtures, and Propositions, looking towards a peace, which might not come accompanied with such a liberty of Conscience, both in Doctrine and Worship, as he knew well could never be admitted by the Ministers of the Catholick King. But the *Calvinians* of all others were most dear unto him. By his encouragement the *Belgick* Confession was drawn up and agreed upon 1567. By his countenance, being then *Burgrave* and Governour of *Antwerp* (as before is said) they set up their Consistory in that City, as afterwards in many others of the Dukedom of *Brabant*; and by his favour they attained unto such Authority, and took such deep root in *Holland, Zealand*, and the rest of the Provinces under his command, that they prevailed in fine over all Religious Sects and Sectaries which are therein tolerated.

57. And that they might the better be enabled to retain that power which under him they had acquired, they were resolved not to return again to their first obedience, which they conceived so inconsistent with it, and destructive of it: To this end they commit the Government to some few amongst them, under the name of the Estates, who were to govern all affairs which concerned the publick in the nature of a Common-wealth, like to that of the *Switzers*; so much the more agreeable to them, because it came more neer to that form or Polity which they had erected in the Church. And in this posture they will stand as long as they can; which if they found themselves unable to continue with any comfort, and that they needs must have a Prince, they will submit themselves to the *French* and *English*, or perhaps the *Dane*; to any rather then their own. And to this point it came at last; for the Prince of *Parma* so prevailed, that by the taking of *Gaunt* and *Bruges* he had

reduced all *Flanders* to the Kings obedience, brought *Antwerp* unto terms of yeilding, and carryed on the War to the Walls of *Utrecht*. In which extremity they offered themselves to the French King ; but his affairs were so perplexed by the *Hugonots* on the one side, and the *Guisian* Faction on the other, that he was not in a fit capacity to accept the offer. In the next place they have recourse to the Queen of *England* ; not as before, to take them into her protection, but to accept them for her Subjects ; and that the acceptance might appear with some shew of justice, they insist on her descent from *Philip* Wife to King *Edward* the Third, Sister, and some say Heir of *William* the Third, Earl of *Holland, Haynalt,* &c. Which *Philip*, if she were the Eldest Daughter of the said Earl *William* (as by their Agents was pretended) then was the Queens Title better then that of the King of *Spain*, which was derived from *Margaret* the other Sister : Or granting that *Philip* was the younger, yet on the failer, or other legal interruption of the Line of *Margaret*, (which seemed to be the case before them) the Queen of *England* might put in f r the next Succession : and though the Queen upon very good reasons and considerations refused the Soveraignty of those Countries, which could not without very great injury to publick justice be accepted by her ; yet so far she gave way to her own fears, the ambition of some great persons who were near unto her, and the pretended zeal of the rest, that she admitted them at the last into her protection.

58. The Earl of *Leicester* was at that time of greatest power in the Court of *England*, who being a great favourer of the *Puritan* Faction, and eagerly affecting to see himself in the head of an Army, sollicited the affair with all care aud cunning ; and it succeeded answerably to his hopes and wishes. The Queen consents to take them into h r protection, to raise an army of five thousand Foot and one thousand Horse, to put it under the command of a sufficient and experienced General, and to maintain it in her pay till the War were ended. And it was condescended to on the other side, that the Towns of *Brill* and *Vlushing*, with the Fort of *Ramekins*, should be put into the hands of the *English*; that the Governour whom the Queen should appoint over the Garrisons, together with two other persons of her nomination, should have place and suffrage in the Council of the States United ; that all their own Forces should be ranged under the command of the *English* General ; and that the States should make no peace without her consent. By which transaction, they did not only totally withdraw themselves from the King of *Spain*, but suffered the *English* to possess the Gates of the *Netherlands*, whereby they might imbar all Trade, shut out all Supplies, and hold them unto such conditions as they pleased to give them. But any Yoke appeared more tolerable then that of the *Spaniard* ; and any Prince more welcome to them, then he to whom both God an Nature had made them subject. According unto which agreement, *Vlushing* is put into the hands of Sir *Philip Sidney*, the *English* Army under the Command of the Earl of *Leicester* ; and (which is more then was agreed on) an absolute authority over all Provinces is committed to him, together with the glorious Titles of Governour and Captain-General of *Holland, Zealand*, and the rest of the States United : which how it did displease the Queen ; what course was took to mitigate and appeafe her anger; what happened in the war, betwixt him and the Prince of *Parma*; and what crofs Capers betwixt him and the States themfelves, is not my purpofe to relate. It is fufficient that we have prefented to the eye of the Reader, upon what principles the *Netherlands* were firft embroyled, whofe hands they were by which the Altars were prophaned, the Images defaced, Religious Houfes rifled, and the Churches ruinated: And finally, by what party, and by whofe ftrange practices, the King of *Spain* was totally devefted of all thofe Provinces, which fince have caft themfelves into the form of a Commonwealth.

59. Which being thus fhortly laid together in refpect of their *Politicks*, we muft look back and take another view of them in their *Ecclefiafticks*. In which we fhall find them run as crofs to all Antiquity, as they had done to Order and good Government in their former Actings. And the firft thing we meet with of a Church-concernment, was the publifhing of their Confeffion of their Faith and Doctrine, *Anno* 1565, or thereabouts (as many national and provincial Churches had done before) but differing in many great points from that of *Ausberg*; and therefore the lefs acceptable unto the *Lutheran* party, and the more diftafteful to the *Romifh*. In which Confeffion, to be fure, they muft hold forth a parity of Minifters in the Church of Chrift; they had not elfe come up to the Example and defign of the Mother-City, which was to lay all flat and levil in the publick Government: For in the XXXI Article (*a*) it is faid exprefly, that for as much as concerns the Minifters of Gods holy Word, in what place foever they fhall execute that Sacred Calling, they are all of them to enjoy the fame Power and Authority, as being all of them the Minifters of Jefus Chrift, the onely Univerfal Bifhop, and the onely Head of his Body which is the Church. And for the Government of the Church, it was declared to be moft agreeable to that Sacred and Spiritual Polity by God prefcribed in his Word, that a Confiftory, or Ecclefiaftical Senate fhould be Ordained in every Church, confifting of *Paftors*, *Elders* and *Deacons*, (*b*) to whofe charge and care it fhould belong, that true Religion be preferved, found Doctrine preached, and that all vitious and lewd livers fhould be reftrained and punifhed by the Churches Cenfures. For turning which *Aerian* Doctrines into ufe and practice, they did not only animate all Orders and Degrees of men not to admit their new Bifhops where they were not fetled, or to expel them where they were; but alienated and difmembred all fuch Lands and Rents by which they were to be maintained. This they conceived the readieft way to make fure work with them; /for when the maintainance was gone, the Calling was not like to hold up long after. And this being done, as they had firft fet up their Confiftories in *Antwerp*, and fuch other Cities in which they were confiderable for power and number; fo by degrees they fet up their *Presbyteries* in the leffer Towns, which they united in *Claffes*, and ranged thofe *Claffes* into National and Provincial Synods: In which they made fuch Laws and Canons (if fome of their *irregular* Conftitutions may deferve that name) as utterly fubverted the whole Frame of the ancient Difcipline, and drew unto themfelves the managery of all Affairs which concerned Religion.

(a) Quantum vero attinet divini verbi Miniftros, ubicunque locorum fint, Fandem illi poteftatem & Authoritatem habent, &c. Confeff. Belg. Art. 31. (b) Seniores quoq; fint & Diaconi, qui cum paftoribus Senatum quafi Ecclefiæ conftituant. ut hac rationes vera Religio conffervari poteft, &c. Ibid. Art. 30.

60. But

60. But that they might not be supposed therein to derogate from the Authority of the Civil Magistrate, they are content to give him a coercive power in some matters which were meerly Civil; and therefore in plain terms condemn the *Anabaptists* for seditious persons, Enemies to all good Order and publick Government. But then they clog him with some Duties, in which he was to be subservient to their own designs; that is to say (*a*) the countenancing of the Sacred Ministry; removing all Idolatry from the Worship of God; the ruinating and destroying of the Kingdom of Antichrist. And what they meant by Antichrist, Idolatry, and the Sacred Ministry, is easie to be understood, without the help of a Commentary. Which Duties if the Magistrate shall discharge with care and diligence, he would ease them of much labour, which otherwise they meant to take upon themselves; if not, they must no longer stay his leisure, nor expect his pleasure, but put their own hands unto the work: and so it was delivered for good Doctrine by *Suecanus*, a Divine of *West-Friesland*, for which see *l. 8. num.* 23. Which though it be the the general Doctrine of all the party, yet never was it preached more plainly then by *Cleselius* a *Calvinian* of *Rotterdam*, who openly maintained, that if the Magistrates took no care to reform the Church, (*b*) that then it did belong to the common people: And they, as he informs us, were obliged to do it even by force and violence, not only to the shedding of their own, but their Brethrens blood. (*c*) So principled, it could be no marvail if they turned out the Bishops to make room for their own *Presbyteries*, defaced all Churches that retained any thing in them of the old Idolatries; and finally, pulled down even the Civil Magistrate, when his advancing did not stand with their ends and purposes. *Flacius Ilyricus*, the founder of the Stiff or Rigid *Lutherans*, had led the way unto them in the last particular: By whom it was held forth for a Rule in all Church-Reformations, (*d*) that Princes should be rather terrified with the fear of Tumults, then any thing which seemed to favour of Idolatry or Superstition should either be tolerated or connived at for quietness sake. Concurring with him as they did, in his Doctrines of Predestination, Grace, Freewil, and things indifferent, they were the better fitted to pursue his Principle, in opposition unto all Authority, by which their Councils were controuled, or their Power restrained. And by this means, the publishing of their Confession with these Heads and Articles, they did not only justifie their exorbitancies in the time then past, but made provision for themselves in the times to come.

61. In such other points of their Confession as were meerly doctrinal, and differing from the general current of the Church of *Rome*, they shew themselves for the most part to be *Anti-Lutheran*; that is to say, *Zuinglians* in the point of the Holy Supper, and *Calvinists* in the Doctrine of Predestination. In which last point, they have exprest the Article in such modest terms, as may make it capable of an Orthodox and sober meaning: For presupposing all mankind by the fall of *Adam* to be involved by Gods just judgment in the Gulph of Perdition, they make them only to be (*e*) predestinate to eternal life, whom God by his eternal and immutable counsel hath elected in Christ, and separated from the rest by the said Election. But when the differences were broken

(a) Ut Sacrum Ministerium tueantur, omnem Idolatriam a Dei cultu submoveant, Regnum Antichristi diruant,&c. Ib. Art. 36.

(b) Necesse est tum id facere plebeios Israelitas.
(c) Licet ad Sanguinem usque pro eo pugnent.

(d) Principes potius metu seditionum terrendos, quam vel minimum pacis causa indulgendam. Necess. Respons. p. 83.

(e) Quo Deus immutabili suo consilio, in Christo Elegit ac selegit. Confess. Art. 16.

ken

ken out betwixt them and such of their Brethren which commonly past amongst them by the name of *Remonstrants*, and that it was pretended by the said *Remonstrants* that the Article stood as fair to them as the opposite party ; the words were then restrained to a narrower sence then the generality of the expression could literally and Grammatically comport withal. It was then pleaded, that they only were to expound the Article, who had contributed their assistance to the making of it ; and that it did appear by the succession of their Doctrine from the first Reformation, that no other method of Predestination had been taught amongst them, then as it was maintained by *Calvin* and his Followers in their publick Writings ; under which name, as those of *Beza*'s judgement which embraced the *Supralapsarian* way desired to be comprehended ; so did they severally pretend, that the words of the Confession did either countenance their Doctrine, or not contradict them. But on the other side, it was made as plainly to appear, that such of their first Reformers as were of the old *Lutheran* stamp, and had precedency of time before those that followed *Calvins* judgement, imbraced the *Melancthonian* way of Predestination, and looked upon all such as Innovators in the publick Doctrines, who taught otherwise of it. By them it was declared, that in the year 1530, the Reformed Religion was admitted into the Neighbouring Countrey of *East-Friesland* under *Enno* the First, upon the Preaching of *Harding Bergius* a *Lutheran* Divine of great Fame and Learning, and one of the principal Reformers of the Church of *Embden*, a Town of most note in all that Earldom ; that from him *Clemens Martini* took those Principles, which he afterwards propagated in the *Belgick* Provinces; that the same Doctrine had been publickly maintained in a Book called *Odegus Laicorum*, or the *Lay mans Guide*, published by *Anastatius Velluanus*, *Anno* 1554, which was ten years before the French Preachers had obtruded on them this Confession; that the said Book was much commended by *Henricus Antonides*, Divinity-Reader in the University of *Franaka* ; that notwithstanding this Confession, the Ministers successively in the whole Province of *Utrecht* adhered unto their former Doctrines, not looked on for so doing as the less reformed; that *Gallicus Suecanus*, a man of great Fame for his Parts and Piety in the County of *West-Friesland*, esteemed no otherwise of those which were of *Calvins* judgement in the points disputed, then as of Innovators in the Doctrine which had been first received amongst them; that *Johannus Isbrandi*, one of the old Professors of *Rotterdam*, did openly declare himself to be an *Anti-Calvinian*; and that the like was done by *Holmanuus* Professor of *Leyden*, by *Cornelius Minardi*, and *Cornelius Wiggeri*, men of principal esteem in their times and places. Which I have noted in this place, because it must be in and about these times, namely before the year 1585, in which most of these men lived and writ who are here remembred. What else was done in the pursuance of this controversie between the parties, will fall more properly under consideration in the last part of this History, and there we shall hear further of it.

62. Next, look upon them in their *Tacticks*, and we shall find them as professed enemies to all publick Liturgies and Forms of Prayer, as the rest of their *Calvinian* Brethren. They thought there was no speedier

way

way to deſtroy the *Maſs*, then by aboliſhing the *Miſſals* ; nor any fitter means to exerciſe their own gifts in the acts of Prayer, then by ſuppreſſing all ſuch Forms as ſeemed to put a reſtraint upon the Spirit.   Onely they fell upon the humour of tranſlating *Davids Pſalms* into *Dutch* Meter, and cauſed them to be ſung in their Congregations, as the *French Pſalms* of *Marrots* and *Beza*'s Meter were in moſt Churches of that people.   By which it ſeems, that they might ſing by the Book , though they prayed by the Spirit ; as if their ſinging by the Book in ſet Tunes and Numbers, impoſed not as great a reſtraint upon the Spirit in the acts of Praiſing, as reading out of Book in the acts of Praying.   But they knew well the influence which Muſick hath on the ſouls of Men : and therefore though they had ſuppreſſed the old manner of ſinging, and all the ancient Hymns which had been formerly received in the Catholick Church ; yet ſinging they would have, and Hymns in the Meter, as well to pleaſe their ears, as to cheer their Spirits , and manifeſt their alacrity in the Service of God. And though they would not ſing with Organs , for fear there might be ſomewhat in it of the old ſuperſtition ; yet they retained them ſtill in many of their Churches ; but whether for civil entertainment when they met together, or to compoſe and ſettle their affections for Religious Offices, or to take up the time till the Church were filled , I am not able to determine.   The like they alſo did with all the ancient weekly and ſet-times of Faſting, which (following the example of *Aerius*) they devoured at once, as contrary to that Chriſtian Liberty, or licentiouſneſs rather, to which they inured the people, when they firſt trained them up in oppoſition to the See of *Rome*.   No Faſt obſerved, but when ſome publick great occaſion doth require it of them ; and then but half-Faſt neither, as in other places , making amends , at night for the days forbearance. And if at any time they feed moſt on Fiſh, as ſometimes they do, it rather is for a variety to pleaſe themſelves in the uſe of Gods Creatures , or out of State-craft to encourage or maintain a Trade which is ſo beneficial to them ; and rather as a civil then Religious Faſt.

63. But there is no one thing wherein they more defaced the outward ſtate of the Church, then in ſuppreſſing all thoſe days of publick Worſhip which anciently were obſerved by the name of Feſtivals , together with their Eves or Vigils.   In which they were ſo fearful of aſcribing any honour to the Saints departed , whoſe names were honoured by thoſe days , that they alſo took away thoſe Anniverſary Commemorations of Gods infinite Mercies in the Nativity, Paſſion, Reſurrection and Aſcention of our Saviour Chriſt : which though retained amongſt the *Switzers* , would not down with *Calvin* ; and being diſallowed by him, were reprobated without more ado in all the Churches of his Platform, and in theſe with others.   And though they kept the Lords day, or rather ſome part of it, for Religious meetings ; yet either for fear of laying a reſtraint on their Chriſtian Liberty , in Attributing any peculiar holineſs to it which might entitle them to ſome ſuperſtition , they kept that neither but by halfs ; it was ſufficient to beſtow an hour or two of the morning in Gods publick Service, the reſt of the day ſhould be their own , to be imployed as profit ſhould adviſe , or their pleaſures tempt them.   And whereas in ſome places they ſtill retained thoſe afternoon Meetings to which they had been bound of Duty by the Rules of the

Church

Church of *Rome* ; it was decreed in one of their first Synods (that namely which was held at *Dort* , 1574) (*a*) that in such Churches where publick Evening-Prayers had been omitted , they should continue as they were ; and where they had been formerly admitted, should be discontinued.   And if they had no Evening-Prayers, there is no question to be made but they had their Evening Pastimes, and that the afternoon was spent in such imployment as was most suitable to the condition of each several man.   Nor was the morning so devoted to Religious uses , but that in some of their good Towns they kept upon that day the ordinary Fairs and Markets, (*Kirk-Masses*, as they commonly called them) which must needs draw away a great part of the people to attend those businesses, to which their several Trades and Occupations did most especially oblige them.   What alterations hapned in the change of times, we shall see hereafter.

(a) Publicæ vespertinæ preces non sunt introducendæ ubi non sunt introdutæ, & ubi sunt tollantur. Collat. Hag. cap. 68.

64.   Nor was that portion of the day which they were pleased to set apart for Religious Duties, observed with much more reverence by those in the Church, then it was by others in the Market ; the head uncovered very seldom , and the knee so little used to kneeling , as if God had created it for no such purpose.   And whereas once *Tertullian* did upbraid the Gentiles for their irreverence in sitting before some of those Gods whom they pretended to adore ; so might this people be reproached for using the same posture in all acts of Worship, but that they do it purposely to avoid all outward signs of Adoration : even in the Sacrament of the Supper , in which it cannot be denyed but that our Saviour is more eminently present then in any other Divine Ordinance of what name soever, they are so fearful of relapsing to their old Idolatries (if by that name they may be called) that they chuse rather to receive it in any posture, sitting or standing, yea, or walking , then reverently upon their knees.   For so they have ordained it in another Synod, mentioned by *Daniel Angelocratur* in his Epitome *Consiliorum.*   By the decrees whereof (*b*) it was left at liberty to receive that Sacrament standing, sitting , or walking , but by no means kneeling : And kneeling was prohibited, *Ob ἀποληψίας periculum* , for fear of falling into a new kind of *Idolatry* , (which was never thought of in the World till they found it out) that is to say, *Bread-worship*, or the Adoration of Bread it self.   The *Conference* at *Hampton-Court* had told us somewhat , but obscurely, of these *Ambling Communions* ; but I never understood them rightly till I saw this Canon.   For Canon they will have it called , though most uncanonical.   More of the like stuff might be produced from the Acts of their Synods , but that this little is too much to inform the Reader how different they are, both in their Discipline and Doctrine, in point of speculation, and matter of practice, from that which was most countenanced by the piety of the Primitive times , and recommended to them by the constant and uniform tradition of the ages following.

(b) Liberum est stando, sedendo vel eundo, cœnam celebrare, non autem geniculando, &c. Cap. 13. Art. 8

65.   As is their work , such is the wages they received ; and as the reverence is which they give to Christ in his holy Sacrament, such is the honour which is paid them by the common people. They had abolished the *daily Sacrifice* of Praise and Prayer, which might have been continued, though the *Mass* was abrogated ; disclaimed the hearing of Confessions, the visitation of the Sick, and Sacerdotal Absolution , as inconsistent

with

with the purity of their Profession ; took away all the annual Festivals, with their Eves and Vigils ; and in a word reduced the whole Service of their Ministry to the Sunday-Morning : Which hardly taking up the tenth part of time expended formerly by the Priests on Religious Offices, they were so consciencious as the rest contented with little more then the tenth part of those yearly profits which by the Priest had been received. They had besides so often preached down Tythes as a *Jewish* maintainance improper and unfit for Ministers of the Holy Gospel, when they were paid unto the Clergy of the Church of *Rome*, that at the last the people took them at their word, believe them to be so indeed ; and are spurred on the faster to a change of Religion, in which they saw some glimmering of a present profit. Of these mistakes the Prince of *Orange* was too wise not to make advantage ; giving assurance to the Land-holders and Countrey-Villagers, that if they stood to him in the Wars against the *Spaniard*, they should from thenceforth pay no Tythes unto their Ministers, as before they did. The Tythes in the mean time to be brought into the common Treasury toward the charges of the War, the Ministers to be maintained by contributions at an easie rate. But when the War was come to so fair an issue, that they thought to be exempted from the payment of Tythes, answer was made that they should pay none to the Ministers, as they had done formerly, whereby their Ministers in effect were become their *Masters* ; but that the Tythes were so considerable a Revenue to the Common-wealth, that the State could not possibly subsist without them ; that therefore they must be content to pay them to the States Commissioners, as they had done hitherto ; and that the State would take due care to maintain a Ministry. By means whereof they do not only pay their Tythes as in former times ; but seeing how much the publick allowance of the State doth come short of a competency (though by that name they please to call it) they are constrained, as it were, out of common charity, if not compelled thereto by order, to contribute over and above with the rest of the people, for the improvement and increase of the Ministers maintainance. But as they Bake, so let them Brew, to make good the Proverb. And so I leave them for the present, till we have traced the *Presbyterian* practices and positions both in *England* and *Scotland* (but in *Scotland* first) to that point of time to which we have deduced their successes in these *Belgick* Provinces, and then we shall hear further of them as they come in our way.

The End of the Third Book.

AERIVS REDIVIVVS:

OR THE

HISTORY

OF THE

Presbyterians.

LIB. IV.

Containing

Their beginning, Progreſs and Poſitions ; their dangerous Practices, Inſurrections, and Conſpiracies in Realm of Scotland, from the year 1544 to the year 1566.

 Rroſs we next over into *Scotland,* where the *Genevian* Principles were firſt reduced into uſe and practice. In which reſpect the *Presbyterians* of that Realm ſhould have had precedencie in the preſent ſtory, not only before any of their Brethren in the *Belgick* Provinces, but even before the *French* themſelves, though neareſt both in ſcituation and affection to the Mother City. For though the Emiſſaries of *Geneva* had long been tampering with that active and unquiet people ; yet ſuch a ſtrict hand was held upon them both by *Francis* the Firſt, and *Henry* the Second his Succeſſor, that they durſt not ſtir, till by the death of thoſe two Kings they found the way more free and open to purſue thoſe counſels, which by the induſtry of thoſe men had been put in-

to

I.

to them, before which time the *Scots* had acted over all thoſe Tumults, Riots and Rebellions, in which not long after they were followed by the *French* and *Netherlands*. But howſoever I have purpoſely reſerved them to this time and place, becauſe of that influence which they had on the Realm of *England*, and the connexion of affairs between both the Kingdoms, till they were both united under the command of one Soveraign Prince. And this being ſaid, I ſhall without more preamble proceed to the following Hiſtory.

2. It was about the year 1527, that the Reformation of Religion begun by *Luther*, was firſt Preached in *Scotland*, by the Miniſtry of one *Patrick Hamilton*, a man of eminent Nobility in regard of his birth, as being Brothers Son to *James* Earl of *Arran*; but far more eminent in thoſe times for his parts and piety, then the Nobility of his Houſe: ſpending ſome time at *Wittenberg* in the purſuit of his Studies, he grew into acquaintance with *Martin Luther*, *Philip Melancthon*, and other men of name and note in that Univerſity; and being ſeaſoned with their Doctrine, he returned into *Scotland*, where he openly declared himſelf againſt Pilgrimages, Purgatory, Prayer to the Saints, and for the dead, without going further. And further as he did not go, ſo indeed he could not. For on the noiſe of theſe his Preachings, he was prevailed with by *James Beton* Archbiſhop of S. *Andrews* to repair to that City; but was ſo handled at his coming, that after ſome examinations he was condemned to the fire: which ſentence was inflicted on him on the laſt of *February*. But the Church is never made more fruitful, then when the ſoyl thereof is watered with the blood of Martyrs. For preſently upon the committing of this Fact, moſt men of quality began to look into the Reaſons of ſuch great ſeverities, and were the more inquiſitive after all particulars, becauſe they had not been affrighted with the like Example in the memory of the oldeſt man which then lived amongſt them. By this means the opinions of this man being known abroad, found many which approved, but very few which had juſt reaſon to condemn them; and paſſing thus from hand to hand, gave further cauſe to thoſe of the Popiſh Party to be watchful over them. And for long time they were on the ſuffering hand, patiently yielding up their lives to the Executioners, whereſoever any ſentence of death was paſt upon them. And it ſtood till the deceaſe of King *James* the Fifth, *Anno* 1542, when the unſetledneſs of Affairs, the tender infancy of the young Queen, not above nine days old at the death of her Father, and the conferring of the Regencie after ſome diſputes on *James* Earl of *Arran*, who was thought to favour their opinions, imboldned them to appear more openly in defence of themſelves, and to attempt upon the Chiefs of the contrary party; whereof they gave a terrible Example in the death of Cardinal *David Beton*, immediately or not long after the cruel burning of *George Wiſchart* (whoſe name is mollified by *Buchanan* into *Sofocardius*) a man of great eſteem amongſt them, who having ſpent ſome time in *France*, and being converſant with ſome *Calviniſts* of that Nation, returned into his Native Countrey with ſuch *French* Commiſſioners as were ſent unto the Earl of *Arran*, *Anno* 1544. In little time he had gained unto himſelf ſo many followers, that he became formidable to the greateſt Prelates; but unto none more then unto Cardinal *David Beton*,

Beton, Archbishop of *St. Andrews* also, and Nephew unto *James* his Predecessor. By whose Authority and procurement he was condemned to the like death as *Hamilton* before had suffered, in the year next following.

3. Amongst the followers of this man (the most remarkable in reference to my present purpose) were *Norman Lesly* eldest Son to the Earl of *Rothes*, *John Lesly* Uncle unto *Norman*, *James Melvin*, and the *Kirkaldies* Lairds of *Grange*. By whom and others of that party, a plot was laid to surprise the Castle, and take revenge upon the Cardinal for the death of *Wishart*. Having possest themselves of the Gates of the Castle, they forced their way into his Chamber, and were upon the point of striking the fatal blow, when *James Melvin* told them with great shews of gravity, that the business was not to be acted with such heat and passion. And thereupon holding a Ponyard at his brest, put him in mind of shedding the innocent blood of that famous Martyr Mass *George Wishart*, which now called loud to God for vengeance, in whose name they were come to do justice on him: which said, he made this protestation, That neither hatred to his person, nor love to his Riches, nor the fear of any thing concerning his own particular, had moved him to the undertaking of that execution; but only because he had been, and still remained an obstinate enemy against Christ Jesus and his Holy Gospel. Upon which words, without expecting any answer, or giving the poor man any time of application to the Father of Mercies, he stabbed him twice or thrice into the body with so strong a malice, that he left him dead upon the place. In the relating of which Murder in *Knox* his History, a note was given us in the Margent of the first Edition, Printed at *London* in *Octavo*, which points us to the Godly act and saying of *James Melvin*; for so the Author calls this most wicked deed. But that Edition being stopt at the Press by the Queens command, the History never came out perfect till the year of our Lord 1644, when the word *Godly* was left out of the Marginal Note, for the avoiding of that horrible scandal which had been thereby given to all sober Readers. But to proceed unto my story: it was upon the 29 of *May*, that the Murderers possest themselves of that strong piece, into which many flocked from all parts of the Realm, both to congratulate the Act, and assist the Actors: So that at last they cast themselves into a Congregation, and chose *John Rough*, (who after suffered death in *England*) to be one of their Preachers; *John Knox*, that great incendiary of the Realm of *Scotland*, for another of them. And thus they stood upon their guard till the coming of one and twenty Gallies, and some Land-Forces out of *France*, by whom the Castle was besieged, and so fiercely battered, that they were forced to yield on the last of *July*, without obtaining any better conditions then the hope of life.

4. The Castle being yielded, and the Countrey quieted, the *French* returned with their booty, of which their Prisoners which they brought along with them made the principal part; not made the tamer by their sufferings in the enemies Gallies; insomuch that when the Image of the Virgin *Mary* was offered to them to be kissed on some solemn occasion, one of them snatched it into his hands, flung it into the Sea,

1546

1547.

and

and said unto them that brought it, in a jeering manner, *That her Lady-ship was light enough, and might learn to swim.* Which desperate and un-advised actions (as it was no other) is said by *Knox* to have produced this good effect, that the *Scots* were never after tempted to the like Idola-tries. *Knox* at this time was Prisoner in the Gallies amongst the rest, and with the rest released upon the Peace made between *France* & *Eng-land*, at the delivering up of *Bulloigne*; from whence he past over into *England*, where he was first made Preacher at *Barwick*, next at *New-castle*, afterwards to some Church of *London*; and finally, in some other places of the *South*: so that removing like our late *Itinerants* from one Church to another, as he could meet with entertainment, he kept him-self within that Sanctuary till the death of King *Edward*, and then be-took himself to *Geneva* for his private Studies: From hence he published his desperate Doctrine of Predestination, which he makes not only to be an impulsive to, but the compulsive cause of mens sins and mens wickednesses: From hence he published his Trayterous and seditious Pamphlet, entituled, *The first blast of the Trumpet*, in which he writes most bitterly, amongst other things, against the Regiment of Women, aiming therein particularly at the two *Maries* Queens of *Scotland*, Queen *Mary* of *England*, and *Mary* Queen Dowager of *Hungary*, Governess of the *Low-Countries* for *Charles* the Fifth: and finally, from hence he pu-blished another of the like nature, entituled, *An Admonition to Christians*: In which he makes the Emperour *Charles* to be worse then *Nero*, and *Mary* Queen of *England* nothing better then *Jesabel*. According to which good beginning, he calls her in his History (but not published hence) that *Idolatrous and Mischievous Mary* of the *Spaniards* blood, a *cruel persecutrix* of Gods People, as the Acts of her unhappy Reign did sufficiently witness. In which he comes as close to *Calvin* as could be desired.

5. By this means he grew great with *Calvin*, and the most leading men of the *Consistorians*, who looked upon him as a proper Engine to advance their purposes: But long he had not stayed amongst them, when he received an invitation from some Friends of his of the same temper and affections, as it after proved, to take charge of the Church of *Frankfort*; to which some learned men and others of the *English* Nation had retired themselves in the Reign of Queen *Mary*: which call he first communicated unto *Calvin*, by whose encouragement and perswasion he accepted of it, and by his coming rather multiplyed then appeased the quarrels which he found amongst them: But siding with the incon-formable party, and knowing so much of *Calvins* mind touching the Li-turgie and Rites of the Church of *England*, he would by no means be perswaded to officiate by it; and for that cause was forced by Dr. *Cox*, and others of the Learned men who remained there, to forsake the place, as hath been shewn at large in another place. Outed at *Frankfort*, he returns again to his Friends at *Geneva*; and being furnished with instru-ctions for his future carriage in the cause of his Ministry, he prepares for his journey into *Scotland*, passeth to *Dieppe*, from thence to *England*, and at last came a welcome man to his Native Countrey, which he found miserably divided into sides and factions. *Mary* their Infant-Queen had been trasported into *France* at six years of age; the Regency taken from *James* Earl of *Arran*, given to *Mary* of *Lorraign* the Queens Mo-ther;

1555.

ther ; not well obeyed by many of the Nobility and great men of the
Country, but openly oppofed and reviled by thofe who feemed to be
inclinable to the Reformation.　To thefe men *Knox* applyed himfelf
with all care and cunning, preaching from place to place, and from
houfe to houfe, as opportunity was given him.　In which he gathered
many Churches, and fet up many Congregations, as if he had been the
Apoftle General of the Kirk of *Scotland* ; in all points holding a conformity unto *Calvins* Platform, even to the finging of *Davids Pfalms* in
the *Englifh* Meter, the only Mufick he allowed of in Gods publick
Service.　From Villages and private Houfes, he ventured into fome
of the great Towns and more eminent Cities ; and at the laft appeared
in *Edenborough* it felf, preaching in all, and miniftring the Communion
in many places, as he faw occafion.　This was fufficient to have raifed a
greater ftorm againft him then he could have been able to indure ; but
he muft make it worfe by a new provocation.　For at the perfwafion
of the Earl of *Glencarne*, and fome others of his principal followers, he
writes a long Letter to the Queen Regent, in which he earneftly per-
fwades her to give ear to the Word of God, according as it was then
preached by himfelf and others : which Letter being communicated by
the Queen to the Archbifhop of *Glafco*, and difperfed in feveral Copies by *Xnox* himfelf, gave fuch a hot Alarm to the Bifhops and Clergy, that he was cited to appear in *Blackfryars* Church in *Edenborough*, on
the 15 of *May* : and though upon advertifement that he came accompanied with fo great a train, that it could not be fafe for them to proceed
againft him, he was not troubled at that time ; yet he perceived that
having made the Queen his enemy, he could not hope to remaine
longer in that Kingdom, but firft or laft he muft needs fall in their
hands.

6. But fo it happened, that when he was in the midft of thefe perplex-
ities, he received a Letter from the Schifmatical *Englifh* which repaired to *Geneva*, when they had loft all hope of putting down the *Englifh*
Liturgy in the Church of *Frankfort*, by which he was invited to return
to his former charge : this Letter he communicated to his principal
Friends, refolves to entertain the offer, and prepares all things for his
journey. And to fay truth, it was but time that he fhould fet forwards;
for the danger followed him fo clofe, that within few days after his
departure, he was condemned for not appearing, and burnt in his *Effi-
gies* at the Crofs in *Edenborough*.　But firft he walks his round, vifits all
his Churches, takes a more folemn farewel of his efpecial Friends ; and
having left fufficient inftructions with them for carrying on the Reformation in defpite of Authority, in the latter end of *July* he fets fail for
France.　His party was by this time grown ftrong and numerous, refolved to follow fuch directions as he left behind him.　To which encouraged by the preaching of one *Willock*, whom *Knox* had more efpecially
recommended to them in the time of his abfence, they ftole away the
Images out of moft of their Churches ; and were fo venturous, as to
take down the great Image of St. *Gyles* in the chief Church of *Edenborough*, which they drowned firft in the *North-lake*, and burnt it afterwards.　But this was but a Prologue to the following Comedy.　The
Feftival of St. *Gyles* draws near, in which the Image of that Saint was

to

to be carryed through the chief Streets of *Edenborough* in a solemn Procession, attended by all the Priests, Fryars, and other Religious persons about that City: another Image is borrowed from the *Gray-Fryars* to supply the place; and for the honour of the day, the Queen Regent her self was pleased to make one in the Pageant. But no sooner was she retired to her private repose, when a confused Rabble of the *Knoxian* Brethren brake in upon them, dismounted the Image, brake off his head against the stones, scattered all the Company, pulled the Priests Surplices over their Ears, beat down their Crosses; and, in a word, so discomposed the Order of that mock-Solemnity, that happy was the man who could first save himself in some House or other; neither their Bag-pipes, nor their Banners, their Tabrets, nor their Trumpets, which made a Principal part in that days triumph, though free enough from superstition in themselves, could escape their fury, but ran the same Fortune with the rest. And though no diligence was wanting for finding out the principal actors in that Commotion; yet as the story hath informed us, the Brethren kept themselves together in such companies, singing of *Psalms*, and openly encouraging one another, that no body durst lay hands upon them.

7. Finding by this experiment that they were strong enough to begin the work, it was thought fit to call back *Knox* to their assistance; to which end they dispatched their Letters to him in the *March* next following, to be conveyed by one *James Sym*, whom they had throughly instructed in all particulars touching their affairs. In *May* the Letters are delivered, the contents whereof he first communicateth to his own Congregation, and afterwards to *Calvin*, and the rest of the Brethren of that Consistory, by whom it was unanimously declared unto him, *that he could not refuse that Vocation, unless he would shew himself rebellious unto his God, and unmerciful to his Native Country.* He returned answer thereupon, That he would visit them in *Scotland* with all convenient expe-

1557. dition, and comes accordingly to *Dieppe* in *October* following; where contrary to expectation he is advertised by Letters from some secret Friends, that all affairs there seemed to be at a stand, so that his coming to them at that time might be thought unnecessary. Highly displeased with such a cooling Card as he did not look for, he sends his Letters thence to the Nobility and principal Gentry; in which he lets them know how much he was confounded for travailing so far in their Affairs, by moving them to the most Godly and most Learned men (by which he means *Calvin* and the *Consistorians*) who at that time did live in *Europe*, whose judgements and grave counsels he conceived expedient, as well for the assurance of their own Consciences as of his own; that it must needs redound both to his shame and theirs, if nothing should succeed in such long consultations; that he left his Flock and Family at *Geneva* to attend their service, to whom he should be able to make but a weak account of his leaving them in that condition, if he were asked at his return concerning the impediment of his purposed journey; that he fore-saw with grief of spirit, what grievous plagues, what misery and bondage would most inevitably befal that miserable Realm, and every Inhabitant thereof, if the power of God with the liberty of his Gospel did not deliver them from the same; that though his words might

might feem fharp, and to be fomewhat undifcreetly fpoken, yet wife. men ought to underftand, that a true Friend can be no flatterer, efpecially when the queftion is concerning the Salvation both of body and foul, not onely of a few men, but of States and Nations; that if any perfwade them for fear of dangers which might follow to faint in their intended purpofe, though otherwife he might feem to be wife and friendly, yet was he to be accounted foolifh, and their mortal enemy, in labouring to perfwade them to prefer their worldly reft to Gods Praife and Glory, and the friendfhip of the wicked before the falvation of their Brethren; that they ought to hazard their own lives, be it againft Kings or Emperours, for the deliverance of the people from fpiritual bondage; for which caufe only they received from their Brethren Tribute, Honour and Homage, at Gods Commandment. Finally, having laid before them many ftrong inducements to quicken them unto the work, he ends with this moft memorable Aphorifm, (which is indeed the fum and fubftance of the whole *Confiftorian* Doctrine in the prefent cafe) that the Reformation of Religion, and of publick enormities, doth appertain to more then the Clergy, or chief Rulers called Kings.

8. On the receiving of thefe Letters, they are refolved to proceed in their former purpofe, and would rather commit themfelves and all theirs to the greateft dangers, then fuffer that Religion which they called Idolatry any longer to remain amongft them, or the people to be fo defrauded as they had been formerly, of that which they efteemed to be the only true preaching of Chrifts Gofpel. And to this end they entred into a common Bond or Covenant, in the name of themfelves, their Vaffals, Tenants and Dependants, dated upon the third of *December* and fubfcribed by the Earls of *Arguile, Glencarne* and *Morton,* the Lords *Lerne, Ereskin* of *Dun, &c.* the Tenour of which was as followeth, *viz.*

9. *We perceiving how Satan in his members, the Antichrifts of our time, cruelly do rage, feeking to overthrow and deftroy the Gofpel of Chrift and his Congregation, ought according to our bounden duty, to ftrive in our Mafters caufe, even unto the death, being certain of the victory in him: The which one duty being well confidered, we ao promife before the Majefty of God and his Congregation, that we (by his Grace) fhall with all dilligence continually apply our whole power, fubftance, and our very lives, to maintain, fet forward, and eftablifh the moft bleffed Word of God and his Congregation. And fhall labour according to our power to have faithful Minifters, truely and purely to minifter Chrifts Gofpel and Sacraments to his people: we fhall maintain them, nourifh them, and defend them, the whole Congregation of Chrift, and every Member thereof, according to our whole powers, and waging of our lives againft Satan, and all wicked power that doth intend tyranny or trouble againft the aforefaid Congregation. Unto the which holy Word and Congregation we do joyn us: and fo do forfake and renounce the Congregation of Antichrift, with all the Superftitious Abomination and Idolatry thereof. And moreover, fhall declare our felves manifeft enemies thereto by this our faithful promife before God, teftified to this Congregation by our fubfcription of thefe prefents.*

10. Having

10. Having ſubſcribed unto this Bond, their next care was to iſſue out theſe directions following, for the promoting of the work which they were in hand with : 1. That in all Pariſhes of that Realm, the Common Prayer-Book (that is to ſay, the Common-Prayer book of the Church of *England*) ſhould be read upon the Sundays and Holydays in the Pariſh-Church, together with the Leſſons of the Old and New Teſtament by the ſame appointed : 2. That preaching and interpretation of Scripture be had and uſed in private Houſes, without any great convention of the people at them, till it ſhould pleaſe God to put it into the heart of the Prince to allow thereof in publick Churches. And had they ſtood to that, they had been unblameable ; but finding by the Subſcriptions which they had received from all parts of the Kingdom, that they were nothing inferiour to their Adverſaries in power and number, they were not able to hold long in ſo good an humour. Howſoever it was thought expedient, for the avoiding of Scandal, that they ſhould firſt proceed in the way of ſupplication to the Queen and Council ; in which it was deſired, that it might be lawful for them to meet publickly or privately for having the Common-prayers in the vulgar tongue ; that the Sacrament of Baptiſm might be adminiſtred in the ſame Tongue alſo ; the Sacrament of the Lords Supper in both kinds, according to Chriſts Inſtitution ; and that a Reformation might be made of the wicked lives of Prelates, Prieſts, and other Eccleſiaſtical perſons. The Queen of *Scots* was in the mean time Married to the *Daulphin* of *France*, upon whoſe head it was deſired by the *French* that at the leaſt the Matrimonial Crown ſhould be ſolemnly placed ; and that all the *French* Nation ſhould forthwith be naturalized in the Realm of *Scotland*. For the better effecting whereof, in the following Parliament, the Queen Regent thought it no ill piece of State-craft ſo far to gratifie the Petitioners in their deſires, as to licenſe them to meet in publick or private for the exerciſe of their own Religion, ſo that it were not in the City of *Edenborough*, or the Port of *Leith*, for fear ſome Tumult or Sedition might enſue upon it. But not content with this Indulgence, they were reſolved to move the Parliament for an Abrogation of all former Laws made againſt Sects and Hereſies, by which they might incur the loſs of Life, Land or Liberty ; and that none of their profeſſion ſhould be condemned for Hereſie, unleſs they were firſt convinced by the Word of God to have erred from the Faith which the Holy Spirit witneſſeth to be neceſſary to mans Salvation.

11. But hereunto they could not get the Queens conſent. And thereupon they cauſed a Proteſtation to be drawn, and openly pronounced in the face of the Parliament, in which it was declared, amongſt other things, that neither they, nor any other of the Godly, who pleaſed to joyn with them in the true Faith grounded upon the Word of God, ſhould incur any danger of Life or Lands, or other particular pains, for not obſerving ſuch acts as have paſſed heretofore in favour of their Adverſaries, or for violating ſuch Rites as have been invented by man without the Commandment of God ; that if any Tumult or Uproar ſhould happen to ariſe in the Realm, or that any violence ſhould be uſed in reforming of ſuch things as were amiſs in the ſtate of the Church, the blame ſhould not be laid on them, who had deſired that all things might

be

be rectified by publick Order: And finally, that they pretended to no
other end, but only for the reforming of such abuses as were found in
Religion; and therefore that they might no otherwise be thought of,
then as faithful and obedient Subjects to Supreme Authority. And now
the Scheme begins to open: the Town of *Perth*, by some called Saint
Johnstone, declared in favour of the Lords of the Congregation, which
name they had took unto themselves; the news whereof was so unpleasing to the Queen, that she commanded the Lord *Ruthven*, a man of
principal Authority in the parts adjoyning, to take some order for suppressing those Innovations in Religion which some busie people of that
Town had introduced: To which he answered, That he was able, if she
pleased, to force their bodies, and to seize their goods; but that he had
no power to compel their consciences: which answer did not more displease the Queen, then it encouraged those of the Congregation; who
now from all parts flocked to *Perth*, as a Town strong by situation, well   1559,
fortified, and standing in a fruitful Countrey, from whence they might
receive all necessaries, if any open force or violence should be used against
them.

12. *Knox* in the mean time had retreated to his charge at *Geneva*, not
thinking fit to tempt that danger by an unseasonable return, which he
had so narrowly escaped at his being there. He only waited opportunity to go back with safety, and would not stir, though frequently sollicited by his Friends in *Scotland*. In so much, that means was made
to *Calvin* by especial Letters, to re-ingage him in the Cause: Which
Letters were brought to him in the Moneth of *November*, Anno 1558.
And that it may appear what influence *Calvin* had upon all the counsels and designs of the Congregation, he is advertised from time to time
of their successes, of the estate of their Affairs, whether good or
bad; in so much, that when the Queen Regent had fed them with some
flattering hopes, *Calvin* is forthwith made acquainted with their
happiness in it. And who but he must be desired to write unto her?
that by his *Grave counsel and Exhortation*, she might be *animated* to go
forward constantly in promoting the Gospel. But though these Letters came to *Calvin* in the Moneth of *November*, yet we find not *Knox*
in *Scotland* till the *May* next following, when those of his party had
possessed themselves of the Town of *Perth*: though he loved *Calvin*
well, and the Gospel better, yet all that a man hath he will give for his
life; and *Knox* was dearer to himself then either of them. But unto
Perth he comes at last, on the fifth of *May*. In the chief Church
whereof he Preached such a thundring Sermon against the *Adoration of
Images*, and the advancing of them in places of Gods publick Worship, as suddenly beat down all the Images and Religious Houses within the Precincts of that Town. For presently after the end of the Sermon, when almost all the rest of people were gone home to dinner,
some few which remained in the Church pulled down a glorious Tabernacle which stood on the Altar, broke it in pieces, and defaced the I-
mages which they found therein. Which being dispatched, they did the
like execution on all the rest in that Church; and were so nimble at their
work, that they had made a clear riddance of them, before the tenth
man in the Town was advertised of it. The news hereof causeth the

Rascal Multitude (so my Author calls them) to resort in great numbers to the Church. But because they found that all was done before they came, they fell with great fury on the Monastery of *Carthusian* Monks, and the Houses of the Preaching and *Franciscan* Fryars, beginning with the Images first, but after spoyling them of all their provisions, Bedding, and Furniture of Houshold, which was given for a pray unto the poor. And in the ruinating of these Houses, they continued with much force and eagerness, so that within the compass of two days, they had left nothing standing of those goodly Edifices but the outward Walls.

13. It was reported that the Queen was so inraged when she heard the news, that she vowed utterly to destroy the Town, Man, Woman, and Child, to consume the same with fire, and after, to sow Salt upon it, in sign of perpetual desolation. And it is possible she might have been as good as her word, if the Earl of *Glencarne*, the Lords *Uchiltrie* and *Boyd*, the young Sheriff of *Air*, and many other men of eminent Quality, attended by two thousand five hundred Horse and Foot, had not come very opportunely to the aid of their Brethren. *Perth* being thus preserved from the threatned danger, but forced to receive a Garrison of the Queens appointment; *Knox* leaves the Town, and goes in company with the Earl of *Arguile*, and the Lord *James Steward*, toward the City of St. *Andrews*. In the way to which, he Preached at a Town called *Craile*, inveighs most bitterly against such *French* Forces as had been sent thither under the Command of Monsieur *d'Offelle*, exhorting his Auditors in fine to joyn together as one man, till all strangers were expulsed the Kingdom; and either to prepare themselves to live like men, or to dye victorious. Which exhortation so prevailed upon most of the hearers, that immediately they betook themselves to the pulling down of Altars and Images; and finally, destroyed all Monuments of Superstition and Idolatry which they found in the Town. The like they did the next day at a place called *Anstruther*. From thence they march unto St. *Andrews*, in the Parish Church whereof *Knox* Preached upon our Saviours casting the Buyers and Sellers out of the Temple, and with his wonted *Rhetorick* so inflamed the people, that they committed the like outrages there as before at *Perth*, destroying Images, and pulling down the Houses of the *Black* and *Grey-fryars* with the like dispatch. This happened upon the 11 of *June*. And because it could not be supposed but that the Queen would make some use of her *French* Forces to Chastise the chief Ring-leaders of that Sedition, the Brethren of the Congregation flock so fast unto them, that before *Tuesday* night, no fewer then three thousand able men from the parts adjoyning were come to *Cooper* to their aid. By the accession of which strength, they first secured themselves by a Capitulation from any danger by the *French*, and then proceeded to the removing of the Queens Garrison out of *Perth*, which they also effected. Freed from which yoke, some of the Towns men joyning themselves with those of *Dundee*, make an assault upon the Monastery of *Scone*, famous of long time for the Coronation of the Kings of *Scotland*; and for that cause more sumptuously adorned, and more richly furnished then any other in the Kingdom. And though the Noblemen, and even *Knox* himself,

himself, endeavoured to appeafe the people, and to ftop their fury, that
fo the place might be preferved; yet all endeavours proved in vain, or
were coldly followed. So that in fine, after fome fpoyl made in defacing of Images, and digging up great quantity of hidden goods which
were buried there, to be preferved in expectation of a better day; they
committed the whole Houfe to the mercy of Fire; the flame whereof
gave grief to fome, and joy to others of St. *Johnftones*, fcituate not above
a Mile from that famous Abby.

14. They had no fooner plaid this prize, but fome of the Chiefs of
them were advertifed that Queen Regent had a purpofe of putting fome
French Forces into *Sterling*, the better to cut off all intercourfe and
mutual fuccours which thofe of the Congregation on each fide of the
Fryth might otherwife have of one another. For the preventing of
which mifchief, the Earl of *Arguile* and the Lord *James Steward* were
difpatched away: Whofe coming fo inflamed the zeal of the furious
multitude, that they pulled down all the Monafteries which were in the
Town; demolifhed all the Altars, and defaced all the Images in the
Churches of it. The Abbey of *Cambuskenneth*, near adjoyning to it,
was then ruined alfo: Which good fuccefs encouraged them to go on
to *Edenborough*, that the like Reformation might be made in the capital City. Taking *Linlithgow* in their way, they committed the like
fpoyl there, as before at *Sterling*; but were prevented of the glory
which they chiefly aimed at in the Saccage of *Edenborough*. Upon the
news of their approach, though their whole Train exceeded not three
hundred perfons, the Queen Regent with great fear retires to *Dunbar*;
and the Lord *Seaton* being then Provest of the Town, ftaid not long behind. But he was fcarce gone out of the City, when the *Rafcal Rabble*
fell on the Religious Houfes, deftroyed the Covents of the *Black* and
Gray-fryars, with all the other Monafteries about the Town, and fhared
amongft them all the goods which they found in thofe Houfes: In which
they made fuch quick difpatch, that they had finifhed that part of the
Reformation, before the two Lords and their attendants could come in
to help them.

15. The Queen Regent neither able to endure thefe outrages, nor of
fufficient power to prevent or punifh them, conceived it moft expedient
to allay thefe humours for the prefent by fome gentle Lenitive, that fhe
might hope the better to extinguifh them in the time to come: which
when fhe had endeavoured, but with no effect, fhe caufed a Proclamation to be publifhed in the name of the King and Queen; in which it
was declared, *That fhe perceived a feditious Tumult to be raifed by a part of
the Lieges, who named themfelves the* Congregation, *and under pretence of
Religion had taken Arms; That by the advice of the Lords of the Council, for
fatisfying every mans Confcience, and pacifying the prefent troubles, fhe had
made offer to call a Parliament in* January *then following (but would call it fooner
if they pleafed) for eftablifhing an Univerfal Order in Affairs of Religion; That
in the mean time every man fhould be fuffered to live at liberty, ufing their own
Confciences without trouble until further order; That thofe who called themfelves
of the* Congregation, *rejecting all reafonable offers, had made it manifeft by
their actions, that they did not fo much feek for fatisfaction in point of Religion,
as the fubverfion of the Crown. For proof whereof, fhe inftanced in fome fecret
intelligence*

intelligence which they had in England, *seizing the Iron of the Mint, and Coyning Money, that being one of the principal Jewels of the Royal Diadem.* In *which regard she straightly willeth and commandeth all manner of persons (not being Inhabitants of the City) to depart from* Edenborough *within six hours after publication thereof, and live obedient to her Authority, except they would be holden and reputed Traytors.*

16. This Proclamation they encountred with another, which they published in their own names for satisfaction of the people, some of which had begun to shrink from them at the noise of the former. And therein they made known to all whom it may concern, *That such crimes as they were charged with, never entered into their hearts ; That they had no other intention then to banish Idolatry, to advance true Religion, and to defend the Preachers of it ; That they were ready to continue in all duty toward their Soveraign, and her Mother there Regent, provided they might have the free exercise of their own Religion, In reference to their medling with the Irons of the Mint, and the Coyning of Money, they justified themselves, as being most of them Councellors born, and doing nothing in it but for the good of the people.* To which effect they writ their Letters also to the Regent her self, whom they assured in the close, that if she would make use of her authority for the abolishing of Idolatry and Superstitious abuses which agreed not with the Word of God, she should find them as obedient as any Subjects within the Realm. Which in plain truth was neither more nor less then this, that if they might not have their wills in the point of Religion, she was to look for no obedience from them in other matters: whereof they gave sufficient proof by their staying in *Edenborough*, her command to the contrary notwithstanding ; by pressing more then ever for a toleration, and adding this over and above to their former demands, that such *French* Forces as remained in *Scotland* might be disbanded and sent back to their native Countrey. In the first of which demands they were so unreasonable, that when the Queen offered them the exercise of their own Religion, upon condition that when she had occasion to make use of any of their Churches for her own Devotions, such exercise might be suspended, and the Mass onely used in that conjuncture ; they would by no means yeild unto it : And they refused to yeild unto it for this Reason only, because it would be in her power, by removing from one place unto another, to leave them without any certain Exercise of their Religion, which in effect was utterly to overthrow it. And hereto they were pleased to add, that, as they could not hinder her from exercising any Religion which she had a mind to (but this was more then they would stand to in their better Fortunes) so could they not agree that the Ministers of Christ should be silenced upon any occasion, and much less, that the true Worship of God should give place to Idolatry. A point to which they stood so stifly, that when the Queen Regent had resetled her Court at *Edenborough*, she could neither prevail so far upon the Magistrates of that City, as either to let her have the Church of St. *Gyles* to be appropriated only to the use of the Mass, or that the Mass might be said in it at such vacant times in which they made no use of it for themselves or their Ministers.

17. But in their other demands for sending the *French* Souldiers

out of *Scotland*, they were not like to find any such compliance as had been offered in the former. *Henry* the Third of *France* dyed about that time, and left the Crown to *Francis* the Second, Married not long before to the Queen of *Scots*; the preservation of whose power and prerogative Royal must be his concernment. And he declared himself so sensible of those indignities which had been lately put upon her, as to protest, that he would rather spend the Crown of *France*, then not be revenged of the seditious Tumults raised in *Scotland*: in pursuance of which resolution, he sends over a *French* Captain, called *Octavian*, who brought with him a whole Regiment of Souldiers; great sums of mony, and all provisions necessary to maintain a War. Followed not long after with four Companies more, which made up twenty Ensigns compleat, together with four Ships of War, both to defend the Town of *Leith*, and command the Haven. Incouraged with whose coming, the Queen Regent did not only fortifie that Town, but put a strong Garrison of the *French* into it; which gave a new grievance unto those of the *Congregation*; the Trade and Town of *Edenborough* being like by this means to be brought under her command, and to rest wholly in a manner at her devotion. The breach made wider on the one side by the taking of the Fort of *Boughty Cragg* into the hands of those of the *Congregation*; which was pretended to be done, for fear left otherwise it might have been seized on by the *French*; and on the other side, by the coming of two thousand *French* Souldiers out of *France*, under pretence of being a Convoy to the Bishop of *Amiens*, and some other persons, sent thither to dispute (as it was given out) with the *Scotish* Ministers. Which great accession of *French* Forces so amazed the Lords of the *Congregation*, that they excited the whole Kingdom by a publick Writing to arm against them; requiring all those which were, or desired to be accounted for natural Scotch-men, to judge betwixt the Queen and them, and not abstract the just and dutiful support from their Native Country in so needful a time; assuring them, that whosoever did otherwise, should be esteemed betrayers of their Country to the power of strangers.

18. And that the people might not cool in the midst of this heat, they draw their Forces together, and march toward *Edenborough* on the 18 of *October*; upon the news whereof, the Queen Regent put her self into *Leith* as the safer place, and leaves them Masters of the City: From whence they send a Letter to her, requiring in a peremptory and imperious manner, that the fortifications about *Leith* be forthwith slighted, the Forts about the same to be demolished, and all strange Souldiers to be immediately removed: Which if she not pleased to do, they must bethink themselves of some such other remedies as they thought most necessary. But when their Messenger returned unsatisfied, and that *Lyon* King at Arms was sent presently after him: commanding them amongst other things to remove from *Edenborough*, they then resolve for putting that in execution which had been long before in deliberation; that is to say, the deposing of the Queen Regent from the publick Government. But first, they must consult with their Ghostly Fathers, that by their countenance and authority, they might more certainly prevail upon all such persons as seemed unsatisfied in

the

the point. *Willock* and *Knox* are chosen above all the rest to resolve this doubt, if at the least any of them doubted of it, which may well be questioned. They were both Factors for *Geneva*, and therefore b th obliged to advance her interest. *Willock* declares that albeit God had appointed Magistrates only to be his Lieutenants on Earth, honouring them with his own title, and calling them Gods; yet did he never so establish any, but that for just causes they might be deprived. Which having proved by some Examples out of holy Scripture, he thereupon inferred, that since the Queen Regent had denied her chi f Duty to the Subjects of this Realm, which was to preserve them from invasion of Strangers, and to suffer the Word of God to be freely preached: seeing also she was a maintainer of superstition, and despised the counsel of the Nobility; he did think they might justly deprive h r from all Regiment and Authority over them. *Knox* goes to work more cautiously, but comes home at last: For having first approved whatsoever had been said by *Willock*, he adds this to it, That the iniquity of the Queen Regent ought not to withdraw their hearts fr m the obedience due to their Soveraign; nor did he wish that any such sentence agsinst her should be pronounced, but that when she should change her course, and submit her self to good counsels, there should be place left unto her of regress to the same honours from which for just cause she ought to be deprived.

19. So said the Oracle: and as the Oracle decreed, so the sentence passed; for presently upon this judgment in the case, a publick Instrument is drawn up, in which the most part of the passages in the course of her Government were censured as grievances and oppressions on the Subjects of *Scotland*, to the violating of the Laws of the Land, the Liberty of the Subjects, and the enslaving of them to the power and domination of strangers. In which respect, they declare her to be fallen from the publick Government; discharge all Officers and others from yeilding any obedience to her; subscribing this instrument with their hands, requiring it to be published in all the Head-Boroughs of the Kingdom, and causing it to be proclaimed with sound of Trumpet. Thus they began with the Queen Regent; but we shall see them end with the Queen her self, their anointed Soveraign. This Instrument bears date on the 23 of *October*, a memorable day for many notable occurrences which have hapned on it in our Brittish Stories. Of all these doings, they advertised her by express Letters, sent back by the same Herald who had brought her last message to them; and having so done, they resolve immediately to try their fortune upon *Leith* in the way of *Scalada*. But the worst was, the Souldiers would not fight without present money, and money they had none to pay them on so short a warning. Somewhat was raised by way of Contribution, but would not satisfie. And thereupon it was advised, that the Lords and other great men should bring in their Plate, and cause it to be presently melted, to content the Souldiers. But they who had so long made a gain of Godliness, did not love Godliness so well, as not to value and prefer their gain before it. And therefore some had so contrived it, that the Irons of the *Mint* were missing; and by that handsome fraud they preserved their Plate.

20. It

20. It was not to be thought that the *Scots* durst have been so bold in the present business, if they had not been encouraged underhand from some Friends in *England*; which the Queen Regent well observed, and prest it on them in her Declaration, as before was noted. To which particular, though the Confederates made no reply in their Anti-remonstrance at that time, yet afterwards they both acknowledged and defended their intelligence with the English Nation. For in a subsequent Declaration, *They acknowledge plainly, that many Messages had past betwixt them, and that they had craved some support from thence; but that it was only to maintain Religion, and suppress Idolatry. Aud they conceived that in so doing, they had done nothing which might make them subject unto any just censure; it being lawful for them, where their own power failed, to seek assistance from their Neighbours.* And now or never was the time to make use of such helps, their Contribution falling short, and the Plate not coming to the Mint, as had been projected. In which extremity it was advised to try some secret Friends at *Barwick*, especially Sir *Ralph Sudlier* and Sir *James Crofts*; by whose encouragement it may be thought they had gone so far, that now there was no going back without manifest ruine. By the assistance of these men, they are furnished with four thousand Crowns in ready Money. But the Queen Regent had advertisement of the negotiation, and intercepts it by the way. The news of this ill fortune makes the Souldiers desperate; some of them secretly steal away, others refuse to venture upon any service; so that the Lords and others of the chief Confederates are put upon a necessity of forsaking *Edenborough*. The *French* immediately take possession of it, compel the Ministers, and most of those who protest the Reformed Religion, to desert their dwellings; restore the Mass, and reconcile with many Ceremonies the chief Church of the City (I mean that dedicated unto St. *Gyles*) as having been prophaned by Heretical Preachings. But the abandonning of *Edenborough* proved the ruine of *Glasco*. To which Duke *Hamilton* repairing, he caused all the Images and Altars to be pulled down, and made himself Master of the Castle; out of which, upon the noise of the Bishops coming with some Bands of *French*, he withdraws again, and quits the Town unto the Victor. No way now left to save their persons from the Law, their Estates from forfeiture, their Countrey from the *French*, and their Religion from the Pope, but to cast themselves upon the favour of the Queen of *England*. And to that course as the Lord *James* did most incline, and *Knox* most Preached for, so there might be some probable Reasons which might assure them of failing of not their expectations.

21. No sooner was Queen *Mary* of *England* dead, but *Mary* the young Queen of *Scots*, not long before Married to the *Daulphin* of *France*, takes on her self the name and title of Queen of *England*; the Arms whereof she quarters upon all her Plate, some of her Coyn, and upon no small part of her Houshould-Furniture. Which though she did not (as she did afterwards alledge) of her own accord, but as she was overruled in it by the perswasion of her Husband, and the Authority (which was not in her to dispute) of the King his Father; yet Queen *Elizabeth* looked upon it as a publick opposition to her own Pretensions, an open disallowing of her Title to the Crown of this Realm. She had good reason to presume

fume that they by whose Authority and Counsel she was devested of her Title, would leave no means untryed, nor no stone unmoved, by the rouling whereof she might be tumbled out of her Government, and deprived also of her Kingdom. Which jealousie so justly setled, received no small increase, from the putting over of so many *French*, distributing them into so many Garrisons, but more especially, by their fortifying of the Town of *Leith* ; at which Gate all the strengths of *France* might enter when occasion served : And then how easie a passage might they have into *England*? divided only by small Rivers in some places, and in some other places not divided at all. But that which most assured her of their ill intentions, was the great preparations lately made by the Marquiss of *Elbeuf* one of the Brothers of the Queen Regent, and consequently Uncle to the Queen of *Scots*. For though he was so distressed by tempests, that eighteen Ensignes were cast away on the Coast of *Holland*, and the rest forced for the present to return into *France* ; yet afterwards, with one thousand Foot, and some remainders of his Horse, he recovered *Leith*, and joyned himself unto the rest of that Nation, who were there disposed of. Of all which passages and provocations, the Chief Confederates of the Congregation were so well informed, as might assure them that Queen *Elizabeth* would be easily moved for her own security to aid them in expelling the *French* ; and then the preservation of Religion, and the securing of themselves, their Estates and Families, would come in of course.

22. It was upon this Reason of State, and not for any quarrel about Religion, that Queen *Elizabeth* put her self into Arms, and lent the *Scots* a helping hand to remove the *French*. And by the same she might have justified her self before all the World, if she had followed those advantages which were given her by it, and seized into her hands such Castles, Towns, and other places of importance within that Kingdom, as might give any opportunity to the *French-Scots* to infest her Territories. For when one Prince pretends a Title to the Crown of another, or makes preparations more then ordinary both by Land and Sea, and draws them together to some place ; from whence he may invade the other whensoever he please ; the other party is not bound to sit still till the War be brought to his own doors, but may lawfully keep it at a distance, as far off as he can, by carrying it into the Enemies Country, and getting into his power all their strong Passes, Holds, and other Fortresses, by which he may be hindred from approaching nearer. But this can no way justifie or excuse the *Scots*, which are not to be reckoned for the less Rebels against their own undoubted Soveraign, for being subservient in so just a War to the Queen of *England* ; as neither the *Caldeans* or the wild *Arabians* could be defended in their thieving, or *Nebuchadnezzar* justified in his pride and Tyranny, because it pleased Almighty God for tryal of *Jobs* faith and patience to make use of the one ; and of the other, for chastising his people *Israel*. The point being agitated with mature deliberation by the Councel of *England*, it was resolved that the *French* were not to be suffered to grow strong so near the Border ; that the Queen could not otherwise provide for her own security, then by expelling them out of *Scotland* ; and

                       that

(margin note: 1560.)

that it was not to be compaſſed at a leſs expence of Blood and Treaſure, then by making uſe of the *Scots* themſelves, who had ſo earneſtly ſupplicated for her aid and ſuccours. Commiſſioners are thereupon appointed to treat at *Barwick* : Betwixt whom and the Agents for the Lords of the Congregation all things in reference to the War are agreed upon : The ſum and reſult whereof was this, That the Engliſh with a puiſſant Army entred into *Scotland*, reduced the whole War to the Siege of *Leith*, and brought the French in ſhort time into ſuch extremities, that they were forced in concluſion to abandon *Scotland*, and leave that Country wholly in a manner to the Congregation.

23. Theſe were the grounds, and this the iſſue of thoſe counſels, which proved ſo glorious and ſucceſful unto Queen *Elizabeth* in all the time of her long Reign : For by giving this ſeaſonable Aid to thoſe of the Congregation in their greateſt need, and by feeding ſome of the Chiefs amongſt them with ſmall annual Penſions, ſhe made her ſelf ſo abſolute, and of ſuch Authority over all the Nation, that neither the Queen Regent, nor the Queen her ſelf, nor King *James* her ſon, nor any of their Predeceſſors, were of equal power, nor had the like Command upon them. The Church was alſo for a while a great gainer by it; the *Scots* had hitherto made uſe of the Engliſh Liturgie in Gods publick Worſhip ; the phancy of extemporary Prayers not being then taken up amongſt them, as is affirmed by *Knox* himſelf in his Scottiſh Hiſtory. But now upon the ſenſe of ſo great a benefit, and out of a deſire to unite the Nations in the moſt conſtant bonds of friendſhip, they bind themſelves by their ſubſcription to adhere unto it : For which I have no worſe a Witneſs then their own *Buchanan*. And that they might approach as near unto it in the Form of Government as the preſent condition of the times would bear, as they placed ſeveral Miniſters for their ſeveral Churches, (as *Knox* in *Edenborough*, *Goodman* at Saint *Andrews*, *Aeriot* at *Aberdeen*, &c.) ſo they ordained certain Superintendents for their Miniſters ; all the Epiſcopal Sees being at that time filled with Popiſh Prelates. And happy it had been for both, had they continued ſtill in ſo good a poſture ; and that the *Presbyterian* humour had not ſo far obliterated all remembrance of their old affections, as in the end to proſecute both the Liturgie and Epiſcopacie to an extirmination. And there accrued a further benefit by it to the *Scots* themſelves ; that is to ſay, the confirmation of the Faith which they ſo contended for by Act of Parliament : for by difficulties of Agreement between the Commiſſioners authorized on all ſides to attone the differences, it was conſented to by thoſe for the Queen of *Scots*, that the Eſtates of the Realm ſhould conveue and hold a Parlement in the *Auguſt* following, and that the ſaid Convention ſhould be as lawful in all reſpects, as if it ſhould be ſummoned by the particular and expreſs command of the Kings themſelves. According to which Article they hold a Parlement, and therein paſs an Act for the ratification of the Faith and Doctrine, as it was then drawn up into the Form of a Confeſſion by ſome of their Miniſters. But becauſe this confeſſion did receive a more plenary confirmation in the firſt Parlement of King *James*, we ſhall refer all further ſpeech of it till we come to that.

They

They also passed therein other Acts to their great advantage; first for abolishing the Popes Authority; the second for repealing all former Statutes which were made and maintained of that which they called Idolatry; and the third against the saying or hearing of Mass.

24. It was conditioned in the Articles of the late agreement, that the Queen of *Scots* should send Commissioners to their present Parliament, that the results thereof might have the force and effect of Laws; but she intended not for her part to give their Acts the countenance of Supreme Authority; and the Chief-leading men of the Congregation did not much regard it, as thinking themselves in a capacity to manage their own business without any such countenance: For though they had addressed themselves to the King and Queen for confirmation of such Acts as had passed in this Parliament; yet they declared that what they did was rather to express their obedience to them, then to beg of them any strength to their Religion. They had already cast the Rider, and were resolved that neither King nor Queen should back them for the time to come. The Queen Regent wearied and worn out with such horrid insolencies, departed this life at *Edenborough* on the 10. of *June*; and none was nominated to succeed with like Authority: The *French* Forces were imbarked on the 16 of *July*, except some few which were permitted to remain in the Castle of *Dunb..r*, and the Isle of *Inchkeeth*; so few, that they seemed rather to be left for keeping possession of the Kingdom in the name of the Queen, then either to awe the Country, or command obedience. And that they might be free from the like fears for the times ensuing, *Francis* the Second dyeth on the fifth of *December*, leaving the Queen of *Scots* a desolate and friendless Widdow, assisted only by her Uncles of the House of *Guise*, who though they were able to do much in *France*, could do little out of it. This put the *Scots* (I mean the leading *Scots* of the *Congregation*) into such a stomack, that they resolved to steer their course by another compass, and not to Sail onely by such Winds as should blow from *England*. They knew full well that the breach between the two Queens was not reconcileable, and that their own Queen would be always kept so low by the power of *England*, that they might trample on her as they pleased, now they had her under. And though at first they had imbraced the Common-prayer-Book of the Church of *England*, and afterwards confirmed the use of it by a solemn Subscription; yet when they found themselves delivered from all fear of the *French* by the death of their King, and the breach growing in that Kingdome upon that occasion; they then began to tack about, and to discover their affections to the Church of *Geneva*. *Knox* had before devised a new Book of Discipline, contrived for the most part after *Calvins* platform, and a new Form of Common-prayer was digested also, more consonant to his infallible judgement then the English Liturgie. But hitherto they had both lain dormant, because they stood in need of such help from *England*, as could not be presumed on with so great a confidence, if they had openly declared any dissent or disaffection to the publick Forms which were established in that Church. Now their estate is so much bettered by the death of the King, the sad condition of their Queen, and the assurances which they had from the Court of *England* (from whence the

the Earls of *Morton* and *Glencarne* were returned with comfort) that they refolve to perfect what they had begun ; to profecute the defolation of Religious Houfes, and the fpoyl of Churches ; to introduce their new Forms, and fufpend the old.　For compaffing of which end they fummoned a Convention of the Eftates to be held in *January*.

25. Now in this Book of Difcipline they take upon them to innovate in moft things formerly obferved and practifed in the Church of Chrift, and in fome things which themfelves had fetled, as the ground-work of the Reformation.　They take upon them to difcharge the accuftomed Fafts, and abrogate all the ancient Feftivals, not fparing thofe which did relate particularly unto Chrift our Saviour, as his Nativity, Paffion, Refurrection, &c. They condemned the ufe of the Crofs in Baptifm, give way to the introduction of the New Order of *Geneva*, for miniftring the Sacrament of the Lords Supper, and commend fitting for the moft proper and convenient gefture to be ufed at it. They require that all Churches not being Parochial fhould be forth-with demolifhed, declare all Forms of Gods publick Worfhip, which are not prefcribed in his Word, to be mere Idolatry, and that none ought to adminifter the holy Sacraments but fuch as are qualified for Preaching.　They appoint the Catechifm of *Geneva* to be taught in their Schools, Ordained three Univerfities to be made and continued in that Kingdom, with Salaries proportioned to the Profefors in all arts and Sciences, and time affigned for being graduated in the fame.　They decree alfo in the fame, that Tythes fhould be no longer paid to the *Romifh* Clergy, but that they fhall be taken up by Deacons and Trea-furers, by them to be imployed for maintainance of the poor, the Minifters, and the faid Univerfities.　They complained very fenfibly of the Tyranny of Lay-Patrons and Impropriators in exacting their Tythes, in which they are faid to be more cruel and unmerciful then the Popifh Priefts ; and therefore take upon them to determine as in point of law what commodities fhall be Tythable, what not; and declare alfo that all Leafes and Alienations, which formerly had been made of Tythes, fhould be utterly void.

26. Touching the Miniftration of the Word and Sacraments, and the performance of other Divine Offices, it is therein ordered, That Common prayers (by which they mean the new Form of their own devifing) be faid every day in the greater Towns, except it be upon the days of publick Preaching ; but then to be forborn, that the Preachers own Prayer before and after Sermon may not be defpifed or difrefpected : That Baptifm be Adminiftred only upon the Sundays, and other days of publick Preaching, for the better beating down of that grofs Opinion of the Papifts (fo they pleas'd to call it) concerning the neceffity of it : That the firft Sundays of *March*, *June*, *September* and *December*, fhould be from thenceforth fet apart for the holy Communion, the better to avoid the fuperftitious receiving of it at the Feaft of *Eafter* : That all perfons exercife themfelves in finging *Pfalms*, to the end they may the better perform that fervice in the Congregation : That no finging of *Pfalms*, no reading of Scriptures fhould be ufed at burials : That no Funeral-Sermon fhall be preached, by which any difference may be made between the rich and the poor ; and that no dead body for the

fame

same cause shall be buried in Churches : That Prophesyings and interpreting of the holy Scriptures shall be used at certain times and places, according to the custom of the Church of *Corinth* : That in every Church there shall be one Bell to call the People together, one Pulpit for the Word, and a Bason for Baptism : And that the Minister may the better attend these Duties, it is ordered that he shall not haunt the Court, nor be of the Council, nor bear charge in any Civil Affairs, except it be to assist the Parliament when the same is called.

27. Concerning Ecclesiastical persons, their Function, Calling, Maintainance and Authority, it was ordered in the said Book of Discipline, That Ministers shall from thenceforth be elected by the Congregation where they are to preach : that having made tryal of their Gifts, and being approved of by the Church where they are to preach, they shall be admitted to their charge, but without any imposition of hands as in other Churches : That some convenient pension be assigned to every Minister for the term of life (except he deserve to be deprived) with some provision to be made after his decease for his Wife and Children : That the bounds of the former Diocesses being contracted or enlarged, there shall be ten or twelve Superintendents appointed in the place of the former Bishops, who are to have the visitation of all the Ministers and Churches in their several bounds, to fix their dwellings in the chief Towns or Cities within the same, and to be chosen by the Burgesses of the said Towns or Cities, together with the suffrages of the Ministers of their several Circuits ; and more particularly, that the County or Province of *Lothaine* shall be abstracted from the Diocess of St. *Andrews*, and have a Superintendent of its own, who was to keep his Residence in the City of *Edenborough* (which afterwards in the year 1633 was erected by King *Charles* into a Bishops See, and *Lothaine* assigned him for his Diocess, as was here devised :) That for the better maintainance of the Ministers and Superintendents, as also for defraying of all other publick charges which concerned the Churches, the lands belonging unto the Bishops, as also to all Cathedral and Conventual Churches, and to the House of Monks and Fryars, shall be set apart, not otherwise to be imployed : That in all Churches there be two Elders annually chosen to be associate with the Ministers in the Cognizance of all Ecclesiastical Causes, and in the Censures of the Church : That the said Elders shall have power not only to admonish, but correct their Ministers, if occasion be ; but not to proceed to deprivation without the allowance and consent of the Superintendent ; and that the Deacons shall be joyned as Assistants in judgement with the Elders and Ministers : That no man presume to eat or drink, or otherwise to converse familiarly with excommunicate persons, except those of his own Family only : That their Children should not be Baptised till they came unto the years of discretion : And that all Murtherers, and other Malefactors punishable by death according to the Laws of the Land, though they be pardoned for the same by the supreme Magistrates, shall notwithstanding be esteemed as excommunicate persons, and not received into the Church without such satisfaction and submission as is required of other notorious offenders by the Rules of the Discipline. It appears

pears alfo by this book, that there was one ftanding Supreme Council for ordering the affairs of the Church, and by which all publick grievances were to be redreffed ; but of what perfons it confifted, and in what place it was held, is not mentioned in it.

28. This Book being tendered to the confideration of the Convention of Eftates, was by them rejected ; whether it were becaufe they could not make fuch a manifeft feperation from the Polity of the Church of *England*, or that it concerned them more particularly in their own proper intereft, in regard of the Church-lands and Tythes which they had amongft them, or perhaps for both. Certain it is, that fome of them paft it over by no better Title then that of fome *devout imaginations*, which could not be reduced to practice. This fo offended *Knox* and others, who had drawn it up (if any other but *Knox* only had a hand therein) that they fpared not bitterly to revile them for their coldnefs in it, taxing them for their carnal liberty, their love unto their worldly Commodities, and their corrupt imaginations : Some of them are affirmed to have been licentious ; fome greedily to have griped the poffeffions of the Church, and others to be fo intent upon the getting of Chrifts Coat, that they would not ftay till he was crucified. Of the Lord *Erskin* who refufed to fubfcribe to the Book, it is faid particularly, that he had a very ill woman to his Wife; and that if the Schools, the poor, and the Miniftry of the Church had their own, his Kitchin would have lacked two parts of that which he then poffeffed. Of all of them it was admired, that for fuch a long continuance they could hear the threatnings of God againft Thieves and Robbers, and that knowing themfelves to be guilty of thofe things which were moft rebuked, they fhould never have any remorfe of Confcience, nor intend the reftoring of thofe things which they had fo ftolen. For fo it was (if they may be believed that faid it) that none in all the Realm were more unmerciful to the poor Minifters, then they that had invaded and poffeffed themfelves of the greateft Rents of right belonging unto the Church, and therein verified, as well the old Proverb, *That the Belly hath no ears at all*, as a new obfervation of their own devifing, *That nothing would fuffice a wretch*. Such were the difcontents and evaporations of thefe zealous men, when they were croffed in any thing which concerned them in their power or profit.

29. But in another of their projects they had better Fortune. They had follicited the Convention of Eftates for demolifhing of all Monuments of Superftition and Idolatry, in which number they accounted all Cathedral Churches as well as Monafteries and other Religious Houfes ; which they infifted on the rather, becaufe it was perceived, and perhaps given out, that the Papifts would again erect their old Idolatry and take upon them a command (as before they did) upon the Confciences of the people ; that fo as well the great men of the Realm, as fuch whom God of his Mercy (fo they tell us) had fubjected to them, fhould be compelled to obey their lawlefs appetites. In this, fome hopes were given them that they fhould be fatisfied, but nothing done in execution of the fame, till the *May* next following : And poffibly enough it might have been delayed to a longer time, if the noife and expectation of

the

the Queens return had not spurred it on: For either fearing, or not knowing what might happen to them, if she should interpose her power to preserve those places, whose demolishing they so much desired; they introduce that Discipline by little and little, which they could not settle all at once.   They begin first planting Churches, and nominating Superintendents for their several Circuits; they superinduce their own Ministers over the heads of the old Incumbents; establish their Presbyteries, divide them into several Classes, and hold their general Assemblies without any leave desired of the Queen or Council.   They proceed next to execute all sorts of Ecclesiastical Censures, and arrogate Authority to their selves and their Elders to Excommunicate all such as they found unconformable to their new devices.   For the first tryal of their power, they convened one *Sanderson*, who had been accused to them for Adultery, whom they condemned to be carted, and publickly exposed unto the scorn of Boys and children.   An uproar had been made in *Edenborough* about the chusing of a *Robbinhood* (or a *Whitson-Lord*) in which some few of the preciser sort opposed all the rest; and for this crime they excommunicate the whole multitude; wherein they shewed themselves to be very unskilful in the Canon-law, in which they might have found, that neither the Supreme Magistrate, nor any great multitudes of people are to be subject to that Censure.   They proceed afterwards to the appointing of solemn Fasts, and make choice of Sunday for the day; which since that time hath been made use of for those Fasts, more then any other: and in this point they shewed themselves directly contrary to the practice of the Primitive Church, in which it was accounted a great impiety to keep any Fast upon that day, either private or publick.   They Interdict the Bishops from exercising any Ecclesiastical Jurisdiction in their several Dioceses; and openly quarrel with their Queen, for giving a Commission to the Archbishop of Saint *Andrews* to perform some Acts which seemed to them to favour of the Episcopal power.   Having attained unto this height, they maintain an open correspondence with some Forein Churches, give audience to the Agents of *Berne*, *Basil* and *Geneva*; from whom they received the sum of their Confessions, and signified their consent with them in all particulars, except Festivals only, which they had universally abolished throughout the Kingdom; and finally, they take upon them to write unto the Bishops of *England*, whom they admonished not to vex or suspend their Brethren for not conforming to the Rules of the Church, especially in refusing the Cap and Surplice, which they call frequently by the name of *trifles*, *vain trifles*, and *the old Badges of Idolatry*.   All which they did, and more, in pursuit of their Discipline, though never authorized by Law, or confirmed by the Queen, nor justified by the Convention of Estates, though it consisted for the most part of their own Professors. A Petition is directed to the Lords of secret Council from the *Assemblies of the Church*, in which their Lordships are sollicited to dispatch the business.   But not content with that which they had formerly moved, it was demanded also that some severe course might be taken against the Sayers and Hearers of Mass; that fit provision should be made for their Superintendents, Preachers, and other Ministers; and that they should not be compellable to pay their Tythes as formerly to the Popish Clergy,

with

with other particulars of that nature.   And that they might not trifle in it as they had done hitherto, the Petition carried in it more threats and menaces, then words of humble supplication as became Petitioners: For therein it said expresly, That before those Tyrants and dumb Dogs should have Empire over them, and over such as God had subjected unto them, they were fully determined to hazard both life, and whatsoever they had received of God in Temporal things; that therefore they besought their Lordships to take such order, that the Petitioners (if they may be called so) might have no occasion to take the Sword of just defence into their hands, which they had so willingly resigned, after the Victory obtained, into those of their Lordships; that so doing, their Lordships should perceive they would not only be obedient unto them in all things lawful, but ready at all times to bring all such under their obedience, as should at any time rebel against their Authority; and finally, that those enemies of God might assure themselves, that they would no longer suffer Pride and Idolatry; and that if their Lordships would not take some in the premises, they would then proceed against them of their own Authority after such a manner, that they should neither do what they list, nor live upon the sweat of the brows of such as were in no sort debtors to them.

31. On the receipt of this Petition, an Order presently is made by the Lords of the Council, for granting all which was desired; and had more been desired, they had granted more: so formidable were the Brethren grown to the opposite party.   Nor was it granted in words only which took no effect, but execution caused to be done upon it, and warrants to that purpose issued to the Earls of *Arrane*, *Arguile*, and *Glancarne*, the Lord *James Steward*, *&c.*   Whereupon followed a pitiful devastation of Churches and Church-buildings in all parts of the Realm; no difference made, but all Religious Edifices of what sort soever, were either terribly defaced, or utterly ruinated; the holy Vessels, and whatsoever else could be turned into money, as Lead, Bells, Timber, Glass, *&c.* was publickly exposed to sale; the very Sepulchres of the dead not spared; the Registers of the Church, and the Libraries thereunto belonging, defaced, and thrown into the fire.   Whatsoever had escaped the former tumults, is now made subject to destruction; so much the worse, because the violence and sacrilegious actings of these Church-robbers had now the countenance of Law.   And to this work of spoyl and rapine, men of all Ranks and Orders were observed to put their helping hands; men of most Note and quality being forward in it, in hope of getting to themselves the most part of the booty; those of the poorer sort, in hope of being gratified for their pains therein by their Lords and Patrons.   Both sorts encouraged to it by the Zealous madness of some of their seditious Preachers, who frequently cryed out, that the places where Idols had been worshipped, ought by the Law of God to be destroyed, that the sparing of them was the reserving of things execrable; and that the commandment given to *Israel* for destroying the places where the *Canaanites* did worship their false Gods, was a just warrant to the people for doing the like.   By which encouragements, the madness of the people was transported beyond the bounds which they had first prescribed unto it. In the beginning of the heats, they designed only the destruction of Religious
gious

gious Houfes, for fear the Monks and Friars might otherwife be reftored in time to their former dwellings : But they proceeded to the demolifhing of Cathedral Churches, and ended in the ruine of Parochial alfo ; the Chancels whereof were fure to be levelled in all places, though the Ifles and Bodies of them might be fpared in fome.

32. Such was the entertainment which the *Scots* prepared for their Queens coming over. Who taking no delight in *France*, where every thing renewed the memory of her great lofs, was eafily intreated to return to her native Kingdom, Her coming much defired by thofe of the Popifh party, in hope that by her power and prefence they might be fuffered at the leaft to enjoy the private Exercife of their Religion, if not a publick approbation and allowance of it. Sollicited as earneftly by thofe of the *Knoxian* intereft, upon a confidence that they fhould be better able to deal with her when fhe was in their power, affifted only by the Counfels of a broken Clergy then if fhe fhould remain in *France*, from whence by her Alliances and powerful Kindred fhe might create more mifchief to them then fhe could at home. On the 19 day of *Auguft* fhe arrives in *Scotland*, accompanied by her Uncles the Duke of *Aumales*, the Marquefs of *Elbœuf*, and the Lord grand Prior, with other Noble-men of *France*. The time of her arrival was obfcured with fuch Fogs and Mifts, that the Sun was not feen to fhine in two days before, nor in two days after. Which though it made her paffage fafe from the Ships of *England*, which were defigned to intercept her, yet was it looked upon by moft men as a fad prefage of thofe uncomfortable times which fhe found amongft them. Againft Sunday, being the 24, there were great preprations made for celebrating Mafs in the Chapel-Royal of *Holyrood*-Houfe. At which the Brethren of the Congregation were fo highly offended, that fome of them cryed out aloud, fo as all might hear them, That *the Idolatrous Priefts fhould dye the death according to Gods Law* ; others affirming with lefs noife, but with no lefs confidence, That *they could not abide, that the Land which God by his power had purged of Idolatry, fhould in their fight be polluted with the fame again.* And queftionlefs fome great mifchief muft have followed on it, if the Lord *James Stuart* (to preferve the honour of his Nation in the eye of the *French*) had not kept the door : which he did, under a pretence that none of the *Scotifh* Nation fhould be prefent at the hearing of Mafs, contrary to the Laws and Statutes made in that behalf ; but in plain truth, to hinder them by the power and reputation which he had amongft them, from thronging in tumultuoufly to difturb the bufinefs.

33. For remedy whereof for the time to come, an Order was iffued the next day by the Lords of the Council, and Authorized by the Queen in which it was declared, that no manner of perfon fhould privately or openly take in hand to alter or innovate any thing in the State of Religion which the Queen found publickly and univerfally received at her Majefties arrival in that Realm, or attempt any thing againft the fame upon pain of death. But then it was required withal, that none of the Leiges take in hand to trouble or moleft any of her Majefties Domeftick Servants, or any other perfons which had accompanied her

out

out of *France* at the time then present, for any cause whatsoever, in word, deed, or countenance; and that upon the pain of death, as the other was. But notwithstanding the equality of so just an Order, the Earl of *Arrane* in the name of the rest of the Congregation professed openly on the same day at the Cross in *Edenborough*, *That no protection should be given to the Queens Domesticks, or to any other person that came out of* France, *either to violate the Laws of the Realm, or offend Gods Majesty, more then was given to any other subjects.* And this he did, as he there affirmed, because Gods Law had pronounced death to the Idolater, and the Laws of the Realm had appointed punishment for the sayers and hearers of Mass; from which he would have none exempted, till some Law were publickly made in Parliament, and such as was agreeable to the Word of God, to annul the former. The like distemper had possest all the rest of the Lords at their first coming to the Town to attend her Majesty to congratulate her save arrival; but they cooled all of them by degrees, when they considered the unreasonableness of the Protestation, in denying that liberty of conscience to their Soverain Queen, which every one of them so much desired to enjoy for himself. only the Earl *Arrane* held it out to the last. He had before given himself some hopes of marrying the Queen, and sent her a rich Ring immediately on the death of the King her Husband; but finding no return agreeable to his expectation, he suffered himself to be as much transported to the other extreme, according to the natural Genius of the *Presbyterians*, who never yet knew any mean in their loves or hatred.

34. *John Knox* makes good the Pulpit in the chief Church at *Edenborough* on the Sunday following, in which he bitterly inveighed against Idolatry, shewing what Plagues and Punishments God had inflicted for the same upon several Nations. And then he adds, that one Mass was more fearful to him, then if ten thousand armed Enemies were landed in any part of the Realm on purpose to suppress their whole Religion; that in God there was strength to resist and confound whole multitudes, if unfeignedly they depended on him, of which they had such good experience in their former troubles; but that if they joyned hands with Idolatry, they should be deprived of the comfortable presence and assistance of Almighty God. A Conference hereupon ensued betwixt him and the Queen, at the hearing whereof there was none present but the Lord *James Steward*, besides two Gentlemen which stood at the end of the Room. In the beginning whereof, she charged him with raising Sedition in that Kingdom, putting her own Subjects into Arms against her, writing a Book against the Regiment of Women; and in the end, descended to some points of Religion. To all which *Knox* returned such answers, or else so favourably reports them to his own advantage (for we must take the whole story as it comes from his pen) that he is made to go away with as easie a victory, as when the Knight of the Boot encounters with some Dwarf or Pigmy in the old *Romances.* All that the Queen got by it from the mouth of this Adversary, was, that he found in her *a proud mind, a crafty wit,* and an *obdurate heart against God and his Truth.* And in this Character he thought himself confirmed by her following actions: For spending the rest of the Summer in visiting some of the chief Towns of her Kingdom, she carried the Mass with her into all

places

places wheresoever she came; and at her coming back, gave order for setting out the Mass with more solemnity on *Alhallows* day, then at any time or place before. Of this the Ministers complain to such of the Nobility as were then Resident in the City, but find not such an eagerness in them as in former times. For now some of them make a doubt *whether the Subjects might use force for suppressing the Idolatry of their Prince;* which heretofore had passed in the affirmative as a truth infallible. A Conference is thereupon appointed between some of the Lords, and such of the Ministers as appeared most Zealous against the Mass; the Lords disputing for the Queen, and urging that it was not lawful to deprive her of that in which she placed so great a part of her Religion. The contrary was maintained by *Knox*, and the rest of the Ministers; who seeing that they could not carry it, as before, by their own Authority, desired that the deciding of the point might be referred to the Godly Brethren of *Geneva*; of whose concurring in opinion with them, they were well assured. And though the drawing up of the point, and the Inditing of the Letter, being committed unto *Ledington* the principal Secretary, was not dispatched with such post haste as their Zeal required; yet they shewed plainly by insisting on that proposition, both from whose mouth they had received the Doctrines of making Soveraign Princes subject to the lusts of the people, and from whose hands they did expect the defence thereof.

35. A general Assembly being indicted by them about that time, or not long after, a question is made by some of the Court-Lords, whether such Assemblies might be holden by them without the Queens notice and consent. To which it was answered, that the Assembly neither was nor could be held without her notice, because she understood that there was a Reformed Church within the Realm, by the Orders whereof they had appointed times for their publick Conventions. But as to her allowance of it, it was then objected, that if the Liberty of the Church should stand upon the Queens allowance or disallowance, they were assured that they should not onely want Assemblies, but the Preaching of the Word it self; for if the freedom of Assemblies was taken away, the Gospel in effect must be also suppressed, which could not long subsist without them. The putting in of the demurrer concerning the Authority in calling and holding their Assemblies, prompted them to present the Book of Discipline to her Majesties view, and to sollicite her by all the Friends and means they could for her Royal-Assent: But finding no hope of compassing their desires for that Book in general, it was thought best to try their Fortune in the pursuit of some particulars contained in it. And to that end it was propounded to the Lords of the Council, that Idolatry might be suppressed, the Churches planted with true Ministers, and that certain provision should be made for them according to equity and good conscience. The Ministers till that time had lived for the most part upon such Benevolences as were raised for them on the people; the Patrimony of the Church being seized into the hands of private persons, and alienated in long Leases by the Popish Clergy. The Revenue of the Crown was small when it was at the best, exceedingly impaired since the death of King *James* the Fifth, and not sufficient to defray the necessary charge and expence of the

the Court.   To satisfie all parties it was ordered by the Lords of the Council, that the third part of all the Rents of Ecclesiastical Benefices should be taken up for the use of the Queen; that the other two parts should remain to the Clergy, or to such as held them in their Right; and that the Queen, out of the part assigned to her, should maintain the Ministers.   This Order bears date at *Edenborough*, *December* 20, but gave no satisfaction to the Ministers or their Sollicitors, who challenged the whole Patrimony, by the Rules of the Discipline, or belong only to themselves.   *Knox* amongst others so disliked it, that he affirmed openly in the Pulpit of *Edenborough*, *That the Spirit of God was not the Author of that Order, by which two parts of the Church Rents were given to the Devil, and the third part was to be divided between God and the Devil*: adding withall, *that in short time the Devil would have three parts of the third*, and that a fourth part only should be left to God.

36. But notwithstanding these seditions and uncharitable surmises of their hot-headed Preachers, a Commission is granted by the Queen to certain of her Officers, and other persons of Quality, not only to receive the said third part, but out of it to assign such yearly stipends to their Ministers as to them seemed meet.   They were all such as did profess the Reformed Religion, and therefore could not but be thought to be well affected to the Ministers maintainance; to some of which they allowed one hundred Marks by the year, unto some three hundred; insomuch, that it was said by *Ledington* principal Secretary of Estate, that when the Ministers we paid the Stipends assigned unto them, the rest would hardly find the Queen a new pair of Shooes.   But on the other side the Ministers vehemently exclaimed against these assignments; and openly profest it to be very unreasonable, that such dumb Dogs and Idle-bellies as the Popish Clergy should have a thousand Marks *per annum*; and that themselves (good men) who spent their whole time in Preaching the Gospel, should be put off with two or three hundred.   They railed with no less bitterness against the Laird of *Pittarow*, who was appointed by the Queen for their pay-Master General; and used to say in common Speech, that the good Laird of *Pittarow*, Comptroller of her Majesties Houshold, was a Zealous Professor of Jesus Christ; but that the Pay-Master or Comptroller would fall to the Devil.   And for the Queen, so far they were from acknowledging the receipt of any favour from her, in the true payment of their Stipends, that they disputed openly against that Title which she pretended to the thirds, out of which she paid them.   By some it was affirmed, that no such part had appertained to any of her Predecessors in a thousand years; by others, that she had no better Title thereunto (whether she kept them to her self, or divided them amongst her Servants) then had the Souldiers by whom Christ was crucified to divide his Garments.

37. It hapned not long after these debates, that upon the receiving 1562. of some good news from her Friends in *France*, the Queen appeared to be very merry, betook her self to dancing, and continued in that recreation till after midnight.   The news whereof being brought to *Knox*, who had his Spies upon her at all times to observe her actions; the Pulpit must needs ring of it, or else all was marred.   He chuseth for his Text these

thefe words of the fecond *Pfalm*, viz. *And now underftand O ye Kings, and be learned ye that judge the Earth.* Difcourfing on which Text, he began to tax the ignorance, the vanity, and the defpight of Princes againft all Vertue, and againft all thofe in whom hatred of Vice and love of Vertue appeared. Report is made unto the Queen, and this report begets a fecond Conference betwixt her and *Knox*, in which fhe muft come off with as little credit as fhe did in the firft. *Knox* tells her in plain terms, that it is oftentimes the juft recompence that God gives the ftubborn of the World, that becaufe they will not hear God fpeaking to the comfort of the Penitent, and for the amendment of the wicked, they are oft compelled to hear the falfe reports of others to their great difpleafure. To which immediately he fubjoyned, that it could not chufe but come to the Ears of *Herod*, that our Saviour Jefus Chrift had called him *Fox*; but that the men who told him of it, did not alfo tell him what an odious act he had committed before God, in caufing *John* the *Baptift* to be Beheaded, to recompence the Dancing of an Harlots Daughter. The Queen defired (after much other talk between them) that if he heard any thing of her which diftafted him, he would repair to her in private, and fhe would willingly hear what he had to fay. To which he anfwered with as little reverence and modefty as to all the reft, that he was appointed by God to rebuke the vices and fins of all, but not to go to every one in particular to make known their offences; that if fhe pleafed to frequent the publick Sermons, fhe might then know what he liked or difliked, as well in her felf as any others; but that to wait at her Chamber-door, or elfewhere, and then to have no further liberty then to whifper in her ear what he had to fay, or tell her what others did fpeak of her, was neither agreeable to his vocation, nor could ftand with his confcience.

38. At *Midfummer* they held a general Affembly, and there agreed upon the Form of a Petition to be prefented to the Queen in the name of the Kirk; the fubftance of it was for abolifhing the Mafs, and other fuperftitious Rites of the *Romifh* Religion; for inflicting fome punifhment againft Blafphemy, Adultery, contempt of Word, the Profanation of Sacraments, and other like vices condemned by the Word of God, whereof the Laws of the Realm did not take any hold; for referring all actions of Divorce to the Churches judgement, or as the leaft to men of good knowledge and converfation; for excluding all Popifh Church men from holding any place in Council or Seffion; and finally, for the increafe and more affured payment of the Minifters Stipends, but more particularly for appropiating the Glebes and Houfes unto them alone. This was the fum of their defires, but couched in fuch irreverent, coarfe, and bitter expreffions, and thofe expreffions juftified with fuch animofities, that *Lethington* had much ado to prevail upon them for putting it into a more dutiful and civil Language. All which the Queen knew well enough, and therefore would afford them no better anfwer, but that fhe would do nothing to the prejudice of that Religion which fhe then profeffed; and that fhe hoped to have Mafs reftored, before the end of the year, in all parts of the Kingdom. Which being fo faid, or fo reported, gave *Knox* occafion in his Preachings to the Gentry of *Kyle* and *Galloway* (to which he was commiffioned by the

said

said Assembly) to forewarn some of them of the dangers which would shortly follow; and thereupon earnestly to exhort them to take such order, that they might be obedient unto Authority, and yet not suffer the Enemies of Gods Truth to have the upper-hand. And they, who understood his meaning at half a word, assembled themselves together on the 4 of *Sep.* at the Town of *Air*, where they entred into a common Bond, subscribed by the Earl of *Glencarne*, the Lords *Boyd* and *Uchiltry*, with 130 more of Note and Quality, besides the Provost and Burgesses of the Town of *Air*, which made forty more. The tenour of which Bond was this that followeth.

39. *We whose names are under written, do promise in the presence of God, and in the presence of his Son our Lord Jesus Christ, that we, and every one of us, shall and will maintain the Preaching of his holy Evangel, now of his mercy offered and granted to this Realm; and also will maintain the Ministers of the same against all persons, Power and Authority, that will oppose themselves to the Doctrine proposed, and by us received. And further, with the same solemnity we protest and promise that every one of us shall assist another, yea, and the whole Body of the Protestants within this Realm, in all lawfull and just occasions, against all persons; so that whosoever shall hurt, molest, or trouble any of our bodies, shall be reputed enemies to the whole, except that the offender will be content to submit himself to the Government of the Church now established amongst us. And this we do, as we desire to be accepted and favoured of the Lord Jesus, and accepted worthy of credit and honesty in the presence of the Godly.*

40. And in pursuance of this Bond, they seize upon some Priests, and give notice to others, that they would not trouble themselves of complaining to the Queen or Council, but would execute the punishment appointed to Idolaters in the Law of God, as they saw occasion, whensoever they should be apprehended. At which the Queen was much offended; but there was no remedy. All she could do, was once again to send for *Knox*, and to desire him so to deal with the Barons, and other Gentlemen of the *West*, that they would not punish any man for the cause of Religion, as they had resolved. To which he answered with as little reverence as at other times, That if her Majesty would punish Malefactors according to the Laws, he durst assure her, that she should find peace and quietness at the hand of those who professed the Lord *Jesus* in that Kingdom: That if she thought or had a purpose to illude the Laws, there were some who would not fail to let the Papists understand, that they should not be suffered without punishment to offend their God. Which said, he went about to prove in a long discourse, that others were by God intrusted with the Sword of Justice, besides Kings and Princes; which Kings and Princes, if they failed in the right use of it, and drew it not against Offenders, they must not look to find obedience from the rest of the Subjects.

41. It is not to be doubted, but that every understanding Reader will be able to collect out of all the premises, both of what Judgement *Knox* and his Brethren were, touching the Soveraignty of Kings, or rather
ther

ther the Supreme Power invefted naturally in the people of a State or Nation ; as alfo from what Fountain they derived their Doctrine, and to whofe fentence only they refolved to fubmit the fame. But we muft make a clearer demonftration of it, before we can proceed to the reft of our Hiftory ; that fo it may appear upon what ground, and under the pretence of what Authority fo many Tumults and Difcords were acted on the Stage of *Scotland* by the *Knoxian* Brethren. It pleafed the Queen to hold a Conference with this man, in the purfuit whereof they fell upon the point of refifting Princes by the Sword, the lawfulneffe whereof was denyed by her, but maintained by him. The Quean demands whether Subjects having power may refift their Princes : *Yea, (Madam)* anfwered *Knox ; if Princes do exceed their bounds, and do againft that wherefore they fhould be obeyed, there is no doubt but that they may be refifted even by power.* For (faid he) *there is neither greater honour, nor greater obedience to be given to Kings and Princes, then God hath commanded to be given unto our Fathers and Mothers ; and yet it may fo happen, that the Father may be ftricken with a Phrenfie, and in fome fit attempt the flaying of his Children. In which cafe, if the Children joyn themfelves together, apprehend their Father, take the Sword out of his hand, and keep him in Prifon till his Phrenfie be over paft ; it is not to be thought that God will be offended with them for their actings in it.* And thereupon he doth infer, that fo it is with fuch Princes alfo, as out of a blind Zeal would murther the Children of God which are fubject to them. And therefore to take the Sword from them, to bind their hands, and to caft them into Prifon, till that they may be brought to a more fober mind, is not difobedience againft them, but rather is to be accounted for a juft obedience, becaufe it agrees with the Word of God.

42. The fame man preaching afterwards at one of their General Affemblies, made a diftinction between the Ordinance of God, and the perfons placed by him in Authority ; and then affirmed that men might lawfully and juftly refift the perfons, and not offend againft the Ordinance of God. He added as a Corollary unto his difcourfe, That Subjects were not bound to obey their Princes, if they Command unlawful things ; but that they might refift their Princes, and that they were not bound to fuffer. For which being queftioned by Secretary *Ledington* in the one, and defired to declare himfelf further in the other point ; he juftified himfelf in both, affirming that he had long been of that opinion, and did fo remain. A Queftion hereupon arifing about the punifhment of Kings, if they were Idolaters ; it was honeftly affirmed by *Ledington,* That there was no Commandment given in that cafe to punifh Kings, and that the people had no power to be judges over them, but muft leave them unto God alone, who would either punifh them by death, imprifonment, war, or fome other Plagues. Againft which *Knox* replyed with his wonted confidence, that to affirm that the people, or a part of the people may not execute Gods Judgments againft their King being an offender, the Lord *Ledington* could have no other Warrant, except his own imaginations, and the opinion of fuch as rather feared to difpleafe their Princes then offend their God. Againft which when *Ledington* objected the Authority of fome eminent Proteftants ; *Knox* anfwered, that they fpake of Chriftians fubject to Ty-

rants

rants and Infidels, ſo diſperſed, that they had no other force but only to cry unto God for their deliverance: That ſuch indeed ſhould hazard any further then then thoſe godly men willed them, he would not haſtily be of counſel.　But that his Argument had another ground, and that he ſpake of a people aſſembled in one Body of a Commonwealth unto whom God had given ſufficient force, not only to reſiſt, but alſo to ſuppreſs all kind of open Idolatry ; and ſuch a people again he affirmed were bound to keep their Land clean and unpolluted: that God required one thing of *Abraham* and his Seed, when he and they were ſtrangers in the Land of *Egypt*, and that another thing was required of them when they were delivered from that bondage, and put into the actual Poſſeſſion of the Land of *Canaan*.

43. Finally, that the Application might come home to the point in hand, it was reſolved by this learned and judicious Caſuiſt, that when they could hardly find ten in any one part of *Scotland*, who rightly underſtood Gods Truth, it had been fooliſhneſs to have craved the ſuppreſſion of Idolatry either from the Nobility or the common ſubject, becauſe it had been nothing elſe but the betraying of the ſilly Sheep for a prey to the Wolves.　*But now* (ſaith he) *that God hath multiplyed knowledge, and hath given the victory unto Truth in the hands of his Servants, if you ſhould ſuffer the Land again to be defiled, you and your Prince ſhould drink the cup of Gods inſignation ; the Queen, for her continuing obſtinate in open Idolatry, in this great light of the Goſpel ; and you, for permiſſion of it, and countenancing her in the ſame.　For my aſſertion is* (ſaith he) *that Kings have no priviledge more then hath the people to offend Gods Majeſty ; and if ſo be they do, they are no more exempted from the puniſhment of the Law, then is any other ſubject ; yea, and that ſubjects may not only lawfully oppoſe themſelves unto their Kings, whenſoever they do any thing that expreſly oppugnes Gods Commandments, but alſo that they may execute Judgement upon them according to Gods Laws ; ſo that if the King be a murtherer, Adulterer, or an Idolater, he ſhould ſuffer according to Gods Law, not as a King, but as an Offender.*　Now that *Knox* did not ſpeak all this as his private judgement, but as it was the judgement of *Calvin*, and the reſt of the *Genevian* Doctors, whom he chiefly followed, appears by this paſſage in the ſtory.　It was required that *Knox* ſhould write to *Calvin*, and to the Learned men in other Churches, to know their judgements in the queſtion ; to which he anſwered, that he was not only fully reſolved in conſcience, but had already heard their judgements as well in that, as in all other things which he had affirmed in that Kingdom; that he came not to that Realm without their reſolution, and had for his aſſurance the hand-writing of many ; and therefore if he ſhould now move the ſame queſtions again, he muſt either ſhew his own ignorance, or inconſtancy, or at leaſt forgetfulneſs.

44. Of the ſame Nature, and proceeding from the ſame Original, are thoſe dangerous paſſages ſo frequently diſperſed in moſt parts of his Hiſtory.　By which the Reader is informed, *That Reformation of Religion doth belong to more then the Clergie and the King : That Noblemen ought to reform Religion, if the King will not : That Reformation of Religion belongeth to the Commonalty, who concurring with the Nobility, may compel the Biſhops to ceaſe from their Tyranny, and bridle the cruel Beaſts* (the Prieſts :) *That they*

may

may lawfully require of their King to have true Preachers: and if he be negligent, they juſtly may themſelves provide them, maintain them, defend them againſt all that do perſecute them, and may detain the profits of the Church-livings from the Popiſh Clergy: That God appointed the Nobility to bridle the inordinate appetite of Princes, who in ſo doing cannot be accounted as reſiſters of Authority: and that it is their duty to repreſs the rage and inſolency of Princes: That the Nobility and Commonalty ought to reform Religion: and in that caſe may remove from honours, and may puniſh ſuch as God hath condemned of what eſtate, condition, or honour ſoever they be: That the puniſhment of ſuch crimes as touch the Majeſty of God, doth not appertain to Kings and chief Rulers only, but alſo to the whole body of the people, and to every member of the ſame, as occaſion, vocation, or ability ſhall ſerve, to revenge the injury done againſt God: That Princes for Juſt cauſes may be depoſed: That if Princes be Tyrants againſt God and his Truth, their ſubjects are freed from their Oaths of obedience: And finally, that it is neither Birth-right or propinquity of bloud which makes a King rule over a people that profeſs Jeſus Chriſt; but that it comes from ſome ſpecial and extraordinary diſpenſation of Almighty God.

45. Such is the *plain Song*, ſuch the *Deſcant* of theſe *Sons of Thunder*, firſt *tuned* by the *Genevian* Doctors, by them commended unto *Knox*, and by *Knox* preached unto his Brethren the Kirk of *Scotland*. In which what countenance he received from *Goodman*, and how far he was juſtified, if not ſucceeded by the pen of *Buchanan*, we ſhall ſee hereafter. In the mean time the poor Queen muſt needs be in a very ſorry caſe, when not her people only muſt be poyſoned with this dangerous Doctrine, but that ſhe muſt be baffled and affronted by each ſawcy *Presbyter*, who could pretend unto a Miniſtry in the Church: Of which the dealing of this man gives us proof ſufficient, who did not only revile her perſon in the Pulpit, and traduce her Government, but openly pronounced her to be an Idolatreſs, and therefore to be puniſhed by her Subjects as the Law required. Nothing more ordinary with him in his factious Sermons, then to call her a *Slave to Sathan*, and to tell the people that *Gods vengeance hanged over the Realm, by reaſon of her impiety*: which what elſe was it, but to inflame the hearts of the people, as well againſt the Queen as all of them that ſerved her? For in his publick Prayers he commonly obſerved this Form, *viz. O Lord, if it be thy good pleaſure, purge the Queens heart from the venom of Idolatry, and deliver her from the bondage and thraldom of Sathan, in the which ſhe yet remains for lack of true Doctrine, &c. that in ſo doing, ſhe may avoid the eternal damnation which is ordained for all obſtinate and impenitent to thee, and that this Realm may alſo eſcape that plague and vengeance which inevitably followes Idolatry, maintained in this Kingdom againſt thy manifeſt Word, and the Light thereof ſet forth unto them.* Such in a word was the intemperancie of his ſpirit, his hatred of her perſon, or contempt of her Government, that he oppoſed and croſſed her openly in all her courſes, and for her ſake, fell foul upon all men of more moderate counſels.

46. During the interval between the death of her Father, and her own coming back from *France*, there had been little ſhewn of a Court in *Scotland*, as not much before. But preſently on her return, a greater bravery in Apparel was taken up by the Lords and Ladies, and ſuch as

waited

waited near her perfon, then in former times; never more visibly, then when they waited on her in a pompous manner, as she went to the Parliament of this year. This gives great scandal to the Preachers, to none more then *Knox*. The Preachers boldly in their Pulpits (that I say not malapertly) declared against the superfluity of their Clothes, and against the rest of their Vanities; which they affirmed should provoke Gods vengeance, not only against those foolish Women, but the whole Realm; and especially against those that maintained them in that odious abusing all things which might have better been bestowed. A course is taken principally by their follicitations, that certain Articles were agreed on, and proposed in Parliament, for regulating all excess in Apparel as a great enormity, the *stinking pride of Women*, as *Knox* plainly calls it. Who being sent for to the Court upon the like occasion, could not but pass a scorn upon such of the Ladies whom he found more gorgeously attired then agreed with his liking, by telling them what a pleasant life it was they lived, if either it would always last, or that they might go to Heaven in all that gear. *But fie on that knave Death* (quoth he) *that will come whether we will or not; and when he hath laid an Arrest, then foul Worms will be busie with this flesh, be it never so fair and tender; and the silly Soul I fear will be so feeble, that it can neither carry with it Gold, Garnishing, Furbishing, Pearl, nor precious Stones.* So Zealous was he for a Purity both in Church and State, as not to tolerate *soft Raiment*, though in *Princes Palaces*. The Queen had graced the Parliament with her presence three days together; in one of which she entertains them with Speech, to the great satisfaction of all her good Subjects. *Knox* calls it by the name of a painted Oration, tells us in scorn that one might have heard amongst her flatterers that it was *Vox Diana*, the voice of a Goddese, (for it could not be *Vox Dei*) and not of a Woman; others (as he pursues the Jeer) crying out, *God save that sweet Face; was there ever Orator spake so properly and so sweetly? &c.* And this as much displeased the Preachers, as the pride of the Ladies.

47. The Queen had gained the thirds of all Church-Rents by an Act of State, for the more honourable support of her self and her Family, upon condition of making some allowance out of it to defray the Ministers: How *Knox* approved of this, hath been shewn before. We must now see how he had trained up *Goodman* (if they were not both rather trained up by the same great Master) to pursue the quarrel; and how far he was seconded by the rest of the Brethren. In a general Assembly held this year, the business of the thirds was again resumed by some Commissioners of the *Kirk*. To which no satisfactory answer being given by the Queen and her Council, it was said by those of the Assembly, If the Queen will not, we must; for both second and third parts are rigorously taken from us and our tenants. *Knox* added, that if others would follow his counsel, the Guard and the Papists should complain as long as their Ministers. *Goodman* taken fire upon this strain, and starts a doubt about the Title which the Queen had unto the thirds, or the Papists to the other two parts of the Church-Rents. At which when he was put in mind by *Ledington* that he was a stranger, and therefore was to be no medler; he boldly answered, that

though

though he was a ſtranger in the Civil Policy of that Realm, yet ſtranger he was none in the Church of God ; the care whereof did appertain to him no leſs in *Scotland*, then if he were in the midſt of *England*, his own native Countrey. So little was there got by talking unto any of theſe powerful Zealots. At whoſe exhorbitances when the Lord *James Steward* (not long before made Earl of *Murray*) ſeemed to be offended, and other-wiſe had appeared more favourable to the Queen then agreed with their liking ; *Knox*, who before adored him above all men living, diſcharged himſelf by Letter in a churliſh manner from any further intermedling in his affairs ; in which he *commits him to his own wit* (ſo the Letter words it) *and to the conduct of thoſe men who would better pleaſe him* ; and in the end thereof upbraids him , that his preferment never came by any com-plying with impiety, nor by the maintaining of peſtilent Papiſts.

48. But to proceed to greater matters : the Queen began her Sum-mers Progreſs, and left a Prieſt behind in *Halyrood*-houſe, to execute Di-vine-Offices in the Chappel to the reſt of her Family. Some of the Citizens of *Edenborough* were obſerved to repair thither at the time of Maſs ; whereof the Preachers make complaint, and ſtir the people in their Sermons to ſuch a fury, that they flock in great multitudes to the Palace, violently force open the Chappel-doors, ſeize upon ſuch as they found there, and commit them to Priſon, the Prieſt eſcaping with much difficulty by a privy Poſtern. The news of this diſorder is car-ried poſt to the Queen, who thereupon gives order to the Provoſt of *Edenborough* to ſeize upon the perſons of *Andrew Armſtrong*, or *Patrick Crauſton*, (the chief Ringleaders of the tumult) that they might under-go the Law at a time appointed, for fore-thought Felony, in making a violent invaſion into the Queens Palace, and for ſpoilation of the ſame. This puts the Brethren into a heat, and *Knox* is ordered by the con-ſent of the reſt of the Miniſters, to give notice unto all the Church of the preſent danger, that they might meet together as one man to pre-vent the miſchief. In the cloſe of which Letter he lets them know what hopes he had, that neither flattery nor fear would make them ſo far to decline from Chriſt Jeſus, as that againſt their publick Pro-miſe, and ſolemn Bond, they would leave their dear Brethren in ſo juſt a cauſe. It was about the beginning of *Auguſt* that the tumult hapned, and the beginning of *October* that the Letter was written. A Copy of it comes into the hands of the Lords of the Council ; by whom the writing of it was declared to be Treaſon, to the great rejoycing of the Queen, who hoped on this occaſion to revenge her ſelf upon him for his former inſolencies. But it fell out quite contrary to her expe-ctation. *Knox* is commanded to appear before the Lords of the Coun-cil, and he comes accordingly ; but comes accompanied with ſuch a train of Godly Brethren, that they did not only fill the open part of the Court, but thronged up ſtairs, and preſt unto the doors of the Coun-cil. This makes the man ſo confident, as to ſtand out ſtoutly a-gainſt the Queen and her Council, affirming that the convocating of the People in ſo juſt a cauſe, was no offence againſt the Law ; and boldly tel-ling them, that they who had inflamed the Queen againſt thoſe poor men, were the Sons of the Devil ; and therefore that it was no marvail if they

obeyed

obeyed the defires of their Father, who was a Murtherer from the beginning. Moved with which confidence, or rather terrified with the clamours of the Rafcal Rable, even ready to break in upon them, the whole Nobility then prefent, abfolved him of all the crimes objected to him, not without fome praife to God for his modefty, and for his plain and fenfible anfwers, as himfelf reports it.

49. Worfe fared it with the Queen, and thofe of her Religion in another adventure, then it did in this. At the miniftring of the Communion in *Edenborough* on the firft of *April*, the Brethren are advertifed that the Papifts were bufie at their Mafs; fome of which taking one of the Bayliffs with them, laid hands upon the Prieft, the Mafter of the Houfe, and two or three of the Affiftants; all whom they carryed to the *Tole-booth* or *Common-hall*: The Prieft they re-inveft with his Maffing-Garments; fet him upon the Market-crofs, unto which they tye him, holding a Chalice in his hand, which is tyed to it alfo, and there expofed him for the fpace of an hour to be pelted by the boys with rotten Eggs. The next day he is accufed and convicted in a courfe of Law, by which he might have fuffered death, but that the Law had never been confirmed by the King or Queen. So that inftead of all other punifhments which they had no juft power to inflict upon him, he was placed in the fame manner on the Market-crofs, the common Hangman ftanding by, and there expofed to the fame infolencies for the fpace of three or four hours, as the day before. Some Tumult might have followed on it, but that the Provoft with fome *Halbertiers* difperfed the multitude, and brought the poor Prieft off with fafety. Of this the Queen complains, but without any remedy: Inftead of other fatisfaction, an Article is drawn up by the Commiffioners of the next Afsembly, to be prefented to the Parliament then fitting at *Edenborough*; in which it was defired, *That the Papiftical and blafphemous Mafs, with all the Papiftical Idolatry, and Papal Jurifdiction, be univerfally fuppreft, and abolifhed throughout this Realm, not onely in the fubjects, but the Queens own perfon*, &c. of which more hereafter. It was not long fince nothing was more Preached amongft them, then the great tyranny of the Prelates, and the unmerciful dealing of fuch others as were in Authority, in not permitting them to have the liberty of confcience in their own Religion; which now they denyed unto their Queen.

50. But the affront which grieved her moft, was the perverfe, but moft ridiculous oppofition which they made to her Marriage: fhe had been defired for a Wife by *Anthony* of *Bourbon* King of *Navar*, *Lewis* Prince of *Conde*, Arch-Duke *Charles*, the Duke of *Bavaria*, and one of the younger Sons of the King of *Sweden*. But Queen *Elizabeth*, who endeavoured to keep her low, diffwaded her from all Alliances of that high ftrain, perfwaded her to Marry with fome Noble Perfon of *England*, for the better eftablifhment of her Succeffion in the Crown of this Realm; and not obfcurely pointed to her the Earl of *Leicefter*: Which being made known to the Lady *Margaret* Countefs of *Lenox*, Daughter of *Magaret* Queen of *Scots*, and Grand-child to King *Henry* the Seventh, from whom both Queens derived their Titles to this Crown; fhe wrought upon the Queen of *Scots*, by fome Court-Inftruments, to accept her Eldeft Son the Lord *Henry Stewara* for

her

1564.

her Husband. A Gentleman he was above all exception, of comely personage, and very plausible behaviour, of English Birth and Education, and much about the same age with the Queen her self. And to this Match she was the more easily inclined, because she had been told of the King her Father, that he resolved (if he had dyed without any Issue of his own) to declare the Earl of *Lenox* for his Heir Apparent, that so the Crown might be preserved in the name of the *Stewarts*. But that which most prevailed upon her, was a fear she had left the young Lord, being the next Heir unto her self to the Crown of *England*, might Marry into some Family of Power and Puissance in that Kingdom; by means whereof he might prevent her of her hopes in the succession; to which his being born in *England*, and her being an Alien and an Enemy, might give some advantage. Nor did it want some place in her consideration, that the young Lord, and his Parents also, were of the same Religion with her, which they had constantly maintained, notwithstanding all temptations to the contrary in the Court of *England*. To smooth the way to this great business, the Earl desires leave of Queen *Elizabeth* to repair into *Scotland*, where he is graciously received, and in full Parliament restored unto his native Countrey, from whence he had been banished two and twenty years. The young Lord follows not long after, and find such entertainment at the hands of that Queen, that report voiced him for her Husband before he could assure himself of his own affections. This proved no very pleasing news to those of the Congregation, who thought it more expedient to their Affairs, that the Queen should not Marry at all; or at least, not Marry any other Husband but such as should be recommended to her by the Queen of *England*, on whom their safety did depend. In which regard they are resolved to oppose this Match, though otherwise they were assured that it would make the Queen grow less in reputation both at home and abroad, to Marry with one of her own subjects, of what blood soever.

51. And now comes *Knox* to play his prize, who more desired that the Earl of *Leicester* (as one of his own Faction) should espouse the Queen, then the Earl desired it for himself. If she will Marry at all, let her make choice of one of the true Religion, for other Husband she should never have, if he could help it. And to this end he lays about him in a Sermon Preached before the Parliament, at which the Nobility and Estates were then assembled. And having raved sufficiently, as his custom was, at last he tells them in plain terms (desiring them to note the day, and take witness of it) *That whensoever the Nobility of* Scotland *who profess the Lord Jesus, should consent that an Infidel (and all Papists are Infidels, saith he) should be head to their Soveraign; they did, so far as in them lyes, banish Christ Jesus from this Realm, yea, and bring Gods Judgement upon the Countrey, a Plague upon themselves, and do small comfort to her self.* For which being questioned by the Queen in a private conference, he did not only stand unto it, without the least qualifying or retracting of those harsh expressions; but must intitle them to God, as if they had been the immediate Inspirations of the Holy Ghost: for in a Dialogue with the Queen, he affirmed expresly, that out of the Preaching-place few had occasion to be any way offended with him but there (that

is to say, in the Church or Pulpit) he was not Master of himself, but must obey him that commands him to speak plain, and flatter no flesh upon the face of the Earth.   This insolent carriage of the man put the Queen into passion; insomuch, that one of her Pages (as *Knox* himself reports the story) could hardly find Handkerchiefs enough to dry her eyes; with which the proud fellow shewed himself no further touched, then if he had seen the like tears from any one of his own Boys on a just correction.

52. Most men of moderate spirits seemed much offended at the former passage, when they heard of the affliction it had given the Queen. But it prevailed so far on the generality of the Congregation, that presently it became a matter of Dispute amongst them, *Whether the Queen might chuse to her self an Husband, or whether it were more fitting that the E-states of the Land should appoint one for her.* Some sober men affirmed in earnest, that the Queen was not to be barred that liberty which was granted to the meanest Subject.   But the Chief leading men of the Congregation had their own ends in it, for which they must pretend the safety of the Common-wealth.   By whom it was affirmed as plainly, that in the Heir unto a Crown, the case was different, because, said they, such Heirs in assuming an Husband to themselves, did withal appoint a King to be over the Nation : And therefore that it was more fit, that the whole people should chuse a Husband to one Woman, then one Woman to elect a King to Rule over the whole people.   Others that had the same design, and were possibly of the same opinion, concerning the imposing of a Husband on her by the States of the Realm, disguised their purpose, by pretending another Reason to break off this Marriage : The Queen and the young Noble-man were too near of kindred to be conjoyned in Marriage by the Laws of the Church ; her Father and his Mother being born of the same *Venter,* as our Lawyers phrase it.   But for this blow the Queen did easily provide a Buckler , and dispatched one of her Ministers to the Court of *Rome* for a Dispensation.   The other was not so well warded, but that it fell heavy at the last, and plunged her into all those miseries which ensued upon it.

53. But notwithstanding these obstructions, the Match went forwards in the Court, chiefly sollicited by one *David Rifio,* born in *Piedmont* ; who coming into *Scotland* in the company of an Ambassador from the Duke of *Savoy,* was there detained by the Queen, first in the place of a Musician, afterwards imployed in writing Letters to her Friends in *France.* By which he came to be acquainted with most of her secrets, and as her Secretary for the *French* Tongue to have a great hand in the managing of all Forein transactions. This brought him into great envy with the *Scots,* proud in themselves, and not easie to be kept in fair terms, when they had no cause unto the contrary.   But the preferring of this stranger was considered by them as a wrong to their Nation, as if not able to afford a sufficient man to perform that Office, to which the Educating of so many of them in the Court of *France,* had made them no less fit and able then this Mungrel *Italian.*   To all this *Rifio* was no stranger, and therefore was to cast about how to save himself, and to preserve that Power and Reputation which he had acquired.   Which to redeffect , he labour by all means to promote the Match, that the young

1565.

Lord

Lord being obliged unto him for so great a benefit, might stand the faster to him against all Court-factions, whensoever they should rise against him. And that it might appear to be his work only, *Ledington* the chief Secretary is dispatched for *England*, partly to gain the Queens consent unto the Marriage, and partly to excuse the Earl of *Lenox* and his Son, for not returning to the Court as she had commanded. In the mean time he carries on the business with all care and diligence, to the end that the Match might be made up before his return. Which haste he made for these two Reasons : first, lest the dissenting of that Queen (whose influence he knew to be very great on the Kingdom of *Scotland*) might either beat it off, or at least retard it ; the second, that the young Lord *Darnley*, for so they called him, might have the greater obligation to him for effecting the business, then if it had been done by that Queens consent.

55. To make all sure (as sure at least as humane Wisdom could project it) a Convention of the Estates is called in *May*, and the business of the Marriage is propounded to them. To which some yeilded absolutely without any condition, others upon condition that Religion might be kept indempnified ; only the Lord *Uchiltry*, one who adher'd to *Knox* in his greatest difficulties, maintained the Negative, affirming openly, that he would never admit a King of the Popish Religion. Encouraged by which general and free consent of the chief Nobility then present, the Lord *Darnley* not long after is made Baron of *Ardmonack*, created Earl of *Ross* and Duke of *Rothesay*, titles belonging to the eldest and the second Sons of the Kings of *Scotland*. But on the other side, such of the great Lords of the Congregation as were resolved to work their own ends out of these present differences, did purposely absent themselves from that Convention, that is to say, the Earls of *Murray*, *Glencarne*, *Rothes*, *Arguile*, &c. together with Duke *Hamilton* and his dependants, whom they had drawn into the Faction : and they convened at *Stirling* also, though not untill the Queen and her retinue were departed from thence ; and there it was resolved by all means to oppose the Marriage, for the better avoiding of such dangers and inconveniences which otherwise might ensue upon it. For whose encouragement, the Queen of *England* furnished them with 10000 pounds, that it might serve them for advance-mony for the lifting of Souldiers, when an occasion should be offered to embroyl that Kingdom. Nor was *Knox* wanting for his part to advance the troubles, who by his popular declamations against the Match, had so incensed the people of *Edenborough*, that they resolved to put themselves into a posture of War, to elect Captains to command them, and to disarm all those who were suspected to wish well unto it. But the Queen came upon them in so just a time, that the chief Leaders of the Faction were compelled to desert the Town, and leave unto her mercy both their goods and families ; to which they were restored not long after by her grace and clemency.

55. A general Assembly at the same time was held in *Edenborough*, who falsely thinking that the Queen in that conjuncture could deny them nothing, presented their desires unto her : In the first whereof it was demanded, *That the Papistical and blasphemous Mass, with all Popish Idolatry, and the Popes jurisdictions, should be universally supprest and abolished throughout the whole Realm, not only amongst the Subjects, but in the Queens Majesties own Per-*
son

son and Family. In the next place it was defired, *That the true Religion for-merly received should be professed by the Queen, as well as by the Subjects; and people of all forts bound to refort upon the Sundays, at leaft to the Prayers and Preachings,* as in the former times to Mafs: *That fure provision should be made for fuftentation of the Miniftry, as well for the time prefent, as for the time to come; and their Livings affigned them in the places where they ferved, or at leaft in the parts next adjacent; and that they should not be put to crave the fame at the hands of any others: That all Benefices then vacant, and fuch as had fallen void fince* March 1558, *or should happen hereafter to be void, should be difpofed to perfons of quality for the Miniftry, upon tryal and admiffion by the Superinten-dent;* with many other demands of like weight and quality. To which the Queen returned this anfwer: Firft, *That she could not be perfwa-ded that there was any impiety in the Mafs: That she had been always bred in the Religion of the Church of* Rome, *which she efteemed to be agreeable to the Word of God, and therefore trufted that her subjects would not force her to do any thing againft her confcience: That hitherto she never had, nor did intend hereafter to force any mans confcience, but to leave every one to the free exercise of that Reli-gion which to him feemed beft; which might fufficiently induce them to oblige her by the like indulgence.* She anfwered to the next: *That she did not think it reafonable to defraud her felf of fuch a confiderable part of the Royal Patrimony, as to put the Patronages of Benefices out of her own power; the publick neceffities of the Crown being fuch, that they required a great part of the Church-Rents to defray the fame:* Which notwithftanding, she declared, *that the neceffities of the Crown being firft fupplyed, care should be taken for the fuftentation of the Mi-nifters in fome reafonable and fit proportion, to be affigned out of the neareft and moft commodious places to their feveral dwellings.* For all the reft, she was con-tented to refer her felf to the following Parliament, to whofe determina-tions in the particulars defired, she would be conformable.

56. Not doubting but this anfwer might fufficiently comply with all expectations, she proceeds to the Marriage, publickly folemnized in the midft of *July,* by the Dean of *Reftalrig,* whom I conceive to be the Dean of her Majefties Chappel, in which that fervice was performed; and the next day the Bridegroom was folemnly proclaimed King by the found of Trumpet, declared to be affociated with her in the publick Government, and order given to have his name ufed in all Coyns and Inftruments. But neither the impoffibility of untying this knot, nor the gracious anfwer she had made to the Commiffioners of the late Affembly, could hinder the Confederate Lords from breaking out into action. But firft they publi-fhed a Remonftrance (as the cuftom was) to abufe the people; in which it was made known to all whom it might concern, *That the Kingdom was openly wronged, the liberties thereof oppreffed, and a King impofed upon the people without the confent of the Eftates;* which they pretend to be a thing not practifed in the former time, contrary to the Laws and received Cu-ftoms of the Country: *And thereupon defired all good Subjects to take the mat-ter into confideration, and to joyn with them in refifting thofe beginnings of Tyran-ny.* But few there were that would be taken with thefe Baits, or thought themfelves in any danger by the prefent Marriage; which gave the Queen no power at home, and much lefs abroad. And that they might continue always in fo good a pofture, the young King was perfwaded to fhew himfelf at *Knoxes* Sermon; but received fuch an entertainment

from

from that fiery and seditious spirit, as he little looked for. For *Knox*, according to his custom, neither regarding the Kings presence, not fearing what might follow on his alienating from the cause of the Kirk, fell amongst other things to speak of the Government of wicked Princes, who for the sins of the people were sent as Tyrants and Scourges to plague them ; but more particularly, that people were never more scourged by God, then by advancing boys and Women to the Regal Throne. Which if it did displease the King, and give offence to many Conscientious and Religious men, can seem strange to none.

57. In the mean time the discontented Lords depart from *Stirling* more discontented then they came, because the people came not in to aid them, as they had expected. From *Stirling* they remove to *Paisely*, and from thence to *Hamilton*, the Castle whereof they resolved to Fortifie for their present defence. But they were followed so close by the King and Queen, and so divided in opinion amongst themselves, that it seemed best to them to be gone, and try what Friends and Followers they could find in *Edenborough* : but they found that place too hot for them also ; the Captain of the Castle did so ply them with continual shot, that it was held unsafe for them to abide there longer. From thence therefore they betook themselves to the Town of *Dumfreis*, not far from the City of *Carlisle* in *England*, into which they might easily escape, whatsoever happened, as in time they did. For the King leaving his old Father, the Earl of *Lenox*, to attend them there, march'd with his Forces into *Fife*, where the party of the Lords seemed most considerable ; which Province they reduced to their obedience : some of the great Lords of it had forsook their dwellings, many were taken prisoners and put to Ransome, and some of the chief Towns fined for their late disloyalty: Which done, they march to *Edenborough*, and from thence followed to *Dumfreis*, On whose approach, the Lords, unable to defend themselves against their Forces, put themselves into *Carlisle*, where they are courteously received by the Earl of *Bedford*, who was then Lord Warden of the Marches; from thence Duke *Hamilton*, the Earls of *Glencarne* and *Rothes*, the Lord *Uchiltry*, the Commendator of *Kilvinning*, and divers others of good note, removed not long after to *New-castle*, that they might have the easier passage into *France* or *Germany*, if their occasions so required. The Earl of *Murray* is dispatched to the Court of *England* ; but there he found so little comfort, at least in shew, as brought the Queen under a suspition amongst the *Scots*, either of deep dissimulation, or of great inconstancy. The news whereof did so distract and divide the rest, that Duke *Hamilton* under-hand made his own peace with his injured Queen, and put himself into her power in the *December* following. The falling off of which great person so amazed the rest, that now they are resolved to follow all those desperate counsels, by which they might preserve themselves and destroy their enemies, though to the ruine of the King, the Queen, and their natural Country. But what they did in the pursuance of those counsels, must be reserved for the subject of another Book.

The End of the Fourth Book.

AERIUS REDIVIVUS:

OR THE

HISTORY

OF THE

Presbyterians.

LIB. V.

Containing

A further discovery of their dangerous Doctrines ; their oppositions to Monarchical and Episcopal Government ? their secret Practices and Conspiracies to advance their Discipline ; together with their frequent Treasons and Rebellions in the pursuance of the same, from the year 1565, till the year 1585.

Mongst the many natural Children of King *James* the Fifth, none were more eminent and considerable in the course of these times then *James* Pryor of St. *Andrews*, and *John* Pryor of *Coldingham* ; neither of which were men in Orders, or trained up to learning, or took any further charge upon them, then to receive the profit of their several places, which they enjoyed as Commendators, or Administrators, according to the ill custom of some Princes in *Germany*. *John* the less active of the two, but Father of a Son who created more mischief to King *James* the Sixth, then *James* the other Brother did to

Y   the

the preſent Queen: For having took to Wife a Daughter of the Houſe of *Hepbourn*, Siſter and next Heir of *James Hepbourn* Earl of *Bothwel* (of whom more anon) he was by her the Father of *Francis Stewart*, who ſucceeded in that Earldom on the death of his Unckle. But *James* the other Brother was a man of a more ſtirring ſpirit, dextrous in the diſpatch of his buſineſs, cunning in turning all things to his own advantage; a notable diſſembler of his love and hatred, and ſuch a Maſter in the Art of Inſinuation, that he knew how to work all parties to eſpouſe his intereſt. His preferments lay altogether in Eccleſiaſtical Benefices, deſigned unto him by his Father, or conferred upon him by his Siſter, or the King her Husband. But that all three conjured to the making of him, appears by the Kings Letter on the ſeventeenth day of *July*, upon this occaſion. At what time as the Marriage was ſolemnized between *Francis* then *Daulphin* of *France*, and the Queen of *Scots*; he went thither to attend thoſe tryumphs, where he became a Suiter to the Queen his Siſter, that ſome further Character or Mark of Honour might be ſet upon him then the name of Pryor. But the Queen having been advertiſed by ſome other Friends, that he was of an aſpiring mind, and enterpriſing nature, and of a ſpirit too great for a private Fortune, thought it not good to make him more conſiderable in the eye of the people then he was already; and ſo diſmiſt him for the preſent.

2. The fruſtrating of theſe hopes ſo exceedingly vexed him (as certainly ſome are as much diſquieted with the loſs of what they never had, others with the ruine of a preſent poſſeſſion) that the next year he joyned himſelf to thoſe of the Congregation, took *Knox* into his moſt immediate and particular care, and went along with him hand in hand in defacing the Churches of St. *Andrews*, *Stirling*, *Lithgow*, *Edenborough*, and indeed what not? And for ſo doing, he received two ſharp and chiding Letters from the King and Queen, upbraiding him with former benefits received from each, and threatning ſevere puniſhment, if he returned not immediately to his due obedience. Which notwithſtanding, he continues in his former courſes, applies himſelf unto the Queen and Council of *England*, and lays the plot for driving the French Forces out of *Scotland*: Which done, he cauſed the Parliament of 1560 to be held at *Edenborough*, procures ſome Acts to paſs for baniſhing the Popes Supremacy, repealed all former Statutes which were made in maintainance of that Religion, and ratifies the Confeſſion of the Kirk of *Scotland* in ſuch form and manner as it was afterwards confirmed in the firſt Parliament of King *Iames* the Sixth. Upon the death of *Francis* the young *French* King, he goes over again. And after ſome condolements betwixt him and the Queen, intimates both to her and the Princes of the Houſe of *Guiſe*, how ill the rugged and untractable nature of the *Scots* would ſort with one, who had been uſed to the compliances and affabilities of the Court of *France*; adviſeth that ſome principal perſon of the Realm of *Scotland* might be named for Regent; and in a manner recommends himſelf to them as the fitteſt man. But the worſt was, that his Mother had been heard to brag amongſt ſome of her Goſſips, that her Son was the lawful Iſſue of King *James* the Fifth; to whoſe deſires ſhe had never yeilded, but

on promiſe of Marriage. This was enough to croſs him in his preſent aims, and not to truſt him with a power by which he might be able to effect his purpoſes, if he had any ſuch aſpirings. And ſo he was diſmiſt again, without further honour then the carrying back of a Commiſſion to ſome Lords in *Scotland,* by which they were impowered to manage the affairs of that Kingdom till the Queens return.

3. This ſecond diſappointment adds more Fewel to the former flame ; and he reſolves to give the Queen as little comfort of that Crown, as if it were a Crown of Thorns, as indeed it proved. For taking *England* in his way, he applies himſelf to ſome of the Lords of the Council, to whom he repreſents the dangers which muſt needs enſue to Queen *Elizabeth,* if *Mary* his own Queen were ſuffered to return into her Country, and thereby lay all paſſages open to the powers of *France,* where ſhe had ſtill a very ſtrong and prevailing party. But when he found that ſhe had fortunately eſcaped the Ships of *England,* that the Subjects from all parts had went away extremely ſatisfied with her gratious carriage, he reſolved to make one in the *Hoſanna,* as afterwards he was the Chief in the *Crucifige* ; he applies himſelf unto the Queens humour with all art and induſtry, and really performed to her many ſignal ſervices in gratifying her with the free exerciſe of her own Religion ; in which, by reaſon of his great Authority with the Congregation, he was beſt able to oblige both her ſelf and her ſervants. By this means he became ſo great in the eyes of the Court, that the Queen ſeemed to be governed wholly by him : and that he might continue always in ſo good a poſture, ſhe firſt conferred upon him the Earldom of *Murray,* and after Married him to a Daughter of *Keith,* Earl-Marſhal of *Scotland.* Being thus honoured and allyed, his next care was to remove all impediments which he found in the way to his aſpiring. The Ancient and Potent Family of the *Gourdons* he ſuppeſſed and ruined, though after it refloriſhed in its ancient glory : But his main buſineſs was to oppreſs the *Hamiltons,* as the next Heirs unto the Crown in the common opinion ; the Chief whereof (whom the *French* King had created Duke of *Chaſteau Herald,* a Town in *Poictou*) he had ſo diſcountenanced, that he was forced to leave Court, and ſuffer his Eldeſt Son the Earl of *Arrane* to be kept in Priſon, under pretence of ſome diſtemper in his brain. When any great Prince ſought the Queen in Marriage, he uſed to tell her, that the *Scots* would never brook the power of a ſtranger ; and that whenſoever that Crown had fallen into the hands of a Daughter, as it did to her, a Husband was choſen for her by the Eſtates of the Kingdom, of their own Language, Laws and Parentage. But when this would not ſerve his turn to break off the Marriage with the young Lord *Darnley,* none ſeemed more forward then himſelf to promote that Match which he perceived he could not hinder : Beſides, he knew that the Gentleman was very young, of no great inſight in buſineſs, mainly addicted to his pleaſures, and utterly unexperienced in the affairs of that Kingdom ; ſo that he need not fear the weakning of his Power by ſuch a King, who deſired not to take the Government upon him. And in this point he agreed well enough with *David Riſio,* though on different ends. But when he found the Queen ſo paſſionately affected to this ſecond Husband ; that all Graces and

Court-

Court-favours were to pass by him; that he had not the Queens ear so advantagiously as before he had; and that she had revoked some grants which were made to him and others, during her minority, as against the Law; he thought it most expedient to the furthering of his own concernments, to peece himself more nearly with the Earls of *Morton, Glencarne, Arguile* and *Rothes*, the Lords *Ruthen, Uchiltry, &c.* whom he knew to be zealously affected to the Reformation, and no way pleased with the Queens Marriage to a person of the other Religion. By whom it was resolved, that *Morton* and *Ruthen* should remain in the Court, as well to give as to receive intelligence of all proceedings: The others were to take up Arms, and to raise the people, under pretence of the Queens Marriage to a man of the Popish Religion, not taking with her the consent of the Queen of *England*. But being too weak to keep the Field, they first put themselves into *Carlisle*, and afterwards into *New-Castle*, as before was said; and being in this manner fled the Kingdom, they are all proclaimed Traytors to the Queen; a peremptory day appointed to a publick Tryal; on which if they appeared not at the Bar of justice, they were to undergo the sentence of a condemnation.

4. And now their Agents in the Court begin to bustle: the King was soon perceived to be a meer outside-man, of no deep reach into Affairs, and easily wrought on; which first induced the Queen to set the less value on him; nor was it long before some of their Court-Females whispered into her ears, that she was much neglected by him, that he spent more of his time in Hawking and Hunting, and perhaps in more unfit divertisements (if *Knox* speak him rightly) then he did in her company; and therefore that it would be requisite to lure him in, before he was too much on the Wing, and beyond her call. On these suggestions, she gave order to her Secretaries, and other Officers, to place his name last in all publick Acts, and in such Coyns as were new stamped to leave it out. This happened as they would have wished: For hereupon Earl *Morton* closeth with the King, insinuates unto him how unfit it was that he should be subject to his Wife; that it was the duty of women to obey, and of men to govern; and therefore that he might do well to set the Crown on his own head, and take that power into his hands which belonged unto him. When they perceived that his ears lay open to the like temptations, they then began to buz into them, that *Risio* was grown too powerful for him in the Court, that he out-vied him in the bravery both of Clothes and Horses, and that this could proceed from no other ground then the Queens affection, which was suspected by wise men to be somewhat greater then might stand with honour. And now the day draws on apace, on which Earl *Murray* and the rest were to make their appearance; and therefore somewhat must be done to put the Court into such confusion, and the City of *Edenborough* into such disorder, that they might all appear without fear or danger of any legal prosecution to be made against him. The day designed for their appearance, was the twelfth day of *March*; and on the day before, say some (or third day before, as others) the Conspirators go unto the King, seemed to accuse him of delay, tell him that now or never was the time to revenge his injuries, for that he

should

should now find the fellow in the Queens private Chamber, without any force to make resistance. So in they rush, find *David* sitting at the Queens Table, the Countess of *Arguile* onely between them. *Ruthen* commands him to arise, and to go with him, telling him that the place in which he sate did no way beseem him. The poor fellow runs unto the Queen for protection, and claps his arms about her middle; which the King forcibly unfastneth, and puts him to the power of his mortal enemies, by whom he was dragged down the Stairs, and stabbed in so many places (fifty three saith *Knox*) that his whole body seemed to be like a piece of Cut-work. Which barbarous Murther *Knox* proclaims for an act of Justice, calls it a *just punishment* on that *Paltron and vile Knave* David, for *abusing the Common wealth, and his other villanies*; and heavily complains, that the *Chief Actors* in the same (which he extols for a *just act, and most worthy of all praise,* Pag. 96) *were so unworthily left by the rest their Brethren, and forced to suffer the bitterness of exile and banishment.*

5. The Queen was then grown great with child, and being affrighted at the suddenness of this execution, and the fear of some treasonable attempt against her person, was in no small danger of miscarrying. The Court was full of Tumult, and the noise thereof so alarmed the Town, that the people flocked thither in great multitudes to know the matter; to whom the King signified out of a Window, that the Queen was safe; which somewhat appeased them for the present: But notwithstanding, both the Court and City were in such distraction, that when the Earl of *Murray* and the rest of the Confederates tendered their appearance, and offered themselves unto the tryal of the Law, there was no information made against them, nor any one sufficiently instructed for the prosecution. Which being observed, they address themselves to the Parliament House, and there take instruments to testifie upon Record, that they were ready to answer whatsoever could be charged upon them; but none there to prosecute. And here the Scene begins to change; *Morton* and *Ruthen*, and the rest of their accomplices, betake themselves to *New-Castle*, as the safest Sanctuary; and *Murray* staid behind to negotiate for them. And he applyed himself so dextrously in his negotiation, that first he endears himself to the Queen his Sister, by causing her Guards to be again restored unto her, which had been taken from her at the time of the Murther. She on the other side, to shew how much she valued the affection of so dear a Brother, was easily intreated that *Morton, Lindesay*, and the rest who remained at *New-Castle*, should be permitted to return; but so, that it should rather seem to be done upon the earnest sollicitations of the Earls of *Huntley* and *Arguile*, then at his request. The King in the mean time finds his errour, and earnestly supplicates unto her for a reconcilement; assuring her, that he had never fallen on that desperate action, but as he was forcibly thrust upon it by *Morton* and *Murray*. And that he might regain his reputation in the sight of the people, he openly protested his innocency at the Cross in *Edenborough* by sound of Trumpet, and publickly averred, that his consent had gone no further with the Murtherers, then for the recalling of the banished Lords which were fled into *England*. The young Prince was not so well studied in the School of mischief, as to have learned that

there

there is no safety in committing one act of wickedness, but by proceeding to another; or at the least, by standing stoutly unto that which was first committed, that so his confidence might in time be took for innocency. A lesson which the rest of the Confederates had took out long since, and were now upon the point to practice it upon himself.

6. For by this piece of ostentation and impertinency, the King gained nothing on the people, and lost himself exceedingly amongst the Peers; for as none of the common sort did believe him to be the more innocent of the wicked murther, because he washed his hands of it in the sight of the multitude; so the great men which had the guiding of the Faction, disdained him as a weak and impotent person, not to be trusted in affairs of his own concernment: nor did he edifie better with the Queen, then he did with the Subject; who was so far from suffering any hearty reconciliation to be made between them, that she exprest more favour unto *Murray* then in former times. Which so exasperated the neglected and forsaken Prince, that he resolved on sending *Murray* after *Risio*; with which he makes the Queen acquainted, in hopes she would approve of it as an excellent service; but she disswades him from the fact, and tells *Murray* of it; knowing full well, that which foever of the two miscarried in it, she should either loose an hated Friend, or a dangerous Enemy. *Murray* communicates the Affair with *Morton*, and the rest of his Friends. By whom it is agreed, that they should take into their Friendship the Earl of *Bothwel*, a man of an audacious spirit, apt for any mischief; but otherwise of approved valour and of a known fidelity to the Queen in her greatest dangers. He had before some quarrels with the Earl of *Murray*, of whose designs he was not distrustful without cause; and therefore laboured both by force and practice, either to make him less or nothing. But *Murray* was too hard for him at the weapon of Wit, and was so much too powerful for him, both in Court and Consistory, that he was forced to quit the Kingdom, and retire to *France*. Returning at such time as *Murray* and the rest of the Confederates were compelled to take sanctuary at *New castle*, he grew into great favour with the Queen, whose discontents against the King he knew how to nourish; which made his friendship the more acceptable, and his assistance the more useful in the following Tragedy. Thus *Herod* and *Pilate* are made friends, and the poor King must fall a *peace offering* for their Redintegration.

7. But first they would expect the issue of the Queens delivery, by the success whereof, the principal conspirators were resolved to steer their course. On the 19 day of *July*, she is delivered of a Son in the Castle of *Edenborough*, to the general joy of all the Kingdom, and the particular comfort of the chief Governours of Affairs for the Congregation. There was no more use now of a King or Queen, when God had given them a young Prince to sit upon the Throne of his Fathers; in whose minority they might put themselves into such a posture, that he should never be able to act much against them when he came to age. And now they deal with *Bothwel* more effectually then before they did, incourage him to remove the King by some means or other, to separate himself from his own Wife, (a Daughter of the House of *Huntley*) and Espouse the Queen. Let him but act the first part, as most proper for him,

him, and they would eafily find a way to bring on the faft. For the performance whereof, and to ftand to him in it againft all the World, they bound themfelves feverally and joyntly under Hand and Seal. In which moft wicked practice they had all thefe ends: firft, the difpatching of the King; next, the confounding of *Bothwel*, whom they feared and hated; Thirdly, the weakning of the Queen both in power and credit, and confequently the drawing of all Affairs to their own difpoſing. *Bothwel* in order to the plot makes ufe of *Ledington* to prompt the Queen to Divorce, which he conceived might eafily be effected in the Court of *Rome*; and is himfelf as diligent upon all occafions to work upon the Queens difpleafures, and make the breach wider betwixt her and her Husband. The greatnefs of which breach was before fo vifible, that nothing was more commonly known, nor generally complained of amongft the people: But never was it made fo eminently notorious in the eye of Strangers, as at the Chriftening of the young Prince in *December* following. At which time fhe would neither fuffer the Ambaffadors of *France* or *England* to give him a vifit, nor permit him to fhew himfelf amongft them at the Chriftening Banquet. From *Stirling*, where the Prince was Chriftened, he departs for *Glafco*, to find fome comfort from his Father. To which place he was brought not without much difficulty: for falling fick upon the way, it appeared plainly by fome fymptoms that he had been poyfoned, the terrible effects whereof he felt in all the parts of his body with unfpeakable torments: But ftrength of Nature, Youth and Phyfick did fo work together, that he began to be in a good way of recovery, to the great grief of thofe who had laid the plot. Some other way muft now be taken to effect the bufinefs, and none more expedient then to perfwade the Queen to fee him, to flatter him with fome hopes of her former favour, and bring him back with her to *Edenborough*; which was done accordingly. At *Edenborough* he was lodged at a private houfe, on the outfide of the Town, (an houfe unfeemly for a King, as *Knox* confeffeth) and therefore the fitter for their purpofe: where, on the 9 of *February* at night, the poor Prince was ftrangled, his dead body laid in an Orchard near adjoyning, with one of his Servants lying by it, whom they alfo murthered, and the houfe moft ridiculoufly blown up with powder, as if that blow could have been given without mangling and breaking the two bodies in a thoufand pieces.

8. The infamy of this horrid murther is generally caft upon the Queen, by the arts of thofe whom it concerned to make her odious with all honeft men; nor did there want fome ftrong prefumptions which might induce them to believe that fhe was of the counfel in the fact; and with the good Brethren of the Congregation, every prefumption was a proof, and every weak proof was thought fufficient to convict her of it. But that which moft confirmed them in their fufpition, was her affection unto *Bothwel*, whom fhe firft makes Duke of *Orknay*, and on the 15 of *May* is married to him in the Chappel of *Halyrood*-houfe, according to the form obferved by thofe of the Congregation. But againft thefe prefumptions there were ftronger evidences: *Bothwel* being compelled not long after to flee into *Denmark*, did there moft conftantly profefs, both living and dying, that the Queen was innocent. *Morton* affirmed the

fame

same at his execution above twelve years after, relating that when *Bothwel* dealt with him about the murther, and that he shewed himself unwilling to consent unto it without the Queens Warrant and Allowance; *Bothwel* made answer, that they must not give themselves any hope of that, but that the business must be done without her privity. But that which seems to make most for her justification, was the confession of *Hepbourne*, *Daglish*, and others of *Bothwels* servants, who were condemned for murdering the young King; and being brought unto the Gallows, they protested before God and his Holy Angels, that *Bothwel* had never told them of any other Authors of so lewd a counsel, but only the two Earls of *Morton* and *Murray*. In the mean time the common infamy prevailed, and none is made more guilty of it then this wretched Queen, who had been drawn to give consent to her marriage with *Bothwel*, by the sollicitation and advice of those very men, who afterwards condemned her for it. In order to whose ends *Buchanan* publishes a most pestilent and malicious Libel, which he called, *The defection*, wherein he publickly traduced her for living an adulterous life with *David Rissio*, and afterward with *Bothwel* himself; that to precipitate her unlawful marriage with him, she had contrived the death of the King her husband, projected a Divorce between *Bothwel* and his former Wife, contrary to the Laws both of God and man. Which Libel being printed and dispersed abroad, obtained so much credit with most sorts of people, that few made question of the truth of the accusations. Most true it is, that *Buchanan* is reported by King *James* himself to have confessed with great grief at the time of his death, how falsly and injuriously he had dealt with her in that scandalous Pamphlet: but this confession came too late, and was known to few, and therefore proved too weak a remedy for the former mischief.

9. He published at the same time also that seditious Pamphlet, which he entitled, *De jure Regni apud Scotos*. In which he laboureed to make proof, that the Supreme power of the *Scottish* Nation was in the body of the people, no otherwise in the King but by delegation; and therefore that it was in the peoples power, not only to control and censure, but also to depose and condemn their Kings, if they found them faulty. The man was learned for his time, but a better Poet then Historian, and yet a better Historian then he was a Statesman. For being of the *Genevian* Leven, he fitted all his State-maximes unto *Calvins* Principles, and may be thought in many points to out-go his Master. Now in this Pamphlet we may find these Aphorisms laid down for undoubted truths, which no *true Scot* must dare to question, unless he would be thought to betray his Countrey; that is to say, *That the People is better then the King, and of greater Authority: That the people have right to bestow the Crown at their pleasure: That the making of the Laws doth belong to the People, and Kings are but Masters of the Rolls: That they have the same power over the King, that the King hath over any one man: That it were good that rewards were appointed by the people for such as should kill Tyrants, as commonly there is for those that have killed either Wolves or Bears, or have taken their Whelps: That the people may arraign their Princes; that the Ministers may excommunicate their King; and that whosoever is by Excommunication cast into Hell, is made thereby unworthy to live on Earth.*

10. And

10. And that he might make sure work of it, he takes upon him to reply upon all Objections, which sober and more knowing men had found out the contrary. For whereas it had been objected, *That custom was against such dealing with Princes: That* Jeremiah *commanded obedience to* Nebuchadnezzar: *That God placed Tyrants sometimes for punishment of his people: That the Jews dealt not so with any of their Princes; and that there was no example to be found in Scripture, to shew that subjects may so use their Governours, as is there pretended:* To all these he returns his particular answers; and in this sort he answereth to them, that is to say, *That there is nothing more dangerous to be followed then a common custom: That the example is but singular, and concludeth nothing: That as God placed Tyrants to punish the people, so he appoints private men to kill them: That the Kings of the Jews were not elected by the people, and therefore might not deal with them, as they might in* Scotland, *where Kings depends wholly on the peoples Election: And finally, that there were sundry good and wholesome Laws in divers Countries, of which there is no example in Holy Scripture.* And whereas others had objected, *That by St.* Pauls *Doctrine we are bound to pray for Kings and Princes:* The Argument is avaded by this handsome shift, *That we are bound to pray for those whom we ought to punish.* But these are only velitations, certain preparatory skirmishes to the grand encounter; the main battail followeth. For finally, the principal objection is, *That St.* Paul *hath commanded every soul to be subject to the higher Powers; and that St.* Peter *hath required us to submit our selves to every Ordinance of man, whether it be unto the King as to the Supreme, or unto such as be in Authority by and under him.* And hereunto they frame their Answer in such a manner, as if they knew Gods mind better then the Apostles did, or that of the Apostles better then they did themselves.

11. The answer is, that the Apostles writ this in the Churches infancy, when there were not many Christians, few of them rich and of ability to make resistance: *As if (saith he) a man should write to such Christians as are under the* Turk, *in substance poor, in courage feeble, in strength unarmed, in number few, and generally subject unto all kind of injuries; would he not write as the Apostles did? who did respect the men they writ to, their words not being to be extended to the body or people of the Common wealth.* For imagine (saith he) *that either of the Apostles were now alive, and lived where both the Kings and People did profess Christianity, and that there were such Kings as would have their wills to stand for Laws, as cared neither for God nor Man; as bestowed the Churches Revenues upon Jesters and Rascals, and such as gibed at those who did profess the more sincere Religion; what would they write of such to the Church? Surely except they would dissent from themselves, they would say, That they accounted no such for Magistrates; they would forbid all men from speaking unto them, and from keeping their company; they would leave them to their subjects to be punished; nor would they blame them if they accounted not such men for their Kings, with whom they could have no society by the Laws of God.* So excellent a proficient did this man shew himself in the Schools of *Calvin*, that he might worthily have challenged the place of Divinity-Reader in *Geneva* it self.

12. To put these Principles into practice, a Bond is made at *Stirling* by some of the chief Lords of the Congregation, pretended for the preservation

vation

vation of the Infant-Prince; but aiming also at the punishment of *Bothwel*, and the rest of the Murtherers. The first that entered into this Combination, were the Earls of *Athol*, *Arguile*, *Morton*, *Marre* and *Glencarne*, with the Lords *Lindsay* and *Boyd*; to which were added not long after, the Lords *Hume* and *Ruthen*, (this *Ruthen* being the Son of him who had acted in the Murther of *David Risio*) together with the Lairds of *Drumlanrig*, *Tulibardin*, *Seffourd*, and *Grange*, men of great power and influence on their several Countries; besides many others of good note. The Earl *Murray* having laid the plot, obtained the Queens leave to retire into *France* till the times were quieter, committing to the Government of his whole Estate; that so if his design miscarried, as it possibly might, he might come off without the least hazard of estate or honour. Of this conspiracy the Queen receives advertisement, and presently prepares for Arms, under pretence of rectifying some abuses about the Borders. The Confederates were not much behind; and having got together a considerable power, made an attempt on *Borthwick* Castle, where the Queen and *Bothwel* then remained. But not being strong enough to carry the place at the first attempt, *Bothwel* escaped unto *Dunbar*, whom the Queen followed shortly after in mans apparel. Missing their prey, the Confederates march toward *Edenborough* with their little Army, and make themselves Masters of the Town. But understanding that the Queens Forces were upon their March, they betook themselves unto the Field, gained the advantage of the ground, and thereby gave her such a diffidence of her good success, that having entertained them with a long parley, till *Bothwel* was gone off in safety, she put her self into their hands without striking a blow.

13. With this great prey the Confederates returned to *Edenborough* in the middle of *June*; and the next day order her to be sent as Prisoner to *Lochlevin* house, under the conduct of the Lords *Ruthen* and *Lindsay*, by whom she was delivered in a very plain and sorry attire to the custody of *Murray*'s Mother, who domineered over the unfortunate Lady with contempt enough. The next day after her commitment, the Earl of *Glencarn* passeth to the Chappel in *Halyrood* house, where he defaceth all the Vestments, breaks down the Altar, and destroys the Images. For which though he was highly magnified by *Knox*, and the rest of the Preachers; yet many of the chief Confederates were offended at it, as being done without their consent, when a great storm was gathering towards them, by the conjunction of some other of the principal Lords on the Queens behalf. To reconcile this party to them, and prevent the Rupture, *Knox* with some other of their Preachers are dispatched away with Letters of Credence, and instructions for attoning the difference. But they effected nothing to the benefit of them that sent them, and not much neither to their own, though they had some concernments of self-interest besides the publick, which they made tender of to their considerations. A general Assembly at the same time was held in *Edenborough*, with which upon the coming back of these Commissioners, it was thought necessary to ingratiate themselves by all means imaginable. And thereupon it was agreed, that the Acts of Parliament made in the year 1560, for the suppressing of Popery, should be

be confirmed in the next Parliament then following ; that the assignation of the Shires for the Ministers maintainance , should be duly put in execution , till the whole Patrimony of the Church might be invested in them in due form of Law ; which was conditioned to be done (if it could not be done sooner) in that Parliament also. Some other point of huge concernment to the Church were then also moved ; but they were only promised , without any performance. It was also then agreed between them, that all Noblemen, Barons , and other Professors should imploy their whole Forces, Strength and Power , for the punishment of all and whatsoever persons that should be tryed and found guilty of that horrible Murther of late committed on the King : And further, that all the Kings and Princes which should succeed in following times to the Crown of that Realm , should be bound by Oath before their Inauguration , to maintain the true Religion of Christ, professed then presently in that Kingdom. Thus the Confederates and the Kirk are united together ; and hard it is to say, whether of the two were least excusable before God and Man. But they followed the light of their own principles, and thought that an excuse sufficient , without fear of either.

14. The news of these proceedings alarms all Christendom, and presently Ambassadors are dispatched from *France* and *England* to mediate with the Confederates (they must not be called Rebels) for the Queens Delivery. *Throgmorton* for the Queen of *England* presseth hard upon it, and shewed himself exceeding earnest and industrious in pursuance of it. But *Knox* and self-interest prevailed more amongst them , then all intercessions whatsoever , there being nothing more insisted upon be that fiery spirit , then that she was to be deprived of her Authority and Life together. And this he thundred from the Pulpit with as great a confidence , as if he had received his Doctrine at Mount *Sinai* from the hands of God, at the giving of the Law to *Moses*. Nor was *Throgmorton* thought to be Zealous on the other side , as he outwardly seemed. For he well knew how much it might concern his Queen in her personal safety , and the whole Realm of *England* in its peace and happiness, that the poor Queen should be continued in the same (or a worse) condition, to which these wretched men had brought her. And therefore it was much suspected by most knowing men , that secretly he did more thrust on her deprivation with one hand , that he seemed to hinder it with both. Wherewith incouraged, or otherwise being too far gone to retire with safety , *Lindsay* and *Ruthen* are dispatched to *Lochlevin*-house , to move her for a resignation of the Crown to her Infant-Son. Which when she would by no means yeild to , a Letter is sent to her from *Throgmorton* to perswade her to it ; assuring her, that whatsoever was done by her under that constraint, would be void in Law. This first began to work her to that resolution. But nothing more prevailed upon her , then the rough carriage of the two Lords which first made the motion. By whom she was threatned in plain terms , that if she did not forthwith yeild unto the desires of her people, they would question her for incontinent living, the murther of the King, her tyranny, and the manifest violation of the Laws of the Land, in some secret transactions with the *French*. Terrified wherewith, without so much as reading

reading what they offered to her, she sets her hand to three several Instruments; In the first of which, she gave over the Kingdom to her young Son, at that time little more then a twelve Month old; in the second, she constituted *Murray* Vice-Roy during his minority; and in the third, in case that *Murray* should refuse it, she substitutes the Duke *Hamilton*, the Earls of *Lenox*, *Arguile*, *Athol*, *Morton*, *Glencarne* and *Marre*; all but the two first being sworn Servants unto *Murray*, and the two first made use of only to discharge the matter.

15. Thus furnished an impowered, the Lords return in triumph to their fellows at *Edenborough*, with the sound of a Trumpet; and presently it was resolved to Crown the Infant-King with as much speed as might be, for fear of all such alterations as might otherwise happen. And thereunto they spurred on with such precipitation, that whereas they exhorted those subscriptions from her on St. *James*'s day, being the 25 of *July*, the Coronation was dispatched on the 29. The Sermon, for the greater grace of the matter, must be Preached by *Knox*; but the Superstitious part and Ceremony of it was left to be performed by the Bishop of *Orknay*, another of the natural Sons of *James* the Fifth, assisted by two Superintendents of the Congregation. And that all things might come as near as might be to the Ancient Forms, the Earl of *Morton* and the Lord *Humes* took Oath for the King, that he should maintain the Religion which was then received, and minister Justice equally to all the Subjects. Of which particular the King made afterwards an especial use, in justifying the use of God-fathers and God-mothers at the Baptizing of Infants, when it was questioned in the Conference at *Hampton-Court*. Scarce fifteen days were past from the Coronation, when *Murray* shewed himself in *Scotland*, as if he had dropt down from Heaven for the good of the Nation; but he had took *England* in his way, and made himself so sure a party in that Court, that he was neither affraid to accept the Regencie in such a dangerous point of time, nor to expostulate bitterly with his own Queen for her former actions: not now the same man as before in the time of her glories. For the first handselling of his Government, he calls a Parliament, and therein ratifies the Acts of 1560 for suppressing Popery, as had been promised to the last general Assembly; and then proceeds to the Arraignment of *Hepbourne*, *Hay*, and *Daglish* for the horrible murther of the King: by each of which it was confessed at their execution, that *Bothwel* was present at the murther, and that he had assured them at their first ingaging that most of the Noble-men in the Realm (*Murray* and *Morton* amongst others) were consenting to it.

16. And now or never must the Kirk begin to bear up bravely: In which if they should fail, let *Knox* bear the blame for want of well-tutoring them in the Catechism of their own Authority. They found themselves so necessary to this new Establishment, that it could not well subsist without them; and they resolved to make the proudest he that was, to feel the dint of their spirit. A general Assembly was convented not long after the Parliament, by which the Bishop of *Orknay* was convented and deposed from his Function, for joyning the Queen in Marriage to the Earl of *Bothwel*, though he proceeded by the Form of their own devising. And by the same the Countess of *Arguile* was ordained

(after

(after citation on their part, and appearance on hers) to give ſatisfaction to the Kirk, for being preſent at the Baptiſm of the Infant-King, becauſe performed according to the Rites of the Church of *Rome* : the ſatisfaction to be made in *Stirling* where ſhe had offended, upon a Sunday after Sermon ; the more particular time and manner of it, to be preſcribed by the Superintendent of *Lothian*.   And this was pretty handſome for the firſt beginning, according whereunto it was thought fit by the Chief Leaders to run on till they came to the end of the Race ; of which general King *James* hath given us this deſcription in a Declaration of his publiſhed not long after the ſurpriſing of his perſon by the Earl of *Gowry* 1582, where we finde it thus: The Biſhops having imbraced the Goſpel, it was at firſt agreed even by the Brethren, with the conſent of Regent, that the *Biſhops eſtate ſhould be maintained and authorized.* This endured for ſundry years ; but then there was no remedy, the Calling it ſelf of *Biſhops* was at leaſt become *Anti Chriſtian*, and down they muſt of neceſity: whereupon *they commanded the Biſhops (by their own Authority) to leave their Offices and Juriſdiction.* They decreed in their Aſſemblies, That *Biſhops ſhould have no vote in Parliament* ; and that done, they deſired of the King that ſuch Commiſsioners as they ſhould ſend to the Parliament and Council, might from thenceforth be authorized *in the Biſhops places for the Eſtate.* They alſo *directed their Commiſsioners to the Kings Majeſty*, commanding him and the Council, under pain of the Cenſures of the Church (Excommunication they meant) *to appoint no Biſhops in time to come, becauſe they* (the Brethren) *had concluded that State to be unlawful.* And that it might appear to thoſe of the ſuffering party, that they had not acted all theſe things without better Authority then what they had given unto themſelves, they diſpatched their Letters unto *Beza*, who had ſucceeded at *Geneva* in the Chair of *Calvin* ; from whence they were encouraged and perſwaded to go on in that courſe, and (a) never readmit that plague (he means thereby the Biſhops) to have place in that Church, although it might flatter them, with a ſhew of retaining unity.

(a) Ne unquam illum peſtem admittant, quamvis unitatis retinendæ ſpecie blandentur, Ep, 79.

17. But all this was not done at once, though laid here together ; to ſhew how anſwerable their proceedings were to their firſt beginnings. To cool which heats, and put ſome Water in their Wine, the Queen by practiſing on her Keepers eſcapes the Priſon, and puts her ſelf into *Hamilton* Caſtle ; to which not only the dependants of that powerful Family, but many great Lords, and divers others, did with great cheerfulneſs repair unto her with their ſeveral followers.   Earl *Murray* was at *Stirling* when this news came to him ; and it concerned him to beſtir himſelf with all celerity, before the Queens power was grown too great to be diſputed. He therefore calls together ſuch of his Friends and their adherents as were near unto him, and with them gives battail to the Queen, who in this little time had got together a ſmall Army 4000 men. The honour of the day attends the Regent, who with the loſs of one man only bought an eaſie Victory ; which might have proved more bloudy to the conquered Army, (for they loſt but three hundred in the fight) if he had not commanded back his Souldiers from the execution. The Queen was placed upon a Hill to behold the battail. But when ſhe ſaw the iſſue of it, ſhe poſted with all ſpeed to the Port of *Kerbright*,

took

took Ship for *England*, and landed most fortunately (as it after proved) at *Wickington* in the County of *Cumberland*. From thence she dispatched her Letters to Queen *Elizabeth*, full of Complaints, and passionate bewailings of her wretched fortune ; desires admittance to her presence, and that she might be taken into her protection ; sending withal a Ring which that Queen had given her, to be an everlasting token of that love and amity which was to be maintained between them. But she soon found how miserably she had deceived her self in her Expectations. *Murray* was grown too strong for her in the Court of *England*; and others which regarded little what became of him, were glad of her misfortunes in relation to their own security ; which could not better be consulted, then by keeping a good Guard upon her, now they had her there. And so instead of sending for her to the Court, the Queen gives order by Sir *Francis Knollis* (whom she sent of purpose) to remove the distressed Lady to *Carlisle*, as the safer place, untill the equity of her cause might be fully known. She hath now took possession of the Realm which she had laid claim to, but shall pay dearly for the purchase ; the Crown whereof shall come at last to her Posterity, though it did not fall upon her person.

18. Now that the equity of her cause might be understood, the Regent is required by Letters from the Court of *England* to desist from any further prosecution of the vanquished party, till that Queen were perfectly informed in all particulars touching these Affairs. Which notwithstanding, he thought fit to make use of his Fortune, summoned a Parliament, in which some few of each sort, noble and ignoble, were proscribed for the present ; by the terrour whereof many of the rest submitted, and they which would not were reduced by force of Arms. *Elizabeth* not well pleased with these proceedings, requires that some Commissioners might be sent from *Scotland* to render an account to her, or to her Commissioners, of the severity and hard dealing which they had shewed unto their Queen. And hereunto he was necessitated to conform, as the case then stood : The *French* being totally made against him, the *Spaniards* more displeased then they, and no help to be had from any, but the *English* only. At *York* Commissioners attend from each part in the end of *September*. From Queen *Elizabeth*, *Thomas* Duke of *Norfolk*, *Thomas* Earl of *Sussex*, and Sir *Ralph Sadlier* Chancellor of the Dutchy of *Lancaster*. For the unfortunate Queen of *Scots*, *John Eesly* Bishop of *Rofs*, the Lords *Levington*, *Loyd*, &c. And for the Infant-King, besides the Regent himself, there appeared the Earl of *Morton*, the Lord *Lindsay*, and certain others. After such protestations made on both sides as seemed expedient for preserving the Authority of the several Crowns, an Oath is took by the Commissioners to proceed in the business according to the Rules of Justice and Equity. The Commissioners from the Infant-King present a Declaration of their proceedings in the former troubles ; to which an answer is returned by those of the other side. *Elizabeth* desiring to be better satisfied in some particulars, requires the Commissioners of both sides, some of them at the least, to repair unto her ; where after much fending and proving (as the saying is) there was nothing done which might redound unto the benefit of the Queen of *Scots*.

19. For whilst these matters were in agitation in the Court of *England*, Letters of hers were intercepted, written by her to those which continued of her party in the Realm of *Scotland*. In which Letters she complained, *that the Queen of* England *had not kept promise with her ; but yet desired them to be of good heart, because she was assured of aid by some other means, and hoped to be with them in a short time.* Which Letters being first sent to *Murray*, and by him shewed to Queen *Elizabeth*, prevailed so much for his advantage, that he was not only dismissed with favour, but waited on by her command through every County by the Sheriffs and Gentry, till he came to *Berwick* ; from whence he passed safely unto *Edenborough*, where he was welcomed with great joy by his Friends and Followers. Nothing else memorable in this Treaty which concerns our History, but that when *Murray* and the rest of the *Scots* Commissioners were commanded by Queen *Elizabeth* to give a reason of their proceedings against that Queen, they justified themselves by the Authority af *Calvin* : by which they did endeavour to prove, (as my Author hath it) *That the* Popular Magistrates *are appointed and made to moderate, and keep in order, the excess and unruliness of Kings ; and that it was lawful for them to put the Kings, that the evil and wicked, into prison, and also to deprive them of their Kingdoms.* Which Doctrine, how it relished with Queen *Elizabeth*, may be judged by any that knows with what a Soveraign power she disposed of all things in her own Dominions, without fear of rendring an account to such Popular Magistrates, as *Calvins* Doctrine might encourage to require it of her. But *Calvin* found more Friends in *Scotland*, then in all the world ; there being no Kingdom, Principality, or other Estate, which had therein followed *Calvins* Doctrine, in the imprisoning, deposing, and expelling their own natural Prince, till the *Scots* first led the way unto it in this sad Example.

20 Between the last Parliament in *Scotland*, and the Regents journey into *England*, a general Assembly of the Kirk was held at *Edenborough*. In which they entred into consideration of some disorders which had before been tolerated in the said Assembly, and were thought fit to be redressed. For remedy whereof, it was enacted, *That none should be admitted to have voice in these Assemblies, but Superintendents, Visiters of Churches, Commissioners of Shires and Universities ; together with such other Ministers, to be elected or approved by the Superintendents, as were of knowledge and ability to dispute and reason of such Matters as were there propounded.* It was ordained also, *That all Papists which continued obstinate after lawful admonition, should be Excommunicated ; as also, that the committers of Murther, Incest, Adultery, and other such hainous crimes, should not be admitted to make satisfaction by any particular Church, till they did first appear in the habit of penitents before the general Assembly, and there receive their Order in it.* It was also condescended to, upon the humble Supplication of the Bishop of *Orkney*, that he should be restored unto his place, from which they had deposed him, for his acting in the Queens Marriage : Which favour they were pleased to extend unto him, upon this condition, That for removing of the scandal, he should in his first Sermon acknowledge the fault which he had committed ; and crave pardon of God, the Kirk, and the State, whom he had offended. But their main business

was

was to alter the Book of Diſcipline, eſpecially in that part of it which related to the Superintendents, whom though they countenanced for the preſent by the former Sanction, till they had put themſelves in a better poſture ; yet they reſolve to bring them by degrees to a lower ſtation, and to lay them level with the reſt. In reference whereunto, the Regent is ſollicited by their Petition, that certain Lords of ſecret Council might be appointed to confer with ſome of the ſaid Aſſembly, touching the Polity and Juriſdiction of the Kirk, and to aſſign ſome time and place to that effect, that it might be done before the next Seſſion of Parliament. To which Petition they received no anſwer, till the *July* following : But there came no great matter of it, by reaſon of the Regents death, which ſoon after hapned.

21. For ſo it was, that after his return from *England*, he became more feared by ſome, and obeyed by others, then he had been formerly ; which made him ſtand more highly upon terms of Honor and Advantage, when Queen *Elizabeth* had propounded ſome Conditions to him in favour of the Queen of *Scots*, whoſe cauſe appearing deſperate in the eyes of moſt who wiſhed well to her, they laboured to make their own peace, and procure his Friendſhip. Duke *Hamilton*, amongſt the reſt, negotiated for a Reconcilement, and came to *Edenborough* to that purpoſe ; but unadviſedly interpoſing ſome delays in the buſineſs, becauſe he would not act apart from the reſt of the Queens Adherents, he was ſent Priſoner to the Caſtle. This puts the whole Clan of the *Hamiltons* into ſuch diſpleaſures (being otherwiſe no good friends to the Race of the *Stewarts*) that they reſolved upon his death ; compaſſed not long after by *James Hamilton*, whoſe life he had ſpared once when he had it in his power. At *Lithgoe*, on the 23 of *January*, he was ſhot by this *Hamilton* into the belly ; of which wound he dyed, the Murtherer eſcaping ſafely into *France*. His death much ſorrowed for by all that were affected to the Infant-King, of whom he had ſhewed himſelf to be very tender ; which might have wiped away the imputation of his former aſpirings, if the Kings death could have opened his way unto the Crown, before he had made ſure of the *Hamiltons*, who pretended to it. But none did more lament his death, then his Friends of the Kirk, who in a General Aſſembly which they held ſoon after, decreed, *That the Murtherer ſhould be Excommunicated in all the chief Boroughs of the Realm*; and, *That whoſoever elſe ſhould happen to be afterwards convicted of the Crime, ſhould be proceeded againſt in the ſame ſort alſo.* And yet they were not ſo intent upon the proſecution of the Murtherers, as not to be careful of themſelves and their own Concernments. They had before addreſſed their deſires unto the Regent, that remedy might be provided againſt chopping and changing of Benefices, diminution of Rentals, and ſetting of Tythes into long Leaſes, to the defrauding of Miniſters and their Succeſſors ; That they who poſſeſſed pluralities of Benefices, ſhould leave all but one ; and, That the Juriſdiction of the Kirk, might be made ſeparate and diſtinct from that of the Civil Courts. But now they take the benefit of the preſent diſtractions, to diſcharge the thirds aſſigned unto them from all other Incumbrances then the payment of Five thouſand Marks yearly for the Kings ſupport ; which being reduced to Engliſh mony, would not amount unto the ſum of 300 pound;

and

and ſeems to be no better then the ſticking up a feather (in the ancient By-word) when the Gooſe was ſtollen.

22. As touching the diſtractions which emboldened them to this Adventure, they did moſt miſerably afflict the whole State of that Kingdom. The Queen of *Scots* had granted a Commiſſion to Duke *Hamilton*, the Earls of *Huntley* and *Arguile*, to govern that Realm in her Name, and by her Authority; in which they were oppoſed by thoſe, who for their own ſecurity, more then any thing elſe, profeſsed their obedience to the King. Great ſpoils and rapines hereupon enſued upon either ſide; but the Kings party had the worſt; as having neither hands enough to make good their intereſt, nor any head to order and direct thoſe few hands they had. At laſt the Earl of *Suſſex*, with ſome Souldiers, came toward the borders, ſupplied them with ſuch Forces as enabled them to drive the Lords of the Queens Faction out of all the South; and thereby gave them ſome encouragement to nominate the old Earl of *Lenox* for their Lord-Lieutenant, till the Queens pleaſure it might be further known. And in this Broyl the Kirk muſt needs act ſomewhat alſo: For finding that their party was too weak to compel their Oppoſites to obedience by the Mouth of the Sword, they are reſolved to try what they can do by the Sword of the Mouth: And to that end, they ſend their Agents to the Duke of *Chaſteau Harald*, the Earls of *Arguile, Eglington, Caſſels* and *Crauford*, the Lords *Boyde* and *Ogilby*, and others, Barons and Gentlemen of name and quality; whom they require to return to the Kings obedience, and ordain Certification to be made unto them, that if they did otherwiſe, the Spiritual Sword of Excommunication ſhould be drawn againſt them. By which, though they effected nothing which advanced the cauſe, yet they ſhewed their affections, and openly declared thereby to which ſide they inclined, if they were left unto themſelves. And for a further evidence of their inclinations, they were ſo temperate at that time, or ſo obſequious to the Lords, whoſe cauſe they favoured, that they deſiſted from cenſuring a ſeditious Sermon, upon an Intimation ſent from the Lords of the Council, that the Sermon contained ſome matter of Treaſon, and therefore that the Cognizance of it belonged unto themſelves and the Secular Judges.

23. The Confuſions ſtill encreaſe amongſt them; the Queen of *England* ſeeming to intend nothing more, then to balance the one ſide by the other, that betwixt both ſhe might preſerve her ſelf in ſafety. But in the end ſhe yields unto the importunity of thoſe who appeared in favour of the King, aſsures them of her aid and ſuccours when their needs required, and recommends the Earl of *Lenox* as the fitteſt man to take the Regency upon him. The Breach now widens more then ever: The Lords commiſſionated by the Queen are poſseſt of *Edenborough*, and having the Caſtle to their Friend, call a Parliament thither, as the new Regent doth the like at *Stirling*, and each pretends to have preheminence above the other. The one, becauſe it was aſsembled in the Regal City: the other, becauſe they had the Kings Perſon for their countenance in it. Nothing more memorable in that at *Edenbor.* then that the Queens extorted Reſignation was declared *null* and void in Law, and nothing ſo remarkable in the other, as that the young King made a ſpeech unto them (which had been put into his mouth) at their firſt ſetting down. In each they

1579

they forfeit the Estates of the opposite party; and by Authority of each, destroy the Countrey in all places in an hostile manner. The Ministers had their parts also in these common sufferings; compelled in all such places where the Queen prevailed, to recommend her in their Prayers by her Name or Titles, or otherwise to leave the Pulpit unto such as would. In all things else the Kirk had the felicity to remain in quiet; care being taken by both parties for the Preservation of Religion, though in all other things, at an extream difference amongst themselves. But the new Regent did not long enjoy his Office, of which he reaped no fruit, but cares and sorrows. A sudden Enterprize is made on *Stirling* by one of the *Hamiltons*, on the third of *September*, at what time both the Parliament and Assembly were there convened : And he succeeded so well in it, as to be brought privately into the Town, to seize on all the Noblemen in their several Lodgings, and amongst others, to possess themselves of the Regents person : But being forced to leave the place, and quit their Prisoners, the Regent was unfortunately kill'd by one of *Hamiltons* Souldiers, together with the Gentleman himself unto whom he had yeilded.   The Earl of *Marre* is on the fifth of the same moneth proclaimed his Successor : His Successor indeed, not only, in his cares and sorrows, but in the shortness of his Rule ; for having in vain attempted *Edenborough* in the very beginning of his Regency, he was able to effect as little in most places else, more then the wasting of the Conntry, as he did *Edenborough*.

1571.

24. The Subjects in the mean time were in ill condition, and the King worse : They had already drawn their Swords against their Queen, first forced her to resign the Crown, and afterwards drove her out of the Kingdom.   And now it is high time to let the young King know what he was to trust to ; to which end, they command a piece of Silver of the value of Five shillings to be coyned and made currant in that Kingdom; on the one side whereof was the Arms of Scotland, with the Name and Title of the King, in the usual manner ; on the other side, was stamped an Armed hand, grasping a naked Sword, with this Inscription ; *viz. Si bene, pro me, si male, contra me* : By which the people were informed, that if the King should govern them no otherwise then he ought to do, they should then use the Sword for his preservation; but if he governed them amiss, and transgressed their Laws, they should then turn the point against him.   Which words being said to have been used by the Emperor *Trajan*, in his delivering of the Sword unto one of his Courtiers, when he made him Captain of his Guard, have since been used by some of our Presbyterian Zealots, for justifying the Authority of inferior Officers, in censuring the actions, and punishing the persons of the Supreme Magistrate. It was in the year 1552, that this learned piece of Coyn was minted, but whether before or after the death of the Earl of *Marre*, I am not able to say : for he having but ill success in the course of his Government, conrracted such a grief of heart, that he departed this life on the eighth of *October*, when he had held that Office a little more then a year; followed about seven weeks after, by that great Incendiary *John Knox*, who dyed at *Edenbor.* on the 27 of *Nov.* leaving the State imbroyled in those disorders, which by his fire and fury had been first occasioned.

25. *Morton* succeeds the Earl of *Marre* in this broken Government, when

when the affairs of the young King ſeemed to be at the worſe ; but he had ſo good fortune in it, as by degrees to ſettle the whole Realm in ſome Form of peace : He underſtood ſo well the eſtate of the Country, as to aſſure himſelf, that till the Caſtle of *Edenborough* was brought under his power, he ſhould never be able to ſuppreſs that party, whoſe ſtubborn ſtanding out (as it was interpreted) did ſo offend the Queen of *England*, that ſhe gave order unto *Drury*, then Marſhal of *Berwick*, to paſs with ſome conſiderable Forces into *Scotland* for his preſent aſſiſtance. With theſe Auxiliaries he lays ſiege to the Caſtle, battering it, and reduceth it to ſuch extremity, that they were compelled to yield to mercy. Of which, though many of them taſted, yet *Grange* himſelf, who firſt or laſt had held the place againſt all the four Regents, together with one of his Brothers, and two Goldſmiths of *Edenborough*, were hanged at the Market-Croſs of that City. By which ſurrender of the Caſtle, the Queens Faction was ſo broke in pieces, that it was never able to make head again ; all of them labouring to procure their own peace by ſome Compoſition. For now the Regent being at leiſure to enquire after the miſcarriages of the years preceding, he ſends his *Juſtices in Eyre* into all parts of the Countrey, who exerciſed their Commiſſions with ſufficient Rigour ; people of all ſorts being forced to compound, and redeem themſelves, by paying ſuch ſums of money as by theſe Juſtices were impoſed. Some of the Merchants alſo were called in queſtion, under colour of Tranſporting Coyn ; fined in great ſums, or elſe committed to the Caſtle of *Blackneſs*, till they gave ſatisfaction. By which proceedings he incurred the cenſure of a covetous man, though he had other ends in it then his own enriching. For by theſe rigorous exactions, he did not only puniſh ſuch as had been moſt active in the late diſtempers, but terrified them from the like attempts againſt the preſent Government for the times enſuing. To ſuch Confuſions and Diſorders, ſuch miſerable Rapines, Spoils and Devaſtations, ſuch horrible Murthers and Aſſaſſinates, was this poor Realm expoſed for ſeven years together, by following the *Genevian* Doctrines of Diſobedience which *Knox* had preached and *Buchanan* in his Seditious Pamphlets had diſperſed amongſt them. Not to ſay any thing of that indeleable reproach and infamy, which the whole Nation had incurred in the eye of Chriſtendom, for their barbarous dealings towards a Queen, who had ſo graciouſly indulged unto them the exerciſe of that Religion which ſhe found amongſt them, without diſturbance unto any.

26. Which matters being thus laid together, we muſt proceed to ſuch affairs as concern the Kirk, abſtracted from the troubles and commotions in the Civil State. In reference whereunto, we may pleaſe to know, that after divers Sollicitations made by former Aſſemblies, for ſetling a Polity in the Church, certain Commiſſioners were appointed to advize upon it. The Earl of *Marre* then Regent, nominated for the Lords of the Council, the Earl of *Morton* Chancellor, the Lord *Ruthen* Treaſurer, the Titular Abbot of *Dumferling* principal Secretary of Eſtate in the place of *Ledington*, *Mackgil* chief Regiſter, *Bullenden* the then Juſtice Clerk, and *Colen Camphil* of *Glenarchy*. The Aſſembly then ſitting at *Leith*, named for the Kirk, *John Ereskin* of *Dun* Superintendent of *Angus*, *John Winram*, Superintendent of *Fife*, *Andrew Hay* Commiſſioner of *Cladiſdale*,

David

David Lindesay Commissioner of the West, *Robert Pont* Commissioner of *Orknay*, and Mr. *John Craige* one of the Ministers of *Edenborough*. The Scots were then under some necessity of holding fair quarter with the English; and therefore to conform (as near as conveniently they might) to the Government of it in the outward Polity of the Church. Upon which reason, and the prevalency of the Court-Commissioners, those of the Kirk did condescend unto these Conclusions; and condescended the more easily, because *Knox* was absent, detained by sickness from attending any publick business. Now these Conclusions were as followeth; 1. *That the Archbishopricks and Bishopricks presently void, or should happen hereafter to be void, should be disposed to the most qualified of the Ministry.*: 2. *That the Spiritual Jurisdictions should be exercised by the Bishops in their several Dioceses*:3.*That all Abbots, Priors, and other inferiour Prelates, who should happen to be presented to Benefices, should be tried by the Bishop and Superintendent of the bounds, concerning their qualification and aptness to give voice for the Church in Parliament; and upon their Collation be admitted to the Benefice, and not otherwise*: 4. *That the nomination of fit persons for every Archbishoprick and Bishoprick should be made by the King or Regent, and the Election by the Chapters of the Cathedrals. And because divers persons were possessed of places in some of the said Chapters, which did bear no Office in the Church*, It was ordered, *That a particular nomination of Ministers in every Diocess should be made, to supply their rooms until their Benefices in the said Churches should fall void*: 5. *That all Benefices of Cure under Prelacies, should be disposed to actual Ministers, and no others*: 6.*That the Ministers should receive Ordination from the Bishop of the Diocess; and where no Bishop was then placed, from the Superintendent of the bounds*: 7. *That the Bishops and Superintendents at the Ordination of the Ministers should exact of them an Oath for acknowledging his Majesties Authority, and for obedience to their Ordinary in all things lawful according to a Form then condescended*; Order was also taken for disposing of Provestries, Colledge-charges, Chaplanaries, and divers other particulars most profitable for the Church, which were all ordained to stand in force until the Kings minority, or till the States of the Realm should determine otherwise. How happy had it been for the Isles of *Britain*, if the Kirk had stood to these Conclusions, and not unravelled all the Web to advance a Faction, as they after did.

1572.   27. For in the next general Assembly held in *August* at the Town of *Perth*, where these conclusions were reported to the rest of the Brethren, some of them took offence at one thing, some at another: some took exception at the Title of *Archbishop* and *Dean*; and others at the name of *Archdeacon*, *Chancellor* and *Chapter* not found in the *Genevian* Bibles, and otherwise Popish, and offensive to the ears of good Christians. To satisfie whose queazie stomachs, some of the Lay-Commissioners had prepared this Lenitive; that is to say, That by using of these Titles, they meant not to allow of any Popish Superstition in the least degree; and were content they should be changed to others which might seem less scandalous. And thereupon it was proposed, that the name of *Bishop* should be used for *Archbishop*, that the *Chapter* should be called the *Bishops Assembly*, and the *Dean* the Moderator of it. But as for the Titles of *Archdeacon, Chancellor, Abbot*, and *Prior* it was ordered that some should be appointed to consider how far these Functions did

did extend, and give their opinion to the next Assembly for the changing of them, with such others, as should be thought most agreeable to the Word of God, and the Polity of the best Reformed Churches. Which brings into my mind the fancy of some people in the Desarts of *Affrick*, who having been terribly wasted with Tygers, and not able otherwise to destroy them, passed a Decree that none should thenceforth call them Tygers; and then all was well. But notwithstanding all this care, and these qualifications, the conclusions could not be admitted, but with this Protestation, that they received those Articles for an interim only, till a more perfect Order might be attained at the hands of the King, the Regent, or the States of the Realm. And it was well that they admitted them so far: For presently upon the rising of this Assembly, Mr. *John Douglass*, Provost of the new Colledge in St. *Andrews*, was preferred to the Archbishoprick of that See; Mr. *James Boyd*, to the Archbishoprick of *Glasco*; Mr. *James Paton* to the Bishoprick of *Dunkeld*; and Mr. *Andrew Grahame* to the See of *Dumblane*; the rest to be disposed of afterwards as occasion served.

28. But long it was not that they held in so good a Posture. *Morton* **1573.** succeeding in the Regencie to the Earl of *Marre*, entered into a consideration of the injury which was done the King by the invading of his Thirds, and giving onely an allowance yearly of five thousand Marks. These he brings back unto the Crown, upon assurance that the Pensions of the Ministers should be better answered then in former times, and to be payable from thenceforth by the Parish in which they served. But no sooner had he gained his purpose, when to improve the Kings Revenue, and to increase the Thirds, he appointed to one Minister two or three Churches; in which he was to Preach by turns; and where he did not Preach, to appoint a Reader. Which Reader for the most part was allowed but twenty or forty pounds yearly; each pound being valued at no more then one shilling eight pence of our English money. And in the payment of these Pensions, they found their condition made worse then before it was: for, whereas, they could boldly go to the Superintendents, and make their poor Estates known unto them, from whom they were sure to receive some relief and comfort; they were now forced to dance attendance at the Court, for getting Warrants for the payment of the sums assigned, and supplicating for such augmentations as were seldom granted. And when the Kirk desired to be restored unto the Thirds, as was also promised in case the assignations were not duly paid, it was at last told them in plain terms, *That since the Surplus of the Thirds belonged to the King, it was fitter the Regent and Council should modifie the Stipends of Ministers, then that the Kirk should have the appointment and designation of a Surplus.* Nor did the Superintendents speed much better, if not worse, when they addressed themselves to any of the Court-Officers for the receiving the Pensions assigned unto them; which being greater then the others, came more coldly in. And if they prest at any time with more importunity then was thought convenient, it was told them that the Kirk had now no use of their services, in regard that Bishops were restored in some places to their Jurisdictions.

29. And now the Discipline begins to alter, from a mixed to a plain Presbytery. Before the confirming of Episcopacy by the late conclusions,

fions, the Government of the Kirk had been by Superintendents, affifted by Commiffioners for the Countries, as they called them then. The Commiffioners changed, or new Elected at every general Afsembly; the Superintendents fetled for term of life. To them in appertained to approve and admit the Minifters; they prefided in all Synods, and directed all Church cenfures within their bounds; neither was any Excommunication pronounced without their Warrant. To them it alfo was referred to proportion the Stipends of all Minifters; to appoint the Collectors of the Thirds, (as long as they were chofen by the general Afsembly) to make payment of them, after fuch form and manner as to them feemed beft; and to difpofe of the Surplufage, if any were, toward the charges of the State. And to this *Knox* confented with the greater readinefs, becaufe in an unfetled Church, the Minifters were not thought of parts fufficient to be trufted with a power of Jurifdiction; and partly becaufe fuch men as were firft defigned for Superintendents, were for the moft part pofsefsed of fome fair Eftate, whereby they were not only able to fupport themfelves, but to afford relief and comfort to the poor Minifters. But when thefe men grew old or dyed, and that the entertaining of the Reformed Religion in all parts of the Realm had given incouragement to men of Parts and Learning to enter into the Miniftry, they then began more univerfally to put in practice thofe reftrictions with which the Superintendents had been fettered, and the power of the Minifters extended by the Book of *Difcipline*, according to the Rules whereof the Minifter and Elders of every Church, with the affiftance of their Deacons, if occafion were, were not alone enabled to exercife moft part of Ecclefiaftical Jurifdiction over their feveral Congregations, but alfo to joyn themfelves with the chief Burgeffes of the greater Towns for cenfuring and depofing their own Superintendents. In which refpect the Government may be faid to be a mixt, not a plain Presbytery, as before was noted; though in effect, Presbytery was the more predominant, becaufe the Superintendents by the Book of Difcipline were to be fubject to the Cenfures of their own Presbyterie.

30. But thefe Presbyteries, and the whole power afcribed unto them by the Book of Difcipline, were in a way to have been crufhed by the late conclufions, when they flew out again upon occafion of the hard dealing of the Earl of *Morton*, in putting them befides their *Thirds*. And then withal, becaufe the putting of fome Minifters into Bifhops Sees, had been ufed by him for a pretence to defraud the Superintendents of their wonted means, the Bifhops were inhibited by the general Affembly which next followed, from exercifing any Ecclefiaftical Jurifdiction within the bounds which they had formerly affigned, to their Superintendents, without their confent and approbation. Which opportunity was both efpied and taken by *Andrew Melvin*, for making fuch an innovation in the Form of Government, as came moft near unto the Pattern of *Geneva*, where he had ftudied for a time, and came back thence more skilful in Tongues and Languages then any other part of Learning. And being hot and eager upon any bufinefs which he took in hand, emulous of *Knoxes* greatnefs, and hoping to be Chronicled for his equal in the Reformation; he entertained all fuch as reforted to him, with the continual commendations of that Difcipline which he found at *Geneva*,

where

where the Presbyteries carried all, without acknowledging any Bishop or Superintendent in power above them. Having by this means much infinuated into divers Minifters, he dealt with one *John Drury*, one of the Preachers of *Edenborough*, to propound a queftion in the general Affembly which was then convened, touching the lawfulnefs of the Epifcopal Function, and the Authority of Chapters in their Election. Which queftion being put according as he had directed, he firft commends the Speakers Zeal (as if he had been unacquainted with the motion) and then proceeds to a long and well framed difcourfe, touching the flourifhing Eftate of the Church of *Geneva*, and the opinions of thofe great and eminent men, *Calvin* then dead, and *Theodore Beza* then alive, in the point of Church-Government. After which premifes, he fell upon this conclufion, *That none ought to bear any Office in the Church of Chrift, whofe titles were not found in the Holy Scipture : That though the name of Bifhop did occur in Scripture, yet was it not to be taken in that fence in which it was commonly underftood : That no Superiority was allowed by Chrift amongft the Minifters of the Church ; all of them being of the fame degree, and having the fame power in all Sacred Matters : That the corruptions crept into the Eftate of Bifhops were fo great and many, that if they fhould be removed, Religion would not long remain in Purity.* And fo referred the whole matter to their confideration.

31. The Game being thus ftarted and purfued by fo good a Huntfman, it was thought fit by the Affembly, to commend the chafe thereof to fix chofen Members, who were to make report of their diligence to the reft of the Brethren. Of which, though *Melvin* took a care to be named for one, and made ufe of all his wit and cunning to bring the reft of the Referrees to his own opinion, yet he prevailed no further at that time, then under colour of a mannerly declining of the point in hand, to fay fome further reftrictions upon the Bifhops in the exercife of their Power and Jurifdictions, then had been formerly impofed. The fum of their report was to this effect ; *Viz. That they did not hold it expedient to anfwer the Queftions propounded for the prefent ; but if any Bifhop was chofen, that had not qualities required by the Word of God, fhe fhould be tryed by the general Affembly : That they judged the name of a Bifhop, to be common to all Minifters who had the charge of a particular flock ; and that by the Word of God, his chief function confifted in the Preaching of the Word, the Miniftration of the Sacraments, and the exercife of Ecclefiaftical Difcipline with the confent of the Elders : That from amongft the Miniftry, fome one might be chofen to overfee and vifit fuch reafonable bounds befides his own flock, as the General Affembly fhould appoint : That the Minifter fo elected, might in thofe bounds appoint Preachers, with the advice of the Minifters of that Province, and the confent of the flock which fhould be admitted ; and that he might fufpend Minifters from the exercife of their Office, upon reafonable caufes, with the confent of the Minifters of the bounds.* This was the fum of the Report ; and that thus much might be reported to begin the game with, great care was took by *Melvin* and his Adherents, that neither any of the Bifhops nor Superintendents which were then prefent in the Affembly (being eight in number) were either nominated to debate the points propofed, nor called to be prefent at the Conference. But fomewhat further muft be done, now their hand was in : And therefore, that the reft might fee what they were to truft to, if

this

this World went on, they depofed *James Patton* Bifhop of *Dunkelden* from his place and dignity, without confulting the Lord-Regent, or any of the fecret Council in fo great a bufinefs.

32. The next Affembly makes fome alteration in propounding the queftion, and gives it out with a particular reference to their own concernment, in this manner following ; that is to fay, *Whether the Bifhops, as they were in* Scotland, *had their Function warranted by the Word of God?* But the determining of this queftion was declined as formerly. Only it was conceived expedient for a further preparative, both to approve the opinions of the Referrees in the former Meeting, and to add this now unto the reft, *That the Bifhops fhould take to themfelves the fervice of fome one Church within their Diocefs, and nominate the particular flock whereof they would accept the charge.* News of which laft addition being brought to the Regent, he required by a fpecial Meffage, either to ftand to the conclufions before mentioned, which were made at *Leith,* or elfe devife fome other Form of Church Government which they would abide. And this fell out as *Melvin* and his Tribe would have it : For after this, there was nothing done in the Afsemblies for two years together, but hammering, forming and reforming a new Book of Difcipline, to be a ftanding Rule for ever to the Kirk of *Scotland.* But poffible it is, that the defign might have been brought to perfection fooner, if the Regent had not thought himfelf affronted by them, in the perfon of his Chaplain Mr. *Patrick Adamfon,* whom he had recommended to the See of St. *Andrews.* For the Election being purpofely delayed by the Dean and Chapter, till the fitting of the next Affembly ; *Adamfon* then prefent, was interrogated whether he would fubmit himfelf unto the tryal, and undertake that Office upon fuch conditions as the Affembly fhould prefcribe. To which he anfwered, That he was commanded by the Regent not to accept thereof upon any other terms, then fuch as had been formerly agreed upon between the Commiffioners of the Kirk and the Lords of the Council. On this refufal they inhibit the Chapter from proceeding in the faid Election ; though, afterwards, for fear of the difpleafure of fo great a man, their command therein was difobeyed, and the party chofen. Which fo provoked thofe meek and humble fpirited men, that at their next Meeting they difcharged him from the exercife of all Jurifdiction, till by fome general Affembly he were lawfully licenfed. And this did fo exafperate the Regent on the other fide, that he refolved to hinder them from making any further Innovation in the Churches Polity as long as he continned in his place and Power.

33. But the Regent having fomewhat imprudently difmiffed himfelf of the Government, and put into the hands of the King, in the beginning of *March,* Anno 1577, they then conceived they had as good an opportunity as could be defired to advance their Difcipline, which had been hammering ever fince in the Forge of their Fancies. And when it hapned (as it was not long before it did) they ufher in the Defign with this following Preamble ; *viz. The General Affembly of the Kirk finding univerfal corruption of the whole Eftates of the body of this Realm, the great coldnefs and flacknefs in Religion in the greateft part of the Profeffors of the fame, with the daily increafe of all kind of fearful fins and enormities ; as Incefts, Adulteries, Murthers (committed in* Edenborough *and* Sterling) *curfed Sacriledge,*

ledge, ungodly Sedition and Division within the bowels of the Realm, with all manner of disordered and ungodly living; which justly hath provoked our God, although long suffering and patient, to stretch out his arm in his anger to correct and visit the iniquity of the Land; and namely, by the present penury, famine and hunger, joyned with the Civil and Intestine Seditions: Whereunto doubtless greater judgements must succeed, if these his corrections work no Reformation and amendment in mens hearts: Seeing also the bloody exclusions of the cruel counsels of that Roman Beast, tending to extermine and rase from the face of all Europe the true light of the blessed Word of Salvation: For these causes, and that God of his mercy would bless the Kings Highness, and his Regiment, and make him to have a happy and prosperous Government, as also to put in his Highness heart, and in the hearts of his Noble Estates of Parliament, not only to make and establish good politick Laws for the Weal and good Government of the Realm, but also to set and establish such a Polity and Discipline in the Kirk, as is craved in the Word of God, and is contained and penned already to be presented to his Highness and Council; that in the one and in the other God may have his due praise, and the age to come an example of upright and Godly dealing. Which Act of the Assembly pass'd on the 24 of *April* 1578.

34. The Discipline must be of most excellent use, which could afford a present remedy to so many mischiefs; and yet as excellent as it was, it could obtain no Ratification at that time of the King or Parliament; which therefore they resolve to put in practise by the strength of their party, without insisting any further on the leave of either. In which respect, it will not be unnecessary to take a brief view of such particulars in which they differ from the ancient Government of the Church of Christ, or the Government of the Church of *England* then by Law established; or finally, from the former Book of Discipline which themselves had justified. Now by this Book it is declared, *That none that bear Office in the Church of Christ ought to have Dominion over it, or be called Lords: That the Civil Magistrates are so far from having any power to Preach, administer the Sacraments, or execute the Censures of the Church, that they ought not to prescribe any Rule how it should be done: and that as Ministers are subject to the judgement and punishment of Magistrates in External things, if they offend; so ought the Magistrates to submit themselves to the Discipline of the Church, if they transgress in matter of Conscience and Religion: That the Ministers of the Church ought to govern the same by mutual consent of Brethren, and equality of power, according to their several Functions: That there are only four ordinary Office bearers in the Church; that is to say, The Pastor, Minister or Bishop, the Doctor, the Elder, and the Deacon; and that no more ought to be received in the Word of God; and therefore that all ambitious Titles invented in the Kingdom of Antichrist and his usurped Hierarchy, which are not of these* 4 *sorts, together with the Offices depending thereupon (that is to say,* Archbishops, Patriarchs, Chancellours, Deans, Archdeacons, &c.) *ought in one word to be rejected: That all which bear Office in the Church, are to be elected by the Eldership, and consent of the Congregation to whom the person presented is appointed, and no otherwise. That the Ordination of the person so elected, is to be performed with Fasting, Prayer, and the Imposition of the hands of the Eldership* (Remember that *Imposition of hands* was totally rejected in the former Book:) *That all Office bearers in the Church should have their own particular flocks, amongst whom they ought to exercise their charge, and keep their residence.*

35. But

35. But more particularly it declares, *That it is the Office of the Pastor, Bishop or Minister, to Preach the Word of God, and to administer the Sacraments in that particular Congregation unto which he is called: and it belongs unto them, after lawful proceeding of the Eldership, to pronounce the sentence of binding and loosing ; as also to solemnize Marriage between persons contracted, being by the said Eldership thereunto required: That it is the Office of the Doctor, simply to open the mind of the Spirit of God in the Scriptures, without making any such application as the Minister useth ; and that this Doctor being an Elder, ought to assist the Pastor in the Government of the Church, by reason that the Interpretation of the Word, which is the onely Judge in Ecclesiastical matters, is to him committed: That it is the Office of the Elder (that is to say, The Lay-Elder, for so they mean) both privately and publickly, to watch with all diligence over the flock committed to them, that no corruptions of Religion or manners grow amongst them ; as also to assist the Pastor or Minister in examining those that come to the Lords Table, in visiting the Sick, in admonishing all men of their duties according to the Rule of the Word ; and in holding Assemblies with the Pastors and Doctors, for establishing good order in the Church, the Acts whereof he is to put in execution: That it is the Office of the Deacon to collect and distribute the goods of the Church at the appointment of the Elders, amongst which he is to have no voyce in the common Consistory ;* contrary to the Rules of the former Book: *That all Ecclesiastical Assemblies have a power lawfully to convene together for that effect: That it is in the power of the Eldership to appoint Visitors for their Churches within their bounds ; and that this power belongs not to any single person, be he Bishop or otherwise: That every three, four or more Parishes, may have an Eldership to themselves ; but so that the Elders be chosen out of each in fit proportion: That it is the Office of these Elderships to enquire of naughty and unruly Members, and to bring them into the way again, either by Admonition, and threatning of Gods Judgement, or by Correction, even to the very Censure of Excommunication ; as also to admonish, censure, and (if the case require) to depose their Pastor, if he be found guilty of any of those grievous crimes (among which* Dancing *goes for one) which belongs to their cognizance: The Errors committed by the Eldership to be corrected by Provincial Assemblies, and those in the Provincials by the General. The maintainance and assisting of which Discipline, and the inflicting of Civil punishments upon such as do not obey the same, without confounding one jurisdiction with another, is made to be the chief Office of Kings and Princes. And that this Discipline might be executed without interruption, it was required that the Name and Office of Bishops, as it then was, and had been formerly exercised in the Church of* Scotland ; *as also the Names and Offices of* Commendators, Abbots, Priors, Deans, Deans and Chapters, Chancellors, Archdeacons, &c. *should from thenceforth be utterly abolished, and of no effect.* Which point, and all the rest therein contained, being granted to them, all right of Patronages destroyed, that the popular Elections may proceed in all their Churches; and finally the whole Patrimony of the Church in Lands, Tythes or Houses, permitted to the distribution of the Deacons in every Eldership, they then conceive that such a right Reformation may be made as God requires.

36. This Book of Discipline being presented to the King in Parliament, and the approving of the same deferred to a further time ; they took this not for a delay, but a plain denial ; and therefore it was agreed in the next general Assembly (as before is said) to put the same in execution

execution by their own Authority, without expecting any further confirmation of it from the King or Council. Which that they might effect without fear of diſturbance, they firſt diſcharge the Biſhops and Superintendents from intermedling in Affairs which concerned Religion, but onely in their own particular Churches; that ſo their Elderſhips (according to this new eſtabliſhment) might grow up and flouriſh. And then they took upon them, with their own adherents, to exerciſe all Eccleſiaſtical Juriſdiction, without reſpect to Prince or Prelate; they altered the Laws according to their own appetite; they aſſembled the Kings Subjects, and Injoyned Eccleſiaſtical pains unto them; they made Decrees, & put the ſame in execution; they preſcribed Laws to the King and State; they appointed Faſts throughout the whole Realm, eſpecially when ſome of their Faction were to move any great enterpriſe; they uſed very traytorous, ſeditious and contumelious words in the Pulpits, Schools, and otherwiſe, to the diſdain and reproach of the King; and being called to anſwer the ſame, they utterly diſclaimed the Kings Authority, ſaying he was an incompetent Judge, and that matters of the Pulpit ought to be exempted from the judgement and correction of Princes. And finally, they did not only animate ſome of thoſe that adhered unto them, to ſeize upon the Kings perſon, and uſurp his power; but juſtified the ſame in one of their general Aſſemblies held at *Edenborough* for a lawful Act; ordaining all thoſe to be excommunicated which did not ſubſcribe unto the ſame. This we take up by *whole ſale* now, but ſhall return it by *retail* in that which follows.

37. And firſt they begin with Mr. *James Boyd*, Archbiſhop of *Glaſco*, a man of a mild and quiet nature, and therefore the more like to be conformable to their commands; requiring him to ſubmit himſelf to the Aſſembly, and to ſuffer the corruptions of the Epiſcopal Order to be reformed in his perſon. To which proud intimation of their will and pleaſure he returned this Anſwer, which, for the modeſty or piety thereof, deſerves to be continued to perpetual memory: *I underſtand* (ſaith he) *the Name, Office and Reverence given to a Biſhop to be lawful, and allowed by the Scripture of God; and being elected by the Church and King to be Biſhop of* Glaſco, *I eſteem my Office and Calling lawful, and ſhall endeavour with all my power to perform the duties required, (ſubmitting my ſelf to the judgement of the Church, if I ſhall be tryed to offend; ſo as nothing be required of me, but the performance of thoſe duties which the Apoſtle preſcribeth.* Finding him not ſo tractable as they had expected, they Commiſſionate certain of their Members to require his ſubſciption to the Act made at *Sterling*, for reformation of the State Epiſcopal; by which it was agreed, that every Biſhop ſhould take charge of ſome flock in particular. And this they preſt upon him with ſuch heat and violence, that they never left proſecuting the poor man, till they had brought him to his Grave. By none more violently purſued then by *Andrew Melvin*, whom he had brought to *Glaſco*, and made Principal of the Colledge there, gave him a free acceſs to his Houſe and Table, or otherwiſe very liberally provided for him. But *Scots* and *Presbyterians* are not won by favours, nor obliged by Benefits: For *Melvin* ſo diſguiſed his nature, that when he was in private with him at his Table or elſewhere, he would uſe him with all reverence imaginable, giving him the title

of

of his *Lordship*, with all the other Honours which pertained unto him; but in all particular Meetings, whatsoever they were, he would only call him Mr. *Boyd*, and otherwise carried himself most despitefully towards him.

38. Their rough and peremptory dealing with this Reverend Prelate discouraged all the rest from coming any more to their Assemblies: Which hapned as they could have wished. For thereupon they agree amongst themselves upon certain Articles, which every Bishop must subscribe, or else quit his place; that is to say, 1. *That they should be content to be Ministers and Pastors of a flock:* 2. *That they should not usurp any criminal jurisdiction:* 3. *That they should not vote in Parliament in the name of the Church, unless they had a Commission from the general Assembly:* 4. *That they should not take up for maintaining their ambitions the Rents which might maintain many Pastors, Schools and Poor, but content themselves with a reasonable portion for discharge of their Offices:* 5. *That they should not claim the title of Temporal Lords, nor usurp any Civil Jurisdiction, whereby they might be drawn from their charge:* 6. *That they should not Empire over Presbyteries, but be subject to the same:* 7. *That they should not usurp the power of Presbyteries, nor take upon them to visit any bounds that were not committed to them by the Church:* 8. *That if any more corruptions should afterwards be tryed, the Bishop should agree to have them reformed.* These Articles were first tendered to *Patrick Adamson*, Archbishop of St. *Andrews*, and Metropolitan of all *Scotland*; against whom they had a former quarrel, not only because he was preferred, elected, and admitted to that eminent Dignity without their consent, but had also exercised the Jurisdiction which belonged unto it, in express and direct opposition unto their commands. And first they quarrelled with him for giving Collation unto Benefices, and for giving voice in Parliament, not being authorized thereunto by the Kirk. They quarrelled with him afterwards for drawing or advising the Acts of Parliament, *Anno* 1584, which they conceived to be so prejudicial to the Rights of the Kirk; and held the King so hard unto it, that he was forced to counsel the poor Prelate to subscribe some Articles, by which he seemed in a manner to renounce his Calling; of which more hereafter. They quarrelled with him again in the year 1589, for marrying one of the Daughters of the late Duke of *Lenox* to the Earl of *Huntly* without their consent; wherein the King was also fain to leave him to their discretion. And finally, they so vexed and persecuted him from one time to another, upon pretence of not conforming to their lawless pleasures, that they reduced him in the end to extreme necessity, published a false and scandalous Paper in his name, as he lay on his death-bed, containing a *Recantation* (as they called in) or rather a renouncing of his Episcopal Function; together with his approbation of their Pres-Presbyteries: which Paper he disowned at the hearing of it. By which, and many such unworthy courses, they brought his gray hairs (as they did some others of his Order) with shame and sorrow to the Grave.

39. Mention was made before of an Act of Parliament made in the time of the *Interregnum*, before the Queens coming back from *France*, for demolishing all Religious Houses, and other Monuments of Superstition and Idolatry. Under which name all the Cathedrals were interpreted

to be contained, and by that means involved in the general ruine; only the Church at *Glasco* did escape that storm, and remained till this time undefaced in its former glory: But now becomes a very great eye-sore to *Andrew Melvin*, by whose practices and sollicitations it was agreed unto by some Zealous Magistrates, that it should forth with be demolished; that the materials of it should be used for the building of some lesser Churches in that City for the ease of the people; and that such Masons, Quarriers, and other Workmen, whose service was requisite thereunto, should be in readiness for that purpose at the day appointed. The Arguments which he used to perswade those Magistrates to this Act of Ruine, were the resorting of some people to that Church for their private Devotions; the huge vastness of the Fabrick, which made it incommodious in respect of hearing; and especially the removing of that old Idolatrous Monument, which only was kept up in despite of the Zeal and Piety of their first Reformers. But the business was not carried so closely, as not to come unto the knowledge of the Crafts of the City, who, though they were all sufficiently Zealous in the cause of Religion, were not so mad as to deprive their City of so great an Ornament. And they agreed so well together, that when the Workman were beginning to assemble themselves to speed the business, they made a tumult, took up Arms, and resolutely swore, that whosoever pulled down the first stone, should be buried under it. The Work-men upon this are discharged by the Magistrates, and the people complained of to the King for the insurrections. The King upon the hearing of it, receives the actors in that business into his protection, allows the opposition they had made, and lays command upon the Ministers (who had appeared most eager in the prosecution) not to meddle any more in that business, or any other of that nature; adding withall, that too many Churches in that Kingdom were destroyed already, and that he would not tolerate any more abuses of such ill example.

40. The King for matter of his Book had been committed to the institution of *George Buchanan*, a most fiery and seditious *Calvinist*; to moderate whose heats, was added Mr. *Peter Young*, (father of the late Dean of *Winchester*) a more temperate and sober man, whom he very much esteemed, and honoured with Knighthood, and afterwards preferred to the Mastership of St. *Cross* in *England*. But he received his Principles for matter of State from such of his Council as were most tender of the publick interest of their Native Country. By whom, but most especially by the Earl of *Morton*, he was so well instructed, that he was able to distinguish between the Zeal of some in promoting the Reformed Religion, and the madness or follies of some others, who practised to introduce their innovation, under that pretence. Upon which grounds of State and Prudence, he gave order to the general Assembly, sitting at this time, not to make any alteration in the Polity of the Church, as then it stood, but to suffer things to continue in the state they were till the following Parliament, to the end that the determinations of the three Estates might not be any way prejudiced by their conclusions. But they neglecting the command, look back upon the late proceedings which were held at *Stirling*, where many of the most material points in the Book of Discipline were demurred upon. And thereupon it was ordained;

1580.

dained, that nothing should be altered in Form or Matter, which in that Book had been concluded by themselves. With which the King was so displeased, that from that time he gave less countenance to the Ministers then he had done formerly. And to the end that they might see what need they had of their Princes favour, he suffered divers sentences to be past at the Council Table, for the suspending of their Censures and Excommunications, when any matter of complaint was heard against them. But they go forwards howsoever, confirmed and animated by a Discourse of *Theodore Beza* which came out this year, entituled, *De Triplici Episcopatu.* In which he takes notice of three sorts of Bishops; *the Bishop of Divine Institution,* which he makes to be no other then the ordinary Minister of a particular Congregation; *the Bishop of humane Constitution,* that is to say, the President or Moderator in the Church-assemblies; and last of all, *the Devils Bishop,* such as were then placed in a perpetual Authority over a Diocess or Province in most parts of Christendome; under which last capacity they beheld their Bishops in the Kirk of *Scotland.* And in the next Assembly, held at *Dundee* in *July* following, it was concluded, *That the office of a Bishop, as it was then used and commonly taken in that Realm had neither foundation, ground, nor warrant in the holy Scriptures.* And thereupon it was decreed, *That all persons either called unto that Office, or which should hereafter be called unto it, should be required to renounce the same, as an Office unto which they are not warranted by the Word of God.* But because some more moderate men in the next Assembly held at *Glascow,* did raise a scruple touching that part of the Decree in which it was affirmed, *That the calling of Bishops was not warranted by the Word of God,* it was first declared by the Assembly, that they had no other meaning in that Expression, then *to condemn the estate of Bishops as they then stood in* Scotland. With which the said moderate men did not seem contented, but desired that the conclusion of the matter might be respited to another time, by reason of the inconvenience which might ensue. They are cryed down by all the rest with great heat and violence; insomuch, that it was proposed by one *Montgomery* Minister of *Stirling, that some Censure might be laid on those who had spoken in defence of that corrupted estate.* Nay, such was the extream hatred to that Sacred Function in the said Assembly at *Dundee,* that they stayed not here; They added to the former, a Decree more strange, inserting, *That they should desist and cease from Preaching, Ministring the Sacraments, or using in any sort the Office of a Pastor in the Church of Christ, till by some General Assembly they were* De Novo *Authorized and Admitted to it; no lower censure then that of Excommunication, if they did the contrary.* As for the Patrimony of the Church, which still remained in their hands, it was resolved that the next General Assembly should dispose thereof.

49. There hapned at this time an unexpected Revolution in the Court of *Scotland,* which possibly might animate them to these high presumptions. It had been the great Master-piece of the Earl of *Morton* in the time of his Regency, to fasten his dependance most specially on the Queen of *England*; without which he saw it was impossible to preserve the Kings Person, and maintain his Power against the practices and attempts of a prevalent Faction, which openly appeared in favour of his Mothers pretensions. And in this course he much desired to keep the

King,

King, when he had took the Government upon himself, as before was said, prevailing with him, much against the mind of most of the Lords, to send an Embassador for that purpose. Which put such fears and jealousies into the heads of the *French*, on whom the *Scots* had formerly depended upon all occasions, that they thought fit to countermine the English party in the Court, and so blow them up. No better Engine for this purpose then the Lord *Esme Stuart*, Seignieur of *Aulgny* in *France*, and Brothers Son to *Matthew* the late Earl of *Lenox* the Young Kings Grandfather. By him it was conceived that they might not only work the King to the party of *France*, but get some ground for re-establishing the old Religion, or at least to gain some countenance for the Favourers and Professors of it. With these Instructions he prepares to the Court of *Scotland*, makes himself known unto the King, and by the affability of his conversation wins so much upon him, that no Honour or Preferment was thought great enough for so dear a Kinsman. The Earldom of *Lenox* being devolved upon the King by the death of his Grandfather, was first conferred on *Robert* Bishop of *Orkney*, one of the Natural Sons of King *James* V. Which he, to gratifie the King, and oblige the Favorite, resigned again into his hands ; in recompence whereof, he is preferred unto the title of Earl of *March*. As soon as he had made this Resignation of the Earldom of *Lenox*, the King confers it presently on his Cosin *Aubigny*, who studied to appear more serviceable to him every day then other. And that his service might appear the more considerable, a report is cunningly spread abroad, that the Earl of *Morton* had a purpose to convey the King into *England*, by means whereof the *Scots* would forfeit all the Priviledges which they held in *France*. *Morton* sufficiently clear'd himself from any such practice. But howsoever, the suspition prevailed so far, that it was thought fit by those of the Adverse party to appoint a Lord-Chamberlain, who was to have the care of His Majesties Person ; and that a Guard of twenty four Noblemen should be assigned to the said Lord-Chamberlain for that end and purpose. Which Trust and Honor was immediately conferred on the Earl of *Lenox*, who had been sworn to the Council much about that time, and within less then two years after was created Duke.

  50. The sudden Preferments of this man, being well known to be a professed Votary of the Church of *Rome*, encouraged many Priests and Jesuits to repair into *Scotland* ; who were sufficiently practical in propagating the Opinions, and advancing the interest of that Church. Which gave occasion to the Brethren to exclaim against him, and many times to fall exceeding foul on the King himself. The King appears sollicitous for their satisfaction ; and deals so effectually with his Kinsman, that he was willing to receive instruction from some of their Ministers, by whom he is made a real Proselyte to the Religion then established ; which he declared, by making profession of his Faith in the great Church of *Edenborough*, and his diligent frequenting the Church at their Prayers and Sermons. But it hapned very unfortunately for him, that some Dispensations sent from *Rome* were intercepted, whereby the Catholicks were permitted to promise, swear, subscribe, and do what else should be required of them, if still they kept

1581.

their

their hearts, and secretly imployed their counsels for the Church of *Rome.* Against this blow the Gentleman could find no buckler, nor was there any ready way either to take off the suspicions, or to still the clamours which by the Presbyterian Brethren were raised against him. Their out-cries much encreased, by the severities then shewed to the Earl of *Morton,* whom they esteemed to be a most assured Friend (as indeed he was) to their Religion, though indeed in all points not corresponding with them to the Book of Discipline. For so it was, that to break off all hopes of fastning a dependance on the Realm of *England, Morton* was publickly accused at the Council Table for being privy to the Murther of His Majesties Father, committed to the Castle of *Edenborough* on the second of *January,* removed to *Dunbritton* on the twentieth: Where having remained above four Moneths, he was brought back to *Edenborough* in the end of *May,* condemned upon the first of *June,* and the next day executed: His capital Accuser being admitted to sit Judge upon him.

51. This news exceedingly perplexed the Queen of *England:* she had sent *Bows* and *Randolph* at several times to the King of *Scots,* who were to use their best endeavours as well to lessen the Kings favour to the Earl of *Lenox,* as to preserve the life of *Morton.* For the effecting of which last, a promise was made by *Randolph* unto some of his Friends, both of Men and Money. But as *Walsingham* sent word from *France,* she had not took the right course to effect her purpose. She had of late been negligent in paying those persons which had before confirmed the *Scots* to the *English* interest; which made them apt to tack about, and to apply themselves to those who would bid most for them. And yet the buness at the present was not gone so far, but that they might have easily been reduced unto her devotion, if we had now sent them ready money instead of promises; for want whereof, that Noble Gentleman, so cordially affected to Her Majesties service, was miserably cast away. Which quick advice, though it came over late to preserve his life, came time enough to put the Queen into a way for recovering Her Authority amongst the *Scots;* of which more hereafter. Nor were the Ministers less troubled at it then the Queen of *England,* imputing unto *Lenox* the contrivance of so sad a Tragedy. Somewhat before this time he had been taxed in the Pulpit by *Drury,* one of the Brethren of *Edenborough,* for his unsoundness in Religion, and all means used to make him odious with the people. For which committed by the Council to the Castle of *Edenborough,* he was, not long after, at the earnest intreaty of his Fellow Ministers, and some promise on his own part for his good behaviour, restored again unto his charge. But after *Mortons* death (some other occasions coming in) he breaks out again, and mightily exclaims against him; insomuch, that the King gave order to the Provost of *Edenborough* to see him removed out of the Town. The Magistrate advises him to leave the Town of his own accord: But he must first demand the pleasure of the Kirk, convened at the same time in an Assembly. Notwithstanding whose Mediation he was forced to leave the Town a little while, to which he was brought back in Triumph within few Moneths after. A Fast was also kept by order of the said Assembly: For the ground whereof they alledged, amongst other things, not onely the oppression

preffion

preſſion of the Church in general, but the danger wherein the Kings Perſon ſtood, by a company of wicked men, who laboured to corrupt him in Religion as well as manners.

52. But no man laid more haſtily about him, or came better off then *Walter Belcanqual*, another Preacher of that City. Who in a Sermon by him Preached, uſed ſome words to this purpoſe, *That within this four years Popery had entered into the Countrey and Court, and was maintained in the Kings Hall, by the Tyranny of a great Champion, who has called* Grace (which Adjunct they gave ordinarily to their Dukes in *Scotland*;) *but that if his Grace continued in oppoſing himſelf to God and his Word, he ſhould come to little Grace in the end.* The King at the firſt hearing of it, gives order to the General Aſſembly to proceed therein. Which being ſignified to *Belcanqual*, he is ſaid to have given thanks to God for theſe two things; firſt, *For that he was not accuſed for any thing done againſt his Majeſty and the Laws*: But principally, *Becauſe he perceived the Church had obtained ſome Victory*. And for the laſt he gave this reaſon, *That for ſome quarrel taken at a former Sermon, the Council had took upon them to be Judges of a Miniſters Doctrine; but now that he was ordered to appear before the Aſſembly, he would moſt joyfully ſubmit his Doctrine to a publick Tryal.* But thoſe of the Aſſembly ſending word to the King, that they could not warrantably proceed againſt him, without the buſineſs were proſecuted by ſome Accuſer, and made good by witneſſes; the King was forced, for fear of drawing any of his Servants into their diſpleaſures, to let fall the cauſe. But *Belcanquel* would not ſo give over: The Kings deſiſting from the proſecution would not ſerve his turn, unleſs he were abſolved alſo by the whole Aſſembly, who had been preſent at the Sermon. This was conceived to be moſt reaſonable and juſt; for having put it to the vote, his Doctrine was declared to be ſound and Orthodox, and that he had delivered nothing which might give juſt offence unto any perſon. The King begins to ſee by theſe particulars what he is truſt to. But they will preſently find out another expedient, as well for tryal of their own power, as his utmoſt patience.

53. A corrupt Contract had been made betwixt *Montgomery* before mentioned, and the Duke of *Lenox*; by which it was agreed, That *Montgomery* ſhould be advanced, by the Dukes Interceſſion, to the Archbiſhoprick of *Glaſco*; and that *Montgomery*, in requital of ſo great a favour, ſhould grant unto the Duke and his Heirs for ever, the whole Eſtate and Rents of the ſaid Archbiſhoprick, upon the yearly payments of one thouſand pound *Scotch*, with ſome Horſe, Corn and Poultry. No ſooner had the Kirk notice of this Tranſaction, but without taking notice of ſo baſe a Contract, they cenſured him for taking on him in the Epiſcopal Function. The King reſolves to juſtifie him in the Acceptation unleſs they could be able to charge him with unſoundneſs of Doctrine, or corruption of manners. Hereupon certain Articles are preferred againſt him; and amongſt others, it was charged, that he had ſaid, *The Diſcipline was a thing indifferent, and might ſtand the one way or the other; That to prove the lawfulneſs of Biſhops in the Church, he had uſed the Examples of* Ambroſe *and* Auguſtine: *That at another time, he called the Diſcipline, and the lawful Calling of the Church, the trieſles of Police: That he ſaid the Miniſters were captious, and men of curious brains: That he charged them with ſedition,*

1573.

sedition, and warned them not to meddle in the disposing of Crowns, and that if they did, they should be reproved: That he accused them of Pasquils, Lying, Backbiting, &c. *And finally, he denyed that any mention of Presbytery or Eldership was made in any part of the New Testament.* For which and other Errours of like nature in point of Doctrine, though none of them sufficiently proved when it came to tryal, it was resolved by the Assembly, that he should stand to his Ministry in the Church of *Stirling,* and meddle no further with the Bishoprick, under the pain of Excommunication. But not content with ordering him to give off the Bishoprick, they suspend him on another quarrel from the use of his Ministry. To neither of which sentences when he would submit, as being supported by the King on one side, and the Duke on the other, they cited him to appear before the Synod of *Lothian* to hear the sentence of Excommunication pronounced against him. This moved the King to interpose his Royal Authority, to warn the Synod to appear before him at the Court at *Stirling,* and in the mean time to desist from all further Process. *Pont* and some others make appearance in the name of the rest; but withal make this protestation, *That though they had appeared to testifie their obedience to his Majesties Warrant, yet they did not acknowledge the King and Council to be competent Judges in that matter; and therefore that nothing done at that time should either prejudge the Liberties of the Church, or the Laws of the Realm.* Which Protestation notwithstanding, they were inhibited by the Council from using any further proceedings against the man, and so departed for the present.

54. But the next general Assembly would not leave him so, but prosecute him with more heat then ever formerly; and were upon the point of passing their judgement on him, when they were required by a Letter Missive from the King, not to trouble him for any matter about the Bishoprick, or any other cause preceding, in regard the King resolved to have the business heard before himself. But *Melvin* hereupon replyed, *That they did not meddle with any thing belonging to the Civil Power; and that for matters Ecclesiastical, they had Authority enough to proceed against him, as being a Member of their Body.* The Master of the Requests, who had brought the Letter, perceiving by these words, that they meant to proceed in it, as they had begun, commanded a Messenger at Arms, whom he had brought along with him, to charge them to desist upon pain of Rebellion. This moves them as little as the Letter, and he is summoned peremptorily to appear next morning, that he might receive his sentence. Next morning he appears by his Procurator, and puts up an appeal from them to the King and Council; the rather, in regard that one who was his principal Accuser in the last Assembly, was now to sit amongst his Judges. But neither the Appeal it self, nor the Equity of it, could so far prevail, as to hinder them from passing presently to the Sentence; by which, upon the specification and recital of his several crimes, he was ordained to be deprived, and cast out of the Church. And now the courage of the man begins to fail him. He requires a present Conference with some of the Brethren, submits himself to the decrees of the assembly, and promiseth neither to meddle further with the Bishoprick, nor to exercise any Office in the Ministry, but as they should license him thereunto. But this inconstancie he makes worse, by another

as bad ; for finding the Kings countenance towards him to be very much changed, he resolves to hold the Bishoprick ; makes a journey to *Glasco*, and entering into the Church with a great train of Gentlemen which had attended him from the Court, he puts by the ordinary Preacher, and takes the Pulpit to himself. For this disturbance, the Presbytery of the Town send out Process against him, but are prohibited from proceeding by his Majesties Warrant, presented by the Mayor of *Glasco*. But when it was replyed by the Moderator, *That they would proceed in the cause notwithstanding this Warrant*, and that some other words were multiplyed upon that occasion ; the Provost pulled him out of his Chair, and committed him Prisoner to the *Tolebooth*. The next *Assembly* look on this action of the Provost as a foul indignity, and prosecute the whole matter unto such extremity, that notwithstanding the Kings intercession, and the advantage which he had against some of their number ; the Provost was decreed to be excommunicated ; and the Excommunication formerly decreed against *Montgomery*, was actually pronounced in the open Church.

55. The Duke of *Lenox* finds himself so much concerned in the business, that he could not support the man, who for his sake had been exposed to all these affronts ; he entertains him at his Table, and hears him Preach, without regard unto the Censures under which he lay. This gives the general Assembly a new displeasure. Their whole Authority seemed by these actions of the Duke to be little valued ; which rather then they would permit, they would proceed against him in the self-same manner. But first it was thought fit to send some of their Members, as well to intimate unto him that *Montgomery* was actually excommunicated ; as also to present the danger in which they stood by the Rules of the Discipline, who did converse with excommunicated persons, The Duke being no less moved then they, demanded in some choler, *Whether the King or Kirk had the Supreme Power* ; and therewith plainly told them, *That he was commanded by the King to entertain him, whose command he would not disobey for fear of their Censures*. Not satisfied with this defence, the Commissioners of the general Assembly presented it unto the King amongst other grievances ; to which it was answered by the King, that the Excommunication was illegal, and was declared to be so upon very good Reasons to the Lords of the Council ; and therefore that no manner of person was to be lyable to censure upon that account. The King was at this time at the Town of *Perth*, to which many of the Lords repaired, who had declared themselves in former times for the Faction of *England*, and were now put into good heart by supplies of money, (according unto *Walsinghams* counsel) which had been secretly sent unto them from the Queen. Much animated, or exasperated rather, by some Leading-men, who managed the Affairs of the late Assemblies, and spared not to inculcate to them the apparent dangers in which Religion stood by the open practices of the Duke of *Lenox*, and the Kings crossing with them upon all occasion. To which the Sermons of the last Fast did not add a little ; which was purposely indicted, as before was said, in regard of those oppressions which the Kirk was under ; but more, because of the great danger which the company of wicked persons might bring to the King ; whom they endeavoured to corrupt both in

Religion

Religion and Manners. All which inducements coming together, produced a resolution of getting the King into their power, forcing the Duke of *Lenox* to retire into *France*, and altering the whole Government of the Kingdom as themselves best pleased.

56. But first, the Duke of *Lenox* must be sent out of the way. And to effect this, they advised him to go to *Edenborough*, and to erect there the Lord Chamberlains Court, for the reviving of the ancient Jurisdiction which belonged to his Office. He had not long been gone from *Perth*, when the King was solemnly invited to the House of *William* Lord *Ruthen* (not long before made Earl of *Gowry*) where he was liberally feasted: but being ready to depart, he was stayed by the eldest Son of the Lord *Glammis*, (the Master of *Glammis*, he is called, in the Scottish Dialect) and he was stayed in such a manner, that he perceived himself to be under a custody. The apprehensions whereof, when it drew some tears from him, it moved no more compassion nor respect from the froward *Scots*, *but that it was fitter for boys to shed tears then bearded Men.* This was the great work of the 23 day of *August*; to which concurred at the first, to avoid suspition, no more of the Nobility but the Earls of *Marre* and *Gowry*, the Lords *Boyd* and *Landsay*, and to the number of ten more of the better sort; but afterwards the Act was owned over all the Nation, not onely by the whole Kirk party, but even by those two were of contrary Faction to the Duke of *Lenox*, who was chiefly aimed at. The Duke, upon the first advertisement of this surprize, dispatched some men of Noble Quality to the King, to know in what condition he was, whether free or captive. The King returned word that he was a captive, and willed him to raise what force he could to redeem him thence. The Lords on the other side declared, That they would not suffer him to be misled by the Duke of *Lenox*, to the oppression of Himself, the Church, and the whole Realm; and therefore the Duke might do well to retire into *France*, or otherwise they would call him to a sad account for his former actions. And this being done, they caused the King to issue out a Proclamation on the 28. In which it was declared, *That he remained in that place of his own free-will: That the Nobility then present had done nothing which they were not in duty obliged to do: That he took their repairing to him for a service acceptable to himself, and profitable to the Commonwealth: That therefore all manner of persons whatsoever which had levied any Forces, under colour of his present restraint, should disband them within six hours, under pain of Treason.* But more particularly, they cause him to write a Letter to the Duke of *Lenox* (whom they understood to be grown considerably strong for some present action) by which he was commanded to depart the Kingdom, before the 20 of *September* then next following. On the receipt whereof, he withdraws himself to the strong Castle of *Dunbritton*, that there he might remain in safety whilst he staid in *Scotland*, and from thence pass safely into *France* whensoever he pleased.

57. The news of this Surprize is posted with all speed to *England*: And presently the Queen sends her Embassadors to the King, by whom he was advertised to restore the Earl of *Angus*, who had lived an exile in *England* since the death of *Morton*, to his Grace and Favour; but most especially, that in regard of the danger he was fallen into by the perverse

verse counsels of the Duke of *L nox*, he would interpret favourably whatsoever had been done by the Lords which were then about him. The King was able to discern, by the drift of this Embassie, that the Queen was privy to the practice ; and that the Embassadors were sent thither rather to animate and encourage the Conspirators, then advise with him. But not being willing at that time to displease either her or them, he absolutely consents to the restoring of the Earl of *Angus* ; and to the rest gave such a general answer, as gave some hope, that he was not so incensed by this Surprize of his person, but that his displeasure might be mitigated on their good behaviour.   And that the Queen of *Scots* also had the same apprehensions concerning the encouragement which they had from the Queen of *England*, appears by her Letter to that Queen, bearing date at *Sheffield*, on the 8 of *November*. In which she intimates unto Her, *That She was bound in Religion, Duty and Justice, not to help forwards their Designs, who secretly conspire His ruine and Hers, both in* Scotl. *and* Eng. And thereupon did earnestly perswade her, by their near Alliance, *to be careful of her Sons welfare, not to intermeddle any further with the affairs of* Scotland, *without her privity or the French Kings ; and to hold them for no other then Traytors, who dealt so with Him at their pleasures.* But as Q. *Eliz.* was not moved with her complaints, to recede from the business, so the Conspirators were resolved to pursue their advantage. They knew on what terms the King stood with the people of *Edenborough*, or might have known it, if they did not, by their Triumphant bringing back of *Dury* their excluded Minister, as soon as they heard the first news of the Kings Restraint. In confidence whereof, they bring him unto *Halyrood-* House on the 8 of *October* : the rather, in regard they understood, that the General Assembly of the Kirk was to be held in that Town on the next day after : of whose good inclinations to them, they were nothing doubtful, nor was there reason why they should.

58. For having made a Formal Declaration to them, concerning the necessity of their repair unto the King, to the end they might take him out of the hands of his *Evil Counsellors*, they desired the said Assembly to deliver their opinion in it.   And they, good men, pretending to do *all things in the fear of God, and after mature deliberation* (as the act importeth) first *justifie them* in that horrid Enterprize, *to have done good and acceptable service to God, their Soveraign, and their Native Countrey.* And that being done, they gave order, *That all Ministers should publickly declare to their several flocks, as well the danger into which they were brought, as the deliverance which was effected for them by those Noble Persons ; with whom they were exhorted to unite themselves, for the further deliverance of the Kirk, and perfect Reformation of the Commonwealth.* Thus the Assembly leads the way and the Convention of Estates follows shortly after.   By which it was declared, in favour of the said Conspirators, *That in their repairing to the King the Three and twentieth of* August *last, and abiding with him since that time, and whatsoever they had done in pursuance of it, they had done good, thankful and necessary service to the King and Country ; and therefore they are to be exonerated of all actions Civil or Criminal that might be intended against them, or any of them in that respect, inhibiting thereby all the Subjects to speak or utter any thing to the contrary, under the pain to be esteemed Calumniators and Dispersers of false Rumors, and to be punished for the same accord-ingly.*

ingly. The Duke perceives by these proceedings, how that cold Country, even in the coldest time of the year, would be too hot for him to continue any longer in it ; and having wearied himself with an expectation of some better fortune, is forced at last on the latter end of *December* to put into *Berwick*, from whence he passeth to the Court of *England*, and from thence to *France*, never returning more unto his Natural, but Ingrateful Countrey. The Duke had hardly left the Kingdom, when two Embassadors came from *France* to attone the differences, to mediate for the Kings deliverance, and to sollicite that the Queen (whose liberty had been negotiated with the Queen of *England* might be made Co-partner with Her Son in the Publick Government. Which last was so displeasing to some zealous Ministers, that they railed against them in their Pulpits, calling them Embassadors of that bloody Murtherer the Duke of *Guise* ; and foolishly exclaiming, that the White-Cross which one of them wore upon his shoulders (as being a Knight of the Order of the Holy Ghost) was a Badge of Antichrist. The King gives order to the Provost and other Magistrates of the City of *Edenborough*, that the Embassadors should be feasted at their going away ; and care is taken in providing all things necessary for the entertainment. But the good Brethren of the Kirk, in further manifestation of their peevish Follies, Indict a Fast upon that day, take up the people in their long-winded Exercises from the morning till night, rail all the while on the Embassadors ; and with much difficulty, are disswaded from Excommunicating both the Magistrates, and the Guests to boot.

1583.   **59.** The time of the Kings deliverance drew on apace, sooner then was expected by any of those who had the custody of his person. Being permitted to retire with his Guards to *Falkland*, that he might recreate himself in Hunting, which he much affected, he obtained leave to bestow a visit on his Uncle the Earl of *March*, who then lay in St. *Andrews*, not far off. And after he had taken some refreshment with him, he procures leave to see the Castle : Into which he was no sooner entred, but Col. *Stewart* the Captain of his Guard (to whom alone he had communicated his design) makes fast the gates against the rest ; and from thence makes it known to all good Subjects, that they should repair unto the King, who by Gods great mercy had escaped from the hands of his enemies. This news brings thither on the next morning the Earls of *Arguile, Marshal, Montross* and *Rothess* : and they drew after them, by their example, such a general concourse, that the King finds himself of sufficient strength to return to *Edenborough* ; and from thence, having shewed himself to be in his former liberty, he goes back to *Perth.* Where first by Proclamation, he declares the late restraint of his Person to be a most treasonable act : but then withall, to manifest his great affection to the peace of his Kingdom, he gives a Free and General Pardon to all men whatsoever which had acted in it ; provided that they seek it of him, and carry themselves for the time coming like obedient subjects. The Kings escape was made in the end of *June* ; and in *December* following, he calls a Convention of the Estates, in which the subject of his Proclamation was approved and verified, the fact declared to be *Crimen laesa Majestatis*, or Treason in the highest degree. For

which

which, as ſome were executed, and others fled ; ſo divers of the Miniſters that had been dealers in that matter, pretending they were perſecuted, had retired into *England*. For notwithſtanding his Majeſties great clemency in pardoning the Conſpirators on ſuch eaſie conditions, they preferred rather the purſuing of their wicked purpoſes, then the enjoying of a peaceable and quiet life. For whether it were that they preſumed on ſupplies from *England*, of which they had received no improbable hopes, as afterwards was confeſſed by the Earl of *Gowry*; or that they built upon the Kirk Faction to come in to aid them, as the General Aſſembly had required ; they begin in all places to prepare for ſome new Commotion ; but being deceived in all their hopes and expectations, they were confined to ſeveral Priſons, before the Convention of Eſtates ; and after it, upon a further diſcovery of their preparations and intentions, compelled to quit the Kingdom, and betake themſelves for their protection unto ſeveral Nations. Only the Earl of *Gowry* ſtaid behind the reſt, and he paid well for it. For being ſuſpected to be hammering ſome new deſign, he was took Priſoner at *Dundee* in the *April* following, 1584, thence brought to *Edenborough*, and there condemned and executed, as he had deſerved.

In the mean time the Kirk-men were as troubleſome as the Lay-Conſpirators. *Drury*, ſo often mentioned, in a Sermon at *Edenborough*, had juſtified the fact at *Ruthen* ; for which being cited to appear before the Lords of the Council, he ſtood in maintainance of that which he had delivered; but afterwards ſubmitting himſelf unto the King on more ſober thoughts, he was kept upon his good behaviour, without further puniſhment. But *Andrew Melvin* was a man of another metal ; who being commanded to attend their Lordſhips for the like offence, declined the judgement of the King and Council, as having no cognizance of the cauſe. To make which good, he broached this Preſbyterian Doctrine, *That whatſoever was ſpoken in the Pulpit, ought firſt to be tryed by the Presbyterie ; and that neither the King nor Council were to meddle with it, though the ſame were treaſonable, till the Presbyterie had firſt taken notice of it.* But finding that the King and Council did reſolve to proceed, and had entred upon examination of ſome Witneſſes which were brought againſt him, he told the King (whether with greater Confidence or Impudence is hard to ſay) *That he preached the Laws both of God and man.* For which undutiful Expreſſion, he was commanded Priſoner to the Caſtle of *Blackneſs*. Inſtead whereof, he takes Sanctuary in the Town of *Berwick*, where he remained till way was made for his return ; the Pulpits in the mean time ſounding nothing, but *that the Light of the Country for Learning and Piety, was forced for ſafety of his life to forſake the Kingdom.* In which Exile he was followed within few moneths after by *Palvart* Sub-Dean of *Glaſco*, *Galloway*, and *Carmichiel*, two inferiour Miniſters ; who being warned to tender their appearance to the King and Council and not appearing at the time, were thereupon pronounced Rebels, and fled after the other. Nor was the General Aſſembly held at *Edenborough* of a better temper then theſe Preachers were, in which thr Declaration made at the laſt Convention of Eſtates, was ſtoutly croſſed and encountred. The King, with the advice of his Eſtates, had reſolved the Fact of ſurprizing His Majeſties perſon to be treaſonable. But the Bre-

thren

thren in the ſaid Aſſembly *did not only authorize and avow the ſame, but alſo(eſteeming their own judgement to be the Soveraign judgement of the Realm) did ordain all them to be excommunicated that would ſubſcribe unto their opinion.*

61. The King perceiving that there was no other way to deal with theſe men, then to husband the preſent opportunity to his beſt advantage, reſolved to proceed againſt them in ſuch a way, as might diſable them from committing the like inſolencies for the time to come. The chief Incendiaries had been forced to quit the Kingdom, or otherwiſe deſerted it of their own accords, the better to eſcape the puniſhment which their crimes had merited. The great Lords, on whoſe ſtrength they had moſt preſumed, were either under the like exile in the neighbouring Countries, or elſe ſo weakned and diſanimated, that they durſt not ſtir. So that the King being clearly Maſter of the Field, his Counſellors in good heart, and generally the Lords and Commons in good terms of obedience, it was thought fit to call a Parliament, and therein to enact ſuch Laws, by which the honour of Religion, the perſonal ſafety of the King, the peace and happineſs of the Kingdom, and the proſperity of the Church might be made ſecure. In which Parliament it was enacted amongſt other things, (the better to encounter the proceedings of the Kirk, and moſt Zealous Kirkmen) *That none of his Highneſs Subjects in time coming, ſhould preſume to take upon them by word or writing, to juſtifie the late treaſonable attempt at* Ruthen; *or to keep in Regiſter or ſtore any Books approving the ſame in any ſort.* And in regard the Kirk had ſo abuſed his Majeſties goodneſs, by which their Presbyterial Seſſions, the general Aſſemblies, and other meetings of the Kirk, were rather connived at then allowed; an Act was made to regulate and reſtrain them for the times enſuing: for by that Act it was ordained, *That from thenceforth none ſhould preſume or take upon them to Convocate, Convene, or aſſemble themſelves together for holding of Councils, Conventions, or Aſſemblies; to treat, conſult, or determine in any matters of Eſtate, Civil or Eccleſiaſtical, (excepting the ordinary judgements) without the Kings ſpecial commandment.*

62. In the next place, the Kings lawful Authority in cauſes Eccleſiaſtical, ſo often before impugned, was approved and confirmed; and it was made treaſon for any man to refuſe to anſwer before the King, though it were concerning any matter which was Eccleſiaſtical. The third Eſtate of Parliament (that is, the Biſhops) were reſtored to the ancient dignity; and it was made treaſon for any man, after that time, to procure the innovation or diminution of the Power and Authority of any of the three Eſtates. *And for as much as through the wicked, licentious, publick and private Speeches, and untrue calumnies of divers his Highneſs ſubjects* (I ſpeak the very words of the Act) *to the diſdain, contempt, and reproach of his Majeſty, his Council and proceedings; ſtirring up his Highneſs ſubjects thereby to miſliking, ſedition, unquietneſs; to caſt off their due obedience to his Majeſty: Therefore it is ordained, that none of his ſubjects ſhall preſume or take upon them privately or publickly, in Sermons, Declarations, or familiar Conferences, to utter any falſe, ſcandalous, and untrue Speeches, to the diſdain, reproach and contempt of his Majeſty, his Council, and proceedings; or to meddle in the affairs of his Highneſs, under pain of treaſon.* And laſtly, an Act was

paſs'd

pafs'd for calling in of *Buchanans* Hiftory , that Mafter-piece of Sedition, intituled, *De jure Regni apud Scotos* ; and that moft infamous libel, which he called *The Detection* : by which laft Acts his Majefty did not onely take care for preventing the like fcandalous and feditious practices for the time to come, but fatisfied himfelf by taking fome revenge upon them in the times foregoing.

63. The Minifters could not want intelligence of particulars before they were paffed into Acts. And now or never was the time to beftir themfelves, when their dear *Helena* was in fuch apparent danger to be ravifhed from them. And firft, it was thought neceffary to fend one of their number to the King, to mediate either for the total difmiffing of the *Bills* prepared, or the fufpending of them at the leaft for a longer time ; not doubting, if they gained the laft, but that the firft would eafily follow of it felf. On this Errand they imploy Mr. *David Landfay*, Minifter of the Church of *Leith* ; a man more moderate then the reft, and therefore more efteemed by the King then any other of that body. And how far he might have prevailed, it is hard to fay: But Captain *James Stewart* (commonly called the Earl of *Arran*) who then governed the Affairs of that Kingdom , having notice of it, caufed him to be arrefted, under colour of maintaining intelligence with the Fugitive Minifters in *England* ; imprifoned him for one night in *Edenborough*, and fends him the next day to the Caftle of *Blacknefs*, where he remained almoft a year. Upon the news of his commitment , *Lawfon* and *Belcanqual*, two of the Minifters of *Edenborough* , forfake their Churches, and joyn themfelves unto their Brethren in *England* ; firft leaving a Manifeft behind them , in which they publifhed the Reafons of their fudden departure. *John Dury*, fo often before mentioned, had lately been confined at *Montrofs* ; fo that no Preacher was now left in *Edenborough*, or the Port adjoyning , to intercede for themfelves and the Kirk in that prefent exigent. By means whereof the Acts were paffed without interruption. But when they were to be proclamed , as the cuftom is , Mr *Robert Pont* , Minifter of Saint *Cutberts*, and one of the Senators of the Colledge of Juftice , (for the good Minifters might act in Civil Matters, though the Bifhops might not) took Inftruments in the hands of a publick Notary , and openly protefted againft thofe Acts, n.ver agreed to by the Kirk ; and therefore that neither the Kirk, nor any of the Kirk-men, were obliged to be obedient to them. Which having done, he fled alfo into *England* to the reft of his Brethren ; and being proclaimed Rebel loft his place in the Seffions.

64. The flying of fo many Minifters , and the noife they made in *England* againft thofe Acts, encreafed a fcandalous opinion which themfelves had raifed, of the Kings being inclined to Popery: and it began to be fo generally believed , that the King found himfelf under a neceffity of rectifying his reputation in the eye of the World by a publick *Manifeft*. In which he certified as well to his good fubjects, as to all others whatfoever whom it might concern, as well the juft occafion which had moved him to pafs thofe Acts , as the great Equity and Reafon which appeared in them. And amongft thefe occafions , he reckoneth the juftifying of the fact at *Ruthen* by the publick fuffrage of the Kirk ; *Melvins* declining of the judgment of the King and Council; the Fact indicted

at the entertainment of the *French* Embassadors; their frequent general Fast, proclaimed and kept in all parts of the Realm by their Authority, without his privity and consent; the usurping of the Ecclesiastical jurisdiction by a certain number of Ministers, and unqualified Gentlemen, in the Presbyteries and Assemblies; the alteration of the Laws, and making new ones at their pleasure, which must bind the Subject; the drawing to themselves of all such causes, though properly belonging to the Courts of Justice, in which was any mixture of scandal: On which account they forced all those also to submit to the Churches Censures, who had been accused in those Courts, for Murther, Theft, or any like enormous crimes, though the party either were absolved by the Court it self, or pardoned by the King after condemnation. But all this could not stop the Mouths, and much less stay the Pens of that Waspish Sect; some flying out against the King in their scurrilous Libells, bald Pamphlets, and defamatory Rythmes; others with no less violence inveighing against him in their Pulpits, but most especially in *England*, where they were out of the Kings reach, and consequently might rail on without fear of punishment. By them it was given out, to render the King odious both at home and abroad; That the King endeavoured to extinguish the light of the Gospel, and to that end had caused those Acts to pass against it: That he had left nothing of the whole ancient Form of Justice and Polity in the Spiritual Estate, but a naked shadow: That Popery was immediately to be established, if God and all good men came not in to help them: That for opposing these impieties, they had been forced to flee their Countrey, and sing the Lords Song in a strange Land; with many other reproachful and calumnious passages of like odious nature.

65. But *losers may have leave to talk*, as the saying is; and by this barking they declared sufficiently that they could not *bite*. I have now brought the *Presbyterians* to their lowest fall; but we shall see them very shortly in their resurrections. In the mean time it will be seasonable to pass into *England*, that we may see how things were carried by their Brethren there, till we have brought them also to this point of time, and then we shall unite them all together in the course of their story.

The End of the Fifth Book

AERIUS REDIVIVUS:
OR THE
HISTORY
OF THE
Presbyterians.

LIB. VI.

Containing

The beginning, progress and proceedings of the Puritan Faction *in the Realm of* England*, in reference to their Innovations both in Doctrines and Forms of Worship; their Opposition to the Church, and the Rules thereof; from the beginning of the Reign of King* Edward *VI.* 1548, *to the Fifteenth year of Queen* Elizabeth, *Anno* 1572.

He Reformation of the Church of *England* was put into so good a way by King *Henry* the Eighth, that it was no hard matter to proceed upon his beginnings. He had once declared himself so much in favour of the Church of *Rome,* by writing against *Martin Luther,* that he was honored with the Title of *Defensor Fidei* (or the *Defender of the Faith*) by Pope *Leo* X. Which Title he afterwards united by Act of Parliament to the Crown of this Realm, not many years before his death. But a breach hapning betwixt him and Pope *Clement* VII.
concerning

I.

concerning his deſired Divorce, he firſt prohibits all appeals and other occaſions of reſort to the See of *Rome*; procures himſelf to be acknowledged by the Prelates and Clergy in their Convocation, for *Supream Head* on Earth of the Church of *England*; obtained a promiſe of them *in verbo Sacerdotii* (which was then equal to an Oath) neither to make, promulge, nor execute any Eccleſiaſtical conſtitutions, but as they ſhould be authorized thereunto by his Letters Patents; and then proceeds unto an Act for extinguiſhing the uſurped Authority of the Biſhop of *Rome*. But knowing what a ſtrong party the Pope had in *England*, by reaſon of that huge multitudes of Monks and Fryers which depended on him, he firſt diſſolves all Monaſteries and Religious Houſes, which were not able to diſpend three hundred Marks of yearly Rent; and after draws in all the reſt upon Surrendries, Reſignations, or ſome other Practices. And having brought to work ſo far, he cauſed the Bible to be publiſhed in the Engliſh Tongue, indulged the private reading of it to all perſons of quality, and to ſuch others alſo as were of known judgement and diſcretion; commanded the Epiſtles and Goſpels, the Lords Prayer, the Creed, and the Ten Commandments, to be rehearſed openly to the people on every Sunday and Holy Day in the *Engliſh* Tongue; and ordered the Litany alſo to be read in *Engliſh* upon *Wedneſdays* and *Fridays*. He had cauſed moreover many rich Shrines and Images to be defaced, ſuch as had moſt notoriouſly been abuſed by Oblations, Pilgrimages, and other the like acts of Idolatrous Worſhip; and was upon the point alſo to aboliſh the Maſs it ſelf, concerning which he had ſome ſecret communication with the *French* Embaſſador, if *Fox* ſpeak him rightly.

2. But what he did not live to do, and perhaps never would have done, had he lived much longer, was brought to paſs in the next Reign of King *Edward* VI. In the beginning whereof, by the Authority of the Lord Protector, the diligence of Archbiſhop *Cranmer*, and the endeavours of many other learned and Religious men, a Book of *Homilies* was ſet out to inſtruct the people; Injunctions publiſhed for the removing of all Images formerly abuſed to Superſtition, or falſe and counterfeit in themſelves. A Statute paſt in Parliament for receiving the Sacrament in both kinds, and order given to the Archbiſhop of *Canterbury*, and ſome other Prelates, to draw a Form for the Adminiſtration of it accordingly, to the honour of God, and the moſt Edification of all good people. The news whereof no ſooner came unto *Geneva*, but *Calvin* muſt put in for a ſhare; and forthwith writes his Letters to Archbiſhop *Cranmer*, in which he offereth his aſſiſtance to promote the ſervice, if he thought it neceſſary. But neither *Cranmer*, *Ridley*, nor any of the reſt of the *Engliſh* Biſhops could ſee any ſuch neceſſity of it, but that they might be able to do well without him. They knew the temper of the man, how buſie & pragmatical he had been in all thoſe places in which he had been ſuffered to intermeddle; that in ſome points of Chriſtian Doctrine he differed from the general current of the Ancient Fathers; and had deviſed ſuch a way of Eccleſiaſtical Polity, as was deſtructive in it ſelf to the Sacred Hierarchy, and never had been heard of in all Antiquity. But becauſe they would give him no offence, it was reſolved to carry on the work by none but *Engliſh* hands, till they had perfected the compoſing of the Publick Liturgy, with all the Rites and Ceremonies in the ſame contained.

And

And that being done, it was conceived not to be improper if they made use of certain learned men of the Protestant Churches for reading the Divinity-Lectures, and moderating Disputations in both Universities ; to the end that the younger Students might be trained up in sound Orthodox Doctrine. On which account they invited *Martin Bucer* and *Peter Martyr*, two men of eminent parts and learning, to come over to them ; the one of which they disposed in *Oxon*, and the other at *Cambridge*. This might have troubled *Calvin* more then his own repulse, but that he thought himself sufficiently assured of *Peter Martyr*, who by reason of his long living amongst the *Switzers*, and his near Neighbourhood to *Geneva*, might possibly be governed by his Directions. But because *Bucer* had no such dependence on him, and had withal been very much conversant in the *Lutheran* Churches, keeping himself in all his Reformations in a moderate course : he practiseth to gain him also, or at least to put him into such a way as might come nearest to his own. Upon which grounds he posts away his Letters to him, congratulates his invitation into *England* : but above all, adviseth him to have a care that he endeavoured not there, as in other places, either to be the Author or Approver of such moderate counsels, by which the parties might be brought to a Reconcilement,

3. For the satisfaction of these strangers, but the last especially, the Liturgie is translated into Latine by *Alexander Alesius*, a right Learned *Scot*. A Copy of whose Translation, or the sum thereof, being sent to *Calvin*, administred no small matter of offence unto him ; not so much because any thing in it could be judged offensive, but because it so much differed from those of his own conception. The people of *England* had received it as an heavenly treasure sent down by Gods great mercy to them ; all moderate men beyond the Seas applauded the felicity of the Church of *England*, in fashioning such an excellent Form of Gods Publick Worship ; and by the Act of Parliament which confirmed the same, it was declared to have been done *by the special aid of the Holy Ghost*. But *Calvin* was resolved to think otherwise of it, declaring his dislike thereof in a long letter written to the Lord Protector : In which he excepteth more particularly against Commemoration of the dead (which he acknowledgeth notwithstanding to be very ancient ;) as also against *Chrism*, or Oyl in Baptism, and the Form of Visiting the sick : and then adviseth, that as well these, as all the rest of the Rites and Ceremonies, be cut off at once. And that this grave advice might not prove unwelcome, he gives us such a Rule or Reason, as afterwards raised more trouble to the Church of *England* then his bare advice. His Rule is this, *That in carrying on the work of a Reformation, there is not any thing to be exacted, which is not warranted and required by the Word of God : That in such cases there is no Rule left for worldly wisdom, for moderation and compliance : but all things to be ordered as they are directed by his will revealed.* What use his Followers made of their Masters Rule, in crying down the Rites and Ceremonies of this Church (as *Superstitious, Antichristian*, and what else they pleased) because not found expresly and particularly in the Holy Scriptures, we shall see hereafter.

In the mean time, we must behold him in his Applications to the King and Council, his tampering with Archb. *Cranmer*, his practising on men

of

of all conditions to encrease his party. For finding little benefit to redound unto him by his Letter to the Lord Protector, he sets upon the King himself; and tells him plainly, that there were many things amiss which required Reformation. In his Letters unto the King and Council, as he writes to *Bullinger*, he had excited them to proceed in the good work which they had begun; that is to say, that they should so proceed as he had directed. With *Cranmer* he is more particular, and tells him in plain terms, *That in the Liturgie of this Church, as then it stood, there remained a whole mass of Popery, which did not only blemish, but destroy Gods Publick Worship.* But fearing he might not edifie with the Godly King, assisted by so wise a Council, and such Learned Prelates, he hath his Emissaries in the Court, and amongst the Clergie; his Agents in the City and Country, his Intelligencers (one Monsieur *Nicholas* amongst the rest) in the University. All of them active and industrious to advance his purposes, but none more mischievously practical then *John Alasco*, a *Polonian* born, but a profest *Calvinian* both in Doctrine and Forms of Worship; who coming out of *Poland* with a mixed Congregation; under pretence of being forced to fly their Countrey for professing the Reformed Religion, were gratified with the Church of *Augustine*-Fryers in *London* for their publick use; and therein suffered to enjoy their own way, both in Worship and Government, though in both exceeding different from the Rules of this Church. In many Churches of this Realm the Altars were left standing as in former times, and in the rest the holy Table was placed Altar-wise at the East-end of the Quire. But by his party in the Court, he procures an Order from the Lords of the Council, for causing the said Table to be removed, and to be placed in the middle of the Church or Chancel, like a common Table. It was the usage of this Church to give the holy Sacrament unto none but such as kneeled at the participation, according to the pious order of the primitive times. But *John Alasco* coming out of *Poland*, where the *Arrians* (who deny the Divinity of Christ our Saviour) had introduced the use of sitting, brought that irreverend custom into *England* with him. And not content with giving scandal to this Church by the use thereof in his own Congregation, he publisheth a Pamphlet in defence of that irreverend and sawcy gesture, because most proper for a Supper. The Liturgie had appointed several Offices for many of the Festivals observed in the most regular times of Christianity: Some of the Clergy in the Convocation must be set on work to question the conveniency, if not the lawfulness of those observations, considering that all days are alike, and therefore to be equally regarded in a Church Reformed. And some there were which raised a scruple touching the words which were prescribed to be used in the delivery of the Bread and Wine to the Congregation

5. Not to proceed to more particulars, let it suffice that these Emissaries did so ply their work, by the continual solliciting of the King, the Council, and the Convocation, that at the last the Book was brought to a review. The product or result whereof was the second Liturgie, confirmed in Parliament *Anno* 5, 6 *Edw.* 6. By the tenour of which Act it may appear, first, that there was nothing contained in the said Book, but *what was agreeable to the Word of God, and the Primitive Church, very*

com-

comfortable to all good people desiring to live in Christian conversation, and most profitable to the Estate of this Realm. And secondly, That such doubts as had been raised in the use and exercise thereof, proceeded rather from the curiosity of the Minister and Mistakers, then of any other worthy cause. And thereupon we may conclude, that the first Liturgie was discontinued, and the second superinduced upon it after this review, to give satisfaction unto *Calvins* Cavils, the curiosities of some, and the mistakes of others of his Friends and Followers. But yet this would not serve the turn ; they must have all things modelled by the Form of *Geneva*, or else no quiet to be had : Which since they could not gain in *England*, in the Reign of King *Edward* (who did not long outlive the setling of the second Liturgie) they are resolved more eagerly to pursue the project in a forein Country, during their exile and affliction in the Reign of Queen *Mary*. Such of the English as retired to *Embden*, *Strasburg*, *Basil*, or any other of the Free and Imperial Cities, observed no Form of Worship in their Publick Meetings, but this second Liturgie. In contrary whereof, such as approved not of that Liturgy when they were in *England*, united themselves into a Church or Congregation in the City of *Frankfort*, where they set up a mixt Form of their own devising, but such as carried some resemblance to the Book of *England*. *Whittingham* was the first who took upon himself the charge of this Congregation ; which after he resigned to *Knox*, as the fitter man to carry on the work intended, who having retired to *Geneva* on the death of King *Edward*, and from thence published some tedeous Pamphlets against the Regiment of Women, and otherwise defamatory of the Emperour and the Queen of *England*, was grown exceeding dear to *Calvin* and the rest of that Consistory. By his indeavours, and the forwardness of too many of the Congregation, that little which was used of the English Liturgy was quite laid aside, and all things brought more near the Order which he found at *Geneva* ; though so much differing from that also, as to intitle *Knox* for the Author of it.

6. The noise of this great Innovation brings *Gryndal* and *Chambers* from the Church of *Strasburg* to set matters right. By whom it was purposed, that the *substance* of the English Book being still retained, there might be a forbearance of some Ceremonies and Offices in it. But *Knox* and *Whittingham* were as much bent against the substance of the Book, as against any of the Circumstantials and Extrinsecals which belonged unto it. So that no good effect following on this interposition, the Agents of the Church of *Strasburg* return back to their brethren, who by their Letters of the 13 of *December* expostulate in vain about it. To put an end to these Disputes, no better way could be devised by *Knox* and *Whittingham*, then to require the countenance of *Calvin*, which they thought would carry it. To him they send an Abstract of the Book of *England*, that by his positive and determinate Sentence (which they presumed would be in favour of his own) it might stand or fall. And he returns this Answer to them. (a) *That in the Book of* England, *as by them described, he had observed many* tolerable Fooleries ; *that though there was no manifest impiety, yet it wanted much of that purity which was to be desired in it ; and that it contained many Reliques of the dregs of Popery : and finally, that though it was lawful to begin with such beggerly Rudiments, yet it be-*

howed

(a) *In Liturgia Anglicana qualem mihi describitis, multos video tolerabiles ineptias.*

hoved the Learned, Godly and Grave Miniſters of Chriſt, to ſet forth ſome-
thing more refined from Filth and Ruſtineſs. Which letter ſee at large in
the firſt Book of this Hiſtory, Numb. 17. This Anſwer ſo prevailed
upon all his Followers, that they who ſometimes had approved, did
now as much diſlike the Engliſh Liturgie ; and thoſe who at firſt had conceived a diſlike thereof, did afterwards grow into an open deteſtation
of it.   In which condition of Affairs. Dr. Richard Cox, Dr. Horne, and
others of great Note and Quality, put themſelves alſo into Frankfort,
where they found all things contrary to their expectation. Cox had been
Almoner to King Edward VI, Chancellor of the Univerſity of Oxon,
Dean of Weſtminſter, one that had a chief hand in compoſing the Engliſh Liturgie ; which made him very impatient of ſuch Innovations, a-
mounting to no leſs then a total rejection of it, as he found amongſt
them.   By his Authority and appointment the Engliſh Litany is firſt
read, and afterwards the whole Book reduced into uſe and practice.
Againſt which when Knox began to rail in a publick Sermon, (according to his wonted cuſtom) he is accuſed by Cox to the Senate of Frankfort for his defamatory writings againſt the Emperour and the Queen of
England.   Upon the news whereof, Knox forſakes the Town, retires
himſelf unto his Sanctuary at Geneva, and thither he is followed by a
great part of his Congregation, who made foul work in England at
their coming home.

   7. But this about the Liturgy, though it was the greateſt, was not the
onely quarrel which was raiſed by the Zuinglian or Calvinian Zealots.
The Church preſcribed the uſe of Surplices in all Sacred Offices, and
Coapes in the officiating at the holy Altar.   It preſcribed alſo a diſtinct
habit in the Clergy from the reſt of the people ; Rochets and Chimeres
for the B.ſhops ; Gowns, Tippets, and Canonical Coats for the reſt of the
Clergy ; the ſquare Cap for all.   Their oppoſition in the uſe of the Surplice much confirmed and countenanced, as well by the writings, as
the practice of Peter Martyr ; who kept a conſtant intercourſe with Calvin at his being here.   For in his Writings he declared to a Friend of
his, (who required his judgement in the caſe) that ſuch Veſtments being in themſelves indifferent, could make no man godly or ungodly,
either by forbearance or the uſe thereof ; but that he thought it more
expedient to the good of the Church, that they and all others of that
kind ſhould be taken away, when the next convenient opportunity ſhould
preſent it ſelf.   Which judgement as he grounds upon Calvins Rule,
that nothing ſhould be acted in a Reformation which is not warranted
expreſly by the Word of God ; ſo he adds this to it of his own, that
where there is ſo much contending for theſe outward matters, there
is but little care of the true Religion. And he aſſures us of himſelf (in
point of practice) that though he were a Canon of Chriſt-Church, and
diligent enough in attending Divine Service as the others did, yet he
could never be perſwaded to uſe that Veſtment ; which muſt needs a-
nimate all the reſt of the Genevians to forbear it alſo   The like was
done by John Alaſco, in crying down the Regular habit of the Clergy
before deſcrib'd. In which prevailing little by his own authority, he
writes to M. Bucer to declare againſt it ; and for the ſame was moſt ſeverely reprehended by that moderate and learned man, and all his cavils

vils and objections very ſolidly anſwered.　Which being ſent unto him in the way of a Letter, was afterwards printed and diſperſed, for keeping down that oppoſite humour, which began then to over-ſwell the Banks, and threatned to bear all before it.　But that which made the greateſt noiſe, was the carriage of Mr. *John Hooper*, Lord Elect of *Glouceſter*, who having lived amongſt the *Switzers* in the time of King *Henry*, did rather chooſe to be denied his Conſecration, then to receive it in that habit which belonged to his Order.　At firſt the Earl of *Warwick* (who after was Duke of *Northumberland*) interceded for him, and afterwards drew in the King to make one in the buſineſs.　But *Cranmer, Ridley*, and the reſt of the Biſhops who were moſt concerned, craved leave not to obey His Majeſty againſt his Laws ; and in the end prevailed ſo far, that *Hooper* for his contumacy was committed Priſoner ; and from the Priſon writes his Letters to *Martin Bucer* and *Peter Martyr*, for their opinion in the caſe.　From the laſt of which, who had declared himſelf no Friend to the Engliſh Ceremonies, he might preſume of ſome encouragement ; the rather, in regard that *Calvin* had appeared on his behalf, who muſt needs have a hand in this quarrel alſo.　For underſtanding how things went, he writes unto the Duke of *Somerſet* to attone the difference ; not by perſwading *Hooper* to conform himſelf to the received Orders of the Church, but to lend the man a helping hand, by which he might be able to hold out againſt all Authority.

8. But *Hooper* being deſerted by the Earl of *Warwick*, and not daring to relie altogether upon *Calvins* credit, which was unable to ſupport him, ſubmits at laſt unto the pleaſure of his Metropolitan, and the Rules of the Church. So that in fine the buſineſs was thus compromiſed ; that is to ſay, *That he ſhould receive his Conſecration attired in his Epiſcopal Robes : That he ſhould be diſpenſed withal from wearing them at ordinary times as his daily habits ; but that he ſhould be bound to uſe them whenſoever he preached before the King in his own Cathedral, or any other place of like publick nature.* According to which Agreement, being appointed to preach before the King, he ſhewed himſelf apparelled in his Biſhops Robes ; viz. A long Scarlet *Chimere* reaching down to the ground for his upper Garment (changed in Queen *Elizabeths* time to one of black Sattin) and under that a white Linen *Rochet*, with a Square Cap on his head.　This *Fox* reproacheth by the name of a *Popiſh Attire*, and makes it to be a great *carſe of ſhame and contumelie to that godly man*. But notwithſtanding the ſubmiſſion of this Reverend Prelate, too many of the inferiour Clergie were not found ſo tractable in their conformity to the Cap and Tippet, the Gown, and the Canonical Coat ; the wearing whereof was required of them, whenſoever they appeared in publick : Being decryed alſo by *Alaſco* and the reſt of the *Zuinglians* or *Calvinians*, as a *Superſtitious* and *Popiſh Attire*, altogether as unfit for Miniſters of the holy Goſpel, as the Chimere and Rochet were for thoſe who claimed to be the Succeſſors of the Lords Apoſtles. So *Tyms* replied unto Biſhop *Gardiner*, when being asked whether a Coat, with ſtockins of divers colours, were a fit apparel for a Deacon : He ſawcily made anſwer, that his *Veſture did not ſo much vary from a Deacons, as his Lordſhips did from that of an Apoſtle.* Which paſſage, as well concerning the debates about the Liturgie, as about the Veſtments, I have here abbreviated leaving

E e　　　　　　　the

the Reader for his further satisfaction to the History of the Reformation not long since published, in which they are laid down at large in their times and places.

9. Nor did they work less trouble to the Church in those early days, by their endeavouring to advance some *Zuinglian* Doctrines, by which the blame of all mens sins was either charged upon Gods will, or his Divine Decree of Predestination. These men are called in Bishop *Hoopers* Preface to the Ten Commandments by the name of *Gospellers*, for making their new Doctrines such a necessary part of our Saviours Gospel, as if men could not possibly be saved without it. These Doctrines they began to propagate in the Reign of King *Edward*; but never were so busie at it, as when they lived at *Geneva*, or came newly thence. For first *Knox* publisheth a book against an *Adversary of Gods Predestination*; wherein it is declared, *That whatsoever the Ethnicks and ignorant did attribute to Fortune, by Christians is to be assigned to Gods heavenly Providence: That we ought to judge nothing to come of Fortune, but that all cometh by the determinate counsel of God: And finally, that it would be displeasing unto God, if we esteem any thing to proceed from any other; and that we do not only behold him as the principal cause of all things, but also the Author, appointing all things to one or the other by his only Counsel.* After came out a Book first written in French, and afterwards by some of them translated into English, which they called, *A brief Declaration of the Table of Predestination:* In which is put down for a principal Aphorism, *That in like manner as God hath appointed the end, it is necessary that he should appoint the causes leading to the same end; but more particularly, That by virtue of Gods will all things are done, yea even those things which are evil and execrable.*

10. At the same time came out another of their books, pretended to be writ *Against a privy Papist*, as the Title tells us; wherein is maintained more agreeably to *Calvins* Doctrine, *That all evil springeth of Gods Ordinance, and that Gods Predestination was the cause of* Adams *fall, and of all wickedness.* And in a fourth book published by *Robert Cowley*, who afterwards was Rector of the Church of S. *Giles* near *Cripplegate*, intituled, *The confutation of Thirteen Articles*; it is said expresly, *That* Adam *being so perfect a creature that there was in him no lust to sin, and yet so weak that of himself he was not able to resist the assault of the subtile Serpent; that therefore there can be no remedy, but that the only cause of his fall must needs be the Predestination of God.* In which book it is also said, *That the most wicked persons that have been, were of God appointed to be wicked even as they were: That if God do predestinate a man to do things rashly, and without any deliberation, he shall not deliberate at all, but run headlong upon it be it good or evil: And in a word, That we are compelled by Gods Predestination to do those things for which we are damned.* By which Defenders of the absolute Decree of Reprobation; as God is made to be Author of sin, either in plain terms, or undeniable consequence; so from the same men, and the *Genevian* Pamphlets by them dispersed, our English *Calvinists* have borrowed all their Grounds and Principles on which they build the absolute and irrespective Decree of Predestination, contrary to the Doctrines publickly maintained and taught in the Church of *England* in the time of King *Edward*, and afterwards more clearly explicated under Queen *Elizabeth*.

11. Such

11. Such was the posture of affairs at Queen *Elizabeths* first coming to the Crown of *England*, when to the points before disputed both at home and abroad, was raised another of more weight and consequence then all the rest ; and such, as (if it could be gained) would bring on the other.   Such as had lived in exile amongst the *Switzers*, or followed *Knox* at his return unto *Geneva*, became exceedingly enamoured of *Calvins* Platform ; by which they found so much Authority ascribed unto the Ministers in the several Churches, as might make them absolute and independant, without being called to an account by King or Bishop. This Discipline they purposed to promote at their coming home ; and to that end, leaving some few behind them to attend the finishing of the Bible with the *Genevian* Notes upon it, which was then in the Press, the rest return amain for *England* to pursue the Project. But *Cox* had done their errand before they came ; and she had heard so much from others of their carriage at *Frankfort*, and their untractableness in point of Decency and comely Order in the Reign of her brother, as might sufficiently forwarn her not to hearken to them. Besides, she was not held to be told with what reproaches *Calvin* had reviled her Sister, nor how she had been persecuted by his followers in the time of her Reign ; some of them railing at her person in their scandalous Pamphlets ; some practising by false, but dangerous allusions, to subvert her Government ; and others openly praying to God, *That he would either turn her heart, or put an end to her days.* And of these men she was to give her self no hope, but that they would proceed with her in the self-same manner, whensoever any thing should be done (how necessary and just soever) which might cross their humours. The consideration whereof was of such prevalency with those of her Council, who were then deliberating about the altering of Religion, that amongst other remedies which were wisely thought of to prevent such dangers as probably might ensue upon it, it was resolved to have an eye upon these men, who were so hot in the pursuit of their flattering hopes, that out of a desire of Innovation (as my Author tells me) they were busied at that very time in setting up a new Form of Ecclesiastical Polity, and therefore were to be supprest with all care and diligence before they grew unto a head.

12. But they were men of harder metal then to be broken at the first blow which was offered at them. Queen *Maries* death being certified to those of *Geneva*, they presently dispatched their Letters to their Brethren at *Frankfort* and *Arrow* ; to which Letters of theirs, an answer is returned from *Frankfort* on the third, from *Arrow* on the 16 of *January* : And thereupon it is resolved to prepare for *England*, before their party was so sunk, that it could not without much difficulty be buoyed up again. Some of their party which remained all the time in *England*, being impatient of delay, and chusing rather to anticipate then expect Authority, had set themselves on work in defacing Images, demolishing the Altars, and might have made foul work, if not stopped in time.   Others began as hastily to preach the Protestant Doctrine in private Houses first, and afterwards as opportunity was offered, in the open Churches : Great multitudes of people resorting to them without Rule or Order. To give a check to whose forwardness, the Queen sets out her Proclamation in the end of *December* ; by which she gave command, *That no Inno-*

vation

vation should be made in the State of Religion, and that all persons should conform themselves for the present to the practices of Her Majesties Chappel, till it was otherwise appointed. Another Proclamation was also issued, by which all Preaching was prohibited, but by such only as were licensed by her Authority; which was not like to countenance any men of such turbulent spirits. The news whereof much hastned the return of those Zealous Brethren, who knew they might have better fishing in a troubled water, then in a quiet and composed. *Calvin* makes use also of the opportunity, directs his Letters to the Queen and Mr. Secretary *Cecil*, in hope that nothing should be done but by his advice. The contrary whereof gave matter of cold comfort both to him and them, when they were given to understand, that the Liturgie had been revised and agreed upon : That it was made more passable then before with the Roman Catholicks; and that not any of their number was permitted to act any thing in it, except *Whitehead* only, who was but half theirs neither, and perhaps not that. All they could do in that Conjecture, was to find fault with the Translation of the Bible which was then in use, in hope that their *Genevian* Edition of it might be entertained ; and to except against the paucity of fit men to serve the Church, and fill the vacant places of it, on the like hopes that they themselves might be preferred to supply the same.

1559.   13. And it is possible enough, that either by the mediation of *Calvin*, or by the intercession of *Peter Martyr* (who wrote unto the Queen at the same time also) the memory of their former Errors might have been obliterated, if *Knox* had not pulled more back with one hand, then *Calvin*, *Martyr*, and the rest could advance with both. For in a Letter of his to Sir *William Cecil*, dated *April* the 24, 1559, he first upbraids him *with consenting to the suppressing of Chrifts true Evangel, to the erecting of Idolatry, and to the shedding of the bloud of Gods most dear children, during the Reign* of Mischievous *Mary*, that professed Enemy of God, as he plainly calls her. Then he proceeds to justifie his treasonable and seditious book against the Regiment of Women. Of the truth whereof he positively affirmeth *that he no more doubteth, then that he doubted that was the voyce of God which pronounced this sentence upon that Sex, That in dolour they should bear their children.* Next he declares in reference to the Person of Queen *Elizabeth, That he could willingly acknowledge her to be raised by God for the manifestation of his glory, although not Nature only, but Gods own Ordinance did oppugn such Regiments.* And thereupon he doth infer, *That if Queen* Elizabeth *would confess, that the extraordinary Dispensations of Gods great mercy did make that lawful in her, which both Nature and Gods Laws did deny in all women besides, none in* England *should be more ready to maintain her lawful Authority then himself.* But on the other side he pronounceth this Sentence on her, *That if she built her Title upon Custom, Laws and Ordinances of men, such foolish presumption would grievously offend Gods Supreme Majesty, and that her ingratitude in that kind should not long lack punishment.* To the same purpose he writes also to the Queen her self, reproaching her withal, *That for fear of her life she had declined from God, bowed to Idolatry, and gone to Mass, during the persecution of Gods Saints in the time of her Sister.* In both his Letters he complains of some ill offices which had been done him, by means whereof he was denyed the

the liberty of Preaching in *England*: And in both Letters he endeavoured to excuse his flock of late *assembled in the most Godly and Reformed Church and City of Geneva*, from being guilty of any offence by his publishing of the Book; the blame whereof he wholly takes upon himself. But this was not the way to deal with Queens and their Privy Counsellors; and did effect so little in relation to himself and his flock, that he caused a more watchful eye to be kept upon them, then possibly might have been otherwise, had he scribled less.

14. Yet such was the necessity which the Church was under, that it was hardly possible to supply all the vacant places in it, but by admitting some of the *Genevian* Zealots to the Publick Ministry. The Realm had been extreamly visited in the year foregoing with a dangerous and contagious Sickness, which took away almost half the Bishops, and occasioned such Mortality amongst the rest of the Clergy, that a great part of the Parochial Churches were without Incumbents. The rest of the Bishops, twelve Deans, as many Archdeacons, Fifteen Masters of Colleges and Halls, fifty Prebendaries of Cathedral Churches, and about eighty Beneficed men were deprived at once, for refusing to submit to the Queens Supremacy. For the filling of which vacant places, though as much care was taken as could be imagined to stock the Church with moderate and conformable men, yet many past amongst the rest, who either had not hitherto discovered their disaffections, or were connived at in regard of their parts and learning. Private opinions not regarded, nothing was more considered in them then their zeal against Popery, and their abilities in Divine and Humane studies to make good that zeal. On which account we find the Queens Professor in *Oxford* to pass amongst the *Non-Conformists*, though somewhat more moderate thee the rest; and *Cartwright* the Lady *Margarets* in *Cambridge*, to prove an unextinguished fire-brand to the Church of *England*; *Wittingham*, the chief Ring-leader of the *Frankfort* Schismaticks, preferred unto the Deanry of *Durham*, from then encouraging *Knox* and *Goodman* in setting up Presbytery and sedition in the Kirk of *Scotland*. *Sampson* advanced unto the Deanry of Christs Church, and not long after turned out again for an *incorrigible Non-Conformist*. *Hardiman*, one of the first twelve Prebends of *Westminster*, deprived soon after, for throwing down the Altar, and defacing the Vestments of the Church. And if so many of them were advanced to places of note and eminence, there is no question to be made, but that some numbers of them were admitted unto Country cures; by means whereof, they had as great an opportunity as they could desire, not onle to dispute their *Genevian* Doctrines, but to prepare the people committed to them for receiving of such Innovations both in Worship and Government, as were resolved in time convenient to be put upon them.

15. For a preparative whereunto they brought along with them the *Genevian* Bible, with their Notes upon it, together with *Davids Psalms in English* Metre; that by the one they might effect an Innovation in the points of Doctrine, and by the other bring this Church more neer to the Rules of *Geneva* in some chief acts of publick Worship. For to omit the incongruities of the Translation, which King *James* judged to be the worst that he had ever seen in the English Tongue, the Notes upon the

1560.

same

same in many places favour of Sedition , and in some of Faction, destructive of the Persons and Powers of Kings , and of all civil intercourse
and humane society.   That learned King hath told us in the Conference at *Hampton-Court*, that the Notes on the *Genevian* Bible were *partial, untrue, seditions, and favouring too much of dangerous and trayterous conceits.*   For proof whereof he instanced in the Note of *Exod.* 1. *ver.* 19.
where they allow of disobedience unto Kings and Soveraign Princes :
And secondly, in that on 2 *Chron,* 8. 15, 16. where *Asa* is taxed for not
putting his Mother to death , but deposing her onely from the Regency
which before she executed.   Of which last note the *Scotish* Presbyterians
made especial use, not only in deposing *Mary* their lawful Queen,but prosecuting her openly and under hand till they had to k away her life.
And to this too he might have added that on *Matth.* 2. 12. where it is
said , that *Promise ought not be kept where Gods honour and Preaching of his
truth is hindred, or else it ought not to be broken.*   Which opens a wide gap
to the breach of all Oaths, Covenants, Contracts and Agreements, not
only between man and man, but between Kings and their Subjects. For
what man can be safe , or King secure ; what Promise can oblige , or
what Contract bind ; or what Oath tye a man to his Faith and Duty, if
on pretence of *Gods Honour* , or the *propagating of his Truth* , he may lawfully break it ?   And yet this Doctrine passed so currantly amongst the
French, that it was positively affirmed by *Eusebius Philadelphus* , whosoever he was , *That Queen* Elizabeth *was no more bound to keep the League
which she had made and sworn with* Charles IX,(because forsooth the *Preaching of the Gospel* might be hindred by it) *then* Herod *was obliged to keep the
Oath which he had sworn to the Dancing Harlot.* Follow them to *Rev.* 9. and
they will tell us in their Notes upon that Chapter, that by the *Locusts
which came out of the smack,* are meant *false Teachers, Hereticks, and worldly
subtle Prelates, with Monks, Fryers, Cardinals, Patriarchs, Archbishops, Bishops,
Doctors, Batchelors and Masters,*   To which though they subjoyn these
words, *viz. Which forsake Christ to maintain false Doctrine* ; yet lays it a
disgrace on all Archbishops and Bishops , and on all such as take Aca-
demical degrees, by bringing them under the name of *Locusts*, and joyning them with *Monks* and *Fryers ,* whom they beheld no otherwise then
as *Limbs of Antichrist.*   Which being the design of their Annotations,
agreeable to *Calvins* Doctrine in reference to Civil and Ecclesiastical
Government, there is no doubt but that they come up roundly to him in
reference to Predestination, and the points appendant : for which I shall
refer the Reader to the Notes themselves ; observing only in this place,
that they exclude Christ and all his sufferings from being any way considerable in mans Election, which they found onely on the absolute will
and pleasure of Almighty God ; but are content to make him an *inferiour
cause* (and only an *inferiour cause*) of a mans salvation : For which consult
them on *Rom.* 9.15.

16.   Now with this Bible, and these Notes, which proved so advantagious to them in their main projectments, they also brought in *Davids
Psalms* in English Metre, of which they served themselves to some tune
in the time succeeding.   Which device being first taken up by *Clement
Marot,* and continued afterwards by *Beza ,* as before is said, was followed here in *England* by *Thomas Sternhold* in the Reign of King *Edward,* and
afterwards

afterwards by *John Hopkins* and some others, who had retired unto *Geneva* in the time of Queen *Mary*. Being there finished, and Printed at the end of their Bibles, they were first recommended to the use of private Families; next brought into the Church for an entertainment before the beginning of the Morning and Evening Service: And finally, published by themselves, or at the end of the *Psalter*, with this Declaration, that they were *set forth and allowed to be sung in all Churches before and after Morning and Evening Prayer, as also before and after Sermons*. But first, no such allowance can be found as is there pretended, nor could be found when this allowance was disputed in the *High Commission*, by such as have been most industrious and concerned in the search thereof. And then whereas it is pretended that the said Psalms should be sung *before and after Morning and Evening Prayer*, as also *before and after Sermons* (which shews they were not to be intermingled with the Publick Liturgie) in very little time they prevailed so far in most Parish Churches, as to thrust out the *Te Deum*, and the *Benedicite*, the *Benedictus*, the *Magnificat*, and the *Nunc Dimittis*, quite out of the Church. And thirdly, by the practices and endeavours of the *Puritan* party (who had an eye upon the usage of *Geneva*) they came to be esteemed the most Divine part of Gods publick service; the reading *Psalms*, together with the first and second Lessons, being heard in many places with a covered head; but all men sitting bare-headed when the *Psalm* is sung. And to that end, the Parish Clerk must be taught to call upon the people to sing it *to the Praise and Glory of God*; no such preparatory Exhortation being used at the naming of the Chapters or the daily Psalms.

17. By these preparatives they hoped in time to bring in the whole body of *Calvinism*, as well in reference to Government, and forms of Worship, as to points of Doctrine. But then they were to stay their time, and not to shew too much at once of the main design, but rather to divert on some other counsels. The Liturgy was so well fortified by the Law, and the Bishops so setled in their jurisdictions, that it had been a madness to attempt on either, till they should find themselves increased both in power and number, and that they had some friend in Court not only to excuse, but defend their actions. In which respect nothing seemed more expedient to them, then to revive the Quarrels of King *Edwards* time about Caps and Tippits, and other Vestments of the Clergy, which had not the like countenance from the Laws of the Land. In which as they assured themselves of all help from the hands of *Peter Martyr*, so they despaired not of obtaining the like from *Calvin* and *Beza*, whensoever it should be required. But as one Wave thrusts another forwards, so this dispute brings in some others, in which the judgement of *Peter Martyr* was demanded also; that is to say, concerning the Episcopal Habit, the Patrimony of the Church, the manner of proceedings to be held against Papists, the Perambulation used in the Rogation Week; with many other points of the like condition. Which quarrels they pursued for five years together, till the setling of that business by the Book of *Advertisements, Anno* 1565. They also had begun to raise their thoughts unto higher matters then Caps and Tippets: In order whereunto, some of them take upon them in their private Parishes, to ordain set Fasts; and others, to neglect the observation of the Annual Festivals

Feſtivals which were appointed by the Church; ſome to remove the Holy Table from the place of the Altar, and to tranſpoſe it to the middle of the Quire or Chancel, that it might ſerve the more conveniently for the poſture of ſitting; and others, by the help of ſome ſilly Ordinaries, to impoſe Books of Forein Doctrine on their ſeveral Pariſhes; that by ſuch Doctrine they might countenance their Actings in the other particulars. All which, with many other innovations of the like condition, were preſently took notice of by the Biſhops, and the reſt of the Queens Commiſſioners; and remedies provided for them in a Book of *Orders*, publiſhed in the year 1561; or the *Advertiſements* before mentioned, about four years after. Such as proceeded in their oppoſitions after theſe *Advertiſements*, had the name of *Puritans*; as men that did profeſs a greater *Purity* in the Worſhip of God, a greater deteſtation of the ceremonies and corruptions of the Church of *Rome*, then the reſt of their Brethren: under which name were comprehended, not onely thoſe which hitherto had oppoſed the Churches Veſtments, but alſo ſuch as afterwards endeavoured to deſtroy the Liturgy, and ſubvert the Government.

18. In all this time they could obtain no countenance from the hands of this State, though it was once endeavoured for them by the Earl of *Leiceſter* (whom they had gained to their Patron.) But it was onely to make uſe of them as a counterpoiſe to the Popiſh party, at ſuch time as the Marriage was in agitation between the Lord *Henry Stewart* and the Queen of *Scots*, if any thing ſhould be attempted by them to diſturb the Kingdom; the fears whereof, as they were onely taken up upon politick ends, ſo the intended favours to the oppoſite Faction vaniſhed alſo with them. But on the contrary, we find the State ſevere enough againſt their proceedings, even to the deprivation of Dr. *Thomas Sampſon*, Dean of *Chriſt-Church*. To which dignity he had been unhappily preferred in the firſt year of the Queen; and being looked upon as head of this Faction, was worthily deprived thereof by the Queens Commiſſioners. They found by this ſeverity what they were to truſt to, if any thing were practiſed by them againſt the Liturgy, the Doctrine of the Church, or the publick Government. It cannot be denyed, but *Goodman, Gilbie, Whittingham*, and the reſt of the *Genevian* Conventicle, were very much grieved, at their return, that they could not bear the like ſway here in their ſeveral Conſiſtories, as did *Calvin* and *Beza* at *Geneva*; ſo that they not onely repined and grudged at the Reformation which was made in this Church, becauſe not fitted to their phancies, and to *Calvins* Platform; but have laboured to ſow thoſe Seeds of Heterodoxy and Diſobedience, which afterwards brought forth thoſe troubles and diſorders which enſued upon it. But being too wiſe to put their own fingers in the fire, they preſently fell upon a courſe which was ſure to ſpeed, without producing any danger to themſelves or their party. They could not but remember thoſe many advantages which *John Alaſco* and his Church of ſtrangers afforded to the *Zuinglian* Goſpellers in the time of King *Edward*; and they deſpaired not of the like, nor of greater neither, if a *French* Church were ſetled upon *Calvin's* Principles in ſome part of *London*.

19. For the advancement of this project, *Calvin* directs his Letters
unto

unto Bishop *Grindal*, newly preferred unto that See, that by his countenance or connivance, such of the *French* Nation as for their Conscience had been forced to flee into *England*, might be permitted the Free Exercise of their Religion : whose leave being easily obtained, for the great reverence which he bares to the name of *Calvin*, they made the like use of some Friends which they had in the Court. By whose sollicitation they procured the Church of St. *Anthony*, not far from *Merchant-Taylors-Hall*, then being of no present use for Religious Offices, to be assigned unto the *French*, with liberty to erect the *Genevian* Discipline, for ordering the Affairs of their Congregation, and to set up a Form of Prayer which had no manner of conformity with the English Liturgy. Which what else was it in effect, but a plain giving up of the Cause at the first demand, which afterwards was contended for with such opposition ? what else but a Foundation to that following Anarchy which was designed to be obtruded on the Civil Government ? For certainly, the tolerating of Presbytery in a Church founded and established by the Rules of Episcopacy, could end in nothing but the advancing of a Commonwealth in the midst of a Monarchy. *Calvin* perceived this well enough, and thereupon gave *Grindal* thanks for his favour in it, of whom they after served themselves upon all occasions ; a *Dutch* Church being after setled on the same Foundation in the *Augustine Fryars*, where *John Alasco* held his Congregation in the Reign of King *Edward*. The inconveniences whereof were not seen at the first ; and when they were perceived, were not easily remedied. For the obtaining of which ends, there was no man more like to serve them with the Queen, then Sir *Francis Knollis* ; who having Married a Daughter of the Lord *Cary* of *Hunsdon*, the Queens Cousin-German, was made Comptroller of the Houshold, continuing in good Credit and Authority with her upon that account. And being also one of those who had retired from *Frankfort* to *Geneva* in the time of the Schism, did there contract a great acquaintance with *Calvin*, *Beza*, and the rest of the Consistorians, whose cause he managed at the Court upon all occasions ; though afterwards he gave place to the Earl of *Leicester*, as their principal Agent.

20. But the *Genevians* will find work enough to imploy them both, and having gained their ends, will put on for more. The Isles of *Guernsey* and *Jarsey*, the only remainder of the Crown of *England* in the Dukedom of *Normandy*, had entertained the Reformation in the Reign of King *Edward* ; by whose command the publick Liturgy had been turned into *French*, that it might serve them in those Islands for their Edifications. But the Reformed Religion being suppressed in the time of Queen *Mary*, revived again immediately after her decease, by the diligence of such *French* Ministers as had resorted thither for protection in the day of their troubles. In former times these Islands belonged unto the jurisdiction of the Bishop of *Constance*, who had in each of them a Subordinate Officer, mixt of a Chancellor and Arch-Deacon, for the dispatch of all such business as concerned the Church : which Officers intituled by the name of Deans, had a particular Revenue in Tythes and Corn allotted to them, besides the Perquisites of their Courts, and the best Benefices in the Islands. But these *French* Ministers desiring

to

to have all things modelled by the Rules of *Calvin*, endeavoured by all the friends they could to advance his Difcipline; to which they were incouraged by the Brothers here, and the Governours there. The Governours in each Ifland advanced the project out of a covetous intent to inrich themfelves by the fpoil of the Deanries; the Brethren have hereupon a hope to gain ground by little and little, for the erecting of the fame in moft parts of *England*. And in purfuance of this plot both Iflands joyn in confederacy to Petition the Queen for an allowance of this Difcipline, *Anno* 1563. In the year next following, the *Signiour de St. Owen*, and *Monfieur de Soulemount* were delegated to the Court to follicite in it; where they received a gratious anfwer, and full of hopes returned to their feveral homes. In the mean time, the Queen being ftrongly perfwaded that this defign would much advance the Reformation in thofe Iflands, was contented to give way unto it, in the Towns of St. *Peters Port* and St. *Hillaries* onely, but no further. To which purpofe there were Letters decretory from the Council, directed to the *Bayliff*, the *Jurates*, and others of each Ifland; fubfcribed by *Bacon* Lord Keeper of the Great Seal, the Marquefs of *Northampton*, the Earl of *Leicefter*, the Lord *Clynton*, afterwards Earl of *Lincoln*, *Rogers*, *Knollis*, and *Cecil*. The Tenour of which letter in relation to the Ifle of *Jarfey*, was this that followeth.

21. *After our very hearty commendations unto you; where the Queens moft excellent Majefty underftandeth, that the Ifles of* Guernfay *and* Jarfey *have anciently depended on the Diocefs of* Conftance, *and that there be certain Churches in the fame Diocefs well reformed, agreeable throughout in the Doctrine as is fet forth in this Realm; knowing therewith, that they have a Minifter, which ever fince his arrival in* Jarfey *hath ufed the like Order of Preaching and Adminiftration, as in the faid Reformed Churches, or as it is ufed in the* French Church *of* London: *her Majefty, for divers refpects and confiderations, moving her Highnefs, is well pleafed to admit the fame Order of Preaching and Adminiftration to be continued at Saint* Hillaries, *as hath been hitherto accuftomed by the faid Minifter. Provided always, that the refidue of the Parifhes in the faid Ifle, fhall diligently put afide all fuperftitions ufed in the faid Diocefs; and fo continue there the Order of Service ordained within this Realm, with the Injunctions necessary for that purpofe. Wherein you may not fail diligently to give your aids and affiftance, as beft may ferve for the advancement of Gods Glory. And fo farewel. From* Richmond *the* 7. *of* Auguft, *Anno* 1565.

22. Where note, that the fame letter, the names onely of the places being changed, and fubfcribed by the fame men, was fent alfo unto thofe of *Guernfey*, for the permiffion of the faid Difcipline in the *Port* of St. *Peters*. In which, though there be no exprefs mention of allowing their Difcipline, but only of their form of Prayer and Adminiftation of Sacraments; yet they prefumed fo far on the general words, as to put in prefently in practice. In profecution of which Counfels the Minifters and Elders of both Churches held their firft Synod in the Ifle of *Guernfey*, on the 2 of *September*, *Anno* 1567, where they concluded to advance it by degrees in all the reft of the Parifhes as opportunity fhould

ſerve, and the condition of Affairs permit : to the great joy, no queſtion, of their great Friends in *England*, who could not but congratulate their own good Fortune in theſe fair beginnings.

23. At home they found not ſuch ſucceſs as they did abroad ; not a few of them being deprived of their Benefices, and other preferments in the Church, for their inconformity, expreſt in their refuſing to officiate by the publick Liturgy, or not ſubmitting to the directions of their Ordinaries in ſome outward matters, as Caps and Surplices, and the like. The news of which ſeverity flies to *France* and *Scotland* ; occaſioning *Beza* in the one, and *Knox* and his Comrades in the other, to interpoſe themſelves in behalf of their brethren. With what authority *Beza* acted in it, we ſhall ſee anon.   And we may now take notice, that in *Knox's* Letter, ſent from the general Aſſembly of the Kirk of *Scotland*, the Veſtments in diſpute are not only called *Trifles* and *Rags* of *Rome*, but are diſcountenanced and decryed, *for being ſuch Garments as Idolaters in time of greateſt darkneſs, uſed in their Superſtitious and Idolatrous ſervice* : and thereupon it is inferred, *That if Surplice, Cap, and Tippet have been badges of Idolaters in the very act of their Idolatry, that then the Preachers of Chriſtian Liberty, and the Rebukers of Superſtition, were to have nothing to do with the dregs of that Romiſh beaſt.* Which inference is ſeconded by this requeſt, *viz. That the Brethren in* England *which refuſed thoſe* Romiſh Rags, *might find of them (the* B ſhops) *who uſe and urge them, ſuch favour, as their Head and Maſter commandeth each one of his Members to ſhew to another.* And this they did *expect to receive of their courteſie, not only becauſe they hoped that they, the ſaid* Biſhops, *would not offend God in troubling their Brethren for ſuch* Vain trifles : *but becauſe they hoped that they would not refuſe the requeſt of them, their Brethren and fellow-Miniſters ; in whom, though there appeared no* worldly Pomp, *yet they aſſured themſelves, that they were eſteemed the* ſervants of God, *and ſuch as travelled to ſet forth Gods Glory againſt the* Antichriſt of Rome, *that conjured enemy of true Religion, the Pope. The days, ſay they, are evil, iniquity abounds, charity (alaſs) waxeth cold ; and therefore that it concerned them all to walk diligently, becauſe it was uncertain at what hour the Lord would come, to whom they were to render an account of their Adminiſtration.* After which Apoſtolical Admonition, they commit them to the Mighty protection of the Lord Jeſus Chriſt. And ſo we conclude their Zealous Letter, dated *Dec.* 27. 1566.

24. With more Authority writes *Beza*, as the greater Patriarch; and he writes too concerning things of greater conſequence then Caps and Surplices. For in a Letter of his to *Grindal*, bearing date *July*, anno 1566, he makes a ſad complaint concerning certain Miniſters, *unblameable (as he ſaith) both in Life and Doctrine, ſuſpended from the Miniſtry by the Queens Authority, and the good liking of the Biſhops, for not ſubſcribing to ſome new Rites and Ceremonies impoſed upon them.* Amongſt which Rites he ſpecifies the *wearing of ſuch Veſtments as were then worn by* Baals *Prieſts in the Church of* Rome ; *the Croſs in Baptiſm, kneeling at the Communion, and ſuch Rites, as had* degenerated (*as he tells us*) into moſt filthy Superſtition. But he ſeems more offended *that Women were ſuffered to baptize in extreme neceſſities : That power was granted to the Queen for ordaining ſuch other Rites and Ceremonies as ſhould ſeem convenient ; but moſt eſpecially,* (which was indeed the point moſt grieved at) *that the Biſhops were inveſted with a ſole*

Autho-

Authority for all matters of the Church, without consulting with the Pastors of particular flocks. He was too well versed in the Writings of the Ancient Fathers, as not to know that all the things which he complains of, were aprroved and practiced in the best and happiest times of Christianity; as might be otherwise made apparent out of the Writings of *Tertullian, Cyprian, Hierome, Chrysostome*; and indeed who not? But *Beza* has a word for this. For first he blames the Ancient Fathers for borrowing many of their Ceremonies from the Jews and Gentiles, though done by them out of a good and honest purpose; that *bring all things to all men*, they might gain the more. And thereupon he gives this rule, *That all such Rites as had been borrowed either from the Jew or Gentile without express Warrant from Christ or the holy Apostles, as also all other significant Ceremonies, which had been brought into the Church against right and reason, should be immediately removed, or otherwise the Church could never be restored to her Native Beauty.* Which Rule of his, if once admitted, there must be presently an end of all external Decency and Order in the Worship of God, and every man might be left to serve him, both for time and place, and every particular circumstance in that Sacred action, as to him seemed best. And what a horrible confusion must needs grow thereby, not only in a whole National Church, but in every particular Congregation, be it never so small, is no hard matter to conceive.

25. At the Reforming of this Church, not only the Queens Chappel, and all Cathedrals, but many Parochial Churches also had preserved their Organs; to which they used to sing the appointed Hymns; that is to say, the *Te Deum*, the *Benedictus*, the *Magnificat*, the *Nunc Dimittis, &c.* performed in an Artificial and Melodious manner, with the addition of Cornets, Sackbuts, and the like, on the Solemn Festivals. For which as they had ground enough from the holy Scripture, if the Practice and Authority of *David* be of any credit; so were they warranted thereunto by the godly usage of the primitive times, after the Church was once restored to her peace and freedom. Certain I am, that S. *Augustine* imputes no small part of his Conversion to that heavenly Melodie which he heard very frequently in the Church of *Millaine,* (a) professing that it did not only draw tears from him, though against his will, but raised his soul unto a sacred Meditation on spiritual matters. But *Beza* having turned so many of the *Psalms* into Metre, as had been left undone by *Marot,* gave an example unto *Sternhold* and *Hopkins* to attempt the like. Whose Version being left unfinished, but brought unto an end by some of our English Exiles which remained at (b) *Geneva*; there was a purpose for imposing them upon the Church by little and little, that they might come as close as might be in all points to their Mother-City. At first, they sung them only in their private houses, and afterwards (as before said) adventured to sing them as a part of the Service it self. For so I understand that passage in the *Church-Historian,* in which he tells us, That Dr. *Gervis* being then Warden of *Merton* Colledge, had abolished certain Latine superstitious Hymns which had been used on some of the Festivals, appointing the same *Psalms* in English to be sung in their place; and that as one *Leech* was ready to begin the *Psalm,* another of the Fellows called *Hall,* snatched

(a) *Vt flev' ad cantus Ecclesiae tuae, &c.* Confes. lib.

(b) *Vt per oblectamentarium assurgit animns, ad pietatis assertum.* Conf. lib.

ed

ed the Book out of his hands, and told him, *That they could no more dance after his Pipe*. But whatsoever *Hall* thought of them, *Beza* and his Disciples were persuaded otherwise. And that he might the better cry down that Melodious Harmony which was retained in the Church of *England*, and so make way for the *Genevian* fashion even in that point also; he tells us in the same letter to Bishop *Gryndal*, *That the Artificial Musick then retained in the Church of England, was fitter to be used in Masks, and Dancings, then Religious Offices; and rather served to please the ear, then to move the affections*. Which censure being pass'd upon it by so great a *Rabby*, most wonderful it was how suddenly some men of good note and quality, who otherwise deserved well enough of the Church of *England*, did bend their wits and pens against it; and with what earnestness they laboured to have their own Tunes publickly introduced into all the Churches. Which that they might the better do, they procured the Psalms in English Metre to be bound in the same Volum with the publick Liturgy, and sometimes with the Bible also; setting them forth, as being *allowed* (so the Title tells us) *to be sung in all Churches before and after Morning and Evening Prayer, as also before and after Sermons*; but with what truth and honesty, we have heard before.

16. In fine, he tells the Bishops *how guilty they would seem to God and his Holy Angels, if they chuse rather to deprive the Ministers of their Cures and Benefices, then suffer them to go apparelled otherwise then to them seemed good: And rather to deprive many hungry souls of their Heavenly food, then give them leave to receive it otherwise then upon their knees*. And this being said, he questions the Authority of the Supreme Magistrate, as contrary to the Word of God, and the Ancient Canons, for ordaining any new Rites and Ceremonies in a Church established; but much more the Authority ascribed to Bishops, in ordering any thing which concerned the Church, without calling the Presbytery to advise about it, and having their approbation in it. This was indeed the point most aimed at. And to this point his followers take the courage to drive on amain; the Copies of this letter being presently dispersed for their greater comfort, if not also Printed. Some of the Brethren, in their zeal to the name of *Calvin*, preferred him once before St. *Paul*; and *Beza* out of question would have took it ill, if he had been esteemed of less Authority then any of those who claimed to be Successors to St. *Peter*. And therefore it were worth the while to compare the Epistles of these men, with those of Pope *Leo*; and then to enter seriously into consideration, whether of the two took more upon him; either Pope *Leo*, where he might pretend to some command; or *Beza*, where he had no authority to act at all. How much more moderate and discreet were the most eminent men for learning amongst the *Switzers*, may appear by the example of *Gualter* and *Bullinger*, no way inferior unto the other, but in Pride and Arrogancy; who being desired by some of the English Zealots to give their judgement in the point of the Churches Vestments, returned their approbation of them; but sent it in a letter directed to *Horn*, *Sandys* and *Grindal*, to let them see, that they would not intermeddle in the affairs of this Church without their privity and advice. Which whether it were done with greater moderation or discretion, it is hard to say.

27. So good a Foundation being laid, the building could not chuse   1567.

but

but go on apace. But first they must prepare the matter, and remove all doubts which otherwise might interrupt them in the course of their building. And herein *Beza* is consulted as the Master Workman. To him they send their several scruples; and he returns such answer to them, as did not onely confirm them in their present obstinacy, but fitted and prepared them for the following Schism. To those before, they add the calling of the Ministers, and their ordaining by the Bishops; neither the Presbytery being consulted, nor any particular place appointed for their Ministration. Which he condemns as contrary to the Word of God and the ancient Canons; but so that he conceives it better to have such a Ministry, then none at all; praying withal, that God would give this Church a more lawful Ministry (the Church was much beholding to him for his zeal the while) in his own good time. Concerning the *Interrogatories* proposed to Infants in their Baptism, he declares it to be only *a corruption of the ancient Form*, which was used in the baptizing persons of riper years. And thereupon desires as heartily as before, *That as the Church had laid aside the use* of Oyl, *and the old Rite of* Exorcising, *though retained at* Rome; *so they would also abdicate those* foolish and unnecessary Interrogations *which are made to Infants*. And yet he could not chuse but vaunt, that there was somewhat in one of St. *Augustines* Epistles which might seem to favour it; and that such questions were proposed to Infants in the time of *Origen*, who lived above two hundred years before St. *Augustine*. In some Churches, and particularly in *Westminster* Abby, they still retained the use of Wafers made of Bread unleavened; to which we can find nothing contrary in the publick Rubricks. This he acknowledgeth of it self for a thing indifferent; but so, that ordinary leavened bread is preferred before it, as being more agreeable to the Institution of our Lord and Saviour. And yet he could not chuse but grant, that Christ administred the Sacrament in unleavened bread, no other being to be used by the Law of *Moses* at the time of the Passover. He dislikes also the deciding of civil causes (by which he means those of Tythes, Marriages, and the last Wills or Testaments of men deceased) in the Bishops Courts; but more, that the Bishops Chancellors did take upon them to decree any Excommunication without the approbation and consent of the Presbyters. Whose acts therein, he Majestically pronounceth to be void and *null*, not to oblige the Conscience of any man in the sight of God; and otherwise to be a soul and shamefull prophanation of the Churches Censures.

28. To other of their Queries, *Touching the Musick in the Church; Kneeling at the Communion; The Cross in Baptism;* and the rest, he answers as he did before, without remitting any thing of his former censure. Which letter of his, bearing date on the 24 of *October*, 1567, was superscribed, *Ad quosdam Anglicanum Ecclesiarum fratres, &c.* To certain of the Brethren of the Church in *England*, touching some points of Ecclesiastical Order and concernment which were then under debate: by the receiving whereof they found themselves so fully satisfied and encouraged, that they fell into an open Schism in the year next following. At 1568. which time *Benson, Button, Hallingham, Coleman*, and others, taking upon them to be of a more Ardent zeal then others in professing the true Reformed Religion, resolved to allow of nothing in Gods Publick Service

vice (according to the Rules laid down by *Calvin* and *Beza*) but what was found expresly in the Holy Scriptures.   And whether out of a desire of Reformation (which pretence had gilded many a rotten post) or for singularity sake and Innovation, they openly questioned the received Discipline of the Church of *England*; yea, condemned the same, together with the Publick Liturgy, and the calling of Bishops, as favouring too much of the Religion of the Church of *Rome*.   Against which they frequently protested in their Pulpits; affirming, *That it was an impious thing to hold any correspondency with the Church*; and labouring with all diligence to bring the Church of *England* to a conformity in all points with the Rules of *Geneva*.   These, although the Queen commanded to be laid by the heels, yet it is incredible how upon a sudden their followers increased in all parts of the Kingdom; distinguished from the rest by the name of *Puritans*, by reason of their own perverseness, and most obstinate refusal to give ear to more sound advice.   Their numbers much encreased on a double account; first, by the negligence of some, and the connivance of other Bishops, who should have looked more narrowly into their proceedings: And partly, by the secret favour of some great men in the Court, who greedily gaped after the Remainder of the Churches Patrimony.

29. It cannot be denied, but that this Faction received much encouragement underhand, from some great persons near the Queen; from no man more then from the Earl of *Leicester*, the Lord *North*, *Knollis*, and *Walsingham*; who knew how mightily some numbers of the *Scots*, both Lords and Gentlemen, had in short time improved their fortune, by humoring the *Knoxian* Brethren in their Reformation; and could not but expect the like in their own particulars, by a compliance with those men, who aimed apparently at the ruine of the Bishops and Cathedral Churches.   But then it must be granted also, that they received no small encouragement from the negligence and remisness of some great Bishops, whom *Calvin* and *Beza* had cajoled to a plain connivance.   Of *Calvins* writing unto *Grindal* for setting up a *French* Church in the middle of *London*, we have seen before.   And we have seen how *Beza* did address himself unto him, in behalf of the Brethren who had suffered for their inconformity to establisht Orders.   But now he takes notice of the Schism, a manifest defection of some members from the rest of the body; but yet he cannot chuse but tamper with him to allow their doings, or otherwise to mitigate the rigour of the Laws in force.   For having first besprinkled him with some commendation for his zeal to the Gospel, and thanked him for his many favours to the new *French* Church, he begins roundly, in plain terms, to work him to his own perswasions.   He lays before him first how great an obstacle was made in the course of Religion, by those petit differences; not onely amongst weak and ignorant, but even learned Men.   And then adviseth that some speedy remedy be applied to so great a mischief, by calling an Assembly of such Learned and Religious men as were least contentious; of which he hoped to be the chief, if that work went forwards: With this Proviso notwithstanding, That nothing should be ordred and determined by them; with reference unto Ancient or Modern usages; but that all Popish Rites and Ceremonies being first abolished, they should proceed

to

to the Establishment of such a Form of Ministration in the Church of *England*, as might be grounded on some express Authorities of the Word of God. Which as he makes to be a Work agreeable unto *Grindals* piety, so *Grindal* after this (and this bears date in *July* 1560) appeared more favourable every day then other to those common Barretters, who used their whole endeavours to embroyl the Church.

30. Nor were these years less fatal to the Church of *England*, by the defection of the Papists, who till this time had kept themselves in her Communion, and did in general as punctually attend all Divine Offices in the same, as the vulgar Protestants. And it is probable enough, that they might have held out longer in their due obedience, if first the scandal which was given by the other Faction, and afterwards the separation which ensued upon it, had not took them off. The Liturgie of the Church had been exceedingly well fitted to their approbation, by leaving out an offensive passage against the Pope; restoring the old Form of words, accustomably used in the participation of the holy Sacrament; the total expunging of a Rubrick, which seemed to make a Question of the *Real presence*; the Situation of the holy-Table in the place of the Altar; the Reverend posture of kneeling at it, or before it, by all Communicants; the retaining of so many of the ancient Festivals; and finally by the Vestments used by the Priest or Minister in the Ministration. And so long as all things continued in so good a posture, they saw no cause of separating from the rest of their Brethren in the acts of Worship. But when all decency and order was turned out of the Church, by the heat and indiscretion of these new Reformers; the holy-Table brought into the midst of the Church like a common-Table; the Communicants in some places sitting at it with as little Reverence as at any ordinary Table; the ancient Fasts and Feasts deserted, and Church-Vestments thrown aside, as the remainders of the Superstition of the Church of *Rome*: they then began visibly to decline from their first conformity. And yet they made no general separation, nor defection neither, till the *Genevian* brethren had first made the Schism, and rather chose to meet in Barns and Woods, yea and common Fields, then to associate with their brethren, as in former times. For, that they did so, is affirmed by very good Authors, who much bemoaned the sad condition of the Church, in having her bowels torn in pieces by those very Children which she had cherished in her bosom. By one of which, who must needs be of years and Judgement at the time of this Schism, we are first told what great contentions had been raised in the first ten years of her Majesties Reign, through the peevish frowardness, the out-cryes of such as came from *Geneva* against the Vestments of the Church, and such like matters. And then he adds, That being crossed in their desires touching those particulars, they separated from the rest of their Congregations; and meeting together in Houses, Woods, and common Fields, kept there their most unlawful and disorderly Conventicles.

31. Now at such time as *Bution*, *Billingham*, and the rest of the *Puritan* Faction had first made the Schism, *Harding* and *Sanders*, and some others of the Popish Fugitives, imployed themselves as busily in perswading those of that Religion to the like temptation: For being licensed by the Pope to exercise Episcopal jurisdiction in the Realm of *England*, they take

upon

upon them to absolve all such in the Court of Conscience, who should return to the Communion of the Church of *Rome*; as also to dispence in Causes of irregularity, except it were incurred by wilful murther; and finally, from the like irregularities incurred by Heresie, if the party who desired the benefit of the Absolution, abstain'd from Ministring at the holy Altar for three years together. By means whereof, and the advantages before mentioned which were given them by the *Puritan Faction*, they drew many to them from the Church, both Priests and People; their numbers every day increasing, as the scandal did. And finding how the Sectaries inlarged their numbers by erecting a *French* Church in *London*, and that they were now upon the point of procuring another for the use and comfort of the *Dutch*; they thought it no ill piece of Wisdom to attempt the like in some convenient place near *England*, where they might train up their Disciples, and fit them for imployment upon oll occasions. Upon which ground, a Seminary is established for them at *Doway* in *Flanders Anno* 1568; and another not long after at *Rhemes* a City of *Champaigne* in the Realm of *France*. Such was the benefit which redounded to the Church of *England* by the perversness of the Brethren of this first separation, that it occasioned the like Schism betwixt her and the Papists, who till that time had kept themselves in her Communion, as before was said. For that the Papists generally did frequent the Church in these first ten years, is positively affirmed by Sir *Edward Coke* in his Speech at the Arraignment of *Garnet* the Jesuit, and afterward at the charge which was given by him at the general Assizes held in *Norwich*. In both which he speaks on his own certain knowledge, not on vulgar hearsay; affirming more particularly, that he had many times seen *Bedenfield*, *Cornwallis*, and some other of the Leading *Romanists*, at the Divine Service of the Church, who afterwards were the first that departed from it. The like averred by the most learned Bishop *Andrews*, in his Book called *Tortura Torti, pag.* 130. and there asserted undeniably against all opposition. And which may serve instead of all, we find the like affirmed also by the Queen her self, in her Instructions given to *Walsingham*, then being her Resident with the *French* King, *Anno* 1570. In which Instructions, bearing date on the 11 of *August*, it is affirmed expresly of the Heads of that party, and therefore we may judge the like of the Members also, that *they did ordinarily resort, from the beginning of her Reign, in all open places, to the Churches, and to Divine Service in the Church, without any contradiction, or shew of misliking.*

32. The parallel goes further yet. For as the *Puritans* were encouraged to this separation by the Missals and Decretory Letters of *Theodore Beza*, whom they beheld as the chief Patriarch of this Church: So were the Papists animated to their defection by a Bull of Pope *Pius* the Fifth, whom they acknowledged most undoubtedly for the Head of theirs. For the Pope being thrust on by the importunity of the House of *Guise*, in favour of the Queen of *Scots*, whose Title they preferred before that of *Elizabeth*; and by the Court of *France*, in hatred to the Queen her self, for aiding the *French Hugonots* against their King, was drawn at last to issue out this Bull against her, dated at *Rome*, *Feb.* 24. 1569. In which Bull he doth not onely Excommunicate her person,

1569.

deprive

deprive her of her Kingdoms, and absolve all her Subjects from their Oaths of Allegeance ; but commands all her Subjects of what sort soever not to obey her Laws, Injunctions, Ordinances, or Acts of State. The Defection of the Papists had before been voluntary, but is now made necessary ; the Popes command being superadded to the scandal which had before been given them by the *Puritan Faction*. For after this, the going or not going to Church was commonly reputed by them for a sign distinctive, by which a Roman Catholick might be known from an English Heretick. And this appears most plainly by the Preamble to the Act of Parliament *against bringing or executing of Bulls from* Rome, 13 *Eliz.* 2. Where it is reckoned amongst the effects of those Bulls and Writings, *That those who brought them, did by their lewd practices and subtile perswasions work so far forth, that sundry people, and ignorant persons have been contented to be reconciled to the Church of* Rome, *and to have withdrawn and absented themselves from all Divine Service, most godlily exercised in this Realm.* By which it seems, that till the roaring of those Bulls, those of the Popish party did frequent the Church, though not so generally in the last five years (as our Learned *Andrews* hath observed) as they did the first, before they were discouraged by the Innovations of the *Puritan Faction*.

33. But for their coming to our Churches for the first ten years, that is to say, before the first beginning of the *Puritan Schism*, there is enough acknowledged by some of their own. *Parsons* himself confesseth, in his Pamphlet which he calls by the name of *Green Coat, That for twelve years together the Court and State was in great quiet, and no question made about Religion.* *Brierly* in his *Apologie* speaks it more at large ; by whom it is acknowledged, *That in the beginning of the Queens Reign most part of the Catholicks for many years did go to the Heretical Churches and Service : That when the better and truer opinion was taught them by Priests and Religious men from beyond the Seas as more perfect and necessary, there wanted not many which opposed themselves of the elder sort of Priests of Queen* Maries *days : and finally, That this division was not onely favoured by the Council, but nourished also for many years by divers troublesome people of their own, both in teaching and writing.* On which the Author of the Reply, whomsoever he was, hath made this Descant, viz. *That for the Catholicks going to Church, it was perchance rather to be lamented then blamed, before it came to be a sign* Distinctive, *by which a Catholick was known from one who was no Catholick.* Thus as the Schisms began together, so are they carried on by the self same means, by Libelling against the State : the Papists, in their *Philopater* ; the Puritans, in *Martin Mar-Prelate*, and the rest : by breeding up their novices beyond the Seas ; the Roman Catholicks, at *Rheims* and *Doway* ; the Presbyterians, at *Geneva, Amsterdam* or *Saumure* : by raising sedition in the State, and plotting Treason against the person of the Queen ; the Papists, by *Throgmorton, Parry, Tichbourn, Babington,* &c. the Puritans, by *Thacker, Penry, Hacket, Coppinger,* &c. And finally, by the executions made upon either part ; of which, in reference to the Presbyterians, we shall speak hereafter. But as none of *Plutarchs* Parallels is so exact, but that some difference may be noted, and is noted by him, betwixt the persons and affairs of whom he writes ; so was there a great difference in one particular between

the fortunes of the Papifts and the contrary faction. The Presbyterians were obferved to have many powerful Friends at Court, in which the Papifts had fcarce any but mortal Enemies. Spies and Intelligencers were employed to attend the Papifts, and obferve all their words and actions; fo that they could not ftir without a difcovery: But all mens eyes were fhut upon the other party, fo that they might do what they lifted without obfervation. Of which no reafon can be given, but that the Queen being ftartled at the Popes late Bull, and finding both her Perfon and Eftate indangered, under divers pretences, by many of the *Romifh* party, both at home and abroad, might either take no notice of the leffer mifchief, or fuffer that faction to grow up to confront the other.

34. And now comes *Cartwright* on the Stage, on which he acted more then any of the *Puritan* Faction, till their laft going off again in the Reign of this Queen. It was upon a difcontent that he firft left *Cambridge*; and in purfuance of the fame, that he left the Church. For being appointed one of the Opponents at the Divinity-Act in *Cambridge*, *Anno* 1564, at fuch time as the Queen was pleafed to honor it with her Royal prefence; he came not off fo happily in her efteem, but that *Prefton* of *Kings Colledge* for action, voyce, and elocution, was preferred before him. This fo afflicted the proud man, that in a fudden humour he retires from the Univerfity, and fets up his ftudies in *Geneva*, where he became as great with *Beza*, and the reft of that Confiftory, as ever *Knox* had been with *Calvin* at his being there. As foon as he had well acquainted himfelf with the Form of their Difcipline, and ftudied all fuch points as were to be reduced to practice at his coming back, well ftocked with Principles, and furnifhed with Inftructions, he prepares for *England*, and puts himfelf into his Colledge. Before, upon the apprehenfion of the faid neglect, he had begun to bufie himfelf with fome difcourfes againft the Ecclefiaftical Government then by Law eftablifhed; and feemed to entertain a great opinion of himfelf, both for Learning and Holinefs; and therewithal a great contemner of fuch others as continued not with him. But at his coming from *Geneva*, he became more practical, or pragmatical rather, condemning the Vocation of Archbifhops, Bifhops, Archdeacons, and other *Ecclefiaftical* Officers; the Adminiftration of our holy Sacraments, and obfervations of our Rites and Ceremonies. And buzzing thefe conceits into the Heads of divers young Preachers and Scholars of the Univerfity, he drew after him a great number of Difciples and Followers. Amongft whom he prevailed fo far by his fecret practices, but much more by a Sermon which he Preached one Sunday-morning in the Colledge-Chappel; that in the afternoon all the Fellows and Scholars threw afide their Surplices (which by the Statutes of the Houfe they were bound to ufe) and went to the Divine Service only in their Gowns and Caps. Dr. *John Whitgift* was at that time Mafter of *Trinity* Colledge, and the Queens Profeffor for Divinity; a man of great temper and moderation, but one withal that knew well how to hold the Reins, and not fuffer them to be wrefted out of his hand by an Headftrong beaft. *Cartwright* was Fellow of that College, emulous of the Mafters Learning, but far more envious at the credit and authority which he had acquired: for which caufe he procured himfelf to be chofen the Profeffor for the Lady *Margaret*, that he might come as near to him as he
could

could, both in place and power. But not content with that which he had done in the Colledge, he puts up his Difciples into all the Pulpits in the Univerfity, where he and they inveigh moft bitterly againft the Government of the Church, and the Governours of it; the Ordination of Priefts and Deacons, the Liturgie eftablifhed, and the Rites thereof. And though *Whitgift* Preached them down as occafion ferved with great applaufe unto himfelf, but greater fatisfaction to all moderate and fober men; yet *Cartwright* and his Followers were now grown unto fuch a head, that they became more violent by the oppofition.

32. It happeneth commonly, as a Learned man hath well obferved, That *thofe fervent Reprehenders of things eftablifhed by publick Authority, are always confident and bold-fpirited men*; and fuch as will not eafily be taken off from their profecutions by any fair and gentle ufage. Which *Whitgift* found at laft, after all his patience; infomuch, that having many times in vain endeavoured, by gentle Admonitions and fair perfwafions, to gain the man unto himfelf, or fo to moderate and reftrain him, as that he fhould no longer trouble both that Colledge and the whole Univerfity with his dangerous Doctrines; he was neceffitated in the end to expel him out of the Houfe, and after to deprive him alfo of the *Margaret*-Lecture. Which laft he acted as Vice-chancellor upon this account, that he had delivered divers errors in his Lectures, which he had neither recanted as he was required, nor fo expounded as to free himfelf from that imputation; and that withal he had exercifed the Function of a Minifter, without being able to produce any Letters of Orders. Hereupon *Cartwright* and his Followers began to mouth it, complaining that the man had been mightily wronged, in being deprived of his preferments in the Univerfity, without being called unto his anfwer; that *Cartwright* had made many offers of Difputation for tryal of the points in Queftion, but could never be heard; and therefore that *Whitgift* fupplyed this by excefs of power, which he was not able to make good by defect of Arguments. To ftop which clamour, *Whitgift* not onely offered him the opportunity of a Conference with him, but offered it in the prefence of fufficient witneffes; and put the man fo hard unto it, that he not only declined the Conference at the prefent, but confeft that *Whitgift* had made him the like offers formerly, and that he had refufed the fame, as he now did alfo. All which appears by a Certificate, fubfcribed by eight fufficient Witneffes, and a publick Notary, dated the 18 of *March* 1570. But this difgrace was followed by a greater, much about that time: for finding himfelf in a neceffity to depart from *Cambridge*, he would have taken the degree of Doctor along with him for his greater credit, but was denyed by the major part of the Regent Mafters and others which had votes therein; which fo difpleafed both him and all his adherents, that from this time the Degrees of Doctors, Batchellors and Mafters were efteemed unlawful, and thofe that took them reckoned for the Limbs of Antichrift, as appears by the *Geneviffn* Notes on the *Revelation*. But for this, and all the other wrongs which he had fuffered (as was faid) in the Univerfity, he will revenge himfelf upon the Church in convenient time; and in convenient time we fhall hear more of it.

36. In

36. In the mean feafon, we muft make a ftep to *Banfteed* in *Surrey*, where we fhall find a knot of more Zealous *Calvinifts*, then in other places; fo Zealous and conceited of their own dear Sanctity, that they feparated themfelves from the reft of their Brethren, under the name of *the Anoynted*, The Bond of Peace was broken by the reft before, and thefe men meant not to retain the unity of fpirit with them, as they had done formerly. Their Leader was one *Wright*; their Opinions thefe, *viz. That no man is to be accufed of fin, but he that did reject the truths by them profeffed. That the whole New Teftament contained nothing but predictions of things to come; and therefore that Chrift (whom they grant to have appeared in the flefh before) fhall come before the Day of Judgement, and actually perform thofe things which are there related: That he whofe fins are once pardoned cannot fin again: And that no credit was to be afforded to men of Learning, but all things to be taught by the Spirit only.* Of thefe men *Sanders* tells us in his Book *De vifibile Monarchia*, Fol. 707, and placeth them in this prefent year 1570. But what became of them, I find not there, or in any others. And therefore I conceive, that either they were foon worn out for want of company, or loft themfelves amongft the *Anabaptifts*, *Familifts*, or fome other. And this I look upon as one of the firft Factions amongft the *Puritans* themfelves, after they had begun their feparation from the Church of *England*: Which feparation, fo begun as before is faid, was clofed again about this time by the hands of thofe who firft had laboured in the breach.

37. For fo it was, that either out of love to their own profit, or the publick peace, fome of them had confulted *Beza* touching this particular; that is to fay, *Whether he thought it more expedient for the good of the Church, That the Minifters fhould chufe rather to forfake their Flocks, then to conform unto fuch Orders as were then prefcribed.* Whereunto he returns this Anfwer: *That many things both may and ought to be obeyed, which are not warrantably commanded: That though the Garments in difpute were not impofed upon the Church by any Warrant from the Word of God; yet having nothing of impiety in them, he conceived that it were fitter for the Minifters to conform themfelves, then either voluntarily to forfake their Churches, or be deprived for their refufal: That in like manner the people were to be advifed to frequent the Churches, and hear their Paftors fo apparelled as the Church required, rather then utterly to forfake that Spiritual food, by which their fouls were to be nourifhed to eternal life: But fo, that firft the Minifters do difcharge their Confciences, by making a modeft proteftation againft thofe Veftments, as well before the Queens Majefty, as their feveral Bifhops? and fo apply themfelves to fuffer what they could not remedy.* This might have ftopt the breach at the firft beginning, if either the *Englifh Puritans* had not been too hot upon it, to be cooled fo fuddenly, or that he had not made his own good counfel ineffectual in the clofe of all: In which he tells them in plain terms, *That if they could no otherwife preferve their ftanding in the Church, then either by fubfcribing to the lawfulnefs of the Orders, Rites and Ceremonies which were then required, or by giving any countenance to them by a faulty filence; they fhould then finally give way to that open violence which they were not able to refift*; that is to fay, (for fo I underftand his meaning) that they fhould rather leave their Churches, then fubmit themfelves to fuch conditions. But this direction being given toward the end of *October, Anno* 1567, feems to be

qualified

qualified in his Epistle to the Brethren of the Forein Churches which were then in *England*, bearing date *June* the fifth in the year next following; in which he thus resolves the case proposed unto him: *That for avoiding all destructive ruptures in the body of Christ, by dividing the members thereof from one another, it was not lawful for any man, of what Rank soever, to separate himself, upon any occasion, from the Church of Christ, in which the Doctrine is preserved, whereby the people are instructed in the ways of God, and the right use of the Sacraments ordained by Christ is maintained inviolable.*

38. This might, I say, have stopped the breach in the first beginning, had not the English *Puritans* been resolved to try some conclusions before they hearkned to the Premises. But finding that their party was not strong enough to bear them out, or rich enough to maintain them on their private purses, they thought it not amiss to follow the directions of their great Dictator. And hereunto the breaking out of those in *Surry* gave some further colour, by which they say, that nothing but confusion must needs fall upon them; and that so many Factions, Subdivisions, and Schismatical Ruptures, as would inevitably ensue on the first separation, must in fine crumble them to nothing. And on these grounds it was determined to unite themselves to the main body of the Church, to reap the profit of the same; and for their safer standing in it, to take as well their Orders as their Institution from the hands of the Bishops. But so, that they would neither wear the Surplice oftner then meer necessity compelled them, or read more of the Common-prayers then what they thought might save them harmless if they should be questioned; and in the mean time by degrees to bring in that Discipline, which could not be advanced at once, in all parts of the Kingdom. Which half conformity they were brought to on the former grounds; and partly by an Act of Parliament which came out this year, 13 *Eliz. Cap.* 12. for the reforming of disorders amongst the Ministers of the Church. And they were brought unto no more then a half-Conformity, by reason of some clashing which appeared unto them, between the Canons of the Convocation, and that Act of Parliament; as also in regard of some interposings which are now made in their behalf, by one of a greater Title, though of no more power, then *Calvin, Martyr, Beza,* or the rest of the Advocates.

39. The danger threatned to the Queen, by the late sentence of Excommunication which was past against her, occasioned her to call the Lords and Commons to assemble in Parliament, the Bishops and Clergy to convene in their Convocation. These last accordingly met together in the Church of St. *Paul,* on the 5 of *April* 1571. At which time Dr. *Whitgift,* Master of *Trinity*-College in *Cambridge,* Preached the Latine Sermon. In which he insisted most especially upon the Institution and Authority of Synodical Meetings, on the necessary use of Ecclesiastical Vestments, and other Ornaments of the Church; the opposition made against all Orders formerly Established, as well by *Puritans* as *Papists*; touching in fine on many other particularities, in rectifying whereof the care and diligence of the Synod was by him required. And as it proved, his counsel was not given in vain. For the first thing which followed the conforming of the Prolocutor, was a command given by the Archbishop

bishop, *That all such of the lower House of Convocation, who not had formerly subscribed unto the Articles of Religion agreed upon* Anno 1562, *should subscribe them now; or on their absolute refusal, or procrastination, be expelled the House.* Which wrought so well, that the said Book of Articles being publickly read, was universally approved, and personally subscribed by every Member of both Houses, as appears clearly by the *Ratification* at the end of those Articles. In prosecution of which necessary and prudent course, it was further ordered, *That the Book of Articles so approved, should be put into Print, by the appointment of the Right Reverend Dr.* John Jewel *then Bishop of* Sarum; *and that every Bishop should take a competent number of them to be dispersed in their Visitations, or Diocesan Synods, and to be read four times in every year in all the Parishes of their several and respective Dioceses.* Which questionless might have settled a more perfect Conformity in all parts of the Kingdom, some Canons of the Convocation running much that way, if the Parliament had spoke as clearly in it as the Convocation; or if some sinister practice had not been excogitated to pervert those Articles, in making them to come out imperfect, and consequently deprived of life and vigour, which otherwise they would have carried.

40. The Earl of *Leicester* at that time was of great Authority, and had apparently made himself the head of the Puritan Faction. They also had the Earl of *Huntingdon,* the Lord *North,* and others in the House of Peers; Sir *Francis Knollis, Walsingham,* and many more in the House of Commons. To which (if *Zanchy* be to be believed, as perhaps he may be) some of the Bishops may be added; who were not willing to tye the Puritans too close to that Subscription by the Act of Parliament, which was required of them by the Acts and Canons of the Convocation. It had been ordered by the Bishops in their Convocation, *That all the Clergy then assembled should subscribe the Articles.* And it was ordered by the unanimous consent of the Bishop and Clergy, *That none should be admitted from thenceforth unto Holy Orders, till he had first subscribed the same, and solemnly had obliged himself to defend the things therein contained, as consonant in all points to the Word of God,* Can. 1571. *Cap. de Episcop.* But by the first Branch of the Act of Parliament, Subscription seemed to be no otherwise required, then to *such Articles alone as contained the Confession of the true Christian Faith, and the Doctrine of the Holy Sacraments.* Whereby all Articles relating to the Book of *Homilies,* the Form of Consecrating Archbishops and Bishops, the Churches power for the imposing of new Rites and Ceremonies, and retaining those already made, seemed to be purposely omitted, as not within the compass of the said Subscription. And although no such Restriction do occur in the following Branches, by which Subscription is required indefinitely unto all the Articles; yet did the first Branch seem to have such influence upon all the rest, that is was made to serve the turn of the *Puritan* Faction, whensoever they were called upon to subscribe to the Episcopal Government, the Publick Liturgie of the Church, or the Queens Supremacy. But nothing did more visibly discover the designs of the Faction, and the great power their Patrons had in the Publick Government, then the omitting the first clause in the twentieth Article: In which it was declared, *That the Church had power to Decree Rites and Ceremonies, and Authority in Contro-*
versies

verſies of Faith. Which Clauſe, though extant in the Regiſters of the Convocation as a part of that Article, and printed as a part thereof both in Latine and Engliſh, *Anno* 1562, was totally left out in this new Impreſſion ; and was accordingly left out in all the Harmonies of *Confeſſions*, or other Collections of the ſame, which were either printed at *Geneva*, or any other place where *Calviniſm* was of moſt predominancy. And ſo it ſtood with us in *England* till the death of *Leiceſter.* After which, in the year 1593 the Articles were reprinted, and that Clauſe reſumed, according as it ſtands in the Publick Regiſters. By which Clauſe it was after publiſhed in the third year of King *James*, and in the tenth year of the ſaid King, *Anno* 1512, and in all following Impreſſions from that time to this. Once cunningly omitted in a Latine Impreſſion which came out at *Oxon*, *Anno* 1536. but the forgery was ſoon diſcovered, and the Book call'd in ; the Printer checked, and ordered to reprint the ſame with the Clauſe prefixed. Which makes it the more ſtrange, and almoſt incredible, that the *Puritans* ſhould either plainly charge it as an Innovation on the late Archbiſhop ; or that any other ſober or indifferent man ſhould make a queſtion, whether the Addition of that Clauſe were made by the Prelates, or the Subtraction of it by the *Puritans*, for their ſeveral purpoſes.

41. There alſo paſt a Book of Canons in this Convocation, by which it was required, *That all ſuch as were admitted unto Holy Orders, ſhould ſub-ſcribe the Book of Articles,* as before was ſaid : *That the* Gray Amice, *ſtill retained (as it ſeems) by ſome of the old Prieſts of Queen* Maries *time, ſhould be from thenceforth laid aſide, and no longer uſed: That the Deans and Reſidentiaries of Cathedral Churches ſhould admit no other Form of ſaying or ſinging Divine Service of the Church, or adminiſtring the holy Sacraments, then that which was preſcribed in the Publick Liturgie : That if any Preacher in the ſame ſhould openly maintain any point of Doctrine contrary to any thing contained in the Book of Articles, or the Book of Common-Prayer, the Biſhop ſhould be adver-tiſed of it by the Dean and Prebendaries, to the end he might proceed therein as to him ſeemed beſt : That no man be admitted to preach, in what Church ſoever, till he be licenſed by the Queen, or the Archbiſhop of the Province, or the Biſhop of the Dioceſs in which he ſerveth : And that no Preacher being ſo licenſed, ſhould preach or teach any thing for Doctrinal, to be believed by the people, but what was conſonant to the Word of God in Holy Scripture ; or by the* Ancient Fathers *or* Orthodox Biſhops of the Church *had been gathered from it . That no Par-ſon, Vicar, or Curate ſhould from thenceforth read the Common Prayers in any Chappl, Oratory, or Private Houſe, unleſs he were licenſed by the Biſhop under hand and ſeal : And that none of the perſons aforeſaid ſhould deſert his Miniſtry, or carry himſelf in his apparel or kind of life like to one of the Laity : That the ſaid Parſons, Vicars and Curates, ſhould yearly certifie to their ſeveral Ordina-ries, the names and Sirnames of all perſons of fourteen years of age and upwards, who had not received the Communion, or did refuſe to be inſtructed in the Pub-lick Catechiſm ; or that they ſhould not ſuffer any ſuch perſons to be God-Father or God-Mother to any child, or to contract any Marriage, either between themſelves or with any other.* It was alſo ordered in thoſe Canons, *That every Biſhop ſhould cauſe the Holy Bible in the largeſt Volume to be ſet up in ſome convenient place of his Hall or Parlour ; that as well thoſe of his own Family, as all ſuch ſtrangers as reſorted to him, might have recourſe to it if they pleaſed : And that*

all Bishops, Deans and Archdeacons should cause the Book called, The Acts and Monuments, *to be disposed of in like sort for the use aforesaid.* The first of which Injunctions seems to have been made for keeping up the Reputation of the English Bibles publickly Authorized for the use of this Church. The credit and authority of which Translation, was much decayed by those of the *Genevian* Faction, to advance their own. By the other there was nothing aimed at, but to gain credit to the Book, which served so seasonably to create an *odium* in all sorts of people, against the Tyrannies and Superstitions of the Pope of *Rome,* whose plots and practices did so apparently intend the ruine of the Queen and Kingdom. No purpose either in the Bishops or Clergie to justifie all or any of the passages in the same contained, which have been since made use of by the Disciplinarians, either to countenance some strange Doctrine, or decry some Ceremony; to which he shewed himself a Friend or Enemy, as the case might vary.

42. Fortified with these Canons and Synodical Acts, the Prelates shew themselves more earnest in requiring Subscription, more zealous in pressing for Conformity then before they did; but found a stiffer opposition in the *Puritan* Faction, then could be rationally expected. For whether it were, that they relyed upon their Friends in Court, or that some Lawyers had informed them that by the Statute no Subscription was to be required of them, but only unto points of Doctrine; certain it is, that they were now more insolent and intractable then they had been formerly. For now, the better to disguise their Projects to wound the Discipline, the quarrels about Surplices and other Vestments (which seemed to have been banished awhile) are revived again; complaints made of their sufferings in it to the Forein Churches; and the report is spread abroad (to gain the greater credit to their own perverseness) that many of the Bishops did as much abominate those Popish Vestments as any of the brethren did. For so writes *Zanchy,* a Divine of *Heidelburg,* in his Letters unto Queen *Elizabeth* of *September* the 2, and writes so by direction from the Prince Elector (whom they had engaged in the cause) out of an hope to take her off from giving any further countenance to the Bishops in that point of Conformity. To the same purpose he writes also to Bishop *Jewel* on the 11 of *Septemb.* Where he informs (as he had been informed himself) *That many of the Ecclesiastical Order would rather chuse to quit their station in the Church, and resign their Offices, then yeild to the wearing of those Vestments which had been formerly defiled by such gross Superstition.* He also signifies what he had writ unto the Queen, of whose relenting he could give himself no great assurance; and that he had also been advised to write to some of the Clergie, to the end that they might be perswaded to a present Conformity, rather then deprive the Church of their future Ministry. The prosecution of which work he commends to *Jewel,* that by the interposing of his Authority, they might be brought to yield to the points proposed, and thereby be continued in the exercise of their Vocation. Which last clause could not chuse but be exceeding acceptable to that Reverend Prelate, who had shewed himself so earnest for Conformity in a Sermon preached by him at the Cross, that he incurred some censure for it amongst the brethren. Which put him to this Protestation before his death, *That his last Sermon at S.* Pauls

Cross, and Conference about the Ceremonies and state of the Church, was not to please any man living, nor to grieve his Brethren of a contrary opinion ; but only to this end, that neither party might prejudice the other. But he was able to act nothing in pursuance of *Zanchy's* motion, by reason of his death within few days after, if not some days before he received that Letter. For on the 22 of the same Moneth, it pleased God to take him to himself ; and thereby to deprive the Church of the greatest Ornament which she could boast of in that age.

The End of the sixth Book.

AERIVS REDIVIVVS:
OR THE
HISTORY
OF THE
Presbyterians.

LIB. VII.

Containing

A Relation of their secret and open Practices ; the Schism and Faction by them raised for advancing the Genevian Discipline in the Church of England, from the year 1572, to the year 1584.

THe English *Puritans* had hitherto maintained their Quarrel by the Authority of *Calvin*, the sawciness of *Knox*, the bold activities of *Beza*, and the more moderate interposing of some Forein Divines, whose name was great in all the Churches of the Reformation. But now they are resolved to try it out by their proper valour ; to fling away their Bulrushes, and lay by their Crutches, or at the best to make no other use of Out-landish Forces, then as Auxiliaries and Reserves, if the worst should happen. And hitherto they had appeared only against Caps and Surplices, or questioned some Rites and Ceremonies in the publick Liturgie which might be thought to have been

I.

been borrowed from the Church of *Rome*: But now they are resolved to venture on the Episcopal Government, and to endeavour the erecting of the *Presbyterian*, as time and opportunity should make way unto it. Amongst which Undertakers none more eminent, because none more violent then *Cartwright*, formerly remembred : *Snape* of *Northampton*, a great stickler for the holy Discipline ; and *Feild* a Lecturer in *London*, as ridiculously zealous to advance *Presbytery*, as the most forward in the pack. But *Cartwright* was the man upon whose Parts and Learning they did most depend, and one who both by private Letters, and some Printed Pamphlets, had gained more credit to the side then all the rest. And yet it was amongst his own only that he gained such credit : For when his Papers had been shewn unto Bishop *Jewel*, and that the Judgment of that Reverend and Learned Prelate was demanded of them, he is said to have returned this answer, That the Arguments therein contained *were too flight to build up, and too weak to pull down*. And so it proved in the event, when *Cartwrights* whose discourses against the Forms of Government and Publick Worship, here by Law established, came to be seriously debated.

2. For having been long great with Child of some new design, the Babe comes forth in the beginning of the Parliament which was held in the year 1572, intituled by the name of an *Admonition* ; in which complaint was made of their many grievances, together with a Declaration of the only way to redress the same ; which they conceived to be no other then the setling of the *Genevian* Platform in all parts of the Kingdom. But the Parliament was so little pleased with the Title, and so much displeased with the matter of the *Admonition*, that the Authors and Preferrers of it were imprisoned by them. But this imprisonment could lay no Fetters on their spirits, which grew the more exasperated, because so restrained. For towards the end of the Parliament out comes the *second Admonition*, far more importunate then the first ; and it comes out with such a flash of Lightning, and such claps of Thunder, as if Heaven and Earth were presently to have met together. In the first he had amassed together all those several Arguments which either his reading could afford, or his wit suggest, or any of that party could excogitate for him against the Government of Bishops, the whole body of the English Liturgie, and almost all the particular Offices in the same contained. And in the second, he not only justified whatsoever had been found in the first, but challenged the Parliament for not giving it a more gracious welcome : For there he tells them in plain terms, *That the State did not shew it self upright, alledge the Parliament what it will. That all honest men should find lack of equity, and all good Consciences condemn that Court : That it should be easier for* Sodom *and* Gomorrha *in the day of Judgement, then for such a Parliament : That there is no other thing to be looked for, then some speedy vengeance to light upon the whole Land, let the Politick* Machiavils *of* England *provide as well as they can, though God do his worst : And finally, that if they of that Assembly would not follow the advice of the first* Admonition, *they would infallibly be their own carvers in it ; the Church being bound to keep Gods Order, and nothing to be called Gods Order but their present Platform.*

3. About this time *Clark, Travers, Gardiner, Barber, Cheston*, and lastly, *Crook*

Crook and *Egerton*, joyned themselves to the Brotherhood. Amongst whom the handling of such points as concerned the Discipline became very frequent, many motions being made, and some conclusions setled in pursuance of it; but more particularly, it was resolved upon the question, *That for as much as divers Books had been written, and sundry Petitions exhibited to her Majesty, the Parliament, and their Lordships, to little purpose, every man should therefore labour by all means possible to bring the Reformation into the Church.* It was also then and there resolved, *That for the better bringing in of the said holy Discipline, they should not only, as well publickly as privately teach it, but by little and little, as well as possibly they might draw the same into practice.* According to which Resolution a Presbytery was erected on the 20 of *November*, at a small Village in *Sarrey* called *Wandsworth*, where *Field* had the Incumbencie, or cure of Souls; a place conveniently scituate for the *London* Brethren, as standing near the Bank of the *Thames*, but four miles from the City, and more retired and out of sight then any of their own Churches about the Town. This first Establishment they indorsed by the name of the *Orders of Wandsworth*. In which the Elders names are agreed on, the manner of the Election declared, the Approvers of them mentioned, their Offices agreed on also, and described. And though the Queen might have no notice of this first Establishment, yet she knew very well both by their Preachings and Writings, that they had defamed the Church of *England*, that many of them refused to be present at that Form of Worship which had the countenance of the Laws, and had set up a new Form of their own devising: Which moved the Queen to look upon them as men of an unquiet and seditious spirit, greedy of change, intent on the destruction of all things which they found established, and ready once again to break out into open Schism. For the preventing whereof, she gave command, *That the severity of the Laws for keeping up the Uniformity of Gods Publick Worship should be forthwith but in execution: And that all such scandalous Books and Pamphlets (the first and second Admonition amongst the rest) should either be immediately delivered to some Bishop in their several Dioceses, or to some one or other of the Lords of the Council, upon pain of imprisonment.*

4. This Proclamation much amazed the Disciplinarians, who were not only more sollicitous in searching into the true Cause and Originial of It, then ready to execute their vengeance upon all such Counsellors as they suspected for the Authors. Sir *Christopher Hatton* was at that time in especial favour, Vice-chamberlain, Captain of the Guard, and afterwards Lord-Chancellor also; in the whole course of his preferments, of a known aversness to the Earl of *Leicester*, and consequently no friend to the *Puritan* Faction. This obstacle must be removed one way or other, according to that Principle of the Ancient *Donatists*, for murthering any man of what Rank soever which opposed their Practices. This Office *Burchet* undertakes, and undertakes the Office upon this Opinion, that it was lawful to assassinate any man who opposed the Gospel. But being blind with too much light, he mistook the man; and meeting in the Street with *Hawkins*, one of the greatest Sea Captains of the times he lived in, he stabbed him desperately with a Ponyard, conceiving that it had been *Hatton* their professed Enemy. For which

which committed to the Tower, he was there examined, found to hold many dangerous and erroneous Tenents; and thereupon sent Prisoner to the *Lollards* Tower. From thence being called into the Consistory of St. *Pauls*, before the Bishop of *London* and divers others, and by them examined, he still persisted in his errors, till the sentence of death was ready on the fourth of *November* to be pronounced against him as an Heretick. Through the perswasions of some men, who took great pains with him, he made a shew as if he had renounced and abjured those Opinions for erroneous and damnable, which formerly he had imbraced with so strong a passion. From thence returned unto the Tower by the Lords of the Council, he took an opportunity when one of his Keepers was withdrawn, to murther the other; intending the like also to his fellow, if he had not happily escaped it. For which fact he was arraigned and condemned at *Westminster* on the morrow after; and the next day he was hanged up in the very place where he wounded *Hawkins*, his right hand being first cut off, and nailed to the Gibbet: a piece of Justice not more safe then seasonable; the horridness of the Fact, and the complexion of the times, being well considered.

5. The Regular Clergy slept not in so great a tempest as was then hanging over their heads; but spent themselves in censuring and confuting *Cartwrights* Pamphlets, which gave the first Animation to those bold attempts. What censure Bishop *Jewel* past upon *Cartwrights* Papers, hath been shewn before; and he will give you his opinion of the Author also, of whom it is reported that he gave this Character, *viz. Stultitia nata est in corde pueri, sed virga Disciplinae fugabit eam*: That is to say, *That folly had been bred in the heart of the young man, and nothing but a Rod of correction would remove it from him.* But *Jewel* had onely seen some scattered Papers intended for materials in the following Pamphlet, which *Whitaker* both saw and censured when it was compleat. For writing of it unto *Whitgift*, he reports him thus: *Quem* Cartwrightus *nuper emisit libellum, &c. I have read over* (saith he) *a great part of the Book which* Cartwright *hath lately set forth. Let me never live, if I ever saw any thing more loose, and almost more childish. As for words indeed, he hath store of them, trim and fresh enough; but as for matter, none at all. Besides which, he not only holds some peevish opinions derogatory to the Queens Authority in causes Ecclesiastical; but had revolted also in that point to the Popish party, from whom he would be thought to fly with such deadly hatred.* He adds in fine, *That he complied not with the Papists in that point alone, but borrowed from them most of his own weapons, wherewith he did assault the Church:* And in a word (as Jerome *did affirm* of Ambrose) (a) *that he was in words, but a Trifler; and for his matter, but a Dreamer; and altogether unworthy to be refuted by a man of Learning.* But these were only some preparatory drops, to the following Tempest which fell upon him from the Pen of the learned *Whitgift*; who punctually dissected the whole *Admonition*, and solidly discoursed upon the Errors and Infirmities of it. Which Book of his, intituled, *An Answer to the Admonition*, followed so close upon the heels of the other, that it was published in the same year with it, 1572. To which Answer *Cartwright* sets out a *Reply* in the year next following; and *Whitgift* presently rejoyns in his *Defence of the Answer*, *Anno* 1574. against which *Cartwright* never stirred, but left him Master of the Field, possest

(a) Verbis ludit, & in sententiis dormitat, & plane indignus est qui a quopiam docto refutetur.

of

of all the figns of an abfolute Victory. And not long after, on the apprehenfion of his foil therein, he withdraws to *Guernfey* firft, and to *Antwerp* afterwards ; erecting the Presbytery in thofe Forein Nations, which he could not compafs in his own.

7. For though the Brotherhood had attempted to advance their Difcipline, and fet up their Presbyterie in the Church of *Wandfworth* ; yet partly by the terror of the Proclamation, and partly by the feafonable execution of *Burchet*, they were reftrained from practifing any further at the prefent on the Church of *England.* But what they durft not do directly, and in open fight, they found a way to act obliquely, and under the difguife of fetting up another Church of Strangers in the midft of *London.* Many of the Low Countrey men, both Merchants, Gentlemen and others, had fled their Countrey at the coming in of the Duke of *Alva*, fettled their dwellings in the Ports and Sea Towns of *England* which lay neareft to them, and in good numbers took up their abode in *London.* Nor did they only bring Families with them, but their Factories alfo : Their feveral Trades and Manufactures ; as the making of all forts of Stuffs, rich Tapiftries, and other Hangings of lefs worth ; and by their diligence therein, not only kept many poor Englifh families in continual work, but taught the Englifh the fame Arts which they brought hither with them. Such welcome Guefts muft needs have fome Encouragement to remain here always. And what Encouragement could be greater and more welcome to them, then to enjoy the liberty of their own Religion, according to fuch Government and Forms of Worfhip as they had exercifed at home ? King *Edward* had indulged the like priviledges to *John Alafco*, and Queen *Elizabeth* to the *French*, neither of which were fo confiderable as the Flemifh Inmates. A fuit is therefore made by their friends in Court, for granting them the Church of *Auguftin Fryars*, where *John Alafco* formerly held his Dutch Congregation ; and granting it with all fuch Priviledges, and Immunities as the Dutch enjoyed. And that they might proceed in fetting up their Presbyteries and new forms of Worfhip, they obtain not only a Connivance or Toleration, but a plain Approbation of their actings in it. For in the Letters which confirmed this new Church unto them, it is exprefly fignified by the Lords of the Council, *That they knew well, that from the firft beginning of the Chriftian Faith, different Rites and Ceremonies had been ufed in fome parts thereof, which were not practifed in the other : That whilft fome Chriftians worfhipped God upon their knees, others erect upon their feet, and fome again groveling on the ground ; there was amongft them all but one and the fame Religion, as long as the whole action tended to the honour of God, and that there was no Superftition and Impiety in it : That they contemned not the Rites which thefe* Dutch *brought with them, nor purpofed to compel them to the practice of thofe which were ufed in* England ; *but that they did approve and allow their Ceremonies, as fitted and accommodated to the nature of the Countrey from whence they came.* Which priviledges they enlarged by their Letter of the 29 of *June*, in the year next following, *Anno* 1574 ; extending them to all fuch of the *Belgick* Provinces as reforted hither, and joyned themfelves unto that Church, though otherwife difperfed in feveral parts and Sea-Towns for their own conveniences; which gave the firft beginning to the new *Dutch* Churches in *Canterbury*, *Sandwich*, *Yarmouth*, *Norwich*, and fome other places in the

the North; to the great animation of the *Presbyters*, and the difcomfart of all fuch who were of judgment to foreſee the fad confequents of it.

8. With like felicity they drove on their defigns in *Jerfey* and *Guernfey*; in the two principal Towns whereof, the Difcipline had been permitted by an Order of the Lords of the Council, as before was faid. But not content with that allowance which the Lords had given them by His Majefties great grace and favour; their Preachers, being for the moſt part natural Frenchmen, had introduced it by degrees into all the Villages; furthered therein by the Sacrilegious Avarice of the feveral Governors, out of a hope to have the fpoil of the poor Deanries, to ingrofs all the Tythes unto themfelves, and then put off the Miniſters with fome forry ftipends, as in fine they did. But firſt thofe Iſlands were to be diffevered by fome Act of State, from being any longer Members of the Diocefs, or fubject to the Jurifdiction of the Bifhops of *Conſtance*. And that being eafily obtained, it was thought fit that *Snape* and *Cartwright*, the great Supporters of the caufe in *England*, fhould be fent unto them to put their Churches in a pofture, and fettle the Difcipline amongſt them in fuch form and manner as it was practifed in *Geneva*, and amongſt the *French*. Which fell out happily for *Cartwright*, as his cafe ftood; who being worſted in the laſt Encounter betwixt him and *Whitgift*, had now a handfome opportunity to go off with credit; not as if worſted in the fight, but rather called away to another tryal. Upon this Invitation they fet fail for the Iſlands, and take the charge thereof upon them; the one of them being made the titular Paſtor of the Caſtle of *Mount Orgueil*, in the Iſle of *Jerfey*; and the other of *Caſtle Cornet*, in the Rode af *Guernfey*. Thus qualified they convene the Churches of each Iſland, communicate unto them a rude Draught of the Holy Difcipline; which afterwards was polifhed, and accommodated to the ufe of thofe Iſlands: but not agreed upon and exercifed until the year next following; as appears by the Title of it, which is this, *viz. The Eccleſiaſtical Difcipline obſerved and practiſed by the Churches of* Jerfey *and* Guernfey, *after thé Reformation of the fame by the Miniſters, Elders and Deacons of the Iſles of* Guernfey, Jerfey, Sark, *and* Alderney; *confirmed by the Authority, and in the prefence of the Governors of the fame Iſles, in a Synod holden in* Guernfey *the* 28 *of* June 1576; *and afterwards revived by the faid Miniſters and Elders, and confirmed by the faid Governors in a Synod holden in* Jerfey *the* 11, 12, 13, 14, 15 *and* 17 *days of* October 1577.

9. With worfe fuccefs, but lefs diligence, did *Travers* labour in the caufe; who being one of the fame fpirit, publifhed a Book in maintainance of the Holy Difcipline; which he caufed to be Printed at *Geneva*, and was thus Intituled; *viz. Eccleſiaſticæ Difciplinæ, & Anglicanæ Eccleſia ab illa aberrationis, plena e verbo Dei & dilucida Explicatio*: that is to fay, *A full and perfect Explication of Eccleſiaſtical Difcipline, according to the Word of God; and of the Church of* Englands *departing from it*. In which Book he advanced the Difcipline to fo great a height, as made it neceffary for all Chriſtian Kings and Princes (a) to fubmit unto it, and lay down their Crowns and Sceptres at the Churches feet, even to the very licking up of the duft thereof, if occafion were. But *Travers* fojourned in *Geneva* when he wrote this Book, and was to frame it to the palat of *Beza*, and the

(a) *Hæic Diſciplinæ omnes Reges & Principes fafces ſuas ſubmittere neceſſe eſt. &c.* Traverf. de Diſcipl. Ecc.

the rest of that Consistory; who had by this time made the Discipline as essential to the true being of a Church, as either the Preaching of the Word, or the Administration of the holy Sacraments. *Beza* had so declared it in a Letter to *Knox*, *An.* 1572. In which he reckons it as a great and signal blessing from Almighty God, that they had introduced in *Scotland*, not only the true Worship of God, but the Discipline also, which was the best Preservative of the truth of Doctrine. Which therefore he desires him so to keep together, as to be sure, that if the one be lost (that is, laid aside) the other is not like to continue long. And *Cartwright* leading in the same path also, heightned it above all which had gone before, or that followed after him. Some of the Brethren have extolled it to the very Skies, as being *the onely Bond of Peace; the Bane of Heresie; the Punisher of Sin, and maintainer of Righteousnesse: A Discipline full of all goodness, for the peace and honour of Gods people, ordained for the joy and happiness of all the Nations.* But *Cartwright* sets them such a leap, as they durst not reach at, not only telling us in his last Book against Learned *Whitgift*, *That the want of the Elderships is the cause of all evil, and that it is not to be hoped that any Commonwealth can flourish without it;* but also, *that it is no small part of the Gospel, yea, the substance of it.*

9 And if it proved to be a part of our Saviours Gospel, what could the brethren do less then pretend some Miracles for Confirmation of the same? and to what Miracles could they pretend with more shew of Sanctity, and manifestation of the Spirit, then to the casting out of Devils? *Cambden* informs us in this year, that the credulity of some *London* Ministers had been abused by a young Wench, who was pretended at at that time to be possessed of the Devil. But I rather think that the *London*-Ministers were confederate with this Wench, then abused by her; considering the subsequent practice in that kind of casting out Devils by the *Puritan* Preachers, to gain the greater credit to their Cause: for in this very year they practised the casting of a Devil out of one *Mildred*, the base Daughter of *Alice Norrington* of *Westwell* in *Kent*. Which for all the godly pretences made by *Roger Newman*, and *John Brainford*, two of the Ministers of that County, who were parties to it, was at the last confessed to be but a false Impostor. Dr. *Harsnet*, (who afterward dyed Archbishop of *York*) informs us also in his Book against *Darrel*, that there were at this time two Wenches in *London*, that is to say, *Agnes Bridges*, and *Rachel Pindeo*, who publickly were given out to be possessed; and it is possible that one of them may be she whom *Cambden* speaks of. Under which head may be also ranged the dispossessing of one *Margaret Cooper* at *Ditchet* in the County of *Sommerset*, about ten years after, 1584. But all inferiour to the Pranks which were played by *Darrel*, with whom none of the *Puritan Exorcists* is to hold comparison; of which we are to speak hereafter in its proper place; The Papists have been frequently and justly blamed for their impostures in this thing, and no terms are thought vile enough to express their falshoods. But they were only *pious frauds* in the *Presbyterians*, because conducing to such godly and religious ends, in the advancing of the Scepter and Throne of Christ, by the holy Discipline. And it is strange that none of all their Zealots have endeavoured to defend them in it, as well as *Cartwright* laboureth to excuse their unlawful meetings from the

name

name of Conventicles ; that being, as he tells us, too light a word to exprefs the Gravity and Piety of thofe Affemblies, in which Sacraments are Adminiftred, and the Gofpel Preached.   If fo, all other Sectaries whatfoever may excufe themfelves from the holding of Conventicles, or being obnoxious to any penal Laws and Sanctions upon that account, becaufe they hold their Cactious and Schifmatical Meetings for the felf fame ends. And then the Queen muft be condemned for executing fome feverity on a Knot of *Anabaptifts*, whom fhe found holding the like lawlefs Meetings in the year next following.

1575.   10. For fo it was, that many of thofe Foreiners, which reforted hither from the *Belgick* Provinces, and were incorporated into a diftinct Society or Congregation, differing both in Government and Forms of Worfhip from the Church of *England*, did by degrees withdraw themfelves from her Communion, and held their Conventicles apart from the reft of that body.   Of thefe, fome openly declared themfelves for the Sect of the *Anabaptifts* ; others would needs be Members of the Family of *Henry Nicholas*, (who had been once a Member of the *Dutch Church* under *John Alafco*) called commonly the *Family of Love* ; of which we have fpoken in the Hiftory of the *Belgick* troubles, (*Lib.* 3. *Numb.* 46.) And not content to entertain thofe new Opinions and devices amongft themfelves, they muft draw in the Englifh alfo to participate with them ; who having deviated from the paths of the Church, were like enough to fall into any other, and to purfue thofe crooked ways, in which the cunning Hereticks of thofe times did, and had gone before them.   But fuch a diligent eye was had upon all their practices, that they were croffed in the beginning.   For upon *Eafter-day*, about nine in the Morning, was difclofed a Conventicle of thefe *Anabaptifts*, *Dutch-men*, at an Houfe without the *Bars* of *Aldgate* ; whereof twenty feven were taken and fent to prifon, and four of them bearing Fagots at St. *Pauls* Crofs, recanted in form following, *viz. Whereas I,* NN, *being feduced by the fpirit of Error and by falfe Teachers his Minifters, have fallen into many damnable and deteftable Herefies, viz.* 1. *That Chrift took not flefh of the fubftance of the Bleffed Virgin* Mary : 2. *That Infants born of faithful Parents ought to be Rebaptized* : 3. *That no Chriftian man ought to be a Magiftrate, or bear the Sword or Office of Authority* : 4. *And that it is not lawful for a Chriftian man to take an Oath.   Now by the Grace of God, and through Conference with good and Learned Minifters of Chrift his Church ; I do underftand and acknowledge the fame to be moft damnable and deteftable Herefies , and do ask God here before his Church mercy for my faid former Errors, and do forfake them, recant, and renounce them, and abjure them from the very bottom of my heart. And further I confefs, that the whole Doctrine and Religion eftablifhed in this Realm of* England, *as alfo that which is received and practifed in the* Dutch Church *here in this City, is found, true, and according to the Word of God ; whereunto in all things I fubmit my felf, and will moft gladly be a Member of the faid* Dutch Church *; from henceforth utterly abandoning and forfaking all and every* Anabaptiftical *Error.*

11. This gave a ftop to many of them at their firft fetting out. But fome there were, who neither would be terrified with the fear of punifhment, or edified by the Retractation which thofe four had made ; continued in their former courfes with great pertinacity ; infomuch, that on

the

the 21 of *May*, being *Whitson-Eve*, no fewer then eleven of that Sect, all *Dutch*, (that is to say, one man and ten Women) were condemned in the Consistory at St. *Pauls*, to be burned in *Smithfield*. And though great pains was taken to reclaim them from those wicked Errors; yet such was their obstinacy and perverseness, that one Woman onely was converted. The rest had so much mercy shewed them, as to be banished the Realm without further punishment; which gave the greater resolution to the rest of their company to be more practical then before in promoting their Heresies. Which put the State upon a just necessity of proceeding more severely against some of them, then by Bonds and banishments: Two of the same Nation and Opinions being burnt in *Smithfield* on the second of *July*, where they dyed with great horror, exprest by many roarings and cryings, but without any sign or shew of true repentance. Before the executing of which sentence *John Fox* the English Martyrologist addrest his Letters to the Queen, in which he supplicated for the lives of those wretched men, and offered many pious and prudential reasons for the reversing of that sentence; or at the least, for staying it from execution. By which he so prevailed upon her, that she consented to a gracious sparing of their lives, if on a moneths Reprieve, and Conference in the mean time with Learned men, they could be gained unto a retractation of their damnable Heresies. But that expedient being tryed, and found ineffectual, the forfeiture of their lives was taken, and the sentence executed. Nor had the *Dutch* Church of *Norwich* any better Fortune, or could pretend to be more free from harbouring some Phanatical spirits, then the *Dutch* Congregation in the *Augustine Fryars*. From some of which it may be probably supposed, that *Matthew Hamant*, a poor Plow-wright of *Featherset*, within three Miles of *Norwich*, took his first impressions, which afterwards appeared in more horrid blasphemies then any English ever had been acquainted with in the times preceding. For being suspected to hold many dangerous and unsound Opinions, he was convented before the Bishop of that City; at what time it was charged upon him, that he had publickly maintained these Heresies following; that is to say, *That the new Testament or Gospel was but meer foolishness, and a story of men, or rather a mere Fable: That he was restored to Grace of the free Mercy of God, without the means of Christ his Blood and Passion: That Christ is not God, or the Saviour of the World, but a sinful man, a mere man, and an abominable Idol; and that all they that worship him are abominable Idolaters: That Christ did not rise again from death to life by the power of his Godhead, neither that he ascended into Heaven: That the Holy Ghost is not God, and that there is no such thing as an Holy Ghost: That Baptism is not necessary in the Church of God, nor the use of the Sacrament of the Body and Blood of Christ.* For which he was condemned for an Heretick in the Bishops Consistory on the Fourteenth of *April*; and being thereupon delivered to the Sheriff of the City, he was burnt in the Castle-Ditch on the Twentieth of *May* 1579. As a preparative to which punishment, his ears had been cut off on the Thirteenth of that Moneth for base and slanderous words against the Queen and Council.

12. About the same time that the *Anabaptists* were first brought to censure, there spawned another fry of Hereticks, who had its first Original

amongst

amongst the *Dutch*, and from thence came for *England* with the rest of their brethren. These called themselves the *Family of Love*, as before is said ; and were so well conceited of their own great holiness, that they thought none to be Elected to Eternal life, but such as were admitted into their Society. The particulars of their Opinions, and the strange manner of Expressions, have been insisted on before. Let it suffice, that by their seeming Sanctity, and other the like deceitful arts of Dissimulation, they had drawn some of the English to them; who having broke the bond of peace, could not long keep themselves to the Spirit of Unity. Some of them being detected, and convented for it, were condemned to do Penance at S. *Pauls* Cross ; and there to make a Retractation of their former Errors. According to which Sentence five of them are brought thither on the 12 of *June* ; who there confest themselves utterly to detest, as well the Author of that Sect *H. N.* as all his damnable Heresies. Which gentle punishment did rather serve to multiply then decrease the Sect ; which by the diligence of the Hereticks, and the remisness of the new Archbishop, came to such an height, that course was taken at the last for their apprehension, and for the severe punishing of those which were so apprehended. For the Queen seriously considering how much she was concerned, both in honor and safety, to preserve Religion from the danger threatned by such desperate Hereticks, published her Proclamation on the ninth of *October*, *Anno* 1580, for bringing their persons unto Justice, and causing their pestilent Pamphlets to be openly burnt. And to that end she gave a strict command to all Temporal Judges, and other Ministers of Justice, to be assistant to the Bishops and their under-Officers, in the severe punishing of those Sects and Sectaries, by which the happiness of the Church was so much endangered. By which severities, and a Formal Abjuration prescribed unto them by the Lords of the Council, these Sects were seasonably suppressed, or had the reason to conceal themselves amougst such of the Brethren as did continue in their Separation from the Church of *England*.

13. In the mean time, there happened a great alteration in the state of the Church, by the death of one, and the preferment of another, of the greatest Prelates. Archbishop *Parker* left this life on the 17 of *May*, *Anno* 1575. To whom succeeded Dr. *Edmond Grindal*, Translated from the See of *York* unto that of *Canterbury*, on the 15 of *February*. The first a Prelate of great parts, and no less Eminent for his zeal in the Churches cause; which prompted him to keep as hard a hand on all Sects and Sectaries, and more particularly on those of the *Genevian* Platform, as the temper of the times could bear. But *Grindal* was a man of another spirit, without much difficulty wrought upon by such as applied themselves to him. And having maintained a correspondence when he lived in Exile with *Calvin*, *Beza*, and some others of the Consistory ; he either could not shake off their acquaintance at his coming home, or was as willing to continue it as they could desire. Being advanced unto the Bishoprick of *London*, he condescends to *Calvins* motion touching the setling of a French Church in that City on *Genevian* Principles ; and received thanks from him for the same. And unto whom but him must *Beza* make his Applications, when any of the brethren were suspended,

depri-

deprived or sequestred, for not conforming to the Vestments then by Law required? Being Translated unto *York*, which was upon the 22 of *May* 1570, he entertains a new Intelligence with *Zanchy* a Divine of *Heidelburg*, somewhat more moderate then the other; but no good friend neither to the Church of *England*, as appears by his interposings in behalf of the Brethren, when they were under any censure for their inconformity. To this man *Grindal* renders an account of his Preferment both to *York* and *Canterbury*: To him he sends Advertisement how things went in *Scotland*, at his Advancement to the first; and of the present state of affairs in *England*, when he came to the other. The like Intelligence he maintained with *Bullinger*, *Gualter*, and some of the chief Divines amongst the *Switzers*; taking great pride in being courted by the Leading men of those several Churches, though they had all their ends upon him for the advancing of Presbytery and Inconformity in the Church of *England*.

14. Upon these grounds the Presbyterians gave themselves good hopes of the new Archbishop; and they soon found how plyant he was like to prove to their expectation. He entred on this great Charge in in the Moneth of *February* 1575; at which time the Prelates and Clergy were assembled in a Convocation; by whom a Book of Articles was agreed upon for the better Reiglement of the Church. In the end whereof this Article was superadded by their procurement; *viz. That the Bishops should take order, that it be published and declared in every Parish Church within their Dioceses, before the first day of* May *then next following, That Marriages might be solemnized at all times in the year; so that the Banes on their several Sundays or Holidays, in the Service time, were openly asked in the Church, and no impediment objected; and so that also the said Marriage be publickly solemnized in the face of the Church at the aforesaid time of Morning Prayer.* But when the Book was offered to the Queens perusal, she disliked this Article, and would by no means suffer it to be Printed amongst the rest; as appears by a Marginal Note in the Publick Register of that Convocation. Which though it might sufficiently have discouraged them from the like Innovations, yet the next year they ventured on a business of a higher nature, which was the falsifying and corrupting of the Common-Prayer-Book. In which, being then published by *Richard Jugge* the Queens Majesties Printer, and published *Cum Privilegio Regiæ Majeslatis*, as the Title intimates; the whole Order of *Private Baptism*, and *Confirmation of Children* was quite omitted. In the first of which it had been declared, *That Children being born in Original sin, were by the Laver of Regeneration in Baptism ascribed unto the number of* Gods *Children, and made the Heirs of Life Eternal*; and in the other, *That by the Imposition of hands and Prayer, they receive strength against sin, the World and the Devil.* Which grand omissions were designed to no other purpose, but by degrees to bring the Church of *England* into some Conformity to the desired Orders of *Geneva*. This I find noted in the Preface of a Book writ by *William Reynolds*, a virulent Papist I confess but one that may be credited in a matter of Fact, which might so easily have been refuted by the Book it self, if he had any way belyed it.

15. Nothing being done for punishing of this great abuse, they enter upon another Project: Which seemed to tend onely to the encrease of

Piety

1579.

1577.

Piety in the Proffeffors of the Gofpel ; but was intended really for the furtherance of the Holy Difcipline. The defign was, that all the Minifters within fuch a Circuit fhould meet upon a day appointed to exercife their gifts, and expound the Scriptures ; one being chofen at each meeting for the Moderator to govern and direct the Action ; the manner whereof was this that followeth : *The Minifters of fome certain Precinct did meet on fome week-days in fome principal Town ; of which Meeting fome ancient grave Minifter was Prefident, and an Auditory admitted of Gentlemen, and other perfons of Leifure. There every Minifter fucceffively (the youngeft ftill beginning) did handle one and the fame piece of Scripture, fpending feverally fome quarter of an hour and better ; but in the whole, fome two hours. And the Exercife being begun and concluded with prayer, the Prefident giving them another Theme for the next Meeting (which was every Fortnight) the faid Affembly was diffolved.* The Exercife they called by the name of *Prophecying*, grounded upon thofe words of the Apoftle, 1 *Cor.* 14. 13. viz. *For ye may all prophecy one by one, that all may learn, and all be comforted.* But finding that the Text was not able to bear it out, they added thereunto fuch pious and prudential Reafons, as the beft Wits amongft them could devife for the prefent. And though this Project was extremely magnified and doted on with no lefs paffion by fome Countrey Gentlemen, who were enamored of the beauty and appearance of it ; yet was it found upon a diligent enquiry, that there was fomething elfe intended then their Edification. For it was eafie to be proved, that under colour of thofe Meetings for Religious Exercifes, the Brethren met together and confulted of the common bufinefs, and furioufly declaimed againft Church and State.

1579.   16. Thefe Meetings *Grindal* firft connived at when he fate at *York*, under pretence of training up a Preaching Miniftry for the Northern parts. But afterwards he was fo much poffeffed with the phancy of it, that he drew many of the Bifhops in the Province of *Canterbury* to allow them alfo. By means whereof, they came to be fo frequent in moft parts of the Kingdom, that they began to look with a face of danger, both on Prince and Prelate. For having once fettled themfelves in thefe new Conventions with fome fhew of Authority, the Leading Members exercifed the Jurifdiction over all the reft, intrenching thereby on the power of their feveral Ordinaries. And they incroached fo far at laft on the Queens Prerogative, as to appoint days for folemn Fafts, under pretence of Sanctifying thofe Religious Exercifes to the good of the Nation, as afterwards in their Claffical and Synodical Meetings, which took growth from hence. Three years thefe Prophefyings had continued in the Province of *Canterbury*, before the Queen took notice of them. But then they were prefented to her with fo ill a complexion, that fhe began to ftartle at the firft fight of them. And having ferioufly weighed all inconveniences which might thence enfue, fhe fends for *Grindal* to come to her ; reproves him for permitting fuch an Innovation to be obtruded on the Church, and gave him charge to fee it fuddenly fuppreffed. She complained alfo, that the Pulpit was grown too common, invaded by unlicenfed Preachers, and fuch as Preached fedition amongft the people ; requiring him to take fome order, that the *Homilies* might be read more frequently, and fuch Sermons Preached

more

more sparingly then of late they had been. But this was hard meat not so easily chewed; therefore not like to be digested by so weak a stomach. Instead of acting any thing in order to the Queens commands, he writes unto her a most tedeous and voluminous Letter; in which he first presents her *with a sad remembrance of the Discourse which past between them, and the great sorrow which he had conceived on the sense thereof.* Which said, he falls into a *commendation of Sermonizing; of the great benefit thereby redounding unto all her Subjects; the manifold advantages which such Preachings had above the Homilies; of what necessary use those* Prophesyings *were toward the training up of Preachers.* In fine, he also lets her know, *that by the example of St.* Ambrose, *and his proceedings toward* Theodosius *and* Valentinian, *two most mighty Emperors, he could not satisfie his conscience in the discharge of the great trust committed to him, if he should not admonish her upon this occasion, not to do any thing which might draw down Gods displeasure upon her and the Nation, by stopping the free Exercise of Gods true Religion, and his promoting of his Gospel.*

17. These Premises being laid together, he comes at last to this conclusion, as to assure her in plain terms, but with all humility, *That he could not with a safe Conscience, and without the offence of the Majesty of God, give his assent to the suppressing of the said Exercises, much less send out any Injunction for the utter and universal subversion of the same: that he might say with the Apostle, That he had no power to destroy, but onely to edifie; that he could do nothing against the Truth, but for it: And therefore finally, that if it were her Majesties pleasure, for this or any other cause to remove him out of his place, he would with all humility yeild thereunto, and render again unto her Majesty that which he had received from her.* For to what purpose, as he said, *should he endeavour to retain a Bishoprick, or to gain the World, with the loss and hazard of his Saul? considering that he which doth offend against his Conscience, doth but digg out his own way to Hell.* In which respect he humbly desires her to bear with him, *if he rather chuse to offend her Earthly Majesty, then the Heavenly Majesty of Almighty God.* But not content with such an absolute refusal, and setting her at such a distance from Almighty God, he takes upon him to advise her to discharge her self of the concernments of the Church, or not to manage it at the least with so high a hand as she had done hitherto. Fitter it was, as he conceived it, *That all Ecclesiastical matters which concerned Religion, the Doctrine and Discipline of the Church, should be referred unto the Bishops, and the Divines of this Realm, according to the example of all Christian Emperours, and the Godly Princes of all ages, in the times before her.* And this he further pressed upon her, by her own Example, in not deciding any questions about the Laws of the Realm in her Court or Palace; but sending them to be determined by her Judges in the Courts of *Westminster*; and therefore by the self-same Reason, when any question did arise about the Discipline and Doctrine of the Church within her Dominions, the ordinary way must be to refer the same to the Decision of the Bishops, and other chief Ministers of the Church in Synodicall Meetings, and not to determine of them in the Court by the Lords of her Council.

18. But notwithstanding his refusal to conform to her will and pleasure on the one side, and this harsh Counsel on the other, which must needs

1580.

needs be unwelcome to a Prince that loved and understood her own Authority so well as his Mistress did, he might have kept his Bishoprick, with her Majesties favour, which he appeared so willing to resign unto her. He might, I say, have kept them both having so many great Friends about the Queen, who approved his doings, if a breach had not happened about this time betwixt him and *Leicester*, the mighty Patron and Protector of the *Puritan Faction*, occasion'd by his denying at the Earls request to alienate his goodly House and Mannor of *Lambeth*, that it might serve for a retiring place to that mighty Favourite. And hereunto he did contribute further, as was said by others, for refusing to grant a Dispensation to marry one which was too near of kindred to him, clearly within the compass of those degrees which seemed to him to be prohibited by the Word of God. This *Leicester* thought he might command, and was exceedingly vexed not to find obedience, in one who had been raised by him, and depended on him. Upon which ground all passages, which before were shut against his Enemies, were now left free and open for them; and the Queens ears are open to their informations, as the passages were unto her person. By them she comes to understand, what a neglect there was of the publick Liturgy in most parts of the Kingdom, what ruine and decay of Churches, what innovations made already, and what more projected; by which she would be eased in time of all cares of Government, and find the same to be transferr'd to the *Puritan* Consistories. She was told also of the general disuse of all weekly Fasts, and those which annually were required by the Laws of the Realm; and that instead thereof, the Brethren had took upon them, according to the *Arrian Doctrine*, to appoint solemn and occasional Fasts in several places, as at *Leicester*, *Coventry*, &c. in defiance of the Laws and her own Prerogative. Touching which last, she gave another hot Alarm to Archbishop *Grindal*, who in a long Letter did excuse the matter, as not being done by his allowance or consent; though it could not be denyed but that it had been done by his connivance, which came all to one: so that the Accusation being strong, his Defences weak, and no friend left about the Queen who durst mediate for him (for who durst favour him on whom *Leicester* frowned?) the Archiepiscopal Jurisdiction was sequestred from him, conferred upon four Suffragans of the Province of *Canterbury*, and he himself confined to one of his Countrey-houses till the Queens further pleasure should be signified to him. Which sequestration must needs happen before the beginning of the Convocation which was held this year; the Presidency whereof was then devolved on the Bishop of *London*, by reason of *Grindals* incapacity to perform that Service.

19. For on the sixteenth day of *January* it pleased the Queen to call a Parliament to be held at *Westminster*, in which some things occurred of great importance in order to the *Presbyterian* History which we have in hand. The *Puritans* following the *Arrians* in that particular, as in many others, had openly decryed all set and determinate Fasts; but then ascribed more merit unto those of their own appointing, then any Papists do to those of the Popes Ordaining. They had also much took off the edge of the people from the Common-Prayer-Book, but most especially from the Litany (none of the meanest Pieces in it) which till that time

was

was read accustomably in the House of Commons, before the Members setled upon any businiss. But in the beginning of this Parliament, it was moved by one *Paul Wentworth* in the House of Commons, that there might be a Sermon every Morning before they sate, and that they would nominate some day for a solemn Fast. How the first motion sped, I have no where found ; but may conclude by the event, that it came to nothing, because I never heard that any thing was done in pursuance of it till the late Long Parliament, where the like Toy was taken up for having Sermons every Morning in the Abbey-Church. But that about the Fast being made when more then half the Members were not present at it, was carried in the Affirmative by fifteen voices. And thereupon it was ordered, as the Journal telleth us, *That as many of the House as conveniently could, should on the Sunday fortnight following assemble and meet together in the* Temple-Church, *there to have Preaching, and to joyn together in Prayer with Humiliation and Fasting for the assistance of Gods Spirit in all their consultations during this Parliament, and for the preservation of the Queens Majesty and her Realms.* And though they were so cautious in the choice of their Preachers, to refer the naming of them to the Lords of the Council, which were then Members of the House, in hope to gain them also to avow the action ; yet neither could this satisfie the Queen, or affect their Lordships. For some of them having made the Queen acquainted with their purpose in it, she sends a Message to them by Sir *Christopher Hatton,* who was then Vice-Chamberlain ; by which he lets them know, *That her Majesty did much admire at so great a rashness in that House, as to put in execution such an Innovation, without her privity and pleasure first made known unto them.* Which Message being so delivered, he moved the House *to make humble submission to her Majesty, acknowledging the said offence and contempt, craving the remission of the same, with a full purpose to forbear the committing of the like hereafter.* Which motion being hearkned to (as there was good reason) Mr. *Vice-Chamberlain* is desired to present their submission to the Queen, and obtain her pardon ; which he accordingly performed.

20. This practice gave the Queen so fair a Prospect into the counsels of the Faction, that she perceived it was high time to look about her, and to provide for the preserving of her power and Prerogative Royal, but more for the security of her Realm and Person. To which end she procured a Statute to be made in that very Parliament, by which it was Enacted, *That if any person or persons, forty days after the end of that Session, should advisedly devise, or write, or print, or set forth any manner of Book, Rhyme, Ballad, Letter or Writing, containing any false, seditious, or slanderous matter, to the Defamation of the Queens Majesty, or to the encouraging, stirring or moving of any Insurrection or Rebellion within this Realm, or any of the Dominions to the same belonging : Or if any person after the time aforesaid, as well within the Queens Dominions, as in any other place without the same, should procure such Book, Rhyme, Ballad, &c. to be written, printed, published or set forth, &c. (the said offence not being within the compass of Treason by vertue of any former Statute) that then the said Offenders, upon sufficient proof thereof by two lawful witnesses, should suffer death and loss of goods, as in case of Felony.* And that the Queen may be as safe from the Machinations of the *Papists,* as she was secured by this Act from the plots of the

the Puritans, a Law was paſt, *To make it Treaſon for any Prieſt or Jeſuit to ſeduce any of the Queens Subjects to the Romiſh Religion ; and for the Sub- jects to be reconciled to the Church of* Rome. This Act, intituled, *An Act for retaining the Queens Subjects in their due obedience* ; the other, *For the puniſhing ſeditious words againſt the Queen*, 23 Eliz. c.1,2. Which Statutes were contrived of purpoſe to reſtrain the Inſolency of both Factions ; and by which, many of them were adjudged to death in times enſuing : Some of them, as in caſe of Treaſon ; and others, as the Authors or the Publiſhers of Seditious Pamphlets. But the laſt Statute being made with Limitation to the life of the Queen, it expired with her. And had it been revived (as it never was) by either of the two laſt Kings, it might poſſibly have prevented thoſe dreadful miſchiefs which their poſterity for ſo long a time have been involved in.

21. Together with this Parliament, was held a Convocation, as the Cuſtom is. In the beginning whereof, an Inſtrument was produced un- der the Seal of Archbiſhop *Grindal,* for ſubſtituting Dr. *John Elmore* then Biſhop of *London* (a Prelate of great parts and ſpirit, but of a con- trary humour to the ſaid Archbiſhop) to preſide therein ; which in the incapacity of the other, he might have challenged as of right belonging to him. Nothing elſe memorable in this Convocation, but the admitting of Dr. *William Day* then Dean of *Windſor,* to be Prolocutor of the Cler- gy; the paſſing of a Bill for the grant of Subſidies ; and a motion made unto the Prelates, in the name of the Clergy, for putting the late Book of Articles in execution. Nothing elſe done within thoſe walls, though much was agitated and reſolved on by thoſe of *Grindals* party in their private Meetings. Some of the hotter heads amongſt them had propo- ſed in publick, *That the Clergy ſhould decline all buſineſs, even the grant of Subſidies, till the Archbiſhop were reſtored to his place and ſuffrage.* But this could find no entertainment amongſt wiſer men. Others adviſed, *That a Petition ſhould be drawn in the name of both Houſes, by which Her Majeſty might be moved to that reſtitution.* And though I find nothing to this purpoſe in the Publick Regiſters (which may ſufficiently evince, that it never paſſed as an Act of the Convocation) yet I find that ſuch a Petition was agreed upon and drawn into form by Dr. *Tobie Matthews* then Dean of *Chriſt-Church,* and by ſome Friends preſented to Her Majeſties ſight. *Mat- thews* was maſter of an elegant and fluent ſtile, and moſt pathetically had bemoaned thoſe ſad misfortunes which had befallen that Prelate, and the Church in him, by ſuffering under the diſpleaſure of a gratious Sove- raign. The mitigation whereof was the rather hoped for, in regard he had offended more out of the tenderneſs of his Conſcience, then from the obſtinacy of his will. But no ſuch anſwer being given unto this Peti- tion, as by his Friends might be expected, *Grindal* continued under his Suſpenſion till the time of his death. Once it was moved, *to have a Co- adjutor impoſed upon him, who ſhould not only exerciſe the Juriſdiction, but re- ceive all the Rents and profits which belonged to his Biſhoprick.* And ſo far they proceeded in it, that Dr. *John Whitgift* (who had been preferred to the See of *Worc.* 1576.) was nominated for the man, as one ſufficiently furniſhed with abilities to diſcharge the truſt. But he moſt worthily declined it, & would not ſuffer the poor man to be ſtript of his clothes, though for the apparelling of his own body with the greater honor, till death had laid him in the bed of Eternal reſt.

22. But

22. But the troubles of this year were not ended thus.   For neither those good Laws before remembred, nor the Executions done upon them, could prevail so far, as to preserve the Church from falling into those distractions, which both the Papists and the Presbyterians had projected in it.   The Jesuits had hitherto been content to be lookers on, and suffered the Seminary Priests to try their Fortunes in the reduction in this Kingdom to the See of *Rome*.   But finding how little had been done by them in twenty years : so little, that it came almost to less then nothing, they are resolved to take the honor to themselves.   To which end, *Heywood, Parsons* and *Campian* first set foot in *England,* and both by secret practices and printed Pamphlets, endeavoured to withdraw the subjects from their due obedience.   Nothing more ordinary in their mouths, or upon their Pens, then *that the Crown belonged of right to the Queen of* Scots *: That* Elizabeth *was to be deprived : That if the Pope commanded one thing, and the Queen another, the Popes commands were to be obeyed, and not the Queens :* And in a word, *That all the Subjects were absolved from their Allegiance, and might declare as much when they found it necessary.* Which that it might be done with the greater safety, Pope *Gregory* the XIII is desired to make an Explication of the former Bull.   By which it should be signified to the English Catholicks, that the said former Bull of Pope *Pius* V should remain obligatory unto none but the Hereticks only ; but that the Romish Catholicks should not be bound by it, as the case then stood, till they should find themselves in a fit capacity to put the same in execution without fear of danger.   And presently upon their first entrance, a Book is published by one *Howlet,* containing many reasons for deterring the Papists from joyning in any Act of Worship with the English Protestants ; the going, or not going to Church, being from henceforth made a sign *distinctive,* as they commonly phrased it.   In this year also *Beza* published his Schismatical Pamphlet, intituled, *De triplici Episcopatu* ; of which see *lib.* 1, *num.* 47. *lib.* 5. *numb* 40. first written at the request of *Knox* and other of the Presbyterians of the Kirk of *Scotl.* that they might have the better colour to destroy Episcopacy; translated afterwards into English for the self same reason, by *Field* of *Wandsworth.* Against this book, Dr. *John Bridges* Dean of *Sarum* writ a large Discourse intituled, *A Defence of the Government established in the Church of England* ; not published till the year 1587, when the Authority thereof was most highly stood on.   The like done afterward by Dr. *Hadrian Savaria* : of which we shall speak more in its proper place.

23. And now the waters are so troubled, that *Cartwright* might presume of gainful fishing at his coming home.   Who having setled the Presbytery in *Jersey* and *Guernsey,* first sends back *Snape* to his old Lecture at *Northampton,* there to pursue such Orders and Directions as they had agreed on ; and afterwards put himself into the Factory of *Antwerp,* and was soon chosen for their Preacher.   The news whereof brings *Travers* to him ; who receives Ordination (if I may so call it) by the Presbytery of that City, and thereupon is made his Partner in that charge. It was no hard matter for them to perswade the Merchants to admit that Discipline, which in their turns might make them capable of voting in the Publick Consistory: and they endeavoured it the rather, that by their help they might effect the like in the City of *London,* whensoever they

should

should find the times to be ready for them. The like they did also in the English Church at *Middleborough* the chief Town in *Zealand*, in which many English Merchants had their constant residence : To which two places they drew over many of the English Nation, to receive admission to the Ministery in a different Form from that which was allowed in the Church of *England*. Some of which following the example of *Cartwright* himself, renounced the Orders which they had from the hands of the Bishops, and took a new Vocation from these Presbyters ; as, *Fennor*, *Arton*, &c. and others there admitted to the rank of Ministers, which never were ordained in *England*; as *Hart*, *Guisin*, &c. not to say any thing of such as were elected to be Elders or Deacons in those Forein Consistories, that they might serve the Churches in the same capacity at their coming home. And now at last they are for *England*, where *Travers* puts himself into the service of the Lord Treasurer *Burleigh*, by whose Recommendation he is chosen Lecturer of the *Temple* Church ; which gave him opportunity for managing all affairs which concerned the Discipline with the *London* Ministers. *Cartwright* applies himself to the Earl of *Leicester*, by whom he is sent down to *Warwick*, and afterwards made Master of an Hospital of his Foundation. In the chief Church of which Town, he was pleased to preach, as often as he could dispence with his other business. At his admission to which place, he faithfully promised, if he might be but tolerated to Preach, not to impugne the Laws, Orders, Policy, Gnvernment, nor Governours in this Church of *England*; but to perswade and procure, so much as he could, both publickly and privately, the estimation and peace of this Church.

24. But scarce was he setled in the place, when he made it manifest by all his actions, how little care he took of his words and promises: for so it was, when any Minister, either in private Conferences, or by way of Letters, required his advice in any thing which concerned the Church, he plainly shewed his mislike of the Ecclesiastical Government then by Law Established, and excepted against divers parts of the Publick Liturgie ; according to the Tenour of the two *Admonitions*, by him formerly published. By means whereof, he prevailed with many, who had before observed the Orders of the Common-prayer-book, now plainly to neglect the same ; and to oppose themselves against the Government of Bishops, as far as they might do it safely, in relation to the present times. And that he might not press those points to others, which he durst not practice in himself, he many times inveighed against them in his Prayers and Sermons : The like he also did against many passages in the Publick Liturgie, as namely, *The use of the Surplice ; the interrogatories to God-fathers in the name of Infants ; the Cross in Baptism ; the Ring in Marriage ; the Thanksgiving after Child-birth ; Burials by Ministers ; the kneeling at Communions ; some points of the Litany ; certain Collects and Prayers ; the reading of Portions of Scripture for the Epistle and Gospel ; and the manner of singing in Cathedral Churches.* And for example unto others, he procured his Wife not to give thanks for her Delivery from the peril of Childbirth, after such Form, and in such place and manner as the Church required. Which as it drew on many other women to the like contempt, so might he have prevailed upon many more, if he had not once

once difcoursed upon matters of Childbirth with fuch in difcretion, that ſome of the good Wives of *Warwick* were almoſt at the point to ſtone him as he walked the ſtreets. But that he might not ſeem to pull down more with one hand, then he would be thought ſufficiently able to build up with both ; he highly magnified in ſome of his Sermons the Government of the Church by Elderſhips in each Congregation, and by more Publick Conferences in *Claſſical* and *Synodical* Meetings ; which he commended for the onely lawful Church-Government, as being of Divine Inſtitution, and ordained by Chriſt. A Form whereof he had drawn up in a little Book : Which having paſt the approbation of ſome private Friends, was afterwards recommended to the uſe of the reſt of the Brethren, aſſembled together by his means for ſuch ends and purpoſes, by whom it was allowed of as moſt fit to be put in practice. For being a new nothing, and of *Cartwrights* doing, it could not but find many beſides women and children to admire the Workmanſhip.

25. This was the ſum of *Cartwrights* Actings in order to the Innovations, both in Government, and Forms of Worſhip, which heretofore he had projected. Not that all this was done at once, or in the firſt year only after his return ; but by degrees, as opportunity was offered to him. Yet ſo far he prevailed in the firſt year only, that a meeting of ſixty Miniſters out of the Counties of *Eſſex, Cambridge,* and *Norfolk,* was held at a Village called *Corkvil,* where *Knewſtubs* (who was one of their number) had the cure of the Souls. Which Meeting was held *May 8 Anno* 1582, there to confer about ſome paſſages in the Common-Prayer-Book, what might be tolerated in the ſame, and what refuſed ; as namely, Apparel, Matter, Form, Holy days, Faſtings, Injunctions, &c. The like Meeting held at the Commencement in *Cambridge* then next enſuing. And what they did reſolve in both, may be gathered partly from a paſſage in the Preface to a Book publiſhed in the year next following by *William Reynods* before mentioned. In which he tells us, *That it had been appointed by the firſt Book of Common-Prayer, That the Miniſter in the time of his Miniſtration ſhould uſe ſuch Ornament in the Church, as were in uſe by Authority of Parliament in the ſecond year of the Reign of King* Edward *the Sixth. And then* (ſaith he) *I appeal to the knowledge of every man, how well that Act of Parliament is obſerved throughout the Realm ; in how many Cathedrals or Pariſh Churches thoſe Ornaments are reſerved : Whether every private Miniſter, by his own Authority, in the time of his Miniſtration, diſdain not ſuch Ornaments, uſing only ſuch Apparel as is moſt vulgar and prophane ; to omit other particular differences, of Faſts, of Holy-days, Croſſing in Baptiſm, the viſitation of the Sick,* &c. *In which their alterations are well known,* ſaith he, *by their daily practice, and by the difference betwixt ſome Common-Prayer-Books which were laſt Printed (as namely that of* Richard Jugg *before remembred) from thoſe which were firſt publiſhed by Supreme Authority.* In all which deviations from the Rule of the Church, the Brethren walked on more ſecurely, becauſe the State was wholly exerciſed at this time in executing the ſeverity of the late Statute on ſuch Prieſts and Jeſuits is laboured to pervert the Subjects and deſtroy the Queen, thereby to re-advance the Pope to his former Tyranny. In which reſpect it was conceived to be a good Rule in the School of Policy, to grant a little more liberty to the

1582.

the *Puritan* Faction ; though poffibly it were done on no other fcore, then that of their notorious enmity to the Popifh party.

26. About this time it alfo was , that by the practices of *Cartwright* and his adherents , their Followers began to be diftinguifhed by their names and titles, from the reft of the people. Firft, in relation to their Titles. Thus thofe of his Faction muft be called *the Godly, the Elect, the Righteous* ; all others being looked upon as *carnal Gofpellers, the Prophane, the Wicked.* And next, in reference to their names. Their children muft not be Baptized by the names of their Anceftors, as *Richard, Robert,* and the like ; but by fome name occurring in the Holy Scriptures , but more particularly in the Old Teftament, becaufe meerly *Hebrew,* and not prophaned with any mixture of the *Greek* or *Roman* : concerning which there goes a ftory, that an Inhabitant of *Northampton,* called *Hodgking-fon,* having a child to be Baptized , repaired to *Snape,* before mentioned, to do it for him ; and he confented to the motion, but with promife that he fhould give it fome name allowed in Scripture. The holy action be-ing fo far forwards , that they were come to the naming of the Infant, they named it *Richard*, which was the name of his Grand-father by the Mothers fide. Upon this a ftop was made , nor would he be perfwaded to Baptize the child, unlefs the name of it were altered. Which when the God-father refufed to do , the child was carried back Unchriftened. It was agreed by him and *Cartwright*, in the Book of Difcipline which they impofed upon the Iflands , *That the Minifter in Baptizing Children fhould not admit of any fuch names as had been ufed in the time of* Paganifm *the names of Idols, and the like.* Which Rule though calculated like a com-mon Almanack, for the Meridian of thofe Iflands only, was afterwards to be obferved on the like occafions , in all the Churches of Great *Bri-tain.* Such was their humour at that time: but they fell fhortly after on another Fancy. For taking it for granted, becaufe they thought fo, that the Englifh Tongue might be as proper and fignificant as the Holy *Hebrew* ; they gave fuch names unto their children , as many of them when they came to age were afhamed to own. Out of which Forge came their *Accepted, Afhes, Confolation, Duft, Deliverance, Difcipline, Earth, Freegift , Fight the good fight of Faith , From above, Joy again, Kill-fin, More Fruit, More Tryal, Praife God , Reformation , Tribunal , The Lord is neer, Thankful,* with many others of like nature , which only ferved to make the Sacrament of Baptifm as contemptible , as they had made themfelves ridiculous by thefe new inventions.

27. Some ftop they had in their proceedings, which might have ter-rified them at the prefent from adventuring further , but that they were refolved to break through all difficulties , and try the patience of the State to the very utmoft. The Queen had entertained a treaty of Mar-riage, *Anno* 1581, with *Francis* Duke of *Anjou,* the youngeft Son of *Hen-ry* the Second, and the only furviving brother of *Henry* the Third , then Reigning in *France.* For the negotiating whereof, *Monfieur Simier,* a moft compleat Courtier,was fent Embaffador from that King.By whom the bufinefs was follicited with fuch dexterity , that the Match was ge-nerally conceived to be fully made. The *Puritans* hereupon begin to clamour,as if this Match did aim at nothing but the reduction of Popery, and

and the deftruction of Religion here by Law eftablifhed. But fearing more the total ruine of their hopes and projects, then any other danger which could happen by it. The Queen took care to tye the Duke to fuch conditions, that he could hardly be permitted to hear Mafs in his private Clofet; and had caufed *Campian* to be executed at his being here, to let him fee how little favour was to be expected by him for the Catholick party. Yet all this would not fatisfie the zealous Brethren, who were refolved to free themfelves from their own fears, by what means foever. Firft, therefore it was fo contrived, that as *Simere* paffed between *Greenwich* and *London*, before the coming of the Duke, a fhot was made at him from a Ship, with which one of the Watermen was killed, but the Embaffador therewith more amazed then hurt. The Gunner afterwards was pardoned, by the great power of the Earl of *Leicefter* had in Court; it being pretended, that the Piece was difcharged upon meer accident, and not upon malice or defign. After this, follows a feditious Pamphlet, writ by one *Stubs* of *Lincolns*-Inn, who had married one of the Sifters of *Thomas Cartwright*; and therefore may be thought to have done nothing in it without his privity. This Book he led, *The Gaping Gulf*; in which *England* was to have been fwallowed, the wealth thereof confumed, and the Gofpel irrecoverably drown'd, writ with great bitternefs of fpirit and reproachful language, to the difgrace of the *French* Nation, the difhonor of the Dukes own perfon; and not without fome vile reflections on the Queen her felf, as if fhe had a purpofe to betray her Kingdom to the power of Strangers.

28. For publifhing this Book, no fuch excufe could be pretended, as was infifted on in defence of the former fhot; nor could the Queen do lefs in Juftice to her felf and her Government, as the caufe then ftood, then to call the Authors and the Publifhers of it to a ftrict account. To which end the faid *Stubs*, together with *Hugh Singleton* and *William Page*, were on the 13 day of *October* arraigned at *Weftminfter*, for Writing, Printing and difperfing that Seditious Pamphlet; and were all then and there condemned to lofe their right hands for the faid offence. Which Sentence was executed on the third of *November* upon *Stubs* and *Page*, as the chief offenders; but *Singleton* was pardoned as an Acceffary, and none of the Principals in the crime. Which execution gave great grief to the *Difciplinarians*; becaufe they faw by that Experiment that there was no dallying with the Queen, when either the honour of her Government, or the peace of her Dominions feemed to be concerned. And they were moft afflicted at it in regard of *Cartwright*, whofe inability to preferve fo near a friend from the feverity and fhame of fo great a punifhment, was looked on a ftrong prefumption that he could be as little able to fave himfelf, whenfoever it was thought expedient upon reafon of State to proceed againft him. But now they are engaged in the fame bottom with him, they were refolved to fteer their courfe by no other Compafs, then that which this grand Pilot had provided for them. Not terrified from fo doing, by the open Schifm which was the next year made by one *Robert Brown*, once a Difciple of their own, and one who built his Schifm upon *Cartwrights* Principles; nor by the hanging of thofe men who had difperfed his Factious and Schifmatical Pamphlets. For the better clearing

ing

ing of which matter, we must fetch the story of this *Brown* a little higher, and carry it a little lower then this present year.

29. This *Robert Brown* was born at *Tolethorp* in the County of *Rutland*, the Grand-child of *Francis Brown* Esquire, priviledged in the 18 year of King *Henry* VIII, to wear his Cap in the presence of the King himself, or any other Lords Spiritual or Temporal in the Land ; and not to put it off at any time, but onely for his own ease and pleasure. He was bred sometimes in *Corpus Christi* Colledge (commonly called *Bennet* Colledge) in the University of *Cambridge*. Where, though he was not known to take any degree, yet he would many times venture into the Pulpit. It was observed, that in his Preaching he was very vehement ; which *Cartwrights* Followers imputed onely to his zeal, as being one of their own number. But other men suspected him to have worse ends in it. Amongst many, whom rather curiosity then Devotion had brought to hear him, Dr. *John Still* (though possibly not then a Doctor) hapned to be one. Who being afterwards Master of Trinity Colledge, and finally Lord Bishop of *Bath* and *Wells*, was used to say, *That he discerned something extraordinary in him at the very first, which he presaged would prove a disturbance to the Church, if it were not seasonably prevented.* Being well verst and conversant in *Cartwrights* Books, and other the like Pamphlets of that time, he became more and more estranged from the Church of *England*: Whose Government he found to be defamed for Anti-christian ; her Sacraments affirmed to be defiled with Superstition ; her Liturgy reproached for Popish, and in some part Heathenish ; and finally, her Ordinations to be made no better then those of *Baals* Priests amongst the Jews. Not able to abide longer in a Church so impure and filthy, he puts himself over into *Zealand*, and joyns with *Cartwrights* new Church in the City of *Middleborough*. But finding there some few remainders of the old impiety, he resolves to constitute a new Church of his own Projectment, which should have nothing in it but what was most pure and Holy. The Draught whereof, he comprehended in a Book which he Printed at *Middleborough*, *Anno* 1582, intituled, *A Treatise of Reformation* : and having sent as many of them into *England* as might serve his turn, he followed after in pursuit of his new Plantation.

1583.
    30. The *Dutch* had then a Church at *Norwich*, as before was said, more numerous then any other Church or Congregation within the Precincts of that City. Many of which enclining of themselves to the *Anabaptists*, were apt enough to entertain any new Opinions which he d Conformity with that Sect. Amongst them he begins, and first begins with such amongst them as were most likely to be ruled and governed by him ; he being of an imperious nature, and much offended with the least dissent or contradiction, when he had uttered any Paradox in his discourses. Having gotten into some Authority amongst the *Dutch*, whose Language he had learned when he lived in *Middleborough*, and grown into a great opinion for his Zeal and Sanctity, he began to practise with the English; using therein the service and assistance of one *Richard Harrison*, a Country School-master, whose ignorance made him apt enough to be seduced by so weak a Prophet. Of each Nation he began to gather Churches to himself, of the last especially ; inculcating nothing more to his simple Auditors, then that the Church of *England* had so much of *Rome*,
that

that there was no place left for Christ, or his Holy Gospel. But more particularly he inveighed against the Government of the Bishops, the Ordination of Ministers, the Offices, Rites and Ceremonies of the publick Liturgy, according as it had been taught out of *Cartwrights* Books; descending first to this Position, *That the Church of* England *was no true and lawful Church.* And afterwards to this conclusion, *That all true Christians were obliged to come out of* Babylon, *to separate themselves from those impure and mixt Assemblies, in which there was so little of Christs institution; and finally, that they should joyn themselves to him and his Disciples, amongst whom there was nothing to be found which favoured not directly of the Spirit of* God; *nothing of those impurities and prophanations of the Church of* England. Hereupon followed a defection from the Church it self; not as before amongst the *Presbyterians*, from some Offices in it. *Browns* Followers (which from him took the name of *Brownists*) refusing obstinately to joyn wit any Congregation, with the rest of the people, for hearing the Word preached, the Sacraments administred, and any publick act of Religious Worship. This was the first gathering of Churches which I find in *England*; and for the justifying hereof, he caused his Books to be dispersed in most parts of the Realm. Which tending as apparently to Sedition, brought both the dispersers of them within the compass of the Statute 23 *Eli.c.*2. Of which we are informed by *Stow*, that *Elias Thasker* was hanged at *Bury* on the 4 of *June*; and *John Copping*, on the 6 of the same month, for spreading certain books, seditiously penned by *Robert Brown* against the Book of Common-prayer established by the Laws of this Realm; as many of their Books as could be found, being burnt before them.

31. As for the Writer of the Books, and the first Author of Schism, he was more favourably dealt with then these wretched instruments, and many other of his Followers in the times succeeding. Being convented before Dr. *Edmond Freak*, then Bishop of *Norwich*, and others of the Queens Commissioners in conjunction with him; he was by them upon his refractory carriage committed to the custody of the Sheriff of *Norwich*. But being a near kinsman by his Mother to the Lord Treasurer *Burleigh*, he was at his request released from his imprisonment, and sent to *London*, where some course was taken to reclaim him, if it might be possible, totally, or in part at least, as God pleased to bless it. *Whitgift* by this time had attained to the See of *Canterbury*; a man of excellent patience and dexterity in dealing with such men as were so affected. By whose fair usage, powerful reason, and exemplary piety, he was prevailed upon so far, as to be brought unto a tolerable compliance with the Church of *England*. In which good humour he was favourably dismist by the Archbishop, and by the Lord Treasurer *Burleigh*, to the care of his father, to the end that being under his eye, & dealt with in a kind and temperate manner, he might in time be well recovered, and finally withdrawn from all the Reliques of his fond opinions. Which letters of his bear date on the 8 of *Oct.* 585. But long he had not staid in his fathers house, when he *returned unto his vomit*, and proving utterly incorrigible, was dismist again; the good old Gentleman being resolved, that he would not own him for a Son, who would not own the Church of *England* for his Mother. But at the last, though not till he had passed through 32. prisons, as he used to brag, by the perswasions of some friends, and his own necessities (the more

powerful

powerful Orators the two) he was prevailed with to accept of a place called *A Church* in *Northamptonshire*, beneficed with cure of Souls; to which he was presented by *Thomas* Lord *Burleigh*, after Earl of *Exon*, and thereunto admitted by the Bishop of *Peterborough*, upon his promise not to make any more disturbances in the proceedings of the Church: A Benefice of good value, which might tempt him to it, the rather, in regard that he was excused as well from Preaching, and from performing any other part of the publick Ministry; which Offices he discharged by an honest Curate, and allowed him such a competent maintainance for it, as gave content unto the Bishop, who had named the man. And on this Benefice he lived to a very great age, not dying till the year 1630; and then dying in *Northampton* Gaol, not on the old account of his inconformity, but for breach of the Peace. A most unhappy man to the Church of *England*, in being the Author of a Schism which he could not close; and most unfortunate to many of his Friends and Followers, who suffered death for standing unto those conclusions, from which he had withdrawn himself divers years before.

32. But it is time that we go back again to *Cartwright*, upon whose principles and positions he first raised this Schism. Which falling out so soon upon the Execution which was done on *Stubs*, could not but put a great rebuke upon his spirit; and might perhaps have tended more to his discouragement, had not his sorrows been allayed and sweetned by a Cordial which was sent from *Beza*, sufficient to revive a half dying brother. Concerning which there is no more to be premised, but that *Geneva* had of late been much wasted by a grievous pestilence, and was somewhat distressed at this time by the Duke of *Savoy*. Their peace not to be otherwise procured, but by paying a good sum of money, and money not to be obtained but by help of their Friends. On this account he writes to *Travers*, being then Domestick Chaplain to the Lord Treasurer *Burleigh*; but so, that *Cartwright* was to be acquainted with the Tenour of it; that by the good which the one might do upon the Queen by the means of his Patron, and the great influence which the other had on all his party, the contribution might amount to the higher pitch. But as for so much of the said letter as concerns our business, it is this that followeth; *viz. If as often, dear Brother, as I have remembred thee and our* Cartwright, *so often I should have written unto thee, you had been long since overwhelmed with my Letters; no one day passing, wherein I do not onely think of you and your matters; which not only our ancient Friendship, but the greatness of those affairs wherein you take pains, seems to require at my hands. But in regard that you were fallen into such times, wherein my silence might be safer far then my writing, I have, though most unwillingly, been hitherto silent. Since which time, understanding that by Gods Grace the heats of some men are abated, I could not suffer this my Friend to come unto you without particular Letters from me, that I may testifie my self to be the same unto you as I have been formerly; as also, that at his return I may be certified of the true state of your affairs.* After which Preamble, he acquaints him with the true cause of his writing, the great extremities to which that City was reduced, and the vast debts in which they were plunged; whereby their necessities were grown so grievous, that except they were relieved from other parts, they could not be able to support
them:

them : And then he adds, *I beseech thee, my dear Brother , not only to go on in health with thy daily Prayers ; but that if you have any power to prevail with some persons , shew us by what honest means you can , how much you love us in the Lord.* Finally, having certified him of other Letters which he had writ to certain Noblemen , and to all the Bishops, for their assistance in that case ; not without some complaints of a disrespect which he had found to some of his late Addresses, he concludes it thus ; *viz. Farewel my dear Brother ; the Lord Jesus every day more and more bless thee , and all that earnestly desire his glory.*

33. This Letter dated in the beginning of *October,* 1582. came very seasonably both to comfort *Cartwright ;* who could not but be much afflicted with his late misfortunes, and encouraged him to proceed in pursuit of that business in which they had took such pains. This was enough to make them hasten in the work, who wanted no such Spurs to set them forwards. Till this time they had no particular Form , either of Discipline or Worship , which generally was allowed of for the use of their Churches ; But every man gathered some directions out of *Cartwrights* Books, as seemed most proper for that purpose. But *Cartwright* having now drawn up his form of Discipline , mentioned before amongst the rest of his practices, 1580, that Book of his was looked on as the only Rule, by which they were to regulate their Churches in all publick duties. But in regard of the great scandal given by *Brown,* the execution done at *Bury* upon *Thacker* and *Copping* , and the severity of the Laws in that behalf ; it was thought fit to look before them, and so to carry on the business as to make no rupture in the Church, and to create no eminent danger to themselves. In reference to which ends, they held a General Assembly , wherein they agreed upon some order for putting the said Discipline in execution, but with as little violation of the peace of the Church as they could possibly devise : And therefore that they might proceed with the greater safety, it was advised and resolved on, 1. *That such as are called unto the Ministery of any Church, should be first approved by the Classis , or some greater Assembly , and then commended to the Bishop by their special Letters , to receive their Ordination at his hands,* 2. *That those Ceremonies in the Book of Common-Prayer which seemed to have been used in the times of Popery , were totally to be omitted, if it might be done without being deprived of their Ministery ; or otherwise the matter to be left to the consideration of the Classis, or other greater Assembly , that by the judgement thereof it might be determined what was most fitting to be done.* 3. *That if Subscription to the Articles of Religion and the Book of Common-Prayer should be urged again, that they might be then subscribed unto , according to the Statute of* 13 *Elizabeth, that is to say, to such of them only as contain the sum of Christian Faith, and the Doctrine of the Sacraments. But* 4. *That for many weighty causes, neither the rest of the said Articles, nor the Book of Common-Prayer were to be subscribed ; no, though a man should be deprived of his Ministery upon such refusal.*

34. A Consultation was held also in the said Assembly, *That without changing of the names , or any sensible alteration in the state of the Church, the Church Wardens and Collectors of every Parish might serve in the place of Elders and Deacons; and to that end, that notice might be given of their election about the space of fifteen days before the times appointed for it by the Law of*

the

the Land: To the intent that the Church might joyn in Prayer to God to be so directed, as to make choice of fit men to supply those Ministeries. It was advised also, That before the ordinary times of the said Elections, the Ordinance of Christ should be publickly intimated to the Congregation, concerning the appointment of Watchmen and Overseers in the Church; it being their duty to foresee that no offence or scandal arise in the Church; and that if any such offence or scandal should happen, it might be seasonably remedied and abolished by them: as also that the names of the parties chosen be published on the next Lords Day; their duties toward the Church, and the said Churches duty toward them, being then declared; and then the said Officers to be admitted to their several Ministeries, with the general Prayers of the whole Church. Orders were also made for a division of the Churches into Classical and Synodical Meetings, according to the tenor of the Book of Discipline; for keeping a Registry of the Acts of the Classis and Synods; for dealing with Patrons to present fit men, when any Church fell void belonging to their Presentations; for making Collections at the General Assemblies (which were then held for the most part at the Act in *Oxon*, or the Commencement in *Cambridge*) towards the relief of the poor, but most especially of those who had been deprived of their Benefices for their not subscribing; as also of such Ministers of the Kirk of *Scotland*, as for their factiousness and disobedience had been forced to abandon that Kingdom: and finally, for nominating some set time at the end of each Provincial Synod, in which the said Provincial Synod was to sit again; as also for the sending of fit men to the General Synods, which were to be held either in times of Parliament, or at such other times as seemed most convenient.

35. By these disguisings it was thought that they might breed up their Presbytery under the Wing of Episcopacy, till they should find it strong enough to subsist of it self, and bid defiance to that power which had given it shelter. It was resolved also, that instead of Prophesying, which now began to be suppreft in every place, Lectures should be set up in some chief Towns in every County: to which the Ministers and Lay-brethren might resort securely, and thereby prosecute their design with the like indemnity. But no disguise could fit them in their alterations of the Forms of Worship; of which nothing was to be retained by *Cartwrights* Rules, but that which held conformity with the Church of *Geneva*. According to the Rules whereof, the Minister had no more to do on the days of Worship, but to Preach his Sermon, with a long Prayer before it, and another after it, of his own devising; the people being entertained both before and after with a *Psalm* in Meter, according to such Tune or Tunes as the Clerk should bid. For having distributed the whole Worship of God into these three parts; that is to say, Prayers, Praises, and Prophesyings; the singing of the *Psalms* (which they conceived to be the onely way of giving praise) became in fine, as necessary as the Prayers or Preachings. Their other aberrations from the publick Liturgy in Sacraments and Sacramentals, may best be found in *Cartwrights* practice, as before laid down; it being not to be supposed that he would practise one thing and prescribe another, or that his own practice might not be a sufficent Canon, to direct all the Churches of this Platform. But these alterations being so gross, that no Cloak conld cover them;

them; another expedient was devised somewhat more chargeable then the other, but of greater safety. For neither daring to reject the publick Liturgy, and being resolved not to conform themselves unto it; they fell upon a course of hiring some Lay brother, (as *Snape* did a Lame Soldier of *Barwick*) or possibly some ignorant Curate, to read the Prayers to such as had a mind to hear them; neither themselves, nor their Disciples coming into the Church, till the singing of the *Psalm* before the Sermon. Concerning which, one of the brethren writes to *Field*, (a) *That having nothing to do with the prescribed form of Common-prayer, he preached every Lords day in his Congregation; and that he did so by the counsel of the Reverend Brethren; by whom (such was Gods goodness to him) he had been lately called to be one of the Classis, which once a week was held in some place or other.*

(a) *Ego singulis sabbatis cum præscripta Formula nihil habens commercii, in Cætu Concionem habeo, &c.* Dat. April. 14.

36. In this condition stood the Affairs, when the Reverend *Whitgift* came to the See of *Canterbury*. A man that had appeared so stoutly in the Churches quarrels, that there could be no fear of his *Grindallizing*, by winking at the plots and practices of the *Puritan Faction*. So highly valued by the Queen, that when she first preferred him to the See of *Worcester, Anno* 1576, she gave him the disposing of all the Prebendaries of that Church, to the end he might be served with the ablest and most Learned men. Nor was he less esteemed for his civil prudence, which moved Sir *Henry Sidney* to select him before all others to be his Vice-President in *Wales*, at such time as he was to go Lord-Deputy for the Realm of *Ireland*. Upon this man the Queen had always kept her eye since *Grindal* fell into disfavour, and willingly would have made him his Co-adjutor, if he could have been perswaded to accept the offer. Which moderation altered nothing of the Queens mind toward him, who was so constant in her choice and designations of fit men to serve her, that upon *Grindals* death, which happened on the 6 of *July* 1583, she preferred *Whitgift* to the place. To which he was actually translated before *Michaelmas* following, that he might have the benefit of the half-years rent. Which as it was another Argument of the Queens good affection to him (who otherwise was sufficiently intent on her personal profit) so for a further demonstration of it, she caused 100 pounds to be abated in his Tenths and first Fruits, which had been over-charged on his Predecessor. And, which was more then both together, she suffered him to Commence a Suit against Sir *James Crofts*, Comptroller of her Houshold, Governour of the Town of *Barwick*, and a privy Councellor, for the recovery of some Lands, to the quantity of 1000 Acres, which had been first alienated to the Queen, and by the Queen was given to *Crofts* on a Court-petition. Which suit, as he had courage enough to take in hand, so had he the felicity of an happy Issue, in the recovering of those Lands from such Potent Competitors, without losing any part of her Majesties favour. But these things are not pertinent to my present business, unless it be to shew upon what ground he stood, and that he was resolved to abate of nothing which concerned the honour of the Church, who was so vigilant and intent (without fear of envy or displeasure) on the profit of it.

37. The Queen was set upon a point of holding her Prerogative-Royal at the very height; and therefore would not yield to any thing in

Civil matters, which feemed to tend to any fenfible diminution of it. And in like fort fhe was refolved touching her Supremacy, which fhe confidered as the faireft Jewel in the Regal Diadem ; and confequently, could as little hearken to fuch Propofitions as had been made in favour of the *Puritan* Faction by their great Agents in the Court, though fhe had many times been follicited in it. To eafe her felf of which Sollicitations for the time to come, fhe acquaints *Whitgift* at his firft coming to the place, that fhe determined to difcharge her felf from the trouble of all the Church-concernments, and leave them wholly to his care: That he fhould want no countenance and encouragement for carrying on the great truft committed to him : That fhe was fenfible enough into what diforder and confufion the affairs of the Church were brought, by the connivance of fome Bifhops, the obftinacy of fome Minifters, and the power of fome great Lords both in Court and Countrey ; but that notwithftanding all thefe difficulties, he muft refolve, not only to affert the Epifcopal Power, but alfo to reftore that Uniformity in Gods Publick Worfhip, which by the weaknefs of his Predeceffor was fo much endangered. Thus authorized and countenanced, he begins his Government. And for the firft Effay thereof, he fends abroad three Articles to be fubfcribed by all the Clergy of his Province. The Tenour of which Articles, becaufe they afterwards created fo much trouble to him, I fhall here fubjoyn. Firft therefore, he required the Clergy to fubfcribe to this, *That the Queen had Supreme Authority over all perfons born within her Dominions, of what condition foever they were ; and that no other Prince, Prelate or Potentate, either had, or ought to have any jurifdiction Civil or Ecclefiaftical within her Realms and Dominions. 2. That the Book of Commonprayer, and the Ordination of Bifhops, Priefts and Deacons, contained nothing contrary to the Word of God, but might lawfully be ufed ; and that they would ufe that and no other. 3. That he allowed the Articles of Religion, agreed in the Synod holden at* London, *in the year of our Lord* 1562, *and publifhed by the Queens Authority ; and did believe them to be confonant to the Word of God.*

38. It is not eafie to imagine what clamours were raifed amongft the Brethren upon this occafion ; how they moved Heaven and Earth, the Court and Country, and all the Friends they had of the Clergy or Laity, to come to their affiftance in this time of their tryal. By means whereof, they raifed fo ftrong an oppofition againft his proceedings, that no man of lefs courage then *Whitgift*, and none but *Whitgift* fo well backed and countenanced by a gratious Miftrefs, could have withftood the violence and fury of it. But by the Queens conftancy on the one fide, who gave *Semper Eadem* for her Motto, to fhew that fhe was always one ; and by his moft invincible patience on the other fide, whofe *Motto* being *Vincet qui patitur*, declared what hopes he had, that by a difcreet patience he might get the Victory ; he had the happinefs to fee the Church reduced to her former luftre, by the removing of all obftacles which lay before him. The firft of which was laid by fome of his own Diocefs, who being required by him to fubfcribe for an Example to others, not only refufed fo to do, but being thereupon fufpended for their contumacy in due Form of Law, they petitioned to the Lords of the Council for relief againft him : the like Petition was prefented to them

by

by some Ministers of the Diocess of *Norwich*, against Dr. *Edmond Freak* their Bishop ; to whom the planting of so many Dutch Churches in the principal City, and other of the chief Towns of his Diocess, had given trouble enough. To the Petition of the *Kentish* Ministers, which concerned himself, he was required to answer at the Council-Table, on the Sunday following. Instead whereof, he lays before them in the Letter, *That the Petitioners, for the most part, were ignorant and raw young men, few of them licensed Preachers, and generally disaffected to the present Government: That he had spent the best part of two or three days in labouring to reduce them to a better understanding of the points in question ; but not being able to prevail, he had no otherwise proceeded then the law required : That it was not for him to sit in that place, if every Curate in his Diocess might be permitted so to use him ; nor possible for him to perform the Duty which the Queen expected at his hands, if he might not proceed to the execution of that power by her Majesty committed to him, without interruption : That he could not be perswaded, that their Lordships had any purpose to make him a party, or to require him to come before them to defend those actions, wherein he supposed that he had no other Judge but the Queen her self ; and therefore in regard that he was called by God to that place and function, wherein he was to be their Pastor, he was the rather moved to desire their assistance in matters pertaining to his Office, for the quietness of the Church, the credit of Religion, and the maintainance of the Laws in defence thereof, without expecting any such attendance on them as they had required, for fear of giving more advantage to those wayward persons, then he conceived they did intend.* And thereunto he added this protestation, *That the three Articles whereunto they were moved to subscribe, were such, as he was ready by Learning to defend, in manner and form as there set down, against all opponents, either in* England *or elsewhere.*

39. In reference to the paper of the *Suffolk* Ministers, he returns this answer : *It seemeth something strange to me, that the Ministers of* Suffolk *finding themselves agrieved with the doings of their Diocesans should leave the ordinary course of proceeding by the Law, (which is to appeal unto me) and extraordinarily trouble your Lordships in a matter not so incident (as I think) to that honourable Board, seeing it hath pleased her Majesty her own self in express words to commit these causes Ecclesiastical to me, as to one who is to make answer unto God and her Majesty in this behalf ; my Office also and place requiring the same. In answer unto their complaint ; touching their ordinary proceedings with them, I have herewith sent your Lordships a Copy of a Letter lately received from his Lordship, wherein I think that part of their Bill to be fully answered. Touching the rest, I know not what to judge of it ; but in some points it talketh (as I think) modestly and charitably. They say, they are no Jesuits sent from* Rome *to reconcile, &c. True it is, neither are they charged to be so ; but notwithstanding, they are contentious in the Church of* England, *and by their contentions minister occasion of offence to those which are seduced by* Jesuits ; *and give the Sacraments against the form of publick Prayer used in this Church, and by Law established, and thereby increase the number of them, and confirm them in their wilfulness. They also make a Schism in the Church, and draw many other of her Majesties Subjects to a misliking of her Laws and Government in Causes Ecclesiastical. So far are they from perswading them to obedience, or at the least, if they perswade them to it in the one part of her Authority, it is in Causes Civil ; they disswade them from it as much in the other, that is, in Causes Ecclesiastical:*

cal:

cal : so that indeed they pluck down with the one hand, that which they seem to build with the other.

40. More of which Letter might be added, were not this sufficient, as well to shew how perfectly he understood both his place and power as with what courage and discretion he proceeded in the maintenance of it. Which being observed by some great men about the Court, who had ingaged themselves in the *Puritans* quarrels, but were not willing to incur the Queens displeasure by their opposition ; it was thought best to stand a while behind the Curtain, and set *Beal* upon him, of whose impetuosity and edge against him they were well assured. This *Beal* was in himself a most eager *Puritan*, trained up by *Walsingham* to draw dry-foot after Priests and Jesuits ; his extream hatred to those men, being looked on as the only good quality which he could pretend to. But being over-blinded by zeal and passion, he was never able to distinguish rightly between truth and falshood ; between true Sanctity, and the counterfeit appearance of it. This made him first conceive, that whatsoever was not *Puritan*, must needs be *Popish* ; and that the Bishops were to be esteemed no otherwise then the sons of Antichrist, because they were not looked upon as Fathers by the holy Brotherhood. And so far was he hurried on by these dis-affections, that though he was preferred to be one of the Clerks of the Council, yet he preferred the interest of the Faction before that of the Queen. Insomuch, that he was noted to jeer and gibe at all such Sermons as did most commend her Majesties Government, and move the Auditory to obedience ; not sparing to accuse the Preachers upon such occasions to have broached false Doctrine, and falsly to alledge the Scriptures in defence thereof. This man had either writ or countenanced a sharp Discourse against Subscription, inscribed to the Archbishop, and presented to him ; and thereupon caused speeches to be cast abroad, that the three Articles to which Subscription was required, should shortly be revoked by an Act of the Council: which much encreased the obstinacy of the self-willed Brethren. But after, fearing lest the Queen might have a sight of the Papers, he resolved to get them out of his hands ; and thereupon went over to *Lambeth*, where he behaved himself in such a rude and violent manner, as forced the Archbishop to give an account thereof by Letter to the Lord Treasurer *Burleigh*, who hitherto had stood fair towards him, in these following words:

41. *I have born* (saith he) *with Mr, Beals intemperate speeches, unseemly for him to use, though not in respect of my self, yet in respect of Her Majesty whom he serveth, and of the Laws established, whereunto he ought to shew some duty. Yesterday he came to my house, as it seems to demand the Book he delivered unto me. I told him, That the book was written unto me, and therefore no reason why he should require it again, especially seeing I was assured that he had a Copy thereof, otherwise I would cause it to be written out for him: Whereupon he fell into very great passions with me (which I think was the end of his coming) for proceeding in the execution of the Articles, &c. and told me in effect, that I would be the overthrow of this Church, and a cause of tumult, with many other bitter and hard speeches, which I heard patiently, and wished him to consider with what spirit he was moved to say so: For I said, it could not be by the Spirit*

of

of God, which worketh in men Patience, Humility and Love ; and your words declare (ſaid I) that you are very Arrogant, Proud, Impatient and Uncharitable. Moreover, the Spirit of God, &c. And all this while (ſaith he) I talked with him in the upper end of my Gallery : My Lord of Wincheſter and divers ſtrangers being in the other part thereof. But Mr. Beal beginning to extend his voice that all might hear, I began to break off. Then he being more and more kindled, very impatiently uttered very proud and contemptuous ſpeeches in the juſtifying of his Book, and condemning the Orders eſtabliſhed, to the offence of all the hearers. Whereupon, being very deſirous to be rid of him, I made ſmall anſwer ; but told him that his ſpeeches were intolerable, that he forgot himſelf, and that I would complain of him to Her Majeſty : whereof he ſeemed to make ſmall account, and ſo he departed in great heat. Which ſaid, he lets his Lordſhip know, That though he was never more abuſed by any man in his life, then ſince his coming to that place he had been by Beal, and that upon no other ground but for doing his duty, yet that he was not willing to do him any ill office with the Queen about it, or otherwiſe to proceed any further in it then his Lordſhip ſhould think moſt convenient.

42. Finding by theſe Experiments how little good was to be done upon him either way, it was reſolved to make ſome tryal on the oppoſite party, in hope to bring them by degrees unto ſome attonement. The Lord Burleigh ſhall firſt break the Ice ; who upon ſome complaint made againſt the Liturgy by ſome of the Brethren, required them to compoſe another, ſuch as they thought might generally be accepted by them. The firſt Claſſis thereupon deviſed a new one, agreeable in moſt things to the Form of Geneva. But this Draught being offered to the conſideration of a ſecond Claſſis, (for ſo the wiſe States-man had of purpoſe contrived the plot) there were no fewer then ſix hundred exceptions made againſt it, and conſequently ſo many alterations to be made therein, before it was to be admitted. The third Claſſis quarrelled at thoſe Alterations, and reſolved therefore on a new Model, which ſhould have nothing of the other : And againſt this, the fourth was able to pretend as many Objections as had been made againſt the firſt. So that no likelyhood appearing of any other Form of Worſhip, either better or worſe, to be agreed upon between them, he diſmiſt their Agents for the preſent ; with this aſſurance, that whenſoever they could agree upon any Liturgy which might be univerſally received amongſt them, they ſhould find him very ready to ſerve them in the ſetling of it. Juſt ſo Pacuvius dealt with the people of Capua, when they reſolved to put all their Senators to death. For when he had adviſed them not to execute that ſentence upon any one Senator, till they were agreed upon another to ſupply the place, there followed ſuch a diviſion amongſt them in the choice of the new, and ſo many exceptions againſt every man which was offered to them, that at the laſt it was reſolved to let the old Senate ſtand in force, till they could better their condition in the change of the perſons. Walſingham tries his fortune next, in hope to bring them to allow of the Engliſh Liturgy, on the removal of ſuch things as ſeemed moſt offenſive. And thereupon he offered in the Queens name, that the three Ceremonies at which they ſeemed moſt to boggle ; that is to ſay, Kneeling at the Communion ; The Surplice ; and, The Croſs in Baptiſm, ſhould be expunged out of the Book of Common-Prayer, if that would content them. But thereunto it was replied

in

in the words of *Mofes*, *Ne ungulam effe relinquendum* ; That they would not leave fo much as a hoof behind. Meaning thereby, that they would have a total abolition of the Book, without retaining any part or Office in it in their next new-nothing. Which peremptory anfwer did much alienate his affeſtion from them ; as a terwards he affirmed to *Knewſtubs*, and *Knewſtubs* to Dr. *John Burges* of *Colſhil* ; from whoſe pen I have it.

43. The Brethren on the other ſide, finding how little they had gotten by their application to the Lords of the Council, began to ſteer another courſe, by practiſing upon the temper of the following Parliaments, into which they had procured many of their chief Friends to be retained for Knights or Burgeſſes, as they could prevail. By whoſe means (notwith-ſtanding that the Queen had charged them not to deal in any thing which was of concernment to the Church) they procured a Bill to paſs in the Houſe of Commons 1585, for making tryal of the ſufficiency of ſuch as were to be ordained or admitted Miniſters by twelve Lay-men ; whoſe approbation and allowance they were firſt to paſs, before they were to receive *Inſtitution* into any Benefice. Another Bill was alſo paſt, for making Marriage lawful at all times of the year ; which had been formerly attempted by the Convocation, and tendred to the Queen amongſt other Articles there agreed upon, but was by her difrelliſhed and rejeſted, as before was ſaid. They were in hand alſo with a third, concerning Eccleſiaſtical Courts, and the Epiſcopal Viſitations ; pretending only a redreſs of ſome Exorbitances in exceſſive Fees, but aiming plainly at the overthrow of the Juriſdiſtion. Of which particulars, *Whitgift* gives notice to the Queen ; and the Queen ſo far ſignified her diſlike of all thoſe proceedings, that all thoſe Projeſts dyed in the Houſe of Commons, without ever coming into Aſts. The like attempt were made in ſome following Seſſions ; in which ſome Members ſhewed themſelves ſo troubleſome to ſober men, ſo alienated from the preſent Government, and ſo difreſpeſtive toward the Queen, that ſhe was fain to lay ſome of them by the heels, and deprive others of their places, before ſhe could reduce them to a better temper. Of which we ſhall ſpeak more hereafter, in the courſe of this Hiſtory.

The End of the ſeventh Book.

AERIVS REDIVIVVS:
OR THE
HISTORY
OF THE
Presbyterians.

L I B. VIII.

Containing

The Seditious Practises and Positions of the English Puritans, their Libels, Railing, and Reviling, in order to the setting up of the Holy Discipline, from the Year 1584, *to the Year* 1589. *The undutiful Carriage of the* French, *and the horrible Insolencies of the* Scotch *Presbyteries, from the Year* 1585, *to the Year* 1592.

HAving thus prosecuted the Affairs of the *Presbyterians* in *England*, to the same point of time where before we left the *Scots*, the *French*, and those of the same Party in the *Belgick* Provinces : we shall hereafter treat of them as they come before us with reference to the Practises and Proceedings of their *English* Brethren.   And first, beginning with the *Scots*, it is to be remembred, that we left them at a very low ebb ; the Earl of *Goury* put to death, many of the Nobility exiled into Forein Countries, and the chief Zealots of the Faction amongst

1584.

mongſt the Miniſters, putting themſelves into a voluntary Baniſhment, becauſe they could not have their wills on the King and Council. *England*, as neareſt hand, was the common Sanctuary, to which ſome Lords, and almoſt all the Refractory Miniſters had retired themſelves. Much countenanced by Mr. Secretary *Walſingham*, who had ſet them on work; and therefore was obliged to gratifie them in ſome fit proportion. To ſuch of the Nobility as had fled into *England*, he aſſigned the Iſle of *Lindisfarm*, (commonly called the *Holy Iſland*) not far from *Berwick*; with order to the Lord *Hundſdon*, who was then Governour of that Town, to give them the poſſeſſion of it. But *Hundſdon*, though he had leſs Zeal, had ſo much knowledge of his Duty, as to diſobey him; conſidering the great conſequence of the place, and that there was no impoſſibility in it, but that the *Scots* might make uſe of it to the common prejudice, if they ſhould prove enemies to this Crown, as perhaps they might. A matter, which the Secretary would not have paſſed over in ſo light a manner, but that an Embaſſador was ſent at the ſame time from the King of *Scots*, by whom it was deſired that the Fugitives of that Nation, whatſoever they were, might either be remitted home, or elſe commanded not to live ſo near the Borders, where they had opportunity, more than ſtood with the good of that Kingdom, to pervert the Subjects. Which reaſonable deſire being yeelded unto, the Lords and Great men of that Nation were ordered to retire to *Norwich*, and many of the Miniſters, permitted to prepare for *London*, *Oxon*, *Cambridge*, and ſome other places; where ſome of them procured more miſchief to the Church of *England*, than all of them could have done to their own Countrey, had they ſtaid at *Berwick*.

2. At *London* they are ſuffered, by ſome zealous Brethren, to poſſeſs their Pulpits, in which they rail, without comptroll, againſt their King, the Council of that Kingdom, and their natural Queen; as if by the practiſes of the one, and the connivance of the other, the Reformed Religion was in danger to be rooted out. Some Overtures had been made at that time by the Queen of *Scots*, by which it was deſired that ſhe might be reſtored unto liberty of her perſon, aſſociating with the young King in the Government of the Realm of *Scotland*; and be ſuffered to have the Maſs ſaid in her private Cloſet, for her ſelf and her Servants. The news whereof being brought to *London*, filled all the Pulpits which the *Scots* were ſuffered to invade, with terrible complaints and exclamations; none of them ſparing to affirm, That her liberty was inconſiſtent with Queen *Elizabeth*'s Safety: That both Kingdoms were undone if ſhe were admitted to the joynt-Government of the Realm of *Scotland*; and, That the Reformed Religion muſt needs breath its laſt, if the *Popiſh* were permitted within the Walls of the Court. Which points they preſſed with ſo much vehemence and heat, that many were thereby inflamed to join themſelves in the Aſſociation againſt that Queen, which ſoon after followed. Againſt their King they railed ſo bitterly, and with ſuch reproach, (one *Davinſon* more than any other) that upon complaint made by the *Scottiſh* Embaſſador, the Biſhop of *London* was commanded to ſilence all the *Scots* about the City; and the like Order given to the reſt of the Biſhops, by whom they were inhibited from Preaching in all other places. But the leſs noiſe they made in the Church, the more cloſely and

and dangerously they practised on particular persons, in whom they endeavoured to beget an ill opinion of the present Government, and to engage them for advancing that of the *Presbyterian* in the place thereof. But this they had followed more successfully at the Act in *Oxon*, where they are liberally entertained by *Gelibrand* and the rest of the Brethren ; amongst which, *Wilcox*, *Hen*, and *Ackton*, were of greatest note. And at this time a question was propounded to them concerning the proceeding of the Minister in his duty, without the assistance or tarrying for the Magistrate. How they resolved this question, may be easily guessed, partly by that which they had done themselves when they were in *Scotland* ; and partly by the Actings of their *English* Brethren, in pursuance of it.

3. For presently after, *Gelibrand* deals with divers Students in their several Colledges, to put their hands unto a paper, which seemed to contain somewhat in it of such dangerous nature, that some did absolutely refuse, and others required further time of deliberation : of which *Gelibrand* thus writes to *Field*, on the 12 of *January* then next following : *I have already (saith he) entred into the matters whereof you write, and dealt with three or four several Colledges, concerning those amongst whom they live. I find that men are very dangerous in this point, generally favouring Reformation ; but when it comes to the particular point, some have not yet considered of the things for which others in the Church are so much troubled : others are afraid to testifie any thing with their hands, left it breed danger before the time : and many favour the Cause of the Reformation, but they are not Ministers, but young Students ; of whom there is good hope, if they be not cut off by violent dealing before the time. As I hear by you, so I mean to go forward where there is any hope, and to learn the number, and certifie you thereof,* &c. But that these secret practises might not be suspected, they openly attend the *Parliament* of this year, as at other times, in hope of gaining some advantage against the Bishops, and the received Orders of the Church : For in the *Parliament* of this year, which began on the Twenty third of *November*, they petitioned, amongst other things, That a Restraint might be laid upon the Bishops, for granting of Faculties, conferring of Orders, as also in the executing of Ecclesiastical Censure, the Oath *Ex officio*, permitting Non-residence, and the like. But the Queen would not hearken to it, partly because of the dislike she had of all Innovations, which commonly tend unto the worse ; but chiefly, in regard that all such Applications as they made to the *Parliament*, were by her looked on as derogatory to her own Supremacy. So that instead of gaining any of those points at the hands of the *Parliament*, they gained nothing but displeasure from the Queen, who is affirmed by *Stow* to have made a Speech at the end of their Session, and therein to have told the Bishops, That if they did not look more carefully to the discharge of their Duties, she must take order to deprive them, Sharp words ! and such as might necessitate the Bishops to look well about them.

4. It happened also, that some of the great Lords at Court whom they most relyed on, began to cool in their affections to the Cause, and had informed the Queen of the weakness of it, upon this occasion. The Earl of *Leicester*, *Walsingham*, and some others of great place and

power, being continually prest unto it by some Leading men, prevailed so far on the Arch-Bishop of *Canterbury*, as to admit them (in their hearing) to a private Conference: To which the Arch-Bishop condescends; and having desired the Arch-Bishop of *York*, and the Bishop of *Winchester*, to associate with him, that he might not seem to act alone in that weighty business; he was pleased to hear such Reasons as they could alledge for refusing to conform themselves to the Orders of the Church established. At which time though the said most Reverend Prelate sufficiently cleared all their Doubts, and satisfied all Exceptions which they had to make; yet at the earnest request of the said great persons, he gave way unto a second Conference to be held at *Lambeth*; at which such men were to be present, whose Arguments and Objections were conceived unanswerable, because they had not yet been heard. But when the points had been canvased on both sides for four hours together, the said great persons openly professed before all the Company, That they did not believe the Arch-bishops Reasons to have been so strong, and those of the other side so weak and trivial, as they now perceived them. And having thanked the Lord Arch-Bishop for his pains and patience, they did not only promise him to inform the Queen in the truth of the business; but endeavoured to perswade the opposite Party to a present Conformity. But long they did not stay in so good a humour; of which more hereafter.

5. With better fortune sped the Lords of the *Scotish* Nation, in the advance of their Affairs: Who being admitted to the Queens presence, by the means of *Walsingham*, received such countenance and support, as put them into a condition of returning homewards, and gaining that by force and practise, which they found impossible to be compassed any other way. All matters in that Kingdom were then chiefly governed by the Earl of *Arran*, formerly better known by the name of Captain *Jones*, who being of the House of the *Stuarts*, and fastening his dependence on the Duke of *Lenox*, at his first coming out of *France*, had on his instigation undertaken the impeaching of the Earl of *Morton*: after which, growing great in favour with the King himself, he began to ingross all Offices and Places of Trust, to draw unto himself the managery of all Affairs, and finally to assume the Title of Earl of *Arran*, at such time as the Chiefs of the *Hamiltons* were exiled and forfeited. Grown great and powerful by these means, and having added the Office of Lord Chancellor to the rest of his Honours, he grew into a general hatred with all sorts of people: And being known to have no very good affections to the Queen of *England*, she was the more willing to contribute towards his destruction. Thus animated and prepared, they make toward the Borders, and raising the Countrey as they went, marched on to *Sterling* where the King then lay. And shewing themselves before the Town with Ten thousand men, they publish a Proclamation in their own terms, touching the Reasons which induced them to put themselves into Arms. Amongst which it was none of the least, " That " Acts and Proclamations had not long before been published against " the Ministers of the Kirk, inhibiting their Presbyteries, Assemblies, " and other Exercises, Priviledges, and Immunities, by reason whereof
" the

" the moſt Learned and Honeſt of that number were compelled for ſafe-
" ty of their Lives and Conſciences, to abandon their Country.   To
" the end therefore that all the afflicted Kirk might be comforted, and
" all the ſaid Acts fully made in prejudice of the ſame, might be can-
" celled, and for ever aboliſhed, they commanded all the Kings Subjects
" to come in to aid them.

6 The King perceiving by this Proclamation what he was to truſt
to, firſt thinks of fortifying the Town : but finding that to be untena-
ble, he betakes himſelf unto the Caſtle, as his ſureſt ſtrength. The Conquerors having gained the Town on the firſt of *October*, poſſeſt themſelves alſo of the Bulwarks about the Caſtle; which they inviron on
all ſides, ſo that it was not poſſible for any to eſcape their hands : In
which extremity the King makes three Requeſts unto them, *viz.* That
his Life, Honour, and Eſtate, might be preſerved.   That the Lives of
certain of his Friends might not be touched.   And that all things might
be tranſacted in a peaceable manner.   They, on the other ſide, demand
three things for their ſecurity and ſatisfaction, *viz.* 1. " That the King
" would allow of their intention, and ſubſcribe their Proclamation, un-
" till further Order were eſtabliſhed by the Eſtates, &c. and that he
" would deliver into their hands all the Strong-holds in the Land. 2. That
" ſuch as had diſquieted the Common-wealth, might be delivered to
" them, and abide their due tryal by Law. And, 3. That the old Guard
" might be removed, and another placed, which was to be at their diſ-
" poſal.   To which Demands the King conſents at laſt, as he could
not otherwiſe; though in their Second they had purpoſely run a-croſs
to the ſecond of his, wherein he had deſired that the Lives of ſuch as
were about him, might not be endangered.   Upon the yeilding of
which points, which in effect was all that he had to give unto them, he
puts himſelf into their hands, hath a new Guard impoſed upon him, and
is conducted by them whereſoever they pleaſe.   And now the Miniſters
return in triumph to their Widowed Churches, where they had the
Pulpits at command, but nothing elſe agreeable to their expectation.
For the Lords having ſerved their own turns, took no care of theirs ;
inſomuch that in a Parliament held in *Lithgoe*, immediately after they
had got the King into their power, they cauſed an Act to paſs for ratifying the appointment betwixt them and the King ; by which they provided well enough for their own Indempnity.   But then withal, they
ſuffered it to be Enacted, *That none ſhould either publickly declare, or privately ſpeak or write in reproach of his Majeſties Perſon, Eſtate, or Government.*
Which came ſo croſs upon the ſtomacks of the Miniſters, whom nothing elſe could ſatisfie but the repealing of all former Statutes which
were made to their prejudice, that they fell foul upon the King in a
ſcandalous manner : inſomuch that one *Gibſon* affirmed openly in a Sermon at *Edenborough*, That heretofore the Earl of *Arran* was ſuſpected
to have been the *Perſecutor*, but *now they found it was the King*; againſt
whom he denounced the Curſe that fell on *Jeroboam*, *That he ſhould dye
Childleſs, and be the laſt of his Race.*   For which, being called to an account before the Lords of the Council, he ſtood upon his juſtification
without altering, and was by them ſent Priſoner to the Caſtle of
Blackroſs.

7. OF

7. Of the same temper were the rest ; who notwithstandiug the late Acts of Parliament inhibiting all Assembly and Classical Conventions, without leave from the King, held a new Synod at *St. Andrews*, in the *April* following, consisting (for the most part) of Barons and Lay-Gentlemen, Masters of Colledges, and ignorant School-Masters. Which Synod (if it may be called so) was purposely indicted by *Andrew Melvin*, for censuring the Archbishop of that City, whom they suspected and gave out to be the chief Contriver of the Acts of Parliament made in 1584, so prejudicial to the Kirk ; and to have penned the Declaration in defence thereof. And hereunto he found the rest so ready to conform themselves, that they were upon the point of passing the Sentence of Excommunication against him, before he was cited to appear ; most of them crying aloud, *It was the Cause of God* ; and, *That there needed no citation, where the iniquity was so manifest.* But being cited, at the last, he appears before them, puts up his Protestation concerning the unlawfulness of that Convention, and his disowning any Jurisdiction which they challenged over him ; and so demanded of them, What they had to say ? His Accusation was, That he had devised the Acts of Parliament in --84, to the subversion of the Kirk, and the Liberties of it. To which he answered, That he only had approved, and not devised the said Acts ; which having past the approbation of the Three Estates, were of a nature too Supreme for such Assemblies ; and thereupon appealed unto the King, the Council, and the following Parliament. But notwithstanding this Appeal, the Sentence of Excommunication is decreed against him, drawn into Writing, and subscribed. Which when neither the Moderator, being a meer Layick, nor any of the Ministers themselves, had confidence enough to pronounce and publish ; one *Hunter*, a Pedagogue in the House of *Andrew Melvin*, (professing that he had the Warrant of the Spirit for it) took the charge upon him, and with sufficient audacity pronounced the Sentence.

8. The informality and perversness of these proceedings, much displeased the King ; but more he feared what would be done in the next Assembly, appointed to be held at *Edenborough*, and then near at hand. *Melvin* intended in the same, not only to make good whatsoever had been done at the former Meeting, but to dispute the nature and validity of all Appeals which should be made against them on the like occasions. To break which blow, the King could find no other way, but to perswade the Arch-bishop to subscribe to these three points, *viz.* That he never publickly professed or intended to claim any Superiority, or to be judge over any other Pastors and Ministers, or yet avowed the same to have any warrant in Gods Word : That he never challenged any Jurisdiction over the late Synod at St. *Andrews* ; and must have erred, by his contempt of the said meeting, if he had so done And thirdly, That he would behave himself better for the time to come ; desiring pardon for the oversight of his former Actions ; promising to be such a Bishop from thenceforth, as was described by St. *Paul*: And finally, submitting both himself and Doctrine, to the Judgement of the said Assembly, without appealing from the same in the times to come. To such unworthy Conditions was the poor man brought, only to gain the King

some peace, and to reserve that little Power which was left unto Him ; though the King lost more by this Transaction, than possibly He could have done by his standing out. For, notwithstanding the Submissions on the part of the Bishop, the Assembly would descend no lower then to declare, That they would hold the said Sentence for not pronounced, and thereby leave the Bishop in the same estate in which they found him , and not this neither, but upon some hopes and assurance given them, that the King would favourably concur with them in the building of the House of God. Which Agreement did so little satisfie the adverse party, that they justified their former process, and peremptorily confirmed the Sentence which had been pronounced. Which when it could not be obtained from the greater part of the Assembly, who were not willing to lose the glory of so great a Victory ; *Hunter* stands up, by the advice of *Andrew Melvin*, and publickly protested against it ; declaring further, That notwithstanding any thing which had been done to the contrary, the Bishop should be still reputed for an Excommunicated person, and one delivered unto Satan. It was moved in this Assembly also, That some Censure should be laid upon the Ministers, who had subscribed the Acts of Parliament made in ˙˙84. But their number proved so great, that a Schism was feared ; and they were wise enough to keep all together, that they might be the better able upon all occasions to oppose the King. Somewhat was also done concerning the Establishment of their *Presbyteries*, and the defining of their Power, of which the King would take no notice, reserving his disgust of so many insolencies, till he should find himself in a condition to do them Rea on.

9. In these Exorbitances, they are followed by the *English Puritans*, who had been bad enough before, but henceforth shewed themselves to have more of the *Scot* in them, than in former times. For presently upon the news of the good success which their *Scottish* Brethren had at *Sterling*, a scandalous Libel, in the nature of a *Diologue*, is published, and dispersed in most parts of *England* : in which the state of this Church is pretended to be laid open in a Conference between *Diotrephes*, (representing the person of a Bishop) *Tertullus*, (a *Papist* brought in to plead for the Orders of our Church) *Demetrius*, an Usurer, (signifying such as live by unlawful Trades) *Pandocheus*, an Inn-keeper, (a receiver of all, and a soother of every man for his Gain) and *Paul*, (*a Preacher of the Word of God*) sustaining the place and person of the *Consistorians*). In the contrivance of which piece, *Paul* falls directly on the Bishop, whom he used most proudly, spightfully, and slanderously. He condemneth both the Calling of Bishops as *Antichristian*, and censureth their proceedings as Wicked, Popish, Unlawful, and Cruel. The Bishop is supposed to have been sent out of *England* into *Scotland*, for suppressing the *Presbyteries* there, and is made upon his return homewards, to be the Reporter of the *Scotish* Affairs ; and withal, to signifie his great fear lest he, and the rest of the Bishops in *England*, should be served shortly as the Bishops had lately been in *Scotland*, viz. at *Edenborough*, St. *Andrews*, &c. *Tertullas*, the *Papist*, is made the Bishops only Counsellor in the whole course of the Government of the Church ; by whose Advice the Bishops are made to bear with the *Popish Recusant*, and that so many ways are sought to suppress the *Puritans* : And he, together with

Pando-

Pandocheus the Host, and *Demetrius* the Usurer, relate unto the Bishop such Occurrences as had happened in *England* during his stay amongst the *Scots*. At which when the Bishop seemed to wonder, and much more marvelled that the Bishops had not yet suppressed the *Puritans* some way or other; *Pandocheus* is made to tell him, That one of their Preachers had affirmed in the Pulpit, That there were one hundred thousand of them in *England*; and that their number in all places did encrease continually.

10. By this last brag about their Numbers, and somewhat which escaped from the mouth of *Paul*, touching his hopes of seeing the Consistorian Discipline, erected shortly; it may be gathered, That they had a purpose to proceed in their Innovations, out of a hope to terrifie the State to a compliance, by the strength of their Party. But if that failed, they would then do as *Penry* had advised and threatned; that is to say, they would present themselves with a Petition to the Houses of Parliament, to the delivering whereof, one hundred thousand Hands should be drawn together. In the mean time, it was thought fit to dissemble their purposes, and to make tryal of such other means as appeared less dangerous. To which end they present with one hand a Petition to the Convocation, in which it was desired, That they might be freed from all Subscriptions; and with the other, publish a seditious Pamphlet, entituled, *A Complaint of the Commons for a Learned Ministry*. But, for the putting of their Counsels in execution, they were for the present at a stand. The Book of Discipline, upon a just examination, was not found so perfect, but that it needed a review; and the review thereof is referred to *Traverse*. By whom being finished, after a tedious expectation, it was commended to the Brethren, and by them approved. But the worst was, it was not so well liked of in the Houses of Parliament, as to pass for current; which so incensed those meek-spirited men, that they fell presently to the threatning and reviling all who opposed them in it. They had prepared their way to the Parliament then sitting, *Anno* 1586, by telling them, ‘That if the Reformation they desired, were ‘not granted, they should betray God, his Truth, and the whole King-‘dom, that they should declare themselves to be an Assembly, where-‘ in the Lords Cause could not be heard, wherein the felicity of misera-‘ble men could not be respected; wherein Truth, Religion, and Piety, ‘could bear no sway; an Assembly that willingly called for the Judge-‘ments of God upon the whole Realm; and finally, that not a man of ‘their seed should prosper, be a Parliament man, or bear rule in *England* ‘any more.

11. This necessary preparation being thus premised, they tender to the Parliament, A Book of the form of Common-Prayer by them desired, containing also in effect the whole pretended Discipline, so revised by *Traverse*; and their Petition in behalf thereof, was in these words following, *viz. May it therefore please your Majesty, &c. that the Book hereunto annexed, &c. Entituled,* A Book of the Form of Common-Prayers, and Administration of Sacraments, &c. *and every thing therein contained, &c. may be from henceforth put in use, and practised through all your Majesty's Dominions, &c.* But this so little edified with the Queen, or that the Grave Assembly, that in the drawing up of a General Pardon

to be passed in Parliament, there was an exception of those that committed any offence against the Act for the uniformity of Common-Prayers, or that were Publishers of Seditious Books, or Disturbers of Divine Service.　And to say the truth, the Queen had little reason to approve of that Form of Discipline in which there was so little consideration of the Supreme Magistrate in having either vote or place in any of their Synodical Meetings, unless he be chosen for an Elder, or indicting their Assemblies, either Provincial or National, or what else soever; or insomuch as nominating the particular time or place, when and where to hold them; or finally, in requiring his assent to any of their Constitutions.　All which, they challenge to themselves with far greater arrogancy than ever was exercised by the Pope, or any Bishop or inferior Minister under his command, during the times of greatest Darkness.　But the Brethren not considering what just reason the Queen had to reject their Bill, and yet fearing to fall foul upon her, in regard of the danger; they let flye at the Parliament in this manner; that is to say, That they should be in danger of the terrible Mass of Gods wrath, both in this life, and that to come; and that for their not abrogating the *Episcopal* Government, they might well hope for the favour and entertainment of *Moses*, that is, the curse of the Law: the Favour and loving Countenance of Jesus Christ, they should never see.

12. It may seem strange that Queen *Elizabeth* should carry such a hard hand on her *English Puritans*, as well by severe Laws and terrible executions, as by excluding them from the benefit of a General Pardon; and yet protect and countenance the *Presbyterians* in all places else.　But that great Monster in Nature, called *Reason of State*, is brought to plead in her defence; by which she had been drawn to aid the *French Hugonots* against their King; to supply the Rebel *Scots* with Men, Money, Arms and Ammunition, upon all occasions; and hitherto support those of the *Belgick* Provinces against the *Spaniard*.　Now she receives these last into her protection, being reduced at that time unto great extremities, partly by reason of the death of the Prince of *Orange*; and partly in regard of the great Successes of the Prince of *Parma*.　In which extremity they offered her the Soveraignity of *Holland, Zealand,* and *West Friesland*; to which they frame for her an unhandsome Title, grounded on her descent from *Philippa*, Wife of *Edward* the Third, Sister of *William* the Third, Earl of *Heynalt, Holland,* &c.　But she not harkning to that offer about the Soveraignty, as a thing too invidious, and of dangerous consequence; cheerfully yeelded to receive them into her protection, to raise an Army presently toward their defence, consisting of five thousand Foot, and one thousand Horse, with Money, Ammunition, Arms, and all other necessaries; and finally, to put the same Arms so appointed, under the Command of some Peson of Honour, who was to take the charge and trust of so great a business.　The Confederates, on the other side, being very prodigal of that which was none of their own, delivered into her hands the Keys of the Country, that is to say, the Towns of *Brill* and *Flushing*, with the Fort of *Ramekins*.　And more then so, as soon as the Earl of *Leicester* came amongst them, in the Head of this Army, which most ambitiously he affected for some other ends; they put into his hands the absolute Government of these

Pro-

Provinces, gave him the Title of His Excellency, and generally submitted to him with more outward cheerfulness than ever they had done to the King of *Spain*. It is not to be thought, but that the *Presbyterian* Discipline went on succesfully in those Provinces , under this new Governor ; who having countenanced them in *England* against the Laws, might very well afford them all his best assistances, when law and liberty seemed to speak in favour of it. But being there was nothing done by them , which was more than ordinary ; as little more than ordinary could be done amongst them, after they had betrayed their Countrey to the Power of Strangers ; We shall leave him to pursue their Wars, and return for *England*,where we shall find the Queen of *Scots* upon the point of acting the last part of her Tragedy.

13. Concerning which, it may not be unfit to recapitulate so much of Her story as may conduct us fairly to the knowledge of her present condition. Immediately on the death of Queen *Mary*, she had taken on her self the Title and Arms of *England* ; which though she did pretend to have been done by the command of her Husband, and promised to disclaim them both in the Treaty of *Edenborough* ; yet neither were the Arms obliterated in her Plate and Hangings , after the death of that Husband ; nor would she ever ratifie and confirm that Treaty, as had been conditioned. On this first grudg, Queen *Elizabeth* furnisheth the *Scots* both with Men and Arms, to expel the *French* ; affords them such a measure both of Money and Countenance , as made them able to take the Field against their Queen , to take her Prisoner , to depose her ; and finally, to compel her to forsake the Kingdom. In which extremity , she lands in *Cumberland* , and casts her self upon the favour of Queen *Elizabeth* ; by whom she was first confined to *Carlisle* , and afterwards committed to the custody of the Earl of *Shrewsbury*. Upon the death of *Francis* the Second , her first Husband , the King of *Spain* designed her for a Wife to his Eldest Son. But the ambition of the young Prince spurred him on so fast , that he brake his Neck in the Career. The Duke of *Norfolk* was too great for a private Subject ; of the Revenue not inferior to the Crown of *Scotland* : insomuch that the Queen was counselled , when she came first to the Throne , either to take him for her Husband, or to cut him off. He is now drawn into the Snare, by being tempted to a hope of Marriage with the captive Queen ; which *Leicester* and the rest, who had moved it to him , turned to his destruction. Don *John* of *Austria* Governour of the *Netherlands* for the King of *Spain*, had the like design, that by her Title he might raise himself to the Crown of *England*. To which end he recalled the *Spanish* Soldiers out of *Italy* , to whose dismission he had yeelded when he first came to that Government ; and thereby gave Queen *Elizabeth* a sufficient colour to aid the Provinces against him. But his aspirings cost him dear; for he fell soon after. The *Guisards* and the *Pope* had another project, which was, To place her first on the Throne of *England*,and then to find an Husband of sufficient Power to maintain her in it. For the effecting of which Project, the *Pope* commissionated his Priests and Jesuits; and the *Guisards* employed their Emissaries of the *English* Nation , by Poyson, Pistol, open War, or secret practises, to destroy the one, that so they might advance the other to the Regal Diadem.

14. With

14. With all these Practises and designs, it was conceived that the Imprisoned Queen could not be ignorant; and many strong presumptions were discovered to convict her of it: Upon which grounds the Earl of *Leicester* drew the form of an *Association*, by which he bound himself, and as many others as should enter into it, *To make enquiry against all such persons as should attempt to invade the Kingdom, or raise Rebellion, or should attempt any evil against the Queens Person, to do her any manner of hurt, from, or by whomsoever that layed any claim to the Crown of England. And that, that Person by whom, or for whom they shall attempt any such thing, shall be altogether uncapable of the Crown, shall be deprived of all manner of Right thereto, and persecuted to the death by all the Queens Loyal Subjects, in case they shall be found guilty of any such Invasion, Rebellion, or Treason, and should be so publickly declared.* Which Band or Association, was confirmed in the Parliament of this year, ending the 29 of *March, Anno* 1585, exceedingly extolled for an Act of Piety, by those very men who seemed to abominate nothing more, than the like Combination made not long before between the Pope, the *Spaniard*, and the House of *Guise*, called the *Holy League*; which League was made for maintenance of the Religion then establish'd in the Realm of *France*, and the excluding of the King of *Navarre*, the Prince of *Conde*, and the rest of the House of *Bourbon*, from their succession to the Crown, as long as they continued enemies to that Religion. The Brethren in this case not unlike the *Lamiæ* who are reported to have been stone-blind when they were at home, but more than Eagle-sighted when they went abroad. But that they might not trust to their own strength only, Queen *Elizabeth* tyes the *French* King to her, by investing him with the Robes and Order of Saint *George*, called the Garter: She draws the King of *Scots* to unite himself unto her in a League Offensive and Defensive against all the World; and under colour of some danger to Religion by that *Holy League*; she brings all the Protestant Princes of *Germany* to confederate with her.

15. And now the Queen of *Scots* is brought to a publick Tryal, accelerated by a new Conspiracy of *Babington, Tichborn*, and the rest; in which nothing was designed without her privity. And it is very strange to see how generally all sorts of people did contribute toward her destruction; the *English* Protestants, upon an honest apprehension of the Dangers to which the Person of their Queen was subject by so many Conspiracies: the *Puritans*, for fear lest she should bring in *Popery* again, if she came to the Crown: the *Scots*, upon the like conceit of over-throwing their Presbyteries, and ruinating the whole *Machina* of their Devices, if ever she should live to be Queen of *England*. The Earl of *Leicester* and his Faction in the Court, had their Ends apart; which was, To bring the Imperial Crown of this Realm, by some means or other, into the Family of the *Dudley's*. His Father had before designed it, by marrying his Son *Guilford* with the Lady *Jane*, descended from the younger Sister of K. *Henry* the Eighth. And he projects to set it on the Head of the Earl of *Huntington*, who had married his Sister, and looked upon himself as the direct Heir of *George* Duke of *Clarence*. And that they might not want a Party of sufficient strength to advance their Interest, they make themselves the Heads of the *Puritan* Faction

Faction; the Earl of *Leicester* in the Court, and the Earl of *Huntingdon* in the Countrey. For him, he obtaineth of the Queen the command of the *North*, under the Title of *Lord President of the Councel in York*, to keep out the *Scots*: and for himself, the Conduct of the *English* Armies which served in the Low-Countreys, to make sure of all. He takes a course also to remove the Imprisoned Queen from the Earl of *Shrewsbury*, and commits her to the custody of *Paulet*, and *Drury*, two notorious *Puritans*, though neither of them were so base as to serve his turn, when he practised on them to assassinate her in a private way. I take no pleasure in recounting the particulars of that Horrid Act, by which a Soveraign Queen, lawfully Crowned and Anointed, was brought to be arraigned before the Subjects of her nearest Kinswoman, or how she was convicted by them; what Artifices were devised to bring her to the fatal Block; or what dissimulations practised to palliate and excuse that Murther.

16. All I shall note particularly in this woful story, is the behaviour of the *Scots*, (I mean the *Presbyters*) who being required by the King to recommend her unto God in their publick Prayers, refused most unchristianly so to do, except only *David Liadesay* at *Leith*, and the Kings own Chaplains. And yet the Form of Prayer prescribed, was no more then this, *That it might please God to illuminate her with the Light of his Truth, and save her from the apparent danger wherein she was cast.* On which default, the King appointed solemn Prayers to be made for her in *Edenborough*, on the third of *February*; and nominates the Arch-bishop of St. *Andrews* to perform that Office. Which being understood by the Ministers, they stirred up one *John Cooper*, a bold young man, and not admitted into Orders, of their own conferring to invade the Pulpit, before the Bishop had an opportunity to take the place: Which being noted by the King, he commanded him to come down, and leave the Pulpit to the Bishops, as had been appointed; or otherwise, to perform the Service which the Day required. To which the sawcy Fellow answered, That he would do therein, *according as the Spirit of God should direct him in it.* And then perceiving that the Captain of the Guard was coming to remove him thence, he told the King with the same impudence as before, *That this day should be a witness against him in the Great Day of the Lord*: And then denouncing a Woe to the Inhabitants of *Edenborough*, he went down, and the Bishop of St. *Andrews* entring the Pulpit, did the Duty required. For which intollerable Affront, *Cooper* was presently commanded to appear before the Lords of the Council, and he took with him *Watson* and *Belcanqual*, two of the Preachers of *Edenborough*, for his two Supporters: Where they behaved themselves with so little reverence, that the two Ministers were discharged from preaching in *Edenborough*, and *Cooper* was sent Prisoner to the Castle of *Blackness*. But so unable was the King to bear up against them, that having a great desire that *Montgomery*, Arch-bishop of *Glascow*, might be absolved from the Censures under which he lay, he could no otherwise obtain it, than by releasing this *Cooper*, together with *Gibson* before mentioned, from their present Imprisonment: which, though it were yeelded to by the King, upon condition that *Gibson* should make some acknowledgment of his Offence in the face of the Church; yet, after many triflings,

flings, and much tergiverfation, he took his flight into *England*, where he became a ufeful Inftrument in the Holy Caufe.

17. For fo it was, that notwithftanding the Promife made to Arch-bifhop *Whitgift*, by *Leicefter*, *Walfingham*, and the reft, as before is faid, they gave fuch encouragements under-hand to the *Presbyterians*, that they refolved to proceed toward the putting of the Difcipline in execution, though they received fmall countenance in it from the Queen and Parliament. Nor were thofe great Perfons altogether fo unmindful of them, as not to entertain their Clamours, and promote their Petitions at the Council-Table, croffing and thwarting the Arch-bifhop whenfoever any Caufe which concerned the Brethren, had been brought before them. Which drew from him feveral Letters to the Lords of the Council, each fyllable whereof, (for the great Piety and Modefty which appears in them) deferves to have been written in Letters of Gold. Now the fum of thefe Letters, as they are laid together by Sir *George Paul*, is as followeth.

18. *God knows, (faith he) how defirous I have been from time to time, to have my doings approved by my ancient and honourable Friends : for which caufe, fince my coming to this place, I have done nothing of importance againft thefe Sectaries, without good Advice. I have rifen up early, and fate up late, to yield Reafons, and make Anfwer to their Contentions, and their Seditious Objections. And fhall I now fay, I have loft my labour ? Or, fhall my juft dealing with difobedient and irregular perfons, caufe my former profeffed and ancient Friends to hinder my juft proceedings, and make them fpeak of my doings, yea, and of my felf, what they lift ? Solomon faith,* An old Friend is better then a new : *I truft thofe that love me indeed, will not fo lightly caft off their old Friends, for any of thefe new fangled and factious Sectaries, whofe fruits are to make divifion, and to feparate old and affured Friends. In my own private Affairs, I know I fhall ftand in need of Friends ; but in thefe publick Actions, I fee no caufe why I fhould feek any, feeing they to whom the care of the Commonwealth is committed, ought of duty therein to joyn with me. And if my honourable Friends fhall forfake me (efpecially in fo good a Caufe) and not put their helping hand to the redrefs of thefe Enormities, (being indeed a matter of State, and not of the leaft moment) I fhall think my coming unto this Place to have been for my punifhment ; and my hap very hard, that when I think to deferve beft ; and in a manner, confume my felf to fatisfie that which God, Her Majefty, and the Church, requireth of me, I fhould be evilly rewarded.* Sed meliora fpero. *It is objected, by fome, that my defire of Uniformity, by way of fubfcription, is for the better maintenance of my Book. They are mine Enemies that fay fo ; but I truft my Friends have a better opinion of me. Why fhould I feek for any confirmation of my Book, after twelve years approbation ? Or what fhall I get thereby, more than already I have ? Yet, if Subfcription may confirm it, it is confirmed long ago, by the Subfcription of almoft all the Clergy of England, before my time. Mine Enemies likewife, and the flanderous Tongues of this uncharitable Sect, report that I am revolted, become a Papift, and I know not what. But it proceedeth from their Leudnefs, and not from any defert of mine.*

29. *I am further burthened with Wilfulnefs : I hope my Friends are better perfwaded of me, to whofe Confciences I appeal. It is ftrange that a man of my*
place

place, dealing by so good a warrant as I do, should be so encountred ; and, for not yeilding, counted wilful.   But I must be content, Vincet qui patitur. *There is a difference betwixt Wilfulness and Constancy.   I have taken upon me, by the Place which I hold under Her Majesty, the defence of the Religion and the Rites of the Church of* England, *to appease the Schisms and Sects therein, to reduce all the Ministers thereof to Uniformity, and to due Obedience, and not to waver with every wind; which also, my place, my Person, the Laws, Her Majesty, and the goodness of the Cause, do require of me ; and wherein the Lords of her Highness Privy Council, (all things considered) ought in duty to assist and countenance me.   But, how is it possible that I should perform what I have undertaken, after so long Liberty and lack of Discipline, if a few persons so meanly qualified, (as most of these Factious Sectaries are) should be countenanced against the whole state of the Clergy, of greatest account both for Learning, Years, Stayedness, Wisdom, Religion, and Honesty; and open Breakers and Impugners of the Law, young in Years, proud in Co ceit, contentious in D. sposition, should be maintained against their Governours, seeking to reduce them to Order and Obedience?* Hæc sunt initia Hæreticorum, & ortus, atque conatus Schismaticorum male cogitantium, ut sibi placeant, ut præpositum superbo tumore contemnant : sic de Ecclesia receditur, sic altare profanum foris collocatur, sic contra Pacem Christi & Ordinationem, atque Veritatem Dei Rebellatur.   *The first Fruits of Hereticks, and the first Births and Endeavours of Schismaticks, are, To admire themselves, and in their swelling pride to contemn any that are set over them.   Thus do men fall from the Church of God; thus is a Forein Unhallowed Alter erected; and thus is Christs Peace, and Gods Ordination and Unity, rebelled against.*

20. *For my own part, I neither have done, nor do any thing in these matters, which I do not think my self in Conscience and Duty bound to do, and wh ch Her Majesty hath not with earnest charge committed unto me, and which I am not well able to justifie to be most requisite for this Church and State ; whereof, next to Her Majesty, (though most unworthy, if not most unhappy) the ch ef Care is committed to me ; which I w ll not (by the Grace of God) neglect, whatsoever come upon me there-for.   Neither may I endure their notorious Contempts, unless I will become* Æsop's *Block ; and undo all that which hitherto hath been done.   It is certain, that if way be given unto them, upon their unjust Surmises and Clamours ; it will be the cause of that confusion which hereafter the State will be sorry for.   I neither care for the honour of this Place I hold, (which is* onus *unto me) nor the largeness of the Revenue, neither any Worldly thing (I thank God) in respect of doing my duty, neither do I fear the displeasure of man nor the evil Tongue of the uncharitable, who call me Tyrant, Pope, Knave, and lay to my charge things that I never did or thought.* Scio enim hoc esse opus Diaboli, ut servos Dei mendaciis laceret, & opinionibus falsis gloriosum nomen infamet ; ut, qui Conscientiæ suæ luce clarescunt, alienis Ruoribus sordidentur: *For I know, that this is the work of that Accuser the Devil, that he may tear in pieces the Servants of God with Lyes, that he may dishonour their glorious Name, with false surmises, that they who through the clearness of their own Consciences are shining bright, may have the filth of other mans slanders cast upon them.   So was* Cyprian *himself used, and oth r Godly Bishops, to whom I am not comparable.   But that which most of all grieveth me, and is to be wondered at and lamented, is, That some of those who give countenance to these men, and cry out for a Learned M nistry, should watch their opportunity, and be*

Instruments

Instruments and Means to place most unlearned men in the chiefest Places and Livings of the Ministry, thereby to make the state of the Bishops and Clergy contemptible, and I fear, salable. This Hypocrisie and Dissembling with God and Man, (in pretending one thing, and doing another) goeth to my heart, and maketh me think, that Gods Judgements are not far off. The day will come, when all mens hearts shall be opened. In the mean time, I will depend upon him who never faileth those that put their trust in him.

21. It may be gathered from this Abstract, what a hard Game that Reverend Prelate had to play, when such great Masters in the Art, held the Cards against him: For at that time the Earls of *Huntington* and *Leicester,* *Walsingham* Secretary of Estate, and *Knolls* Comptroller of the Houshold (a professed *Genevian,*) were his open Adversaries; *Burleigh,* a Neutral at the best; and none but *Hatton* (then Vice-Chamberlain, and afterwards Lord Chancellor) firmly for him. And him he gained but lately neither; but gained him at the last by the means of Dr. *Richard Bancroft,* his Domestick Chaplain, of whom we shall have cause to speak more hereafter. By his procurement he was called to the Council-table, at such time as the Earl of *Leicester* was in *Holland*; which put him into a capacity of going more confidently on (without checks or crosses, as before) in the Churches cause. A thing which *Leicester* very much stomacked at his coming back; but knowing it was the Queens pleasure, he disguised his trouble, and appeared fair to him in the publick, though otherwise he continued his former favours to the *Puritan* Faction. Sure of whose countenance, upon the perfecting and publishing of the Book of Discipline, they resolved to put the same in practise in most parts of the Realm, as they did accordingly. But it was no where better welcome, than it was in *London,* the Wealth and Pride of which City was never wanting to cherish and support those men which most apparently opposed themselves to the present Authority, or practised the introducing of Innovations, both in Church and State. The several Churches or Conventicles rather, which they had in that City, they reduced into one great and general Classis, of which *Cartwright,* *Egerton,* or *Traverse,* were for the most part Moderators; and whatsoever was there ordered, was esteemed for current: from thence the Brethren of other places did fetch their light; and as doubts did arise, thither they were sent to be resolved; the Classical and Synodical Decrees of other places, not being Authentical indeed, till they were ratified in this, which they held the Supreme Consistory and chief Tribunal of the Nation. But in the Countrey, none appeared more forward than they did in *Northamptonshire,* which they divide into three *Classes*; that is to say, the Classis of *Northampton,* *Daventry,* and *Kettring:* and the device forthwith is taken up in most parts of *England,* but especially in *Warwickshire,* *Suffolk,* *Norfolk,* *Essex* &c. In these *Classes* they determined in points of Doctrine, interpreted hard places of Scripture, delivered their Resolution in such cases of conscience as were brought before them, decided doubts and difficulties touching Contracts of Marriage. And whatsoever was concluded by such as were present (but still with reference to the better judgement of the *London* Brethren) became forthwith binding to the rest; none being admitted into any of the aforesaid *Classes,* before he hath

promised

ptomifed under his hand, That he would fubmit himfelf, and be obedient unto all fuch Orders and Decrees as are fet down by the Claffis to be
obferved. At thefe Claffis they enquired into the Life and Doctrine of all
that had fubfcribed unto them ; cenfuring fome, depofing others, as they
faw occafion ; in nothing more fevere than in cenfuring thofe who had
formerly ufed the Crofs in Baptifm, or otherwife had been conformable
to the Rules of the Church. And unto every Claffis there belonged a
Regifter, who took the Heads of all that paffed, and faw them carefully
entred in a Book for that purpofe, that they might remain upon Record.

22. It may feem ftrange , that in a conftituted Church, backed by
Authority of Law, and countenanced by the favour of the Supreme Magiftrate ; a diftinct Government and Difcipline fhould be put in practife
in contempt of both : but more, that they fhould deal in fuch weighty
matters as were deftructive of the Government by Law eftablifhed.
Some queftions had before been ftarted at a Meeting in *Cambridge* , the
final decifion whereof, was thought fit to be referred to the *Claffis* of *Warwick*, where *Cartwright* governed as the perpetual Moderator : And they
accordingly affembling on the tenth day of the fourth Moneth , (for fo
they phrafed it) did then and there determine in this manner following :
*That private Baptifm is unlawful : That it is not lawful to read Homilies in the
Church : and that the fign of the Crofs is not to be ufed in Baptifm : That the
Faithful ought not to communicate with unlearned Minifters, although they may
be prefent at their Service , in cafe they come of purpofe to hear a Sermon (the
reading of the Service being looked on as a Lay-mans Office :) That the calling
of Bifhops, &c. is unlawful : That as they deal in caufes Ecclefiaftical, there is no
duty belonging to them, nor any publickly to be given them : That it is not lawful to
be ordained by them into the Miniftry, or to denounce either Sufpenfions or Excommunications fent by their Authority : that it is not lawful for any man to reft in
the Bifhops deprivation of him from his Charge , except upon confultation it feem
good unto his Flock and the Neighbouring Minifters ; but that he continue in the
fame, until he be compelled to the contrary by Civil Force. That it is not lawful to
appear in a Bifhops Court , but with a Proteftation of their unlawfulnefs. That
Bifhops are not to be acknowledged either for Doctors, Elders, or Deacons, as having no ordinary calling in the Church of Chrift. That touching the reftauration
of the Ecclefiaftical Difcipline, it ought to be taught to the people (data occafio-
ne) as occafion fhould ferve ; and that as yet the people are not to be follicited
publickly to practife the Difcipline, till they be better inftructed in the knowledge
of it. And finally, that men of better underftanding are to be allured privately
to the prefent allowing the Difcipline, and the practife of it, as far as they fhall be
well able with the* Peace of the Church.

23. But here we are to underftand, that this laft caution was fubjoined in the clofe of all ; not that they had a care of the *Churchs Peace*, but
that they were not of fufficient ftrength to difturb the fame, without
drawing ruine on themfelves ; which fome of the more hot headed Brethren were refolved to hazzard : of which they had fome lofs this year,
by the Imprifonment of *Barrow* , *Greenwood, Billet, Boudler,* and *Studley* ;
who building on their Principles, and following the Example of *Robert
Brown*, before remembred, had brake out into open Schifm, when their
more cunning Brethren kept themfelves within the Pale of the Church.
But thefe we onely touch at now , leaving the further profecution of
them

them to a fitter place : Suffice it that their present sufferings did so little moderate the heats of some fiery spirits, that they resolved to venture all for the Holy Discipline, as appears by *Pain's* Letter unto *Field*. *Our zeal to Gods Glory,* (saith he) *our love to his Church ; and the due planting of the same in this Foreheaded Age, should be so warm and stirring in us, as not to care what adventure we give, or what censures we abide,* &c. *For otherwise the Diabolical boldness of the Jesuits and Seminaries will cover our faces with shame,* &c. And then he adds, *It is verily more then time to register the names of the fittest and hottest Brethren round about our several dwellings, whereby to put the Godly Counsel of* Specanus *in execution,* (Note that *Specanus* was one of the first Presbyterian Ministers in the *Belgick* Churches) that is to say, *Si quis objiciat,* &c. *If any man object, That the setting up the lawful practise of the Discipline in the Church be hindred by the Civil Magistrate ; let the Magistrate be freely and modestly admonished of his duty in it ; and if he esteem to be accounted either a Godly or Christian Magistrate, without doubt he will admit wholesome Counsels : but if he do not, yet let him be more exactly instructed, that he may serve God in fear, and lend his Authority in defence of Gods Church and his Glory. Marry if by this way there happen no good success, then let the Ministers of the Church execute their Office according to the appointment of* Christ : *for they must rather obey God than Men. In which last point* (saith Pain) *we have dolefully failed, which now or never stands us in hand to prosecute with all celerity, without lingring or staying so long for Parliaments.* But this counsel of *Pain* being thought too rash, in regard they could not find a sufficient number of Brethren to make good the action, it was thought fit to add the caution above mentioned. The hundred thousand hands which they so much bragged of, were not yet in readiness ; and therefore it was wisely ordered, that as yet the whole multitude were not to be allured publickly to the practise of it, until men were better instructed in the knowledge of so rare a Mystery : till when, it could not be safe for them to advance their Discipline in the way of force.

24. Now to prepare the people for the entertainment of so great a change, it was found necessary in the first place to return an answer to some Books which had been written in defence of Episcopal government: and in the next to make the Bishops seem as odious and contemptible in the eyes of their Proselytes, as Wit and Malice could devise. Dr. *John Bridges* Dean of *Sarum,* and afterwards Bishop of *Oxford,* published a Book in the year 1587, entituled *A Defence of the Government of the Church of England;* intended chiefly against *Beza,* but so that it might serve to satisfie the doubts and cavils which had been made against that Government by the *English Puritans.* To which an answer is returned by some zealous Brethren, under the name of *A Defence of the Godly Ministers, against the slanders of Dr.* Bridges. *Bridges* replies, and his Reply produceth a Rejoynder, *Anno* 1588, bearing this Inscription, *viz. A Defence of the Ecclesiastical Discipline against the Reply of Mr.* Bridges. Dr. *Some* Master of *Peter-House* in *Cambridge,* to check the sawciness of *Penrie,* a most fiery *Puritan,* published a discourse at the same time, to detect his Follies : and presently comes out a Libel, entituled, *Mr. Some laid open in his Colours.* The Brethren had been malepert enough with Dr. *Bridges,* and might be thought to have been malepert enough with Dr. *Some,* if they had not carried themselves with far more irreverence towards the Archbishop

and

and the reſt of the Sacred Hierarchy: For now, in proſecution of the other part of their deſign, which was, To make the Biſhops odious and contemptible in the eyes of their Proſelytes; four of the moſt ſeditious of all the Pack, (that is to ſay, *Penrie, Throgmorton, Udal,* and *Fenner*) lay their heads together. From which conjunction there proceeded ſuch a ſwarm of peſtiferous Libels, that the like miſchief (neither in nature nor in number) did never exerciſe the patience of a Chriſtian State. The Authors of them maſked under the borrowed name of *Martin Mar-Prelate*; which Title they had taken on themſelves, not without good cauſe, as may appear unto any which have looked into theſe particulars; that is to ſay, *The Epiſtle to the Convocation Houſe: The Epitome: The Demonſtration of Diſcipline: The Supplication: Diotrephes: Martins Minerals: Have you any work for a Cooper:* Penry's *Epiſtles ſent from* Scotland: *Theſes Martiniana,* or *Martin Junior: The Proteſtation of Martin: Martin Senior: More work for the Cooper: A Dialogue, ſetting forth the Tyrannical dealing of the Biſhops againſt Gods Children.* Read over Dr. *Bridges,* &c. with many others of the like ſtrain, of which it is hard to ſay, whether their malice or uncharitableneſs had the moſt predominancy. In all which doings, *Cartwright* was either of the council in the firſt deſign, or without doubt a great approver of them upon the poſt-fact; and thereupon he is affirmed to have uſed theſe words, *That ſince the Biſhops lives would not amend by grave Books and Advertiſements, it was fit they ſhould be ſo dealt with to their further ſhame.*

25. For Printing theſe peſtiferous Libels, they chiefly made uſe of *Walgrave*'s Preſs, which he removed from place to place, for his greater ſafety; that is to ſay, at *Moulſey,* near *Kingſton* upon *Thames,* thence to *Fauſly* in *Northamptonſhire,* ſo to *Norton;* afterwards to *Coventry* and ſo to *Welſtome* in *Warwickſhire;* and from thence, finally to the Town of *Mancheſter,* where both the Workmen and the Preſs were ſeized on by the Earl of *Darby,* as they were Printing the bold Pamphlet, called *More Work for Cooper.* For the diſperſing of theſe Libels, they made uſe of one *Newman* a Cobler, a fellow fit for ſuch a buſineſs; and it had been great pity if they had employed any other Inſtrument. But for their countenance and ſupport, eſpecially as to the bearing of their charges) they had the Purſe of *Knightly* of *Fauſley,* (at whoſe Houſe ſome of them were Printed) being a Gentleman of good Note, but of greater Zeal, whom *Snape* and other leading men of that County had inveigled to them. But he and all the reſt might have payed dear for it, if he whom they moſt wronged, had not ſtood their Friend: For, being called into the Star-Chamber, and there deeply cenſured, they were upon ſubmiſſion, at the humble and moſt earneſt ſuit of the Archbiſhop, releaſed from their Impriſonment, and their Fines remitted. And it is worth the obſervation, That the *Puritans* were then moſt buſie, as well in ſetting up their Diſcipline, as in publiſhing theſe Railing and Seditious Pamphlets, when the *Spaniards* were hovering on the Seas with their terrible Navy. At what time they conceived, and that not improbably, that the Queen and Council would be otherwiſe buſied, than to take notice of their practiſes, or ſuppreſs their doings; or rather that they durſt not call them into queſtion for their words and actions, for fear of alienating the affections of ſo ſtrong a party as they had raiſed to themſelves. The
ſerious

serious apprehension of which mischievous Counsels, prevailed so far on *Leicester* and *Walsingham*, that they did absolutely renounce any further intercession for them; professing, That they had been horribly abused with their Hypocrisie; which possibly might happen better for themselves, than it did for the Church; the Earl of *Leicester going to his own Place*, before the end of this year; and *Walsingham* being gathered to his Fathers within two years after.

26 I am ashamed to rake in these filthy Puddles, though it be necessary that the bottom of the Cinque be opened, that notice may be taken of that stinch and putrefaction which proceeded from them. In which respect I hope the *Reader* will excuse me, if I let him know, that they could find no other Title for the Arch-Bishop of *Canterbury*, then *Belzebub* of *Canterbury*, *Pope of Lambeth*, the *Canterbury-Caiaphas*, *Esau*, *a Monstrous Antichristian Pope*, *A most bloody Opposer of Gods Saints*, *A very Antichristian Beast*, *A most vile and cursed Tyrant*. They tell us further of this humble and meek-spirited man, that *no Bishop ever had such an aspiring and ambitious mind as he*; *no*, *not Cardinal* Wolsey: *None so proud as he*, *no*, *not* Stephen Gardiner *of* Winchester: *None so tyrannical as he*; *no*, *not* Bonner *the Butcher of* London. In general, he tells us both of him, and the rest of the Bishops, That they are *Unlawful: Unnatural, False, and Bastardly Governours of the Church, the Ordinances of the Devil, Petty Popes Petty Antichrists, Incarnate Devils, Bishops of the Devil, Cogging, Cozening Knaves, and will lye like Dogs.* That they are *Proud, Popish, Presumptuous, Prophane, Paltry, Pestilent, Pernicious Prelates and Usurpers; Enemies of God, and the most pestilent Enemies of the State*; and, *That the worst* Puritan *in* England, *is an Honester man than the best Lord Bishop in Christendom.* Nor do they speak any better of the Inferior Clergy, than they do of the Bishops; of whom they tell us in like manner, That *they are Popish Priests, or Monks, or Friars, or Ale-haunters, or Boys and Lads, or Drunkards and Dolts, That they will wear a Fools Hood for a Living-sake: That they are Hogs, Dogs, Wolves, Foxes, Simoniacks, Usurpers, Proctors of Antichrists Inventions, Popish Chap-men, halting Neutrals, greedy Dogs to fill their Paunches, a multitude of desperate and forlorn Atheists, a Cursed, Uncircumcised, Murthering Generation, a Crew or Hoop of Bloudy Soul-Murtherers, and Sacrilegious Church-Robbers, and Followers of Antichrist.*

27. Behold the Bishops and Clergy in their Convocation, and we shall see them termed by one of the Captains of this Crew. *Right Puissant, poysoned, persecuting, and terrible Priests, Clergie-Masters of the Convocation-House, the Holy League of subscription, the Crew of monstrous and ungodly Wretches, that mingle Heaven and Earth together: Horned Monsters of the Conspiration-House, An Antichristian Swinish Rabble, Enemies of the Gospel, most covetous wretched Popish Priests, and the Convocation-House of Devils, and* Belzebub of Canterbury *the chief of these Devils.* The like Reproaches they bestow on the Common-Prayer, of which they say, That *it is full of Corruption*; and that *many of the Contents thereof, are against the Word of God, the Sacraments wickedly mangled and prophaned therein, the Lords Supper not eaten, but made a Pageant or Stage-play, and that the Form of publick Baptism, is full of Childish Superstitious toys.* So that we are not to admire, if the *Brownists* please themselves in their separation from

a Church so polluted and unreformed, from men so wicked and prophane, from *such a Sink of Satan*, such a *Den of Devils*. But much less can we wonder that the Papists should make use of these horrible Slanders, not only to confirm, but encrease their Party, by shewing them from the Pens of their greatest Adversaries, what ugly Monsters had the Government of the Church of *England*, from what Impieties they were preserved, by not joyning with them. One, I am sure, that is, *Parsons* in his Book of *Three Conversions*, reports these Calumnies and Slanders for undoubted Truths: That *Martin Mar-Prelate* is affirmed by Sir *Edwine Sandys*, to pass in those times for unquestion'd Credit in the Court of *Rome* his Authority much insisted on to disgrace this Church; and finally, that (*a*) *Kellison*, one of later date, doth build as much upon the Credit of these Libels, to defame the Clergy, as if they had been dictated by the same Infallible Spirit which the Pope pretends to. Such excellent Advantages did these Saints give unto the Devil that all the *Locusts* in the *Revelation* which *came out of the pit*, never created so much scandal to the Primitive times.

(a) Apellant Episcopum Cantuariensem, PseudoEpiscopum, principem Dæmoniorum, Caipham, Esauum, Monstrosum, Antichristianum Papam, & Bestiam, alios autem Episcopos Angliæ degeneres, perniciosos, usurpatores, deteriores Monachis, Latrones, Lupos Episcopos Diaboli, &c. Mason. l.3.c.16.

28. To still these Clamours, or at the least to stop the mouths of these Railing *Rabshecha's*, that so the abused people on all sides might be undeceived, as good a course was took by *Whitgift* and the rest of the Prelates, as Humane Wisdom could devise. For first a grave discourse is published in the year next following, entituled, *An Admonition to the people of England*, in answer to the slanderous Untruths of *Martin* the Libeller: But neither this nor any other grave Refutal, would ever put them unto silence, till they were undertaken by *Tom Nash*, a man of a Sarcastical and jeering Wit: who by some Pamphlets written in the like loose way, which he called *Pasquill*, and *Marforius*, *The Counter-Scuffle*, *Pappe with a Hatchet*, and the like, stopped their mouths for ever, none of them daring to deal further in that Commodity, when they saw what coyn they should be paid in by so frank a Customer. Mention was made before of a sorry Pamphlet, entituled, *The Complaint of the Commons for a Preaching-Ministry*, which *Penry* seconded by another called by the Name of, *A Supplication* for Preaching in *Wales*: In both which it was intimated to all sorts of people, That the Gospel had no free passage amongst us: That there was no care taken for Preaching the Word of God for the instruction of the people; for want whereof they still remained in darkness and the shadow of death. For the decrying of which scandalous and leud suggestions, Order was given unto the Bishops to take the Names and Number of the Preachers in their several Diocesses, and to present a true and perfect Catalogue of them in the Convocation, which was then at hand. By which Returns it will appear, That at this time when so much noise was made for want of Preaching, there were within the Realm of *England*, and the Dominion of *Wales*, no fewer then Seven thousand four hundred sixty three Preachers and Catechisers; which last may be accounted the best sort of Preachers for the instruction of the people. Of which great Number there were found to be no fewer then one hundred forty five Doctors in Divinity, three hundred forty eight Batchellors of Divinity, thirty one Doctors of both Laws, twenty one Batchellors of the

the same ; Eighteen hundred Masters in Arts, Nine hundred forty six
Batchelors of Arts, and two thousand seven hundred forty six Catechisers. So that neither the number of bare Reading-Ministers was so great,
nor the want of Preaching so deplorable, in most parts of the Kingdom,
as those Pamphlets made it ; the Authors whereof ought rather to have
magnified the Name of God for sending such a large Encrease of La-
bourers in his Heavenly Husbandry, as could not any where be parallel'd
in so short a time ; there passing no more than thirty years between the
first beginning of Queen *Elizabeths* Reign, and the rendring of this account to the Convocation.

29. And that the Parliament might receive the same satisfaction, a
most excellent and judicious Sermon was Preached at St. *Pauls* Cross, on
Sunday the ninth of *February*, being the first *Sunday* after their Assembling, by Dr. *Richard Bancroft*, being then Chaplain to the Lord Chancellor *Hatton*, preferred within some few years after to the See of *London*, and from thence to *Canterbury*. In the performance of which Service
he selected for the Theam or Subject of his Discourse, 1 *John* 4. 1. viz.
*Dearly beloved, believe not every spirit, but try the spirits whether they be of
God : for many false prophets are gone out into the world.* In canvasing which
Text, he did so excellently set forth the false Teachers of those times
in their proper colours, their Railing against Bishops, their Ambition,
their self-love, their Covetousness, and all such Motives as had spurred them on to disturb this Church, as satisfied the greatest part of that
huge Congregation, touching the Practises and Hypocrisies of these
holy Brethren. He also shewed on what a weak Foundation they had
built their Discipline, of which no tract or footsteps could be found in
the Church of Christ from the Apostles days to *Calvin* ; and with what
Infamy the *Aerian* Hereticks were reproached in the Primitive times,
for labouring to introduce that Parity which these men designed. He
further laid before them the great danger which must needs ensue, if
private men should take upon them to deny or dispute such matters
as had been setled in the Church by so good Authority : Against which
troublesome Humour many Provisions had been made by the Canons of
Councils, and the Edicts of Godly and Religious Emperors. To which
he added, the necessity of requiring Subscription, in a Church well
constituted, by all the Ministers of the same ; which he justified by the
example of *Geneva*, and the Churches of *Germany*, to be the best way
to *try the spirits whether they be of God or not*, as his Text required. Next,
he insisted on the excellency of the Common-Prayer-Book, applauded
by the Divines of Foreign Churches, approved by *Bucer, Fox, Alessus,*
the Parliaments and Convocations of this Kingdom ; and after justified by Arch-bishop *Cranmer* against the Papists, by Bishop *Ridley* a-
gainst *Knox*, and by divers others : shewing withal, the many gross Absurdities found in *extemporary* Prayers, to the great dishonour of God,
and the shame of Religion. Hence he proceeds to justifie the Superiority of Bishops, and the Supremacy of the Queen, together with the
dangerous Practices and Designs of the Disciplinarians, exemplified by
their Proceedings in *Scotland*, and their Positions in *England*, of which
more anon. All which particulars, with many more upon the by, he
proved with such evidence of demonstration, such great variety of Learning,

ning, and ſtrength of Arguments, that none of all that party could be found to take Arms againſt them, in defence either of their leud *Doctrine*, or more ſcandalous *Uſes*. And this being done, he cloſed up all with a grave and ſerious Application, in reference to the prevalency and malignity of the preſent Humours : which wrought ſo much upon his Auditors of both Houſes of Parliament, that in the paſſing of a general Pardon at the end of the Seſſions, there was Exception *of Seditious Books, Diſturbances of Divine Service, and Offences againſt the Act of Uniformity in the Worſhip of God.*

30. And yet it is not altogether improbable, but that this Exception was made rather at the Queens Command, or by ſome Caveat interpoſed by the Houſe of Peers, than by the ſole Advice, or any voluntary Motion of the Houſe of Commons ; in which the Puritans at that time had a very ſtrong Party. By whoſe Endeavour, a ſmart Petition is preſented to the Lords, in the Name of the Commons, for rectifying of many things which they conceived to be amiſs in the ſtate of the Church. The whole Petition did conſiſt of Sixteen particulars, of which the firſt Six did relate to a Preaching-Miniſtry ; the want of which, was much complained of in a Supplication which had been lately Printed and preſented to them ; but ſuch a Supplication, as had more in it of a Factious and Seditious Libel, then of a Dutiful Remonſtrance. In the other ten it was deſired, *That no Oath or Subſcription might be tendred to any at their entrance into the Miniſtry, but ſuch as was preſcribed by the Statutes of the Realm, and the Oath againſt corrupt entring.* 2. *That they may not be troubled for omiſſion of ſome Rites or Offices preſcribed in the Book of Common Prayer.* 3. *That ſuch as had been ſuſpended or deprived for no other offence, but only for not ſubſcribing, might be reſtored.* 4. *That they may not be called and urged to anſwer before the Officials and Commiſſaries, but before the Biſhops themſelves.* 5. *That they might not be called into the High Commiſſion, or Moot of the Dioceſs where they lived, except for ſome notable offence.* 6. *That it might be permitted to them, in every Arch-Deaconry, to have ſome common Exerciſes and Conferences amongſt themſelves, to be limited and preſcribed by the Ordinaries.* 7. *That the high Cenſure of Excommunication may not be denounced or executed for ſmall matters.* 8. *Nor by Chancellors Commiſſioners or Officials, but by the Biſhops themſelves, with the aſſiſtance of grave perſons.* 9. *That Non-reſidency may be quite removed out of the Church.* Or, 10. *That at leaſt, according to the Queens Injunctions* (Art. 44.) *no Non-reſident having already a Licenſe or Faculty, may enjoy it, unleſs he depute an able Curate, that may weekly Preach and Catechiſe, as was required by Her Majeſty in the ſaid Injunctions.* Againſt the violence of this Torrent, Arch-biſhop *Whitgift* interpoſed both his Power and Reaſon ; affirming with a ſober confidence in the Houſe of Peers, not only that *England* flouriſhed more at that time with able Miniſters, than ever it had done before ; but that it had more able men of eminent Abilities in all parts of Learning, than the reſt of *Chriſtendome* beſides. But, finding that the Lord *Gray*, and others of that Houſe, had been made of the Party, he drew the reſt of the Biſhops to joyn with him in an humble Addreſs to Her Sacred Majeſty ; in which they repreſented to Her the true eſtate of the Buſineſs, together with thoſe many Inconveniences which muſt needs ariſe to the State preſent and to come, to the two Univerſities, to

all

all Cathedral Churches, and the Queen her felf, if the Commons might have had their will, though in no other Point than in that of Pluralities. All which they preft with fuch a dutiful and Religious Gravity, that the Queen put an end to that Difpute, not only for the prefent, but all Parliaments following.

31. Somewhat there muft be in it, which might make them fo a-fraid of that Subfcription which was required at their hands to the Queens Supremacy, as well to the Confecration of Archbifhops and Bifhops, to the Liturgy, and to the Articles of Religion by Law eftablifh-ed: and therefore it will not be amifs (as we have done already in all places elfe) to touch upon the Principles and Pofitions of our *Englifh Puritans*, that we may fee what harmony and confent there is betwixt them and their dear Brethren of the Difcipline in other Nations: For if we look into the Pamphlets which came out this Year, we fhall find thefe Doctrines taught for more Sacred Truths, *viz. That if Princes do hinder them that feek for this Difcipline, they are Tyrants both to the Church and Minifter ; and being fo, may be depofed by their Subjects. That no Civil Magiftrate hath preeminence by ordinary Authority, either to determine of Church caufes, or to make Ecclefiaftical Orders and Ceremonies. That no Civil Magiftrate hath fuch Authority, as that without his confent it fhould not be lawful for Ecclefiaftical perfons to make and publifh Church Orders. That they which are no Elders of the Church, have nothing to do with the Government of it. That if their Reformation be not haftned forward by the Magiftrate, the Subjects ought not any longer to tarry for it, but muft do it themfelves. That there were many thoufands which defired the Difcipline: And that great troubles would enfue if it were denied them. That their Presbyteries muft prevail: And that if it be brought about by fuch ways and means as would make the Bifhops hearts to ake, let them blame themfelves.* For explication of which laft paffage, *Martin Mar-Prelate* in his firft Book threatens onely *fifts* ; but in the fecond he advifeth the Parliament then affembled, *to put down Lord Bifhops, and bring in the Reformation which they looked for, whether Her Majefty would or not.*

32. But thefe perhaps were only the Evaporations of fome idle heads, the freaks of difcontent and paffion, when they were crofsed in their defires : Let us fee therefore what is taught by *Thomas Cartwright*, the very *Calvin* of the *Englifh* ; as highly magnified by *Martin*, and the reft of that Faction, as the other was amongft the *French*. Dr. *Harding* in his anfwer to Bifhop *Jewel* affures us, That the Office of a King is the fame in all places, not only amongft Chriftians, but amongft the Heathen. Upon which premifes he concludes, That a Chriftian Prince hath no more to do in deciding of Church matters, or in making Ceremonies and Orders for the fame, than hath a Heathen. *Cartwright* affirms himfelf to be of the fame opinion; profeffing ferioufly his diflike of all fuch Writers as put a difference between the rights of a Prophane and a Chriftian Magiftrate. *Specanus*, a ftiff *Presbyterian* in the the *Belgick* Provinces, makes a diftinction between *poteftas Facti*, and *poteftas Juris* ; and then infers upon the fame, That the Authority of determining what is fit to be done, belongs of right unto the Minifters of the Church, though the execution of the fact in Civil caufes doth properly appertain to the Supreme Magiftrate. And more than this, the greateft Clerks amongft themfelves

would not give the Queen. If ſhe aſſume unto her ſelf the exerciſe of her farther Power, in ordering matters of the Church according to the lawful authority which is inherent in the Crown, ſhe ſhall preſently be compared unto all the wicked Kings, and others, of whom we read in the Scriptures; that took upon them, unlawfully to intrude themſelves into the Prieſts Office; as unto *Saul*, for his offering of Sacrifice; unto *Oſias* for burning Incenſe upon the Altar; unto *Gideon*, for making of an *Ephod*: and finally, to *Nadab* and *Abihu*, for offering with ſtrange fire unto the Lord.

33. According to theſe Orthodox and ſound reſolves, they hold a Synod in St. *John*'s Colledge in *Cambridge*, taking the opportunity of *Sturbridge* Fayr, to cloak their Meeting for that purpoſe. At which Synod (*Cartwright* and *Perkins* being preſent amongſt the reſt) the whole Book Diſcipline, reviewed by *Traverſe*, and formally approved of by the Brethren in their ſeveral Claſſes, received a more Authentick approbation: inſomuch, that firſt it was decreed amongſt them, That all which would might ſubſcribe unto it, without any neceſſity impoſed upon them ſo to do. But not long after it was made a matter neceſſary, ſo neceſſary, as it ſeems that no man could be choſen to any Eccleſiaſtical Office amongſt them, nor to be of any of their Aſſemblies, either Claſſical, Provincial, or National, till he had firſt ſubſcribed to the Book of Diſcipline. Another Synod was held at *Ipſwich*, not long after, and he reſults of both confirmed in a Provincial and National Synod held in *London*, which gave the Book of Diſcipline a more ſure eſtabliſhment than an Act of State. It is reported, that the night before the great Battel in the Fields of *Theſſaly*, betwixt *Cæſar* and *Pompey*, the *Pompeyan* party was ſo confident of their good ſucceſs, that they caſt Dice amongſt themſelves for all the great Offices and Magiſtracies of the City of *Rome*, even to the Office of the chief Prieſthood, which then *Cæſar* held. And the like vanity or infatuation had poſſeſſed theſe men, in the opinion which they had of their their ſtrength and numbers: Inſomuch that they entered into this conſideration, how Archbiſhops, Biſhops, Chancellors, Deans, Canons, Arch-Diacons, Commiſſaries, Regiſters, Apparitors, &c. (all which by their pretended Reformation muſt have been thruſt out of their Livings) ſhould be provided for, that the Common-wealth might not be thereby peſtered with Beggars. And this they did upon the confidence of ſome unlawful aſſiſtance to effect their purpoſes, if neither the Queen, nor the Lords of the Council, nor the Inferior Magiſtrates in their ſeveral Counties (all which they now ſollicited with more heat than ever) ſhould co operate with them. For about this time it was, that *Cartwright* in his Prayer before his Sermon was noted to have uſed theſe words, *viz. Becauſe they* (meaning the Biſhops) *which ought to be Pillars in the Church, combine themſelves againſt Chriſt and his Truth; therefore, O Lord, give us Grace and Power, all as one man, to ſet our ſelves againſt them.* Which words he uſed frequently to repeat, and to repeat with ſuch an earneſtneſs of ſpirit, as might ſufficiently declare that he had a purpoſe to raiſe Sedition in the State, for the impoſing of that Diſcipline on the Church of *England*, which was not likely to be countenanced by any lawful Authority; which put the Queen to a neceſſity of calling him, and all the reſt of them, to a better

account;

account ; to which they shall be brought in the year next following.

33. In the mean-time we must pass over into *France*, where we find *Henry* the Third, the last King of the House of *Valoise*, most miserably deprived of his Life and Kingdom ; driven out of *Paris* first by the *Guisian* Faction ; and afterwards assassinated by *Jaques Clement*, a Dominican Fryar, as he lay at St. *Cloud*, attending the reduction of that stubborn City. Upon whose death the Crown descended lineally on *Henry* of *Bourbon*, King of *Navarre*, and Duke of *Vendosme*, as the next Heir Male : For the excluding of which Prince, and the rest of that House, the *Holy League* was first contrived, as before is said. There was at that time in the late Kings Army, a very strong Party of *French Catholicks*, who had preferred their Loyalty to their natural Prince, before the private Interest and designs of the House of *Guise* ; and now generally declare in favour of the true Successor. By their assistance, and the concurring Forces of the *Hugonot* Faction, it had been no hard matter for him to have Mastered the Duke of *Mayne*, who then had the command of the *Guisian Leagues*. But in the last he found himself deceived of his expectation. The *Hugonots*, which formerly had observed with so much cheerfulness under his command their King, would not now serve him in his just and lawful Wars against his enemies : Or if they did, it shall be done upon conditions so intolerable, that he might better have pawned his Crown to a Forein Prince, then on such terms to buy the favour of his Subjects. They looked upon him as reduced to a great necessity most of the Provinces, and almost all the principal Cities, having before engaged against *Henry* the Third, and many others falling off when they heard of his death. So that they thought the new King was not able to subsist without them ; and they resolved to work their own ends out of that necessity. Instead of leading of their Armies, and running cheerfully and couragiously towards his defence, who had so often defended them, they sent Commissioners or Delegates to negotiate with him, that they may know to what conditions he would yeeld for their future advantage, before they acted any thing in order to his preservation: and their conditions were so high, so void of all respects of Loyalty, and even common honesty, that he conceived it safer for him, and far more honourable in it self, to cast himself upon the favour of the Queen of *England*, then condescend to their unreasonable and unjust demands. So that in fine the *Hugonots* to a very great number, forsook him most disloyally in the open Field, drew off their Forces, and retired to their several dwellings, inforcing him to the necessity of imploring succours from the professed enemies of his Crown and Nation. Nor did he find the Queen unwilling to supply him both with Men and Money on his first desires. For which she had better reason now, than when she aided him and the rest of the *French Hugonots*, in their former quarrel. And this she did with such a cheerful openness both of heart and hand, as did not only make him able to keep the Field, but to gain ground on the untractable and insulting Rebels. Which when the *Hugonots* observed, and saw that he was like enough to do well without them, they then came freely to his aid, and were content to take such terms as he pleased to give them.

34. And

1587.   34. And now again we are for *Scotland,* where we shall find the Kings Affairs grown from bad to worse.   We left him in a great vexation, for not being able to prevail in any thing in behalf of *Montgomery,* unless he relinquished his pursuit against *Gibson* and *Cooper.*   For so it was, that he must do and suffer more than he had done hitherto, before he could give himself any hopes of living peaceably amongst them. A Parliament is therefore summoned to be held at *Edenborough* in the end of *July.* In which he was contented to pass some Acts for ratifying all Laws made in his Minority, in favour of the Kirk of *Scotland,* for trying and censuring the Adversaries of true Religion; as also for the punishing of such as did menace or invade the Ministers. But that which gave them most content, was an Act of Parliament for annexing of all the Temporalties of Bishopricks, Abbeys, and other Religious Houses, which had not otherwise been disposed of to the Crown of that Realm ; which they promoted under colour of improving the Royal Patrimony, that the King might have means to bear forth the Honour of his Estate, and not trouble his Subjects with Taxations; but in plain truth to overthrow the Calling and Estate of Bishops, which they presumed that no man of Quality would accept, when the Lands were aliened.   And this the King was the more willing to consent to, in regard that he had been perswaded by some about him, that the Episcopal Houses being reserved out of that Grant, together with the Tythes of the Churches formerly annexed to their Benefices, would be sufficient to maintain their Dignity in some fit proportion. But the King soon found himself abused : for the rest of the temporalties which formerly had been disposed of amongst the Laity, being settled and confirmed upon them in the present Parliament, there remained so little to the Crown by this Annexation, as left him nothing behind, but the envy of so high a Sacriledge, the gain and benefit whereof was injoyed by others. And of that little which remained unto him by the Annexation, he received very small contentment, most of it being squandered away by some begging Courtiers till he had left himself unable to reward or gratifie a deserving Minister. But this he did not find till it was too late ; though the disease was past all remedy, had he found it sooner.   But what he could not do himself when he lived in *Scotland,* he first commended to the doing of his Son Prince *Henry,* in his Book called *Basilicon Doron* ; and after lived to see it remedied, in part, when he reigned in *England.*

    35. There hapned also a Dispute in the present Parliament betwixt the Ministers of the Kirk, and such of the Gentry as formerly had possessed themselves of Abbeys and Priories, and thereby challenged to themselves a place in Parliament : concerning which we are to know, that most of the Monasteries and Religious Houses had been founded upon Tythes and Impropriations, though not without some good proportion of Demesnes, which were laid unto them.   But when the *Scots* were set upon the humour of Reformation, and set upon it in a way which shewed them rather to proceed upon private ends, than the publick Interest of Religion ; the principal men amongst them seized on all which they could lay hands on, and after kept it to themselves by no better Title then that of the first Usurpation only, and no more then so.   Some of the Bishops and Abbots also seeing how things were like to go, and
that

that the Churches Patrimony was not like to hold in the same Successions which had conveyed it unto them, difmembred the beſt Tythes and Mannors from them, or otherwiſe reſigned the whole to the hands of of ſuch as appeared moſt able to protect them. And ſo it ſtood, till *Murrey* was made Regent of the Realm in the Kings firſt Infancy, who did not only wink at thoſe Uſurpations, (the queſtioning whereof would moſt infallibly have eſtranged the Occupants from adhering to him) but ſuffered many of the Layards and Gentlemen to invade the Tythes, which had not formerly been appropriated to Religious Houſes, and to annex them to the reſt of their own Eſtates. By means whereof, ſome of them were poſſeſſed to ſix, ten, twelve, or 20 Tythings, united into one Eſtate, as they lay moſt convenient for them. The Miniſters being put off with beggerly ſtipends, amounting in few places to ten pounds *per annum* of good *Engliſh* mony. Theſe, with the reſt, they called the *Lords of new Erection*, and they did Lord it over the poor people with pride and tyranny enough: For, neither would they ſuffer the Occupant or Landholder to carry away his nine parts of the Fruits, till they had taken off their Tenth; and ſometimes out of ſpight, or ſelf-will, or any other peſſant humour, would ſuffer their tenth part to lye at waſte in the open Field, that the poor Labourer of the Earth might ſuffer the more damage by it. But that which did moſt grieve the Miniſters in the preſent exigent, was, That ſuch Lairds and Gentlemen as had robbed the Church, and plumed their own Neſts with the Feathers of it, ſhould ſit and vote in Parliament as Spiritual perſons, and they themſelves be quite excluded from thoſe publick Councils. A great heat hereupon was ſtruck in the preſent Seſſion by *Pont* and *Lindſey*, commiſſionated by the Kirk for that employment; who openly propounded, in the Name of the Kirk, That the ſaid pretended Prelates might be removed at the preſent, and diſabled for the time to come, to ſit in Parliament, as having no Authority from the Church, and moſt of them no Function or Calling in it. *Bruce*, Commendator of *Kinloſſe*, was choſen for the mouth of the reſt; and he appeared ſo ſtrongly in it, that the Petition of the Miniſters was referred to the Lords of the Articles, and by them rejected; though afterwards they had their ends in it by a following Parliament.

36. Being made ſecure from any further fear of Biſhops, by reaſon of the Poor Submiſſion which was made by *Montgomery*, and the annexing of Arch-biſhops Lands to the Royal Patrimony, the Miniſters became more inſolent and imperious then they had been formerly; and in that jolly humour they ſo vexed and terrified him, that he could find no other way in point of King-craft to preſerve himſelf againſt their inſolencies and attempts, but by giving ſome encouragement to the Popiſh party. The exerciſe whereof brought out many Prieſts and Jeſuits; ſome of them more particularly to negotiate in behalf of the King of *Spain*, who was then a ſetting forward his great *Armada*. But the King, well knowing of what conſequence that imployment was, and how deſtructive of his Intereſt to the Crown of *England*, commanded them by publick Proclamation to avoid the Kingdom. But withal gave them day till the firſt of *January*, that they might not complain of being taken unprovided: Which ſmall Indulgence ſo offended the unqniet brethren

thren, that they called a number of Noble-men, Barons, and Commissioners of *Burgley* (without so much as asking the Kings leave in it) to meet at *Edenborough* on the fixt of *February*, to whom they represented the Churches dangers, and thereupon agreed to go all together in a full body to the Court, to attend the King ; to the end that by the terror of so great a company, they might work him to their own desires. But the King hearing of their purpose, refused to give access to so great a multitnde ; but signified withal that he was ready to give audience unto some few of them which should be chosen by the rest. But this affront the King was forced to put up also, to pass by the unlawfulnes of that Convention, to acknowledge their grievances to be just, and to promise a redress thereof in convenient time. Which drew him into Action against *Maxwell* and some others of the Popish Lords and for the same received the publick thanks of the next Affembly, that being no ordinary favour in them ; and was so far gratified withall, as to be suffered to take Mr. *Patrick Galloway* from his Charge in *Perth*, to be one of the Preachers at the Court. Of which particular I had perhaps took little notice, but that we are to hear more of him on some other occassion.

37. The next fine pranck they plaid, relates to the Crowning of Queen *Ann*, with whom the King landed out of *Denmark* at the Port of *Leith*, on the 20 of *May* 1590. and designed her Coronation on the morrow after None of the Bishops being at hand, the King was willing to embrace the opportunity to oblige the Kirk, by making choice of one of their own Brethren, to perform that ceremony ; to which he nominated Mr. *Robert Bruce*, a Preacher at *Edenborough*, and one of the most moderate men in a whole Affembly. But when the fitnes of it came to be examined by the rest of the Brethren, it was resolved to pretermit the Unction (or anointing of her) as a *Jewish* Ceremony, abolished by Chrift, restored into Chriftian Kingdoms by the Popes Authority, and therefore not to be continued in a Church Reformed. The Doubt firft started by one *John Davinson*, who had then no Charge in the Church, though followed by a Company of ignorant and seditious people, whom *Andrew Melvin* set on work to begin the Quarrel, and then stood up in his defence to make it good. Much pains was taken to convince them by the Word of God, That the Unction, or Anointing of Kings, was no *Jewish* Ceremony : but *Melvins* will was neither to be ruled by Reafon, nor subdued by Atonement, and he had there sc strong a Party, that it passed in the Negative. Infomuch, that *Bruce* durft not proceed in the Solemnity, for fear of the Censures of the *Kirk*. The King had notice of it, and returus this word, That if the Coronation might not be performed by *Bruce*, with the wonted Ceremonies, he would stay till the coming of the Bishops, of whose readiness to conform therein, he could make no question. Rather then so, said *Andrew Melvin*, let the Unction pass : better it was that a Minifter should perform that honourable Office, in what Form soever, than that the Bishops should be brought again unto the Court upon that occafion. But yet, unwilling to prophane himself by confenting to it, he left them to agree about it, as to them seemed beft ; and he being gone, it was concluded by the major part of the Voices, That the Anointing should be used. According where-

whereunto, the Queen was Crowned and Anointed on the Sunday following, with the wonted Ceremonies, but certainly with no great State; there being fo fhort an interval betwixt Her Landing, and the appointed day of Her Coronation.

38. It was not long before, that they had a quarrel with the Lords of the Seffion, touching the Jurifdiction of their feveral Courts; but now the Affembly would be held for the chief Tribunal. One *Graham* was conceived to have fuborned a publick Notary to forge an Inftrument, which the Notary confeffed on Examination, to have been brought to him ready drawn, by one of the faid *Grahams* Brethren. *Graham* enraged thereat, enters an Action againft *Sympfon*, the Minifter of *Sterling*, as one who had induced the man, by fome finifter Practifes, to make that Confeffion. The Action being entred, and the Procefs formed, *Sympfon* complains to the Affembly, and they give Order unto *Graham* to appear before them, to anfwer upon the fcandal raifed on one of their Brethren. *Graham* appears, and tells them, That he would make good his Accufation before competent Judges, which he conceived not them to be. And they replyed, That he muft either ftand to their judgment in it, or elfe be cenfured for the flander. The Lords of the Seffion hereupon interpofe themfelves, defiring the Affembly not to meddle in a Caufe which was then dependent in their Court in due form of Law. But the Affembly made this Anfwer, That *Sympfon* was a Member of theirs: That they might proceed in the purgation of one of their own number, without intrenching on the Jurifdiction of the Civil Courts; and therefore, that their Lordfhips fhould not take it ill, if they proceeded in the Tryal. But let the Lords of the Seffion, or the party interefted in the Caufe, fay what they pleafed, the Affembly vote themfelves to be Judges in it, and were refolved to proceed to a Sentence againft him as a falfe Accufer. In fine, the bufinefs went fo high on the part of the Kirk, that the Lords of the Seffion were compelled to think of no other Victory than by making a drawn battel of it; which by the Mediation of fome Friends was at laft effected.

39. The Kirk is now advancing to the higheft pitch of her *Scotch* Happinefs, in having her whole Difcipline, that is to fay, their National and Provincial Affemblies, together with their Presbyteries and Parochial Seffions, confirmed by the Authority of an Act of Parliament. In order whereunto they had ordained in the Affembly held at *Edenborough*, on the 4 of *Auguft, Anno* 1590. That *all fuch as then bore Office in the Kirk, or from thenceforth fhould bear any Office in it, fhould actually fubfcribe to the Book of Difcipline.* Which Act being fo material to our prefent Hiftory, deferves to be exemplified *verbatim*, as it ftands in the Regifters, and is this that followeth, *viz.*

40. " Forafmuch that it is certain, That the Word of God
" cannot be kept in the own fincerity, without the *Holy Difcipline*
" be had in obfervance: It is therefore by the common confent of
" the whole Brethren and Commiffioners prefent, concluded,
" That whofoever hath born Office in the Miniftry of the Kirk
" within this Realm, or that prefently bears, or fhall hereafter
" bear Office therein, fhall be charged by every particular Presbytery,

" bytery, where their refidence is, to fubfcribe the Heads of the
" Difcipline of the Kirk of their Realm, at length fet down and
" allowed by Act of the whole Affembly, in the Book of Polity,
" which is regiftred in the Affembly-Books, and namely the
" Heads controverted by Enemies of the Difcipline of the Re-
" formed Kirk of this Realm, betwixt this and the next Syno-
" dical Affemblies of the Provinces, under the pain of Excom-
" munication to be executed againft the Non-fubfcribers : and
" the Presbyteries which fhall be found remifs and negligent
" herein, to receive publick rebuke of the whole Affembly. And
" to the effect the faid Difcipline may be known as it ought to
" be, to the whole Brethren ; it is ordained, That the Modera-
" tor of each Presbyrery fhall receive from the Clerk of the Af-
" fembly a Copy of the faid Book, under his Subfcription, upon
" the Expences of the Presbytery, betwixt this and the firft day
" of *September* next to come, under the pain of being openly ac-
" cufed in the face of the whole Affembly.

41. This Preparation being made, they prefent their whole defires
to the King, in the following Parliament, convened at *Edenborough*, in
the Month of *June*, 1592. In which it was propofed, 1. ' That the Acts
' of Parliament made in the year 1584, againft the Difcipline of the Kirk,
' and the Liberty thereof, fhould be abrogated and annulled ; and a Ra-
' tification of the Difcipline granted, whereof they were then in practife.
' 2. That the Act of Annexation fhould be repealed, and reftitution made
' of the Churches Patrimony.   3.   That the Abbots, Priors, and other
' Prelates, bearing the Titles of Kirk-men, and giving Voices for the
' Kirk without Power and Commiffion from the fame, fhould not be
' permitted in the time coming, to give voice in Parliament, or convene
' in the Name of the Kirk.   And, 4. That a folid Order might be taken
' for purging the Realm of Idolatry and Blood, wherewith it was mife-
' rably polluted.   On the fecond and third of thefe Defires the King
took longer time of deliberation, as being points of great concernment
to himfelf and others, touching the main of their Eftates.   But he refolved to give them fatisfaction in the firft and laft.   It was anfwered
therefore to the firft part of the Article, *That faying of Mafs, receiving of*
Jefuits, Seminary Priefts, and Trafficking Papifts, againft the Kings Majefty
and Religion prefently profeffed, fhould be a juft caufe to infer the pain of Trea-
fon: with this Provifo notwithftanding, *That if the Jefuits and Seminary*
Priefts did fatisfie the Prince and the Church, the forefaid Penalty fhould not be
laid on the Receivers.   And to the fecond part thereof, concerning Blood
it was anfwered, That the fame fhould be remitted to the Courts of Juftice.   In like manner it was anfwered to the firft branch of their firft
Propofal, *That the faid Statutes fhould be no ways prejudicial, nor derogatory*
to the Priviledges that God had given to the fpiritual Office-bearer in the Church,
concerning Heads of Religion, matters of Herefie, Excommunication, Collation,
or Deprivation of Minifters, or any fuch Ecclefiaftical Cenfures, grounded and
having warrant of the Word of God.   But to the fecond branch thereof he
gave his Plenary affent, according to the tenor of the Act here following ; which in regard it contains the fum of all their Projects for life-
time

time then paft, and the ground of all their Infolencies for the times enfuing ; it fhall not grieve me to fubjoyn, nor be troublefome to the *Reader*
to pafs it over, if he have not patience enough to go thorow with it. Now
the tenor of the faid Act is as followeth.

At the Parliament holden at Edenborough, June 5.
in the Year of God 1592.

42. 'Our Soveraign Lord, and Eftates of this prefent Parlia-
'ment, following the Laudable and Good Example of their Pre-
'deceffors, hath ratified and approved, and by the tenor of this
'prefent Act ratifies and approves all Liberties, Priviledges, Im-
'munities, and Freedoms, whatfoever, given and granted by His
'Highnefs, his Regents in His name, or any of His Predeceffors,
'to the True and Holy Kirk, prefently eftablifhed within this
'Realm and declared in the firft Act of His Highnefs Parliament,
'the 20*th* day of *Octob.* 1579. And all and whatfoever Acts of Par-
'liaments and Statutes made of before by His Highnefs and His
'Regents, anent the Liberty and Freedom of the faid Kirk, and
'fpecially the firft Act of Parliament holden at *Edenborough*, the
'24*th*. of *October*, in the year of God 1581, with the whole particu-
'lar Acts there mentioned ; which fhall be as fufficient as if the
'fame were here mentioned : and all other Acts of Parliament
'made fince, in favour of the true Kirk, and fuch like ; ratifies
'and approves the general Affemblies appointed by the faid Kirk
'and declares, That it fhall be lawful to the Kirk and Minifters
'every year, at leaft, or oftner, *pro re nata*, as occafion and neceffity
'fhall require, to hold and keep general Afemblies, providing,
'that the King's Majefty, or His Commiffioners with Him, to be
'appointed by His Highnefs, be prefent at ilk general Afembly,
'before the difsolving thereof, to nominate and appoint time and
'place, when and where the next general Afembly fhall be hold-
'en. And in cafe neither His Majefty nor His Commiffioners be
'prefent for the time, in that Town where the next general Af-
'fembly is holden ; then, and in that cafe, it fhall be lefum to the
'faid general Afembly, by themfelves to nominate and appoint
'time and place where the next general Afembly of the Kirk
'fhall be kept and holden, as they have been ufed to do in times
'by-paft. And alfo, ratifies and approves the Provincial and Sy-
'nodal Afsemblies, to be holden by the faid Kirk and Minifters
'twice ilk year, as they have been, or prefently are in ufe to do,
'within every Province of this Realm. And ratifies and approves
'thefe Presbyteries, and particular Seffions appointed by the faid
'Kirk, with the whole Difcipline and Jurifdiction of the fame,
'agreed upon by His Majefty, in conference had by His Highnefs,
'with certain of the Minifters convened to that effect; of the which
'Articles the tenour followeth.

1. *Matters to be intreated in Provincial Assemblies.*

43. ‘ Their Assemblies are constitute for weighty matters,
‘ necessary to be intreated by mutual consent and assistance of
‘ Brethren within the Province, as need requires. This Assem-
‘ bly hath Power to handle, order, and redress, all things omit-
‘ ted or done amiss in the particular Assemblies. It hath Power
‘ to depose the Office-bearers of the Province, for good and just
‘ causes deserving deprivation. And generally these Assemblies
‘ have the whole Power of the particular Elderships, whereof they
‘ are collected.

2. *Matters to be intreated in the Presbyteries.*

‘ The power of the Presbyteries is, To use diligent labours in
‘ the bounds committed to their charge, that the Kirks be kept in
‘ good order : To enquire diligently of naughty and ungodly
‘ persons, and to travel to bring them into the way again, by ad-
‘ monition or threatening of Gods Judgements, or by correction.
‘ It appertains to the Eldership to take heed that the Word of
‘ God be purely Preached within their bounds, the Sacraments
‘ rightly Ministred, the Discipline entertained, and Ecclesiastical
‘ goods uncorruptly distributed. It belongeth to this kind of
‘ Assemblies, To cause the Ordinances made by the Assemblies
‘ Provincial, National, and General, to be kept and put in exe-
‘ cution : To make constitutions which concern τὸ πρέπον in the
‘ Kirk , for decent order in the particular Kirk where they go-
‘ vern ; providing that they alter no Rules made by the Provin-
‘ cial and General Assemblies : and that the Provincial As-
‘ semblies aforesaid, be privy to the Rules that they shall make,
‘ and to abolish Constitutions tending to the hurt of the same.
‘ It hath power to excommunicate the obstinate, formal process
‘ being had, and due interval of times observed. Anent parti-
‘ cular Kirks , if they be lawfully ruled by sufficient Ministers,
‘ and Session, they have Power and Jurisdiction in their own Con-
‘ gregation, in matters Ecclesiastical : and decrees and declares
‘ the Assemblies, Presbyteries, and Sessions Jurisdiction , and
‘ Discipline aforesaid, to be in all times coming most just, good,
‘ and Godly in it self; notwithstanding whatsoever Statutes, Acts,
‘ Canons, Civil and Municipal Laws made to the contrary : to
‘ which and every one of them , these Present shall make express
‘ derogation.

44. ‘ And because there are divers Acts of Parliament made
‘ in favour of the Papistical Church , tending to the prejudice
‘ of the liberty of the true Kirk of God, presently professed with-
‘ in this Realm , Jurisdiction and Discipline thereof, which stand
‘ yet in the Books of the Acts of Parliament not abrogated nor
‘ annulled : Therefore his Highness and Estates foresaid , hath
‘ abrogated, casted, and annulled, and by the tenour hereof
‘ abrogates,

' abrogates, casts, and annuls all Acts of Parliament made by any
' of his Highness Predecessors for maintenance of Superstition
' and Idolatry ; with all, and whatsoever Acts, Laws, and Sta-
' tutes, made at any time before the day and date hereof, against
' the liberty of the true Kirk, Jurisdiction and Discipline there-
' of, as the same is used and exercised within this Realm.   And
' in special, that Act of Parliament holden at *Sterling*, the 4th. of
' *November* 1543, commanding obedience to be given to *Eugenius*
' the Pope for the time : the Act made by King *James* the 3d,
' in his Parliament holden at *Edenborough*, the 24th of *February*,
' in the year of God 1480. And all other Acts whereby the Pope's
' authority is established.   The Act of the said King *James* in
' his Parliament holden at *Edenborough*, the 20th of *November*
' 1469, anent the *Saturday*, and other Vigils, to be Holy-day from
' Even-song to Even-song.   *Item*, That part of the Act made by
' the Queen Regent, holden at *Edenborough* the first day of *Februa-*
' *ry* 1551, giving specially License for holding of *Pasch*, and
' *Zuil*.

45. ' And further, the Kings Majesty and Estates aforesaid,
' declare, That the 129th Act of Parliament holden at *Edenbo-*
' *rough* the 22d of *May*, in the year of God 1584, shall no ways be
' prejudicial, or derogate any thing from the Priviledge that God
' hath given the Spiritual Office-bearers in the Kirk, concerning
' Heads of Religion, Matters of Heresie, Excommunication, Col-
' lation, or Deprivation of Ministers, or any such like Ecclesia-
' stical Censures, specially grounded, and having warrant of the
' Word of God.   *Item*, Our Soveraign Lord and Estates of Par-
' liament foresaid, abrogates, casts, and annihilates the Acts of
' the same Parliament holden at *Edenborough* the same year 1584;
' granting Commission to Bishops and other Judges, constitute
' in Ecclesiastical Causes, to receive his Highness Presentation
' to Benefices, to give Collation thereupon, and to put Order
' to all Causes Ecclesiastical, which his Majesty and Estates
' foresaid, declares to be expired in the self, and to be null in
' time coming, of none avail, force or effect.   And therefore or-
' dains all Presentations to Benefices to be direct to the particular
' Presbyteries in all time coming, with full power to give Col-
' lation thereupon, and to put order to all matters and causes Ec-
' clesiastical within their bounds, according to the Discipline of
' the Kirk : providing the foresaid Presbyters be bound and
' astricted to receive and admit whatsoever qualified Minister
' presented by His Majesty or Laick Patrons.

46. Such was the Act by which the Presbyterian Discipline was
setled in the Kirk of *Scotland*.   They had given him trouble enough before, when they had no authority of Law to confirm their actions. But
now he must expect much more; and they will see his expectation satisfied to the very full.   So that it may be much admired that he yeelded to it, the rather in regard the reasons of it are not certainly known,
nor very easie to be guessed at.   Whether it were, that he were not well
                                                                    enough

enough informed touching the low condition which the *English Puritans* were at this time brought to, or that he stood so much in fear of the Earl of *Bothwell*, (whose treacherous practises threatned him with continual danger) that he was under a necessity of conforming to them for his own preservation; or that he thought it his best way to let them have their own Wills, and pursue their own Counsels, till they had wearied both themselves and the rest of the Subjects, by the misgovernment of that Power which he had given them; or whether it were all, or none of these, it is hard to say. Nor is it less to be admired, that the Nobility of *Scotland*, who had found the weight of that heavy yoke in the times foregoing, should take it so easily on their necks, and not joyn rather with the King to cast it off. But they had gotten most of the Church Lands into their possession, and thought it a greater piece of wisdom to let the Presbytery overtop them in their several Consistories, than that the Bishops, Deans, and Chapters, or any other who pretended unto their Estates, should be restored again to their power and places, and thereby brought to a capacity of contending with them for their own. In which respect they yielded also to another Act against the everting of Church lands and Tenths into Temporal Lordships: for, To what purpose should they strive for such empty Titles, as added little to their profit, and not much to their pleasures? There also passed some other Acts which seemed much to favour both the Kirk and the Kirk men; as namely, For the ratification of a former Act 1587, in favour of the Ministers, their Rents and Stipends; for enabling Lay Patrons to dispose of their Prebendaries and Chaplinaries unto Students; and that no Benefices with Cure pay any Thirds. There passed another Act also which concerned the Glebes and Manses in Cathedral Churches, preserved of purpose by the King (though they thought not of it) that when he found it necessary to restore Episcopacy, the Bishops might find Houses, and other fit accommodations, near their own Cathedrals.

47. Thus have the Presbyterians gained two Acts of great importance; The one for settling their Presbyteries in all parts of the Kingdom: The other for repressing all thoughts of restoring Episcopacy, by passing over the Church lands to the use of the Crown. And to make as sure of it as they could, (because a three-fold Cord is not easily broken) they had before called upon the King to reinforce the Band, or National Covenant, which had been made for their adhæsion to the true Religion, and renouncing Popery. For so it was, that some suspitions had been raised by the Presbyterians, That the King was miserably seduced, and enclined to Popery; and that the Earl of *Lenox* had been sent from *France* for no other purpose, but to work him to it. And thereupon the King gave order unto Mr. *J. Craige*, being then a Preacher in the Court, to form a short Confession of Faith; wherein not onely all the corruptions of the Church of *Rome* in point of Doctrine, but even those also which related unto Discipline and Forms of Worship, were to be solemnly abjured. Which Confession (for example of others) the King himself with all his Court and Council, did publickly both subscribe and swear *Anno* 1580. And the next year he required the like Oath and Subscription from all his Subjects, for the securing

ring

ring of those fears and jealousies which the Kirk had of him. But in regard this general Confession was not found sufficient to hinder the increase of Popery, for want of some strict Combination amongst the Subjects which professed the Reformed Religion ; it was desired, that a *Solemn League or Band* might be authorized, by which they should be bound to stand to one another in defence thereof , that is to say, both of their Covenant and Religion, against all Opponents. The *Gurfian* Papists had projected the like League in *France*, to suppress the Gospel ; and why should they in *Scotland* be less zealous for the true Religion than the *Guisian Papists* for the false ? Upon which ground the King was easily entreated to consent unto it : and first subscribed the Band himself, with all his Family, *An.* 1589 ; which the next year he caused to be subscribed by all sorts of people, as the General Assembly had desired.

48. Now in this Covenant and Confession, they did not only bind themselves to renounce the Pope, together with all the Superstitions and Corruptions of the Church of *Rome* ; but in particular, *to continue in obedience to the Doctrine and Discipline of the Kirk of* Scotland *; and to defend the same according to their vocation and power all the days of their lives.* And though it cannot be conceived that under those general words of *Doctrine* and *Discipline*, there could be any purpose to abjure the Episcopal Government, which was in being when that Confession was first framed, and for many years after : yet being now received and subscribed unto, and their Presbyteries established by Act of Parliament, it was interpreted by the *Covenanters* of succeeding times, *Anno* 1638, to contain in it an express renouncing of Episcopacy, as also of such Rites and Ceremonies as had been introduced amongst them by the Synod of *Perth, Anno* 1618. The sad effects whereof, the King foresaw not at the present ; but he took order to redress them in the time to come : For now the Temporal Estates of Bishops being alienated and annexed to the Crown by Act of Parliament, *Anno* 1587. *Episcopacy* tacitly abjured by Covenant, and that Covenant strengthened by a Band or Association, *Anno* 1590. And finally, their *Presbyteries* setled by like Act of Parliament in this present year *Anno* 1592. it was not to be thought that ever Bishops or Episcopacy could revive again, though it otherwise happened. It cannot be denied, but that King *James* did much despise this Covenant, (commonly called the Negative Confession) when he came into *England* : for, taking occasion to speak of it in the Conference of *Hampton Court*, he lets us know, That Mr. *Craige* (the Compiler of it) *with his renouncings and abhorrings, his detestations and abrenunciations, did so amaze the simple people, that few of them being able to remember all the said particulars, some took occasion thereby to fall back to* Popery, *and others to remain in their former ignorance.* To which he added this short note, *That if he had been bound to that Form of* Craige's, *the Confession of his Faith must have been in his Table-Book, and not in his Head.* But what a mean opinion soever King *James* had of it, the *Puritans* or *Presbyterians* of both Kingdoms, made it serve their turns for raising a most dangerous Rebellion against his Son, and altering the whole Frame of Government both in Church and State, which they new-molded at their pleasure : and sure I

am,

am, that at the first entring into this Band, the *Presbyterians* there grew so high and insolent, that the King could get no Reason of them in his just demands. The King had found by late experience, how much they had encroached upon his Royal Prerogative, defamed the present Government, and reviled his Person. And thereupon, as he had gratified them in confirming their Discipline, so he required them not long after to subscribe these Articles ; that is to say, *That the Preacher should yield due obedience unto the Kings Majesty. That they should not pretend any priviledge in their Allegiance. That they should not meddle in matters of State. That they should not publickly revile His Majesty. That they should not draw the people from their due obedience to the King. That when they are accused for their Factious Speeches, or for refusing to do any thing, they should not alledge inspiration of the Spirit, nor feed themselves with colour of Conscience, but confess their faults like Men, and crave pardon like Subjects.* But they were well enough, they thanked him ; and were resolved to hold their own Power, let him look to his.

The End of the Eighth Book.

AERIVS REDIVIVVS:

OR THE

HISTORY

OF THE

Presbyterians.

LIB. IX.

Containing

Their Disloyalty, Treasons, and Seditions in France, the Country of East-Friesland, and the Isles of Britain ; but more particularly in England. Together with the severe Laws made against them, and the several Executions in pursuance of them, from the year 1589 to the year 1595.

 Hus have we brought the *Presbyterians* to their highest pitch in the Kirk of *Scotland*, when they were almost at their lowest fall in the Church of *England:* these being at the very point of their *Crucifixion*, when the others were chanting their *Hosannas* for their good success. The *English* Brethren had lost their principal Support by the death of *Leicester*, though he was thought to have cooled much in his affections towards their affairs. But what they lost in him they studied to repair by the Earl of *Essex*, whose Fathers Widow he had

1.

had married, trained him up for the most part under *Puritan* Tutors, and married him at the last to *Walsinghams* Daughter. Upon these hopes they made their applications to him, and were chearfully welcomed ; the Gentleman being young, ambitious, and exceeding popular, and therefore apt enough to advance their Interest, and by theirs his own. And he appeared the rather for them at the first, to cry quits with *Whitgift* ; who, when he might have been elected Chancellor of the University of *Oxon*, on the death of *Leicester*, chose rather to commend his dear Friend, the Lord Chancellor *Hatton*, to the place, than to assume it on himself ; and after *Hattons* death, to nominate the Lord *Buckhurst* to them, who was also chosen. The young Earl had an eye upon that great Office, that he might be as powerful amongst men of the Gown, as he was amongst Gentlemen of the Sword ; and took it for an high affront, that the Archbishop should presume to commend any other to that Honour, which he designed unto himself. But the Queen easily took him off, and made him so far Friends with *Whitgift*, as not to make any open profession of displeasure toward him, by which the opposite Faction might be animated to their former Insolencies, which notwithstanding the Arch-bishop kept a vigilant eye upon all his actions, as one that was not to be told of his private practises, the secret intelligence which he had with the Heads of that Party, and saw that most of his Allies and Kindred were engaged that way. For, though upon the reconciliation which was made between them, the Earl had offered him to run a course in Clergy-Causes, according to his directions and advice ; yet what he did therein, proceeded rather from a fear of the Queens displeasure, than from any love to *Whitgift*, or the Church it self ; as afterwards appeared most evidently in the course of his actions.

2. But that which gave the Brethren their greatest blow, was the death of *Walsingham*, who dyed on the sixth of *April* 1590. The Queen had lately been more sensible of those manifold dangers which both the Principles and Practises of the *Disciplinarians* did most apparently threaten to her whole Estate ; more now than ever, by the coming out of a Pamphlet, called *The humble Motion* : In which it was affirmed, That thousands did sigh for the Discipline, ten thousands had sought it ; and that the most worthy men of every Shire had consented to it : That the *Eldership* was at hand : That the people were inflamed with a zeal to have it ; and, that it was hard, dangerous, and impossible to stand against it. Incensed thereat, and fearing the sad consequences of such pestilent Pamphlets, She resolved upon some speedy course to prevent the mischief : and therefore gave the greater countenance to the Archbishops, Bishops, and their subordinate Officers, for proceeding with them. On which encouragement, the seeming Neutrality of the Earl of *Essex*, and the sickness of *Walsingham*, *Snape*, and some others of their principal Leaders, were called before the High-Commission at *Lambeth*, in the first beginning of *Easter* Term : which, though it seemed both strange and unwelcome to them, yet there was no remedy. Appear they did, because they must ; but were resolved, that their appearance should conduce as little as might be to their disadvantage. For, being required to take their Oaths, according to the use of the Court,

to anſwer punctually to all ſuch Interrogatories as were to be propounded to them ; the Oath is abſolutely refuſed, unleſs the Interrogatories might be ſhewed unto them. Firſt, therefore, they were made acquainted with the ſubſtance of them, but that would not ſerve. They were aſſured in the next place, That they ſhould be required to anſwer no further unto any of them, than they were bound to do by the Laws of the Land. But that ſerved as little. In fine, it was reſolved, That the Interrogatories ſhould be ſhewed unto them, (here contrary to the practiſe of all Courts in Criminal Cauſes) which ſerved leaſt of all: For now *Snape* finding what was like to be charged upon them, gave notice of the ſame to the reſt of the Brethren, and did not only refuſe the Oath, as before he did ; but put the reſt upon a courſe of premeditation, both whether it were fit to anſwer upon Oath or not, and then what anſwer they would make, if they were put to it. But ſo it hapned, that his Letters, being intercepted, were produced againſt him ; upon which he was clapped up in Priſon, and a great terror thereby ſtruck into all the Brethren, who now began to apprehend the dangers they were fallen into by their former Inſolencies.

3. It may be gathered by thoſe Letters, that no ſmall diligence had been uſed by ſuch as had employed themſelves in it, to ſearch into the bottom of their deepeſt Counſels, and moſt ſecret Purpoſes ; and that ſo perfect a diſcovery had been made thereof, as might warrant the high Commiſſioners to proceed ſeverely, without the leaſt fear of being foyled in their undertakings. For *Snape* confeſſeth in thoſe Letters, *That they had the knowledge not only of Generals, but of Specials, and Particulars alſo* ; that is to ſay, touching the places where they met, *Oxford, London, Cambridge*, &c. the times of their accuſtomed Meetings, as, *Sturbridg-Faire, Acts, Terms*, &c. the perſons which aſſembled at them, as *Cartwright, Perkins, Travers, Chark*, &c. and finally, the very matters which they dealt in, and agreed upon. Much troubled the good man ſeemed to be, in gueſſing at that falſe Brother who had made the diſcovery : but, that they were diſcovered, he is ſure enough ; for he affirmeth, that their Actings neither were, or could be any longer concealed ; and therefore, that the Lord called upon them to be reſolute in the preſent caſe. And thereupon it was propounded, *Whether it were better and more ſafe, that one man (with the conſent of the reſt) ſhould boldly, freely, and wiſely confeſs, and lay open*, &c. or, *that ſome weak or wicked man ſhould without conſent, and in evil ſort, acknowledge*, &c. He tells them, That the matter aimed at by High Commiſſioners, was To bring them within danger of Law for holding *Conventicles*: That in Cauſes of Murther, and the like, it was commonly asked, Whether the Party fled upon it ; and therefore, that they ſhould do well to conſider of it, in reference to the preſent caſe, and ſo adviſing, That *T. C.* ſhould be ſent to with all ſpeed, he concludes his Letter.

4. This Letter coming up ſo cloſe to the former diſcoveries, brings *Cartwright* into play in *September* following. But firſt, a conſultation muſt be had amongſt them, at the Houſe of one *Gardiner*, Whether, and if at all, how far it might be fit for him to reveal all or any of the matters which had paſſed in conference or diſputation in any of their former aſſemblies. And, as it ſeems, it was determined in the *Negative*, (according

to

to the Doctrine of the old *Priscilianists*) that he should not do it. For, when the Oath was offered to him, he refused to take it. The High-Commission-Court was at that time held in the Bishop of *Londons Consistory*, in the Church of St. *Paul.* At which were present amongst others the Lord Bishop of *London*, the two Chief Justices, Serjeant *Puckering*, afterwards Lord Keeper of the Great Seal, Mr. Justice *Gaudie*, and *Popham* then Attorney General, but afterwards Chief Justice of the Common-Pleas. All which did severally and distinctly assure him upon their credits, That by the Laws of the Realm he was bound to take the Oath required, for making a true answer unto the Interrogatories which were to be propounded to him. To which he made no other Answer, but that he could find no such thing in the law of God; and so continuing in his obstinacy, was committed also. But the Commissioners having spent some time in preparing the matter, and thinking the cognizance thereof more fitter for the Star-Chamber, referred both the Persons and the cause to the care of that Court. In which an Information was referred against them by the Queens Attorney, for setting forth and putting in practise (without warrant and authority) a new form of Common-Prayer and Administration of the Sacraments, together with the Presbyterial Discipline not allowed by Law. Upon the news whereof the Brethren enter into consultation, as well about some course to be presently taken for relief of the Prisoners, as for the putting of their Discipline into further practise: What the result was, may be gathered from a Letter of *Wiggingtons,* (one of the hottest heads amongst them) in which he thus writes to *Porter* of *Lancaster,* viz. Mr. Cartwright *is in the* Fleet *for refusing the Oath* (*as I hear*) *and Mr.* Knewstubs *is sent for, and sundry worthy Ministers are disquieted, who have been spared long: So that we look for some bickering ere long, and then a Battel, which cannot long endure.*

5. But before any thing could be done upon either side, in order to the proceedings of the Court, or the release of the Prisoners, there brake out such a dangerous Treason, as took up all the thoughts of the Lords of the Council, and the Brethren too. The Brethren had so fixed their fancies on the Holy Discipline, and entertained such strange devices to promote the same, beyond the warrant of Gods Word, and the Rule of Law; that at the last God gave them up to strong delusions, and suffered them to be transported by their own ill spirits to most dangerous downfalls. One *Coppinger,* a Gentleman of a very good Family, had been so wrought upon by some of the chief Factors to the *Presbyterians,* that he became a great admirer of their Zeal and Piety: and being acquainted with one *Arthington,* a Lay-*Genevian,* but very zealous in the cause, he adviseth with him of some means for the good of the Prisoners. But upon long deliberation they could think of no course at all, unless it would please God by some extraordinary calling to stir up some zealous Brethren to effect their desires: and if God pleased to take that way, why might not one or both of them be chosen, as fit Instruments in so great a service; then whom they knew of none more able, and of few more zealous. On these Preparatories they betake themselves to Prayer and Fasting, hold a strict Fast together on the 15*th* of *December,* and then began to find themselves extraordinarily exercised, as appears by their letters writ to *Lancaster,* in whose House they held it. Immediately

diately upon this Fact, *Coppinger* takes a journey into *Kent*, and fancies (by the way) that he was admitted to a familiar Conference with God himself, that he received from him many strange Directions, to be followed by him whensoever God should please to use his service for the good of his Church ; and more particularly, that he was shewed a way to bring the Queen to repentance, and to cause all the Nobles to do the like out of hand ; or else to prove them to be Traytors to Almighty God. Another Fast is held by him and *Arthington* at his coming back, in which he finds himself more strongly stirred to a matter of some great importance, then he was before : of which he gives notice unto *Gibson* in *Scotland*, by his Letter of the last of *December*, and afterward to *Wiggington* above-mentioned, by them to be communicated to the rest of the brethren. Another Fast follows upon this, at which *Wiggington* and some others did vouchsafe their presence, who had before confirmed them in the fancy of some such extraordinary Calling as he seemed to drive at. With the intention of this last, *Cartwright* and other of the Prisoners were made acquainted before-hand, to the intent that by the benefit of their secret prayers, the Action might be crowned with an end more glorious. And the same night, *Coppinger* finds himself in Heaven, exceedingly astonished at the Majesty of Almighty God, but very much comforted by the Vision ; and every day more and more encouraged to some great work ; which he communicates at several times, and by several Letters to *Cartwright*, *Travers*, *Clark*, &c, amongst the Preachers ; and from the Lay-Brethren, unto *Lancaster*, and Sir *Peter Wentworth*.

6. And now we must make room for another Actor, a greater Zealot than the other, and one that was to rob them of the glory of their dreams and dotages ; *Hacket*, an inconsiderable Fellow both for Parts and Fortune, pretends to a more near Familiarity with Almighty God, than either of the other durst aspire to. A Wretch of such a desperate Malice, that bearing an old grudge to one that had been his School-Master, he bit off his Nose. And when the poor man humbly prayed him to let him have it again, to the end it might be sowed on before it was cold, he most barbarously chewed it with his teeth, and so swallowed it down. After this, having wasted that small Estate which he had by his Wife, he becomes a Proselyte, pretends at first to more than ordinary zeal for a Reformation, and afterwards to extraordinary Revelations for the compassing of it. This brings him into the acquaintance of some zealous Ministers, who were then furiously driving on for the Holy Discipline ; but none more than *Wiggington* before remembred, who brings him presently to *Coppinger*, at such time as the poor man was raised to the height of his Follies. *Hacket* had profited so well in the School of Hypocrisie, that by his counterfeit-holiness, his fervent and continual praying *ex tempore*, fasting upon the Lords days, making frequent brags of his Conflicts with *Satan*, and pretending to many personal Conferences with the Lord himself, that he became of great esteem with the rest of the Brethren; insomuch that some of them did not stick to say, not only that he was one of Gods beloved, but greater in His Favour than *Moses*, or *John the Baptist*. And he himself made shew, That he was a Prophet, sent to foretell Gods Judgments, where his mercies were neglected ; prophesying, That there should be no more Popes ; and, that *England* this

present

present Year fhould be afflicted with Famine, War, and Peftilence, unlefs the Lords Difcipline and Reformation were forthwith admitted.
Thefe men, being both governed by the fame ill fpirit, were mutually
over-joyed at this new acquaintance, and forthwith entered into counfel for freeing *Cartwright, Snape,* and the reft of the Minifters, not only
from the feveral Prifons in which they lay, but from the danger of their
Cenfure in the *Star-Chamber,* which was then at hand.

7. It was expected that the Cenfure would have paffed upon them
on the laft day of *Eafter* Term ; of which *Coppinger* gives *Hacket* notice, and fends him word withall, That he meant to be at the hearing
of it ; and that if any Severity fhould be ufed towards them, *he fhould
be forced in the Name of the Great and Fearful God of Heaven and Earth to
proteft againft it.* The like expectation was amongft them in the Term
next following, at what time *Coppinger* was refolved on fome defperate
act to divert the Sentence. For thus he writes to *Lancafter* before-re-
membred, *That if our Preachers in Prifon do appear to morrow in the Star-
Chamber, and if our great men deal with them fo as it is thought they will ; and
that if then God did not throw fome fearful Judgment amongft them,* &c. that
is to fay, (for fo we muft make up the fenfe) let him give no more credit
unto him or his Revelations But the Hearing being deferred at that
time alfo, and nothing like to be done in it till after *Michaelmas,* the Confpirators perceived they had time enough for new Confultations. And
in thefe Confultations they refolve amongft them to impeach the two
Archbifhops of High Treafon, that fo they might be made uncapable
of proceeding in a Legal way againft the Prifoners, or otherwife to af-
faffinate both together, with the Lord Chancellor *Hatton,* (whom they
deadly hated) if any fevere Sentence was pronounced againft them. But
Hacket was for higher matters. The Spirit of Infatuation had fo wrought
upon him, that he conceived himfelf to partake of the fame Divine
Nature with Almighty God. That he was appointed by his God to
be King of *Europe* ; and therefore looked upon all Kings (but the Queen
efpecially) as the Ufurpers of the Throne which belonged unto him. And
againft her he carried fuch a bitter hatred, that againft her he often caft
forth dangerous fpeeches, That fhe had loft her Right to the Crown ;
and fpared not to do execution upon her in her Arms and Pictures, by
ftabbing his Dagger into both whenfoever he faw them. The people
alfo muft be dealt with, to make ufe of their Power, according unto that
Maxim of the Difciplinarians, *That if the Magiftrate will not reform the
Church and State, then the People muft.* And that he might wind them to
this height, he fcatter'd certain Rhimes or Verfes amongft them ; by
which it was infinuated, That a true Chriftian, though he were a Clown
or poor Countrey-man, (which was *Hackets* own cafe) might teach Kings
how to manage their Sceptres ; and that they might depofe the Queen, if
fhe did not zealoufly promote the Reformation.

8. Finding to what an admiration he had raifed himfelf in the efteem
of *Coppinger* and his Fellow *Arthington,* he looks upon them as the fitteft Inftruments to advance his Treafons, perfwading them, That they
were endued not only with a Prophetical, but an Angelical Spirit. And
they, believing what he faid, performed all manner of obedience to
him, as one that was appointed to reign over them, by God himfelf ;

setting themselves from that time forward to raise some Sedition, in which the people might be moved unto what they pleased. Being thus possest, they intimate to *Wiggington* fore-mentioned, That Christ appeared to them the night before, not in his own body as he sits in Heaven; but in that especial Spirit by which he dwelt in *Hacket* more than in any other. They added also, That *Hacket* was the very Angel which should come before the Day of Judgement, with his Fan in the one hand, and his Shepherds Crook in the other, to distinguish the Sheep from the Goats; to tread down *Satan*, and ruine the Kingdom of *Antichrist*. What counsel they received from *Wiggington* is not certainly known, though it may be judged by the event. For presently on their going from him, which was on the sixteenth of *July*, they repair to *Hacket*, whom he found lazing in his bed in a private House at *Broken Wharf*; and casting themselves upon their knees, as if they were upon the point of Adoration; *Arthington* suddenly ariseth, and adviseth *Coppinger*, in the Name of the Lord Jesus Christ to annoint their King. But *Hacket* cunningly declines it, telling them that he was already annointed by the Holy Ghost, and therefore that they were to do what he should command them. Which said, he ordains *Coppinger* to be his Prophet of Mercy, and *Arthington* to be his Prophet of Justice; and gives them their Mission in this manner: ' Go now (saith he) and tell up and down the City, That ' Jesus Christ is come with his Fan in his hand to judge the World: if ' any ask you where he is, direct them to this place: if they will not be-' lieve you, let them come and see if they can kill me. As sure as God ' is in Heaven, no less assuredly is Christ now come to judge the worlds With this Commission flye the two new Prophets from one street to another, till they came to *Cheapside*, crying out, *Christ is come*, *Christ is come*, all the way they went; and adding with as loud a voice, *Repent*, *Repent*. In *Cheapside* they mount into a Cart, (a proper Pulpit for such Preachers) proclaiming thence, that *Hacket* participated of Christs glorified Body, by his especial Spirit, and was now come with his Fan to propagate the Gospel, to *settle the Discipline*, (for that was the impulsive to all this madness) and to establish in *England* a new Common-wealth: They added further, that themselves were two Prophets, the one of Mercy, and the other of Justice; the truth whereof they took upon their Salvation. That *Hacket* was the only Supreme Monarch of the World; and that all the Kings of *Europe* held of him as his Vassals: That therefore he onely ought to be obeyed, and the Queen deposed; and that vengeance should shortly fall from Heaven, not only on the Archbishop of *Canterbury*, but the Lord Chancellor *Hatton*.

9. Infinite were the throngs of people which this strange Novelty had drawn together to that place; but they found none so mad as themselves, none so besotted as to cry, God save King *Hacket*: so that not able to be heard by reason of the noise, nor to go forward in their Mission, because of the Throng; they dismounted their Chariot, and by the help of some of their Friends conveyed themselves to *Hacket's* Lodging. They had not staid there long, when they were all three apprehended, and brought before the Lords of the Council; to whom they shewed so little reverence, that they never moved their Hats unto them; and told them that they were above all Magistrates, of what rank soever. *Hacket*

is afterward arraigned *July* 26. and two days after drawn to his execution, which was to be done upon him in that part of *Cheapſide* in which his two Prophets had proclaimed him. Neither the Sentence paſt upon him, nor the fear of death, mitigated any thing of that Spirit of Infatuation with which the Devil had poſſeſt him. Infomuch, that he exclaimed moſt horribly (as he was drawn upon the *Hurdle*) all the way he paſſed, crying out in theſe words, *Jehovah the Meſſias, Jehovah the Meſſias: behold, Heaven is opened; behold, the Son of the moſt High is coming down to deliver me.* With the like ill ſpirit he was governed when he came to the Gallows; at which he is affirmed to have made this Imprecation, (for I can by no means call it Prayer) *viz. Almighty Everlaſting God, Jehovah, Alpha and Omega, Lord of Lords, King of Kings, the Everlaſting God, thou knoweſt that I am the true Jehovah whom thou haſt ſent. Shew ſome Miracle from the Clouds, for the converſion of theſe Infidels, and deliver me from my Enemies.* The reſt, too horrid and blaſphemous to be imparted to the eyes of a ſober Chriſtian, I forbear to add. Let it ſuffice, that after ſome ſtrugling with the Hangman, and many fearful Execrations againſt God and man, he was turned off the Ladder, and preſently cut down, ript up and quartered, according unto the Law in that behalf. Unto ſuch dangerous Precipices do men caſt themſelves, when they forſake the rule of the Church, and will not be content with that ſobriety in the things of God, which makes men wiſe unto ſalvation. But as for his two Prophets, they found different ends, though they had ſteered the ſame courſe with him. *Coppinger* by a wilful abſtinence, ſtarved himſelf in Priſon within few days after. But *Arthington* lived to ſee his errors, was pardonned upon his repentance, and publiſhed a Retractation of his follies, as became a Chriſtian.

10. Many endeavours have been uſed for freeing *Cartwright* and the reſt of the chief *Presbyterians*, from having any hand in theſe damnable practiſes. And it is true enough, that many of them were ſo wiſe, as neither to admit them to a perſonal Conference, nor return anſwer to thoſe Letters which were ſent unto them from the parties. But then it is as true withall, that *Coppinger* had communicated his firſt thoughts touching his extraordinary calling, by ſeveral Letters writ to *Cartwright, Egerton, Travers, Clark, Gardiner, Cooper, Philips,* and others; not to ſay any thing of *Penry* or *Wiggington,* who ſeemed to have been of counſel with them in the whole deſign. And it is alſo true, that when he deſcended to particulars in reference to the courſe which he meant to take in the preſent Exigent, they would by no means entertain any Meſſages from him, by which they might be made acquainted with the Plot in hand. But then it cannot be denied, that knowing them to be intent upon ſome courſe which they could not juſtifie, they neither revealed it to the State, nor laboured to diſwade them from it, but ſeemed content to let them run their full career, and then to take ſuch benefit of it as the iſſue and ſucceſs thereof ſhould afford unto them. And in this caſe it may be ſaid too juſtly in the Orators language, that there was little difference between the adviſing of a Fact, and the rejoycing at it when it was once executed: and how they then could take the benefit of ſuch a miſchief, with which they had been pre-acquainted in the general notion, and either not be joyful at it, and conſequently be in the ſame caſe with ſuch as had adviſed unto it, let them judge that liſt.

                                                      11. The

11. The dangers growing to the State by thefe odious practifes, may be fuppofed to haften the Arraignment of *Udal* , one of the four which had a hand in thofe fcurrilous Libels which fwarmed fo numeroufly in all parts of the Kingdom *Anno* 1588, and the times fince following. But more particularly he ftood charged for being the Author of a Book called, *The Demonftration of Difcipline which Chrift hath prefcribed in his Word for the Government of his Church , in all times and place until the Worlds end.* In the Preface whereof occurreth thefe paffages : Firft, He infcribes the fame not to the Governours, but *to the fuppofed Governours of the Church of* England. And then he flyes upon them in thefe following words, viz. *Who can deny you without blufhing , to be the caufe of all Ungodlinefs ? feeing feeing your Government is that which giveth leave to a man to be any thing, faving a found Chriftian.* For certainly, *it is more free in thefe days to be a* Papift, Anabaptift, *of the* Family of Love ; *yea, as any moft wicked whatfoever, then that which we fhould be.* And I could live thefe twenty years, as well as any fuch in England, (yea in a Bifhops Houfe it may be) and never be molefted for it: *So true is that which you are charged with in a Dialogue lately come forth againft you, and fince burn'd by you, That you care for nothing but the maintainance of your Dignities, be it to the damnation of your own fouls, and infinite millions more.* For which whole Book, but more efpecially for this paffage in the Preface of it, he was indicted at an Affizes held in *Croydon* for the County of *Surrey*, on the 23d of *July Anno* 1590 ; and by fufficient evidence found guilty of it. The Prifoner pleaded for himfelf, That his Indictment was upon the Statute of 23 *Eliz. Cap.* 2. for punifhing Seditious words againft the Queen ; but that the Book for which he ftood accufed, contained no offenfive paffages againft the Queen, but the Bifhops only, and therefore could not come within the compafs and intent of that Statute. But it was anfwered by the Judges, and refolved for Law, *That they who fpeak againft her Majefties Government in cafes Ecclefiaftical, her Laws, Proceedings, or Ecclefiaftical Officers, which ruled under her, did defame the Queen.* Which refolution being given and the evidence heard , he had fo much favour fhewed him by confent of the Court , as to be put unto this queftion, that is to fay , Whether he would take it either on his confcience or his credit , that he was not the Author of that Book : Which if he would or could have done , it was conceived that both the Judges and Jurors would have refted fatisfied. But he not daring to deny it, the Jurors could not otherwife do , than pronounce him *Guilty* , upon fuch evident proofs, and fo many Witneffes as were brought againft him. But the Archbifhop being then at his Houfe in *Croydon* , prevailed fo far in his behalf, that the Judges did fufpend the Sentence of his condemnation. This Tryal hapned in the interval between the feveral Commitments of *Snape* and *Cartwright* before mentioned , when the State had taken up a refolution to proceed feverely againft the Difturbers of her Peace ; which gave fome occafion of offence to the Lord Chancellor *Hatton*, that the Archbifhop, who feemed moft concerned in the prefent cafe, fhould fhow fuch favour to a man whom the Law condemned, and by whofe feafonable execution, a ftop might poffibly be made to all further troubles.

12. But *Snape* and *Cartwright* ftill continued obftinate in refufing the Oath , and the fufpition growing ftrong of fome new defigns , he was

brought again unto the Bar at *Southwark*, in the *March* next following, and there received the Sentence of death in a due form of Law. But such was the exceeding lenity of the good Archbishop, that he looked more upon the parts of the man, than upon his Passions, upon his learning and abilities, though too much abused, then the ill use that he made of them in those stirring times. And so far he engaged himself with his Royal Mistress, (who used to call him her Black Husband) that she gave way to a Reprieve, though she could not easily be induced to grant a Pardon. Which notwithstanding the Archbishop could not scape the lash of some virulent Tongues, by whom he stood more accused for the condemnation, than he was magnified for the Reprieve of the man condemned. And therefore it was after pleaded in his justification, That *Udal*'s Book was clearly within the compass of the Statute 23 *Elizab. Cap.* 2. for punishing *Seditious words against the Queen*, according to the resolution of the Judges before laid down. That divers Seditious Sermons might have been objected against him, as well as the making of that Book, which would have rendred him more culpable in the sight of his Judges; and that whereas one *Catsfield* could have spoken more materially against him, than any of the rest of the witnesses, he was never called unto the Bar to give in his evidence, the Jurors being fully satisfied in the former proofs. So that the whole Indictment being rightly grounded, the Prosecution favourable, and the evidence full, the man remained a living Monument of the Archbishops extraordinary goodness to him, in the preserving of that life which by the Law he had forfeited. But how long he remained alive, I am not able to say; and therefore shall add only this, That he left a Son behind, called *Ephraim*, who afterwards was beneficed at the Church of St. *Augustines*, near St. *Paul*'s Church-yard, and proved as great a Zealot for conformity, in the time of King *Charles*, as his Father was reputed for his Non-conformity in the times we write of. And he paid almost as dear for it, as his Father did, being sequestred about the year 1643, not submitting to some Oaths and Covenants then required of him; his bed-rid Wife turned out of doors, and left most unmercifully in the open Streets.

13. Now whilst the State was taken up in these criminal Processes, the learned men and others interessed on each side, were no less busied in defence of their own concernments. *Adrian Savaria* born in the *Lower Germany*, but better studied in the Fathers than the most of his Rank, had found by search into their Writings, of what Antiquity and necessity the Calling of Bishops had been reckoned in the Primitive times, even in the days of the Apostles; but finding no encouragement to maintain any such opinion in his Native Countrey, where the *Presbyteries* governed all, and Parity of Ministers was received as an Article of their publick Confession; he put himself upon the favour and Protection of
1590. the Church of *England*. He had before fashioned his Reply to *Beza*'s Book, entituled, *De Triplici Episcopatu*, as before was said. But the first Piece published by him on his coming hither, was a right learned Work, entituled, *De diversis gradibus Ministrorum Evangelii*: In which he proved by undeniable Arguments, That Bishops were a different Order, as well as by Degrees superior to all other *Presbyters*. This Book he dedicates to the Ministers of the *Belgick* Churches, as appears by his Epistle
dated

dated *March* 26, *Anno* 1590. Amongſt whom though he could not hope for much approbation, yet he received but little or no oppoſition. But ſo it prov'd not at *Geneva*, where *Beza* governed, backed by *Danæus*, and the reſt of the *Conſiſtorians*, who looked upon it as deſtructive to their whole Contrivements. *Beza* had other work in hand, and therefore leaves him for the preſent to the laſh of *Danæus*, who falls upon him with Reproaches inſtead of Arguments (as *Saravia* complained in his Reply) reckoning his Corpulency for a Crime, calling him *Swineherd, Hog*, a man born only for the ſtuffing of a filthy paunch; with many like ſcurrilous ſtrains of *Genevian* Rhetorick. *Beza* comes ſlowly on, but he comes at laſt; not publiſhing his Anſwer to it, till the third year after: to which *Saravia* replies in the year next following, *Anno* 1594. In which he made an exact parallel (amongſt other things) betwixt the practiſes of *Hacket* and the *Puritan* Faction on the one ſide, and thoſe of *John* of *Leyden* and the *Anabaptiſts* when they reigned in *Munſter*. In the end *Beza* gave him over; which raiſed him to ſuch eminent note with the *Engliſh* Prelates, that he was made a Prebendary of Church of *Weſtminſter*, and otherwiſe well provided for to his full contentment.

14. In the mean time the Miniſter of the *Italian* Church in the City of *London* could not reſt ſatisfied with the enjoying the ſame Priviledges which the *French* and *Dutch* Churches had before procured; but publiſhed a Book in maintainance and commendation of the Holy Diſcipline: which gave a juſt occaſion to Dr. *Matthew Suttliff*, then Dean of *Exon*, to ſet out a judicious Work in *Latin* touching the nature of the *De vera Catruely* Catholick and Chriſtian Church; wherein he grated ſomewhat *tholica &* hard on the Point of *Presbytery*, and was the firſt *Engliſh* man that did ſo in *Ecleſia.* the *Latin* Tongue. And though he named *Beza* only, and no more than named him; yet *Beza* thought his name ſo ſacred, or himſelf ſo high, that he conceived himſelf to be much diſhonoured; reproaches him by the name of a petulant Railer, and complains of the affront in an Epiſtle *Convitiatorem* to the Archbiſhop of *Canterbury*. But he got nothing by the *Bargain*: *petulantem vo-* For as he was handſomly ſhaked up for it by *Saravia* in his Replicati-*cari doleo. Sa-* on, ſo the Archbiſhop in an anſwer to the ſaid Epiſtle, dated in *January*, *rav. Repl.* 1593, ſeverely reprehends him for his intermedling with the Church of *England*, and plainly lays before him all thoſe diſturbances which by his means had been occaſioned in the ſame: ſo that being learnedly refuted by *Saravia* on the one ſide, and gravely reprehended on the other by that Reverend Prelate, he grows wiſe at laſt, leaving the *Engliſh Puritans* to their own defences. And more then ſo in his Reply to his laſt Letter he gives him his due Titles, of the *moſt Reverend Father in Chriſt*, and *His Honoured Lord*; aſſuring him, *That in all his writings touching Church-Government, he impugned only the Romiſh Hierarchy, but never intended to touch the Eccleſiaſtical Polity of this Church of England, nor to exact of us to frame our ſelves or our Church to the pattern of their Presbyterian Diſcipline.* And thereunto he added this ſafe Concluſion, *That as long as the ſubſtance of Doctrine was uniform in the Church of Chriſt, they may lawfully vary in other matters, as the circumſtance of time, place, and perſons, requires, and as Preſcription of Antiquity may warrant.* And, to that end he wiſhed and hoped, that the Sacred and Holy Colledges of Biſhops (for ſo he calls them) *would for ever continue and maintain ſuch their Right*

and

and Title in the Churches Government , with all Equity and Christian Moderation.

15. At this time grew the Heats also betwixt *Hooker* and *Travers:* the first being Master of the *Temple* , and the other Lecturer : *Hooker* received his Education in *Corpus Christi Colledge* in *Oxon*, from whence he came well stocked in all kind of Learning, but most especially in Fathers, Councils, and other approved Monuments of Ecclesiastical Antiquity. *Travers* was bred in *Trinity Colleage* in *Cambridge*, well skilled in the Oriental Tongues, and otherwise better studied in words than matter, being Contemporary with *Cartwright*, and of his affection :He sets up his studies in *Geneva*, and there acquaints himself with *Beza*, and the rest of that Consistory , of whom and their new Discipline he grew so enamoured , that before his coming into *England* he was made Minister (as well at the least as such hands could make him)by the Presbytery of *Antwerp*, as appears by their Certificate , (for I dare not call them Letters of Orders) dated *May 14*, 1578. Thus qualified, he associates himself with *Cartwright* whom he found there at his coming, in Preaching to the Factory of *English* Merchants, and follows him not long after into *England* also. By the commendation of some Friends he was taken into the House of *William* Lord *Burleigh*, whom he served first in the nature of a Pedagogue to his younger Son, and after as one of his Chaplains. Preferments could not chuse but come in his way, considering the greatness of his Master, whose eminent Offices of Lord Treasurer, chief Secretary, and Master of the Wards, could not but give him many opportunities to prefer a Servant to the best places in the Church. But *Travers* knew his incapacity to receive such favours, as neither lawfully ordained, according to the Form prescribed by the Church of *England* , nor willing to subscribe to such Rites and Ceremonies as he found were used in the same. But being a great Factor for promoting the Holy Discipline, he gets himself into the Lecture of the *Temple* ; which could not easily be denyed , when the Chaplain of so great a Councellor was a Suitor for it.

16. In this place he insinuates himself, by all means imaginable, into the good affections of many young Students, and some great Lawyers of both Houses, on whom he gained exceedingly by his way of Preaching, graced with a comely Gesture , and a Rhetorical manner of Elocution. By which advantages he possest many of the long Robe with a strong affection to the devices of *Geneva*, and with as great a prejudice to the *English Hierarchy* ; the fruits whereof discovered themselves more or less in all following Parliaments, when any thing concerning the Church came in agitation. And by the opportunity of this Place, he had the chief managing of the affairs of the *Disciplinarians* , presiding for the most part in their Classical Meetings , and from hence issuing their Directions to the rest of the Churches. And so it stood till *Hooker*'s coming to be Master, who being a man of other Principles, and better able to defend them in a way of Argument ; endeavoured to instruct his Auditors in such Points of Doctrine as might keep them in a right perswasion of the Church of *England*, as well in reference to her Government, as her Forms of Worship. This troubled *Travers* at the heart, as it could not otherwise, to see that fine Web which he had been so long in weaving , should be thus unravell'd. Rather than so *Hooker* shall tell them nothing in the

Morning,

Morning, but what he laboured to confute in the afternoon ; not doubting but that a great part of the Auditors would pass Sentence for him, though the truth might run most apparently on the other side. *Hooker* endured it for time ; but being weary at the last of the opposition, he complains thereof to the Archbishop, who had (deservedly) a very great opinion of him ; and this complaint being seasonably made in that point of time when *Cartwright*, *Snape*, and other Leading-men of the *Puritan* Faction, were brought into the High Commission ; it was no hard matter for him to procure an Order to suppress his Adversary, silenced from Preaching in the *Temple*, and all places else. Which Order was issued upon these grounds, that is to say, *That he was no lawfully ordained Minister according to the Church of* England : *That he took upon him to Preach without being licensed*: and, *That he had presumed openly to confute such Doctrine as had been publickly delivered by another Preacher, without any notice given thereof to the lawful Ordinary, contrary to a Provision made in the Seventh year of the Queen for avoiding Disturbances in the Church*

17. But *Travers* was too stiff, and too well supported, to sit down on the first assault : He makes his supplication therefore to the Lords of the Council, where he conceived himself as strong and as highly favoured as *Hooker* was amongst the Bishops and the High Commissioners. In this Petition he complains of some obliquity in the proceedings had against him for want of some Legalities in the conduct of it. But when he came to answer to the Charges which were laid upon him, his Defences appeared very weak and flat, and could not much conduce his justification, when they were seriously examined in the scale of Judgment. His exercising the Ministry without lawful *Orders*, he justified no otherwise then that by the Communion of Saints all Ordinations were of like Authority in a Christian Church. The Bishop of *London* had commended him by two letters unto that Society, to be chosen Lecturer ; and that he took for a sufficient License, as might enable him to Preach to that Congregation. And as for his confuting in the Afternoon what had been Preached by Mr. *Hooker* in the morning before, he conceived that he had warrant for it from S. *Paul*'s example, in withstanding S. *Peter* to his face, for fear lest otherwise Gods Truth might receive some prejudice. The weakness and insufficiency of which Defences was presently made known in *Hooker*'s Answer to the Supplication. Which wrought so much upon the Lords, and was so strongly seconded by the Archbishop himself, that all the Friends which *Travers* had amongst them could not do him good ; especially when it was represented to them how dangerous a thing it was, that a man of such ill Principles, and of worse affections, should be permitted to continue in his former Lectures ; which, what else were it, in effect, but to *retain* almost half the Lawyers of *England* to *be of Council* in all Causes which concerned the Church, whensoever those of the *Genevian* or *Puritan* Faction should require it of them. But so it hapned, (and it hapned very well for *Travers*) that the Queen had erected an University at *Dublin*, in the year foregoing 1591 ; Founding therein a Colledge dedicated to the *Holy Trinity*: to the Provostship whereof he was invited by the Archbishop of *Dublin*, who had been once a Fellow of the same House with him. Glad of which opportunity to go off with credit, he prepares for *Ireland*. But long he had not dwelt on his new Preferment, when

either

either he proved too hot for the Place, or the Countrey (by reason of the following Wars) grew too hot for him: Which brought him back again to *England*; where he lived a very great age in a small Estate, more comfortably than before, because less troublesome to the Church than he had been formerly.

18. Thus have we seen *Travers* taken off, and *Beza* quieted; nor was it long before *Cartwright* was reduced to a better temper: But first, it was resolved to try all means for his delivery, both at home and abroad. Abroad, they held intelligence with their Brethren in the Kirk of *Scotland*, by means of *Penry* here, and of *Gibson* there; two men as fit for their designs, as if they had been made of purpose to promote the mischief. Concerning which, thus *Gibson* writes in one of his letters to *Coppinger* before remembred; whereby it seems that he was privy to his practises also. *The best our Ministers* (saith he) *are most careful of your estate; and had sent for that effect a Preacher of ours the last Summer, of purpose to confer with the best affected of your Church, to lay down a plot how our Church might best travel for your relief. The Lord knows what care we have of you, both in our publick and private Prayers,* &c. *For, as feeling members of one body, we reckon the affliction of your Church to be our own.* This showed how great they were with child of some good affections; but there wanted strength to be delivered for the burthen. They were not able to raise Factions in the Court of *England*, as Queen *Elizabeth* had done frequently on their occasions in the Realm of *Scotland*. All they could do, was to engage the King in mediating with the Queen in behalf of *Cartwright*, *Udal*, and some others of the principal Brethren then kept in Prison for the contumacy in refusing the Oath. And they prevailed so far upon him, who was not then in a condition to deny them any thing, as to direct some lines unto her in this tenour following.

19. R Ight Excellent, High and Mighty Princess, Our dearest
   'Sister and Cousin, in Our heartiest manner we recom-
' mend us to you. Hearing of the Apprehension of Master *Udal*,
' and Master *Cartwright*, and certain other Ministers of the Evan-
' gel, within your Realm, of whose good Erudition, and Faith-
' full Travel in the Church, We hear a very credible commen-
' dation, however that their diversity from the Bishops and other
' of your Clergy, in matters touching their delation to work them
' your misliking: at this time we cannot (weighing the duty which
' we owe to such as are afflicted for their conscience in that Pro-
' fession) but by our most effectuous and earnest letter, interpone
' us at your hands, to stay any harder usage of them for that
' cause. Requesting you most earnestly, That for our cause
' and Intercession, it may please you to let them be relieved of
' their present strait, and whatsoever further Accusation or pur-
' suit depending upon that ground, respecting both their former
' Merit in setting forth the Evangel, the simplicity of their con-
' science in this Defence, which cannot well be, their lett by com-
' pulsion, and the great slander which would not fail to fell out
' upon their further straitning for any such occasion. Which
' we assure us, your Zeal to Religion, besides the expectation we
                                       ' have

' have of Your good will ro pleafure Us, will willingly accord to
' Our Requeft, having fuch proofs from time to time, of our like
' difpofition to you, in any matter which You recommend unto
' Us. And thus, Right Excellent, Right High, and Mighty
' Princefs, Our dear Sifter and Coufin, We commit You to Gods
' Protection.

Edenborough, June
12. 1591.

20. This Letter was prefented to the Queen by the hands of one
Johnfon, a Merchant of that Nation then remaining in *London*. But it
produced not the effect which the Brethren hoped for : For the Queen
looked upon it as extorted rather by the importunity of fome which were
then about him, than as proceeding from himfelf, who had no reafon
to be too indulgent unto thofe of that Faction. This Project therefore
not fucceeding, they muft try another ; and the next tryal fhall be made
on the High Commiffion, by the Authority whereof, *Cartwright*, and
Snape, and divers others, were committed Prifoners. If this Commiffion could be weakned, and the Power thereof reduced to a narrower compafs, the brethren might proceed fecurely in the Holy Difcipline, the Prifoners be releafed, and the Caufe eftablifhed. And for the queftioning
thereof, they took this occafion : One *Caudreys*, Parfon of *North-Luffeng-
ham*, in the County of *Rutland*, had been informed againft, about 40 years
fince, in the High Commiffion, for preaching againft the Book of Common-Prayer, and refufing to celebrate Divine Service, according to the
Rules and Rubricks therein prefcribed. For which, upon fufficient
proof, he was deprived of his Benefice by the Bifhop of *London*, and
the reft of the Queens Commiffioners for Ecclefiaftical Caufes. Four
years together he lay quiet, without acting any thing againft
the fentence of the Court. But now it was thought by fome of thofe
Lawyers, whom *Travers* had gained unto the fide, to queftion the Authority of that Commiffion, and confequently the illegality of his Deprivation. In *Hillary* Term, *Anno* 1591, the Caufe was argued in the *Exchequer* Chamber, by all the Judges, according to the ufual cuftom in all
cafes of the like importance ; and it was argued with great Learning, as
appears by the fum and fubftance of their feveral Arguments, drawn up
by *Coke*, then being the Queens Sollicitor-General, and extant amongft
the reft of his Reports, both in *Englifh* and *Latin*, infcribed *De Jure Regis
Ecclefiaftico* ; but known moft commonly by the name of *Cawdreys Cafe*.
In the debating of which Point, the Refult was this, That the Statute
of 10 of the Queen, for *reftoring to the Crown the ancient Jurifdiction*, &c.
was not to be accounted *introductory* of a new Authority, which was not
in the Crown before ; but only *declaratory* of an old, which naturally and
originally did belong to all Chriftian Princes, and amongft others alfo,
to the Kings of *England*. For proof whereof, there wanted not fufficient evidence in our *Englifh* Hiftories, as well as in fome old Records of
unqueftioned Credit, exemplifying the continual practife of the Kings
of *England*, before and fince the *Norman* Conqueft, in ordering and directing matters which concerned the Church : In which they ruled fometimes

times abfolutely, without any difpute: and fometimes relatively, in reference to fuch oppofition as they were to make againft the Pope, and all
Authority derived from the See of *Rome*.

21. Againft this Cafe fo folidly debated, and fo judicioufly drawn up,
when none of the *Puritan* Profeffors could make any Reply, *Parfons* the
Jefuit undertook it ; but fpent more time in fearching out fome contrary Evidence, which might make for the Pope, than in difproving that
which had been brought in behalf of the Queen. So that the ftrugling on both fides much confirmed the Power which they endeavoured
to deftroy ; the Power of that Commiffion being better fortified both
by Law and Argument, than it had been formerly. For, by the over-
ruling of *Cawdreys* Cafe, in confirmation of the Sentence which was paft
againft him, and the great pains which *Parfons* took to fo little purpofe ;
the Power of that Commiffion was fo well eftablifhed in the Courts of
Judicature, that it was afterwards never troubled with the like Difputes. The Guides of the Faction therefore are refolved on another
courfe, To ftrike directly at the Root, to queftion the *Epifcopal* Power,
and the Queens Authority, the Jurifdiction of their Courts, the exacting of the Oath called the Oath *Ex Officio*, and their other proceedings in the fame. And to this purpofe it was publifhed in Print by fome
of their Lawyers, or by their directions at the leaft, That men were heavily oppreffed in the Ecclefiaftical Courts, againft the Laws of the
Realm : That the Queen could neither delegate that Authority which
was vefted in it, nor the Commiffioners to exercife the fame by her delegation : That the faid Courts could not compel the taking of the Oath
called the Oath *Ex Officio*, fince no man could be bound in Reafon to accufe himfelf : That the faid Oath did either draw men into wilful Per-
jury, to the deftruction of their fouls ; or to be guilty, in a manner, of
their own condemnation, to the lofs both of their Fame and Fortunes.
And finally, That the ordinary *Epifcopal* Courts were not to meddle in
any Caufes whatfoever, but only Teftamentary and Matrimonial : by
confequence, not in matter of Tythes, all Mifbehaviours in the Church,
or punifhing of Incontinency, or Fornication, Adultery, Inceft, or any
the like grievous or enormous Crimes : but on the contrary, it was affirmed by the Profeffors of the Civil laws, That to impugn the Authority which had been vefted in the Queen by Act of Parliament was nothing in effect but a plain Invafion of the Royal Prerogative, the opening of a way to the violation of the Oath of Allegeance, and confequently to undermine the whole Frame of the prefent Government. It
was proved alfo, That the ordinary *Epifcopal* Courts had kept themfelves
within their bonnds ; that they might lawfully deal in all fuch caufes
as were then handled in thofe Courts ; that their proceedings in the
fame by the Oath *Ex Officio* was neither againft Confcience, Reafon,
nor the laws of the land ; and therefore, that the Clamours on the o-
ther fide were unjuft and fcandalous. In which, as many both Divines
and Civilians, deferved exceeding well both of the Queen and the
Church ; fo none more eminently then Dr. *Richard Cofins*, Dean of the
Arches, in a learned and laborious Treatife by him writ and publifhed,
called, *An Apology for Proceedings in Courts Ecclefiaftical*, &c. Printed in
the year 1593.

22. But notwithstanding the legality of these Proceedings, the punishing of some Ring-leaders of the *Puritan* Faction, and the imprisonment of others, a Book comes out under the name of *A Petition to her Majesty*: The scope and drift whereof was this, 'That the Ecclesiastical 'Government of the Church of *England*, was to be changed : That the 'Eldership, or Presbyterial Discipline was to be established, as being the 'Government which was used in the Primitive Church, and commanded 'ded to be used in all Ages. That the Disciplinarian Faction hath not 'offended against the Statute 23 *Eliz.* cap. 2. And, That *John Udal* was 'unjustly condemned upon it. That the Consistorial Patrons are unjustly 'slandered with desire of Innovation, and their Doctrine with Disorder and Disloyalty. And this being said the Author of the Pamphlet makes it his chief business by certain Questions and Articles therein propounded, to bring the whole Ecclesiastical State into envy and hatred. This gave the Queen a full assurance of the restless spirit wherewith the Faction was possessed ; and that no quiet was to be expected from them till they were utterly supprest. To which end She gives Order for a Parliament to begin in *February*, for the Enacting of some Laws to restrain those Insolencies with which the Patience of the State had been so long exercised. The *Puritans* on the other side are not out of hope to make some good use of it for themselves ; presuming more upon the strength of their Party, by reason of the Pragmaticalness of some Lawyers in the House of Commons, than they had any just ground for, as it after proved. To which end they prepared some Bills sufficiently destructive of the Royal Interest, the Jurisdiction of the Bishops, and the whole Form of their Proceedings in their several Courts. With which the Queen being made acquainted before their meeting, or otherwise suspecting, by their former practises, what they meant to do ; She thought it best to strangle those Conceptions in the very Womb. And to that purpose she gave order for the signification of her pleasure to the Lords and Commons, at the very first opening of the Parliament, That they should not pass beyond their bounds ; That they should keep themselves to the redressing of such Popular Grievances as were complained of to them in their several Countreys : but, that they should leave all Matters of State to Her self and the Councill ; and all Matters which concerned the Church unto Her and Her Bishops.

23. Which Declaration notwithstanding, the Factors for the *Puritans* are resolved to try their Fortune, and to encroach upon the Queen and the Church at once. The Queen was always sensible of the Inconveniences which might arise upon the nominating of the next Successor, and knew particularly how much the Needle of the *Puritans* Compass pointed toward the North: Which made her more tender in that point, then she had been formerly. But Mr. *Peter Wentworth*, whom before we spake of, a great Zealot in behalf of the Holy Discipline, had brought one *Bromley* to his lure ; and they together deliver a Petition to the Lord Keeper *Puckering*, desiring that the Lords would joyn with them of the Lower House, and become Suppliants to the Queen for entailing of the Succession of the Crown, according to a Bill which they had prepared. At this the Queen was much displeased, as being directly contrary to

her

her strict command; and charged the Lords of the Council to call the said Gentlemen before them, and to proceed against them for their disobedience. Upon which signification of Her Majesties Pleasure Sir *Thomas Heanage*, then Vice Chamberlain, and one of the Lords of the Privy Council, convenes the Parties, reprehends them for their Misdemeanour, commands them to forbear the Parliament, and not to go out of their several Lodgings, until further Order. Being afterwards called before the Lord Treasurer *Burleigh*, the Lord *Buckhurst*, and the said Sir *Thomas*; *Wentworth* is sent unto the Tower, *Bromley* committed unto the Fleet, and with him *Welsh* and *Stevens*, two other Members of that House, were committed also, as being privy to the Projects of the other two. In whose behalf when it was moved by one Mr. *Wroth*, That the House should be humble Suitors to Her Majesty for the releasing of such of their Members as were under restraint; it was answered by such of the Privy Councellors as were then Members of the House, *That Her Majesty had committed them for causes best known to her self; and, that to press Her Highness with this Suit, would but hinder those whose good it sought. That the House must not call the Queen to an account for what she did of her Royal Authority. That the Causes for which they are restrained may be high and dangerous. That Her Majesty liketh no such Questions, neither did it become the House to deal in such matters.* Upon which words the House desisted from interposing any further in their behalf, but left them wholly to the Queen, by whom *Wentworth* was continued Prisoner for some years after.

24. In the same Parliament one *Morrise*, Chancellor of the Dutchy of *Lancaster*, proposed unto the House, That some course might be taken by them against the hard courses of Bishops Ordinaries, and other Ecclesiastical Judges, in their several Courts, towards sundry godly Ministers, and painful Preachers, who deserved more encouragement from them. They also spake against *Subscription*, and the Oath *Ex Officio*, and offered a Bill unto the House against the imprisonment of such as refused the same. Of this the Queen had present notice, and thereupon sends for *Coke*, then Speaker of the House of Commons, (but afterwards successively Chief Justice of either Bench) to whom she gave command to deliver this Message to the House; that is to say, *That it was wholly in Her Power to call, to determine, to assent, or dissent, to any thing done in Parliament. That the calling of this, was only that the Majesty of God might be more Religiously observed, by compelling, with some sharp Laws, such as neglect that Service; and, that the safety of her Majesties Person, and the Realm might be provided for: That it was not meant they should meddle with matters of State, or Causes Ecclesiastical: That she wondered that any should attempt a thing so contrary to her Commandment: and, that She was highly offended at it: and finally, that it was her pleasure, That no Bill touching any matters of State, or for the Reformation of Causes Ecclesiastical, should be there exhibited.* On the delivery of which Message *Morrise* is said to have been seized on in the House by a Serjeant at Arms; but howsoever, seized on and committed Prisoner, kept for some years in *Tutbury* Castle, discharged from his Office in the Dutchy, and disabled from any Practice in his Profession as a common Lawyer. Some others had prepared a Bill to this effect, That in lieu of Excommunication, there should be given

ven

ven fome ordinary Procefs, with fuch fute and coertion as thereunto might appertain ; that fo the Dignity of fo high a Sentence being retained, and the neceffity of mean Procefs fupplied, the Church might be reftored to its ancient fplendor. Which Bill though recommended fomewhat incogitantly by one of the Graveft Councellors of State which was then in the Houfe, was alfo dafhed by Her Majefties exprefs command, upon a Refolution of not altering any thing (the quality of the times confidered) which had been fettled in the Church, both by Law and Practice. Which conftancy of hers in the preferving of Her own Prerogative and the Churches Power, kept down that fwelling humour of the *Puritan* Faction, which was even then upon the point of overflowing the banks, and bearing down all oppofition which was made againft them.

25. And, that they might be kept the better in their natural Chanel, fhe caufed an Act to be prepared and paffed in this prefent Parliament, for retaining them, and others of Her Subjects, in their due obedience: By which it was Enacted, ' For the preventing and avoiding of fuch In-
' conveniencies and Perils as might happen and grow by the wicked and
' dangerous Practices of Seditious Sectaries, and Difloyal perfons ;
' That if any perfon or perfons above the age of fixteen years, fhould
' obftinately refufe to repair to fome Church, Chapel, or ufual place of
' Common Prayer, to hear Divine Service eftablifhed, or fhall forbear
' to do the fame by the fpace of a moneth, without lawful caufe ; or
' fhould move or perfwade any other perfon whatfoever, to forbear and
' abftain from coming to the Church to hear Divine Service, or to re-
' ceive the Communion, according to the Laws and Statutes aforefaid;
' or to come or be prefent at any unlawful Affemblies, Conventicles, or
' Meetings, under pretence of Religious Exercife, contrary to the Laws
' and Statutes made in that behalf; or fhould at any time after 40 days
' from the end of that Seffion, by Printing, Writing, or exprefs Words
' or Speeches, advifedly and purpofely go about to move or perfwade a-
' ny of Her Majefties Subjects, or any other within Her Highnefs Realms
' and Dominions, to deny, withftand, or impugn Her Majefties Power
' and Authority in caufes Ecclefiaftical, united and annexed to the Im-
' perial Crown of the Realm : That then every perfon fo offending,
' and convicted of it, fhould be committed unto Prifon without Bail or
' Main-prife, till he or they fhould teftifie their Conformity, by coming
' to fome Church, Chapel, or other place of Common Prayer, to hear
' Divine Service, and to make open fubmiffion and declaration of the
' fame in fuch form and manner, as by the faid Statute was provided. Now that we may the better fee what great care was taken, as well by the two Houfes of Parliament, as by the Queen Her felf, for preferving the Honour of the Church, the Jurifdiction of the Bifhops, and the Royal Prerogative in both ; it will not be amifs to reprefent that Form to the eye of the *Reader*, in which the faid Submiffion was to be delivered. The tenour whereof was as followeth, *viz.*

26. ' I, *A. B.* do humbly confefs and acknowledge, That I have
' grevoufly offended God in contemning her Majefties godly and
' lawful Government and Authority, by abfenting my felf from
Church,

' Church & from hearing Divine Service, contrary to the Godly
' Laws & Statutes of this Realm; & in using and frequenting dif-
' ordered and unlawful Conventicles and Assemblies, under pre-
' tence and colour of exercise of Religion. And I am heartily
' sorry for the same, and do acknowledge and testifie in my Con-
' science, That no person or persons hath, or ought to have, any
' Power or Authority over Her Majesty. And I do promise and
' protest without any dissimulation, or any colour of means of
' any Dispensation, That from henceforth I will from time to
' time obey and perform Her Majesties Laws and Statutes in re-
' pairing to the Church, and hearing Divine Service, and do mine
' utmost endeavour to maintain and defend the same.

27. This Declaration to be made in some Church or Chapel, before
the beginning of Divine Service, within three moneths after the con-
viction of the said Offenders, who otherwise were to abjure the Realm,
and to depart the same, at such time and place as should be limited and
assigned unto them; with this Proviso superadded, That if any of the
said persons so abjuring, should either not depart the Realm at the time
appointed, or should come back again unto it without leave first granted; that then every such person should suffer death as in case of Felony, without the benefit of his Clergy. And to say the truth, there was
no reason why any man should have the benefit of his Clergy, who should
so obstinately refuse to conform himself to the Rules and Dictates of
the Church. There also was a penalty of ten pounds by the moneth imposed upon all those who harboured any of the said *Puritan Recusants*, if
the said *Puritan Recusants* (not being of their near Relations) or any of
them, should forbear coming to some Church or Chapel, or other place
of Common Prayer, to hear the Divine Service of the Church, for the
space of a moneth. Which Statute being made to continue no longer
then till the end of the next Session of Parliament, was afterwards kept
in force from Session to Session till the death of the Queen; to the great
preservation of the Peace of the Kingdom, the safety of Her Majesties
Person, and the tranquillity of the Church, free from thenceforth from
any such disturbances of the *Puritan* Faction, as had before endangered the Foundations of it.

1593.   28. And yet it cannot be denied, but that the seasonable execution
of the former Statute on *Barrow*, *Penry*, and some others of these common Barreters, conduced as much to the promoting of this general calm,
as the making of this. It was in the moneth of *November*, 1587, that
Henry Barrow, Gentleman, and *John Greenwood*, Clerk, (of whose commitment, with some others, we have spoke before) were publickly convened by the High Commissioners, for holding and dispersing many
Schismatical Opinions, and Seditious Doctrines, of which the principal
were these, *viz.* That our Church is no true Church. That the Worship of the *English* Church is flat Idolatry. That we admit into our
Church unsanctified persons. That our Preachers have no lawful Calling. That our Government is ungodly. That no Bishop or Preacher prea-
cheth Christ sincerely or truly. That the people of every Parish ought to
chuse their Bishop. And, That every Elder, though he be no Doctor or
Pastor,

Pastor, is a Bishop,   That all of the Precifer fort, who refufe the Ceremonies of the Church, ftrain at a Gnat, and fwallow a Camel, and are clofe Hypocrites, and walk in a left handed Policy, as *Cartwright, Wiggington,* &c. That all which make, teach, or expound Printed or 'Written Catechifms, are idle Shepherds, as *Calvin, Urfin, Nowell,* &c. 'That the Children of ungodly Parents ought not to be baptized, us of 'Ufurers, Drunkards, *&c* and finally, that Set-prayer is blafphemous. On their Convention, and fome fhort reftraint for fo many dotages, they promifed to recant, and were enlarged upon their Bonds.   But being fet at liberty, they brake out again into further Extremities, and drew fome others to the fide, almoft as mifchievous as themfelves, and no lefs Pragmatical: the principal whereof (not to take notice of the Rabble of befotted people who became their followers) were *Saxio Billet,* Gentleman; *Daniel Studley,* Girdler; *Robert Bouler,* Fifh-monger; committed Prifoners to the Fleet, with their principal Leaders, in the *July* following.

29. The times were dangerous, in regard of the great Preparations of the King of *Spain* for the invading of this Kingdom : which rendred the imprifonment of thefe furious Sectaries as necefsary to the prefervation of the publik fafety, as the fhutting up of fo many of the Leading *Papifts* into *Wisbich* Caftle. But fo it was, that the State being totally taken up with the profecutirn of that war on the Coafts of *Spain,* and the quenching of the fire at home, which had heen raifed by *Cartwright, Udal,* and the reft of the *Difciplinarians,* there was nothing done againft them, but that they were kept out of harms way, as the faying is, by a clofe Imprifonment. During which time *Cartwright,* who was their fellow-Prifoner, had a Conference with them, the rather, in regard it had been reported from *Barrows* mouth, That he had neither acted nor written any thing, but what he was warranted to do by *Cartwrights* Principles. The Conference was private, and the refult thereof not known to many, but left to be conjectured at by this following ftory. The Reverend *Whitgift* had a great defire to fave the men from that deftruction in which they had involved themfelves by their own perverfenefs ; and to that end fends Dr. *Thomas Ravis,* then one of his Chaplains, (but afterwards Lord Bifhop of *London*) to confer with *Barrow.* At whofe requeft, and fome directions from the Archbifhop, in purfuance of it, *Cartwright* is dealt with to proceed to another Conference : but no perfwafions would prevail with him for a fecond Meeting. Which being fignified to *Barrow,* by the faid Dr. *Ravis,* in the prefence of divers perfons of good account, the poor man fetched a great figh, faying, *Shall I be thus forfaken by him ? Was it not he that brought me firft into thefe briars, and will he now teave me in the fame ? Was it not from him alone that I took my grounds ? Or, did I not out of fuch Premifes as he pleafed to give me infer thofe Propofitions, and deduce thofe Conclufions for which I am now kept in Bonds ?* Which faid, the company departed, and left the Prifoners to prepare for their following Tryal. By the Imprifonment of *Cartwright,* the Condemnation of *Udal,* and the Execution of *Hacket,* the times had been reduced to fo good a temper, that there could be no danger in proceeding to a publick Arraignment.   The Parliament was then alfo fitting ; and poffible it is, that the Queen might pitch upon that time for

their

their condemnation, to let them see, that neither the sitting of a Parliament, nor any Friends they had in both or either of the Houses, could either stay the course of Justice, or suspend the Laws. Certain it is, that on the 21 of *March*, 1592, they were all indicted at the Sessions Hall without *Newgate*, before the Lord Mayor, the two Chief Justices, some of the Judges, and divers other Commissioners of *Oyer* and *Terminer*, for writing and publishing sundry Seditious Books, tending to the slander of the Queen and State. For which they were found guilty, and had the Sentence of Death pronounced upon them, *March* 23. Till the Execution of which Sentence they were sent to *Newgate*.

30. The fatal Sentence being thus passed, Dr. *Lancelot Andrews*, afterwards Lord Bishop of *Ely*; Dr. *Henry Parrey*, afterwards Lord Bishop of *Worcester*; Dr. *Philip Bisse*, Arch-Deacon of *Taunton*; and Dr. *Thomas White*, one of the Residentiaries of St. *Pauls*; were sent to *Barrow*, to advise him to recant those Errors, which otherwise might be as dangerous to his soul, as they had proved unto his body. Who having spent some time to this purpose with him, were accosted thus : ‘You are not ‘ (saith he) the men whom I most dislike in the present differences: For, ‘ though you be out of the way, yet you think you are in the Right, and ‘ walk according to that light which God hath given you. But I can- ‘ not but complain of Mr. *Cartwright*, and all others of his Opinion, ‘ from whom we have received the truth of these things, and by whose ‘ Books we have been taught, that your Calling is *Antichristian*. And yet ‘ these men, saith he, forsake us in our Sufferings, against their consci- ‘ ences, and rather chuse to save their lives, than go out of *Babylon*. To which when Dr. *White* objected, That those Callings, which he reproached as *Antichristian*, had been embraced by Archbishop *Cranmer*, Bishop *Ridley*, and divers other godly persons, who suffered Martyrdom for their Religion in Queen *Maries* days. *Barrow* thus gloriously replies, *Most true it is* (quoth he) *that they and others were Martyrs in Queen* Maries *days; but these holy Bands of mine* (and therewith shook his Fetters) *are much more glorious then any of theirs, because they had the Mark of Antichrist in their hands.* Such was the Fortune of these men, that these learned Doctors could do as little good upon them, as *Cartwright* and his Fellows had done before ; though, to say the truth, it had not been in *Cartwrights* power to have changed their minds, unless he had first changed his own. And thereupon it was very well said by Dr. *John Burges*, (who had been once one of *Cartwrights* Followers) ‘ That he was, and e- ‘ ver had been of that opinion, That no just confutation could be made ‘ of the *Separatists*, by any of the *Non-Conformists*, who had given them ‘ their Principles. That though he had seen some endeavours that way, ‘ yet did they never satisfie him in point of Conscience. That the Ar- ‘ guments published in his time against Conformity were pretended ‘ for the grounds of the Separation. That the *Separatists* did pretend ‘ their Pedigree from none but the *Puritans* ; which no man can deny ‘ (saith he) that hath any Modesty. And finally, that therefore the ‘ *Puritans* might well call them their *dear Brethren of the Separation*, as ‘ *Dighton* and some others had began to do. To bring this business to an end. *Barrow* and *Greenwood* were brought to *Tiburn* in a Cart, on the last

laſt of *March* ; and having been expoſed for ſome time to the ſight of the people, were carried back again to *Newgate*. But no repentance following on the ſenſe of ſo great a mercy, they were both hanged at *Tiburn* on the ſixth of *April*. The other three being reprieved, with ſome hope of pardon, as being only acceſſary to the Crimes of the other.

31. In *May* next following *Penry* is brought upon his Tryal ; a man of moſt Seditious Malice, and one of the chief Penners of thoſe ſcurrilous Libells which had paſſed under the name of *Martin Mar-Prelate*. But not content with having a hand in thoſe Peſtilent Pamphlets, but muſt needs take upon him to be the *Inter-Nuncio*, or common Agent, between the *Presbyters* of *Scotland*, and the *Engliſh Puritans*. Having enflamed the *Scots* unto ſome Seditions, he remained Leiger there till the beginning of *Hacket*'s Treaſons, and thereupon writes to *Arthington* to this effect, *That Reformation muſt be ſhortly erected in* England : And thereupon he makes for *London*, to have play'd his pranks, if their Deſign had took effect ; it being his hope, as poſſibly it was the hope of all the reſt of that Faction, That on the Proclamations which were made by *Hacket*'s Prophets, the people would have been incited to an Inſurrection. But when he ſaw thoſe hopes deluded, and *Hacket* executed, his guilty Conſcience prompted him to fear the like cruel death, which hurried him again to *Scotland* ; where he remained till the beginning of the Parliament before remembred. At what time ſtealing privately back again towards *London*, he was diſcovered at *Stebunheth*, (commonly called *Stepny*) apprehended by the Vicar there, committed Priſoner, tryed at the Kings-Bench-Barr, at *Weſtminſter-Hall*, condemned of Felony on the Statute of 23, *Eliz.* and executed not long after at St. *Thomas* of *Waterings* ; but executed with a very thin company attending on him, for fear the Fellow might have raiſed ſome Tumult, either in going to the Gallows, or upon the Ladder. But what he could not do when he was alive, was put into a way of being affected when the Hang-man had done his office, by publiſhing one of his Seditious Pamphlets, entituled, *The Hiſtory of* Corah, Dathan, *and* Abiram, *applied to the Prelacy and Miniſtry of the Church of* England ; *by Mr.* John Penry, *a Martyr of Jeſus Chriſt*, as the Pamphlet calls him. The Work not finiſhed at the time of his Apprehenſion, but was Printed however by ſome zealous Brother, that he might poyſon the Queen's Subjects as well dead as living.

32. To which end we are told in the Preface of it, by the zealous, or rather Seditious Publiſher, ' That the Author, Mr. *John Penry*, was ' a Godly man, Learned, Zealous, and of a moſt Chriſtian Carriage ' and Courage. That he was born and bred in the Mountains of *Wales*, ' and with all godly care and labour, endeavoured to have the Goſpel ' preached amongſt his Countrey-men, whoſe caſe he greatly ſeemed ' to pity, wanting all the ordinary means for their ſalvation. That ' being uſed by God for a ſpecial Inſtrument in the manifeſtation of his ' Truth, he was hardly entreated, impriſoned, condemned, and execu- ' ted ; and ſo ſuffered Martyrdom for the Name of Chriſt. But more ' particularly, That he was adjudged at the King's-Bench by Sir *John* ' *Popham*, Lord Chief Juſtice, and the reſt of the Judges then aſſembled,

' on

‘on the 25th of the fifth Moneth, and executed at St. *Thomas* of *Wate-*
‘*rings*, near *London*, on the 29th of the fame, in the year of our God
‘1593. And finally, That he was not brought to execution the next
‘fecond or third day, as moft men expected ; but, that when men did
‘leaft look for it, he was taken while he was at dinner, carried in a
‘clofe manner to his Execution, and haftily bereaved of his life, with-
‘out being fuffered (though he much defired) to make a declaration
‘of his Faith towards God, or his Allegeance to the Queen. And in
‘a Poftfcript to the fame he concludes it thus. *viz.* That he was ap-
‘prehended, adjudged, and executed, for writing for the Truth of
‘ *Chrift*, whatfoever other things were pretended againft him. Let
us no longer blame the *Papifts* for making Martyrs of fuch Priefts and
Jefuits as fuffered death according to the Law of the Land, for their
feveral Treafons : the *Puritans*, or *Presbyterians*, have their Martyrs alfo, *Penry* and *Hacket*, and the reft, condemened by the fame Laws, for
their Treafons and Felonies. And if thefe men, with *Barrow, Green-*
wood, and the reft, who had gone before them, muft pafs in our account
for Martyrs, becaufe they fuffered in purfuance of the Holy Difcipline;
there is no queftion to be made, but *Cartwright, Snape* with fuch as
fuffered only by Imprifonment, or the lofs of their Benefices, muft be
marked for *Confeffors*, in the next fetting out of *Gellibrand*'s Calendar,
whenfoever it be. Which, as it was the higheft honour that any of
Cartwright's Friends can pretend to for him ; fo in himfelf he feemed
not very ambitious of thofe glorious Attributes, which could not otherwife be purchafed then at *Penry*'s Price.

33. For now perceiving, when too late, to what calamitous and
miferable Ends he had brought his Followers, what horrible Confufions had difturbed the whole Church by his obftinate Follies ; he was
contented to knock off, and to give way to thofe Prudential Confiderations which the complexion of Affairs did fuggeft unto him. He faw
too clearly, that there were no more *Walfinghams* or *Leicefters* at the
Council-Table. That the Archbifhops little finger moved more powerfully there, then thofe few Friends which durft fpeak for him being put together. That the Chief Juftice *Popham* was a man of a ridg-
ed nature, not to be trifled with, or took off from the profecution, if
he fhould come within the compafs of the Law. And finally, that
though the Statute made in the laft Seffion feemed chiefly to relate unto the Brethren of the Separation ; yet there might be fome way or o-
ther to hook in all the Zealots for the Difcipline alfo, if they did any
thing in derogation of the prefent Government. Of thefe Relentings
fome intelligence had been given to Archbifhop *Whitgift*, who thereupon refolved to work fome impreffion on him, when he found him like a
piece of *Wax* well warmed, and thereby fitted to receive it. In which
Refolution he applies himfelf unto the Queen, from whofe Clemency
he not only obtained for him a Releafe from Prifon, but made it the
more comfortable by a gracious Pardon for all Errors paft. He fuffered
him moreover to return to *Warwick*, where he was Mafter of the Hofpital founded by the Earl of *Leicefter*, as before is faid, and there permitted him to preach ; though with this condition, That he fhould neither Write, nor Preach, nor Act in any thing to the difturbance of the
Church,

Church, either in reference to her Government, or Forms of Worship:
And though it be affirmed, That *Cartwright* kept himself within those
Restrictions ; yet when the Queen had notice of it, she was much displeased, and not a little blamed the Archbishop for it : But he beheld
not *Cartwright*, as he had done *Travers*, though both pretending to the
Ordination of a Forein Presbytery. For *Travers* never had any other
Hands imposed on him, then those of the Presbytery of *Antwerp*, which
might stand for nothing. But *Cartwright* was first lawfully ordained in
the Church of *England* ; the Character whereof could not be obliterated, though it might possibly be defaced, either by the Rescinding of
his Letters of Orders (which some say he did) or by the super-addition
of such other Hands as were laid upon him, after the fashion of *Geneva*.
Neither was *Cartwright* so insensible of the Obligation, as not to know
and to acknowledge by whose Favour he received that Freedom; carrying himself for that time forwards to the Archbishop, both in his Letters and Addresses, with as much respect as any of the Regular and
Conformable Clergy ; continuing in that peaceable disposition, till the
time of his death ; which hapned about ten years after his enlargement,
that is to say, on the 27th day of *December*, Anno 1603.

34. But the Archbishop stayed not here ; he knew right well, that
Punishment without Instruction would not edifie much with men of
common understandings ; and therefore carefully employed both himself and others in giving satisfaction to all doubting judgments. For his
own part, he wrote this year his long and learned Letter to *Theodore Beza*,
which before we spake of ; and therein calmly laid before him that
deplorable Rupture which not without his privity had been made in
the Church of *England*. Which point he prest upon him with such
Christian Modesty, and did withall so clearly justifie this Church in her
whole proceedings, that *Beza* could not but confess himself to be conquered by his future carriage, which from thenceforth breathed nothing
else but Peace to the Church it self, and dutiful respects to that Reverend
Prelate. And for the satisfaction of all Parties interested amongst our
selves, a Book was published this year also by Dr. *Thomas Bilson*, then
Warden of the College near *Winchester*, concerning *The perpetual Government of the Church of Christ*; proving therein, That from the time of Christ
himself till these later days, neither the Universal Church, nor any National or Provincial Church, in what place soever, had been governed o-
therwise then by Bishops and their Under-Officers. True, other Books
were published at the same time also, by Dr. *Richard Bancroft*, so often
mentioned ; the one for the undeceiving of the people, (who had been
miserably abused by such counterfeit Wares) entituled, *A Survey of the
pretended Holy Discipline.* The other to inform them in the *Dangerous
Positions and Proceedings published and practised in this Island of* Britain, *under pretence of* Reformation, *&c.* which was the Title of the Book. The
like course was also taken for the justification of the Bishops Courts, by
publishing the *Apology* of Dr. *Cosens* before remembered. And because
Hacket's Treasons had been built on no other Foundation, then that the
Holy Discipline might be raised upon them, a Narrative thereof is
penned by Dr. ———— ——— a Doctor of Civil Laws, collected for
the most part out of the Letters and Confessions of some Disciplina-
ians,

rians, which either had been intercepted, or perfwaded from them. A courfe exceeding profperous to all thofe whom it moft concerned. For the Archbifhop by this means went in peace to his Grave, *Beza* was gratified by him with a liberal Penfion, *Bilfon* within a fhort while after made Bifhop of *Winchefter* ; *Bancroft* preferred about the fame time ro the See of *London* ; *Cofens*, for his encouragement, made Dean of the Arches.

35. And though we find not any Preferment to be given to *Cartwright*, yet was it a Preferment to him to enjoy his Miniftry ; by means whereof he is affirmed to have grown very wealthy, partly by the Revenues of his Place in the Hofpital, and partly by the Bounty and Munificence of his conftant Auditors. Only it is reported of him, that towards his end he was afflicted with many infirmities ; infomuch, that he could not otherwife apply himfelf unto his Studies, then upon his knees ; which fome were willing to impute as a judgment on him, for having fo bitterly inveighed againft all fuch men as in that reverend and religious pofture did receive the *Sacrament*. Some alfo have informed us of him, That notwithftanding all his Clamours, and Tumultuous manner of proceedings againft the Church, he could not chufe but confefs there was more Difcipline exercifed in the Church of *England*, then in any of thofe Churches beyond Seas which himfelf had feen. Which words, as he is faid to have fpoken to one Mr. *Woods*, then Parfon of *Freckenham* in *Norfolk*, during the time of his imprifonment in the Fleet ; fo the faid *Woods* reported them to Dr. *John Burges*, before-mentioned, and from him I have them. But I had brought the man to his Grave before, and fhould not have difturbed his reft by thefe fad remembrances, if the Honour of the Church of *England* were not fome way vindicated as well by the one as by the other. Thus, as before we brought the *Presbyterians* in *Scotland* to their greateft height, in feeing their Difcipline eftablifhed by Laws, and confirmed by Leagues : fo have we brought the *Englifh Puritans* to their loweft fall, by divers fharp Laws made againft them, fome fevere Executions done upon them for their tranfgreffing of thofe Laws, their principal Leaders humbled, or cut off by the Sword of Juftice, and the whole *Machina* of their Devices brought to utter ruine : not the lefs active for all this to advance the Caufe, though after a more peaceful and more cunning way; fo much the more dangerous to this Church, becaufe lefs fufpected, but not fo clofely carried as to fcape difcovery. And the firft practife which they fell upon was this that followeth.

36. It hath been an ancient Cuftom in the City of *London*, to have three folemn Sermons preached on *Monday*, *Tuefday*, and *Wednefday*, in the *Eafter* Week, at the place commonly called the *Spittle* ; being a diffolved Hofpital not far from *Bifhops-gate* ; at which the Lord Mayor and Aldermen ufed to be prefent in their Robes, befides a great concourfe of Divines, Gentlemen, and other Citizens : For the performance of which Work a decent Pulpit was erected in an open place, which had been part of the Church-yard ; the ordinary Hearers fitting upon Forms before the Pulpit ; the Lord Mayor, Aldermen, and their Wives, with other Perfons of Quality, in two handfome Galleries ; to which was added, in the year 1594, a fair large Houfe for the reception of the Governours and Children of the Hofpital, founded in the *Grey Friars*, who from thenceforth were tied to attend thofe Sermons. At what time alfo

1594.

also the old Pulpit was taken down, and a new set up, with the Preachers face turned toward the South, which had before been towards the West; for so in former times the Pulpits were generally placed in all Churches of *England*, to the end that the peoples faces, in all acts of Worship, might look toward the East, according to the custom of the Primitive times. Which alteration seemed to be made upon design, that without noise, or any notice taken of it, they might by little and little change the posture of Adoration from the East to the West, or any other point of the Compass, as their humour served. In which first they were shewed the way by Sir *Walter Mildmay*, in his Foundation of the Chapel of *Emanuel* College, 1585. Who being a great favourer of the *Puritan Faction*, gave order for this Chapel to stand North and South, and thereby gave example unto others to affect the like. Which brings into my mind a Project of *Tiberius Gracchus*, one of the most Seditious of the *Roman Tribunes*, for transferring the Supreme Power of the Commonwealth, from the Lords of the Senate, to the People: for, whereas formerly all Orators in the Publick Assemblies, used to address their speeches to the Lords of the Senate, as the Supreme Magistrates, this *Gracchus* turned his face to the common people; and by that Artifice, (saith *Plutarch*) transferred unto them the Supreme Majesty of the *Roman* Empire, without Noise or Tumult.

37. But it is now time to look back towards *Scotland*, where we left them at their highest, and the poor King so fettered or intangled by his own Concessions, that he was not able to act any thing in the Kirk, and very little in the State. He had not very well digested their Refusal to subscribe to his Articles, mentioned in the close of the former Book, when he held an Assembly at *Dundee*, in the end of *April*, 1593; at what time the King, being well informed of the low condition of the *English Puritans*, sent Sir *James Melvin* to them with these two Articles, amongst many others. In the first of which it was declared, ‘ That He would ‘ not suffer the Privilege and Honour of his Crown to be diminished, ‘ and Assemblies to be made when and where they pleased ; therefore ‘ willed them, before the dissolution of the present Assembly, to send ‘ two or three of their number, by whom they should know His mind ‘ touching the time and place of the next Meeting. And in the second it ‘ was required, That an Act should be made, inhibiting Ministers to de-‘ claim in the Pulpit against the proceedings of His Majesty, and the ‘ Lords of his Council; which He conceived he had good reason to desire, ‘ in regard that his Majesties good intentions were well known to them-‘ selves, for maintaining Religion and Justice, and of the easie access ‘ that divers of the Ministry had unto him, by whom they might signifie ‘ their Complaints and Grievances. To the first of which two Articles, they returned this Answer, ‘ That in their Meetings they would follow ‘ the Act of Parliament made by Him in the year preceding. And to the second, they replyed, ‘ That they had made an Act, prohibiting all ‘ Ministers to utter in the Pulpit any rash or irreverent speeches against ‘ His Majesty, or His Council ; but to give their Admonitions upon just ‘ and necessary Causes, in fear, love, and reverence. Which seeming to the King to serve then rather for a colour to excuse their Factiousness,

then

then to lay any juſt reſtraint upon it, he turned a deaf Ear to their Petitions, as well concerning his proceeding with the Popiſh Lords, as againſt the erecting of the Tythes into Temporal Lordſhips. In this Aſſembly alſo they paſſed an Act, prohibiting all ſuch as profeſſed Religion, to traffick in any part of the Dominions of the King of *Spain*, where the Inquiſition was in force. And this to be obſerved under the pain of Excommunication, till His Majeſty could obtain a free Trade for them, without fear of any danger to their Goods or Conſciences. Which being complained of to the King, and by him looked upon as an Intrenchment upon the Royal Prerogative, the Merchants were encouraged to proceed as formerly. In oppoſition whereunto, the Miniſters fulminate their Cenſures, till the Merchants generally made offer to forbear that Trade, as ſoon as their Accounts were made, and that their Creditors in thoſe parts had diſcharged their Debts. They paſs'd another Order alſo in the ſaid Aſſembly, for putting down the *Monday's* Market in the City of *Edenborough*, under pretence that the Sabbath was thereby prophaned. Which ſo diſpleaſed the Shoo-makers, and other Artificers, that they came tumultuouſly to the Miniſters Houſes, and threatned to turn them out of the City, without more ado, if ever that Act were put into execution. For fear whereof, that Project was daſhed for ever after; and thereby an occaſion given unto the Court to affirm this of them, *That Raſcals and Sowters could obtain that at the Miniſters hands, which the King was not able to do in matters far more juſt and reaſonable.* To ſuch audaciouſneſs were they grown upon the ſilly confidence of their own eſtabliſhment, as to put limits upon Trade, diſpoſe of Markets, and proſtitute both King and Coucil, to the luſt of their Preachers. But we will let them run unto the end of their Line, and then pull them back.

38. And firſt, We will begin with the Conſpiracies and Treaſons of *Francis Steward*, Earl of *Bothwell*, Son of *John*, Prior of *Coldingham*, one of the many Baſtards of K. *James* the Fifth; who, by the Daughter and Heir of *James* Lord *Hepborn*, the late Earl of *Bothwell*, became the Father of this *Francis*. A man he was of a ſeditious and turbulent nature, principled in the Doctrines of the *Presbyterians*, and thereby fitted and diſpoſed to run their courſes. At firſt he joyned himſelf to the baniſhed Lords, who ſeized upon the King at *Sterling*; not becauſe he was any way engaged in their former Practiſes, for which they had been forced to flye their Countrey; but becauſe he would ingratiate himſelf with the Lords of that Faction, and gain ſome credit with the Kirk. But being a man alſo of a diſſolute Life, gave ſuch ſcandal to all Honeſt and Religious men, that in the end to gain the Reputation of a Convert, he was contented to be brought to the Stool of Repentance, to make Confeſſion of his Sins, and promiſe Reformation for the time to come. Preſuming now upon the Favour of the Kirk, he conſults with Witches, enquires into the Life of the King, how long he was to Reign, and what ſhould happen in the Kingdom after his deceaſe; & more then ſo, deals with the witch of *Keith*, particularly, to employ her Familiar to diſpatch the King, that he might ſet on foot ſome title to the Crown of that Realm. For which notorious crimes, (& ſo eſteemed by all the Laws both of God & Man) he was committed unto ward, & breaking Priſon was confiſcated, proclaimed traytor & all Intelligence & Commerce interdicted with him. After this, he projects

1585.

1590.

jects a Faction in the Court it self, under pretence of taking down the Power and Pride of the Lord Chancellor then being. But finding himself too weak to atchieve the Enterprise, he departs secretly into *England*. His Faction in the Court being formed with some more Advantage, he is brought privily into the Palace of *Haly-Rood* House, makes himself Master of the Gates, secureth the Fort, and violently attempts to seize the King. But the King hearing of the noise, retired himself to a strong Tower, and caused all the Passages to be locked and barred. Which *Bothwell* not being able to force, he resolves to burn the Palace and the King together. But before Fire could be made ready, the Alarm was taken, the *Edenbourgers* raised, and the Conspiration compelled, with the loss of some of their Lives, to quit the place.

39. The next year he attempts the like at *Falkland*, where he showed himself with a Party of six-score Horse ; but the rest of the Conspirators not appearing, he retires again, is entertained privately by some eminent Persons ; and having much encreased his Faction, lives concealed in *England*. The Queen negotiates his return ; and by the Lord *Burrough* her Ambassador, desires the King to take him to Grace and Favour. Which being denyed, a way is found to bring him into the King's Bed chamber, together with one of his Confederates, with their Swords in their hands, followed immediately by many others of the Faction, by whom the King is kept in a kind of Custody, till he had granted their Desires. At last, upon the Mediation of the *English* Ambassador, and some of the Ministers of *Edenborough*, who were of Counsel in the Plot, the King is brought to condescend to these Conditions; that is to say, *That Pardon should be given to* Bothwell, *and his Accomplices, for all matters past* ; *and that this Pardon should be ratified by Act of Parliament, in* November *following*: *That, in the mean time, the Lord Chancellor, the Lord* Hume, *the Master of* Glammir, *and Sir* George Hume, (who were all thought to favour the Popish Lords) *should be excluded from the Court*. And finally, *That* Bothwell *and all his Party, should be held good Subjects*. But these Conditions being extorted, were not long made good ; Agreed on *August* the 14th, and declared void by a Convention of Estates at *Sterling*, on the 7th of *September*. Some Troubles being raised upon this occasion, and as soon blown over ; *Bothwell* is cited to appear at *Edenborough* ; and failing of his day, is declared Rebel; which only served to animate him to some greater Mischief : For, being under hand assisted by the *English* Ambassador, he prepares new Forces, desires the Lords which were of his Confederacy to do the like, under pretence of banishing the Popish Lords ; but in plain truth to make the King of no signification in the Power of Government. Accompanied with Four hundred Horse, he puts himself into *Leith*, to the great affrightment of the King, who was then at *Edenborough*. But understanding that the rest of his Associates were not drawn together, it was thought good to charge upon him with the Bands of that City, and some Artillery from the Castle, before his numbers were encreased. Which Counsel sped so well, that he lost the day, and therewith all his hopes in *Scotland*, and in *England* too.

40. For Queen *Elizabeth* being sensible at the last of the great Dishonour which she had drawn upon her self by favouring such an Infamous Rebel,

1592.

1593.

1594.

Rebel, caused Proclamation to be made, That no man should receive or harbour him within her Dominions. And the Kirk, moved by her example, and the King's Request, when they perceived that he could be no longer serviceable to their Ends and Purposes, gave Order that the Ministers in all Places should diswade their Flocks from concurring with him for the time to come, or joyning with any other in the like Insurrections against that Authority which was divested by God in His Majesty's Person. The Treasons and Seditious practises of which man I have laid together, the better to express those continual Dangers which were threatned by him to the King; by which he was reduced to the necessity of complying with the desires of the Kirk, settling their Discipline, and in all points conforming to them for his own preservation. But nothing lost the Rebel more, then a new Practise which he had with the Popish Lords, whereby he furnished the King with a just occasion to lay him open to the Ministers, and the rest of the Subjects, in his proper colours, as one that was not acted by a Zeal to Religion, though under that disguise he masked his Ambitious Ends. In fine, being despised by the Queen of *England,* and Excommunicated by the Kirk for joyning with the Popish Lords, he was reduced to such a miserable condition, that he neither knew whom to trust, nor where to flye. Betrayed by those of his own Party, (by whom his Brother *Hercules* was impeached, discovered, and at last brought to Execution in the Streets at *Edenborough*) he fled for shelter into *France,* where finding sorry entertainment, he removed into *Spain,* and afterwards retired to *Naples*; in which he spent the short remainder of his Life in Contempt and Beggery.

41. About this time one of the Ministers, named *Rosse,* uttered divers Treasonable and Irreverent speeches against His Majesty, in a Sermon of his preached at *Perth*; for which the King craved Justice of the next Assembly : and he required this also of them, *That to prevent the like for the times ensuing, the Ministers should be inhibited by some Publick Order, from uttering any irreverent speeches in the Pulpit, against His Majesty's Person, Council, or Estate, under the pain of Deprivation.* This had been often moved before, and was now hearkened to with as little care as in former times. All

1595. which the King got by it, was no more but this, that *Rosse* was only admonished to speak so reverently of His Majesty for the time to come, as might give no just cause of complaint against him. As ill success he had in the next Assembly; to which he recommended some Conditions about the passing of the Sentence of Excommunication; two of which were to this effect: 1. 'That none should be excommunicated for Civil causes, for any Crimes of light importance, or for particular wrongs 'offered to the Ministers, lest the Censure should fall into contempt. '2. That no Summary Excommunication should be thenceforth used, but 'that lawful citations of the Parties should go before, in all manner of 'Causes whatsoever. To both which he received no other Answer, but that the Points were of too great weight to be determined on the sudden, and should be therefore agitated in the next Assembly. In the mean time it was provided, that no Summary Excommunication should be used, but in such occasions in which the Safety of the Church seemed to be in danger. Which Exception much displeased the King, knowing that they
1596. would serve their turn by it, whensoever they pleased. Nor sped he better

ter

ter with them, when he treated ſeverally, then when they were in the
Aſſembly. The Queen of *England* was grown old, and he deſired to be
in good terms with all his Subjects, for bearing down all oppoſition
which might be made againſt his Title after her deceaſe. To which end
he deals with *Robert Bruce*, a Preacher of *Edenborough*, about the calling
home the Popiſh Lords, men of great Power and Credit in their ſeveral
Countreys, who had been baniſhed the laſt year for holding ſome intelligence with the Catholick King. *Bruce* excepts only againſt *Huntley*,
whom the King ſeemed to favour above all the reſt ; and poſitively declared *That the King muſt loſe him, if he called home* Huntley ; *for that it was
impoſſible to keep them both.* And yet this *Bruce* was reckoned for a Moderate man, one of the quieteſt and beſt-natur'd of all the Pack. What
was the iſſue of this buſineſs, we ſhall ſee hereafter.

42. In the mean time let us paſs over into *France*, and look upon the
Actions of the *Hugonots* there, of whoſe deſerting their new King we
have ſpoke of before. And though they afterwards afforded him ſome
Supplies both of Men and Money, when they perceived him backed by
the Queen of *England*, and thereby able to maintain a defenſive War
without their aſſiſtance ; yet they did it in ſo poor a manner, as made
him utterly deſpair of getting his deſired peace by an abſolute Victory.
In which perplexity he beholds his own ſafe condition, his Kingdom
waſted by a long and tedeous War ; invaded, and in part poſſeſſed by the
Forces of *Spain*; new Leagues encreaſing every day both in ſtrength and
number, and all upon the point of a new Election, or otherwiſe to divide the Provinces amongſt themſelves. To prevent which, he reconciles himſelf to the Church of *Rome*, goes perſonally to the Maſs ; and
in all other publick Offices which concerned Religion, conformed himſelf unto the directions of the Pope. And for ſo doing he gives this
account to *Wilks*, the Queens Embaſſador, ſent purpoſely to expoſtulate
with him upon this occaſion ; that is to ſay, That 800 of the Nobility,
and no fewer then nine Regiments of the Proteſtant Party, who had put
themſelves into the Service of his Predeceſſor, returned unto their ſeveral homes, and could not be induced to ſtay with him upon any perſwa-
ſions. That ſuch of the Proteſtants as he had taken at the ſame time to
his Privy Council, were ſo intent on their own buſineſs, that they ſeldom vouchſafed their preſence at the Council Table : ſo that being already forſaken by thoſe on whom he relyed, and fearing to be forſaken
by the Papiſts alſo, he was forced to run upon that courſe which unavoidable neceſſity had compelled him to : and finally, that being thus
neceſſitated to a change of Religion, he rather choſe to make it look like
his own free Act, that he might thereby free the Doctrine of the Proteſtants from thoſe Aſperſions which he conceived muſt otherwiſe needs
have fallen upon it, if that Converſion had been wrought upon him by
Diſpute and Argument ; for hearkening whereunto he had bound
himſelf when he firſt took the Crown upon him. If by this means the *Hugonots* in *France* ſhall fall to as low an ebb as the Fortunes of their Brethren did in *England* at the ſame time ; they can lay the blame on nothing but their own Ingratitude, their Diſobedience to their King, and
the *Genevian* Principles that were rooted in them, which made them e-
nemies to the Power and Guidance of all Soveraign Princes. But the
King

King being still in heart of his own Religion, or at least exceeding favourable to all those that professed the same ; he willingly passed over all unkindness which had grown between them : and by his countenance or connivence; gave them such advantages as made them able to dispute the point with his Son and Successor, whether they would continue Subjects to the Crown, or not.

43. In the *Low-Countreys* all things prospered with the *Presbyterians*, who then thrive best when they involve whole Nations in Blood and Sacrilege. By whose example the *Calvinians* take up Arms in the City of *Embden*, renounce all obedience to their Prince, and put themselves into the Form of a Commonwealth. This *Embden* is the principal City of the Earl of *East-Eriesland*, (situate on the mouth of the River *Emns*, called *Amasus* by *Latin* Writers) and from thence denominated. Beautified with a Haven so deep and large, that the greatest Ships with full sail are admitted into it. The People rich, the Buildings generally fair, both private and publick ; especially the Town-Hall, and the stately Castle : Which last being situate on a rising-ground, near the mouth of the Haven, and strongly fortified toward the Town, had for long time been the Principal Seat of the Earls of that Province. The second Earl hereof, called *Ezard*, when he had governed this Countrey for the space of 60 years, or thereabouts, did first begin to introduce the Doctrines of *Luther* into his Estates, *Anno* 1525. But being old, he left the Work to be accomplished by *Enno* his eldest Son, who first succeeded in that Earldom ; and using the assistance of *Hardimbergius*, a Moderate and Learned man, established the *Augustine* Confession in the City of *Embden*; and afterwards in all places under his command, prohibiting the exercise of all Religion, but the *Lutheran* only. Which Prohibition notwithstanding some *Anabaptists* from the Neighbouring *Westphalia*, found way to plant themselves in *Embden*, where liberty of Trade was freely granted to all comers ; which allured thither also many Merchants and Artificers, with their Wives and Families, out of the next adjoyning Provinces of *Holland*, *Zealand*, and *West-Friesland*, then subject to the King of *Spain*. Who being generally *Calvinians* in point of Doctrine, were notwithstanding suffered to plant there also, in regard of the great benefit which accrued unto it by their Trade and Manufactures. But nothing more encreased the Power and Wealth of that City, than the Trade of *England*, removed from *Antwerp* thither, on occasion of the *Belgick* Troubles, and the great fear they had conceived of the Duke of *Alva*, who seemed to breathe nothing but destruction unto their Religion. And though the *English* Trade was removed not long after unto *Hambourgh*, upon the hope of greater Priviledges and Immunities then they had at *Embden*, yet still they kept a Factory in it, which added much to the improvement of their Wealth and Power : insomuch that the Inhabitants of this Town only are affirmed to have sixty Ships of 100 Tun a piece, and 600 lesser Barks of their own, besides 700 Busses and Fishing-Boats, maintained for the most part by their Herring-fishing on the Coast of *England*.

44. Having attained unto this Wealth, they grew proud withal, and easily admitting the *Calvinian* Doctrines, began to introduce also the *Genevian* Discipline, connived at by *Ezardus* the second, the Son of *Enno*,

in respect of the profit which redounded by them to his Exchequer, though they began to pinch upon him to the diminution of his power. In which condition it remained till his marriage with *Catharine* the Daughter of *Guſtavus Ericus*, King of *Sweden*, who being zealouſly addicted to the *Lutheran* Forms, and ſenſible of thoſe great incroachments which had been made upon the Earls Temporal Juriſdiction by the *Conſiſtorians*, perſwaded him to look better to his own Authority, and to regain what he had loſt by that Connivence.　Something was done for the recovering of his Power, but it went on ſlowly, hoping to compaſs that by time and diſſimulation, which he could not eaſily obtain by force of Arms. After whoſe death, and the ſhort Government of *Enno* the ſecond, the matter was more ſtoutly followed by *Rodolphus*, the Nephew of *Catharine* who did not only curb the *Conſiſtorians* in the exerciſe of their Diſcipline, but queſtioned many of thoſe Priviledges which the unwarineſs of his Predeceſſors had indulged unto them.　The *Calvinians* had by this time made ſo ſtrong a Party, that they were able to remonſtrate againſt their Prince, complaining in the ſame, That the Earl had violated their Priviledges, and infringed their Liberties: That he had interpoſed his power againſt Right and Reaſon, in matters which concerned the Church, and belonged to the Conſiſtory. That he aſſumed unto himſelf the power of diſtributing the Alms or publick Collections by which they uſe to bind the poor to depend upon them.　That he prohibited the exerciſe of all Religions, except only the Confeſſion of *Auſberg*: And that he would not ſtand to the Agreement which was made betwixt them, for interdicting all Appeals to the Chamber of *Spires*.　Having prepared the way by this Remonſtrance, they take an opportunity when the Earl was abſent, arm themſelves, and ſeize by force upon his Caſtle, demoliſhed part of it which looks toward the Town, and poſſeſt themſelves of all the Ordnance, Arms, and Ammunition, with an intent hereafter to employ them againſt him. And this being done, they govern all Affairs in the Name of the Senate, without relation to their Prince; making themſelves a Free-Eſtate, or Commonwealth, like their *Belgick* Neighbors.

45. Extreamly moved with this affront, and not being able otherwiſe to reduce them to a ſenſe of their duty, he borrows Men and Arms from *Lubeck*, to compel them to it.　With which aſſiſtance he erects a Fort on the further ſide of the Haven, to ſpoil their Trade, and, by impoveriſhing the people, to regain the Town.　The Senate hereupon ſend abroad their Edicts to the Nobility and Commons of *Eaſt-Friesland* it ſelf, requiring them not to aid their own lawful Prince, with Men, Arms, or Mony; threatning them, if they did the contrary, to ſtop the courſe of all Proviſions which they had from their City; and, by breaking down their Dams and Sluces, to let the Ocean in upon them, and drown all their Country.　Which done, they make their Applications to the States of *Holland*, requiring their aſſiſtance in that common Cauſe, to which they had been moſt encouraged by their Example; not doubting of their Favour to a City of their own Religion, united to them by a long intercourſe of Trade, and reſemblance of Manners; and not to be deſerted by them, without a manifeſt betraying of their own Security. All this the States had under their conſideration.　But they conſider this withall, That if they ſhould aſſiſt the *Embdeners* in a publick way, the

[margin: 1594.]

the Earl would prefently have recourfe for fome aid from the *Spaniard*, which might draw a War upon them on that fide where they lay moft open. Therefore they fo contrived the matter, with fuch Art and Cunning, that carrying themfelves no otherwife then as Arbiters and Umpires between the Parties, they difcharged fome Companies of Soldiers which they had in *Weft-Friefland*, who prefently put themfelves into the Pay of the *Embdens*, and thereby caufed the Earl to defift from his Intrenchments on the other fide of the Haven. After which followed nothing but Wars and Troubles between the City and the Earl, till the year 1606. At what time, by the Mediation of the *Englifh* Embafsador, and fome other Honourable Friends, the differences were compromifed to this effect: That all the Ordnance, Arms, and Ammunition, which were found in the Caftle, fhould be reftored unto the Earl. That he fhould have to his own ufe the whole Profit of the Impofts which were laid on Wine, and half the benefit of thofe Amercements or Fines which fhould be raifed upon Delinquents, together with the fole Royalties both of Fifhing and Hunting. And on the other fide, That the *Embdeners* fhould have free Trade, with all the Profits and Emoluments belonging to it, which fhould be granted to them by Letters Patents. But for admitting him to any part of the Publick Government, or making reftitution of his Houfe or Caftles, the ancient Seat of his abode, as there was nothing yeelded or agreed on then, fo could he never get poffeffion of them from that time to this. Which faid, we muft crofs over again into the Ifle of *Brittain*, where we fhall find the *Englifh Puritans* climbing up by fome new devices, and the *Scottifh Presbyterians* tumbling down from their former height, till they were brought almoft to as low a fall as their *Englifh* Brethren.

The End of the Ninth Book.

AERIUS REDIVIVUS:
OR THE
HISTORY
OF THE
Presbyterians.

LIB. X.

Containing

A Relation of their Plots and Practises in the Realm of England: *Their horrible Insolencies, Treasons, and Seditions in the Kingdom of* Scotland; *from the Year* 1595 *to the Year* 1603.

THE *English Puritans* having sped so ill in a course of violence, were grown so wise as to endeavour the subverting of that Fort by an undermining, which they had no hope to take by storm or Battery. And the first course they fell upon, besides the Artifices lately mentioned, for altering the posture of the Preacher, in the *Spittle* Sermons; and that which was intended as a consequent to it, was the Design of Dr. *Bound,* (though rather carried under his Name, then of his devising) for lessening, by degrees, the Reputation of the ancient Festivals. The Brethren had tryed many ways to suppress them formerly,

formerly, as having too much in them of the Superſtitions of the Church of *Rome* ; but they had found no way ſucceſsful till they fell on this ; which was, To ſet on foot ſome new Sabbath-Doctrine ; and by advancing the Authority of the Lords-Day Sabbath, to cry down the reſt. Some had been hammering on this Anvil ten years before ; and had procured the Mayor and Aldermen of *London* to preſent a Petition to the Queen for the ſuppreſſing of all Plays and Interludes on the Sabbath-day, (as they pleaſed to call it) within the Liberties of their City. The gaining of which point, made them hope for more, and ſecretly to retail thoſe Speculations which afterward *Bound* ſold in groſs, by publiſhing his Treatiſe of the Sabbath, which came out this year 1595. And as this Book was publiſhed for other Reaſons, ſo more particularly for decrying the yearly Feſtivals, as appears by this paſſage in the ſame, viz. *That he ſeeth not where the Lord hath given any Authority to his Church, ordinarily and perpetually, to ſanctifie any day, except that which he hath ſanctified himſelf* : And makes it an eſpecial Argument againſt the goodneſs of Religion in the Church of *Rome,* That to the Seventh day they had joyned ſo many other days, and made them equal with the Seventh, if not ſuperior thereunto, as well in the ſolemnity of Divine Offices, as reſtraint from labour. So that we may perceive by this, what their intent was from the very beginning, To cry down the Holy-days as ſuperſtitious, Popiſh Ordinances, that ſo their new-found Sabbath being left alone, (and Sabbath now it muſt be called) might become more eminent: Some other ends they might have in it, as, the compelling of all perſons of what rank ſoever, to ſubmit themſelves unto the yoke of their Sabbath-rigors, whom they deſpaired of bringing under their *Presbyteries* : Of which more hereafter.

2. Now for the Doctrine, it was marſhalled in theſe Poſitions ; that is to ſay, That the Commandment of ſanctifying every Seventh day, as in the *Moſaical* Decalogue, is Natural, Moral, and Perpetual. That when all other things in the Jewiſh Church were ſo changed, that they were clean taken away, this ſtands, the obſervation of the Sabbath. And though Jewiſh and Rabinical this Doctrine was, it carried a fair ſhew of Piety, at the leaſt in the opinion of the common people, and ſuch as did not ſtand to examine the true grounds thereof, but took it up on the appearance ; ſuch as did judge thereof, not by the workmanſhip of the Stuff, but the gloſs and colour. In which it is not ſtrange to ſee how ſuddenly men were induced not only to give way unto it, but without more ado to abet the ſame ; till in the end, and that in very little time, it grew the moſt bewitching error, the moſt popular infatuation, that ever was infuſed into the people of *England* : For what did follow hereupon, but ſuch monſtrous Paradoxes, and thoſe delivered in the Pulpit, as would make every good man tremble at the hearing of them : It being preached at a Market-Town, (as my Author tells me) *That to do any ſervile work or buſineſs on the Lords day, was as great a ſin as to kill a man, or commit Adultery.* In *Somerſetſhire, That to throw a Bowl on the Lords day, was as great a ſin as to kill a man.* In *Norfolk, That to make a Feaſt, or dreſs a Wedding-dinner on the ſame, was as great a ſin as for a Father to take a knife and cut his childs throat.* And in *Suffolk, That to ring more Bells then one on the Lords day, was as great a ſin as might be.* Some of which Preachers being complained of.

of, occasioned a more strict enquiry into all the rest; and not into their Persons only, but their Books and Pamphlets; insomuch that both Archbishop *Whitgift*, and Chief Justice *Popham*, commanded these Books to be called in, and neither to be Printed nor made common for the time to come. Which strict proceedings notwithstanding, this Doctrine became more dispersed then can be imagined, and possibly might encrease the more for the opposition; no System of Divinity, no Book of Catechetical Doctrine, from thenceforth published, in which these Sabbath Speculations were not pressed on the Peoples Consciences.

3. Endearing of which Doctrines as formerly to advance their Elderships, they spared no place or Text of Scripture where the Word Elder did occurre; and without going to the Heralds, had framed a Pedigree thereof from *Jethro*, from *Noahs* Ark, and from *Adam* finally. So did these men proceed in their new Devices; publishing out of Holy Writ, both the Antiquity and the Authority of their Sabbathday. No passage of Gods Book unransacked, where there was mention of a Sabbath; whether the Legal Sabbath charged upon the *Jews*, or the Spiritual Sabbath of the Soul from sin, which was not fitted and applied to the present purpose; though if examined as it ought, with no less reason then *Paveant illi, & non paveam ego*, was by an ignorant Priest alledged from Scripture, to prove that his Parishioners ought to *pave* the Chancel. And on the confidence of those Proofs they did presume exceedingly of their success, by reason of the general entertainment which those Doctrines found with the common people, who looked upon them with as much regard, and no less reverence, then if they had been sent immediately from the Heavens themselves, for encrease of Piety. Possest with which, they greedily swallowed down the Hook which was baited for them.

4. A Hook indeed, which had so fastened them to those men who love to fish in troubled waters, that by this Artifice there was no small hope conceived amongst them, to fortifie their Side, and make good that Cause, which till this trim Device was so thought of, was almost grown desperate. By means whereof, they brought so great a bondage on all sorts of people, that a greater never was imposed on the *Jews* themselves, though they had pinned their Consciences on the Sleeves of the Scribes and Pharisees. But then withall, by bringing all sorts of people into such a bondage, they did so much improve their power, and encrease their Party, that they were able at the last to oppose Edicts of the two next Kings, for tolerating lawful sports upon that day, and to confirm some of their Sabbatarian Rigours by Act of Parliament.

5. From this Design let us proceed to the next, which was briefly this. When the *Genevian-English* resolved to erect their Discipline, it was thought requisite to prepare the way unto it, by introducing the *Calvinian* Doctrines of *Predestination*, that so mens Judgments being formed & possessed by the one, they might the more easily be enclined to embrace the other, so long connived at by the Supream Governours of the Church and State, to which they were exceeding serviceable against the Pope; that in the end those Doctrines which at first were counted *Aliens*, came by degrees to be received as *Denizons*, and at last as *Natives*. For being supposed to contain nothing in them contrary to Faith and Manners,

ners, they were first commended to the Church as *probable*, next imposed as *necessary*; and finally, obtruded on the people as her Natural
Doctrines.　And possibly they might in time have found a general entertainment beyond exception, if the *Calvinian*-spirit (being impatient
of the least opposition) could have permitted other men to enjoy that
liberty which they had took unto themselves, and not compelled them
to Apologize in their own defences, and thereby shew the Reasons of
dissenting from them.　One of the first Examples whereof, (for I pass
by the branglings between *Champney* and *Crowley*, as long since forgotten) was the complaint of *Travers* to the Lords of the Council, a-
gainst incomparable *Hooker*.　In whom he infaulteth this, amongst o-
ther things, *That he had taught another Doctrine of Predestination, then what
was laid down in the Word of God, as it was understood by all the Churches which
professed the Gospel.* to which it was replyed, by that learned man " That
" the matter was not uttered by him in a blind Ally, where there was
" none to hear it who either had judgment or authority to comptroul the
" same; or covertly insinuated by some gliding sentence; but that it
" was pulickly delivered at St. *Pauls Cross* : not hudled in amongst o-
" ther matters, to the end it might pass without observation; but, that
" it was opened, proved, and for some reasonable time insisted on.　And
" therefore, that he could not see how the Lord Bishop of *London*, that
" was present at it, could neither excuse so great a fault, or patiently
" hear without rebuke then, and controulment afterwards, that any
" man should preach doctrine *contrary to the Word of God*; especially if the
" word of God be so understood, not by the private interpretation of
" some, as two or three men, or by a special construction received in
" some few Books; but as it is understood *by all Churches professing the*
" *Gospel*, and therefore even by our own Church amongst the rest.

6. This hapned in the year 1591 or thereabouts, somewhat before
the breakings out of the stirrs at *Cambridge*, occasioned by a Treatise
published by *William Perkins*, a well-known Divine, (but withall, a
professed *Presbyterian*) entituled, *Armilla Aurea*, or *The Golden Chain*;
*containing the Order of the Causes of Salvation and Damnation, according to
the Word of God.*　Maintaining in this Book the Doctrine of the *Supra-
lapsarians*, and countenanced therein by Dr. *Whitacres* the Queen's Professor; some opposition was soon made by Dr. *Baroe*, Professor for the
Lady *Margaret* in the same University.　Which *Baroe* being by birth a
French-man, but being very well studied in the Writings of the Ancient
1595. Fathers, had constantly for the space of more then twenty years maintained a different Doctrine of Predestination, from that which had been
taught by *Calvin* and his Disciples; but he was never quarrelled for it
till the year 1595, and then not quarrelled for it, but in the person of
one *Barret*, who in a Sermon at St. *Maries* Church, had preached such
Doctrines as were not pleasing unto *Perkin*, *Whitacre*, and the rest of that
Party.　For which being questioned and condemned to a Recantation,
he rather chose to quit his place in the University, then to betray his
own Judgment and the Church of *England* by a Retraction.　The rest
of *Baroe*'s Followers not well pleased with these harsh proceedings, begin
to shew themselves more publickly then before they did; which made
Baroe think himself obliged to appear more visibly in the head of his

Company, and to encounter openly with Dr. *Whitacre*, whom he beheld as the Chief Leader of the opposite Forces, And the heats grew so high at last, that the *Calvinians* thought it necessary in point of Prudence, to effect that by Power and Favour, which they could not obtain by force of Argument.   To which end they first addressed themselves to the Lord Treasurer *Burleigh* then being their Chancellor, with the disturbances made by *Barret*, thereby preparing him to hearken to such further motions as should be made by them in pursuit of that Quarrel.

7. But finding little comfort there, they resolved to steer their course by another Compass. And having pre-possest the most Reverend Archbishop *Whitgift* with the turbulent carriage of those men, the affronts given to Dr. *Whitacre*, whom (for his learned and laborious Writings against Cardinal *Bellarmine*) he most highly favoured ; and the great Inconveniences like to grow by that publick Discord ; they gave themselves good hope of composing those differences, not by way of an accommodation, but an absolute Conquest.   And to this end they dispatched to him certain of their number, in the name of the rest, such as were interested in the Quarrels, (Dr. *Whitacre* himself for one, and therefore like to stir hard for obtaining their ends.)   The Articles to which they had reduced the whole state of the business, being ready drawn, and there wanting nothing to them but the Face of Authority, wherewith, as with *Medusas* head, to confound their Enemies, and turn their Adversaries into stones.   And that they might be sent back with the Face of Authority, the most Reverend Archbishop, calling unto him Dr. *Flecher* Bishop of *Bristol*, then newly elected unto *London* ; and Dr. *Richard Vaughan*, Lord Elect of *Bangor* ; together with Dr. *Trindal*, Dean of *Ely*; Dr. *Whitacre*, and the rest of the Divines which came from *Crambridge*; proposed the said Articles to their consideration, at his House in *Lambeth*, on the tenth of *November* ; by whom these Articles (from thenceforth called the *Nine Articles of Lambeth*)were presently agreed upon, and sent down to *Cambridge*, not as the Doctrines of the Church, but as a necessary expedient to compose those differences which had been raised amongst the Students of that Uuiversity.   And so much was acknowledged by the Archbishop himself, when he was questioned by the Queen for his actings in it.   For so it was, that the Queen being made acquainted with all that passed, became exceedingly offended at the Innovation ; and was upon the point of causing all of them to be attainted in a *Præmunire* ; but by the mediation of some Friends of *Whitgift's*, and the high opinion which she had of his Parts and Person, she was willing to admit him to his defence.   And he accordingly declared, in all humble manner, ' That he and his Associates had not made any Canons, ' Articles, or Decrees, with an intent that they should serve hereafter ' for a standing-Rule to direct the Church ; but only had resolved on ' some Propositions to be sent to *Cambridge*, for quieting some unhappy ' differences in that University.   With which Answer Her Majesty being somewhat pacified, commanded notwithstanding, That he should speedily recall and suppress those Articles : Which was performed with such Care and Diligence, that a Copy of them was not to be found for a long time after.

8. As

8. As for the Articles themselves, they were so contrived, that both the *Subbatarians*, and the *Supra-lapsarians*, (very considerably at odds amongst themselves) might be sheltered under them, to the intent that both may be secured from the common Adversary. Which Articles I find translated in these following words. *viz.*

I. *God from Eternity hath predestinated certain men unto life ; certain men he hath reprobated.*

II. *The moving or efficient Cause of Predestination unto life is not the fore-sight of Faith, or of Perseverance, or of Good Works, or of any thing that is in the person predestinated ; but only the Good Will and Pleasure of God.*

III. *There is predetermined a certain number of the Predestinate, which can neither be augmented nor diminished.*

IV. *Those who are not predestinate to salvation, shall be necessarily damned for their sins.*

V. *A true, living, and justifying faith, and the Spirit of God justifying, is not extinguished, falleth not away, it vanisheth not away in the Elect, either totally, or finally.*

VI. *A man truly faithful, that is, such an one who is endued with a justifying faith ; is certain, with the full assurance of Faith, of the remission of his Sins, and of his everlasting salvation by Christ.*

VII. *Saving Grace is not given, is not granted, is not communicated to all men, by which they may be saved if they will.*

VIII. *No man can come unto Christ, unless it be given unto him, and unless the Father shall draw him ; and all men are not drawn by the Father, that they may come to the Son.*

IX. *It is not in the will or power of every one to be saved.*

9. Such were the Articles of *Lambeth*, so much insisted on by those of the *Calvinian* Faction in succeeding times, as comprehending in them the chief Heads of *Calvins* Doctrine, in reference to the points of Divine Election and Reprobation ; of Universal Grace, and the impossibility of a total or a final falling from the true justifying-faith ; which were the subject of the Controversies betwixt *Baroe* and *Whitacre*. Some have adventured hereupon to ranck this most Reverend Archbishop in the List of these *Calvinists*; conceiving that he could not otherwise have agreed to those Articles, if he had not been himself of the same Opinion. And possible it is, that he might not look so far into them, as to consider the ill consequenses which might follow on them ; or that he might prefer the pacifying of some present Dissenters, before the apprehension of such Inconveniences as were more remote ; or else, according to the custom of all such as be in Authority, he thought it necessary to preserve *Whitacre* in power and credit against all such as did oppose him ; the Merit and Abilities of the man being very eminent. For if this Argument wer good, it might as logically be inferred, That he was a *Jesuit* or a *Melanchthonian* at the least in these points of Doctrine, because he countenanced those men who openly and professedly had
oppofed

opposed the *Calvinian*. In which respect, as he took part with *Hooker* at the Council Table against the Complaints and Informations of *Travers*, as before is said; so he received into his service Mr. *Samuel Harsnet*, then being one of the Fellows of *Pembroke* Hall; who in a Sermon preached at St. *Pauls Cross* the 27*th* of *October* 1584, had so diffected the whole *Zuinglian* Doctrine of Reprobation, as made it feem ugly in the ears of his Auditors, as afterwards in the eyes of all Spectators when it came to be Printed.   Which man he did not only entertain as his Chaplain at large, but used his Service in his House as a Servant in ordinary, employed him in many of his Affairs; and finally commended him to the care of King *James*; by whom he was first made Master of *Pembroke* Hall, and afterwards preferred to the See of *Chichefter*, from thence tranflated to *Norwich*, and at laft to *York*.

10. No lefs remarkable was this year for the repairing of the Crofs in *Cheapside*; which having been defaced in the year 1581, and fo continued ever fince, was now thought fit to be reftored to its former beauty.   A Crofs it was of high efteem, and of good Antiquity, erected by K. *Edward* the firft, *Anno* 1290, in honour of Queen *Elienor* his beloved Wife, whofe Body had there refted, as it was removed to the place of her Burial.   But this Crofs being much decayed, *John Hatherly*, Lord Mayor of *London* in the year 1441, procured leave of King *Henry* the 6*th* to take it down, and to re-edfie the fame in more beautiful manner for the greater honour of the City. Which leave being granted, and two hundred Fodder of Lead allowed him toward the beginning of the Work, it was then curioufly wrought at the charge of divers wealthy Citizens, adorned with many large and maffie Images; but more efpecially advanced by the Munificence of *John Fifher* Mercer, who gave fix hundred Marks for the finifhing of it.   The whole Structure being reared in the fecond year of K. *Henry* the 7*th*, *Anno* 1486, was after gilded over in the year 1522, for the entertainment of the Emperour *Charles* the fifth; new burnifhed againft the Coronation of Q. *Anne Bullen*, *Anno* 1533; as afterwards at the Coronation of King *Edward* the fixth: and finally, at the Magnificent Reception of King *Philip* 1554. And having for fo long time continued an undefaced Monument of Chriftian Piety, was quarrelled by the *Puritans* of the prefent Reign; who being emulous of the Zeal of the *French Calvinians* whom they found to have demolifhed all Croffes wherefoever they came; they caufed this Crofs to be prefented by the Jurors in feveral *Ward-Motes*, for ftanding in the High-way to the hindering of Carts and other Carriages: but finding no remedy in that courfe, they refolved to apply themfelves unto another.   In purfuance whereof they firft fet upon it in the night, *June* 21, *Anno* 1581, violently breaking and defacing all the loweft Images which were placed round about the fame; that is to fay, the Images of Chrift's Refurrection, of the Virgin *Mary*, K. *Edward* the Confeffor, &c.   But more particularly, the Image of the bleffed Virgin was at that time robbed of her Son, and her Arms broke by which fhe held him in her Lap, and her whole Body haled with ropes and left likely to fall. Proclamation prefently was made, with promife of Reward to any one that could or would difcover the chief Actors in it. But without effect.

11. In

11. In which condition it remained till this present year, when the said Image was again faltened and repaired ; the Images of Chrilts Resurrection, and the rest continuing broken as before. And on the East fide of the said Crofs where the fleps had been, was then fet up a curious wrought Tabernacle of gray Marble, and in the fame an Alabafter Image of *Diana*, from whofe naked breafts there trilled continually fome ftreams of Water conveyed unto it from the *Thames*. But the madnefs of this Faction could not fo be ftayed; for the next year (that I may lay all things together which concern this Crofs) a new mifhapen Son, as born out of time all naked was put into the Arms of the Virgin's Image, to ferve for matter of derifion to the common people. And in the year 1599 the Figure of the Crofs erected on the top of the Pile, was taken down by Publick Order, under pretence that otherwife it might have fallen and endangered many ; with an intent to raife a *Pyramis* or Spire in the place thereof : which coming to the knowledge of the Lords of the Council, they directed their Letters to the Lord Mayor then being, whom they required in the Queen's Name to caufe the faid Crofs to be repaired and advanced as formerly. But the Crofs ftill remaining headlefs for a year and more, and the Lords not enduring any longer fuch a grofs Contempt, they re-inforced their Letters to the next Lord Mayor, dated *December* 24, in the year 1600. In which they willed and commanded him, in purfuance of Her Majefties former directions, to caufe the faid Crofs without more delay to be readvanced ; refpecting in the fame, the great Antiquity and Continuance of that ftately Monument erected for an Enfign of our Chriftianity. In obedience unto which Commands, a Crofs was forthwith framed of Timber, cover'd with Lead, and fet up and gilded ; and the whole body of the Pile new cleanfed from filth and rubbifh : Which gave fuch frefh difpleafure to fome zealous Brethren, that within twelve nights after the Image of the Bleffed Virgin was again defaced by plucking off her Crown, and almoft her head; difpoffeffing her of her naked Child, and ftabbing her into the breaft, *&c.* Moft ridiculous Follies.

1596.

12. In the beginning of the year, we find Sir *Thomas Egerton* advanced to the Cuftody of the Great Seal of *England*, Lord Chancellor in effect, under the Title of Lord Keeper ; to which place he was admitted on the fixth of *May*, to the great joy of the Archbifhop, who always looked upon him as a lover of Learning, a conftant favourer of the Clergy, zealous for the eftablifhed Government, and a faithful Friend unto himfelf upon all occafions. Who being now Peered with the Lord Chancellor and the Earl of *Effex*, affured of the good will of the Lord Treafurer *Burleigh*, and ftrengthened with the Friendfhip of Sir *Robert Cicil*, Principal Secretary of State, was better fortified then ever. And at this time Her Majefty laying on his fhoulders the burden of all Church-Concernments, told him, It fhould fall on his Soul and Confcience, if any fell out amifs ; in that by reafon of her age fhe had thought good to eafe her felf of that part of her cares, and looked that he fhould yield an account thereof to Almighty God. So that upon the matter, he was all in all for all Church Affairs, and more efpecially in the difpofing of Bifhopricks, and other Ecclefiaftical Promotions. For his firft entrance on which truft, he prefers Dr. *Thomas Bilfon* to the See of *Worcefter*, who

received

received his Episcopal Confecration on the 13th of *June*, *Anno* 1596.
and by his Favour was tranflated within two years after to the Church
of *Winchefter*. He advanced alfo his old Friend Dr. *Richard Bancroft*
to the See of *London*; whom he confecrated on the 8th of *May*, *Anno*
1597, that he might always have him near him for Advice and Counfel. Which Famous Prelate (that I may note this by the way) was
born at *Farnworth* in the County of *Lancafter*, Baptized *September* 1544.
His Father was *John Bancroft* Gentleman, his Mother *Mary Curwin*,
Daughter of *John* Brother of *Hugh Curwin* Bifhop of *Oxon*, whofe eldeft
Son was *Chriftoper* the Father of Dr. *John Bancroft*, who after dyed Bifhop of that See, *Anno* 1640. But this *Richard* of whom now we fpeak,
being placed by his Unkle Dr. *Curwin* in *Chrift's Colledge* in *Cambridge*,
from thence removed to *Jefus Colledge* in the fame Univerfity, becaufe
the other was fufpected to incline to *Novellifm*; his Unkle Dr. *Curwin*
being preferred to the Archbifhoprick of *Dublin*, made him a Prebend
of that Church: after whofe death he became Chaplain to *Cox* Bifhop
of *Ely*, who gave him the Rectory of *Teverfham* not far from *Cambridge*.
Being thus put into the Road of preferment, he proceeded Batchellor
of Divinity *Anno* 1580, and Doctor in the year 1585: About which
time he put himfelf into the Service of Sir *Chriftopher Hatton*, by whofe
recommendation he was made a Prebend of St. *Peters* in *Weftminfter* 1592.
From whence he had the eafier paffage to St. *Pauls* in *London*.

13. About this time brake out the Juglings of *John Darrel* who without any lawful Calling, had fet up a new Trade of Lecturing in the
Town of *Nottingham*: and, to advance fome Reputation to his Perfon,
pretends an extraordinary Power in cafting out Devils. He practifed
firft on one *Catharine Wright*, *An*, 1586. But finding fome more powerful Practifes to be then on foot in favour of the *Presbyterian* Difcipline,
he laid that Project by till all others failed him. But in the year 1592,
he refumes the Practife, hoping to compafs that by Wit and *Legerde-
main*, which neither *Cartwright* by his Learning, nor *Snape* by his Diligence, *Penry* by his Seditions, or *Hacket* by his damnable Treafons, had
the good fortune to effect. He firft begins with *William Summers*, an
unhappy Boy, whom he firft met at *Afhby de la Zauch* in the County of
————— Him he inftructs to do fuch Tricks, as might make him
feem to be poffeft; acquaints him with the manner of the Fits which
were obferved by *Catharine Wright*, delivers them in writing to him for
his better remembrance, wifhed him to put the fame practife, and told
him, that in fo doing he fhould not want. But either finding no great
forwardnefs in the Boy to learn his Leffon, or being otherwife difcouraged from proceeding with him; he applies himfelf to one *Thomas Darling*, commonly called the Boy of *Burton*, *Anno* 1596, whom he found
far more dexterous in Diffimulations; the Hiftory of whofe Poffeffings
and Difpoffeffings was writ at large by *Jeffe Bee*, a Religious fad Lyar;
contracted by one *Denifon*, a Countrey Minifter; feen and allowed by *Hil-
derfham*, (one of the principal fticklers in the Caufe of *Presbytery*) & Printed
with good leave and liking of *Darrel* himfelf; who growing famous by
this means, remembers *Summers* his firft Scholar; to whom he gives a fecond meeting at the Park of *Afhby*, teacheth him to act better then before
he did; fends him to fee the Boy at *Burton*, that he might learn him to behave

have himself on the like occasions. And finding him at last grown perfect, sends him to *Nottingham*, with intimation that he should make mention of him in his fits. *Darrel* is hereupon made Lecturer of the Town of *Nottingham*, (that beinst the Fish for which he angled) as being thought a marvellous Bug to scare the Devil. And though he had no lawfull Calling in that behalf; yet was this given out to be so comfortable a Vocation, and so warrantable in the sight of God, that very few Ministers have had the like; there being no Preacher setled there(as he gave it out) since her Majesties Reign; as if neither Parsons, nor Vicars, nor any that bear such Popish Names, might pass for Preachers.

14. After this, he pretends occasion for a journey to *Lancashire*; where he finds seven women possest with Devils, and out of every one of them was affirmed to have cast as many as had entred into *Mary Magdalen*. Of this he published a Book, *Anno* 1600, though the Exploit was done in this present year, *Anno* 1597. These things being noised abroad by his Confederates, this extraordinary Faculty of casting out Devils was most highly magnified and cryed up both in Sermons and Printed Pamphlets, as a Candle lighted by God upon a Candlestick in the heart and centre of the Land. And no small hopes were built upon it, that it would prove a matter of as great consequence as ever did any such Work that the Lord gave extraordinarily since the time that he restored the Gospel, and as profitable to all that profess the knowledge of Jesus Christ. Now what this Plot was, may appear by this which is deposed by Mr. *Moor*, one of Mr. *Darrels* great Admirers and Companions, viz. *That when a Prayer was read out of the Common Prayer Book, in the hearing of those which were possessed in* Lancashire, *the Devils in them were little moved with it : but afterwards, when Mr.* Darrel *and one Mr.* Dicon *did severally use such Prayers as for the present occasion they had conceived,* then (saith he) *the wicked Spirits were much more troubled,* (or rather the wicked Spirits did much more torment the Parties:) *So little do premeditated Prayers which are read out of a Book ; and extreamly do* extemporary *and conceived Prayers torment the Devil.*

15. But *Summers*, at the last grown weary of his frequent Counterfeitings, tired out with his possessings, dispossessings, and repossessings; and in that Fit discovers all to be but Forgeries, and to have been acted by Confederacy; *Darrel* deals with him to revoke his said Confession, seeks to avoid it by some shifts, discredits it by false Reports ; and finally, procures a Commission from the Archbishop of *York*, (to whose Province *Nottingham* belongeth) to examine the business. A Commission is thereupon directed to *John Thorald* Esq; Sheriff of the County, Sir *John Byron*, Knight, *John Stanhop*, &c. (most of them being *Darrels* friends) the Commission executed *March* 20. no fewer then seventeen Witnesses examined by it, and the Return is made, That he was no Counterfeit. But the Boy stands to it for all that ; and on the last of the same moneth confesseth before the Mayor of *Nottingham*, and certain Justices of the Peace, the whole contrivement of the Plot ; and within three days after acts all his Tricks before the Lord Chief Justice at the publick Assizes. Upon this news the Boy of *Burton* also makes the like confession : *Darrel* thereupon is convented by the High Commissioners at *Lambeth*, and by them committed; his Friends and Partizens upon that
Commitment

Commitment are in no small Fury; which notwithstanding he and one of his Associates receive their Censure, little or nothing eased by their Exclamations of his Friends and Followers, who bitterly inveighed against the Judgment, and the Judges too. To still whose Clamours, so maliciously and unjustly raised, the story of these leud Impostors is writ by *Harsnet*, then being the Domestick Chaplain of Archbishop *Whitgift*; by whom collected faithfully out of the Depositions of the Parties and Witnesses, and published in the year next following, *Anno* 1599.

16. In the same year brake out the Controversie touching *Christ's Descent*, maintained by the Church of *England* in the literal sense; that is to say, That the Soul of Christ being separated from his Body, did *locally* descend into the nethermost Hell, to the end that he might manifest the clear light of his Power and Glory to the Kingdom of Darkness, triumphing over Satan as before he did over Death and Sin. For which consult the Book of *Articles*, *Art.* 4. the Homily of the Resurrection, *fol.* 195. and *Nowel's* Paraphrase on that Article, as it stands in the *Creed*, published in his authorized Catechism, *Anno* 1572. But *Calvin* puts another sense upon that Article, and the *Genevian English* must do the same: For *Calvin* understands by Christs descending into Hell, that he suffered in his Soul (both in the Garden of *Gethsemane*, and upon the Cross) all the Torments of Hell, even to abjection from God's Presence, and Despair it self. Which horrid Blasphemy, though balked by many of his Followers in the Forein Churches, was taken up and very zealously promoted by the *English Puritans*. By these men generally it was taught in Catechisms, and preached in Pulpits, That true it was, that the death of Christ Jesus on the Cross, and his bloudshedding for the remission of our sins, were the first cause of our Redemption. But then it was as true withall, That he must and did suffer the death of the Soul, and those very pains which the damned do in Hell, before he could be ransomed from the Wrath of God : and that this only was the descent of Christ into Hell, which we are taught by Christ to believe. But more particularly it was taught by *Banister*, That Christ being dead, descended into the place of everlasting Torments, where in his Soul he endured for a time the very Torments which the damned Spirits without intermission did abide. By *Paget*, in his *Latin* Catechism, That Christ alive upon the Cross humbled himself *usque ad Inferni tremenda tormenta,* even to the most dreadful Torments of Hell. By *Gifford* & the *Houshold Catechism*, That Christ suffered the Torments of Hell, the second death, abjection from God, and was made a Curse, *i.e.* had the bitter anguish of Gods Wrath in his Soul and Body, which is the fire that shall never be quenched. *Carlisle* more honestly, not daring to avouch this Doctrine, nor to run cross against the dictates of his Master, affirmed, That Christ descended not into Hell at all; and therefore, that this Article might be thought no otherwise then as an Error and a Fable.

17. The Doctrine of the Church being thus openly rejected, upon some Conference that passed between Archbishop *Whitgift* & Dr. *Thomas Bilson* then Lord Bishop of *Winchester*, it was resolved that Bishop *Bilson* in some Sermons at St. *Pauls Cross*, and other places, should publickly deliver what the Scriptures teach, touching our Redemption by the
death

death and blood-shedding of Christ Jesus the Son of God, and his descending into Hell. This he accordingly performed in several Sermons upon the words of the Apostle, viz. *God forbid that I should glory in any thing but in the Cross of our Lord Jesus Christ, whereby the world is crucified unto me, and I unto the world*, Gal. 6. 14. In prosecuting of which Text he discoursed at large as well concerning the *contents*, as the *effects* of Christs Cross; and brought the point unto this issue, that is to say, *That no Scripture did teach the death of* Christs Soul, *or the Pains of the damned, to be requisite in the Person of Christ before he could be our Ransomer, and the Saviour of the World*. And because the proofs pretended for this point might be three; *Predictions*, that Christ should suffer those pains; *Causes* why he must suffer them; and *Signs* that he did suffer them: He likewise insisted on all three, and shewed, there were no such *Predictions*, *Causes*, or *Signs*, of the true pains of Hell to be suffered in the Soul of Christ before he could save us. And next, as touching Christs descent into Hell, it was declared, *That by the course of the Creed it ought not to be referred to* Christ living, *but to* Christ *being* dead : *shewing thereby the Conquest which Christs Manhood had after death over all the powers of darkness, declared by his Resurrection, when he arose Lord over all his Enemies, in his own Person; Death, Hell, and Satan, not excepted: and had the keys* (that is, all Power) *of* Death *and* Hell *delivered to him by God, that those in Heaven, Earth, and Hell, should stoop unto him, and be subject to the Strength and Glory of his Kingdom*. And this he proved to be the true and genuine meaning of that Article, both from the Scriptures and the Fathers; and justified it for the Doctrine of the Church of *England* by the Book of Homilies.

18. But let the Scriptures, and the Fathers, and the Book of Homilies, teach us what they please, *Calvin* was otherwise resolved, and his Determination must be valued above all the rest. For, no sooner were these Sermons Printed, but they were presently impugned by a Humorous Treatise, the Author whereof is said to have writ so loosly, as if he neither had remembred what the Bishop uttered, or cared much what he was to prove. In answer whereunto the Bishop adds a short conclusion to his Sermons, and so lets him pass. The *Presbyterian* Brethren take a new Alarm, muster their Forces, compare their Notes, and send them to the Author of the former Treatise, that he might publish his *Defence*. Which he did accordingly; the Author being named *Henry Jacob*, a well known Separatist. Which controversie coming to the Queens knowledge, being then at *Farnham*, (a Castle belonging to the Bishop) she signified Her Pleasure to him, That he should neither desert the Doctrine, nor suffer the Function which he exercised in the Church of *England* to be trodden and trampled under foot by unquiet men, who both abhorred the Truth, and despised Authority. On which Command the Bishop sets himself upon the writing of that Learned Treatise, entituled, *A Survey of Christs Sufferings*, &c. although by reason of a sickness of two years continuance it was not published till the year 1604. The Controversie after this was plyed more hotly in both Universities, where the Bishops Doctrine was maintained, but publickly opposed by many of our Zealots both at home and abroad. At home, opposed by *Gabriel Powel*, a stiff *Presbyterian* : Abroad, by *Broughton*,

ton, *Parker*, and some other Brethren of the Separation. After this, justified and defended by Dr. *Hill*, whom *Aumes* replyed unto in his Rejoynder : as also, by another *Parker*, and many more ; till in the end the Brethren willingly surceased from the prosecution of their former Doctrines, which they were not able to maintain. And though the Church received some trouble upon this occasion, yet by this means the Article of Chrifts Descent became more rightly underflood, and more truly stated, according to the Doctrine of the Church of *England* then either by the Church of *Rome*, or any of the Proteftant or Reformed Churches of what Name foever.

19. But while the Prelates of the Church were busied upon thefe and the like Difputes, the *Presbyterians* found themfelves some better work, in making Friends, and faftening on some eminent Patron to fupport their Caufe. None fitter for their purpofe then the Earl of *Effex*, gracious amongft the Military men, popular beyond meafure, and as ambitious of Command as he was of Applaufe. He had his Education in the Houfe of the Earl of *Leicefter*, and took to Wife a Daughter of Sir *Francis Walfingham*, as before is faid, who fitted and prepared him for thofe Applications which hitherto he had neglected, upon a juft fear of incurring the Queens Difpleafure. But the Queen being now grown old, the King of *Scots* not much regarded by the *Englifh*, and very ill obeyed by his natural Subjects ; he began to look up towards the Crown, to which a Title was drawn for him, as the direct Heir of *Thomas of Woodftock*, Duke of *Gloucefter*, one of the younger Sons of King *Edward* the third. This man the *Puritans* cry up with moft infinite Praifes, both in their Pulpits, and in their Pamphlets ; telling him, That he was not only great in Honour, and the love of the people ; but *temporis expectatione major*, far greater in the expectation which his Friends had of him. And he accordingly applies himfelf to thofe of the *Puritan Faction*, admits them to Places of moft Truft and Credit about his Perfon, keeps open Houfe for men of thofe Opinions to refort unto, under pretence of hearing Sermons ; and hearing no Sermons with more zeal and edification, than thofe which feemed to attribute a Power to Inferior Magiftrates for curbing and controlling their undoubted Soveraigns. Which queftionlefs muft needs have ended in great difturbance to the Church and State, if he had not been out-witted by Sir *Robert Cicil*, Sir *Walter Rawleigh*, and the reft of their Party in the Court ; by whom he was firft fhifted over into *Ireland*, and at laft brought upon the Scaffold, not to receive a Crown, but to lofe his Head. Which hapned very opportunely for King *James* of *Scotland*, whofe Entrance might have been oppofed, and his Title queftioned, if this Ambitious man had profpered in his undertakings, which he conducted generally with more heat then judgment.

20. This brings me back again to *Scotland*. In which we left the 　　　**1596.**
King intent upon the expectation of a better Crown, and to that end refolved upon the Reftitution of the banifhed Lords ; who being advertifed of his purppfe, returned as fecretly as might be, offering to give good Security to live conformable to the Laws in all peace and quietnefs. The King feems willing to accept it, and is confirmed by a Convention of Eftates, in thofe good intentions. The News whereof gave
　　　　　　　　　　　　　　　　　　　　　　　　　　　　　fuch

ſuch offence to thoſe of the Kirk, that preſently they aſſembled themſelves at *Edenborough*, gave notice to the ſeveral Miniſters of the preſent dangers, and adviſed them to excite their Flocks to be in readineſs, to the end they might oppoſe theſe Reſolutions of the King and Council, as far as lawfully they might. A day was alſo ſet apart for Humiliation, and Order given to the *Presbyteries* to excommunicate all ſuch as either harboured any of the Popiſh Lords, or kept company with them ; and this Excommunication to be paſſed ſummarily on the firſt Citation, becauſe the ſafety of the Church ſeemed to be in danger , which was the miſchief by the King ſuſpected under that Reſerve. They appointed alſo, that ſixteen of their Company ſhould remain at *Edenborough*, (according to the number of the *Tribunes* at *Paris*) who together with ſome of the Presbytery of that City ſhould be called, *The Council of the Kirk* : That four or five of the ſaid ſixteen ſhould attend monethly on the Service, in their turns and courſes; and that they ſhould convene every day with ſome of that Presbytery, to receive ſuch Advertiſements as ſhould be ſent from other places, and thereupon take counſel of the beſt Expedients that could be offered in the caſe. And for the firſt Eſſay of their new Authority the Lord *Seaton*, Preſident of the Seſſions, appears before them , tranſmitted unto their Tribunal by the Synod of *Lothian*, for keeping intelligence with the Earl of *Huntley*. From which with many affectations having purged himſelf, he was moſt graciouſly diſmiſt. Which though the King beheld as an Example of moſt dangerous conſequence ; yet being willing to hold fair with the Kirk, he connived at it, till he perceived them to be fixed on ſo high a pin, ſo croſs to his Commands and Purpoſes, that it was time to take them down. He therefore ſignifies to them once for all, That there could be no hope of any right underſtanding to be had between them, during the keeping up of two Juriſdictions, neither depending on the other : That in their Preachings they did cenſure the affairs of the State and Council , convocate ſeveral Aſſemblies without his Licenſes, and there conclude what they thought good without his Allowance and approbation : That in their Synods, Presbytertes, and particular Seſſions, they embraced all manner of buſineſs under colour of ſcandal ; and, that without redreſs of theſe Miſdemeanors, there either was no hope of a good agreement, or that the ſaid agreement, when made, could be long kept by either Party.

21. The miniſters on the other ſide had their Grievances alſo ; that is to ſay, the Fovours extended by his Majeſty to the Popiſh Lords, the inviting of the Lady *Huntley* to the Baptiſm of the Princeſs *Elizabeth*, being then at hand ; the committing of the Princeſs to the Cuſtody of the Lady *Levingſton* ; and the eſtrangement of his Countenance from themſelves. And though the King gave very ſatisfactory Anſwers to all theſe complaints, yet could not the ſuſpitions of the Kirk be thereby removed ; every day bringing forth ſome great cry or other, That the Papiſts were favoured in the Court, the Miniſters troubled for the free rebuke of ſin, and the Sceptre of Chriſts Kingdom ſought to be overthrown. In the mean time it hapned, that one *David Blake*, one of the Miniſters of St. *Andrews*, had in a Sermon uttered divers Seditious Speeches of the King and Queen ; as alſo againſt the Council, and the Lords of

of the Session : but more particularly, that *as all Kings were the Devils Barns* ; so the heart of King *James* was full of Treachery : That the Queen was not to be prayed for but for fashion-sake, because they knew that she would never do them good: That the Lords of the Council were corrupt, and takers of Bribes : and, that the Queen of *England* was an *Atheist*, one of no Religion. Notice whereof being given to the *English* Embassador, he complains of it to the King, and *Blake* is cited to appear before the Lords of the Council. *Melvin* makes this a common Cause, and gives it out, That this was only done upon design against the Ministers, to bring their Doctrine under the censure and controlment of the King and Council ; or at the least, a mere device to divert the Ministers from prosecuting their just Suit against the coming and reception of the Popish Lords, and that if *Blake* or any other should submit their Doctrines to the tryal of the King and Council, the Liberties of the Kirk would be quite subverted. By which means he prevailed so far on the rest of the Council, (I mean *the Council of the Kirk*) that they sent certain of their number to intercede in the business, and to declare how ill it might be taken with all sorts of people, if the Ministers should now be called in question for such trifling matters, when the Enemies of the Truth were both spared and countenanced. But not being able by this means to delay the Censure, it was advised, that *Blake* should make his *Declinatour*, renounce the King and Council as incompetent Judges, and wholly put himself upon tryal of his own *Presbytery*. Which though it seemed a dangerous course by most sober men ; yet was it carryed by the major part of the Voices, as *the Cause of God*.

22. Encouraged by this general Vote, and enflamed by *Melvin*, he presents his *Declinatour*, with great confidence, at his next appearance. And when he was interrogated, amongst other things, whether the King might not as well judge in matters of *Treason*, as the Kirk of *Heresie* ? He answered, That supposing he had spoken Treason, yet could he not be first judged by the King and Council, till the Kirk had taken cognizance of it. In maintainance of which proceeding, the Commissioners of the Kirk direct their Letters to all the Presbyteries of the Kingdom, requiring them to subscribe the said *Declinatour*, to recommend the cause in their Prayers to God, and to stir up their several Flocks in defence thereof. This puts the King to the necessity of publishing his Proclamation of the moneth of *November*. In which he first lays down the great and manifold encroachments of this new Tribunal, to the overthrow of his Authority: The sending of the *Declinatour* to be subscribed generally by all the Ministers : The convocating of the Subjects to assist their proceedings, as if they had no Lord or Superiour over them ; and in the mean time, that the Ministers forsake their Flocks, to wait on these Commissioners, and attend their service : which being said, he doth thereby charge the said Commissioners from acting any thing according to their deputation ; commanding them to leave *Edenborough*, to repair to their several Flocks, and to return no more for keeping such unlawful Meetings under pain of Rebellion. He published another Proclamation at the same time also, by which all Barons, Gentlemen, and other Subjects were commanded not to joyn with any of the Ministry, either in their Presbyteries, Synods, or other Ecclesiastical Assemblies, without

his

his Licenfe. Which notwithftanding he was willing to revoke thofe Edicts, and remit his Action againft *Blake*, if the Church would either wave the *Declinatour*, or if they would declare at the leaft, That it was not a general, but a particular *Declinatour*; ufed in the cafe of Mr. *Blake*, as being in a cafe of *Slander*; and therefore appertaining to the Churches Cognizance. But thefe proud men, either upon fome confidence of another *Bothwell*, or elfe prefuming that the King was not of a Spirit to hold out againft them, or otherwife infatuated to their own deftruction, refolved, That both their Pulpits, and their Preachers too, fhould be exempted totally from the Kings Authority. In which brave humour they return this Anfwer to his Propofition, That they refolved to ftand to their *Declinatour*, unlefs the King would pafs from the Summons, and remitting the purfuit to the Ecclefiaftical Judge, That no Minifter fhould be charged for his Preaching, at leaft before the meeting of the next general Affembly, which fhould be in their Power to call, as they faw occafion. Which Anfwer fo difpleafed the King, that he charged the Commiffioners of the Kirk to depart the Town, and by a new Summons citeth *Blake* to appear on the laft of *Nov.* This fills the Pulpit with Invectives againft the King, and that too on the day of the Princefs's Chriftening, at what time many Noble men were called to *Edenborough* to attend that Solemnity. With whofe confent it was declared at *Blakes* next appearance, That the Crimes and Accufations charged in the Bill were Treafonable and Seditious ; and that his Majefty, his Council, and all other Judges fubftitute by his Authority, were competent Judges in all matters, either Criminal or Civil, as well to Minifters as to other Subjects. Yet ftill the King was willing to give over the Chafe, makes them another gracious offer, treats privately with fome Chiefs amongft them, and feems contented to revoke his two Proclamations, if *Blake* would only come before the Lords of the Council, and there acknowledge his offence againft the Queen. But when this would not be accepted, the Court proceeds unto the Examination of Witneffes. And upon proof of all the Articles objected, Sentence was given againft him to this effect : *That he fhould be confined beyond the North water, enter into Ward within fix days, and there remain till his Majefties pleafure fhould be further fignified.* Some Overtures were made after this for an Accommodation. But the King not being able to gain any reafon from them, fends their Commiffioners out of the Town, and prefently commands, That 24 of the moft Seditious perfons in *Edenborough* fhould forfake the City; hoping to find the reft more cool and tractable when thefe Incendiaries were difmiffed.

23. The Preachers of the City notwithftanding take fire upon it, and the next day excite the Noble men, affembled at the Sermon upon Sunday the 15 of *Decemb.* to joyn with them in a Petition to the King, to preferve Religion. Which being prefented in a rude and diforderly manner, the King demands by what Authority they durft convene together without his leave : *We dare do more then this* (faid the Lord of *Lindfey*) and *will not fuffer our Religion to be overthrown.* Which faid, he returns unto the Church, ftirs up the people to a tumult, and makes himfelf the head of a Factious Rabble, who crying out, *The Sword of the Lord, and* Gideon, thronged in great numbers to the place, in which the King had locked himfelf for his greater fafety ; the doors whereof they queftionlefs had

had forced open, and done some out rage to his Person, if a few honest men had not stopt their Fury : The Lord Provost of the City, notwithstanding he was then sick and kept his Bed, applied his best endeavours to appease the Tumult, and with some difficulty brought the people to lay down their Arms ; which gave the King an opportunity to retire to his Palace, where with great fear he passed over all the rest of that day. The next morning he removes with his Court and Council to the Town of *Lintithgoe*, and from thence publisheth a Proclamation to this effect, *viz.* That the Lords of the Session, the Sheriffs, Commissioners, and Justices, with their several Members and Deputies, should remove themselves forth of the Town of *Edenborough*, and be in readiness to go to any such place as should be appointed ; and that all Noblemen and Barons should return unto their Houses, and not to convene in that or in any other place without License, under pain of his Majesty's Displeasure. The Preachers on the contrary are resolved to keep up the Cause to call their Friends together, and unite their Party ; and were upon the point of Excommunicating certain Lords of the Council, if some more sober then the rest had not held their hands.

24　In which confusion of Affairs they indict a Fast, for a preparatory whereunto a Sermon is preached by one *Welch*, in the chief Church of that City : Who taking for his Theme the Epistle sent to the Angel of the Church of *Ephesus*, did pitifully rail against the King, saying, That *he was possessed with a Devil, and that one Devil being put out, seven worse were entered in the place : and that the Subjects might lawfully rise and take the Sword out of his hands.* Which last he confirmed by the Example of a Father, that falling into a *Phrensie*, might be taken by the Children and Servants of the Family, and tyed hand and foot from doing violence. Which brings into my mind an usual saying of that King, to this effect, viz. *That for the twelve last years past of his living in* Scotland, *he used to pray upon his knees before every Sermon, That he might hear nothing from the Preacher which might justly grieve him ; and that the case was so well altered when he was in* England, *that he was used to pray that he might profit by what he heard.* But all exorbitancy of Power is of short continuance, especially if abused to Pride and Arrogance. The madness of the *Presbyterians* was now come to the height, and therefore in the course of Nature was to have a fall; and this the King resolves to give them, or to lose his Crown. He had before been so afflicted with continual Baffles, that he was many times upon the point of leaving *Scotland*, putting himself into the Seigneury of *Venice*, and living there in the capacity of a Gentleman(so they call the *Patricians* of that Noble City.) And questionless he had put that purpose in execution, if the hopes of coming one day to the Crown of *England* had not been some temptation to him to ride out the storm. But now a sword is put into his hands by the Preachers themselves, wherewith he is enabled to cut the *Gordian* knot of their plots & practises, which he was not able to unty. For not contented to have raised the former tumults, they keep the Noblemen together, invite the people to their aid, and write their Letters to the Lord of *Hamilton*, to repair unto them, and make himself the Head of their Association. A Copy of which Letter being shewed unto the King by that Noble Lord, command is given unto the Provost of *Edenborough* to attach the Ministers. But they had

notice

notice of his purpose and escape into *England*, making *Newcastle* their retreat as in former times.

25. It is a true saying of the wise Historian, That every Insurrection of the people when it is suppressed, doth make the Prince stronger, and the Subject weaker. And this the King found true in his own particular. The Citizens of *Edenborough* being pinched with the Proclamation, and the removal of the Court and the Courts of Justice, offered to purge themselves of the late Sedition, and tendered their obedience unto any thing whatsoever which his Majesty and the Council should be pleased to enjoyn, whereby they might repair the huge Indignity which was done to his Majesty; provided that they should not be thought guilty of so great a crime, which from their hearts they had detested. But the King answers, That he would admit of no purgation, that he would make them know that he was their King : And the next day proclaims the Tumult to be Treason, and proclaims all for Traytors who were guilty of it. This made them fear their utter ruine to be near at hand. The ordinary Judicatories were removed to *Leith*, the Sessions ordained to be held at *Perth* ; their Ministers were fled, their Magistrates without regard ; and none about the King but their deadly Enemies. And to make up the full measure of disconsolation, Counsel is given unto the King to raise the Town, and to erect a Pillar in the place thereof for a perpetual Monument of so great an Insolence. But he resolves to travel none but Legal ways; and being somewhat sweetned by a Letter from the Queen of *England*, he gives command unto the *Provost*, and the rest of the Magistrates, to enter their persons at *Perth* on the first of *February*, there to keep ward untill they either were acquitted or condemned of the former uproar. Whilst things remained in this perplexity and suspence, he is advised to make his best use of the conjecture, for setling matters of the Church, and to establish in it such a decent Order as was agreeable to Gods Word. To which end he appoints a National Assembly to be held at *Perth* ; and prepares certain Queries, fifty five in number, to be considered and debated in the said Assembly, all of them tending to the rectifying of such Abuses which were either crept into the Discipline, or occasioned by it. Nothing so much perplexed the principal Ministers, who had the leading of the rest, as, that the Discipline should be brought under dispute which they had taught to be a part of the word of God But they must sing another tune before all be ended.

26. For the King having gained a considerable Party amongst the Ministers of the North, and treated with many of the rest in several, whom he thought most tractable; prevailed so far on the Assembly, that they condescend at the last upon many particulars, which in the pride of their prosperity had not been required. The principal of which were these, *viz.* 'That it should be lawful to his Majesty by himself or his
'Commissioners, or to the Pastors, to propone in general Assembly whatsoever point he or they desired to be resolved in, or reformed in matters
'of external Government, alterable according to circumstances ; providing it to be done in right time and place, *Animo ædificandi non tentandi*.
'2. That no Minister should reprove his Majesty's Laws & Statutes, Acts
'or Ordinances, until such time as he hath first by the advice of his Presbytery, or Synodal, or general Assemblies, complained & sought remedy
'of

' of the same from his Majesty, and made report of his Majesties Answer,
' before any further proceedings. 3. That no mans Name should be ex-
' pressed in the Pulpit, except the Fault be notorious and publick, and
' so declared by an Assize, Excommunication, Contumace, and lawful
' Admonition; nor should he be described so plainly by any other circum-
' stances, then publick Vices, always damnable. 4. That in all great
' Towns the Ministers shall not be chosen without his Majesties consent,
' and the consent of the Flock. 5. That no matter of Slander should be
' called before them, wherein his Majesties Authority is pre-judged,
' Causes Ecclesiastical only excepted. 6. And finally, That no Conven-
' tions shall be amongst Pastors, without his Majesties knowledge, ex-
' cept their Sessions, Presbyteries, and Synods, the Meetings at the Visi-
' tation of Churches, admission or deprivation of Ministers, taking up of
' deadly Feuds, and the like which had not already been found fault
' with by his Majesty. According to which last Article the King confents unto another general Assembly to be held at *Dundee*, and nominates
the 10 of *May* for the opening of it.

27. It was about this time that Dr. *Richard Bancroft*, Bishop of *London*, began to run a constant course of Correspondence with the King of
Scots, whom he beheld as the undoubted Heir and Successor of the Queen
then Reigning. And well considering how conduceable it was to the
Peace of both Kingdoms, that they should both be governed in one
Form of Ecclesiastical Policy; he chalked him out a ready way, by
which he might restore Episcopacy to the Kirk of *Scotland*. To which
end, as the King had gained the liberty in the last Assembly to question
and dispute the Government then by Law established, and gained a power of nominating Ministers in the principal Cities; so in the next they
gratified him in this point, That no man should from thenceforth exercise as a Minister, without having a particular Flock; nor be admitted to
that Flock, without Ordination by the Imposition of hands. He required also in the same, that before the conclusion of any weighty matter,
his Highness advice and approbation should be first obtained. And so far
they consented to the Proposition, as to express how glad they were to
have his Majesties Authority interposed to all Acts of importance which
concerned the Church, so as matters formerly concluded might not be
drawn in question. He gained some other points also in the same Assembly, no less important then the other towards his Designs; as namely,
1. *That no Minister shall exercise any Jurisdiction, either by making of Constitutions or leading of Processes, without advice and concurrence of his Session, Presbytery, Synod, or General Assembly.* 2. *That Presbyteries shall not meddle with a-
ny thing that is not known without all controversie to belong to the Ecclesiastical
judicatory; and that therein Uniformity should be observed throughout the Country.* And, 3. *That where any Presbyters shall be desired by his Majesties Missive
to stay their proceedings, as being prejudicial to the Civil Jurisdiction, or private mens Rights, they should desist until his Majesty did receive satisfaction.* But
that which made most toward his purpose was, the appointing of thirteen of their number to attend his Majesty, as the Commissioners of the
Kirk, whom we may call the High Commissioners of *Scotland*, the
Kings Ecclesiastical Council, the Seminary of the future Bishops, to
whom they gave Authority for the planting of Churches in *Edenborough*,
St.

St. *Andrews*, *Dundee*, &c. as also to present the Petitions and Grievances of the Kirk to his Majesty; and to advise with him in all such matters as conduced unto the peace and welfare of it.

28. It was no hard matter for the King, by Rewards and Promises, to gain these men unto himself, or at the least to raise amongst them such a Party as should be ready at all times to serve his turn. And such a general compliance he found amongst them, that they not only served him in the punishment of *David Blake*, in whose behalf they had stood out so long against him; but in the sentencing of *Wallace*, who in a Sermon at St. *Andrews* had abused his Secretary: both which, upon the cognizance of their several Causes, they deprived of their Churches, and decreed others of more moderation to be placed therein. They served him also in the reformation of that University where *Andrew Melvin* for some years had continued Rector; and thereby gained an excellent opportunity for training up young Students in the Arts of Sedition. To which end he had so contrived it, that instead of Lecturing in Divinity, they should read the Politicks, as namely, *Whether Election or Succession of Kings were the best Form of Government? How far the Royal Power extended? And, Whether Kings were to be Censured and Deposed by the Estates of the Kingdom, in case their Power should be abused?* For remedy whereof, the King not only ordered by the Advice of his Commissioners, That no man from thenceforth should continue Rector of that University above the space of a year; but appointed also on what Books, and after what manner every Professor for the time to come was to read his Lectures. He next proceeds unto a Reformation of the Churches of *Edenborough*, but had first brought the Town to submit to mercy. Failing of their attendance at *Perth*, in so full a number as were appointed to appear, the whole Town was denounced Rebel, and all the Lands, Rents, and other goods, which formerly belonged to the Corporation, confiscate to the use of the King: the news whereof brought such a general disconsolation in that Factious City, that the Magistrates renounced their Charges, the Ministers forsook their Flocks, and all things seemed to tend to a dissolution. But at the end of 15 days his Majesty was graciously inclined, upon the mediation of some Noble men who took pity on them, to re-admit them to his Favour. Upon Advertisement whereof the Provost, Bailiffs, and Deacons of Crafts, being brought unto his presence the 21 of *March*, and falling upon their knees, did with tears beg pardon for their negligence, in not timely preventing that Tumult; beseeching his Majesty to take pity of the Town, which did simply submit it self to his Majesties Mercy.

29. The King had formerly considered of all advantages which he might raise unto himself out of that Submission; but aimed at nothing more then the reduction of the people to a sense of their duty; the curbing of the City-Preachers, and setling some good Order in the Churches of it. In these last times the Ministers had lived together in one common House, situate in the great Church-yard, and of old belonging to the Town; which gave them an opportunity to consult in private, to hatch Seditions, and put their Treasons into form. This House the King required to be given up to him, to the end that the Ministers might be disposed of in several Houses, far from one another, so as they might

not

not meet together without obſervation. The Miniſters of late had preached in common, without conſideration of particular Charges; and
were reduced alſo to a leſs number then in former times, which made
them of the greater Power amongſt the people.   But now the King reſolves upon the dividing of the Town into ſeveral Pariſhes, and fixing e-
very Miniſter in his proper Church, according to the Acts of the laſt
Aſſembly. This had been thought of two years ſince; but the Town oppoſed it. Now they are glad to yield to any thing which the King propounded, and to this point amongſt the reſt. And hereupon the payment of a Fine 20000 pounds to the King, and entring into a Recogni-
zance (as our Lawyers call it) of 40000 marks more, for the indempni-
fying of the Lords of the Seſſion in the time of their ſitting; the City is
reſtored to the good Grace of the King, and the Courts of Juſtice to the
City. His Majeſty was alſo pleaſed, that the Fugitive Preachers of the
City ſhould be reſtored unto their Miniſtry, upon theſe conditions, that
is to ſay, That each of them ſhould take the charge of a ſeveral Flock:
That four new Preachers ſhould be added to the former number, and
each of them aſſigned to his proper Charge: That they ſhould uſe more
moderation in their Preachings for the time to come, and not refuſe to
render an account thereof to the King and Council. And finally, That
ſuch as had not formerly received Ordination by the Impoſition of hands,
ſhould receive it now. In which laſt *Bruce* created no ſmall trouble to
the Kings Commiſſioners (who laboured very zealouſly to advance that
Service;) but he ſubmitted in the end.

30. After theſe preparations, comes a Parliament, which was to take
beginning in the moneth of *December*. Againſt which time the King had
dealt ſo dexterouſly with *Patrick Galloway*, and he ſo handſomly had applied himſelf to his Aſſociates, that the Commiſſioners were drawn to
joyn in a Requeſt to the Lords and Commons, *That the Miniſters, as re-
preſenting the Church, and Third Eſtate of the Kingdom, might be admitted to
give voice in Parliament, according to the ancient Rites and Priviledges of the
Kirk of* Scotland. The King was alſo humbly moved to be-friend them
in it. And he ſo managed the Affair to his own advantage, that he obtained an Act to paſs to this effect, viz. *That ſuch Paſtors and Miniſters as
his Majeſty ſhould pleaſe to provide to the Place, Dignity, and Title of a Biſhop,
Abbot, or other Prelate, at any time ſhould have voice in Parliament, as freely as
any other Eccleſiaſtical Prelate had in the times fore-going; provided, that ſuch
perſons as ſhould be nominated to any Arch-biſhoprick or Biſhoprick within the
Realm, ſhould either actually be Preachers at the time of their nomination, or elſe
aſſume and take upon them to be actual Preachers; and according thereunto ſhould
practiſe and perform that duty: and that neither this Act, nor any thing in the
ſame contained, ſhould prejudice the Juriſdiction of the Kirk eſtabliſhed by Acts
of Parliament; nor any of the Presbyteries, Aſſemblies, or other Seſſions of the
Church.* After which followed another General Aſſembly, appointed to
be held at *Dundee* in the *March* enſuing, the King himſelf being preſent at
it. In which it was concluded, after ſome debate, *That Miniſters lawfully
might give voice in Parliament, and other publick Meetings of the Eſtates; and
that it was expedient to have ſome always of that number preſent, to give voice
in the name of the Church.* It was agreed alſo, *That ſo many ſhould be appointed to have voice in Parliament, as there had been Arch-Biſhops, Biſhops, Ab-*
bots,

bots, and Priors, in the times of Popery: Which coming to the number of 50, or thereabouts, gave every Minister some hopes to be one of that number. It was resolved also, That the Election of the Persons, should belong partly to the King, and in part to the Church. But as for the manner of the Election, the Rents to be assigned unto them, and their continuance in that Trust, for life, or otherwise; these points were left to be considered of at better leisure.

1589.

31. For the dispatch whereof, with the more conveniency, it was appointed, That the matter should be first debated in each Presbytery, and afterwards in Provincial Synods, to be holden all upon one day, that to be the first *Tuesday* of *June*, three men to be selected out of every Synod, to attend the King; and they, together with the Doctors of the Universities, to conclude the business, with reference notwithstanding to the approbation of the next Assembly. Accordingly they meet in Synods, and appoint their Delegates; who being called to *Falkland* in the end of *July*, did then and there conclude upon these particulars. First, for the manner of Elections; That for each Prelacy that was void, the Church should nominate six persons, and the King chuse one; and that if his Majesty should like none of that number, six others should be named by the Church, of which his Majesty was to chuse one without more refusal. Next, for the Rents; That the Churches being sufficiently planted, and no prejudice done to Schools, Colledges, and Universities already erected, he should be put into possession of the rest of that Prelacy to which he was to be preferred. As to the term of his continuance in that trust, there was nothing done, that point being left unto the consideration of the next Assembly. And for the naming of the Child, the Godfathers agreed, that he should be called the *Commissaire* or *Commissioner* of such a place, if the Parliament could be induced by his Majesty to accept that Title, or else the General Assembly to devise some other. But fearing left this *Commissaire* might in time become a Bishop, it was resolved to tye him up to such Conditions, as should disable him from aspiring above the rest of his Brethren. But more particularly it was cautioned and agreed upon, That he should propound nothing in the Name of the Church, without express warrant from the same; or give consent to any thing proposed in Parliament, which tended to the diminution of the Liberties of it. That he should be bound to give an account of his proceedings to the next General Assembly, and to submit himself to their judgment in it without any Appeal. That he should faithfully attend his particular Flock, and be as subject to the Censure of his own Presbytery, or Provincial Synod, as any other Minister which had no Commission. That in the Administration of Discipline, Collation of Benefices, Visitation, and other points of Ecclesiastical Government, he should neither usurp, nor claim to himself any more Power and Jurisdiction then the rest of his Brethren. That if he shall usurp any part of Ecclesiastical Government, the Presbytery, Synod, or General Assembly, protesting against it, whatsoever he should do therein, shall be null and void. That if he chance to be deposed from the Ministry, by the Presbytery, Synod, or Assembly, he should not only lose his Place and Vote in Parliament, but the Prelacy should be also voided for another man. And finally, That he should subscribe to all these Cautions before he was admitted to his Place and Trust.

32. In

32. in the Affembly of *Montrofs*, which began on the 28 of *March*, *Anno* 1599, thefe Cautions were approved, and two new ones added : 1. *That they who had voice in Parliament, fhould not have place in the General Afembly, unlefs they were authorifed by a Commiffion from the Presbyteries whereof they were Members.* 2. *That* Crimen Ambitur. *or any finifter endeavours to procure the Place, fhould be a fufficient reafon to deprive him of it.* As for the term of their continuance in this Truft, the Leading-members were refolved not to make it certain, and much lefs to endure for term of life : all they would yield unto was this, That he who was admitted unto that Commiffion, fhould yearly render an account of his employment to the next General Afembly. That he fhould lay down his Commiffion at the feet thereof, to be continued if they pleafed, or otherwife to give place unto any other whom his Majefty and the faid Afembly fhould think fit to employ. To all which Cautions and Reftrictions the King was willing to confent, that fo the bufinefs might proceed without interruption ; not doubting but to find a way, at fome time or other, in which thefe Rigors might be moderated, and thefe Chains knocked off. Nothing now refted, but the nominating of fome able perfons to poffefs thofe Prelacies which either were vacant at that time, or actually in the Kings difpofing. The Bifhopricks of St. *Andrews* and *Glafcow*, had been given or fold to the Duke of *Lenox* ; the Bifhoprick of *Murray*, to the Lord of *Spinie* ; and that of *Orkney*, to the Earl ; which muft be firft compounded with, before the King would nominate any man to either of them. The Sands of *Galloway* and the *Ifles* were fo delapidated, that there was nothing left to maintain a Prelate, and therefore muft be firft endowed. The Sees of *Aberdeen* and *Argile*, had their Bifhops living, both of them being actual Preachers ; and thofe of *Brechen*, *Dunkeld*, and *Dumblane*, had their Titulars alfo, but no Preaching Minifters. So as there were but two Churches to be filled at the prefent, that is to fay, the Bifhopricks of *Rothes*, and *Cathnefs* ; to which the King prefents Mr. *David Lindefay*, Minifter of *Leith* ; and Mr. *George Gladftaves*, one of the Minifters of St. *Andrews* ; of whofe fobriety and moderation he had good experience. Which two enjoyed their places in their following Parliament, and rode together with the reft in the Pomps thereof.

33. Thus far the bufinefs went on fmoothly in the outward fhew ; but inwardly were great thoughts of heart ; which firft appeared in words of danger and difcontent, and afterwards in acts of the higheft Treafon. The Leading Members of the Kirk, which had fo long enjoyed an Arbitrary Power in all parts of the Realm, could with no patience brook the Limitations which were put upon them in the Afembly at *Dundee* : and much lefs able to endure that fuch a fair Foundation fhould be laid for *Epifcopacy*, which muft needs put a final end to their Pride and Tyranny ; of which fort was a Letter writ by *Davidfon*, to the next Afembly : In which he thus expoftulates with the reft of his Brethren ; *How long fhall we fear or favour Flefh and Blood, and follow the Councel and Command thereof ? Should our Meetings be in the Name of Man ? Are we not to take up our felves, and to acknowledge our former errors, and feeblenefs in the Work of the Lord ? It is time for us now, when fo many of our worthy Brethren are thruft out of their Callings, without all order of juft proceedings ; and* Jefuits, Atheifts, *and* Papifts, *are fuffered, countenanced, and advanced to*
great

great Rooms in the Realm, for the bringing in Idolatry, and Captivity more then Babylonical, with an high hand, and that in our chief City : Is it time for us, I say, of the Ministry, to be inveigled and blindfolded with pretence of the preferment of some small number of our Brethren to have voice in Parliament, and have Titles of Prelacy ? Shall we, with Sampson, *sleep still on* Dalilahs *knees, till she say, the* Philistines *be upon thee* Sampson *? &c.* Which Letter speaks the words of *Davidson,* but the sense of others, who having the like discontentments, privately whispered them in the ears of those who either seemed zealous for Religion, or Factiously inclined to make new Disturbances in this unsetledness of Affairs : In which conjuncture it was no hard matter for them so to work upon mens Affections, as to assure them to themselves, and to be ready to flye out upon all occasions, especially when any powerful Head should be offered to them.

1600.

34. Of the last sort was the Conspiracy and Treason of the Earl of *Goury,* Son of that *William* Earl of *Goury,* who had been executed for surprising the Kings Person at *Ruthen* Castle, *Anno* 1584. And though this Son of his had been restored by the King to his Blood and Honours, one of his Sisters married to the Duke of *Lenox,* another placed in the Attendance of the Queen, and that his Brother *Alexander* was advanced to a Place in the Bed-Chamber ; yet these Favours were not able to obliterate the remembrance of the Execution so justly done upon their Father. By nature he was Proud, Aspiring, and of a Mind greater then his Fortune. Ill principled in the course of his Education ; which made him passionately affected to the *Disciplinarians,* of whom he was ambitious to be thought a Patron. To this man they apply themselves ; who by the loss of their Authority, or Tyranny rather, measured the Fortunes of the Church ; as though Religion could not stand, if their Empire fell. To him they frequently insinuated their Fears and Jealousies, the Kings averseness from the Gospel, his extraordinary Favour to the Popish Lords, his present Practises and Designs to subvert the Discipline, the only Pillar and Support of the Kirk of *Scotland* ; not without some Reflections on the death of his Father, whose Zeal to God was testified by the loss of his Life, which cryed aloud for vengeance both to God and Man. By which insinuations they so wrought upon him, that he began to study nothing but Revenge ; and to that end engaged his Brother *Alexander* (a fierce young man, and of a very daring Spirit) in the practise with him. He also held intelligence with such of the Ministers as were supposed to be most discontented at the present Transactions ; but most especially with the Preachers of *Edenborough,* who could not easily forget the Injuries (so they must be called) which they had suffered from the King for some years last past. The like intelligence he kept with many *Male-contents* amongst the Laicks ; preparing all, but opening his Design to few ; but opening it howsoever to *Logen* of *Restalrig,* in whom he had more confidence then all the rest.

35. Concerning which, it was avered by one *Sprot* a Notary, as well upon Examination before the Lords of the Session, as his Confession at the Gallows, *Anno* 1608, That he had seen a Letter written by this *Logan* to the Earl of *Goury,* in which was signified, *That he would take part with him in revenge of his Fathers death. That to effect it, he must find some way or other to bring the King to* Fast Castle. *That it was easier to be done by Sea then*

Land :

Land : *and they might safely keep him there till they had given advertisement of it to the other Conspirators.* For proof of which Confeffion (being free and voluntary) he told the people on the Ladder, that he would give them a Sign; which he performed by clapping his hands three times after his turning off by the Executioner. It was affirmed alfo by Mr. *William Cowper* (a right godly man) then being Minifter at *Perth*, and afterwards made Bifhop of *Galloway*; That going to the Houfe of the Earl, (the Hereditary Provoft of that Town) not many days before the intended Treafon, he found him reading a Book entituled *De Conjurationibus adverfus principes*, containing a Difcourfe of Treafons and Confpiracies againft feveral Princes; of which he was pleafed to give this cenfure, *That moft of them were very foolifhly contrived, and faulty in fome point or other, which was the reafon that they found not the defired effect.* By which it feems that he intended to out go all former Confpirators in the contrivance of his Treafon; though in the end he fell upon a Plot which was moft ridiculous, not to be parallell'd by any in that Book which be fo much vilified. The defign was to draw the King to his Houfe in the Town of *Perth*, under pretence of coming fecretly to fee a man whom he had lately intercepted with Letters, and fome quantity of Gold from *Rome*; and having brought him to fome remote part of the Houfe, to make fure work of him. The King was then at *Falkland Caftle*; and going out betimes on *Tuefday* the fifth of *Auguft*, to take his pleafure in the Park, he is met by *Alexander*, who tells him of the News of *Perth*, and that a fpeedy pofting thither would be worth his travel. The King comes thither before dinner, accompanied with the Duke of *Lenox*, the Earl of *Marre*, *Evesking* the Captain of his Guard, and fome other Gentlemen, all of them in their Hunting Coats, as minding nothing but a Vifit to the Nobleman. Thus is he brought into the toyl; but they fhall only hunt him to the view, and not pull him down.

36. The Kings own dinner being ended, the Lords fall to theirs, which *Alexander* takes to be the fitteft time to effect the Enterprife; and therefore takes the King along with him to an upper Chamber. But feeing *Evesking* at his heels, he wiled him to ftay behind, & made faft the doors. Being brought into a Chamber on the top of the Houfe, the King perceived a man in a fecret corner, and prefently asked *Alexander* if he were the Party who had brought the Letters and the Gold. But *Alexander* then changed his countenance, upbraided him with the death of his Father, for which he was now brought to make fatisfaction; and therewith left him to the mercy of the Executioner. I fhall not ftand on all particulars of the Story; the fum whereof is briefly this : That the King having by much ftrugling gained a Window, a corner whereof looked toward the Street, cryed out fo loud, that he was heard by all the Lords and Gentlemen of his Retinue, who thereupon prepared themfelves for his affiftance. In the purfuit whereof the Earl himfelf is killed by *Evesking*, as he was making haft to help his Brother; and *Alexander* is difpatched by *Ramfey*, one of the Kings Pages; who being acquainted with the Houfe, came by the back ftairs time enough to preferve his Mafter. Of this great danger and deliverance the King gives notice to all his Subjects, defiring them to joyn with him in thanks to Almighty God for fo great a mercy; which was acordingly performed by all honeft men : but

the whole story disbelieved, discredited, mis-reported by the *Presbyterians*, whom it concerned to wash their hands of so foul a Treason. And how far they were Parties in it, or at least well-wishers to it, may appear by this, That when the Ministers of *Edenborough* were desired to convene their people, and give God thanks for this deliverance of the King, they excused themselves as not being well acquainted with all particulars. And when it was replyed unto them, *That they were only required to make known to the people, That the King had escaped a great danger, and to excite them to thanksgiving for his deliverance* : They answered, *That they were not very well satisfied in the truth of the matter : That nothing was to be delivered in a Pulpit, the truth whereof was not certainly known : and that they were to utter nothing in that place but that which might be spoke in* Faith. On which Refusal it was ordered by the Lords of the Council, That the people should be drawn together into the Market-place, that the Bishop of *Ross* should make a Declaration of the whole design, and therewithall conceive a Prayer of Thanksgiving for the Kings deliverance. Which was performed on his part with a true affection, and entertained by the people with great joy and gladness.

37. But the whole Nation was not so bespotted by the *Presbyterians*, as either to dispute the Story, or despise the Mercy. Which wrought so far upon the Consciences of all honest men, that in a Parliament held at *Edenborough* in *November* following, the Estate of *Goury* was confiscate, his Sons disherited, the Name of *Ruthen* utterly abolished, (but the last dispenced with) the bodies of the two Brothers brought to *Edenborough*, there hanged and quartered, the Heads of both being fixed upon the top of the common Prison : and finally, the fifth of *August* ordained by Act of Parliament for a day of Thanksgiving in all times succeeding. The like done also two years after at a general Assembly of the

1602. Ministers of the Church held in *Haly Rood House* as to the day of thanksgiving, which they decreed to be kept solemnly from thenceforth, in all the Churches of that Kingdom. And it was well they did it then, the King not venturing the Proposal to them in the year foregoing, when they assembled at *Burnt Island*, whether in reference to some indisposition of Mind which he found in them. But now it went clearly for him without contradiction, as did some other things propounded to their consideration. His Eye now looks unto the Crown of *England*, and he resolved to bring the Churches of both Kingdoms to an Uniformity : but so to do it as might make neither noise nor trouble. The solemnizing of Marriage had been prohibited on *Sundays* by the Rules of Discipline : but by an Order made in the present Assembly it was indifferently permitted on all days alike, *Sundays* as well as other days at the will of the Parties. Before this time the Sacrament of Baptism was not administred but only at the times of Preaching, on some opinion which they had of the indifferency, or at the least the non-necessity thereof. But now it was ordained with a joynt consent, *That the Ministers should not refuse the Sacrament of Baptism to Infants, nor delay the same upon whatsoever pretext, the same being required by the Parents, or others in their name.* Which brought them two steps nearer to the Church of *England*, then before they were.

38. In

38. It was not long after the end of this Assembly, when the King received intelligence of Q. *Elizabeth's* death, & of the general acknowledgment of his Succession, both by Peers and People. This puts him on a preparation for a Journy to *Engl.* where he is joyfully received, and found no small contentment in the change of his Fortunes; here sitting *amongst Grave, Learned, and Reverend men ; not as before, a King without State, without Honour, without Order, where Beardless Boys would every day brave him to his face ; where* Jack, *and* Tom, *and* Will, *and* Dick, *did at their pleasures censure the proceedings of him and his Council ; where* Will *stood up and said, he would have it thus: and* Dick *replied, Nay marry, but it shall be so ::* as he describes their carriage in the Conference at *Hampton-Court,* p. 4. and 80. So leaves he *Scotland,* and the *Puritans* there, with this Character of them, recorded in the Preface of his Book, called *Basilicon Doron* ; in which he paints them out, as people which *refusing to be called* Anabaptists, *too much participated of their Humours, not only agreeing with them in their General Rule, the contempt of the Civil Magistrate, and in leaning to their own Dreams, Imaginations, and Revelations ; but particularly in accounting all men prophane that agree not to their Fancies ; in making, for every particular Question of the* Polity of the Church, *or much Commotion as if the Article of the* T*rinity was called in question ; in making the Scripture to be ruled by their Conscience, and not their Conscience by the Scripture ; in accounting every body* Ethnicus & Publicanus, *not worthy to enjoy the benefit of breathing, much less to participate with them in the Sacraments, that denies the least jot of their Grounds: and in suffering King, People, Law, and all, to be trod under feet, before the least jot of their Grounds be impugned ; in preferring such Holy Warrs to an Ungodly Peace ; not only in resisting Christian Princes, but denying to pray for them ; for Prayer must come by Faith, and it is not revealed that God will hear their Prayers for such a Prince.* To which he adds this Clause in the Book it self, *viz.* That they used commonly to tell the people in their Sermons, *That all Kings and Princes were naturally Enemies to the Liberty of the Church, and could never patiently bear the Yoke of Christ.* And thereupon he gives this Counsel to the Prince, To take heed all of such *Puritans,* whom he calls the *very Pests of the Church and Commonwealth ; whom no deserts can oblige, neither Oaths nor Promises bind ; breathing nothing but Sedition and Calumnies ; aspiring without measure, railing without reason, and making their own imaginations the square of their Conscience: protesting before the Great God, That he should never find in any* Highlander *baser Thieves, greater Ingratitude, and more lyes and vile Perjuries, then amongst those* Fanatical *spirits he should meet withall.*

39. But on the contrary, he tells us of the Church of *England* at his first coming thither, ' That he found that Form of Religion which was ' established under Queen *Elizabeth* of famous memory, by the Laws of ' the Land, to have been blessed with a most extraordinary Peace, and of ' long continuance ; which he beheld as a strong evidence of Gods being ' very well pleased with it. He tells us also, That he could find no cause ' at all, on a full debate, for any Alteration to be made in the Com-' mon Prayer Book, though that most impugned ; that the Doctrines ' seemed to be sincere, the Forms and Rites to have been justified out ' of the Practise of the Primitive Church. And finally, he tells us, that

there

'there was nothing in the same which might not very well have been
'born withal, if either the Adverfaries would have made a reafonable
'conftruction of them ; or that his Majefty had not been fo nice, or rather
'jealous, (as himfelf confeffeth) for having all publick Forms in the
'Service of God, not only to be free from all blame, but from any fuf-
'picion. For which confult his Proclamation of the fifth of *March* before
the Book of Common prayer. And herewith he declared himfelf fo highly pleafed, that in the *Conference* at *Hampton Court* he entered into a gra-
tulation to Almighty God, for *bringing him into the Promifed Land,* (fo he
pleafed to call it) where Religion was purely profeft, the Government
Ecclefiaftical approved by manifold bleffings from God himfelf, as well
in the increafe of the Gofpel, as in a glorious and happy Peace : and
where he had the happinefs to fit amongft Grave and Learned men, and
not to be a King (as elfewhere he had been) without State, without Honour, without Order, as before was faid. And this being faid, we fhall
proceed unto the reft of our Story, cafting into the following Book, all
the Succeffes of the *Puritans* or *Presbyterians* in his own Dominions, during the whole time of his Peaceful Government ; and fo much alfo of
their Fortunes in *France* and *Belgium,* as fhall be neceffary to the knowledge of their future actings.

The End of the Tenth Book.

AERIUS REDIVIVUS:
OR THE
HISTORY
OF THE
Presbyterians.

LIB. XI.

Containing

Their Successes whether good or bad, in England, Scotland, Ireland, *and the Isle of* Jersey, *from the Year* 1602 *to the Year* 1623 *; with somewhat touching their Affairs, as well in* France *and* Sweden, *as the* Belgick Provinces.

HE *Puritans* and *Presbyterians* in both Kingdomes were brought so low, when King *James* first obtained the Crown of *England*, that they might have been supprest for ever without any great danger, if either that King had held the Rains with a constant hand, or been more fortunate in the choice of his Ministers, after the old Councellors were worn out, then in fine he proved. But having been kept to such hard meats when he lived in *Scotland*, he was so taken with the Delicacies of the *English* Court, that he abandoned the Severities and Cares of Government, to enjoy the Pleasures of a Crown. Which being

being perceived by such as were most near unto him, it was not long before the Secret was discovered to the rest of the people ; who thereupon resolved to husband all occasions which the times should give them, to their best advantage. But none conceived more hopes of him then some *Puritan* Zealots ; who either presuming on his Education in the Kirk of *Scotland*, or venturing on the easiness of his Disposition, began to intermit the use of the *Common Prayer*, to lay aside the Surplice, and neglect the Ceremonies ; and more then so, to hold some Classical and Synodical Meetings, as if the Laws themselves had dyed, when the Queen expired. But these Disorders he repressed by his Proclamation, wherein he commanded all his Subjects, of what sort soever, not to innovate any thing either in Doctrine or Discipline, till he upon mature deliberation should take order in it.

2. Bnt some more wary then the rest refused to joyn themselves to such forward Brethren, whose actions were interpreted to favour stronger of Sedition then they did of Zeal. And by these men it was thought better to address themselves by a Petition to his Sacred Majesty, which was to be presented to him in the name of certain Ministers of the Church of *England, desiring Reformation of sundry Ceremonies and Abuses* : Given out to be subscribed by a thousand hands, and therefore called the *Millenary Petition*, though there wanted some hundreds of that number to make up the sum. In which Petition deprecating first the imputation of Schism and Faction, they rank their whole Complaints under these four heads ; that is to say, *The Service of the Church, Church-Ministers, the Livings and Maintenance of the Church, and the Discipline of it.* In reference to the first, the Publick Service of the Church, it was desired, 'That the Cross in Baptism, Interrogatories ministred to Infants, ' and Confirmations (as superfluous) might be taken away. That Bap- ' tism might not be administred by Women. That the Cap and Surplice ' might not be urged. That Examination might go before the Commu- ' nion ; and, that it be not administred without a Sermon. That the terms ' of *Priest* and *Absolution*, with the Ring in Marriage, and some others, ' might be corrected. That the length of Service might be abridged. ' Church Songs and Musick, moderated. And, that the Lords Day be ' not prophaned, nor Holy-days so strictly urged. That there might be ' an Uniformity of Doctrine prescribed. That no Popish Opinion be a- ' ny more taught or defended. That Ministers might not be charged to ' teach their people to bow at the Name of *Jesus*. And, that the Cano- ' nical Scriptures be only read in the Church.

3. In reference to Church-Ministers it was propounded, That none ' hereafter be admitted into the Ministry but Able and Sufficient men ; ' and those to preach diligently, especially upon the Lords Day : but ' such as be already entered, and cannot preach, may either be removed, ' and some charitable course taken with them for their Relief ; or else ' to be forced, according to the value of their Livings, to maintain ' Preachers. That *Non-residency* be not permitted. That K. *Edwards* Sta- ' tute for the lawfulness of Ministers marriage might be revived. That ' Ministers might not be urged to subscribe (but according to the Law) ' the Articles of Religion, and the Kings Supremacy. It was desired al- ' so, in relation to the Churches Maintenance, That Bishops might leave

' their

'their *Commendams*, fome holding Prebends, fome Parfonages, fome
'Vicaridges, with their Bifhopricks. That double Beneficed men might
'not be fuffered to hold fome two, fome three Benefices, and as many
'Dignities. That Impropriations annexed to Bifhopricks and Colleges,
'be demifed only to the Preachers Incumbents for the old Rent. That
'the Impropriations of Lay-mens Fee may be charged with a fixth or
'feventh part of the worth, to the maintenance of a Preaching Mini-
'fter. And finally, in reference to the execution of the Churches Difci-
'pline, it was humbly craved, That the Difcipline and Excommunica-
'tion might be adminiftred according to Chrifts own Inftitution ; or
'at the leaft, that Enormities might be redreffed : as namely, That Ex-
'communication might not come forth under the name of Lay-perfons,
'Chancellors, Officials, &c. That men be not excommunicated for Tri-
'fles, and Twelve-penny matters. That none be excommunicated with-
'out confent of his Paftors. That the Officers be not fuffered to extort
'unreafonable Fees. That none having Jurifdiction, or a Regifters
'Place, put the fame to Farm. That divers Popifh Canons for re-
'ftraint of Marriage at certain times be reverfed. That the length of
'Suits in Ecclefiaftical Courts, (which hung fometimes two, three, four,
'five, fix, feven years) may be reftrained. That the Oath *Ex Officio*,
'whereby men are forced to accufe themfelves, be more fparingly ufed.
'That Licenfes for Marriages, without being asked, may be more fpa-
'ringly granted.

4. And here it is to be obferved, that though there was not one word
in this Petition either againft Epifcopal Government, or Set Forms of
Prayer, yet the defign thereof was againft them both. For if fo many
of the Branches had been lopped at once, the Body of the Tree muft
needs have rotted and confumed in a fhort time after. The two Univerfities, on the contrary were no lefs zealous for keeping up the Difcipline and Liturgy of the Church, then by Law eftablifhed. And to
that end it was propofed, and paffed at *Cambridge*, or the ninth of *June*,
That whofoever fhould oppofe by word or writing, either the Doctrine
or the Difcipline of the Church of *England*, or any part thereof whatfoever, within the Verge and Limits of the fame Univerfity (otherwife
then in the way of Difputation) he fhould be actually fufpended from
all Degrees already taken, and utterly difabled for taking any in the
time to come. They refolved alfo to return an Anfwer to the faid Petition ; but underftanding that the Univerfity of *Oxon* was in hand therewith, and had made a good progrefs in the fame, they laid by that purpofe, congratulating with their Sifter-Univerfity for her forwardnefs
in it, as appears plainly by their Letter of the 7 of *October*. All this was
known unto the King, but he refolved to anfwer them in another way;
and to that end defigned a Conference between the parties. A Conference much defired by thofe of the **Puritan** Faction in Queen *Elizabeths*
time, who could not be induced to grant it ; knowing full well, how
much it tended to the ruine of all publick Government, that matters
once eftablifhed in due form of law fhould be made fubject to difputes.
But King *James*, either out of a defire of his own fatisfaction, or to fhew
his great Abilities in Judgment, Oratory, and Difcourfe, refolved
upon it, and accordingly gave Order for it. To which end certain Delegates

legates of each Party were appointed to attend upon him at his Royal Palace of *Hampton Court*, on the 14*th* of *January* then next following, there to debate the Heads of the said Petition, and to abide his Majesties Pleasure and Determination. At what time there attended on behalf of the Church, the Lord Archbishop of *Canterbury*, the Lord Bishop of *London*, the Bishops of *Durham, Winchester, Worcester, St. Davids, Chichester, Carlisle*, and *Peterborough*; the Dean of the Chapel, *Westminster, Christs Church, Pauls, Worcester, Salisbury, Chester*, and *Windsor* : together with Doctor *King*, Archdeacon of *Nottingham*, and Dr. *Feild*, who afterwards was Dean of *Gloucester* : Apparelled all of them in their Robes and Habits, peculiar to their several Orders.

5. There appeared also in the behalf of the *Millenaries* Dr. *John Reynolds*, and Dr. *Thomas Spark* of *Oxford* Mr. *Chattreton*, and Mr. *Knewstubs*, of *Cambridge* : Apparell'd neither in Priests Gowns, or Canonical Coats; but in such Gowns as were then commonly worn (in reference to the form and fashion of them) by the *Turkey* Merchants; as if they had subscribed to the Opinion of old *T. C.* That we ought rather to conform in all outward Ceremonies to the *Turks*, then the *Papists*. Great hopes they gave themselves for settling the *Calvinian* Doctrines in the Church of *England*, and altering so much in the Polity and Forms of Worship, as might bring it nearer by some steps to the Church of *Geneva*. In reference to the first, it was much prest by Dr. *Reynolds*, in the name of the rest, That the Nine Articles of *Lambeth*, (which he entituled by the name of *Orthodoxal Assertions*) might be received amongst the Articles of the Church. But this Request (upon a true account of the state of that business) was by that prudent King rejected, with as great a constancy as formerly the Articles themselves had been suppressed under Queen *Elizabeth*. It was moved also, That these words (*neither totally nor finally*) might be inserted in the Sixteenth Article of the publick Confession, to the intent that the Article so explained, might speak in favour of the *Zuinglian* or *Calvinian* Doctrine, concerning the impossibility of falling from the state of Grace and Justification. Which Proposition gave a just occasion to Bishop *Bancroft* to speak his sense of the *Calvinian* Doctrine of *Predestination*, which he called in plain terms *A desperate Doctrine*. Upon whose interposings in that particular, and a short Declaration made by the Dean of *St. Pauls*, touching some Heats which had been raised in *Cambridge* in pursuit thereof, this second Motion proved as fruitless as the first had done.

6. Nor sped they better in relation to the Forms of Worship, then they had done in reference unto points of Doctrine. Some pains they took in crying down the Surplice, and the Cross in Baptism, the Ring in Marriage, and the Interrogatories proposed to Infants : And somewhat also was observed touching some Errors in the old Translation of the *English Psalter*; as also in the Gospels and Epistles, as they stood in the Liturgy : But their Objections were so stale, and so often answered, that the Bishops and Conformable Party went away with an easie Victory; not only the Kings Majesty, but the Lords of his Council, being abundantly well satisfied in such former scruples as had been raised against the

the Church and the Orders of it. The ſum and ſubſtance of which Conference, collected by the hand of Dr. *Barlow* then Dean of *Cheſter*, can hardly be abreviated to a leſſer compaſs, without great Injury to the King and the Conferrees. Let it ſuffice that this great Mountain, which had raiſed ſo much expectation, was delivered only of a Mouſe : The *Millenary Plaintiffs* have gained nothing by their fruitleſs travel, but the expounding of the word *Abſolution* by *Remiſſion of Sins* ; the qualifying of the *Rubrick* about Private Baptiſm ; the adding of ſome Thankſgivings at the end of the Litany, and of ſome Queſtions and Anſwers in the cloſe of the Catechiſm. But on the other ſide the Brethren loſt ſo much in their Reputation, that the King was very well ſatisfied in the weakneſs of their Objections, and the Injuſtice of their Cavils ; inſomuch that turning his head towards ſome of the Lords, *If this be all* (quoth he) *which they have to ſay, I will either make them conform themſelves, or hurry them out of the Land, or do ſomewhat which is worſe,* p. 85. Which notwithſtanding they gave out, ' That all was theirs ; and that they ' had obtained an abſolute Victory : but more particularly that the King ' gratified Dr. *Reynolds* in every thing which he propoſed ; and that Dr. ' *Reynolds* obtained and prevailed in every thing they did deſire. That if ' any man report the contrary he doth lye ; and that they could give ' him the lye from Dr. *Reynolds* his mouth : that theſe things now obtai- ' ned by the Reformers, were but the beginning of Reformation ; the ' greater matters being yet to come. That my Lord of *Winton* ſtood ' mute, and ſaid little or nothing. That my Lord of *London* called Dr. ' *Reynolds Schiſmatick* ; (he thanks him for it) but otherwiſe ſaid little ' to the purpoſe. That the Kings Majeſty uſed the Biſhops with very ' hard words ; but embraced Dr. *Reynolds*, and uſed moſt kind ſpeeches ' to him. That my Lord of *Canterbury*, and my Lord of *London* falling ' on their knees, beſought his Majeſty to take their Cauſe into his ' own Hands, and to make ſome good end of it, ſuch as might ſtand ' with their Credit.

7. All this and more they ſcattered up and down in their ſurrilous Papers, to keep up the ſpirits of their Party ; two of which coming to the hands of Dr. *Barlow* before mentioned, he cauſed them to be publiſhed at the end of the Conference : The Truth and Honeſty of whoſe Collections, having been univerſally approved above fifty years, hath been impugned of late by ſome ſorry Scriblers of the Puritan Faction ; and a report raiſed of ſome Retractation which he is fabled to have made at the time of his death, of the great wrong which he had done to Dr. *Reynolds*, and the reſt of the *Millenaries*. The ſillineſs of which Fiction hath been elſewhere canvaſed, and therefore not to be repeated in this time and place. But for the clearing of that Reverend perſon from ſo foul a Calumny, we ſhall not make uſe of any other Argument, then the words of King *James*, who tells us in his Proclamation of the fifth of *March*, that he could not conceal, *That the ſucceſs of that Conference was ſuch as hapneth to many other things, which moving great expectations before they be entered into, in their iſſue produce ſmall effects : That he found mighty and vehement Informations ſupported with ſo weak and ſlender Proofs, as it appeared unto him and his Council ; that there was no cauſe why any change ſhould be in that which was moſt impugned, namely, The Book of*

Common Prayer, containing the publick Service of God here established ; nor in the Doctrine, which appeared to be sincere ; nor in the Forms and Rites, which were justified out of the practice of the primitive Church : And finally, that though with the consent of the Bishops and other learned men and then and there assembled, some passages therein were rather explained then altered; yet, that the same might very well have been born amongst such men who would have made a reasonable construction of them.   Which I conceive to be sufficient for the vindication of that Learned Prelate, for clearing him from doing any injury to Dr. *Reynolds*, in the repeating of his words, as is suggested by some *Puritan* Scriblers of these present times.

8. But to proceed : This Conference was followed with the Proclamation of the fifth of *March* ; in which his Majesty having first declared the occasion and success thereof, in the words formerly laid down, proceeds to signifie the present course which he had taken for ‘ causing the Book of Common Prayer to be so explained ; and being ‘ so explained, to be forthwith Printed : not doubting but that all his ‘ Subjects, both Ministers and others, would receive the same with due ‘ reverence, and conform themselves to it. Which notwithstanding he ‘ conceived it necessary to make known his Authorizing of the same by ‘ his Proclamation, and by that Proclamation to require and enjoyn all ‘ men, as well Ecclesiastical as Temporal, to conform themselves there- ‘ unto, as to the only publick Form of serving God, established and al- ‘ lowed in this Realm.   Which said, he lays a strict command on all ‘ Archbishops, and Bishops, and all other publick Ministers, as well ‘ Ecclesiastical as Civil, for causing the same to be observed, and punish- ‘ ing all Offenders to the contrary, according to the Laws of the Realm ‘ made in that behalf. Finally, He admonisheth all his Subjects of what ‘ sort soever, not to expect hereafter any Alteration in the publick Form ‘ of Gods Service, from that which he had then established. And this ‘ he signified (as afterward it followeth in the said Proclamation) be- ‘ cause that he neither would give way to any to presume, that his judg- ‘ ment having determined in a matter of such weight, should be swayed ‘ to any Alteration by the Frivolous Suggestions of any light head ; ‘ nor could be ignorant of the inconveniencies that do arise in Govern- ‘ ment, by admitting *Innovation* in things once settled by mature delibe- ‘ ration ; and how necessary it was to use constancy in the publick De- ‘ terminations of all States : for that (saith he) such is the unquietness ‘ and unstedfastness of some dispositions, affecting every year new Forms ‘ of things, as if they should be followed in their unconstancy, would ‘ make all Actions of State ridiculous and contemptible ; whereas the ‘ steadfast maintaining of things by good Advice established, is the Pre- ‘ servative and Weal of all publick Governments.

9. The main concernments of the Church being thus secured, his Ma- jesty proceeds to his first Parliament; accompanied as the custom is with a Convocation ; which took beginning on the twentieth day of *March* then next ensuing. In the Parliament there passed some Acts which con- cerned the Church; as namely, one for making void all Grants and Leases which should be made of any of the Lands of Archbishops and Bishops, to the Kings Majesty, or any of his Heirs & Successors, for more then one & twenty years, or three lives. Which Act was seasonably procured by Bishop

shop *Bancroft*, to prevent the begging of the *Scots*, who otherwise would have picked the Church to the very bone. There also past an Act for the repealing of a Statute in the Reign of Queen *Mary*, by means whereof the Statute of King *Edward* the sixth, touching the lawfulness of Ministers Marriages, were revived again, as in the *Millenary Petition* was before desired. And either by the Practises of some *Puritan* Zealots, who had their Agents in all corners, or by the carelesness and connivence of his Majesty's Council, learned in the Laws of this Realm, who should have had an eye upon them, that Statute of K. *Edward* was revived also, by which it was enacted, that all Processes, Citations, Judgments, &c. in any of the Ecclesiastical Courts, should be issued in the Kings Name, and under the Kings Seal of Arms; which afterwards gave some colour to the *Puritan* Faction, for creating trouble to the Bishops in their Jurisdiction. The Convocation was more active; some days before the sitting whereof the most Reverend Archbishop *Whitgift* departs this life, and leaves it to the managing of Dr. *Richard Bancroft*, Bishop of *London*, as the President of it : By whose great industry and indefatigable pains a Body of Canons was collected, to the number of one hundred forty one, out of the Articles, Injunctions, and Synodal Acts during the Reigns of Queen *Elizabeth* and K. *Edward* the sixth. Which being methodically digested, approved of in the Convocation, and ratified by his Majesty's Letters Patents in the due form of a w, were stoutly put in execution by the said Dr. *Bancroft*, translated to the See of *Canterbury* in the Moneth of *December, Anno* 1604.

10. And to say truth, it did concern him to be resolute in that prosecution, considering how strict a Bond was made by many of the Brethren, when they agreed unto the drawing of the former Petition : by which they bound themselves not only to seek redress of those particulars which are comprehended in the same ; *but that the state of the Church might be reformed in all things needful, according to the Rule of Gods holy Word, and agreeable to the example of other Reformed Churches, which had restored both their Doctrine and Discipline, as it was delivered by our Saviour Christ and his holy Apostles.* And how far that might reach, none knew better then he ; who in his Note of *Dangerous Positions and Proceedings*, and his *Survey of the pretended holy Discipline*, had founded the depth of their designs, and found that nothing could ensue upon their Positions, but a most unavoidable ruine to the Church and State. He had observed with what a pevish malice they had libelled against Archbishop *Whitgift* (a Prelate of a meek and moderate spirit) after his decease; and could not but expect a worse dealing from them ; which he after found, by how much he had handled them more coursly then his Predecessor. For though the Lords had shewed their zeal unto the memory of that famous Prelate, by the severe punishment of *Pickering* who made the Libell ; yet well he knew, that the terror of that punishment would be quickly over, if a hard hand were not also kept upon all the rest. And for keeping a hard hand upon all the rest he was encouraged by the words of King *James* at the end of the Conference, when he affirmed, *That he would either make the* Puritans *conform themselves, or else would hurry them out of the Land, or do that which was worse.* Upon which grounds he set himself upon the work, requires a strict conformity to the rules of the Church, according

ding to the Laws and Canons in that behalf ; and without ſparing
Non-conformiſts, or Half-Conformiſts, at laſt reduced them to that
point, That they muſt either leave their Churches, or obey the Church.
The *Altar* of *Damaſcus* tells us, if we may believe him, That no fewer
then three hundred Preaching Miniſters, were either ſilenced or deprived upon that account. But the Authors of that Book, whoſoever they
were, who uſe ſometimes to *ſtrain at Gnats, and ſwallow a Camel* ; at
other times can make a Mountain of a Mole-hill, if it ſtand in their
way : For it appears upon the Rolls brought in by Biſhop *Bancroft* before his death, that there had been but 49 deprived upon all occaſions ;
which in a Realm containing 9000 Pariſhes, could be no great matter.
But ſo it was, that by the puniſhment of ſome few of the Principals, he
ſtruck ſuch a general terror into all the reſt, that inconformity grew
out of faſhion in a leſs time then could be eaſily imagined.

11. Hereupon followed a great alteration in the Face of Religion ;
more Churches beautified and repaired in this ſhort time of his Government, then had been in many years before : The Liturgy more ſolemnly
officiated by the Prieſts, and more religiouſly attended by the common
people ; the Faſts and Feſtivals more punctually obſerved by both, then
of later times. Coaps brought again into the Service of the Church, the
Surplice generally worn without doubt or hæſitancy ; and all things in
a manner are reduced to the ſame eſtate in which they had been firſt ſetled under Queen *Elizabeth* : which, though it much redounded to the
Honour of the Church of *England* ; yet gave it no ſmall trouble to ſome
ſticklers for the *Puritan* Faction, expreſt in many ſcandalous Libels, and
ſeditious railings ; in which this Reverend Prelate ſuffered both alive
and dead. Some who had formerly ſubſcribed, but not without ſome
ſecret evaſion, or mental reſervation which they kept to themſelves, are
now required to teſtifie their Conformity by a new ſubſcription, in which
it was to be declared, that they did *willingly* & ex animo, *ſubſcribe to the
three Articles,* (formerly tendred to the Clergy under Archbiſhop *Whitgift*,
but now incorporated into the thirty ſix Canons) *and to all things in the
ſame contained.* Which leaving them no ſtarting-hole either for practiſing thoſe Rites and Ceremonies which they did not approve, or for approving that which they meant not to practiſ ; as they had done formerly ; occaſioned many of them to forſake their Benefices, rather then
to ſubſcribe according to the true intention of the Church in the ſaid
three Articles : Amongſt which, none more eminent then Dr. *John
Burges*, beneficed at that time in *Lincoln* Dioceſs, who for ſome paſſages in a Sermon preached before the King, on the 19 of *Iune*, 1604,
was committed Priſoner : and being then required by the Biſhop of *London* to ſubſcribe thoſe Articles, he abſolutely made refuſal of it ; and
preſently thereupon reſigned his Benefice ; the reaſons whereof, he gives
in a long Letter to Dr. *William Chatterton*, then Biſhop of *Lincoln.* He
applied himſelf alſo, both by Letter and Petition, to his Sacred Majeſty,
clearing himſelf from all intention of preaching any thing in that Sermon which might give any juſt offence ; and humbly praying for a
reſtitution, not to his Church, but only to his Majeſties Favour. Which
gained ſo far upon the King, that he admitted him not long after
to a perſonal Conference, recovered him unto his ſtation in the Church,

from

from which he was fallen: and finally, occasioned his preferring to the Rectory of *Colshill*, in the County of *Warwick*. After which, he became a profest Champion of the Government and Liturgy of the Church of *England*; both which he justified against all the Cavils of the *Non Conformists*, as appears by a Learned Book of his, entituled, *An Answer rejoyned to the applauded Pamphlet*, &c. published in the year 1631.

12. But the gaining of this man did not still the rest: For presently   1605. on the neck of this, comes out a Factious Pamphlet, published by the *Lincoln-shire* Ministers, which they call *The Abridgment*; containing the sum and substance of all those Objections which either then were, or formerly had been made against the Church, in reference to Doctrine, Government, or Forms of Worship: Concerning which, it is observed by the said Dr. *Burges*, That he found the state of the Questions to be very much altered in the same; that *Cartwright*, and the rest, in the times foregoing, though they had sharpned both their Wits and Pens against the Ceremonies, opposed them as inconvenient only, but not unlawful: That therefore they endeavoured to perswade the Ministers rather to conform themselves, then to leave their Flocks; the people, rather to receive the Communion kneeling, then not to receive the same at all: but, that the Authors of that Book, and some other Pamphlets, pronounced them to be simply unlawful, neither to be imposed nor used; some of them thinking it a great part of godliness to cast off the Surplice, and commanded their Children so to do. This made the Bishops far more earnest to reduce them to a present Conformity, then otherwise they might have been, though by so doing they encreased those discontents, the seeds whereof were sown at the end of the Conference. All this the *Papists* well observed, and rejoyced at it, intending in the carrying on of the Gun-powder Treason, to lay the guilt thereof on the *Puritans* only. But the King and his Council mined with them, and undermined them, and by so doing blew them up in their own Invention; the Traytors being discovered, condemned, and executed, as they most justly had deserved. But this Design which was intended for a ruine of the *Puritan* Faction, proved in conclusion very advantagious to their Ends and Purposes: For, the King being throughly terrified with the apprehension of so great a danger, turned all his thoughts upon the *Papists*, and was content to let the *Puritans* take breath, and regain some strength, that they might serve him for a counterpoise against the other: as afterwards he gave some countenance to the *Popish* Party, when he perceived the opposite Faction to be grown too head-strong. Nor were the *Puritans* wanting to themselves upon this occasion, but entertained the Court and Country with continual fears of some new dangers from the *Papists*; and by appearance of much zeal for the true Religion, and no less care for the preserving of their common Liberty against the encroachments of the Court, came by degrees to make a Party in the House of Commons. And hereunto King *James* unwittingly contributed his assistance also; who being intent upon uniting the two Kingdoms by Act of Parliament, suffered the Commons to expatiate in Rhetorical Speeches, to call in question the extent of his Royal Prerogative, to embrue many Church-concernments, and to dispute the

power

power of the High Commiſſion : By means whereof they came at laſt to ſuch an height, that the King was able in the end to do nothing in Parliament, but as he courted and applyed himſelf to this popular Faction.

13. Worſe fared it with the Brethren of the Separation, who had retired themſelves unto *Amſterdam* in the former Reign, then with their firſt Founders and Forefathers in the Church of *England* : For having broken in ſunder the *Bond of Peace*, they found no poſſibility of preſerving the *Spirit of Unity* ; one Separation growing continually on the neck of another, till they were crumbled into nothing. The Brethren of the firſt Seporation had found fault with the Church of *England* for reading Prayers and Homilies as they lay in the Book, and not admitting the *Presbytery* to take place amongſt them. But the Brethren of the ſecond Separation take as much diſtaſte againſt retaining all Set forms of Hymns and Pſalms, committing their Conceptions, both in Praying and Propheſying, to the help of Memory ; and did as much abominate Presbytery, as the other liked it : For firſt, They pre-ſuppoſe for granted, as they ſafely might, that there be three kinds of Spiritual Worſhip, *Praying*, *Propheſying*, and *Singing of Pſalms* ; and then ſubjoyn this Maxim, in which all agreed, that is to ſay, That there is the ſame reaſon of Helps in all the parts of Spiritual Worſhip, as is to be admitted in any one, during the performing of that Worſhip. Upon which ground they charge it home on their fellow-Separatiſts, That, *as in Prayer the Book is to be laid aſide, by the confeſſion of the ancient Brethren of the Separation, ſo muſt it alſo be in Propheſying and Singing of Pſalms : and therefore, whether we pray, or ſing, or propheſie, it is not to be from the Book, but out of the heart.* For *Propheſying*, next, they tell us, that the Spirit is quenched two manner of ways, by Memory, as well as Reading. And to make known how little uſe there is of Memory in the Act of Propheſying or Preaching, they tell us, That the citing of Chapter and Verſe (as not being uſed by Chriſt and his Apoſtles in their Sermons or Writings) is a mark of Antichriſt. And as for *Pſalms*, which make the third part of Spiritual Worſhip, they propoſe theſe Queries : 1. *Whether in a Pſalm a man muſt be tyed to* Meeter, Rythme, *and* Tune ? *and whether* Voluntary *be not as neceſſary in* Tune *and* Words, *as well as* Matter ? And 2. *Whether* Meeter, Rythme, *and* Tune, *be not* quenching the Spirit ?

14. According to which Reſolution of the *New Separation* every man, when the Congregation ſhall be met together, may firſt conceive his own Matter in the Act of Praiſing ; deliver it in Proſe or Meeter, as he liſts himſelf ; and in the ſame inſtant chant out in what Tune ſoever that which comes firſt into his own head : Which would be ſuch a horrible confuſion of Tongues and Voices, that hardly and any howling or gnaſhing of teeth can be like unto it. And yet it follows ſo directly on the former Principles, that if we baniſh all ſet Forms of Common Prayer, (which is but only one part of Gods Publick Worſhip) from the uſe of the Church, we cannot but in Juſtice and in Reaſon both, baniſh all *ſtudied* and *pre-meditated* Sermons from the Houſe of God, and utterly caſt out all King *Davids* Pſalms, (whether in Proſe or Meeter, that comes all to one) and all Divine Hymns alſo into the bargain.

gain. Finally, as to Forms of Government, they declared thus, (or to this purpose, at the least, if my memory fail not) That as they which live under the Tyranny of the Pope and Cardinals, worship the *very Beast* it self; and they which live under the Government of Archbishops and Bishops, do worship the *Image of the Beast*; so they which willingly obey the Reformed Presbytery of Pastors, Elders, and Deacons, worship the *shadow of that Image*. To such ridiculous Follies are men commonly brought, when once presuming on some *New Light* to direct their Actions, they suffer themselves to be misguided by the *Ignis fatuus* of their own Inventions. And in this posture stood the *Brethren of the Separation*, Anno 1606, when *Smith* first published his Book of the present differences between the Churches of the *Separation*, as he honestly calls them. But afterwards there grew another great dispute between *Ainsworth* and *Broughton*, Whether the colour of *Aaron's* Linen *Ephod* were of *Blew*, or a *Sea water Green*: Which did not only trouble all the *Dyers in Amsterdam*, but drew their several Followers into Sides and Factions, and made good sport to all the World, but themselves alone. By reason of which Divisions and Sub-divisions, they fell at last into so many Fractions, that one of them in the end became a Church of himself, and having none to joyn in Opinion with him, baptized himself, and thereby got the name of a *Sea-baptist*; which never any Sectary or Heretick had obtained before.

15. It fell not out much otherwise in the *Belgick* Provinces, with those of the *Calvinian* Judgment, who then began to find some diminution of that Power and Credit wherewith they carried all before them in the times preceding. *Junius*, a very moderate and learned man, and one of the Professors for Divinity in the Schools of *Leyden* departed out of this life in the same year also; into whose Place the Overseers, or *Curators*, as they call them, of that University, made choice of *Jacob Van Harmine*, a man of equal Learning, and no less Piety. He had for fifteen years before, been Pastor (as they love to phrase it) to the great Church of *Amsterdam*, the chief City of *Holland*; during which time he published his Discourse against the Doctrine of *Predestination*, as laid down by *Perkins*, who at that time had printed his *Armilla Aurea*, and therein justified all the Rigours of the *Supra-lapsarians*. Encouraged with his good success in this Adventure, he undertakes a Conference on the same Argument with the Learned *Junius*, one of the *Sub-lapsarian* Judgment; the summe whereof being spread abroad in several Papers, was afterward set forth by the name of *Amica Collatio*. By means whereof, as he attained a great esteem with all moderate men, so he exceedingly exasperated most of the *Calvinian* Ministers, who thereupon opposed his coming to *Leyden* with their utmost power, accusing him of Heterodoxies and unsound Opinions, to the Council of *Holland*. But the *Curators* being constant in their Resolutions, and *Harmin* having purged himself from all Crimes objected before his Judges at the *Hague*; he is dispatched for *Leyden*, admitted by the University, and confirmed by the Estate : Towards which the Testimonial Letters sent from *Amsterdam* did not help a little; in which he stands commended for a man of an * *unblameable life, sound Doctrine, and fair behaviour*; as by their Letters may appear, exemplified in an Oration which was made at his Funeral.

                      16. By

* *Ob vitæ inculpatæ, sanes doctrinæ, & morum sumam integritatem, Hunc, Orat.*

16. By which Attractives he prevailed as much amongst the Students of *Leyden*, as he had done amongst the Merchants at *Amsterdam*. For during the short time of his sitting in the Chair of *Leyden*, he drew unto him a great part of that University; who by the Piety of the man, his powerful Arguments, his extream diligence in that place, and the clear light of Reason which appeared in all his Discourses, became so wedded at the last unto his Opinions, that no time or trouble could divorce them from *Harmin*: Dying in the yeer 1609, the Heat, betwixt his Scholars, and those of a contrary Perswasion, were rather encreased then abated; the more encreased for want of such prudent Moderators as had before preserved the Churches from a publick Rupture. The breach between them growing wider and wider, each side thought fit to seek the countenance of the State; and they did accordingly. For in the year 1610 the Followers of *Arminius* addrefs their *Remonstrance* (containing the Antiquity of their Doctrines, and the substance of them) to the States of *Holland*, which was encountred presently by a *Contra-Remonstrance*, exhibited by those of *Calvins* Party: from hence the Name of *Remonstrants*, and *Contra-Remonstrants*, so frequent in their Books and Writings. Which though it brought some trouble for the present on the Churches of *Holland*, conduced much more to the advantage of the Church of *England*, whose Doctrine in those points had been so over-born, if not quite suppressed, by those of the *Calvinian* Party, that it was almost reckoned for a Heresie to be found and Orthodox, according to the tenour of the Book of Articles, and other publick Monuments of the Religion here by Law established. For being awakened by the noise of the *Belgick* Troubles, most men began to look about them, to search more narrowly into the Doctrines of the Church, and by degrees to propagate, maintain, and teach them against all Opposers, as shall appear more largely and particularly in another place.

17. At the same time more troubles were projected in the Realm of *Sweden*; Prince *Sigismund*, the eldest Son of *John*, and the Grand-child of *Gustavus Ericus*, the first King of that Family, was in his Fathers life time chosen King of *Poland*, in reference to his Mother, the Lady *Catherine*, Sifter to *Sigismund* the second. But either being better pleased with the Court of *Poland*, or not permitted by that people to go out of the Kingdom, he left the Government of *Sweden* to his Uncle *Charles*, a Prince of no small Courage, but of more Ambition. At first he governed all Affairs as Lord Deputy only, but practised by degrees the exercise of a greater Power then was belonging to a Vice-Roy. Finding the *Lutherans* not so favourable unto his Designs, as he conceived that he had merited by his Favours to them, he raised up a *Calvinian* Party within the Realm, according to whose Principles he began first to withdraw his obedience from his Natural Prince, and after to assume the Government to himself. But first he suffers all Affairs to fall into great Disorders, the Realm to be invaded by the *Muscovites* on the one side, by the *Danes* on the other, that so the people might be cast on some necessity of putting themselves absolutely under his protection. In which distractions he is earnestly sollicited by all sorts of people, except only

only thofe of his own Party, to accept the Crown; which he confents to at the laft, as if forced unto it by the neceffity of his Countrey. But he fo play'd his Game withall, that he would neither take the fame, nor protect the Subjects, till a Law was made for entailing the Crown for ever unto his Pofterity, whether *Male* or *Female*, as an Hereditary Kingdom. In all which Plots and Purpofes, he thrived fo luckily, (if to ufurp another Princes Realm may be called *Good luck*) that after a long War, and fome Bloody Victories, he forced his Nephew to defift from all further Enterprifes, and was Crowned King at *Stockholm*, in the year 1607. But as he got this Kingdom by no better Title then of Force and Fraud; fo by the fame, the Daughter of his Son *Guftavus Adolphus*, was divefted of it, partly compelled, and partly cheated out of her Eftate. So foon expired the Race of this great Politician, that many thoufands of that people who faw the firft beginning of it, lived to fee the end.

18. Such Fortune alfo had the *French Calvinians* in their glorious Projects, though afterwards it turned to their deftruction. For in the year 1603, they held a general Synod at *Gappe* in *Daulphine*, anciently the chief City of the *Apencenfes*, and at this time a Bifhop's See. Nothing more memorable in this Synod (as to points of Doctrine) then it was determined for an Article of their Faith, That *the Pope was Antichrift*. But far more memorable was it for their Ufurpations on the Civil Power. For at this Meeting they gave Audience to the Embaffadors of fome Foreign States, as if they had been a Common-wealth diftinct from the Realm of *France*. More then which they audacioufly importuned the King (of whofe affection to them they prefumed too far) by their feveral Agents, for liberty of going wherefover they lifted, or fending whomfoever they pleafed, to the Councils and Affemblies of all Neighbouring-Eftates and Nations which profeft the fame Religion with them. This though it had not been the firft, was looked on as their greateft encroachment on the Royal Authority, which in conclufion proved the ruine of their caufe and Party. For what elfe could this aim at, (as was well obferved by the King then reigning) but to make themfelves a State diftinct and independent, to raife up a new Common-wealth in the midft of a Kingdom, and to make the Schifm as great in Civil, as in Sacred matters: Which wrought fo far upon the Councils of his next Succeffor, who had not been trained up amongft them as his Father was, that he refolved to call them to a fober reckoning on the next occafion, and to drive them all at once of thofe Powers and Priviledges which they fo wantonly abufed unto his difturbance. Of which we fhall fpeak more hereafter in its proper place.

In the mean time let us crofs over into *Scotland*, where all Affairs moved retrograde, and feemed to threaten a relapfe to their old confufions. A general Affembly had been intimated to be held at *Aberdeen*, in the moneth of *July Anno* 1604, which by reafon that the King was wholy taken up with effecting the Union, was adjourned to the fame moneth, in the year next following. In the mean feafon, fome of the more Factious Minifters, hoping to raife no fmall advantage to themfelves and their Party, by the abfence of fo many Perfons of moft Power and Credit, began to entertain new Counfels for the unravelling of that Web　　　　　which

1605.

which the King had lately wrought with such care and cunning. The King hears of it, and gives order to suspend the Meeting till his further Pleasure were declared. Wherein he was so far obeyed by the major part, that of the fifty Presbyteries into which the whole Kingdom was divided, *Anno* 1592, nine only sent Commissioners to attend at *Aberdeen*. When the day came, the meeting was so thin and slender, that there appeared not above one and twenty, when they were at the fullest. But they were such as were resolved to stand stoutly to it, each man conceiving himself able in the Cause of God, to make resistance to an Army. The Laird of *Lowreston* commands them in the Kings Name to return to their Houses, to discontinue that unlawful Assembly, and not to meet on any publick occasion which concerned the Church, but by his Majesty's appointment. They answer, that they were assembled at that time and place, according to the word of God, and the Laws of the Land; and that they would not betray the Liberties of the Kirk of *Scotland*, by obeying such unlawful Prohibitions. Which said, and having desired him to withdraw a while, they made choice of one *Forbes* for their Moderator, and so adjourned themselves to *September* following. *Lowreston* thereupon denounced them Rebels; and fearing that some new affront might be put upon him, and consequently on the King, in whose Name he acted, he seeks for remedy and Prevention to the Lords of the Council: *Forbes* and *Welch*, the two chief sticklers in the Cause, are by them convented; and not abating any thing of their former obstinacy, are both sent Prisoners unto *Blackness*: A day is given for the appearance of the rest, which was the third day of *October*; at what time thirteen of the number made acknowledgment of their offence, and humbly supplicated, that their Lordships would endeavour to procure their pardon: the rest remaining in their disobedience, are by the Lords disposed of into several Prisons.

19. But these proceedings did so little edefie with that stubborn Faction, that the Lords of the Council were condemned for their just severity, and all their Actings made to aim at no other end but by degrees to introduce the Rights and Ceremonies of the Church of *England*. The King endeavours by a Declaration to undeceive his good people, and reclaim these obstinate persons from the ways of ruin; and intimates withall, that new Assembly should be held at *Dundee* in *July* following. But this prevails as little as the former course. Which puts the business on so far, that either the King must be conformable to their present humour, or they submit themselves to the Kings just power. The Lords resolve upon the last, command them to appear at the Council Table, to receive their Sentence, and nominated the 24*th* of *October* for the day of Doom. Accordingly they came, but they came prepared, having subscribed a publick Instrument under all their hands, by which they absolutely decline the Judgment of the King and Council, as altogether incompetent, and put themselves upon the tryal of the next Assembly, as their lawful Judge. Before they were convented only for their disobedience; but by this Declinator, they have made themselves Traytors. The King is certified of all this; and being resolved upon the maintenance of his own Authority, gave order that the Law should pass upon them, according to the Statute made in Parliament, *Anno* 1584. Hereupon

Forbes,

Forbes, *Welch*, *Duncam*, *Sharp*, *Davie*, *Straghan*, are removed from *Blackness*, arraigned at an Assize held in *Linlithgoe*, found guilty by the Jury, and condemned to death ; but all of them returned to their several Prisons till the Kings pleasure should be known for their Execution. The *Melvins*, and some other of the principal Zealots, caused Prayers and Supplications to be made in behalf of the Traytors, though they had generally refused to perform that office when the Kings Mother was upon the point of losing her life, upon a more unwarrantable Sentence of Condemnation. This brought forth first a Proclamation, inhibiting all Ministers to recommend the condemned persons unto God in their Prayers or Sermons ; and afterwards a Letter to some Chiefs amongst them, for waiting on his Majesty at the Court in *England*, where they should be admitted to a publick Conference, and have the King to be their Judge.

20. Upon this Summons there appear in behalf of the Church the Archbishops of St. *Andrews* and *Glasgow*, the Bishops of *Orkney* and *Galloway*, together with *Nicolson* the designed Bishop of *Dunkeeden* ; and for the Kirk the two *Melvins*, *Bolt*, *Carmichall*, *Scot*, *Balfour*, and *Watson*. The place appointed for the Conference was *Hampton Court*, at which they all attended on *Septemb.* 20. But the Kirk Party came resolved neither to satisfie the King nor be satisfied by him, though he endeavoured all fit ways for their information. To which end he appointed four Eminent and Learned Prelates to preach before them in their turns : the first of which was Dr. *Barlow*, then Bishop of *Rochester*, who learnedly asserted the Episcopal Power out of those words to the Elders at *Ephesus*, recorded *Acts* 20. *v.* 28. The second was Dr. *Buckeridge*, then Master of St. *John's* College in *Oxon*, and afterwards preferred to the See of *Rochester* ; who no less learnedly evinced the Kings Supremacy in all concernments of the Church ; selecting for his Text the words of the same Apostle, *Rom.* 13. *v.* 1. Next followed Dr. *Andrews*, then Bishop of *Chichester*; who taking for his Text those words of *Moses*, viz. *Make the two Trumpets of silver,* &c. *Numb.* 10. *v.* 2. convincingly demonstrated out of all Antiquity, that the calling of all General and National Councils had appertained unto the Supreme Christian Magistrate. Dr. *King*, then Dean of *Christs Church* brings up the Rear; and taking for his Text those words of the *Canticles*, Cap. 8. *v.* 11. disproved the calling of Lay-Elders, as men that had no power in governing the Church of Christ, nor were so much as heard of in the Primitive times. But neither the Learned Discourses of these four Prelates, nor the Arguments of the *Scotish* Bishops, nor the Authority and Elocution of the King, could gain at all on these deaf Adders, who came resolved not to hear the voice of those Charmers, *charmed they never so wisely*. Thus have we seen them in their Crimes, and now we are to look upon them in their several punishments. And first the Ministers which had been summoned into *England*, were there commanded to remain until further. The six which were condemned for Treason, were sentenced by the King to perpetual banishment, and never to return to their native Countrey upon pain of death. And as for those which had acknowledged their offence and submitted to mercy, they were confined unto the Isles and Out-parts of the Kingdom, where they may possibly work some good, but could do no harm.

harm. After which, *Andrew Melvin* having made a Seditious Libell
againſt the Altar, and the Furniture thereof, in his Majeſty's Chappel,
was brought into the Star-Chamber by an *Ore tenus*, where he behaved
himſelf ſo malepertly toward all the Lords, and more particularly towards the Archbiſhop of *Canterbury*, that he was ſentenced to impriſonment in the Tower of *London*, and there remained till he was begged
by the Duke of *Bouillon*, and by him made Profeſſor of Divinity in the
School of *Sedan*.

21. During the time that all mens Eyes were faſtned on the iſſue of
this great diſpute, the King thought fit to call a Parliament in *Scotland*,
which he managed by Sir *George Hume*, his right truſty Servant not long
before created Earl of *Dunbar*, and made Lord Treaſurer of that Kingdom. His chief Work was to ſettle the Authority of the King, and
the calling of Biſhops, that they might mutually ſupport each other in
the Government of the Church and State. It was ſuppoſed, that no
ſmall oppoſition would be made againſt him by ſome *Puritan* Miniſters,
who repaired in great numbers to the Town, as on their parts it was reſolved on. But he applyed himſelf unto them with ſuch Art and Prudence, that having taken off their edg, the Acts paſſed eaſily enough
with the Lords and Commons. By the firſt Act, the Kings Prerogative was confirmed over all Perſons, and in all Cauſes whatſoever:
Which made him much more abſolute in all Affairs which had relation
to the Church, then he had been formerly. And by the next entituled,
An Act for Reſtitution of the Eſtate of Biſhops ; the name of *Biſhops* was
conferred upon ſuch of the Miniſters, as by the King were nominated
unto any of the Biſhop-Sees, and thereby authorized to have place in
Parliament : A courſe was alſo taken by it, to repoſſeſs the Biſhops of
the Lands of their ſeveral Churches as well as their Titles and Degree:
not that a Plenary repoſſeſſion of their Lands was then given unto them;
but that by a Repeal of the late Act of Annexation, the King was put
into a capacity of reſtoring ſo much of the Rents as remained in the
1606. Crown, and otherwiſe providing for them out of his Revenues. And
that the like diſtraction might not be made of their Eſtates for the time
to come, an Act was paſſed for reſtraining ſuch Dilapidations as had
impoveriſh'd all the Biſhopricks ſince the Reformation. After which,
and the dooming of the greater Zealots to their ſeveral Puniſhments,
he indicts a general Aſſembly at *Linlithgow* in *December* following : at
which convened one hundred thirty ſix Miniſters, and about thirty
three of the Nobility and principal Gentry, In this Aſſembly it was
offered in behalf of his Majeſty, that all Presbyteries ſhould have their
conſtant Moderators ; for whoſe encouragement his Majeſty would
aſſign to each of them a yearly ſtipend amounting to one hundred
pounds, or two hundred Marks in the *Scots* account : that the Biſhops
ſhould be Moderator of all Presbyteries in the Towns and Cities where
they made their reſidence ; as alſo in Provincial and Dioceſan Synods :
and that the Biſhops ſhould aſſume upon themſelves the charge of
proſecuting *Papiſts*, till they returned to their obedience to the King
and the Church. In the obtaining of which Acts, there was no ſmall
difficulty ; but he obtained them at the laſt, though not without ſome
limitations and reſtrictions ſuper-added to them, under pretence of
keeping

keeping the Commissioners (hereafter to be called *Bishops*) within their bounds.

22. The *Presbyterians* notwithstanding, were not willing to fore go their Power ; but strugling like half-dying men betwixt life and death, laid hold on all advantages which were offered to them, in opposition to the Acts before agreed on. *Gladstanes* Archbishop of St. *Andrews*, taking upon him to preside as Moderator in the Synod of *Fife*, being within his proper Diocess and Jurisdiction, was for a while opposed by some of the Ministers, who would have gone to an Election as at other times. The Presbyteries also in some places refused to admit the Bishops for their Moderators, according to the Acts and Constitutions of the said Assembly. Which though it put the Church into some disorder, yet the Bishops carried it at the last, the stoutest of the Ministers submitting in the end unto that Authority which they were not able to contend with. In which conjuncture the King gives order for a Parliament to be held in *June* ; in which he passed some severe Laws against the *Papists*, prohibiting the sending of their Children to be educated beyond the Seas, and giving order for the choice of Pedagogues or Tutors to instruct them there ; as also against Jesuits, and the Sayers and Hearers of Mass. The cognizance of several Causes which anciently belonged to the Bishops Courts, had of late times been settled in the Sessions or College of Justice : But by an Act of this Parliament, they are severed from it, and the Episcopal Jurisdiction restored as formerly ; the Lords of the Session being in lieu thereof, rewarded with ten thousand pounds yearly, (which must be understood according to the *Scottish* account) out of the Customs of that Kingdom. It was enacted also that the King from thenceforth might appoint such habit as to him seemed best, to Judges, Magistrates and Churchmen. Which Acts being past, Patterns were sent from *London* in a short time after, for the Apparel of the Lords of the Session, the Justice and other inferior Judges ; for the Advocates, the Lawyers, the Commissairs, and all that lived by practise of the Law ; with a command given to every one whom the Statutes concerned, to provide themselves of the Habits prescribed, within a certain space, under the pain of Rebellion. But for the habit of the Bishops and other Churchmen, it was thought fit to respite the like appointment of them, till the new Bishops had received their Consecration ; to which now we hasten.

1609.

23. But by the way, we must take notice of such preparations as were made towards it in the next General Assembly held at *Glasgow Anno* 1610, and managed by the Earl of *Dunbar*, as the former was : in which it was concluded, *That the King should have the indiction of all General Assemblies. That the Bishops or their Deputies, should be perpetual Moderators of the Diocesan Synods. That no Excommunication or Absolution should be pronounced without their approbation. That all presentations of Benefices should be made by them ; and that the deprivation or suspension of Ministers should belong to them. That every Minister at his admission to a Benefice should take the Oath of Supremacy and Canonical Obedience : That the Visitation of the Diocess shall be performed by the Bishop or his Deputy only. And finally, That the Bishop should be Moderator of all Conventions, for Exercisings, or Prophesyings, (call them which you will) which should be held within their bounds.*

bounds. All which conclusions were confirmed by Act of Parliament in the year 1612 : in which the Earl of *Dumfermling* then being Lord Chancellor of that Kingdom sate as chief Commissioner ; who in the same Session also procured a Repeal of all such former Acts (more particularly of that which passed in favour of the Discipline, 1592.) a were supposed to be derogatory to the said conclusions. In the mean time the King being advertised of all which had been done at *Glasgow*, calls to the Court by special Letters under his Sign Manual, Mr. *John Spotswood* the designed Archbishop of *Glasgow*, Mr. *Gawen Hamilton* nominated to the See of *Galloway*, and Mr. *Andrew Lamb* appointed to the Church of *Brechin* ; to the intent that being consecrated Bishops in due Form and Order, they might at their return give consecration to the rest of their Brethren. They had before been Authorized to vote in Parliament, commended by the King unto their several Sees, made the perpetual Moderators of Presbyteries and Diocesan Synods : and finally by the conclusions made at *Glasgow*, they were restored to all considerable Acts of their Jurisdiction. The Character was only wanting to compleat the Work, which could not be imprinted but by consecration according to the Rules and Canons of the Primitive times.

24. And that this Character might be indelebly imprinted on them, His Majesty issues a Commission under the Great Seal of *England*, to to the Bishops of *London*, *Ely*, *Wells*, and *Rochester*, whereby they were required to proceed to the consecration of the said three Bishops, according to the Rules of the *English* Ordination ; which was by them performed with all due solemnity in the Chapel of the Bishop of *Londons* House near the Church of St. *Pauls*, *Octob.* 21. 1610. But first a scruple had been moved by the Bishop of *Ely*, concerning the capacity of the persons nominated for receiving the Episcopal Consecration, in regard that none of them had formerly been ordained Priests : which scruple was removed by Archbishop *Bancroft*, alledging that there was no such necessity of receiving the Order of Priesthood, but that Episcopal Consecrations might be given without it ; as might have been exemplified in the cases of *Ambrose* and *Nectarius* of which the first was made Archbishop of *Millain*, and the other Patriarch of *Constantinople*, without receiving any intermediate Orders, whether of Priest, Deacon, or any other (if there were any other) at that time in the Church. And on the other side the Prelates of *Scotland* also had their Doubts and Scruples, fearing lest by receiving Consecration of the *English* Bishops, they might be brought to an acknowledgment of that Superiority which had been exercised and enjoyed by the *Primates* of *England*, before the first breaking out of the Civil Wars betwixt *York* and *Lancaster*. Against which fear the King sufficiently provided, by excluding the two Archbishops of *Canterbury* and *York* (who only could pretend to that Superiority) out of his Commission, which *Bancroft* very cheerfully condescended to, though he had chiefly laid the plot, and brrought on the work, not caring who participated in the Honour of it, as long as the Churches of both Kingdoms might receive the Benefit.

25. This great work being thus past over, the King erects a Court of *High Commission* in the Realm of *Scotland*, for ordering all matters which concerned that Church, and could not safely be redressed in the

Bishops Courts. He also gave them some Directions for the better exercise of their Authority, by them to be communicated to the Bishops, and some principal Churchmen whom he appointed to be called to *Edenborough* in the following *February*; where they were generally well approved. But as all general Rules have some Exceptions, so some Exceptions were found out against these Commissions, and the proceedings thereupon. Not very pleasing to those great Persons who then sate at the Helm, and looked upon it as a diminution to their own Authority, and could not brook that any of the Clergy should be raised to so great a Power; much more displeasing to the principal sticklers in the Cause of *Presbytery*, who now beheld the downfall of their glorious Throne, which they had erected for themselves in the Name of Christ. One thing perhaps might comfort them in the midst of their sorrows, that is to say, the death of the most Reverend Archbishop *Bancroft*, who left this life upon the second of *November*, not living above thirteen days after the *Scotish* Bishops had recived Consecration. For which great blessing to the Church, he had scarce time to render his just acknowledgment to God and the King, when he is called on to prepare for his *Nunc Dimittis*. And having seen so great a work accomplished for the glory of God, the honour of his Majesty, and the good of both Kingdoms, beseecheth God to give him leave to depart in peace, that with his eyes he might behold that great Salvation, which was ordained to be a Light unto the Gentiles, and to be the Glory of his people *Israel*.

26. *Bancroft* being dead, some Bishops of the Court held a Consultation touching the fittest Person to succeed him in that eminent Dignity: The great Abilities and most exemplary Piety of Dr. *Lancelot Andrews* then Bishop of *Ely*, pointed him out to be the man, as one sufficiently able to discharge a Trust of such main importance; and rather looked on as a Preferment to that See then preferred unto it. Him they commended to King *James*, who had him in a high esteem for his Parts and Piety and settled all things as they thought in so good a posture, that some of them retired to their Countrey-houses, and others slackned their attendance about the Court. Which opportunity being taken by the Earl of *Dunbar*, he puts in for *Abbot*, who had attended him in some of his Negotiations with the Kirk of *Scotland*. Upon the merits of which Service, he was prefered first to the See of *Litchfield*, to which he received his Episcopal Cofecration on the third of *December*, 1609; and within the compass of the year was removed to *London*. But *Dunbar* was resolved to advance him higher. And he put in so powerfully on his behalf, that at last he carried it to the great detriment of the Church, as it after proved. For, as one very well observeth of him, he seemed to be *better qualified with merit to attain that Dignity, then with a spirit answerable to so great a Function.* Which made him slack and negligent in the course of his Government, and too indulgent to that Party, which *Bancroft* had kept under with such just severity. But take his Character in the words of the said Historian, and we shall find that he was a man *too facil and yielding in the exercise of that great Office; that by his extraordinary remisness in not exacting strict conformity to the prescribed Orders of the Church in point of Ceremony, he seemed to resolve those Legal determina-*

tions

tions to their *first indifferency*: and finally, That he brought in *such a habit of Nonconformity*, that the future reduction of *those tender Conscienced men to a long discontinued obedience*, was at the last *interpreted for* an *Innovation*.

27. But to go forwards where we left, *Bancroft* being dead, the *English Puritans* began to put forth again, not pushing at the Liturgy and Episcopal Government (as in former times,) but in pursuance of the *Sabbatarian* and *Calvinian* Rigors : Which having been advanced in the year 1595, as it was there declared, and afterward laid aside till a fitter season, were now thought fit to be resumed as the most proper Mediums for inferring the desired conclusion. In both which they received some countenance from King *James* himself; but more from the connivence (if I may not call it, the incouragement) of a new Archbishop. In reference to the first, the King had published a Proclamation in the first year of his Reign, prohibiting some rude and disorderly Pastimes, (as namely, Ball, Baitings, Bear-baitings, and common Interludes) from being followed on the *Sunday*, because they drew away much people from Gods publick Service. And he had caused the Morality of the Lords-day-Sabbath, to be confirmed among the rest of the *Irish* Articles *Anno* 1615 of which more anon. Which condescentions were so husbanded by the *Puritan* Faction, that by the raising of the Sabbath, they depressed the Festivals, and with the Festivals, all those ancient and Annual Fasts which had been kept upon the Eves. And following close upon the Doctrines of *Aerius*, before remembred, they introduced, by little and little a general neglect of the Weekly Fasts, the holy time of *Lent*, and the Embring-days; reducing all the Acts of Humiliation, to solemn and occasional Fasts, as amongst the *Scots*; and yet this was not all the mischief which ensued on their Sabbath-Doctrines. By which, and by the temper of the present Government, they gave occasion to some Preachers, and not a few publick Ministers of Justice, in their several Countreys to interdict all lawful sports upon that Day. By means whereof, the people were perswaded by some Priests and Jesuits, especially in *Lancashire*, and some others of the Northern Counties, that the Reformed Religion was incompatible with that Christian Liberty which God and Nature had indulged to the sons of men. And having brought them to that point, it was no hard matter to perswade them to fall off to Popery, as a Religion more agreeable to human Society, and such as would permit them all such lawful pleasures as by the *Stoicism* of the other had been interdicted. Which brought the King to a necessity of publishing his Declaration about lawful sports, dated at *Greenwich* on the 24th day of *May*, *Anno* 1620. Which as it put some Water into the Wine of the *Sabbatarians*; so shewed he, within few years after how little he affected the *Calvinian Rigors*.

28. In reference to which last, some of the Zealots in the Cause had took encouragement from his Declaration against *Vorstius*, a Divine of the *Netherlands*, in which he had bestowed some unhandsome Epetheres upon the Followers of *Van Hermine*, in the *Belgick* Provinces. This seemed sufficient to expose all those of the same Perswasions, unto scorn and hatred; and on the other side, to animate all those who favoured *Calvinism*, to act such things as drew upon them at the last the Kings high

high displeasure. *Calvin* had published a blasphemous Fancy touching Chrifts suffering of Hell-torments in the time of his Passion, even to the horrors of despair. Which being touched upon by *Corbet*, one of the Students of *Christ Church*, in a Passion Sermon 1613, he was most sharply reprehended by the *Repetitioner* for so great a sauciness. Dr. *John Houfon*, one of the Canons of that Church, who had most worthily discharged the Office of Vice-Chancellor twelve years before, declared himself somewhat to the prejudice of the *Annotations* which were made on the *Genevian* Bibles; and for so doing is condemned to a Recantation much about that time, though the said *Annotations* had been censured for their partiality and seditiousness by the Tongue of K. *James*. And finally, Dr. *William Laud*, being then President of St. *John's* College, had shewed himself no Friend to *Calvinism* in Doctrine or Discipline; and must be therefore branded for a *Papist*, in a publick Sermon Preached upon *Easter Sunday* by Dr. *Robert Abbot*, then Vice-Chancellor and Doctor of the Chair in that University : Which passages so closely following upon one another, occasioned (as most conceived) the publishing of some directions by his Majesty in the year next following : In which it was enjoyned among other things, *That young Students in Divinity should be directed to study such Books as were most agreeable in Doctrine and Discipline to the Church of* England; *and be excited to bestow their time in the Fathers and Councils, School-men, Histories, and Controversies; and not to insist too long upon Compendiums and Abbreviators, making them the grounds of those Sacred Studies.* Which as it was the first great blow that was given to *Calvinism*, so was it followed not long after by the Kings *Instructions touching Preaching and Preachers.* In which it was precisely cautioned amongst other things, *That no Preacher of what Title soever, under the Degree of a Bishop, or Dean at the least, should from thenceforth presume to preach in any popular Auditory the points of Predestination, Election, Reprobation, or of the Universality, Efficacity, Resistibility, or Irresistibility of Gods Grace; but should rather leave those Theams to be handled by Learned men; as being fitter for Schools and Universities then for simple Auditories.* Which said Instructions bearing date at *Windsor*, on the 10th of *August* 1622, opened the way to the suppression of that heat and fierceness by which the *Calvinists* had been acted in some years foregoing.

29. During which Heats and Agitations between the Parties, a plot was set on foot to subvert the Church, in the undoing of the Clergy; and there could be no readier way to undo the Clergy, then to reduce them unto such a beggerly competency (for by that name they love to call it) as they had brought them to in all the rest of the *Calvinian* or *Genevian* Churches. This the Design of many hands, by whom all passages had been scored in *Cottons* Library, which either did relate to the point of Tythes, or the manner of payment: But the Collections being brought together, and the Work compleated, there appeared no other Name before it, then that of *Selden*, then of great Credit in the World for his known Abilities in the retired Walks of Learning. *The History of Tythes* writ by such an Author, could not but raise much expectation amongst some of the Laity, who for a long time had gaped after the Churches Patrimony, and now conceived and hoped to swallow

it

it down without any chewing. The Author highly magnified, the Book held unanswerable, and all the Clergy looked on but as Pigmies to that great *Goliah*, who in his Preface had reproached them with *Ignorance* and *Laziness*, upbraided them with having nothing to keep up their Credit, but *Beard*, *Title*, and *Habit*; and that their studies reached no further then the *Breviary*, the *Postills*, and the *Polyanthea*. Provoked wherewith he was so galled by *Tillesly*, so gagged by *Mountague*, and stung by *Nettles* ; that he never came off in any of his undertakings with more loss of Credit. By which he found that some of the *Ignorant* and *Lazy* Clergy were of as retired Studies as himself; and could not only match, but overmatch him too in his own Philology. But the chief Governours of the Church went a shorter way, and not expecting till the Book was answered by particular men, resolved to seek for reparation of the wrong from the Author himself, upon an information to be brought against him in the High Commission. Fearing the issue of the business, and understanding what displeasures were conceived against him by the King and Bishops, he made his personal appearance in the open Court at *Lambeth*, on the 28*th* day of *January* 1618, where in a full Court he tendred his submission and acknowledgment, all of his own hand writing, in these following words:

My Lords, I most humbly acknowledge my Error which I have committed, in publishing The History of Tythes ; *and especially in that I have at all, by shewing any Interpretations of Holy Scriptures , by medling with Councils, Fathers, or Canons, or by whatsoever occurrs in it, offered any occasion of Argument against any Right of Maintenance* Jure Divino *of the Ministers of the Gospel; beseeching your Lordships to receive this ingenuous and humble acknowledgment, together with the unfeigned Protestation of my grief, for that through it I have so incurred both His Majesty's and your Lordships Displeasure conceived against me in behalf of the Church of* England.

JOHN SELDEN.

This for the present was conceived to be the most likely Remedy for the preventing of the Mischief, but left such smart Remembrances in the mind of the Author, as put him on to act more vigorously for the *Presbyterians*, (of which more hereafter) by whom he seemed to be engaged in the present Service.

30. But it is now high time for us to cross over St. *George*'s Chanel, and take a short view of the poor and weak Estate of the Church of *Ireland*, where these Designs were carried on with better Fortune. A Church which for the most part had been modelled by the Reformation which was made in *England*. But lying at a greater distance, and more out of sight, it was more easily made a prey to all Invaders ; the *Papists* prevailing on the one side, and the *Puritans* on the other, getting so much ground that the poor *Protestants* seemed to be crucified in the midst between them. Some Order had been taken for establishing the *English* Liturgy, together with the Bible in the *English* Tongue, in all the Churches of that Kingdom : which not being understood by the natural *Irish*, left them as much in Ignorance and Superstition, as in the darkest times

of

of the Papal Tyranny. And for the Churches of the Pale, which very well understood the *English* Language, they suffered themselves to be seduced from the Rules of the Church, and yielded to the prevalency of those zealous Ministers who carried on the *Calvinian* Project with their utmost power. In order whereunto, it was held necessary to expose the Patrimony of the Bishops and Cathedral Churches, to a publick Port-sale; that being as much weakned in their Power as they were in Estate, they might be rendred inconsiderable in the eyes of the people. Hence forward such a general devastation of the Lands of the Church, that some Episcopal Sees were never since able to maintain a Bishop, but have been added to some others; two or three for failing, to make up somewhat like a Competency for an *Irish* Prelate. The Bishoprick of *Ardagh* was thereupon united unto that of *Killmore*; but the Cathedral of the one, together with the Bishops House adjoyning to it, had been levelled with the very ground: the other in some better repair; but neither furnished with Bell, Font, or Chalice. The like union had been also made between the Bishopricks of *Clonfert* and *Killmore*, *Ossery*, and *Kilkenny*, *Down* and *Connour*, *Waterford* and *Lismore*, *Cork* and *Rosse*, &c. and was projected by the late Lord Primate, between the See of *Kilfanore*, and that of *Killallow*: not to descend any more particulars of the like Conjunctions.

31. Such also were the Fortunes of the Rural Clergy, whose Churches in some places lay unrooted, in others unrepaired and much out of order. The Tythes annexed, for the most part, to Religious Houses, fell (by the ruine of those Houses) to the power of the Crown, and by the Kings and Queens of *England*, were aliened from the Church, and by them became Lay-Fees. The Vicaridges generally so ill provided, that in the whole Province of *Connaught*, most of the Vicars Pensions came but to forty shillings *per annum*, and in some places but sixteen only. And of such Vicaridges as appeared to be better endowed, three, four, or five, were many times ingrossed into one mans hands, who neither understood the Language, nor performed the Service. In which respect it was no marvel if the people took up that Religion which came next to hand, such as did either serve most fitly to continue them in their former Errors, or to secure them in the quiet enjoyment of those Estates which they had ravished from the Church, and still possessed by the Title of the first Usurpers. In which estate we find the Church of *Ireland*, at the death of the Queen, not much improved in case it were not made more miserable. In the time of K. *James*, some Propositions had been offered by him in the Conference at *Hampton-Court*, about sending Preachers into *Ireland*, of which he was but half King, as himself complained, their Bodies being subject unto his Authority, but their Souls and Consciences to the Pope. But I find nothing done in pursuance of it, till after the year 1607, where the Earl of *Ter-ownen*, *Ter-connel*, Sir *John Odaghartie*, and other great Lords of the North, together with their Wives and Families, took their flight from *Ireland*, and left their whole Estates to the Kings disposing. Hereupon followed the Plantation of *Ulster*, first undertaken by the City of *London*, who fortified *Colraine*, and built *London-Derrie*, and purchased many thousand Acres of Lands in the parts adjoyning. But it was carried on more vigorous-

ly, as more unfortunately withall, by some Adventurers of the *Scotish* Nation, who procured themselves into this Countrey as the richer Soil : And though they were sufficiently industrious in improving their own Fortunes there, and set up Preaching in all Churches wheresoever they fixed ; yet whether it happened for the better, or for the worse, the event hath shewed : For they brought with them hither such a stock of *Puritanism*, such a contempt of Bishops, such a neglect of the publick Liturgy, and other Divine Offices of this Church, that there was nothing less to be found amongst them, then the Government and Forms of Worship established in the Church of *England*

32. Nor did the Doctrine speed much better, if it sped not worse : For *Calvinism* by degrees had taken such deep root amongst them, that at the last it was received and countenanced as the only Doctrine which was to be defended in the Church of *Ireland.* For not contented with the *Articles* of the Church of *England*, they were resolved to frame a *Confession* of their own ; the drawing up whereof was referred to Dr. *James Usher*, then Provost of the College of *Dublin*, and afterwards Archbishop of *Armagh*, and Lord Primate of *Ireland* : By whom the Book was so contrived, that all the *Sabbatarian* and *Calvinian* Rigors were declared therein to be the Doctrines of that Church. For first the Articles of *Lambeth* rejected at the *Conference* at *Hampton Court*, must be inserted into this *Confession*, as the chief parts of it. And secondly, An Article must be made of purpose to justifie the Morality of the Lords-day-Sabbath, and to require the spending of it wholly in Religious Exercises. Besides which deviations from the Doctrine of the Church of *England*, most grievous Torments immediately in his Soul, are there affirmed to be endured by Christ our Saviour, which *Calvin* makes to be the same with his descent into Hell. The Abstinencies from eating Flesh upon certain days declared not to be Religious Fasts, but to be grounded upon Politick Ends and Considerations. All Ministers adjudged to be lawfully called, who are called unto the work of the Ministry by those that have publick Authority given them in the Church (but whether they be Bishops or not, it makes no matter, so they be Authorized unto it by their several Churches.) The Sacerdotal Power of Absolution made *Declarative* only , and consequently quite subverted. No Power ascribed to the Church in making Canons, or censuring any of those who either carlesly or maliciously do infringe the same. The Pope made Antichrist, according to the like determination of the *French Hugonots* at *Gappe* in *Daulphine.* And finally, such a silence concerning the Consecration of Archbishops and Bishops (expresly justified and avowed in the *English* Book) as if they were not a distinct Order from the common Presbyters. All which being *Usher's* own private Opinions, were dispersed in several places of the Articles for the Church of *Ireland* ; approved of in the Convocation of the year 1615 ; and finally confirmed by the Lord Deputy *Chichester* in the Name of King *James*.

33. What might induce King *James* to confirm these Articles, differing in so many points from his own Opinion, is not clearly known : but it is probable, that he might be drawn to it on these following grounds : For first He was much governed at that time, in

all

all Church concernments, by Doctor *George Abbot* Archbishop of *Canterbury*, and Doctor *James Mountague* Bishop of *Bath* and *Wells*; who having formerly engaged in maintenance of some or most of those Opinions, as before is said, might find it no hard matter to perswade the King to a like approbation of them. And secondly, the King had so far declared himself in the Cause against *Vorstius*, and so affectionately had espoused the Quarrel of the Prince of *Orange* against those of the *Remonstrant* Party in the *Belgick* Churches, that he could not handsomely refuse to confirm those Doctrines in the Church of *Ireland* which he had countenanced in *Holland*. Thirdly, The *Irish* Nation at that time were most tenaciously addicted to the Errors and Corruptions of the Church of *Rome*, and therefore must be bended to the other Extream, before they could be straight and Orthodox in these points of Doctrine. Fourthly and finally, It was an usual practise with that King, in the whole course of his Government, to balance one Extream by the other; countenancing the *Papists* against the *Puritans*, and the *Puritans* against the *Papists*, that betwixt both the true Religion, and Professors of it, might be kept in safety. But whether I hit right or not, certain it is, that it proved a matter of sad consequence to the Church of *England*; there being nothing more ordinary amongst those of the *Puritan* Party, when they were pressed in any of the points aforesaid, then to appeal unto the Articles of *Ireland*, and the infallible Judgment of King *James*, who confirmed the same. And so it stood untill the year 1634, when by the Power of the Lord Deputy *Wentworth*, and the Dexterity of Doctor *John Bramhall*, then Lord Bishop of *Derry*, the *Irish* Articles were repealed in a full Convocation, and those of *England* authorized in the place thereof.

34. Pass we next over to the Isles of *Jersey* and *Guernsey*, where the *Genevian* Discipline had been settled under Queen *Elizabeth*; and being so settled by that Queen, was confirmed by King *James* at his first coming to this Crown: though at the same time he endeavoured a subversion of it in the Kirk of *Scotland*. But being to do it by degrees, and so to practise the restoring of the old *Episcopacy*, as not to threaten a destruction to their new *Presbyteries*; it was thought fit to tolerate that Form of Government in those petit Islands, which could have no great influence upon either Kingdom. Upon which ground he sends a Letter to them of the 8th of *August*, first writ in *French*, and thus translated into *English*; that is to say:

35. JAMES *by the Grace of God, King of* England, Scotland, France, *and* Ireland, &c. *Unto all those whom these Presents shall concern, greeting. Whereas We Our selves, and the Lords of Our Council, have been given to understand, that it pleased God to put into the Heart of the late Queen Our most dear Sister, to permit and allow unto the Isles of* Jersey *and* Guernsey *parcel of the Dutchy of* Normandy, *the use of the Government of the Reformed Churches of the said Dutchy, whereof they have stood possessed until Our coming to*
the

the Crown. For this cause We desiring to follow the pious Example of Our said Sister in this behalf, as well for the advancement of the Glory of Almighty God, as for the edification of his Church; do will and ordain, That Our said Isles shall quietly enjoy their said Liberty in the use of Ecclesiastical Discipline there now established. Forbidding any one to give them any trouble or impeachment, so long as they contain themselves in Our Obedience, and attempt not any thing against the Power and Sacred Word of God. Given at Our Palace at Hampton-Court the 8th of August, in the first year of Our Reign of England, 1603.

36. This Letter was communicated unto all whom it might concern, in a Synod of both Islands held in *Jersey Anno* 1605. But long they were not suffered to enjoy the benefit of this Dispensation : For Sir *John Peiton* who succeeded Governour of *Jersey* in the place of *Raleigh*, had of himself no good affections to that Plat-form, and possibly might be furnished with some secret Instructions for altering it in the Island on the first conveniency. The ground whereof was laid upon this occasion : The Curate of St. *John*'s being lately dead, it pleased the *Colloquie* of that Island, according to their former method, to appoint one *Brevin* to succeed him. Against this course, the Governour, the Kings Attorney, and other the Officers of the Crown, protested publickly, as being prejudicial to the Rights and Profits of the King. Howbeit the Case was over-ruled, and the *Colloquie* for that time carried it. Hereupon a Bill of Articles was exhibited to the Lords of the Council, against the Ministers of that Island, by *Peiton* the Governour, *Marret* the Attorney, and the rest; as, viz. *That they had usurped the Patronage of all Benefices in the Island : That thereby they admitted men to Livings without any Form or Presentation; and by that means deprived his Majesty of Vacancies and First fruits. That by the connivance* (to say no worse of it) *of the former Governours, they exercised a kind of Arbitrary Jurisdiction, making and disannulling Laws at their own most uncertain pleasure.* In consideration whereof, they humbly pray His Sacred Majesty to grant them such a Discipline as might be fittest to the nature of that Place, and less derogatory to the Royal Prerogative.

37. In the pursuance of this Project, Sir *Robert Gardiner* once Chief Justice of *Ireland*; and *James Hussey* Doctor of the Laws, are sent Commissioners unto that Island, though not without the colour of some other business. To these Commissioners the Ministers give in their Answer, which may be generally reduced to these two heads : First, That their appoinment of men into the Ministry, and the exercise of Jurisdiction, being principal parts of the Church-Discipline, had been confirmed unto them by His Sacred Majesty. And secondly, That the payment of First fruits and Tenths, had never been exacted from them since they were freed from their subordination to the Bishops of *Constance*, to whom formerly they had been due. But these Answers giving no just satisfaction unto the Council of *England*, and nothing being done in order to a present Settlement, a foul deformity both of Confusion

fusion and Distraction, did suddenly overgrow the face of those wretched Churches. For in the former times all such as took upon them any publick charge either in Church or Commonwealth, had bound themselves by Oath to cherish and maintain the Discipline : That Oath is now disclaimed as dangerous and unwarrantable. Before it was their custom to exact subscription to their Platform, of all such as purposed to receive the Sacrament : but now the Kings Attorney, and others of that Party, chose rather to abstain from the Communion, then to yield Subscription. Nay, even the very *Elders*, silly Souls, that thought themselves as *sacrosancti* as a *Roman Tribune*, were drawn with Process into the Civil Courts, and there reputed with the vulgar. Nor was the Case much better in the *Sacred Consistory*; the Jurates in their *Cohu* or Town-Hall relieving such by their Authority, whom that (once *paramount*) Tribunal had condemned or censured. And yet this was not all the Mischief which befell them neither : Those of the lower ranck seeing the Ministers begin to stagger in their Chairs, refused to set out their Tythes; and if the Curates mean to exact their Dues, the Law is open to all comers, to try their Title. Their Benefices, which before were accounted as exempt and priviledged, are now brought to reckon for First fruits and Tenths; and that not according to the Book of *Constance* (as they had been formerly) but by the will and pleasure of the present Governour. And to make up the total sum of all misfortunes, one of the Constables preferrs a Bill against them in the common *Cohu*, in which they were accused of Hypocrisie in their Conversation, and Tyranny in the exercise of their Jurisdiction : and finally of holding some secret practises against the Governour, which consequentially did reflect on the King himself.

38. In this Confusion they address themselves to the Earl of *Salisbury*, then being Lord Treasurer of *England*, and in great Credit with King *James*; who seeming very much pleased with their Application, advised them to invite their Brethren of the Isle of *Guernsey*, to joyn with them in a Petition to the King, for a redress of those Grievances which they then complained of. A Counsel which then seemed rational and of great respect; but in it self of greater cunning then it seemed in the first appearance. For by this means (as certainly he was a man of subtile Wit) he gave the King more time to compass his designs in *Scotland*, before he should declare himself in the present business; and by engaging those of *Guernsey* in the same desires, intended to subject them also to the same conclusion. But this Counsel taking no effect by reason of the death of the Counsellor, they fall into another trouble of their own creating. The Parish of St. *Peters* falling void by the death of the Minister, the Governour presents unto it one *Aaron Messering*, one that had spent his time in *Oxon*; and had received the Order of Priesthood from the Right Reverend Doctor *Bridges* then Bishop of that Diocess, but of himself a native of the Isle of *Jersey*. A thing so infinitely stomached by those of the *Colloquy*, that they would by no means yield unto his admission;

1612.

1615.

ſion; not ſo much in regard of his preſentation by the Power of the Governour, as becauſe he had taken Orders from the hands of a Biſhop: For now they thought that Popery began to break in upon them, and therefore that it did concern them to oppoſe it to the very laſt. A new complaint is hereupon preferred againſt them to the Lords of the Council; in which their Lorpſhips were informed, that the Inhabitants generally of the Iſle were diſcontented with the preſent Diſcipline and guidance of the Church, that moſt of them would be eaſily perſwaded to ſubmit to the *Engliſh* Government, that many of them did deſire it.

1618.   39. This brings both Parties to the Court; the Governour and his Adherents to proſecute the Suit, and make good their Intelligence; the Miniſters to anſwer to the complaint, and ſtand to the Pleaſure of his Majeſty in the final Judgment. And at the firſt, the Miniſters ſtood faſt together: but as it always happeneth, that there is no Confederacy ſo well joynted, but one Member of it may be ſevered from the reſt, and thereby the whole practiſe overthrown: ſo was it alſo in this buſineſs. For thoſe who there ſolicited ſome private buſineſs of the Governours, had kindly wrought upon the weakneſs and ambition of *De la Place*, (one of the Miniſters appointed to attend the Service) perſwading him, that if the Government were altered, and the Dean reſtored, he was infallibly reſolved on to be the man. Being faſhioned into this hope, he ſpeedily betrayed the Counſels of his Fellows, and furniſhed their Opponents at their Interviews with ſuch Intelligence as might make moſt for their advantage. At laſt the Miniſters not well agreeing in their own demands, and having little to ſay in defence of their proper cauſe, whereunto their Anſwers were not provided before hand; my Lord of *Canterbury* at the Council Table thus declared unto them the Pleaſure of the King and Council, *viz. That for the ſpeedy redreſs of their diſorders, it was reputed moſt convenient to eſtabliſh amongſt them the Authority and Office of the Dean That the Book of Common Prayer being again Printed in the* French, *ſhould be received into their Churches; but the Miniſters not tyed to the ſtrict obſervance of it in all particulars. That* Meſſervy *ſhould be admitted into his Benefice, and that ſo they might return to their ſeveral Charges.* This ſaid, they were commanded to depart, and to ſignifie to thoſe from whom they came, the full ſcope of His Majeſty's Reſolution, and ſo they did. But being ſomewhat backward in obeying this Decree, the Council intimated to them by Sir *Philip de Carteret*, chief Agent for the Governour and Eſtates of the Iſland. That the Miniſters from among themſelves ſhould make choice of three Learned and Grave Perſons, whoſe Names they ſhould return unto the Board, out of which his Majeſty ſhould reſolve on one to be their Dean.

1619.   40. But this propoſal little edified amongſt the Brethren; not ſo much out of any diſlike of the alteration with which they ſeemed all well enough contented; but becauſe every one of them gave himſelf ſome hopes of being the man: And being that all of them could not be elected, they were not willing to deſtroy their

particular

particular hopes, by the appoinment of another. In the mean time, Mr. *David Bandinell*, an *Italian* born, then being Minister of St. *Maryes*, under pretence of other business of his own, is dispatched for *England*, and recommended by the Governour as the fittest person for that Place and Dignity. And being well approved of by the Archbishop of *Canterbury*, who found him answerable in all points to the Governours Character, he was established in the Place by his Majesties Letters, Patents, bearing date *Anno* 1619, and was accordingly invested in all such Rights as formerly had been inherent in that Office, whether it were in point of Profit, or of Jurisdiction. And for the executing of this Office, some Articles were drawn and ratified by his Sacred Majesty, to be in force until a certain Body of Ecclesiastical Canons should be digested and confirmed: Which Articles he was pleased to call the *Interim*, (a Name devised by *Charles* the fifth, on the like occasion) as appears by his Majesties Letters, Patents, for confirmation of the Canons, not long after **1626.** made. And by this *Interim* it was permitted for the present, that the Ministers should not be obliged to bid the Holy-days, to use the Cross in Baptism, or to wear the Surplice, or not to give the Sacrament of the Lords Supper unto any others but such as did receive it kneeling; but in all other things, it little differed from the Book of Canons; which being first drawn up by the Dean and Ministers, was afterwards carefully perused, corrected, and accommodated for the use of that Island, by the Right Reverend Fathers in God, *George* Lord Archbishop of *Canterbury*, *John* Lord Bishop of *Lincoln*, Lord Keeper of the Great Seal of *England*; and *Lancelot* Lord Bishop of *Winchester*, whose Diocess or Jurisdiction did extend over both the Islands. In which respect it was appointed in the Letters, Patents, (by which His Majesty confirmed these Canons, **1623.** *Anno* 1623,) That the said Reverend Father in God, the Bishop of *Winchester*, should forthwith by his Commission under his Episcopal Seal, as Ordinary of the place, give Authority unto the said Dean to exercise Ecclesiastical Jurisdiction in the said Isle, according to the Canons and Constitutions thus made and established. Such were the Means, and such the Councils, by which this Island was reduced to a full conformity with the Church of *England*.

41. *Guernsey* had followed in the like, if first the breach between King *James* and the King of *Spain*; and afterwards between King *Charles* and the Crown of *France*, had not took off the edg of the prosecution During which time the Ministers were much heartned in their Inconformity, by the Practises of *De la Place*, before remembred: Who stomaching his disappointment in the loss of the Deanry, abandoned his Native Countrey, and retired unto *Guernsey*, where he breathed nothing but disgrace to the *English* Liturgy, the Person of the new Dean, and the change of the Government. Against the first so perversly opposite, that when some Forces were sent over by King *Charles* for defence of the Island, he would not suffer them to have the use of the *English* Liturgy in the Church of St. *Peters*, being the principal of that Island, but upon these conditions; that is to say, *That they should neither use the Liturgy therein, nor receive the Sacrament.* And secondly, *Whereas there was a Lecture weekly every* Thursday, *in the said Church of St.* Peters, *when once the Feast of* Christs Nativity *fell upon that day, he rather chose to disappoint the Hearers, and put off the*

the Sermon, then that the least honour should reflect on that ancient Festival. An Opposition far more superstitious, then any observation of a day, though meerly *Jewish.* By his Example others were encouraged to the like perversness, insomuch that they refused to baptize any Child or Children, though weak, and in apparent danger of present death, but such as were presented unto them on the day of Preaching : And when some of them were compelled by the Civil Magistrate to perform their duty in this kind, a great complaint thereof was made to the Earl of *Darby,* being then Governour of that Island, as if the Magistrate had intrenched on the Ministers Office, and took upon them the administration of the blessed Sacraments. Of these particulars, and many others of that nature, intelligence was given to the late Archbishop Dr. *Laud,* who had proceeded thereupon to a Reformation *Anno* 1637, if the Distraction then arising in the *Realm* of *Scotland,* had not enforced him to a discontinuance of that Resolution.

The End of the Eleventh Book.

AERIVS REDIVIVVS:

OR THE

HISTORY

OF THE

Presbyterians.

LIB. XII.

Containing

Their Tumultuating in the Belgick *Provinces ; their Practises and Insurrections in the* Higher Germany *; the frustrating of their Design on the Churches of* Brandenbourgh*; the Revolts of* Transilvania, Hungary , Austria, *and* Bohemia, *and the Rebellions of the* French, *from the Year* 1610 *to the Year* 1628.

Rom *Guernsey* we set sail for *Holland,* in which we left the Ministers divided into two main Factions ; the one being called the *Remonstrants,* the other taking to themselves the Name of *Contra-Remonstrants.* To put an end to those Disorders, a Conference was appointed between the Parties held at the *Hague,* before the General Assembly of Estates of the *Belgick* Provinces, *Anno* 1610. The Controversie reduced to five Articles only, and the dispute managed by the ablest men who appeared in the Quarrel on either side. In which

which it was conceived, that the *Remonstrants* had the better of the day, and came off with Victory. But what the *Contra Remonstrants* wanted in the strength of Argument, they made good by Power : For, being far the greater number, and countenanced by the Prince of *Orange* as their principal Patron, they prosecuted their Opponents in their several Consistories, by Suspensions, Excommunications, and Deprivations, the highest Censures of the Church. This forced the *Remonstrant* Party to put themselves under the protection of *John Olden Barnevelt*, an *Hollander* by birth, and one of the most powerful men of all that Nation ; who fearing that the Prince of *Orange* had some secret purpose to make himself absolute Lord of those Estates, received them very cheerfully into his protection, not without hope of raising a strong Party by them to oppose the Prince. This draws K. *James* into the Quarrel ; who being displeased with the Election of *Conradus Vorstius* to a Divinity-Readers Place in the Schools of *Leiden*, and not so readily gratified by the Estates in the choice of another ; published a Declaration against this *Vorstius*, and therein falls exceeding foul upon *James Van Harmine*, and all that followed his Opinions in the Present Controversies. Which notwithstanding, *Barnevelt* gains an Edict from the States of *Holland*, *Anno* 1613, by which a mutual Tolleration was indulged to either Party, more to the benefit of the *Remonstrants*, then the contentment of the others. An Edict highly magnified by the Learned *Grotius*, in his *Pietas Ordinum*, &c. Against which some Answers were returned by *Bogerman, Sibrandus*, and some others, not without some reflections on the Magistrates for their actings in it.

1613.

2. This made the breach much wider then it was before; King *James* appearing openly in favour of the Prince of *Orange*, the *Spaniard* secretly fomenting the Designs of *Barnevelt*, as it was afterwards suggested, with what truth I know not. But sure it is, that as K. *James* had formerly aspersed the *Remonstrant* Party in his Declaration against *Vorstius*, before remembred; so he continued a most bitter Enemy unto them, till he had brought them at the last to an extermination. But what induced him thereunto hath been made a question. Some think that he was drawn unto it by the powerful perswasions of Archbishop *Abbot*, and Bishop *Mountague*, who then much governed his Councils in all Church-concernments. Others impute it to his Education in the Church of *Scotland*, where all the *Heterodoxies* of *Calvin* were received as Gospel ; which might incline him the more strongly to those opinions which he had sucked in as it were with his Nurse's Milk. Some say that he was carried in this business, not so much by the clear light of his own understanding, as by a transport of affection to the Prince of *Orange*, to whom he had a dear regard, and a secret sympathy. Others more rationally ascribe it unto Reason of State, for the preventing of a dangerous and uncurable Rupture, which otherwise was like to follow in the State of the *Netherlands*. He had then a great Stock going amongst them, in regard of the two Towns of *Brill* and *Vlushing*, together with the Fort of *Ramekins*, which had been put into the hands of Queen *Elizabeth* for great sums of money. In which regard the Governour of the Town of *Vlushing*, and the Embassador Resident for the Crown of *England*, were to have place in all publick Councils which concerned those

Provinces;

Provinces; on whose Tranquillity and Power he placed a great part of the peace and happiness of his own Dominions. He knew that Concord was the strongest Ligament of their Confederation; and looked on the *Remonstrants* as the breakers of that Bond of Unity, which formerly had held them so close together.

3. Upon this reason he exhorts them in his said Declaration, *To take heed of such infected persons; their own Countrey men being already divided into Factions upon this occasion; which was a matter so opposite to Unity, (the only prop and safety of their State, next under God) as must of necessity by little and little bring them to utter ruine, if wisely and in time they did not provide against it.* And on the same reason he concurred in Counsel and Design with the Prince of *Orange*, for the suppressing of that Party which he conceived to be so dangerous to the common Peace; and sending such of his Divines to the Synod of *Dort*, as were most like to be sufficiently active in their condemnation. For so it happened, that the Prince of *Orange* being animated by so great a Monarch, suddenly puts himself into the head of his Forces, marches from one strong Town to another, changeth the Garrisons in some, the chief Commanders in the rest, and many of the principal Magistrates in most Towns of *Holland, Utrecht,* and the rest of those Provinces. Which done, he seizeth on the person of *Barnevelt,* as also on *Grotius,* and *Lidebrogius;* and then proclaims a National Synod to be held at *Dort* in *November* following, to which the *Calvinists* were invited from all parts of Christendom. And yet not thinking themselves strong enough to suppress their Adversaries, they first disabled some of them by Ecclesiastical Censures from being chosen Members of it; others who had been lawfully chosen, were not permitted to give suffrage with the rest of the Synodists, unless they would renounce their Party. And finally, they took such order with the rest, that they would not suffer them to sit as Judges in the present Controversies, but only to appear before them as Parties Criminal. All which being condescended to, though against all reason, they were restrained to such a method in their disputation, as carried with it a betraying of their Cause & Interest; and for not yielding hereunto they were dismist by *Bogerman* in a most bitter oration, uttered with fiery eyes, & most virulent language.

1618.

4 It might be rationally conceived, that they who did conspire with such unanimity to condemn their opposites, should not fall out amongst themselves: but so it was, that there was scarce a point in difference between the Parties, wherein they had not very frequent and most fearful bickerings with one another; the Provincials many times enterfering with the Forein Divines, and sometimes falling foul on those of different Judgment, though of the same University with them. The *British* Divines, together with one of those that came from *Breme,* maintained an Universality of Redemption of Mankind by the death of Christ. But this by no means would be granted by the rest of the Synod, for fear of yielding any thing in the least degree to the opposite Party. *Martinius,* another of the Divines of *Breme,* declared his dissent from the common Opinion, touching the manner of Christ's being *Fundamentum Electionis:* and that he thought Christ not only to be the Effector of our Election, but also the Author and Procurer of it. But hereupon *Gomarus* flings down his Glove, and openly defies *Martinius* to a Duel, telling the Synod that he

he knew *Martinius* was able to say nothing at all in refutation of that Doctrine. The said *Martinius* had affirmed, that God was *Cauſa Phyſica Converſionis*; and for the truth thereof, appealed unto *Goclenius* a renowned Philoſopher, who was then preſent in the Synod, and confirmed the ſame. But preſently *Sibrandus Lubbertus* takes fire at this, and falls expreſly upon both. And though the controverſie for the preſent was ſtilled by *Bogerman*; yet was it revived by *Gomarus* within few days after; who being backed by ſome of the *Palatine* Divines, behaved himſelf ſo rudely and uncivilly againſt *Martinius*, that he had almoſt driven him to a reſolution of forſaking their company.

5. The General Body of the Synod not being able to avoid the Inconveniences which the *Supra-lapſarian* way brought with it, were generally intent on the *Sub lapſarian*. But on the other ſide the Commiſſioners of the Churches of *South Holland* thought it not neceſſary to determine whether God conſidered man fallen, or not fallen, while he paſſed the decrees of Election and Reprobation. But far more poſitive was *Gomarus*, one of the Four Profeſſors of *Leyden*, who ſtood as ſtrongly to the Abſolute, Irreſpective, and Irreverſible Decree, (excluſive of mans ſin, and our Saviours ſufferings) as he could have done for the Holy Trinity. And not being able to draw the reſt unto his Opinion, nor willing to conform to theirs, he delivered his own Judgment in writing apart by it ſelf, not joyning in ſubſcription with the reſt of the Brethren, for Conformity ſake, as is accuſtomed in ſuch caſes But *Macrovius*, one of the Profeſſors of *Franekar* in *Weſt-Friesland*, went beyond them all, contending with great heat and violence againſt all the reſt, *That God propounds his Word to Reprobates to no other purpoſe, but to leave them wholly inexcuſable. That if the Goſpel is conſidered in reſpect of Gods intention, the proper end thereof, and not the accidental in regard of Reprobates, is to deprive them totally of all excuſe. And finally, That Chriſt knows all the hearts of men; and therefore only knocketh at the hearts of Reprobates, not with a mind of entering in (becauſe he knows they cannot open to him if they would;) but partly, that he might upbraid them for their impotency; and partly that he might encreaſe their damnation by it.* Nor reſted the Blaſphemer here, but publickly maintained againſt *Sibrandus Lubbertus* his Collegue (in the open Synod) *That God wills Sin: That he ordains Sin as it is Sin.* And, *That by no means he would have all men to be ſaved.* And more then ſo, he publickly declared at all adventures, *That if thoſe points were not maintained, they muſt forſake the chief Doctors of the Reformation.* Which whether it were more unſeaſonably, or more truly ſpoken, I regard not now. In the agitation of which Points, they ſuffered themſelves to be tranſported into ſuch extremities, that greater noiſe and tumult hath been ſeldom heard of in a ſober Meeting. Inſomuch that when the Biſhop of *Landaff*, to avoid the ſcandal, put them in mind of Moderation, and to endeavour to retain the *Spirit of Unity in the Bond of Peace*; *Gomarus* ſnapt him up, and told him, *That matters were not to be carried in Synodical Meetings, by the Authority of the Perſon, but the ſtrength of the Argument.* For further proof of which particulars, if more proof be neceſſary, I ſhall refer the *Engliſh* Reader to two Books only; that is to ſay, the *Golden Remains* of Mr. *Hales*; and the *Arcana Anti-Remonſtrantium*, by *Tilenus Junior*.

Non agendum hic eſt in Synodo Authoritate ſed Ratione.

6. **From** Confultation and Debate, let us proceed in the next place to Execution, which we find full of Cruelty and accurfed Rigour. The Acts hereof firft ratified in the blood of *Barnevelt*, for whofe difpatch they violated all the Fundamental Laws of the *Belgick* Liberty; in maintenance whereof, they firft pretended to take Arms againft the *Spaniard*, their moft Rightful Prince. The Party being thus beheaded, it was no hard matter to difperfe the whole Trunk or Body : For prefently upon the ending of the Synod, the *Remonftrants* are required to fubfcribe to their own condemnation ; and for refufing fo to do, they were all banifhed by a Decree of the States-General, with their Wives and Children, (to the number of of feven hundred Families or thereabouts) and forced to beg their bread, even in defolate places. But yet this was no end of their forrows neither ; they muft come under a new *Crofs*, and be calumniated for holding many horrid Blafphemies and grofs Impieties which they moft abhorred. For in the continuation of the Hiftory of the *Netherlands* writ by one *Crofs* a Fellow of neither Judgment nor Learning, and fo more apt to be abufed with a falfe report; it is there affirmed, (whether with greater Ignorance, or Malice, it is hard to fay) *That there was a Synod called at* Dort, *to fupprefs the* Arminians; & *that the faid* Arminians *held amongft other Herefies, firft, That God was the Author of Sin; Secondly, That he created the far greater part of Mankind, for no other purpofe but only to find caufe to dam them.* And to fay truth, it had been well for them in refpect of their Temporal Fortunes, had they taught thofe Herefies, for then they might have fped no worfe then *Macorvius* did, who notwithftanding all his Heterodoxies, and moft horrid Blafphemies, was only looked upon as one of their *Erring-Brethren*; fubjected to no other Cenfure, but an Admonition to forbear all fuch Forms of Speech as might give any juft offence *to tender Ears*, and could not be *digefted by perfons ignorant and uncapable of fo great Myfteries*. As on the other fide it is reported of *Francifcus Auratus*, a right Learned man, and one of the Profeffors for Divinity in the Schools of *Sedan*, (a Town and Seignury belonging to the Dukes of *Bouilton*) *That he was moft difgracefully deprived of his Place and Function, by thofe of the* Calvinian *Party, becaufe he had delivered in a Sermon on thofe words of St.* James, c. 1. v. 13. God tempteth no man, &c. *That God was not the* Author of Sin.

7. But poffibly it may be faid, That thefe Oppreffions Tyrannies, and Partialities, are not to be afcribed to the Sect of *Calvin*, in the capacity of *Presbyterians*, but of *Predeftinarians* ; and therefore we will now fee what they acted in behalf of *Presbytery*, which was as dear to all the Members of that Synod, but the *Englifh* only, as any of the five Points, whatfoever it was : For in the hundred forty fifth Seffion, being held on the 20th of *April*, the *Belgick* Confeffion was brought in to be fubfcribed by the Provincials, and publickly approved by the Forein Divines : In which Confeffion there occurred one Article which tended plainly to the derogation and difhonour of the Church of *England*. For in the Thirty one Article it is faid exprefly, *That forafmuch as doth concern the Minifters of the Church of Chrift, in what place foever, they are of equal* * *Power and Authority with one another, as being all of them the Minifters of Jefus Chrift, who is only the Univerfal Bifhop, and fole Head of his Church.*

1619.

* *Quantum vero attinet divini Verbi miniftros, eandem illi Poteftatem & Authoritatem habent.* Confef. Belg. Art. 31.

Church. Which Article being as agreeable to *Calvin's* Judgment in point of Difcipline, as their determinations were to his Opinion in point of Doctrine, was very cheerfully entertained by the Forein Divines, though found in few of the Confeffions of the Forein Churches. But being found directly oppofite to the government of the Church by Archbifhops and Bifhops, with which a parity of Minifters can have no confiftence, was cordially oppofed by the Divines of the *Britifh* College, but moft efpecially by Dr. *George Clarton* then Lord Bifhop of *Landaff,* and afterwards tranflated to the See of *Chichefter,* who having too much debafed himfelf beneath his calling, in being prefent in a Synod or Synodical Meeting, in which an ordinary Presbyter was to take the Chair, and have precedency before him, thought it high time to vindicate himself, and the Church of *England,* to enter a Legal Proteftation againft thofe proceedings. Which though it was admitted, and perhaps recorded, received no other Anfwer but negleft, if not fcorn withall. Concerning which, he publifhed a Declaration after his return in thefe words enfuing.

8. *When we were to yield our confent to the* Belgick *Confeffion at* Dort, *I made open proteftation in the Synod, That whereas in the Confeffion there was inferted a ftrange conceit of the Parity of Minifters to be inftiuted by Chrift; I declared our diffent utterly in that point. I fhewed, that by Chrift a Parity was never inftituted in the Church: that he ordained Twelve Apoftles, as alfo Seventy Difciples: that the Authority of the Twelve was above the other: that the Church preferved this order left by our Saviour. And therefore, when the extraordinary Power of the Apoftles ceafed, yet this ordinary Authority continued in Bifhops, who fucceeded them, who were by the Apoftles left in the Government of the Church, to ordain Minifters, and to fee that they who were fo ordained, fhould preach no other Doctrine: that in an inferior degree, the Minifters were governed by Bifhops, who fucceeded the Seventy Difciplies: that this Order hath been maintained in the Church from the times of the Apoftles; and herein I appealed to the Judgment of Antiquity, and to the Judgment of any Learned man now living, and craved herein to be fatisfied, if any man of Learning could fpeak to the contrary. My Lord of Salisbury is my Witnefs, and fo are all the reft of my company, who fpeak alfo in the Caufe. To this there was no anfwer made by any; whereupon we conceived that they yielded to the truth of the Proteftation. But it was only he and his Affociates which conceived fo of it : and fo let it go.*

9. His Lordfhip adds, that in a Conference which he had with fome Divines of that Synod, he told them, *Twat the caufe of all their troubles, was becaufe they had no Bifhops amongft them, who by their Authority might reprefs turbulent fpirits, that broached Novelty, every man having liberty to fpeak or write what they lift; and that as long as there were no Ecclefiaftical men in Authority to reprefs and cenfure fuch contentious Spirits, their Church could never be without trouble.* To which they anfwered, That they did much honour and reverence the good Order and Difcipline of the Church of *England,* and with all their hearts would be glad to have it eftablifhed amongft them; but that could not be hoped for in their State: that

that their hope was, That ſeeing they could not do what they deſired, God would be merciful to them, if they did what they could. This was, ſaith he, the ſum and ſubſtance of their Anſwer, which he conceived to be enough to free that people from aiming at an *Anarchy*, and open confuſion ; adding withal, that they groaned under the weight of that burden, and would be eaſed of it if they could. But by his Lordſhips leave, I take this to be nothing but a piece of diſſimulation of ſuch a ſanctified Hypocriſie as ſome of the *Calvinians* do affirm to be in Almighty God : For certainly they might have Biſhops if they would, as well as the Popiſh Cantons of the *Switzers*, or the State of *Venice* ; of which, the one is ſubject to an *Ariſtocracy*, the other to a Government no leſs popular then that of the *Netherlands*. In which reſpect it was conceived more lawful, by the late Lord Primate, for any *Engliſh* Proteſtant to communicate with the Reformed Churches in *France*, who cannot have Biſhops if they would ; then with the *Dutch*, who will not have Biſhops though they may ; there ſtill remaining in their hands 7 Epiſcopal Sees, with all the Honours and Revenues belonging to them ; that is to ſay, the Biſhoprick of *Harlem* in *Holland*, of *Middlebourgh* in *Zealand*, of *Lewarden* in *Frieſland*, of *Groining* in the Province ſo called, of *Deventer* in the County of *Overyſſell*, and of *Ruremond* in the Dutchy of *Gueldreſs* ; all of them, but the laſt, ſubordinate to the Church of *Utreſt*, which they kept alſo in their Power.

10. Somewhat was alſo done in the preſent Synod, in order to the better keeping of the Lords day, then it had been formerly : For till this time they had their Faires and Markets upon this day, their *Kirk-maſſes*, as they commonly called them : Which, as they conſtantly kept in moſt of the great Towns of *Holland, Zealand*, &c. even in *Dort* it ſelf ; ſo by the conſtant keeping of them, they muſt needs draw away much people from the Morning Service, to attend the buſineſs of their Trades. And in the Afternoon (as before was noted) all Divine Offices were interdicted by a conſtitution, which received life here, *Anno* 1574, that time being wholly left to be diſpoſed of as the people pleaſed, either upon their profit, or their recreation. But their acquaintance with the *Engliſh*, brought them to more ſenſe of Piety. And now they took the opportunity to train the people to the Church in the Afternoon, by the Authority and Reputation of the preſent Synod : For, having entertained the *Palatine Catechiſm* in their publick Schools, it was reſolved that it ſhould be taught in all their Churches on *Sunday* in the Afternoon : That the Miniſters ſhould be bound to read and expound that Catechiſm, though none were preſent at the Exerciſes, but thoſe of their own Families, only in hope that others might be drawn after their example ; and that the Civil Magiſtrate ſhould be employed by the Synod to reſtrain all Servile Works, and other Prophanations of that day, wherewith the Afternoons had commonly been ſpent, that ſo the people might repair to the Catechiſings. And though ſome Reformation did enſue upon it in the greater Towns, yet in their leſſer Villages(where men are more intent on their worldly buſineſſes) it remains as formerly.

11. As little of the *Sabbatarian*, had the *Palatine* Churches, which in all points adhered tenaciouſly unto *Calvins* Doctrine: For in thoſe Churches it was ordinary for the Gentlemen to betake themſelves in the Afternoon

noon of the Lords day, unto *Hawking* and *Hunting*, as the season of the year was fit for either ; or otherwise in taking the Air, visiting their Friends, or whatsoever else shall seem pleasing unto them.   As usual it was also with the Husband-man, to spend the greatest part of the Afternoon in looking over his Grounds, ordering his Cattel, and following of such Recreations as are most agreeable to his Nature and Education: no publick Divine Offices being prescribed for any part of that day, but the Morning only.   And so it stood in the year 1612 : At what time the Lady *Elizabeth,* Daughter to King *James,* and Wife to *Frederick* the fifth, Prince Elector of *Palatine,* came first into that Countrey ; who having Divine Service every Afternoon in her Chapel, or Closet, officiated by her own Chaplains, according to the Liturgy of the Church of *England,* gave the first hint unto that Prince to cause the like Religious Offices to be celebrated in his part of the Family ; afterwards by degrees in all the Churches of *Heldenbourgh* ; and finally, in most other Cities and Towns of his Dominions.   Had he adventured no further on the confidence of that Power and Greatness which accrued to him by contracting an Alliance with so great a Monarch, it had been happy for himself and the Peace of Christendom.   But being tempted by *Scultetus,* and some other of the Divines about him, not to neglect the opportunity of advancing the Gospel, and making himself the principal Patron of it, he fell on some Designs destructive to himself and his.   Who, though he were a Prince of a Flegmatick nature, and of small Activity; yet being prest by the continual sollicitation of some eager Spirits, he drew all the Provinces and Princes which profest the *Calvinian* Doctrines, to enter into a strict League or Union amongst themselves, under pretence of looking to the Peace and Happiness of the true Religion.

    12. It much advantaged the design, that the *Calvinians* in all parts of *Germany* had began to stir, as men resolved to keep the Saddle, or to lose the Horse.   In *Aix* (the *Latins* call it *Aquisgranum*) an Imperial City, they first appeared considerable for their Power and Numbers, *Anno* 1605, at what time they shrewdly shaked the Estate thereof.   But being thereupon debarred the exercise of their Religion, and punished for the Misdemeanor, they kept themselves quiet till the year 1614 ; when in a popular Tumult they surprise the City, secure the principal Magistrates of it, and eject the Jesuits.   And though by the Mediation of the *French* Agents, and those of *Juliers,* a Peace was for the present clapt up between them; yet neither Party was resolved to stand longer to it, then might serve their turns.   But whosoever made the reckoning, the *Calvinists* were at last compelled to pay the shot : For the Town being proscribed by *Matthias* the Emperor, and the execution of the *Ban* committed to Arch Duke *Albert* ; he sends the Marquess of *Spinola* with an Army thither, by whom the Town is brought to a surrender, the ancient Magistrates restored, and the *Calvinians* either forced to forsake the place, or to submit themselves unto Fine and Ransome, if they kept their dwellings.   Nor did they speed much better in the City of *Colen,* where their Party was not strong enough to suppress the Catholicks ; and therefore they forsook the City, and retired to *Mulleime,* which they began to build and fortifie for their habitation.   But those of *Colen* fearing that this new Town might in short time overtop that City both in wealth and power,

addrest

dreſt themſelves unto the Emperor *Matthias* : By whoſe Command the Duke of *Newbourgh* falls upon it, deſtroys the greateſt part thereof, and leaves the finiſhing of that Work to the Marqueſs of *Spinola.*

13. In *Haſſia* their Affairs ſucceeded with more proſperous Fortune, where *Lodowick,* of the ſecond Houſe of the *Lantgraves,* who had the City of *Marperge* for his Seat and Reſidence, declared himſelf in favour of their Forms and Doctrines, at ſuch time as the *Calviniſts* of *Aix* (before remembred) firſt began to ſtir, followed therein by *George* his Brother, commonly called the *Lantgrave* of *Darmſtad,* from the place of his dwelling ; half of which Town belonging to the Patrimony of the Prince Elector, had eaſily made way for *Calviniſm* into all the reſt, And though this *Lodowick* was diſturbed in his Government or Poſſeſſion by his Couſin *Maurice,* commonly called the *Lantgrave* of *Caſſels,* from his principal City ; who ſeized upon the Town of *Marperge, An.* 1612 ; yet was he ſhortly after reſtored to his whole eſtate, by the *Palatine* League, which for the time carried a great ſway in thoſe parts of *Germany.* But of greater conſequence were the agitations about *Cleve* and *Gulick,* occaſioned by a difference between the Marqueſs of *Brandenbourgh,* and the Duke of *Newbourgh,* about the partage of the Patrimony and eſtate, of the Duke of *Cleve* : For *John William,* the laſt Duke of *Cleve,* deceaſing without Iſſue in the year 1610, left his Eſtates between the Children of his Siſters ; of which the eldeſt, called *Maria Leonora,* was married to *John Sigiſmund,* the Elector of *Brandenbourgh,* was Mother of *George William,* the young Marqueſs of *Brandenbourgh,* who in her Right pretended to the whole Eſtate. The like pretence was made by *Wolfgangus Guilielmus,* Duke of *Newbourgh,* deſcended from the Electoral Family of the Princes *Palatine,* whoſe Mother *Magdalen* was the ſecond Siſter of the ſaid *John William.* The firſt of theſe Pretenders was wholly of a *Lutheran* Stock, and the other as inclinable to the Sect of *Calvin* ; though afterwards, for the better carrying on of their Affairs, they forſook their Parties.

14. For ſo it happened, that the Duke of *Newbourgh* finding himſelf too weak for the Houſe of *Brandenbourgh,* put himſelf under the protection of the Catholick King ; who having concluded a Truce of Twelve years with the States United, wanted employment for his Army; and, that he he might engage that King with the greater confidence, he reconciles himſelf to the Church of *Rome,* and marries the Lady *Magdalen,* Daughter to the Duke of *Bavaria,* the moſt potent of the *German* Princes of that Religion : which alſo he eſtabliſhed in his own Dominions on the death of his Father. This puts the young Marqueſs to new Counſels, who thereupon calls in the Forces of the *States United* ; the War continuing upon this occaſion betwixt them and *Spain,* though the Scene was ſhifted. And that they might more cordially eſpouſe his Quarrel, he took to Wife the Siſter of *Frederick* the Fifth, Prince Elect or *Palatine,* and Neece of *William* of *Naſſaw,* Prince of *Orange,* by his youngeſt Daughter ; and conſequently Couſin German, once removed to Count *Maurice* of *Naſſaw,* Commander General of the Forces of the *States United,* both by Sea and Land. This kept the Balance even between them ; the one poſſeſſing the Eſtates of *Cleve* and *Mark,* and the other

other, the ureateft part of *Berge* and *Gulick*. But fo it was, that the old Marquefs of *Brandenbourgh* having fettled his abode in the Dukedom of *Prufsia*, and left the management of the Marqueffate to the Prince his Son ; left him withal unto the Plots and Practifes of a fubtile Lady : Who being throughly inftructed in all points of *Calvinifme*, and having gotten a great Empire in her Husbands Affections, prevailed fo far upon him in the firft year of their Marriage, *Anno* 1614, that he renounced his own Religion, and declared for Hers ; which he more cheerfully embraced, in hope to arm all the *Calvinians* both of the Higher and Lower *Germany*, in defence of his Caufe, as his Competitor of *Newbourgh* had armed the *Catholicks* to preferve his intereft.

15. Being thus refolved, he publifheth an Edict in the Moneth of *February, Anno* 1615 ; publifhed in his Fathers Name, but only in his own Authority and fole Command, under pretence of pacifying fome diftempers about Religion ; but tending, in good earneft, to the plain fuppreffion of the *Lutheran* Forms : for, having fpent a tedeous and impertinent Preamble touching the Animofities fomented in the *Proteftent* Churches, between the *Lutherans* and thofe of the *Calvinian* Party, he firft requires that all unneceffary Difputes be laid afide, that fo all grounds of ftrife and difaffection might be alfo buried. Which faid, he next commands all Minifters within the Marqueffate, to preach the Word purely and fincerely, according to the Writings of the Holy Prophets and Apoftles, the Four Creeds commonly received (amongft which the *Te Deum* is to go for one) and the Confeffion of *Ausberg*, of the laft Correction ; and that omitting all new gloffes and interpretations of idle and ambitious men, affecting a Primacy in the Church, and a Power in the State, they aim at nothing in their Preachings, but the Glory of God, and the Salvation of Mankind. He commands alfo, That they fhould abftain from all calumniating of thofe Churches which either were not fubject to their Jurifdiction, nor were not lawfully convicted of the Crime of Herefie ; which he refolved not to connive at for the time to come, but to proceed unto the punifhment of all thofe who wilfully fhould refufe to conform themfelves to his Will and Pleafure. After which, giving them fome good Counfel for following a more moderate courfe in their Preachings and Writings, then they had been accuftomed to in the times fore-going, and in all points to be obedient to their principal Magiftrate, he pulls off the Difguife, and fpeaks plainly thus,

* Ceterum Reformationi in Electoratu Brandenburgico inftituendæ, hæc capita memorantur. Thuan. Contin. lib.1. An, 1614.

' 16. Thefe are * (faith he) the Heads of that Reformation, which ' is to be obferved in all the Churches of *Brandenbourgh* ; that is to fay, ' All Images, Statues, and Croffes, to be removed out of the place of ' publick Meetings ; all Altars, as the Reliques of *Popery*, and purpofely ' erected for the Sacrifices of the Popifh Mafs, to be taken away. That ' in their room they fhould fet up a Table of a long fquare Figure, cove- ' red at all times with a Carpet of Black, and at the time of the Com- ' munion with a Linen Cloth. That Wafers fhould be ufed inftead of ' the former Hofts ; which being cut into long pieces fhould be re- ' ceived and broken by the hands of thofe who were admitted to com- ' municate at the Holy Table. That ordinary Cups fhould be made ufe

' of for the future, inſtead of the old Popiſh Chalice. That the Veſt-
' ments uſed in the Maſs ſhould be forborn ; no Candles lighted in any
' of their Churches at noon-day. No Napkin to be held to thoſe that
' received the Sacrament ; nor any of them to receive it upon their
' knees, as if Chriſt were corporally preſent. The ſign of the Croſs to
' be from thenceforth diſcontinued. The Miniſter not to turn his back
' to the people at the Miniſtration. The Prayers and Epiſtles before
' the Sermon to be from thenceforth read, not ſung ; and the ſaid
' Prayers not to be muttered with a low voice in the Pulpit, or Reading
' Pew, but pronounced audibly and diſtinctly. Auricular Confeſſion
' to be laid aſide, and the Communion not to be adminiſtred to ſick
' perſons in the time of any common Plague, or Contagious Sickneſs.
' No bowing of their knee at the Name of *Jeſus*: Nor Fonts of ſtone
' to be retained in their Churches, the want whereof may be ſupplied by
' a common Baſon. The Decalogue to be repeated wholly without
' mutilation ; and the Catechiſm, in ſome other points no leſs errone-
' ous, to be corrected and amended. The Trinity to be adored, but not
' expreſt in any Images either carved or painted. The words of Con-
' ſecration in the holy Supper to be interpreted and underſtood accor-
' ding unto that Analogy which they held with the Sacrament and o-
' ther Texts of Holy Scripture. And finally, That the Miniſters ſhould
' not be ſo tyed to preach upon the Goſpels and Epiſtles that were ap-
' pointed for the day, but that they might make choice of any other
' Texts of Scripture, as beſt pleaſed themſelves. Such was the tenour
of this Edict ; on which I have inſiſted the more at large, to ſhew the
difference between the *Lutheran* and *Genevian* Churches ; and the great
correſpondence of the firſt with the Church of *England.* But this *Calvinian* Pill did not work ſo kindly, as not to ſtir more humours then it
could remove. For the *Lutherans* being in poſſeſſion, would not deliver up their Churches, or deſert thoſe Uſages to which they had been
trained up, and in which they were principled, according to the Rules
of their firſt Reformation. And hereupon ſome Rupture was like to
grow betwixt the young Marqueſs and his Subjects, if by the intervention of ſome honeſt Patriots it had not been cloſed up in this
manner, or to this effect: That the *Lutheran* Forms only ſhould be uſed
in all the Churches of the *Marqueſſate,* for the contentation of the people ; and, that the Marqueſs ſhould have the exerciſe of his new Religion for Himſelf, his Lady, and thoſe of his Opinion, in their private
Chapels.

17. But the main buſineſs of theſe times were the Commotions raiſed in *Tranſylvania, Hungary, Auſtria,* and *Bohemia,* by thoſe of the *Calvinian* Party ; which drew all the Provinces of the Empire into ſuch
confuſions, as have diſturbed the Peace thereof to this very day. For,
laying down the true Original thereof, we may pleaſe to know, that
Ferdinand, the younger Brother of *Charles* the Fifth, ſucceeding on the
death of *Maximillian* the Emperor in the Dukedom of *Auſtria,* and afterwards attaining by Marriage to the Crown of *Hungary* and *Bohemia,*
which he was not born to, endeavoured to oblige his Subjects in all
thoſe Dominions, by a connivance at ſuch Deviations from the Church
of *Rome,* as were maintained by thoſe who adhered to *Luther,* and held
them-

themfelves to the Confeffion of *Ausberg* : which afterwards was ratified by Imperial Edict. Followed therein by *Maximillian* the fecond, who fucceeded him in his Eftates ; and being a mild and gracious Prince, not only fhewed himfelf unwilling to challenge any Power over Souls and Confciences, but was pleafed to mediate in behalf of his *Proteftant* Subjects with the Fathers at *Trent*, amongft whom he incurred the fufpition of being a *Lutheran.* But *Rodolphus* the eldeft of his Sons, and his next Succeffor, was of a different temper from his Father and Grandfather, a profeft enemy to all that held not a Conformity with the Church of *Rome*, which he endeavoured to promote with fuch terrible Edicts, as threatned nothing but deftruction unto all gain-fayers. He had five Brethren at that time, but none of them the father of any children ; which made him caft his eyes on *Ferdinand* of *Gratts*, Son of *Charles* Duke of *Gratts*, and Nephew of *Ferdinand* the Emperor, before remembred. Who going to *Rome* in the year of *Jubile*, *Anno* 1600, obliged himfelf by Oath to the Pope then being, to extirpate all the Proteftants out of his Dominions ; which upon the inftigation of the *Jefuits* he did accordingly, by pillaging and banifhing all of the *Auguftian Confefsion*, thorough *Styria*, *Carinthia*, and *Carniola*, though they had paid for the Freedom of their Confcience a great fum of Money.

18. This fo endeared him to *Rodolphus*, that he refolved upon him for his next Succeffor, and at the prefent to eftate him in the Realm of *Hungary*, as a ftep unto it. In which Defign as he was feconded by the *Pope* and *Spaniard*, fo queftionlefs it had been effected, if *Matthias* the Emperors Brother, and next Heir, had not countermined them, by countenancing thofe of the *Calvinian* or Reformed Religion, who then began to feem confiderable in the eye of that Kingdom. To carry on which *Spanifh* Plot to the end defired, the Prelates of *Hungary*, in an Affembly held at *Presburgh*, *Anno* 1604, publifhed a Decree without the confent of the Nobility and Eftates of the Kingdom, for the burning
1604. or perpetual banifhment of all fuch as were of the Reformed Religion. Which having been entertained in the Realm of *Poland*, found no great difficulty in croffing the *Carpathian* Mountains, and gaining the like favourable admiffion in this Kingdom alfo. Againft which Edict of the Bifhops a *Proteft* is prefently made by the Eftates of the Realm, under the Seal of the *Palatine*, the chief Officer of it ; by whom it was publickly affirmed, *That they would with juft Arms defend themfelves, if they fhould be queftioned for the caufe of Religion.* Which notwithftanding *Beliojofa* (one of the Emperors chief Commanders in the Realm of *Hungary*) firft got into his hands the ftrong Town of *Caffovia*, ftanding upon the borders of *Tranfylvania*. And that being done, he did not only interdict all thofe of the *Reformed Religion* from making any ufes of them as they had done formerly ; but he inhibits them from having Sermons in their private Houfes, from reading in the Holy Bible, and from the burying of their dead in hallowed places.

19. Nor ftaid he there, but pick'd a needlefs quarrel with *Iftivan Botfcay*, a great man of that Country ; two of whofe Caftles he furprifed and razed, and thereupon provoked him to become his Enemy.
For,

For, being so provoked, he takes upon himself the Patronage of his Native Country, then miserably oppressed by the *German* Soldiers; calls himself Prince of *Transylvania*, confederates himself with the *Turkish Bassa's*, and thrived so well in his Designs, that he compelled the Emperor to recall his Forces out of *Transylvania*, and procured Liberty of Conscience for all his Followers. For, being assisted by the *Turks*, he encountred the said *Beliojosa*, cuts off 6000 of his men, and sends a great part of the enemies Ensigns, to the *Visier Bassa*, as a sign of his Victory. Which Blow he followed by a Proclamation to this effect, viz. *That all such as desired Liberty of Conscience, and to live free from the Corruptions and Iaolatries of the Church of* Rome, *should repair to him as to their Head, and that he would allow to each of them Five Dollars weekly.* Which Proclamation did not only draw unto him many thousands of the common people, together with a great part of the Nobility and Gentry; but tempted many of the Emperors Soldiers to forsake their General, and joyn themselves unto his Party. Strengthened wherewith, he makes himself Master of *Cassovia*; in which he changed not only the Religion, but the Civil Government: insomuch that many of those which were addicted to the Church of *Rome*, were presently slain upon the place, and most of the rest turned out of the City, together with the greatest part of the Church-men, the Bishops, and the Emperors Treasurer. Upon which fortunate Success, a great Party in the *Upper Hungary* declare in favour of his Cause, violently break open the Religious Houses, compel the Fryers to put themselves into fortified places; and finally, to abandon *Presburgh*, the chief Town of that Kingdom, and to flye for shelter to *Vienna*, as their surest refuge.

20. After this, *Basta*, the Lord-General of the Emperors Forces, obtained the better of them in some Fortunate Skirmishes, which rather served to prolong, then to end the War. For *Botscay* was grown to so great strength, and made such spoil in all places whereever he came, that *Pallas Lippa* his Lieutenant, was found to be possessed at the time of his death, of no fewer then Seven hundred Chains of Gold, and one hundred thousand Ducats in ready mony, which he had raked together within less then a year. This Treasure coming into *Botscay*'s hands by the death of *Lippa*, he mightily encreased his Army, with which he took in many strong Towns, and brought in some of the Nobility of the *Upper Hungary*, sending his Forces into *Styria*, *Austria*, and *Moravia*, which he spoiled and wasted. Insomuch that the Emperor, being forced to send Commissioners to him to accord the Differences, could obtain no better Conditions from him, but, *That Liberty of Conscience, and the free exercise of the Reformed Religion, should be permitted to all those who demanded the same; and that himself should be estated in the Principality of* Transylvania, *for the term of his life.* And though the Emperor at first refused to yield to these hard Conditions; yet in the next year, *Anno* 1606, upon a second Treaty with the Estates of that Kingdom, it was agreed upon by the Commissioners on both sides, That the free exercise as well of the *Reformed*, as of the *Romish* Religion, should be permitted to all men in the Realm of *Hungary*, as in the time of *Maximillian* the Father, and *Ferdinand* the Grandfather, of the present Emperor.

Which

1605.

1606.

Which Articles were more fully ratified in the Pacification made at *Vienna*, on the fourteenth of *September* then next following. In which it was expresly cautioned and capitulated, *That the* Calvinian *Religion should from thenceforth be exercised as freely as either the* Lutheran *or the* Romish. In managing which Negation between the Parties, *Matthias* the Arch-Duke, who hitherto had secretly encouraged the *Hungarian Gospellers*, was not only present, but openly gave both countenance and consent unto it.

21. The gaining of this point, put them upon a hope of obtaining greater, even to the abrogating of all Laws and Ordinances for the burning of Hereticks, and whatsoever else were contrary to their Religion ; as also, to the nominating of the *Palatine*, or Principal Officers, and to the making of Confederacies with their neighbour-Nation. During the agitating of which matters, *Botscay* dyes in *Cassovia* ; but leaves his Faction so well found, that they are able to go on without their Leader. An Assembly of the States of *Hungary* is called, by the Emperor, at *Presburgh*, in the middle of *August*, Anno 1607 ; but nothing done, for want of the presence of Arch Duke *Matthias*, who was appointed by the Emperor to preside therein. Which hapned also to the like Assembly of Estates of the Dukedom of *Austria*, and of the whole Empire, the next year, at the City of *Ratisbone*. *Matthias*, in the mean season, had his own Designs apart : For, at such time as the Assembly of the Estates was held at *Ratisbone*, he makes a journey unto *Presburgh*, convocates thither the Estates of *Hungary*, confirms the Pacification made before at *Vienna*, suffers them to confederate with their Neighbours of *Austria*, and makes himself the Head of that Confederation. By vertue whereof, he commands the people of both Countreys to put themselves into Arms, pretending an Expedition into *Moravia*, but aiming directly against *Prague*, the chief Town of *Bohemia*, where the Emperor *Rodolphus* then resided : Whom he so terrified with his coming with an Army of eighteen thousand, that he confented to deliver the Crown of *Hungary* into the hands of *Matthias*, to yeild unto him the possession of all that Kingdom, and to discharge his Subjects from their former Allegiance ; upon condition that the estates of that Realm should chuse no other King but the said Arch Duke. Which Agreement being made the 17*th* of *June*, 1608, *Matthias* is accordingly Crowned King of *Hungary* ; and *Illisachius*, a profest *Calvinian*, and one of the principal Sticklers in these Agitations, is made *Palatine* of it.

1607.

1608.

22. By this Transaction, the whole Dukedom of *Austria*, and so many of the Provinces subordinate to it, as were not actually possessed by the Arch Duke *Ferdinand*, are consigned over to *Matthias*. Many Inhabitants whereof, professing the *Calvinian* Forms and Doctrines, (which only must be called the Reformed Religion) and building on the late Confederation with the Realm of *Hungary*, presumed so far upon the patience of their Prince, as to invade some publick Churches for the exercise of it. But they soon found themselves deceived : For *Matthias* having somewhat of the States-man in him, and being withal exasperated by the Popes *Nuncio*, interdicts all such publick Meetings. He had now served his turn in getting the possession of the Crown of

Hungary

Hungary, and was not willing to connive at those Exorbitances in his *Austrian* Subjects, (over whom he challenged a more absolute *Soveraignty* then over any of the rest) which he had cherrished for self ends in the Kingdom of *Hungary*. The *Austrians* on the other side, who professed the Reformed Religion, refuse to take the Oath of Allegiance to him, if they might not exercise their Religion in as free a manner as the *Hungarians* were permitted to do by the Pacification. And thereupon they presently give Order to their Tenants and Vassals to put themselves into Arms, appoint a General Assembly of the *Protestant* and Reformed States to be held at *Horn*, and there resolve to extort that by way of Force, which they could not hope to gain by Favour. Some pains was took by *Maximilian* the Archduke, another of the Emperors Brothers, to accord the difference; who offered him in the name of the King to tollerate the free exercise of their Religion without the Cities; and that in the bestowing of the publick Offices there should be no exception taken at them in regard of their difference in Religion; and withall gave them many Reasons why such a general Liberty as they desired could not be granted by the King, with reference to his Honour, Conscience, or particular safety.

23. But this reasonable Offer did not satisfie the Reformed Party, (for so the *Calvinians* must be called) by whom the *Hungarians* and *Moravians* are sollicited to associate with them, till they had compassed their desires: And upon confidence thereof refused more obstinately to take the Oath then before they did; levying new Forces for the War, and quartering them in great numbers round about the City of *Crema*, the chief City of the *Upper Austria*. But in the end, upon the intervention of the *Moravian* Ambassadors, the new King was content to yield to these Conditions following, viz. *That the Nobility in their Castles or Towns,*   1609. *as also in their City Houses, should for themselves and their people have the free exercise of their Religion. That the free exercise of Preaching might be used in the three Churches of* Iferdorf, Trihelcuincel, *and* Horn. *That the like freedom of Religion might be also exercised in all those Churches in which they enjoyed the same till the Kings late Edict. And, that the Counsellors of State, and other publick Officers, should from thenceforth be chose promiscuously out of both Religions.* Upon the granting of which Articles, but not before, they did not only take the Oath of Allegiance, but gave him a Magnificent Reception in the Town of *Lintz*; which happened on the 17th of *May*, 1609.

24. No sooner were the *Austrians* gratified in the point of Religion, but the *Bohemians* take their turn to require the like; concerning which we are to look a little backward, as far as to the year 1400 About which time, we find a strong party to be raised amongst them against some Superstitions and Corruptions in the Church of *Rome*; occasioned, as some say, by reading the works of *Wickliff*, and by the diligence of *Piccardus*, a *Flemming* born, as is affirmed by some others, from whom they had the name of *Piccardus*; cruelly persecuted by their own Kings, & publickly condemned in the Council of *Constance*; they continued constant notwithstanding to their own perswasions: distinguished also from the rest of the *Bohemians*, by the name of *Calixtins*, from the use of the Chalice; and *Subutraque*, from communicating in *both kinds*, against

all

all oppofers. Their Adverfaries in the Church of *Rome* reproached them by the name of *Adamites*, and fometimes of *Piccards*; imputing to them many Heterodoxies, and fome filthy Obfcenities, of which they never proved them guilty. In this condition they remained till the preaching of *Luther*, and the receiving of the *Auguftin* Confeffion in moft parts of the Empire; which gave them fo much confidence, as to purge themfelves from all former Calumnies, by publifhing a Declaration of their Faith and Doctrine: Which they prefented at *Vienna* to the Archduke *Ferdinand*, about ten years before chofen King of *Bohemia*, together with a large Apology prefixt before it. By which confeffion it appears, that they afcribe no power to the Civil Magiftrate in the Concernments of the Church. That they had fallen upon a way of Ordaining Minifters amongft themfelves, without recourfe unto the Bifhop, or any fuch Superior Officer, as a Super-intendent. And finally, that they retained the ufe of Excommunication, and other Ecclefiaftical Cenfures, for the chaftifing of irregular and fcandalous perfons. In which laft point, and almoft all the other Branches of the faid Confeffion, though they appeared as found and Orthodox as any others which had feparated from the Church of *Rome*; yet by their fymbolyzing with *Geneva* in fo many particulars, it was no hard matter for the whole Body of *Calvinianifm* to creep in amongft them; the growth whereof inflamed them to fuch defperate courfes as they now purfued.

1609.

25. For this they laid a good Foundation in the former year 1609: when *Matthias* with his great Army was preparing for *Prague*, they found the Emperor in fome fear, from which he could not be fecured, but by their affiftance; and they refolved to husband the conjuncture for their beft advantage. In confidence whereof, they propofe unto him thefe Conditions, viz. *That the free exercife of Religion, as well according to the* Bohemian, *as the* Auguftin Confeffion, *might be kept inviolable; and that they which profeßed the one fhould neither fcoff or defpife the other. That all Archbifhopricks, Bifhopricks, Abbotfhips, and other Spiritual Preferments, fhould be given to the* Bohemians *only; and that Ecclefiaftical Offices fhould be permitted to Proteftant Minifters as in former times. That it fhould be lawful for all men in their own Bounds and Territories, to build Churches for their own Religion: and that the Profeßors and Patrons of the Univerfity of* Prague *fhould be joyned to the Confiftory as in former times. That all Political Offices fhould be indifferently permitted unto men of both Religions.* With many other things of like weight and moment in their Civil Concernments. But the Emperor was not yet reduced to that neceffity, as to confent to all at once. He gratified them at the prefent with a Conformation of their Civil Rights; but put of the Demands which concerned Religion to the next Affembly of Eftates; conniving in the mean time at the exercife of that Religion which he could not tolerate.

26. But the *Calvinian Calixtins*, or *Confeffionifts*, call them which you will, perceiving a ftrong party of the Catholicks to be made againft them, appointed a General Affembly to be holden in the City of *New Prague*, the 4th of *May*, to confult of all fuch matters as concerned their Caufe, protefting publickly (according to the common Cuftom of that kind) that this Affembly, though not called by the Emperors Authority, aimed

aimed at no other End then his *Service* only, and the prosperity of that Kingdom ; that both the Emperor and the Kingdom too might not, through the *Perswafions* of his *Evil Counsellors*, be brought to extream peril and danger. This done, they send their Letters to the new King of *Hungary*, the Prince Elector *Palatine*, the Dukes of *Saxony* and *Brunswick*, and other Princes of the Empire; befeeching them, that by their powerful interceffion with his Imperial Majefty, they might be fuffered to enjoy the exercife of their own Religion, which they affirmed to differ in no material point from the Confeffion of *Ausberg*. Following their blow, they firft remonftrate to the Emperor how much they had been difappointed of their hopes and expectations from one time to another ; and in fine, tell him in plain terms, that they will do their beft endeavour for the raifing of Arms, to the end they might be able with their utmoft power *to defend him their Soveraign*, together with themfelves and the whole Kingdom, againft the practifes of their Forein and Domeftick Enemies. According to which Refolution, they forthwith raifed a great number both of Horfe and Foot, whom they ranged under good Commanders, and brought them openly into *Prague*. They procured alfo, that Ambffadors were fent from the Elector of *Saxony*, and the Eftates of *Silefia*, (a Province many years fince incorporated with the Realm of *Bohemia*) to intercede in their behalf. This gave the Emperor a fair colour to confent to that, which nothing but extream neceffity could have wrefted from him.

27. For thereupon he publifhed his Letters of the 14*th* of *July*, 1610, **1610.** by which it was declared, that all his Subjects communicating under one or both kinds fhould live together peaceably and freely, and without wronging or reviling one another, under the pain and penalty of the Law to be inflicted upon them who fhould do the contrary. That as they who communicated under one kind, enjoyed the exercile of their Religion in all points, throughout the Kingdom of *Bohemia*; fo they which did communicate under both kinds, fhould enjoy the field, without the lett or interruption of any; and that they fhould enjoy the fame till a general union in Religion, and an end of all Controverfies fhould be fully made. That they fhould have the lower Confiftory in the City of *Prague*, with power to conform the fame according to their own Confeffion. That they might lawfully make their Priefts as well of the *Bohemian* as of the *German* Nation ; and fettle them in their feveral Parifhes without lett or moleftation of the Archbifhop of *Prague* : and that befides the Schools and Churches which they had already, it might be lawfull for them to erect more of either fort, as well in Cities as in Towns and Countrey Villages. He declared alfo, that all Edicts formerly publifhed againft the free exercife of Religion fhould be void, fruftrate, and of none effect : and that no contrary Edict againft the States of the Religion fhould either be publifhed by himfelf, or any of his Heirs and Succeffors ; or if any were, they fhould not be efteemed of any force or effect in Law : and finally, that all fuch of his Majefties Subjects that fhould do any thing contrary to thefe his Letters, whether they were Ecclefiaftical or Temporal perfons, fhould be feverely punifhed as the Troublers of the Common Peace.

28. The paffing of this Gracious Edict (which the *Confeffionifts* were
not

not flow of putting into execution) exceedingly exafperated all thofe of the Catholick Party ; who thereupon called in the Arch Duke *Leopold*, Bifhop of *Paffaw*, and one of the Emperors younger Brothers : Which invitation he obeyed, entred the Country with an army of 12000 men, makes himfelf Mafter of *New Prague*, and attempts the *Old*. But he found fuch refiftance there, that King *Matthias*, with a powerful Army, came time enough to their relief, and diflodged the Befiegers. Which Aid he brought them at that time, not out of love to their Religion, or their Perfons either, but only upon fome Advertifement which had been given him of Duke *Leopolds* purpofes, of getting that Kingdom to himfelf, as formerly *Matthias* had extorted the Realm of *Hungary*, in defpight of the Emperor. But meening to make fure work of it, he prevailed fo far, that the Emperor refigned unto him that Kingdom alfo, to which he was cheerfully elected by the Eftates of the Country, before the end of this year, *Anno* 1610. And within two years after, was raifed to the Imperial Dignity on the death of his Brother. Advanced unto which Power and Height, he governed his Dominions with great moderation, till the year 1617. When being Himfelf, and all his Brothers, without hope of Children, he caft his eyes upon his Coufin *Ferdinand*, then Duke of *Gratzi*, (a Prince wholly acted by the Jefuits) whom he adopted for his Son, declared him for his Succeffor in all the Patrimony and Eftates belonging to the Houfe of *Auftria* ; and in the year 1618, put him into the actual poffeffion of the Realms of *Hungary* and *Bohemia* ; but not with any fuch formality of Election unto either of them, as in his own cafe had been obferved.

29. This gave encouragement to fome of the Catholick Party, to take offence at fome Churches lately erected by thofe of the Reformed Religion, and either totally to deface them, or to fhut them up. Complaint hereof is made unto the Emperor, but without any remedy. So that being doubly injured, as they gave it out, they called an Affembly of the States, that order might be taken for the prefervation of Religion, and their Civil Rights, both equally endangered by thefe new encroachments. The Emperor difallows the Meeting, commanding them by Proclamation to diffolve the fame. Which fo exafperated fome hot fpirits, that the Emperors Secretary, and two of his principal Councellors, were caft headlong out of the Caftle-Windows. And though all three miraculoufly efcaped with life, yet the Confpirators conceived the Fact to be fo unpardonable, that they could find no means of doing better, but by doing worfe. For hereupon they fet a Guard of Soldiers on the Baron of *Sterneberge*, Governour of the Caftle and Kingdom ; they fecure *Prague*, difplace all the Emperors old Councellors, and totally clear the Kingdom of all the Jefuits ; and prefently, as well by Letters to *Matthias* himfelf, as by a publick Declaration fcattered in all parts of the Kingdom, they juftifie themfelves and their actings in it. Which done, they nominate two and thirty perfons of their own Perfwafion, to have a fuperintendency over all Affairs which concerned that Kingdome, whom they called by the name of *Directors* ; and enter into a folemn League or Covenant, to defend each other againft all perfons whatfoever, without excepting either King or Emperor. For punifhing thefe infolencies on the one fide ; and preferving the Malefactors, on the other,

from

from the hands of Justice; a terrible Confusion first, and afterwards a more terrible War breaks out amongst them. In the first heats whereof, the Emperor *Matthias* dyes, and *Ferdinand* is lawfully elected to succeed in the Empire. To stop the course of whose good Fortunes, the *Bohemian* Confederates renounce all Allegiance to him, proclaim him for no King of theirs, nor so to be acknowledged by the Princes and Estates of *Germany*.

30. But their new Governours (or *Directors*, as they called them) being generally worsted in the war, and fearing to be called to a strict account for these multiplyed injuries, resolve upon the choice of some Potent Prince, to take that unfortunate Crown upon him. And who more like to carry it with success and honour then *Frederick* the fifth, Prince Elector *Palatine*, the Head of the *Calvinian* Party, Son-in-law to the King of *England*, descended from a Daughter of the Prince of *Orange*, and by his wife allyed to the King of *Denmark*, the Dukes of *Holstein* and *Brunswick*, three great *Lutheran* Princes. These were the motives on their part to invite him to it; and they prevailed as much with him to accept the offer, to which he was pushed forward by the secret instigation of the States United, whose Truce with *Spain* was now upon the point of exspiration; and they thought fit, in point of State-craft, that he should exercise his Army further off, then in their Dominions. And unto these it may be added, He had before incurred the Emperors Displeasure on a double account; first, for projecting the Confederacy of the Chiefs of the *Calvinists*, (whom they called the *Princes of the Union*) for defence of themselves and their Religion. And secondly, for demolishing the Fortifications which were raised at *Udenhaine*, though authorized by the *Placart* of *Matthias* himself, for which he was impleaded in the Chamber of *Spires*. Upon which Motives and Temptations, he first sends forth his Letters to the Estates of *Bohemia*, in which he signified his acceptance of the Honour conferred upon him, and then acquaints King *James* with the Proposition, whose Councel he desired therein for his better direction. But King *James* was not pleased in the precipitancy of this rash adventure, and thought himself unhandsomely handled, in having his Advice asked upon the post-fact, when all his Counsels to the contrary must have come too late. Besides, he had a strong Party of *Calvinists* in his own Dominions, who were not to be trusted with a Power of disposing Kingdoms, for fear they might be brought to practise that against himself, which he had countenanced in others. He knew no Prince could reign in safety, or be established on his Throne with Peace and Honour, if once Religion should be made a Cloak to disguise Rebellions.

31. Upon these grounds of Christian Prudence, he did not only disallow the Action in his own particular, but gave command that none of his Subjects should from thenceforth own his Son-in-law for the King of *Bohemia*, or pray for him in the Liturgy, or before their Sermons, by any other Title then *the Prince Elector*. At which the *English Calvinists* were extreamly vexed, who had already fancied to themselves upon this occasion the raising of a *Fifth Monarchy* in these parts of Christendom, even to the dethroning of the Pope, the setting up of *Calvin* in S. *Peters* Chair,

and

and carrying on the War to the Walls of *Conſtantinople*. No man more zealous in the Cauſe then Archbiſhop *Abbot*, who preſſed to have the news received with Bells and Bonfires, the King to be engaged in a war for the defence of ſuch a *Righteous* and *Religious Cauſe*, and the Jewels of the Crown to be pawned in purſuance of it; as appears plainly by his Letter to Sir *Robert Naunton*, principal Secretary of State. Which Letters bearing date on the 12 of *Decem. An.* 1619, are to be found at large in the Printed *Cabala*, p.169,*&c.* and thither I refer the *Reader* for his ſatisfaction. But neither the Perſwaſion of ſo great a Prelate, nor the ſollicitations of the Princeſs and her publick Miniſters, nor the tronbleſome interpoſings of the Houſe of Commons in a following Parliament, were able to remove that King from his firſt reſolution. By which, though he incurred the high diſpleaſure of the *Engliſh Puritans*, and thoſe of the *Calvinian* Party in other places ; yet he acquired the Reputation of a juſt and religious Prince, with moſt men beſides, and thoſe not only of the *Romiſh*, but the *Lutheran* Churches. And it is hard to ſay which of the two were moſt offended with the Prince Elector, for his accepting of that Crown; which of them had more ground to fear the ruine of their Cauſe and Party, if he had prevailed; and which of them were more impertinently provoked to make Head againſt him after he had declared his acceptance of it.

32. For when he was to be Inaugurated in the Church of *Prague*, he neither would be crowned in the uſual Form, nor by the hands of the Archbiſhop, to whom the performing of that Ceremony did of right belong ; but after ſuch a form and manner as was digeſted by *Scultetus*, his Domeſtick Chaplain, who chiefly governed his Affairs in all Sacred matters. Nor would *Scultetus* undertake the Ceremony of the Coronation, though very ambitious of that honour, till he had cleared the Church of all Carved Images, and defaced all the Painted alſo. In both reſpects alike offenſive to the *Romiſh* Clergy, who found themſelves diſpriviledged, their Churches Sacrilegiouſly invaded, and further ruine threatned by theſe Innovations. A Maſſie Crucifix had been erected on the Bridge of *Prague*, which had ſtood there for many hundred years before ; neither affronted by the *Lutherans*, nor defaced by the *Jews*, though more averſe from Images then all people elſe: *Scultetus* takes offence at the ſight thereof, as if the Brazen Serpent were ſet up and worſhipped ; perſwades the King to cauſe it preſently to be demoliſhed, or elſe he never would be reckoned for an *Hezekiah* ; in which he found Conformity to his Humour alſo. And thereby did as much offend all ſober *Lutherans*, (who retain Images in their Churches, and other places) as he had done the *Romiſh* Clergy by his former Follies. This gave ſome new encreaſe to thoſe former Jealouſies which had been given them by that Prince ; firſt, by endeavouring to ſuppreſs the *Lutheran* Forms in the Churches of *Brandenbourgh*, by the Arts and Practiſes of his Siſter : and ſecondly, by condemning their Doctrine at the Synod of *Dort*, (in which his Miniſters were more active then the reſt of the Foreiners) though in the perſons of thoſe men whom they called *Arminians*. But that which gave them greateſt cauſe of offence and fear, was his determination

mination in a Cause depending between two Sisters, at his first coming to the Crown ; of which the youngest had been married to a *Calvinian*, the eldest to a *Lutheran* Lord. The place in difference was the Castle and Seignury of *Gutscin*, of which the eldest Sister had took possession as the Seat of her Ancestors. But the King passing Sentence for the younger Sister, and sending certain Judges and other Officers to put the place into her actual possession, they were all blown up with Gun-Powder by the *Lutheran* Lady, not able to concoct the Indignity offered, nor to submit unto Judgment which appeared so partial.

33. In the mean time whilst the Elector was preparing for his journey to *Prague*, the Faction of *Bohemia* not being able to withstand such Forces as the Emperour had poured in upon them, invited *Bethlem Gabor* (not long before made Prince of *Transylvania* by the help of the *Turks*) to repair speedily to their succour. Which invitation he accepts, raiseth an Army of Eighteen thousand men, ransacks all Monasteries and Religious Houses wheresoever he came ; and in short time becomes the Master of the *Upper Hungary*, and the City of *Presburgh* ; the Protestants in all places, but most especially the *Calvinians*, submitting readily unto him, whom they looked upon as their deliverer from some present servitude. From thence he sends his Forces to the Gates of *Vienna*, and impudently craves that the Provinces of *Styria*, *Carinthia*, and *Carniola*, should be united from thenceforth to the Realm of *Hungary*, the better to enable the *Hungarians* to resist the *Turk*. And having a design for ruining the House of *Austria*, he doth not only crave protection from the *Ottoman* Emperor, but requires the new King and Estates of *Bohemia*, with the Provinces incorporate to it, to send their Embassadors to *Constantinople*, for entring into a Confederacy with the common Enemy. Hereupon followed a great Meeting of Embassadors from *Bohemia*, *Austria*, *Silesia*, *Lusatia*, *Venice*, *Poland*, and *Turkie*: All which assembled at *Newhasall* in the *Upper Hungary* ; where the *Turk* readily entred into the Association, and the *Venetian* Embassador undertook the like in the Name of that Seignury. Encouraged wherewith the *Transylvanian* is proclaimed King of *Hungary* ; who to make good a Title so unjustly gotten, provides an Army of no fewer then Thirty thousand (others say Fifty thousand) men. With which if he had entred into any part of *Bohemia*, before the new King had lost himself in the Battel of *Prague*, it is most probable that he might have absolutely assured that Kingdom to the Prince Elector, acquired the other for himself, and parted the Estates of *Austria* amongst their confederates.

34. But so it hapned, that some *Lutheran* and *Popish* Princes, being both equally jealous of their own Estates, and careful to preserve the Interest of their several Parties, entred into League with the Emperor *Ferdinand*, for the defence of one another, and the recovery of that Kingdom to the House of *Austria*. In prosecution of which League, *John George*, the Duke Elector of *Saxony*,

1620.

invades

invades *Lufatia* (another of the incorporate Provinces) with a puifsant Army, and in short time reduceth it under his Command. And with like puifsance *Maximillian*, Duke of *Bavaria*, the most potent of the Catholick Princes, falleth into *Bohemia* and openeth all the way before him to the Walls of *Prague*. Joyning with the Imperial Forces under Count *Bucquoy*, they are said to have made up an Army of Fifty thousand. With which they gave battel to the Army of the Prince Elector, consisting of thirty thousand men, under the Conduct of the Prince of *Anhalt*, and the Count of *Thurne*. It is reported, that the Prince Elector was so good a Husband for the Emperor, as to preserve his Treasures in the Castle of *Prague*, without diminishing so much thereof as might pay his Souldiers : which made many of them throw away their Arms, and refuse to fight. But sure it is, that the Imperials gained a great and an easie Victory ; in the pursuit whereof the young Prince of *Anhalt*, together with Count *Thurne*, and *Saxon Weimar*, were taken Prisoners, the *Bohemian* Ordnance all surprised, *Prague* forced to yield unto the Victor, the King and Queen compelled to flye into *Silefia*, from whence by many difficult passages, and untravelled ways, they came at last in safety to the *Hague* in *Holland*. Nor is it altogether unworthy of our observation, That this great Victory was obtained on a *Sunday* morning, being the 8th of *November*, and the 23d *Sunday* after *Trinity*, ; in the Gospel of which day occurred that memorable passage, *Reddite Cæsari quæ sunt Cæsaris* ; that is to say, *Render unto Cæsar the things which are Cæsars* : Which seemed to judge the Quarrel on the Emperors side. Hereupon followed the most Tragical, or rather most Tyrannical Execution of the chief *Directors*, who had a hand in the Design ; the suppressing of the Protestant Reformed Religion, in all the Emperors Estates, the falling back of *Bethlem Gaber* into *Transylvania*, the proscribing of the Prince Elector and his Adherents, the transferring of the Electoral Dignity, together with the Upper *Palatinate*, on the Duke of *Bavaria* ; the Conquest of the lower *Palatinate* by the King of *Spain*, and the setting up of Popery in all parts of both. In which condition they remained till the restoring of *Charles Lodowick*, the now Prince Elector, to the best part of his Estate, by the Treaty of *Munster*, 1648.

1618.   35. Such was the miserable end of the Warr of *Bohemia*, raised chiefly by the Pride and Pragmaticalness of *Calvins* Followers, out of a hope to propagate their Doctrines, and advance their Discipline in all parts of the Empire. Nor sped the *Hugonots* much better in the Realm of *France* ; where by the countenance and connivance of King *Henry* the IV. who would not see it ; and during the minority of *Lewis* the XIII. who could not help it ; they possessed themselves of some whole Countreys, and near Two hundred strong Towns, and fortified places. Proud of which Strength, they took upon them as a Commonwealth in the midst of a Kingdom ; summoned Assemblies for the managing of their own Affairs, when, and as often as they pleased. Gave Audience to the Ministers of Forein Churches ; and impowered Agents of their own to negotiate

ate with them. At the same Meetings they consulted about Religion, made new Laws for Government, displaced some of their old Officers, and elected new ones ; the Kings consent being never asked to the Alterations. In which licentious calling of their own Assemblies, they abused their Power to a neglect of the Kings Authority ; and not dissolving those Assemblies when they were commanded, they improved that Neglect to a Disobedience. Nay, sometimes they run cross therein to those very Edicts which they had gained by the effusion of much Christian Blood, and the expence of many hundred thousand Crowns. For by the last Edict of Pacification the King had granted the free exercise of both Religions, even in such Towns as were assigned for Caution to the *Hugonot* Party. Which liberty being enjoyed for many years, was at last interrupted by those very men who with so much difficulty had procured it. For in an Assembly of theirs which they held at *Loudun*, *Anno* 1619, they strictly commanded all their Governours, Mayors, and Sheriffs, not to suffer any Jesuit, nor those of any other Order, to preach in any of the Towns assigned to them, though licensed by the Bishop of the Diocess in due Form of Law. And when upon a dislike of their proceedings, the King had declared their Meetings to be unlawful, and contrary to the Publick Peace ; and had procured that Declaration to be verified in the Court of Parliament ; they did not only refuse to separate themselves as they were required, but still insisted upon terms of Capitulation, even to a plain justifying of their actings in it.

36. These carriages gave the King such just offence, that he denied them leave to send Commissioners to the Synod of *Dort*, to which they had been earnestly invited by the States of the *Netherlands*. For being so troublesome and imperious, when they acted only by the strength of their Provincial or National Meetings; what danger might not be suspected from a general Confluence, in which the Heads of all the Faction might be laid together ? But then to sweeten them a little after this Refusal, he gave them leave to hold an Assembly at *Charenton*, four miles from *Paris*, there to debate those points, and to agree those differences· which in that Synod had been agitated by the rest of their Party. Which Liberty they made such use of in the said Assembly, that they approved all the Determinations which were made at *Dort*, commanded them to be subscribed, and bound themselves and their Successors in the Ministry by a solemn Oath, * Not only stedfastly and constantly to adhere unto them, but to persist in maintainance thereof to the last gasp of their breath. But to return to the Assembly at *Loudun* : They would not rise from thence, though the King commanded it, till they had taken order for another Assembly to be held at *Rochel*, the chief place of their strength, and the Metropolis or principal City of their Common-wealth. Which General Assembly being called by their own Authority, and called at such a time as had given the King some trouble in composing the Affairs of *Bearn*, was by the King so far disliked, and by especial Edict so far prohibited, that they were

* Non tantum constanter firmiterque sed ad extremum usque halitum perstiturus. Exa. Cens.

all

all declared to be guilty of Treafon, who fhould continue in the fame without further Order. Which notwithftanding they fate ftill, and very undutifully proceeded in their former purpofes. Their bufinefs was to draw up a Remonftrance of their prefent Grievances, or rather of the Fears and Jealoufies which they had conceived on the Kings journey into *Bearn*. This they prefented to the King by their own Commiffioners, and thereunto received a fair and plaufible Anfwer, fent in a Letter to them by the Duke *Des Diguiers*; by whom they were advifed to diffolve the Affembly, and fubmit themfelves unto the King. Inftead whereof they publifhed a Declaration in defence of their former Actions, and fignified a Refolution not to feparate or break up that Meeting, until their Grievances were redrefsed.

37. It happened at the fame time that the Lord of *Privas* (a Town in which the *Hugonots* made the ftrongeft Party) married his Daughter and Heir to the Vifcount of *Cheylane*; and dying, left the fame wholly unto his difpofal. Who being of different perfwafions from the greateft part of his Vaffals, altered the Garrifon, and placed his own Servants and Dependents in it, as by Law he might. This moved the *Hugonots* of the Town, and the Neighbouring villages, to put themfelves into a pofture of War, to feize upon the places adjoyning, and thereby to compel the young Nobleman to forfake his Inheritance. Which being fignified to the King, he prefently fcored this infolence on the account of the *Rochellers*; who ftanding in defiance of his Authority, was thought to have given fome animation unto the Town *Privas*, to commit thofe out-rages. Doubly affronted and provoked the King refolves to right himfelf in the way of Arms: But at the inftant requeft of *Des Diguires*, before remembred, (who had been hitherto a true Zealot to the *Hugonot* Caufe) he was content to give them Four and twenty days of deliberation before he drew into the Field. He offered them alfo very fair and reafonable Conditions; not altogether fuch as their Commiffioners had defired for them, but far better then thofe which they were glad to accept at the end of the War, when all their ftrengths were taken from them. But the *Hugonots* were not to be told, that all the *Calvinian* Princes and Eftates of the Empire had put themfelves into a pofture of War; fome for defence of the *Palatinate*, and others in purfuance of the War of *Bohemia*: Of which they gave themfelves more hopes then they had juft caufe for. In which conjuncture fome hot fpirits then affembled at *Rochel*, blinded with pride, or hurried on by the *fatality* of thofe *Decrees* which they maintained to be refolved upon by God before all Eternity, reject all offers tending to a Pacification, and wilfully run on to their own deftruction. For prefently upon the tendry of the Kings Propofals, they publifh certain Orders for the regulating of their Difobedience; as namely, *That no Agreement fhould be made with the King, but by the confent of a General Convocation of the Chiefs of their Party: About the payment of their Souldiers Wages, and intercepting the Revenues of the King and Clergie toward the maintainance of the*

War

War. They alfo Cantoned the whole Kingdom into feven Divifions; affigned to each of thofe Divifions a Commander in Chief, and unto
each Commander, their particular Lieutenants, Deputy-Lieutenants,
and other Officers, with feveral Limitations and Directions prefcribed to each of them for their proceeding in this fervice.

38. This makes it evident, that the King did not take up Arms   1621.
but on great neceffities. He faw his Regal Authority neglected, his
efpecial Edicts wilfully violated, his Gracious Offers fcornfully
flighted, his Revenues Felonioufly intercepted, his whole Realm
Cantoned before his face, and put into the power of fuch Commanders as he could not truft: So that the War being juft on his part,
he had the more reafon to expect fuch an iffue of it, as was agreeable to the Equity of fo good a Caufe. He had befides, all thofe
Advantages both at home and abroad, which in all probability might
affure him of the end defired. The Prince Elector Palatine had been
worfted in the War of *Bohemia*, and all the Princes of the U-
nion fcattered to their feveral Homes, which they were hardly a-
ble to defend againft fo many Enemies; fo that there was no danger to be feared from them. And on the other fide the King of
Great Britain, whom he had moft caufe to be afraid of, had denied
affiftance to his own Children in the War of *Bohemia*, which feemed
to have more Juftice in it then the War of the *Hugonots*; and
therefore was not like to engage in behalf of ftrangers, who rather
out of wontonnefs then any unavoidable neceffity had took up
Arms againft their Lawful and Undoubted Soveraign. At home the
Rochellers were worfe befriended then they were abroad; I mean
the Commonwealth of Rochel, as King *Lewis* called it. The whole
Confederacy of the *Hugonots* there contrived and fworn to; they
had Cantoned the whole Realm into feven Divifions, which they
affigned to the Command of the Earl of *Chaftillon*, the Marquefs *De
la Force*, the Duke of *Soubize*, the Duke of *Rohan*, the Duke of
Trimoville, the Duke *Des Diguer*, and the Duke of *Bouillon*, whom
they defigned to be the *Generaliffimo* over all their Forces. But neither he, nor *Des Diguers*, nor the Duke of *Trimoville*, nor *Chaftillon*, would act any thing in it, or accept any fuch Commiffions as
were fent unto them: Whether it were that they were terrified with
the ill fuccefs of the War of *Bohemia*, or that the Confcience of
their duty did direct them in it, I difpute not now. So that the *Rochellers* being deferted both at home and abroad, were forced to relye
upon the Power and Prudence of the other three; and to fupply all
other wants out of the Magazine of Obftinacy and Perverfnefs;
with which they were plentifully ftored. Two inftances I fhall only
touch at, and pafs over the reft. The Town of *Clerack* being fummoned the 21 of *July*, 1621, returned this Anfwer to the King, viz.
*That if he would permit them to enjoy their Liberties, withdraw his Ar-
mies, and leave their Fortifications in the fame eftate in which he found them,
they would remain his faithful and obedient Subjects.* More fully
thofe of *Mount Albon* on the like occafion, *That they refolve to live*

and

and dye (not in obedience to the King, as they should have said, but) *in the Union of the Churches.* Most Religious Rebels!

39. Next let us look upon the King ; who being brought to a necessity of taking Arms, first made his way unto it by his Declaration of the second of *April*, published in favour of all those of that Religion who could contain themselves in their due obedience. In pursuance whereof he caused five persons to be executed in the City of *Tours*, who had tumultuously disturbed the *Hugonots*, whom they found busied at the burial of one of their dead. He also signified to the King of *Great Britain*, the Princes of the Empire, and the States of the *Netherlands*, That he had not undertook this war to suppress the Religion, but to chastise the Insolencies of Rebellious Subjects. And what he signified in words, he made good by his deeds : For when the war was at the hottest, all those of the Religion in the City of *Paris* lived as securely as before, and had their accustomed Meetings at *Charenton*, as in times of peace. Which safety and security was enjoyed in all other places, even where the Kings Armies lodged and quartered. Nay, such a care was taken of their preservation, that when some of the Rascality in the City of *Paris*, upon the first tydings of the death of the Duke of *Mayenne* (who had been slain at the Siege of *Mont albon* amongst many others) breathed nothing but slaughter and revenge to the *Hugonot* Party ; the Duke of *Mounbazon*, being then Governour of the City, commanded their Houses and the Streets to be safely guarded, so that no hurt was done to their Goods or Persons. And when the Rabble, being disappointed of their ends in *Paris*, had run tumultuously the next day to *Charenton*, and burned down their Temple ; an Order was presently made by the Court of Parliament for the re-edifying it at the Kings sole Charges, and that too in a far more beautiful Fabrick then before it had. But in the conduct of the War he governed not his Counsels with like moderation , suffering the Sword too often to range at liberty ; as if he meant to be as terrible in his Executions, as he desired to be accounted just in his Undertakings. But possibly this may be excused, though not defended, as being done in hot blood, when the spirits of the Souldiers were enflamed with anger by reason of the loss of so many of their chief Commanders, occasioned by the holding out of the obstinate Party ; or the loss of their Fellows ; and could not easily be quenched but by the blood of their enemies.

1622.   40. I shall not touch upon the particulars of this War, which was quick and violent ; and as successful on the Kings part as he could desire. Let it suffice that within the compass of eighteen moneths, or thereabouts, he stript them of no fewer then one hundred of their strongest places : so that their whole strength was reduced in a manner to two Towns only ; that is to say, the strong Town of *Montalbon*, and the Port of *Rochel* ; the rest submitting one by one at the first demand. A Peace is thereupon concluded before *Montpellier*, agreeable enough to the Will of the Victor, and with security enough to the vanquished Party, if all Conclusions had been kept with as great a conſtancy, as they had been agreed upon with a ſeeming alacrity. By which Accord the ſaid two Towns were to be held in caution for three years only ; and the laſt ſeemed much over-awed by the Fort of King *Lewis*, erected by the Count of *Soiſoons* when he lay before it. For the demoliſhing of which Fort, the King was earneſtly ſollicited by their Commiſſioners ; and for the not granting whereof when it was deſired, he was accuſed for violating the Pacification which he had made with them before *Montpellier*, and ſolemnly confirmed in the Courts of Parliament. And on the other ſide the King complained as ſenſibly againſt the *Hugonots*, in regard they had not ſetled the *Eccleſiaſticks* in their lawful Poſſeſſions, nor admitted thoſe of the *Roman Catholick* Religion unto Civil Offices in any of their Towns and Territories, as by the Articles of that Pacification they were bound to do. So that the Wound ſeemed rather to be skinned then healed ; and ſuddenly became more dangerous then at firſt it was. For thoſe of *Rochel* being ſomewhat blocked up by Fort *Lewis* toward the Land, practiſed with the Duke of *Soubize* to grow ſtrong by Sea, and make up a Fleet conſiſting of Eleven men of War, beſides leſſer Veſſels, enter the large Haven of *Blavet* in *Bretagne*, ſeize upon all the Ships which they found therein ; and amongſt others ſix of great ſtrength and beauty, belonging to the Duke of *Nevers*. By the acceſſion of this Strength they ſeize upon the Iſles of *Rhe* and *Oleron*, with all the Shipping in the ſame ; and having gathered together a Navy of no fewer then Seventy Sail, they infeſt the Seas, and interrupt the courſe of Traffick.

41. For the repreſſing of theſe Pyrates, (for they were no better) the King ſends out the Duke of *Montmorency* with a Naval Power; hires twenty men of War of the States of *Holland*, and borrows eight tall Ships of the King of *England* : With which he gives battel to *Soubize*, beats him at Sea, and forceth him to flye diſhonourably from the Iſle of *Rhe*, which the *French* preſently poſſeſs, and begin to fortifie. For the removal of whoſe Forces from that Iſland, which blockt up their Haven, the *Rochellers* mediate by *Soubize* with King *Charles* of *England*, betwixt whom and his Brother of *France* ſome diſguſt had happened, for ſending back the *French* of both Sexes, whom the Queen brought with her. For hereupon the *French* King ſeizeth upon all the *Engliſh* Ships which traded on the River of *Bourdeaux* ; and the *Engliſh*, to revenge the wrong, ſet out a Fleet of Thirty ſail, all Men of War, commanded by the Earls of *Denbigh* and *Lindſey*, with an intent to ſteer for *Rochel*, and relieve that Town. But being encountred with croſs winds, they came back again, and leave the proſecuting of the Action to the Duke of *Buckingham*. Who the next year ſets forward with a puiſſant Army, conſiſting of Ten thouſand men, and wafted over in One hundred and fifty Sail of Ships, all fit for Service. His Deſign was for the recovering of the Iſle of *Rhe*, and relieving *Rochel*. Both which he might have compaſſed without any great difficulty, if he had not loſt the opportunities which he gained at his landing ; paſſed by the Fort of

La Pre,

1625.

1626.

1627.

La Pre, as not worth the taking, and ſuffering himſelf to be com-
plemented out of the ſtorming of St. *Martins*, when it was at his
mercy. For the *French* Forces entering by the Fort of *La Pre*, compelled him to an unſafe Retreat, cut off a great part of his Army,
and ſent him back with far leſs Honour then he brought along with
him.

1628.   42. But the Relief of *Rochel* is not ſo given over. A ſtrong Fleet
is prepared for the year next following, to be commanded by the
Duke, who gave himſelf more hopes of good Fortune in it then
his Fates aſſigned him. For being villainouſly ſlain at *Portſmouth*,
when he was almoſt ready to embarque his Souldiers, the Conduct of
the Action is committed to the Earl of *Lindſey* ; who very cheerfully and courageouſly undertook the Service. But the *French* had
blockt up the Haven of *Rochel* with Piles and Ramparts, and other
moſt ſtupendious Works in the midſt of the Ocean, that it was utterly impoſſible for the Earl to force his paſſage, though he did moſt
gallantly attempt it. Which being obſerved by thoſe of *Rochel*,
who were then beſieged to Landward by the King in Perſon, and
even reduced unto the laſt extremity by Plagues and Famine ; they
preſently ſet open their Gates, and without making any Conditions
for their preſervation, ſubmitted abſolutely to that Mercy which
they had ſcorned ſo often in their proſperous fortunes. The King
thus Maſter of the Town, diſmantleth all their Fortifications, leaves
it quite open both to Sea and Land, commands them to renounce the
Name of *Rochel*, and to take unto the Town the Name of *Mary Ville*,
or *Bourg de St. Mary*. But herein his Command found but ſmall compliance ; the Name of *Rochel* ſtill remaining, and that of *Mary
Ville*, or *Bourg de St. Mary*, almoſt as ſoon forgotten as it had been
given. After which followed the ſurrendry of *Niſmeſs*, and *Montalbon*, two impregnable places ; the firſt of which had been re-forti-
fied in theſe laſt Commotions. For, What Town could preſume of
ſtanding out againſt the King, when *Rochel* had been forced to ſubmit
to Mercy ?

43. See now to what a low condition theſe hot *Calvinian* ſpirits
have reduced themſelves by their frequent Inſolencies ; how different
their Affairs were at an end of this War from that felicity which
they enjoyed when they firſt began it. Before the beginning of the
War, *Anno* 1620, they were poſſeſſed of well near Two hundred
ſtrong Towns and Caſtles, well fortified for their perſonal ſafety,
beſides many fair Houſes and large Territories which they had in
the Villages, in which their Pleaſures and their Profits were alike
conſulted ; they ſlept all of them under their own Vines, and their
own Fig-trees, neither fearing, nor having cauſe to fear the leaſt diſturbance. With thoſe of the *Catholick* Party they were grown ſo
intimate by reaſon of their frequent inter-marriages with one a-
nother, that in few years they might have been incorporated with
them, and made of the ſame Family, though of different Faiths.
The exerciſe of their Religion had been permitted to them ſince the
paſſing of the Edict of *Nants* 1598, without interruption. And
that

that they might have satisfaction alfo in the Courts of Justice, some Courts were purpofely erected for their eafe and benefit, which they called *Les Chambres de l' Edict*, wherein there were as many Judges and other Officers of their own Perfwafions, as there were of the contrary. In a word, they lived fo fecure and happy, that they wanted nothing to perpetuate their felicities to fucceeding Ages, but Moderation in themfelves, Gratitude to Almighty God, and Good Affections towards their King.

44. Such were the fortunes and fuccefses of the *Presbyterians* in the reft of Chriftendom, during the laft ten years of the Reign of King *James*, and the beginnings of King *Charles*. By which both Kings might fee how unfafe they were, if men of fuch Pragmatical Spirits, and Seditious Principles fhould get ground upon them. But King *James* had fo far fupported them in the *Belgick* Provinces, that his own *Calvinifts* prefumed on the like Indulgence ; which prompted them to fet nought by his Proclamations, to vilifie his *Inftructions*, and defpife his Meffages. Finally, they made tryal of his patience alfo, by fetting up one *Knight* of *Broadgates* (now called *Pembroke* College) to preach upon the Power of fuch popular Officers as *Calvin* thinks to be ordained by Almighty God, for curbing and reftraining the Power of Kings. In which though *Knight* himfelf was cenfured, the Doctrines folemnly condemned, and execution done upon a Book of *Pareus*, which had mifguided the unfortunate and ignorant man ; yet the *Calvinians* moft tenacioufly adhered to their Mafters tendries, with an intent to bring them into ufe and practice when occafion ferved. So that King *James* with all his King-craft could find no better way to fupprefs their Infolencies, then by turning *Mountague* upon them ; a man of mighty Parts, and an undaunted Spirit, and one who knew as well as any how to difcriminate the Doctrines of the Church of *England* from thofe which were peculiar to the Sect of *Calvin* : By which he galled and gagged them more then his Popifh Adverfary ; but raifed thereby fo many Pens againft himfelf, that he might feem to have fucceeded in the ftate of *Ifmael*.

45. In this conjuncture of Affairs, King *James* departs this life, and King *Charles* fucceeds ; who to ingratiate himfelf with this powerful Faction had plunged his Father in a War with the Houfe of *Auftria*, by which he was brought under the neceffity of calling Parliaments, and gave thofe Parliaments the courage to difpute his Actions. For though they promifed to ftand to him with their Lives and Fortunes in profecution of that War ; yet when they had engaged him in it, they would not part with any mony to defray that Charge, till they had ftripped him of the Richeft Jewels in the Regal Diadem. But he was much more punifhed in the confequence of his own Example in aiding thofe of *Rochel* againft their King, whereby he trained up his own Subjects in the School of Rebellion, and taught them to confederate themfelves with the *Scots* and *Dutch*, to feize upon his Forts and Caftles, invade the Patrimony of the Church, and to make ufe of his Revenue againft himfelf. To fuch
Mis-

Misfortunes many Princes do reduce themselves, when either they engage themselves to maintain a Party, or govern not their Actions by the Rules of Justice; but are directed by self-ends, or swayed by the corrupt Affections of untrusty Ministers. These things I only touch at here, which I reserve for the Materials of another History, as I do also all the intermediate passages in the Reign of King *Charles* before the breaking out of the *Scottish* Tumults, and most of the preparatives to the War of *England*.

The End of the Twelfth Book.

AERIVS REDIVIVVS:

OR THE

HISTORY

OF THE

Presbyterians.

LIB. XIII.

Containing

The Insurrections of the Presbyterian *or* Puritan *Faction in the* Realm *of* Scotland: *The Rebellions raised by them in* England: *Their horrid Sacrileges, Murders, Spoils, and Rapines, in pursuit thereof: Their Innovations both in Doctrine and Discipline: And the greatest Alteration made in the Civil Government, from the Year* 1636 *to the Year* 1647, *when they were stript of all Command by the* Independents.

He *Presbyterian Scots*, and the *Puritan English*, were not so much discouraged by the ill successes of their Brethren in *France* and *Germany*, as animated by the prosperous Fortunes of their friends in *Holland*. Who by Rebellion were grown Powerful, and by Rapine Wealthy; and by the Reputation of their Wealth and Power were able to avenge themselves on the opposite Party. To whose

I,

whose felicities, if those in *England* did aspire, they were to entertain those Counsels, and pursue those courses, by which the others had attained them: that is to say, They were by secret practises to diminish the Kings Power and Greatness, to draw the people to depend upon their Directions, to dissolve all the Ligaments of the former Government; and either call in Forein Forces, or form an Army of their own to maintain their doings. And this had been the business of the *Puritan Faction* since the death of *Bancroft*; when by the retirements of King *James* from all cares of Government, and the connivance or remisness of Archbishop *Abbot*, the Reins were put into their hands. Which gave them time and opportunity to grow strong in Parliaments, under pretence of standing for the Subjects Property, against the encroachments of the Court, and for the preservation of the true Religion against the practises of the *Papists*. By which two Artifices they first weakned the Prerogative Royal to advance their own; and by the diminution of the Kings Authority endeavoured to erect the People, whom they represented. And then they practised to asperse with the Name of *Papist* all those who either joyn not with them in their Sabbath Doctrines, or would not captivate their judgments unto *Calvins* Dictates. Their actings in all which particulars, either as Zealots for the Gospel in maintaining *Calvinism*, or Patriots for the Commonwealth in bringing down the Power and Reputation of the two last Kings; shall be at large delivered in the Life of the late Archbishop, and consequently may be thought unnecessary to be here related. And therefore, pretermitting all their former practises, by which their party was prepared, and the Design made ready to appear in publick; we will proceed to a Relation of the following passages, when they had pulled off their Disguise, and openly declared themselves to be ripe for Action.

2. The Party in both Kingdoms being grown so strong that they were able to proceed from Counsel unto Execution, there wanted nothing but a fair occasion for putting themselves into a posture of defence, and from that posture breaking out into open War. But finding no occasion they resolve to make one; and to begin their first Embroilments upon the sending of the new Liturgy and Book 1617. of Canons to the Kirk of *Scotland*. For though the *Scots* in a general Assembly held at *Aberdeen*, had given consent unto the making of a Liturgy for the use of that Kirk, and for drawing up a Book of Canons out of the Acts of their Assemblies, and some Acts of Parliament; yet when those Books were finished by the Care of King *Charles*, and by his Piety recommended unto use and practice, it 1618. must be looked on as a violation of their Rights and Liberties. And though in another of their Assemblies, which was held at *Perth*, they had past five Articles for introducing Private Baptism, communicating of the sick, kneeling at the Communion, Episcopal Confirmation, and the observing of such ancient Festivals as belonged immediately unto Christ: yet when those Articles were incorporated in the Common Prayer Book, they were beheld as Innovations in the worship of God, and therefore not to be admitted in so pure and Reformed a Church

as

as that of *Scotland.* These were the Hooks by which they drew the people to them, who never look on their Superiors with a greater reverence, then when they see them active in the Cause of Religion ; and willing, in appearance, to lose all which was dear unto them, whereby they might preserve the Gospel in its native purity. But it was rather Gain then Godliness which brought the Great men of the Realm to espouse this Quarrel ; who by the Commission of *Surrendries* (of which more elsewhere) began to fear the losing of their Tithes and Superiorities, to which they could pretend no other title then plain usurpation. And on the other side, it was Ambition and not Zeal which enflamed the *Presbyters* ; who had no other way to invade that power which was conferred upon the Bishops by Divine Institution, and countenanced by many Acts of Parliament in the Reign of King *James,* then by embracing that occasion to incense the people, to put the whole Nation into tumult, and thereby to compel the Bishops and the Regular Clergy to forsake the Kingdom. So the *Genevians* dealt before with their Bishop and Clergy, when the Reforming Humour came first upon them : and what could they do less in *Scotland* then follow the Example of their Mother City.

3. These breakings out in *Scotland* smoothed the way to the like in *England,* from which they had received encouragement, and presumed on Succours. The *English Puritans* had begun with Libelling against the Bishops, as the *Scots* did against the King : For which the Authors and Abettors had received some punishment ; but such as did rather reserve them from ensuing mischiefs, then make them sensible of their Crimes, or reclaim them from it. So that upon the coming of the Liturgy and Book of Canons, the *Scots* were put into such heat, that they disturbed the execution of the one by an open Tumult, and refused obedience to the other by a wilful obstinacy. The King had then a Fleet at Sea, sufficiently powerful to have blockt up all the Havens of *Scotland,* and by destroying that small Trade which they had amongst them, to have reduced them absolutely to his will and pleasure. But they had so many of their party in the Council of *Scotland,* and had so great a confidence in the Marquess of *Hamilton,* and many friends of both Nations in the Court of *England,* that they feared nothing less then the Power of the King, or to be enforced to their obedience in the way of Arms. In confidence whereof they despise all his Proclamations, with which Weapons only he encountred them in their first Seditions ; and publickly protested against all Declarations which he sent unto them, in the Streets of *Edenborough.* Nothing else being done against them in the first y ar of their Tumults, they cast themselves into four Tables for dispatch of business ; but chiefly for the cementing of their Combination. For which they could not easily bethink themselves of a speedier course, then to unite the people to them by a League or Covenant Which to effect it was thought necessary to renew the old Confession, excogitated in the year 1580, for the abjuring of the Tyranny and Superstitions of the Church of *Rome* ; subscribed first by the King and His Houshold Servants, and the next year by all the Natives of the Kingdom, as was said before. And it was also said before, that unto this Confession they adjoined a Band, *Anno* 1592, for standing

1637.

ing

ing unto one another in defence thereof against all *Papists*, and other professed Adversaries of their Religion. This is now made to serve their turn against the King: For by a strange interpretation which was put upon it, it was declared, That both the Government of the Church by Bishops, and the Five Articles of *Perth*, the Liturgy, and the Book of Canons, were all abjured by that Confession, and the Band annexed; though the three last had no existency or being in the Kirk of *Scotland*, when that Confession was first formed, or the Band subjoined.

1638. 4. These Insolencies might have given the King a just cause to arm, when they were utterly unprovided of all such necessaries as might enable them to make the least show of a weak resistance. But the King deals more gently with them, negotiates for some fair accord of the present differences, and sends the Marquess of *Hamilton* as his Chief Commissioner for the transacting of the same. By whose sollicitation he revokes the Liturgy and the Book of Canons, suspends the Articles of *Perth*, and then rescinds all Acts of Parliament which confirmed the same; submits the Bishops to the next General Assembly, as their competent Judges; and thereupon gives intimation of a General Assembly to be held at *Glasgow*, in which the point of Church Government was to be debated, and all his Condescentions enrolled and registred. And which made most to their advantage, he caused the *Solemn League or Covenant* to be imposed on all the Subjects, and subscribed by them. Which in effect was to legitimate the Rebellion, and countenance the Combination with the face of Authority. But all this would not do his business, though it might do theirs. For they had so contrived the matter, that none were chosen to have voices in that Assembly, but such as were sure unto the side, such as had formerly been under the Censures of the Church for their Inconformity, and had refused to acknowledge the Kings Supremacy, or had declared their disaffections to Episcopal Government. And that the Bishops might have no encouragement to sit amongst them, they cite them to appear as Criminal persons, Libel against them in a scandalous and unchristian manner; and finally, make choice of *Henderson*, a Seditious *Presbyter*, to sit as Moderator or chief President in it. And though upon the sense of their disobedience the Assembly was again dissolved by the Kings Proclamation, yet they continued, as before in contempt thereof. In which Session they condemned the Calling of Bishops, the Articles of *Perth*, the Liturgy, and the Book of Canons, as inconsistent with the Scripture and the Kirk of *Scotland*. They proceed next to the rejecting of the five controverted points, which they called *Arminianism*: and finally decreed a general subscription to be made to these Constitutions. For not conforming whereunto the Bishops and a great part of the Regular Clergy are expelled the Country, although they had been animated unto that Refusal, as well by the Conscience of their duty as by his Majesties Proclamation, which required it of them.

5. They could not hope that the Kings Lenity so abused might not turn to Fury; and therefore thought it was high time to put themselves into Arms, to call back most of their old Souldiers from the Wars in *Germany*, and almost all their Officers from such Commands in the *Nether-*

len

lands; whom to maintain they intercept the Kings *Revenue*, and the Rents of the Bishops, and lay great Taxes on the people, taking up Arms and Ammunition from the *States United*, with whom they went on Ticket, and long days of payment, for want of ready mony for their satisfaction. But all this had not served their turn if the King could have been perswaded to have given them battel, or suffered any part of that great Army which he brought against them to lay waste their Countrey. Whose tenderness when they once perceived, and knew withall how many friends they had about him, they thought it would be no hard matter to obtain such a Pacification as might secure them for the present from an absolute Conquest, and give them opportunity to provide better for themselves in the time to come, upon the reputation of being able to divert or break such a puissant Army. And so it proved in the event. For the King had no sooner retired his Forces both by Sea and Land, and given his Souldiers a License to return to their several Houses, but the *Scots* presently protest against all the Articles of the Pacification, put harder pressures on the Kings Party, then before they suffered, keep all their Officers in pay; by their Messengers and Letters apply themselves to the *French* King for support and succours. By whom encouraged under hand, and openly countenanced by some Agents of the Cardinal *Richelieu*, who then governed all Affairs in *France*, they enter into *England* with a puissant Army, making their way to that Invasion, by some Printed Pamphlets, which they dispersed into all parts, thereby to colour their Rebellions, and bewitch the people.

6. And now the *English Presbyterians* take the courage to appear more publickly in the defence of the *Scots* and their proceedings, then they had done hitherto. A Parliament had been called on the 13*th* of *April*, for granting Moneys to maintain the War against the *Scots*. But the Commons were so backward in complying with the Kings desires, that he found himself under the necessity of dissolving the Parliament, which else had blasted his Design, and openly declared in favour of the publick Enemies. This puts the discontented Rabble into such a fury, that they violently assaulted *Lambeth-House*, but were as valiantly repulsed; and the next day break open all the Prisons in *Southwark*, and release all the Prisoners whom they found committed for their Inconformities. *Benstead*, the Ringleader in these Tumults, is apprehended and arraigned, condemned and executed; the whole proceeding being grounded on the Statute of the 25*th* of King *Edward* the III. for punishing all Treasons and Rebellions against the King. But that which threatned greater danger to the King and the Church, then either the Arms of the *Scots*, or the Tumults in *Southwark*, was a Petition sent unto the King, who was then at *York*, subscribed by sundry Noblemen of the Popular Faction; concluded on the 28*th* of *August*; carried by the Lord *Mandevil*, and the Lord *Howard* of *Escrigg*; and finally, presented on the third of *September*. In which it was petitioned, amongst other things, *That the present War might be composed without loss of bloud. That a Parliament should be forthwith called for redress of Grievances*, (amongst which, some pretended *Innovations* in Religion must be none of the least) *and that the Authors and Counsellors of such Grievances as are there complained*

plained

1640.

plained of, might be there brought to such a Legal Tryal, and receive such condign punishment as their Crimes required. This haſtened the Aſſembling of the great Council of the Peers at *York*, and put the King upon the calling of a Parliament of his own accord, which otherwiſe might be thought extorted by their importunity.

7. The *Scots*, in the mean time had put by ſuch *Engliſh* Forces as lay on the South ſide of the *Tine*, at the paſſage of *Newborn*, make themſelves Maſters of *Newcaſtle*, deface the goodly Church of *Durham*, bring all the Countreys on the North ſide of the *Tees* under Contribution, and tax the people to all payments at their only pleaſure. The Council of Peers, and a Petition from the *Scots*, prepare the King to entertain a Treaty with them ; the managing whereof was chiefly left unto thoſe Lords who had ſubſcribed the Petition before remembered. But the third day of *November* coming on apace, and the Commiſſioners ſeeming deſirous to attend in Parliament, which was to begin on that day, the Treaty is adjourned to *London* ; which gave the *Scots* a more dangerous opportunity to infect that City, then all their Emiſſaries had obtained in the times foregoing Nor was it long before it openly appeared what great power they had upon their Party in that City ; which animated *Pennington*, attended with ſome hundreds of inferior note, to tender a Petition to the Houſe of Commons againſt the Government of Biſhops here by Law eſtabliſhed. It was affirmed, that this Petition was ſubſcribed by many thouſands ; and it was probable enough to be ſo indeed. But whether it were ſo or not, he gave thereby ſuch an occaſion to the Houſe of Commons, that they voted down the Canons which had paſſed in the late Convocation, condemned the Biſhops and Clergy in great ſums of Money, which had ſubſcribed to the ſame ; decry the Power of all Provincial or National Synods, for making any Canons or Conſtitutions which could bind the Subject, until they were confirmed by an Act of Parliament. And having brought this general terror on the Biſhops and Clergy, they impeach the Archbiſhop of High Treaſon, cauſe him to be committed to the Black Rod, and from thence to the Tower. Which being done, ſome other of the Biſhops and Clergy muſt be ſingled out, informed againſt by ſcandalous Articles, and thoſe Articles printed without any conſideration either true or falſe.

8. And though a Convocation were at that time ſitting ; yet to encreaſe the Miſeries of a falling Church, it is permitted that a private Meeting ſhould be held in the Deanry of *Weſtminſter*, to which ſome Orthodox and Conformable Divines were called, as a foil to the reſt which generally were of *Presbyterian* or *Puritan* Principles. By them it was propoſed, That many paſſages in the Liturgy ſhould be expunged, and others altered to the worſe. That Decency and Reverence in officiating Gods publick Service ſhould be brought within the compaſs of Innovations. That Doctrinal *Calviniſm* ſhould be entertained in all parts of the Church ; and all their Sabbath Speculations, though contrary to *Calvins* Judgment, ſuperadded to it. But before any thing could be concluded in thoſe weighty matters, the Com-

1641.

Commons set their Bill on foot against *Root* and *Branch*, for putting down all Bishops and Cathedral Churches ; which put a period to that Meeting without doing any thing.   And though the Bill, upon a full debate thereon amongst the Peers, was cast out of that House, and was not by the course of Parliaments to be offered again ; yet contrary to all former Custom it was prest from one time to another, till in the end they gained the point which they so much aimed at. Hereupon followed some Petitions from the Universities in favour of Cathedral and Collegiate Churches, without which Learning must be destitute of its chief encouragements ; and some Petitions from whole Counties, in behalf of Episcopacy, without which there was like to be no preservative against Sects and Heresies.   But nothing was more memorable then the inter-pleadings in the House of Commons between Dr. *John Hacket*, one of the Prebendaries of St. *Pauls*, and Archdeacon of *Bedford* ; and Dr. *Cornelius Burges*, a right doubty Disputant ; but better skilled in drawing down his Myrmidons, then in mustering Arguments: the issue of whose Plea was this, *That though Cathedrals were unnecessary, and the Quire-men scandalous ; yet, that their Lands could not be alienated unto private persons without guilt of Sacrilege.*

9 But little did this edifie with the Leading part in the House of Commons, who were resolved to practice on the Church by little and little, and at the last to play at Sweep Stake and take all together. First therefore they began with taking down the Star Chamber, and the High Commission, without which Courts the Subjects could not easily be kept in order, nor the Church from Faction.   And in the Act for taking down the Court of the High Commission a clause is cunningly inserted, which plainly took away all Coercive Power which had been vested in the Bishops and their Under-Officers, disabling them from imposing any pain or penalty ; and consequently from inflicting all Church Censures on notorious sinners.   Their Jurisdiction being thus gone, it was not likely that their Lands should stay long behind ; though in good manners it was thought convenient to strip them first from having any place or suffrage in the House of Peers: And when they once were rendered useless to the Church and State, the Lands would follow of themselves without any great trouble.   And that they might attain the end which they so much aimed at, *Burges* draws down his *Myrmidons* to the Doors of the Parliament, and teacheth them to cry *No Bishops, No Bishops*, with their wonted violence. By which confused Rabble some indignities and affronts are very frequently put upon them, either in keeping them off from landing if they came by water, or offering violence to their persons, if they came by land.   Which multiplied Injuries gave such just cause of fear and trouble, that they withdrew themselves from the House of Peers, but sent withal a *Protestation* to preserve their Rights: In which it was declared, *That all Acts made, or to be made in the time of their absence, considering their absence was inforced, not voluntary, should be reputed void and null to all intents and purposes in the Law whatsoever.*   This *Protestation* being tendred in the House of Peers, communicated to the House of Commons, and the supposed offence extreamly aggravated by the Lord Keeper *Littleton,*

tleton, the Bishops are impeached of Treason, nine of them sent Prisoners to the Tower, and two committed to the custody of the Gentleman Usher.

10. And there we leave them for a while, to look into the Fortunes of the publick Liturgy ; not like to stand when both the *Scots* and *English Presbyterians* did conspire against it. The Fame whereof had either caused it totally to be laid aside, or performed by halfs in all the Counties where the *Scots* were of strength and power ; and not much better executed in some Churches of *London,* wherein that Faction did as much predominate, as if it had been under the protection of a *Scottish* Army. But the first great interruption which was made at the officiating of the publick Liturgy, was made upon a Day of Humiliation, when all the Members of the House of Commons were assembled together at St. *Margarets* in *Westminster.* At what time as the Priest began the second Service at the Holy Table, some of the *Puritans* or *Presbyterians* began a Psalm ; and were therein followed by the rest in so loud a Tune, that the Minister was thereby forced to desist from his duty, and leave the Preacher to perform the rest of that days Solemnity. This gave encouragement enough to the rest of that Party to set as little by the Liturgy in the Country, as they did in the City ; especially in all such usages and rights thereof, as they were pleased to bring within the compass of *Innovations.* But they were more encouraged to it, by an Order of the Lower House, bearing date on the **8th** of *September, Anno,* 1641. By which all Church Wardens were required in their several Parishes to remove the Holy Table from the East end of the Chancel to any other part of the Church , to take away the Rales before it, and not to suffer any Tapers, Candlesticks, or Basons, to be placed upon it. It was required also by the same, That there should be no bowing at the Name of Jesus, nor adoration toward the East, nor any reverence used in mens approaches to the Holy Table. And by the same, all Dancing, and other lawful Recreations, were prohibited on their Lords day Sabbath, after the duties of the day ; and Catechising turned into Afternoon Sermons, directly contrary to His Majesties Declarations and Instructions given in that behalf. And though the Lords refused to joyn with them in that Vote, and sent them back unto an Order of the 16th of *January,* by which they had confirmed and enjoined the use of the Liturgy ; yet *Pym* commands the Order to be put in execution by a Warrant under his own hand only, and that too during the *Recess,* when almost all the Lords and Commons had retired themselves to their several dwellings.

11. Hereupon followed such an alteration in all Churches and Chapels, that the Church Wardens pulled down more in a week or two, then all the Bishops and Clergy had been able to raise in two weeks of years. And hereupon there followed such irreverences in Gods publick Service, and such a discontinuance of it in too many places, that His Majesty was compelled to give new life to it by his Proclamation of the tenth of *December* ; and taking order in the same for *punishing all the wilful Contemners and Disturbers of it.* But this Proclamation being published in that point of time, in which the Commons
were

were intent on the War of *Ireland*, and the *Puritans* as much bu-fied in blowing the Trumpet of Sedition in the Kingdom of *England* ; it only shewed the Kings good meaning, with his want of Power. In which conjuncture happened the Impeachment and Imprisonment of Eleven of the Bishops: Which made that Bench so thin, and the King so weak, that on the *6th* of *February* the Lords consented to the taking away of their Votes in Parliament. The News whereof was solemnized in most places of *London* with Bells and Bonfires. Nothing remained, but that the King should pass it into Act by his Royal Assent, by some unhappy Instrument extorted from him when he was at *Canterbury*; and signified by his Message to the Houses on the fourteenth of that moneth. Which Condescention wrought so much unquietness to his Mind and Conscience, and so much unsecureness to his Person for the rest of his Life, that he could scarce truly boast of one days Felicity, till God was pleased to put a final period to his Griefs and Sorrows. For in relation to the last, we find that the next Vote which passed in Parliament deprived him of his *Negative Voice*, and put the whole *Militia* of the Kingdom into the hands of the Houses. Which was the first beginning of his following Miseries. And looking on him in the first, he will not spare to let us know in one of his Prayers, *That the injury which he had done to the Bishops of* England *did as much grate upon his Conscience, as either the permitting of a wrong way of Worship to be set up in* Scotland *, or suffering innocent bloud to be shed under colour of Justice.*

12. For so it was, that some of the prevailing Members in the House of Commons, considering how faithfully and effectually the *Scots* had served them, not only voted a Gratuity of Three hundred thousand pounds of good *English* Money to be freely given them, but kept their Army in a constant and continual Pay for Nine moneths together. And by the terror of that Army they forced the King to pass the Bill for Trienial Parliaments, and to perpetuate the present Session at the will of the Houses, to give consent for Murthering the Earl of *Strafford* with the Sword of Justice, and suffering the Archbishop of *Canterbury* to be banished from him; to fling away the Star Chamber, and the High Commission, and the Coercive Power of Bishops; to part with all his right to Tonnage and Poundage, to Ship mony, and the Act for Knighthood ; and by retrenching the Perambulation of his Forests and Chases, to leave his Game to the destruction of each Bore or Peasant. And by the terror of this Army they took upon them to engage all the Subjects of the Kingdom in a *Protestation*; first hammered on the third of *May*, in order to the condemnation of the Earl of *Stafford*, for maintainance of the Privileges and Rights of Parliament, standing to one another in pursuance of it, and bringing all persons to condign punishment who were suspected to oppose them. Encouraged also by the same, they took upon them an Authority of voting down the Churches Power in making

of

of Canons, condemning all the Members of the late Convocation, calumniating many of the Bishops and Clergy in most odious manner, and vexing some of them to the Grave. And they would have done the like to the Church it self, in pulling down the Bishops and Cathedral Churches, and taking to themselves all their Lands and Houses, if by the Constancy and Courage of the House of Peers they had not failed of their Design. But at the last the King prevailed so far with the *Scots* Commissioners, that they were willing to retire and withdraw their Forces, upon his Promise to confirm the Acts of the Assembly at *Glasgow*, and reach out such a Hand of Favour unto all that Nation, as might estate them in a happiness above their hopes. On this assurance they march homewards, and He followeth after. Where he consents to the abolishing of Bishops, and alienating all their Lands by Act of Parliament; suppresseth by like Acts the Liturgy, and the Book of Canons, and the five Articles of *Perth*; rewards the chief Actors in the late Rebellion, with Titles, Offices, and Honours; and parts with so much of His Royal Prerogative to content the Subjects, that He left Himself nothing of a King but the empty Name. And to sum up the whole in brief, In one hour He unravelled all that excellent Web, the weaving whereof had took up more then forty years, and cost His Father and Himself so much Pains and Treasure.

13. By this indulgence to the *Scots*, the *Irish Papists* are invited to expect the like, and to expect it in the same way which the *Scots* had travelled; that is to say, by seizing on His Forts and Castles, putting themselves into the Body of an Army, and forcing many of His good Protestant Subjects to forsake the Kingdom. The Motives which induced them to it, their opportunities for putting it in execution, and the miscarriage of the Plot, I might here relate, but that I am to keep my self to the *Presbyterians*, as dangerous Enemies to the King and the Church of *England* as the *Irish Papists*. For so it happened, that His Majesty was informed at His being in *Scotland*, That the *Scots* had neither took up Arms nor invaded *England*, but that they were encouraged to it by some Members of the Houses of Parliament, on a design to change the Government both of Church and State. In which he was confirmed by the *Remonstrance of the state of the Kingdom*, presented to Him by the Commons as his first coming back; the forcible attempt for breaking into the Abby of *Westminster*; the concourse of seditious people to the Dores of the Parliament, crying out, that they would have *no Bishops nor Popish Lords*; and their tumultuating in a fearful manner, even at *White Hall* Gates, where they cryed out with far more horror to the Hearers, *That the King was not worthy to live: that they would have no Porters Lodge between Him and them:* and, *That the Prince would Govern better.* Hereupon certain Members of both Houses, that is to say, the Lord *Kimbolton* of the Upper; *Hollis*, and *Haslerig*, *Hampden*, *Pym*, and *Stroud*, of the Lower House, are impeached of Treason, a Serjeant sent to apprehend them, and command given for sealing up their Trunks and Closets.

14. But

14. But on the contrary the Commons did pretend and declared accordingly, That no Member of theirs was to be impeached, arrested, or brought unto a Legal Tryal, but by the Order of that House ; and that the sealing up of their Trunks or Closets was a breach of Priviledge. And thereupon it was resolved on *Monday, Jan. 3.* being the day of the Impeachment, *That if any persons whatsoever should come to the Lodgings of any Member of the House, or seize upon their persons, that then such Members should require the aid of the Constable to keep such persons in safe custody till the House gave further Order.* And it was then resolved also, *That if any person whatsoever should offer to arrest or detain the person of any Member of their House, without first acquainting the House therewith, and receiving further Order from the House ; that then it should be lawful for such Member, or any person, to resist him, and to stand upon his or their guard of defence ; and to make resistance according to the Protestation taken to defend the Liberties of Parliament.* This brings the King on *Tuesday* morning to the Commons House, attended only by his Guard, and some few Gentlemen, no otherwise weaponed then with Swords ; where having placed himself in the Speakers Chair, He required them to deliver the Impeached Members to the hands of Justice. But they had notice of His Purpose, and had retired into *London* as their safest Sanctuary ; to which the whole House is adjourned also, and sits in the *Guild Hall* as a Grand Committee. The next day brings the King to the City also ; where in a Speech to the Lord Mayor and Common Council He signified the Reasons of his going to the House of Commons ; *That He had no intent of proceeding otherwise against the Members, then in a way of Legal Tryal ; and thereupon desired, That they might not be harboured and protected in despite of Law.* For answer whereunto He is encountred with an insolent and sawcy Speech, made by one *Fowk,* a Member of the Common Council, corcerning the Impeached Members, and the Kings proceedings ; and followed in the Streets by the Rascal Rabble ; by some of which a Virulent and Seditious Pamphlet, entituled, *Every man to his Tents, O Israel* ; is cast into His Coach ; and nothing sounded in His Ears, but *Privileges of Parliament, Privileges of Parliament,* with most horrible out-cries. The same night puts them into Arms, with great fear and tumult, upon a rumour that the King and the *Cavaliers* (for so they called such Officers of the late Army as attended on him for their Pay) had a design to sack the City, who were then sleeping in their beds, and little dreamed of any such Seditious practises as were then on foot for the enflaming of the people.

15. And now comes *Calvins* Doctrine for restraining the Power of Kings to be put in practise. His Majesties going to the House of Commons on the 4th of *Jan.* is voted for so high a breach of their Rights and Priviledges, as was not to be salved by any *Retractation* or *Disclaimer,* or any thing by him alledged in excuse thereof. The Members are brought down in triumph both by Land and Water, guarded with Pikes and Protestations to their several Houses ; and the forsaken King necessitated to retire to *Windsor,* that he might not be an eye witness of his own disgraces. The Lord *Digby* goes to *Kingstone* in a Coach with six

six Horfes, to beftow a vifit upon Collonel *Lundsford*, and fome other Gentlemen ; each Horfe is reckoned for a Troop, and thefe Troops faid to have appeared in a warlike manner. Which was enough to caufe the prevailing party of the Lords and Commons to declare againft it ; and by their Order of the 13th of *January* to give command, *That all the Sheriffs of the Kingdom, affifted by the Juftices and Trained Bands of the Country, fhould take care to fupprefs all unlawful Affemblies, and to fecure the Magazines of their feveral Counties.* The Kings Attorney muft be called in queftion, examined, and endangered, for doing his duty in the impeachment of their Members, that no man might hereafter dare to obey the King. And though His Majefty had fent them a moft Gracious Meffage of the 20th of *January*, in which He promifed them *to equal or exceed all Acts of Favour which any of his Predeceffors had extended to the People of* England ; yet nothing could fecure them from their fears and jealoufies, unlefs the Trained bands, and the Royal Navy, the Tower of *London*, and the reft of the Forts and Caftles, were put into fuch hands as they might confide in. On this the King demurrs a while ; but having Shipped the Queen for *Holland*, with the Princefs *Mary*, and got the Prince into his Power, he denies it utterly. And this denial is reputed a fufficient reafon to take the Militia to themfelves, and execute the Powers thereof without his confent.

1642.　　16. But leaving them to their own Councils, he removes to *York*, affembleth the Gentry of that County, acquaints them with the reafons of His coming thither, and defires them not to be feduced by fuch falfe reports as had been raifed to the difhonour of his Perfon, and difgrace of his Government. By their advice he makes a journey unto *Hull*, in which he had laid up a confiderable Magazine of Canon, Arms, and Ammunition ; intended firft againft the *Scots*, and afterwards defigned for the War of *Ireland* ; but now to be made ufe of in his own defence. And poffibly He might have got it into his poffeffion, if he had kept his own Counfel, and had not let fome words fall from him in a Declaration, which betrayed his purpofe. For hereupon *Hotham*, a Member of their Houfe, and one of the two Knights for the County of *York*, is fent to Garrifon the Town ; who moft audacioufly refufed to give him entrance (though he was then accompanied with no more then his private Guards) and for fo doing is applauded and indempnified by the reft of the Members. This fends him back again to *York*, and there he meets as great a Baffle as he did at *Hull*. For there he is encountred with a new Committee from the Houfe of Commons, confifting of *Ferdinand* Lord *Fairfax*, Sir *Henry Cholmnly*, Sir *Hugh Cholmnly*, and Sir *Philip Stapleton* ; fent thither on purpofe to ferve as Spies upon his actions, to undermine all his proceedings, and to infinuate into the people, that all their hopes of peace and happinefs depended on their adhering to the prefent Parliament. And they applied themfelves to their Inftructions with fuch open Confidence, that the King had not more meetings with the Gentry of that County in his Palace called the Mannor-houfe, then they had with the Yeomanry and Freeholders in the great Hall of the Deanry. All which the King fuffered very ftrangely, and thereby robbed himfelf of the opportunity

portunity of raising an Army in that County, with which he might have marched to *London*, took the Hen sitting on her Nest before she had hatched, and possibly prevented all those Calamities which after followed.

17. But to proceed, during these counter-workings betwixt them and the King, the Lords and Commons plied him with continual Messages for his return unto the Houses ; and did as frequently endeavour to possess the people with their Remonstrances and Declarations to his disadvantage. To each of which His Majesty returned a significant Answer, so handsomly apparelled, and comprehending in them such a strength of Reason, as gave great satisfaction to all equal and unbyassed men. None of these Messages more remarkable then that which brought the Nineteen Propositions to his Majesties hands : In which it was desired, *That all the Lords of his Majesties Council, all the great Officers both of Court and State, the two Chief Justices, and the Chief Baron of the Exchequer, should be from thenceforth nominated and approved by both Houses of Parliament. That all the great Affairs of the Kingdom should be managed by them, even unto the naming of a Governour for his Majesties Children, and for disposing them in Marriage, at the will of the Houses. That no Popish Lord (as long as he continued such) should vote in Parliament.* And amongst many other things of like importance, *That he would give consent to such a Reformation of Church Government and Liturgy as both the Houses should advise.* But he knew well enough, that to grant all this was plainly to divest himself of all Regal Power which God had put into his hands. And therefore he returned such an answer to them as the necessity of his Affairs, compared with those impudent demands, did suggest unto him. But as for their Demand about Reformation, he had answered it in part before they made it, by ordering a Collection of sundry Petitions presented to himself and both Houses of Parliament, in behalf of *Episcopacy*, and for the preservation of the Liturgy, to be printed and published. By which Petitions it appeared, that there was no such general disaffection in the Subjects, unto either of them , (whether they were within the power of the Houses, or beyond their reach) as by the Faction was pretended ; the total number of Subscribers unto seven of them only (the rest not being calculated in the said Collection) amounting to Four hundred eighty two Lords and Knights, One thousand seven hundred and forty Esquires and Gentlemen of Note, Six hundred thirty one Doctors and Divines, and no fewer then Forty four thousand five hundred fifty nine Free-holders of good name and note.

18. And now the War begins to open. The Gentlemen of *Yorkshire* being sensible of that great affront which had been offered to His Majesty at the Gates of *Hull* ; and no less sensible of those dangers which were threatned to him by so ill a Neighbourhood, offered themselves to be a Guard unto his person. The Houses of Parliament upon the apprehension of some fears and jealousies had took a Guard unto themselves in *December* last ; but they conceived the King had so much innocence that he needed none: and therefore his accepting of this Guard of Gentlemen is voted for a levying of War against the Parliament,

and

and Forces muft be raifed in defence thereof. It hapned alfo that fome Members of the Houfe of Commons, many of his Domeftick Servants, and not a few of the Nobility and great men of the Realm, repaired from feveral places to the King at *York*, fo far from being willing to involve themfelves in other mens fins, that they declared the conftancy of their adhefion to his Majefties fervice. Thefe men they branded firft by the Name of *Malignants*, and after looked upon them in the notion of evil Counfellors ; for whofe removing from the King, they pretend to arm, (but now the ftale device muft be taken up) as well as in their own defence. Towards the raifing of which Army the *Presbyterian* Preachers fo beftir themfelves, that the wealthy Citizens fend in their Plate, the zealous Sifters rob'd themfelves of their Bodkins and Thimbles, and fome poor Wives caft in their Wedding Rings, like the Widows Mite, to advance the Service. Befides which they fet forth Inftructions, difperfed into all parts of the Realm, for bringing in of Horfes, Arms, Plate, Mony, Jewels, to be repayed again on the *Publick Faith*; appoint their Treafurers for the War ; and nominate the Earl of *Effex* for their chief Commander, whom fome difgraces from the Court had made wholly theirs. Him they commiffionate to bring the King from his *Evil Counfellors*, with power to kill and flay all fuch as oppofed them in it. And that he might perform the Service with a better Confcience, they laid faft hold on an Advantage which the King had given them, who in his Declaration of the 16*th* of *June*, either by fome incogitancy, or the flip of his Pen, had put himfelf into the number of the Three Eftates ; for thereupon it was inferred, That the Two Houfes were co-ordinate with him in the Publick Government ; and being co-ordinate, might act any thing without his confent, efpecially in cafe of his refufal to co-operate with them, or to conform to their defires. Upon which ground, both to encreafe their Party, and abufe the people, (who ftill held the Name of King in fome veneration) the War is managed in the Name of *King and Parliament*, as if both equally concerned in the Fortunes of it. It was alfo Preached and Printed by the *Presbyterians* to the fame effect, (as *Buchanan*, and *Knox*, *Calvin* and fome others of the Sect had before delivered) *That all Power was Originally in the people of a State or Nation ; in Kings no otherwife then by Delegation, or by way of Truft ; which Truft might be recalled when the People pleafed. That when the underived Majefty (as they loved to phrafe it) of the Common People was by their voluntary act transferred on the Supreme Magiftrate, it refted on that Magiftrate no otherwife then cumulativè ; but privativè by no means, in reference unto them that gave it. That though the King was* Major fingulis, *yet he was* Minor univerfis *; Superior only unto any one ; but far inferior to the whole Body of the People. That the King had no particular property in his Lands, Rents, Ships, Arms, Towers or Caftles ; which being of a publick nature, belorged as much to the people as they did to him. That it was lawful for the Subjects to refift their Princes, even by force of Arms, and to raife Armies alfo if need required, for the prefervation of Religion and the common Liberties.* And finally, (for what elfe can follow fuch dangerous premifes?) *That Kings being only the fworn Officers of the Commonwealth, they might be called to an account, and punifhed in cafe*

of

of Male-Administration, even to Imprisonment, Deposition, and to Death it self, if lawfully convicted of it. But that which served their turns best, was a new distinction which they had coined between the *Personal* and *Political* capacity of the Supreme Magistrate ; alleging that the King was present with the Houses of Parliament in his *Political* capacity, though in his *Personal* at *York.* That they might fight against the King in his *Personal* capacity, though not in his *Politick* ; and consequently might destroy *Charles Stuart,* without hurting the King. This was good *Presbyterian* Doctrine, but not so edifying at *York* as it was at *Westminster.* For his Majesty finding a necessity to defend *Charles Stuart,* if he desired to save the King, began to entertain such Forces as repaired unto him, and put himself into a posture of defence against all his Adversaries.

19. In *Yorkshire* he was countermined, and prevailed but little, not having above Two thousand men when he left that County. At *Nottingham* he sets up his *Standard,* which by an unexpected Tempest was blown down to the ground, and looked on as a sad presage of his following Fortunes. Passing thorough *Staffordshire* he gained some small encrease to his little Party, but never could attain unto the reputation of an Army till he came to *Shrewsbury* ; to which great multitudes flocked unto him out of *Wales* and *Cheshire,* and some of the adjoining Countreys. Encouraged with which supplyes, and furnished as well by the Queen from *Holland,* as by the Countrey Magazines, with Cannon, Arms and Ammunition, he resolves for *London,* gives the first brush unto his Enemies at *Poick* near *Worcester,* and routs them totally at *Edge hill* in the County of *Warwick.* This battel was fought on *Sunday* the 23d of *October, Anno* 1642, being a just twelve moneths from the breaking out of the *Irish Rebellion* : this being more dangerous then that, because the Kings Person was here aimed at more then any other. For so it was, that by corrupting one *Blake,* (once an *English* Factor, but afterwards employed as an Agent from the King of *Morocco*) they were informed from time to time of the Kings proceedings ; and more particularly in what part of the Army he resolved to be, which made them aim with the greater diligence and fury at so fair a Mark. But the King being Master of the Field. possest of the dead Bodies, and withal of the Spoil of some of the Carriages, discovered by some Letters this most dangerous practise. For which, that wretched Fellow was condemned by a Court of War, and afterwards hanged upon the Bough of an Oak not far from *Abington.*

20. In the mean time the King goes forward, takes *Banbury* both Town and Castle, in the sight of the Enemy, and enters triumphantly into *Oxon,* (which they had deserted to his hands) with no fewer then six score Colours of the vanquished Party. But either he stayed there too long, or made so many halts in his way, that *Essex* with his flying Army had recovered *London* before the King was come to *Colebrook.* There he received a Message for an Accommodation, made ineffectual by the Fight at *Brentford* on the next day after. Out of which Town he beat two of their choicest Regiments, sunk many pieces of Cannon, and much Ammunition, put many of them to the Sword in the heat of the Fight, and took about Five hundred Prisoners for a taste of his

Mercy,

Mercy. For knowing well how miserably they had been mis-guided, he spared their Lives, and gave them liberty on no other conditions, but only the taking of their Oaths not to serve against him. But the Houses of Parliement being loth to lose so many good men, appointed Mr. *Stephen Marshall*, (a principal Zealot at that time in the Cause of *Presbytery*) to call them together, and to absolve them from that Oath: Which he performed with so much Confidence and Authority, that the Pope himself could scarce have done it with the like. The next day being *Sunday*, and the 13th of *Nov.* he prepares for *London*, but is advertised of a stop at *Turnham Green*, two miles from *Brentford* ; where both the remainders of the Army under the Earl of *Essex*, and the Auxiliaries of *London* under the Conduct of the Earl of *Warwick*, were in a readiness to receive him. On this Intelligence it was resolved, on mature deliberation in the Council of War, That he should not hazard that victorious Army by a fresh encounter, in which if he should lose the day, it would be utterly impossible for him to repair that ruine. Accordingly he leads his Army over *Kingston-Bridge*, leaves a third part of it in the Town of *Reading*, and with the rest takes up his Winter Quarters in the City of *Oxon*.

21. But long he had not been at *Oxon* when he received some Propositions from the Houses of Parliament, which by the temper and complexion of them might rather seem to have proceeded from a conquering then a losing side. One to be sure must be in favour of *Presbytery* or else *Stephen Marshalls* zeal had been ill regarded. And in relation to *Presbytery* it was thus desired, that is to say, *That his Majesty would give consent to a Bill for the utter abolishing and taking away of all Archbishops, Bishops, their Chancellors and Commissaries, Deans, Subdeans, Deans and Chapters, Archdeacons, Canons, and Prebendaries, and all Chaunters, Chancellors, Treasurers, Subtreasurers, Succentors, and Sacrists, and all Vicars Choral and Choristers, old Vicars and new Vicars of any Cathedral or Collegiate Church, and all other their Under-officers, out of the Church of* England. And that being done, that he would consent to another Bill for consultation to be had with Godly, Religious, and Learned Divines, and then to settle the Church Government in such a way, as upon consultation with the said Divines should be concluded and agreed on by both Houses of Parliament. A Treaty howsoever did ensue upon these Propositions, but it came to nothing : the Commissioners for the Houses being so straitned in point of time, and tyed up so precisely to the Instructions of their Masters, that they could yield to nothing which conduced to the Publick peace. Nor was the North or South more quiet then the rest of the Kingdom : For in the North the Faction of the Houses was grown strong and prevalent, commanded by *Ferdinand* Lord *Fairfax*, who had possest himself of some strong Towns and Castles ; for maintainance whereof he had supplies from *Hull* upon all occasions. The care of *York* had been committed by the King to the Earl of *Cumberland*, and *Newcastle* was then newly Garrisoned by the Earl thereof; whose Forces being joined to those of the Earl of *Cumberland*, gave *Fairfax* so much work, and came off so gallantly, that in the end both Parties came to an accord, and were resolved to stand as Neutrals in the Quarrel. Which coming to the knowledge of the Houses of Par-

Parliament, they found some *Presbyterian* Trick to diffolve that Contract, though ratified by all the Obligations both of Honour and Confcience.

22. But in the South the Kings Affairs went generally from bad to worfe; *Portfmouth* in *Hampfhire* declared for him when he was at *York*; but being befieged, and not fupplied either with Men, Arms, or Victuals, as had been promifed and agreed on, it was furrendred by Col. *Goring*, the then Governour of it, upon Capitulation. *Norton* a Neighbouring Gentleman of a fair Eftate, was one of the firft that fhewed himfelf in Arms againft it for the Houfes of Parliament, and one that held it out to the very laft. For which good Service he was afterward made a Colonel of Horfe, Governour of *Southampton*, and one of the Committee for *Portfmouth*, after the Government of that Town had been taken from Sir *William Lewis*, on whom it was conferred at the firft furrendry. A Party of the Kings commanded by the Lord Vifcount *Grandifon*, was followed fo clofely at the heels by *Brown* and *Hurrey*, two mercenary *Scots* in the pay of the Houfes, that he was forced to put himfelf into *Winchefter* Caftle; where having neither victuals for a day, nor Ammunition for an hour, it was fome favour to his Souldiers to be taken to Mercy. But whatfoever Mercy was expreft to them, the poor Town found but little, and the Church much lefs; the Town being miferably plundered for no other reafon, but that they were not able to keep *Grandifon* out, had they been fo minded. Which though it was fufficient to impoverifh a more Wealthy City; yet *Waller* had two pulls more at it in the courfe of the War, to the undoing of fome Families, and the fpoil of others. But it was more defaced by *Ogle* about three years after, in burning down fome Houfes about the Caftle; but moft of all by pulling down the Bifhops Palace, the Deanry, and no fewer then eight Prebends Houfes, fold by the *Presbyterians*, to make mony of the Lead and Timber, the Iron, Glafs and Stones, which made up thofe Edifices.

23. But for the Church, though it was not the firft Example of their Reformation, according to the practice of the *Hugonot French*, the *Scottifh* and the *Belgick* Zealots; yet fared it worfe in fome refpects then the other Cathedrals, becaufe it fell unto the *Scots* (commanding fome *Scotizing Englifh*) to do execution. For they not only broke the Organs in pieces, and defaced the Carved Work of the Quire, containing the ftory of the Old and New Teftament, in moft excellent Imagery; but threw down the Communion Table, and broke down the Rails (which they burnt afterwards in an Alehoufe) and ftrewed the Pavements of the Quire with the torn leaves and Fragments of the Common prayer Books. Next, they proceeded to the fpoiling of the Tombs and Monuments, erected to the memory of fome eminent Prelates, which had been formerly both an Ornament and an Honour to it; as namely that of Cardinal *Beaufort*, a principal Benefactor to the Church and Hofpital of St. *Crofs*, neighbouring near unto the City; and that of *William Wainflet*, the magnificent and fole Founder of *Magdalen* College in *Oxon*. And whereas the Remainders of the Bodies of fome *Saxon* Kings, and many Bifhops of thofe times, had been gathered into feveral Leaden Chefts by Bifhop *Fox*, who lived and flourifhed in the laft times of

King

King *Henry* the VII. the barbarous Souldiers Sacrilegiouſly threw down thoſe Cheſts, ſcattered the duſt remaining of their Bodies, before the wind, and threw their bones about the Pavements of the Church. They break down as many of the Glaſs Windows as they could reach with Swords and Pikes; and at the reſt they threw the Bones of the dead Kings, or ſhot them down with their Muſquets; the ſpoil of which windows could not be repaired for one thouſand pounds. After all,this, they ſeize upon the Communion Plate, the Surplices of the Prieſts and Quire men, all the rich Hangings and large Cuſhions of Velvet,and the coſtly Pulpit clothes, ſome of which were of Cloth of Silver, and others of Gold. And finding two Brazen Statua's of King *James* and King *Charles*, at the firſt entrance of the Quire, they brake off the two Swords which were placed by their ſides, and with their own, mangled the Crown upon the head of King *Charles*, ſwearing in ſcorn, *That they would bring him back again to his Houſes of Parliament.*

24 This hapned upon *Thurſday* the fifteenth of *December*; and the ſame moneth proved as calamitous to the Church of *Chicheſter*; which City had received ſome Souldiers of His Majeſties Party, who either were too few to keep it, or found it not tenable enough to make any reſiſtance. *Waller* preſents himſelf before it, and without any great diſpute, becomes Maſter of it; by which the Town got little, and the Church loſt more. For upon *Innocents day*, the Souldiers forcibly break into it, where they ſeize upon the Veſtments and Ornaments of the Church, together with the Conſecrated Plate ſerving for the Altar, not leaving ſo much as a Cuſhion for the Pulpit, or a Chalice for the bleſſed Sacrament. But this rich ſpoil being committed by the Marſhal and other Officers, the reſt was left unto the hands and weapons of the common Souldiers, who with their Pole axes did not only break down the Organs, but cut in pieces the Communion Table, with the Rail before it. They defaced the two Tables of the Law at the Eaſt end of the Quire, for fear they ſhould riſe up againſt them in the Day of Judgment; moſt miſerably made havock of the Hiſtory of that Churches Foundation, which they found on the one ſide of the South croſs Iſle, pourtrayed in Artificial manner, with the Statues of the Kings of *England*; and coming to the Portraiture of King *Edward* the VI, they picked out his eyes, ſaying in ſcorn, *That all this miſchief came from him, in eſtabliſhing the Book of Common Prayer.* Which that it might not be officiated as in former times, they break open all the Cheſts and Cupboards in which the Quire-men had laid up their Singing Books, Common Prayer Books, Gowns and Surplices; ſtrewing the Pavements of the Church with the Leaves of the Books, but turning the Gowns and Surplices into ready mony. To all which Acts of Sacrilegious Spoil and Rapine, as *Waller* gave ſome countenance by his perſonal preſence; and in that ſomewhat worſe then *Nero* * as the ſtory tells us: So *Haſlerig* gave much more by his Voice and Actions: For forcing his way into the *Chapter Houſe*, he did not only command the Souldiers to break down the Wainſcot, but ſeized on all the rich Plate which belonged to the Church. And when it was deſired that they would leave one Chalice only for the uſe of the Sacrament, anſwer was moſt prophanely made by one of the *Scots*, (of which Nation the two Houſes had employed too many) *That they might ſerve th turne*

* *Et juſſit ſcelera Nero, non ſpectavit.* Tacit. in vit. Agric.

turn with a Wooden Dish.   Nor were some *Presbyterian* Zealots in the City of *Exeter* more favourable to their own Cathedrals, then the rude Souldiers were to this ; where being incensed by some of their Seditious Preachers,they acted over all those outrages of Spoil and Rapine,which have been formerly recited; and added to them such prodigious and unheard Irreverences, by turning the Church into a Jakes, and leaving their filth on and about the holy Altar, as fills me with Religious horror at the thinking of it.

25. But their first Furies in this kind brake out in the Cathedral Church of *Canterbury*, and that of *Rochester*, under the conduct and command of Colonel *Sandys*, one of the Natives of that County ; who taking some Forces with him to make sure of *Canterbury*,came thither in the end of *August* ; and having got the Keys of the Cathedral into his possession, gave a free entrance to the Rabble which attended on him; forcing their way into the Quire, they overthrew the Communion Table,tore the Velvet Cloth which they found about it,defaced the goodly Screen or Tabernacle work, violated the Monuments of the dead, spoiled the Organs, brake down the ancient Rails and Seats, with the brazen Eagle which did support the Bible, forced open the Cupboards of the Singing-men, rent some of their Surplices, Gowns, and Bibles, & carried away others,mangled all the Service Books,& Books of Common Prayer, bestrewing the whole Pavement with the Leaves thereof. They also exercised their madness on the Arras Hangings which adorned the Quire, representing the whole story of our Saviour.   And meeting with some of his Figures amongst the rest, some of them swore that they would stab him, and others that they would rip up his bowels : which they did accordingly, so far forth at the least as those figures in the Arras Hanging could be capable of it.   And finding another *Statua* of Christ placed in the Frontispiece of the South Gate there, they discharged Forty Musquets at it,exceedingly triumphing when they hit him in the Head or Face.   And it is thought they would have fallen upon the Fabrick, if at the humble suit of the Mayor and Citizens they had not been restrained by their principal Officers.   Less spoil was made at *Rochester*, though too much in that, their Follies being chiefly exercised in tearing the Book of Common Prayer, and breaking down the Rails before the Altar. *Seaton* a *Scot*, and one of some command in the Army afterwards, took some displeasure at the Organs, but his hands were tyed ; whether it were that *Sandys* repented of the Outrages which were done at *Canterbury*, or else afraid of giving more scandal and offence to the *Kentish* Gentry, I am not able to determine.   But sure it is, that he enjoyed but little comfort in these first beginnings, receiving his deaths wound about three weeks after in the fight near *Powick* ; of which within few weeks more he dyed at *Worcester*.

26. But I am weary of reciting such Spoils and Ravages as were not acted by the *Goths* in the sack of *Rome*. And on that score I shall not take upon me to relate the Fortunes of the present War, which changed and varied in the West, as in other places, till the Battel of *Stratton*; in which Sir *Ralph Hopton*, with an handful of his gallant *Cornish*, raised by the reputation of Sir *Bevil Greenvile* and Sir *Nicholas Slaining*, gave such a general defeat to the Western Rebels, as opened him the way towards

wards *Oxon* with small opposition. Twice troubled in his March by *Waller*, grown famous by his taking of *Malmsbury*, and relieving *Glou-cester*, but so defeated in a fight at *Roundway Down*, (*Run away Down* the Souldiers called it) that he was forced to flye to *London* for a new recruit. Let it suffice, that the King lost *Reading* in the Spring, received the Queen triumphantly into *Oxon* within a few weeks after, by whom he was supplied with such a considerable stock of Arms and other Necessaries, as put him into a condition to pursue the War. This Summer makes him Master of the North and West ; the North being wholly cleared of the Enemies Forces, but such as seemed to be imprisoned in the Town of *Hull*. And having lost the Cities of *Bristol* and *Exon*, no Towns of consequence in the West remained firm unto them, but *Pool, Lime* and *Plymouth* : so that the Leading Members were upon the point of forsaking the Kingdom, and had so done (as it was generally reported and averred for certain) if the King had not been diverted from his march to *London* upon a confidence of bringing the strong City of *Glocester* to the like submission. This gave them time to breathe a little, and to advise upon some course for their preservation ; and no course was found fitter for them then to invite the *Scots* to their aid and succour, whose amity they had lately purchased at so dear a rate. Hereupon *Armin* and some others are dispatched for *Scotland* ; where they applied themselves so dextrously to that proud and rebellious people, that they consented at the last to all things which had been desired. But they consented on such terms as gave them an assurance of One hundred thousand pounds in ready mony ; the Army to be kept both with Pay and Plunder ; the chief Promoters of the Service to be rewarded with the Lands and Houses of the *English* Bishops, and their Commissioners ; to have as great an influence in all Councils both of Peace and War as the Lords and Commons.

27. But that which proved the strongest temptation to engage them in it, was an assurance of reducing the Church of *England* to an exact conformity, in Government and Forms of Worship, to the Kirk of *Scotland* ; and gratifying their Revenge and Malice, by prosecuting the Archbishop of *Canterbury* to the end of his Tragedy. For compassing which Ends a Solemn League and Covenant is agreed between them ; first taken and subscribed to by the *Scots* themselves, and afterwards by all the Members in both Houses of Parliament ; as also by the principal Officers of the Army, all the Divines of the Assembly, almost all those which lived within the Lines of Communication, and in the end by all the Subjects which either were within their power, or made subject to it. Now by this Covenant the Party was to bind himself, amongst other things, first, *That he would endeavour in his place and calling to preserve the Reformed Religion in* Scotland, *in Doctrine, Discipline, and Government : That he would endeavour in like manner the Reformation of Religion in the Kingdoms of* England *and* Ireland, *according to the Word of God, and the example of the best Reformed Churches ; but more particularly to bring the Churches of God in all the three Kingdoms to the nearest conjunction and uniformity in Religion, Confession of Faith, Form of Church Government, and Directory for Worship and Catechising.* Secondly, *That without respect of persons they would endeavour to extirpate Popery and Prelacy ; that is to say,*

Church

Church Government by Archbishops, their Chancellors & Commissairs, Deans, Deans and Chapters, Archdeacons, and all other Ecclesiastical Officers depending on it. And thirdly, *That he would endeavour the discovery of such as have been, or shall be Incendiaries, Malignants, and evil Instruments, either in hindering the Reformation of Religion, or in dividing between the King and his people, &c. whom they should bring to condign punishment before the Supream Judicatories of either Kingdom, as their offences should deserve.* Of which three Articles the two first tended to the setting up of their dear Presbyteries ; the last unto the profecution of the late Archbishop, whom they confidered as their greatest and most mortal Enemy.

28. The terror of this Covenant, and the fevere penalty impofed on thofe which did refufe it, compelled great numbers of the Clergy to forfake their Benefices, and to betake themfelves to fuch Towns and Garrifons as were kept under the command of his Majefties Forces ; whofe vacant places were in part fupplied by fuch *Presbyterians,* who formerly had lived as Lecturers or Trencher Chaplains, or elfe beftowed upon fuch Zealots as flocked from *Scotland* and *New England,* like *Vultures* and other Birds of Rapine, to feek after the prey. But finding the deferted Benefices not proportionable to fo great a multitude, they compelled many of the Clergy to forfake their Houfes, that fo they might avoid imprifonment or fome worfe calamity. Others they fent to feveral Gaols, or fhut them up in Ships whom they expofed to ftorms and tempefts, and all the miferies which a wild Sea could give to a languifhing ftomach. And fome again they fequeftered under colour of fcandal, imputing to them fuch notorious and enormous Crimes, as would have rendered them uncapable of Life, as well as Livings, if they had been proved. But that which added the moft weight to thefe Oppreffions, was the publifhing of a malicious and unchriftian Pamphlet, entituled, *The firft Century of Scandalous and Malignant Priefts*: which, whether it were more odious in the fight of God, or more difgraceful to the Church, or offenfive to all fober and religious men, it is hard to fay. And as it feems the fcandal of it was fo great, that the Publifher thereof, though otherwife of a fiery and implacable nature, defifted from the putting forth of a *Second Century,* though he had promifed it in the Firft, and was inclinable enough to have kept his word. Inftructions had been fent before to all Counties in *England,* for bringing in fuch Informations againft their Minifters as might fubject them to the danger of a Deprivation. But the times were not then fo apt for mifchief, as to ferve their turns, which made them fall upon thefe wretched and unchriftian courfes to effect their purpofe. By means whereof they purged the Church of almoft all Canonical and Orthodox men. The greatnefs of which defolation in all the parts of the Kingdom may be computed by the havock which they made in *London,* and the Parifhes thereunto adjoining, according as it is prefented in the Bill of Mortality hereunto fubjoined.

29. *A General Bill of Mortality of the Clergy of* London, *which have been Defunct by reason of the Contagious Breath of the Sectaries of that City, from the year* 1641 *to the year* 1647 : *with the several Casualties of the same.* Or, *A Brief Martyrology and Catalogue of the Learned, Grave, Religious, and Painful Ministers of the City of* London, *who have been imprisoned, plundered, and barbarously used, and deprived of all Livelihood for themselves and their Families ; for their constancy to the* Protestant Religion *established in this Kingdom, and their Loyalty to their Soveraign.*

THe Cathedral Church of S. *Paul,* the Dean, Residentiaries, and other Members of that Church, sequestered, plundered, and turned out.

St. *Albans Woodstreet,* Dr. *Wats* sequestered, plundered, his Wife and Children turned out of doors, himself forced to flye.

Alhallows Barking, Dr. *Layfield* persecuted, imprisoned in *Ely house,* and the Ships, sequestered and plundered ; afterwards forced to flye.

Alhallows Breadstreet ————

Alhallows Great ————

Alhallows Honey lane ————

Alhallows Less ————

Alhallows Lumbardstreet, Mr. *Weston* sequestered.

Alhallows Stainings ————

Alhallows the Wall ————

Alphage, Dr. *Halsie* shamefully abused, his Cap pulled off to see if he were not a shaven Priest, voted out, and forced to flye : dead with grief.

Andrew Hubbard, Dr. *Chambers* sequestered.

Andrew Undershaft, 1. Mr. *Mason* through vexation forced to resign. 2. Mr. *Prichard* after that sequestered.

Andrew Wardrobe, Dr. *Isaacson* sequestered.

Ann Aldersgate, Dr. *Clewet* sequestered.

Ann Black Fryars ————

Antholin's Parish ————

Austins Parish, Mr. *Udal* sequestered,

his Bed-rid Wife turned out of doors, and left in the streets.

Barthol Exchange, Dr. *Grant* sequestered.

Bennet Fink, Mr. *Warfield* sequestered.

Bennet Grace-Church, Mr. *Guelch* sequestered.

Bennet Pauls Wharf, Mr. *Adams* sequestered.

Bennet Shere-hog, Mr. *Morgan* dead with grief.

Botolph Billingsgate, Mr. *King* sequestered and forced to flye.

Chrifts Church ———— turned out and dead.

Christophers, Mr. *Hanslow.*

Clement Eastcheap, Mr. *Stone* shamefully abused, sequestered, sent Prisoner to *Plymouth,* and plundered.

Dionyse Back-Church, Mr. *Humes* sequestered and abused.

Dunstans East, Dr. *Chiderly* reviled, abused, and dead.

Edmonds Lombardstreet, Mr. *Paget,* molested, silenced, and dead.

Ethelborough, Mr. *Clark,* sequestered and imprisoned.

Faiths, Dr. *Brown,* sequestered and dead.

Fosters, Mr. *Batty* sequestered, plundered, forced to flye, and dead.

Gabriel Fenchurch, Mr. *Cook* sequestered.

George Botolphlane ————

Gregories by *Pauls* ————

Hellens, Mr. *Miller* turned out and dead

James

James Duke place, Mr ————— sequestered.

James Garlickhithe, Mr. *Freeman* plundered and sequestered, and Mr. *Anthony* turned out.

John Baptist, Mr. *Weemsly* sequestered.

John Evangelist ——— ———

John Zachary, Mr. *Edlin* sequestered, forced to fly, and plundered.

Katherine Coleman, Dr. *Hill*, and Mr. *Ribbuts* sequestered.

Katherine Creechurch, Mr. *Rush* turned out.

Laurence Jury, Mr. *Lane* sequestered.

Laurence Poutney ——— ———

Leonard Eastcheap, Mr. *Calf* forced to give up to Mr. *Roborow*, Scribe to the Assembly.

Leonard Foster lane, Mr. *Ward* forced to flye, plundered, sequestered, and dead for want of necessaries.

Margaret Lothbury, Mr, *Tabor* plundered, imprisoned in the Kings Bench, his Wife and Children turned out of doors at midnight, and himself sequestered.

Margaret Moses ——— ———

Margaret New-Fishstreet, Mr. *Pory* forced to flye, plundered and sequestered.

Margaret Pattons, Mr. *Megs* plundered, imprisoned in *Ely-house*, and sequestered.

Mary Abchurch, Mr. *Stone* plundered, sent Prisoner by Sea to *Plymouth*, and sequestered.

Mary Aldermanbury ——— ———

Mary Aldermary, Mr. *Brown* forced to forsake it.

Mary le Bow, Mr. *Leech* sequestered and dead with grief.

Mary Bothow, Mr. *Proctor* forced to flye, and sequestered.

Mary Colechurch ——— ———

Mary Hill, 1. Dr. *Baker* sequestered, pursivanted, and imprisoned, 2.

Mr. *Woodcock* turned out, and forced to flye.

Mary Mounthaw, Mr. *Thrall* sequestered, and shamefully abused.

Mary Sommerset, Mr. *Cook* sequestered.

Mary Stainings ———

Mary Woolchurch, Mr. *Tireman* forced to forsake it.

Mary Woolnoth, Mr. *Shute* molested and vext to death, and denied a Funeral-Sermon to be preached by Dr. *Holdsworth*, as he desired.

Martins Ironmonger lane, Mr. *Spark* sequestered and plundered.

Martins Ludgate, Dr. *Jermine* sequestered.

Martins Orgars, Dr. *Walton* assaulted, sequestered, plundered, and forced to flye.

Martins Outwich, Dr. *Pierce*, sequestered and dead.

Martins Vintry, Dr. *Ryves* sequestered, plundered, and forced to flye.

Matthew Friday street, Mr. *Chestlin* violently assaulted in his House, imprisoned in the Counter, thence sent to *Colchester* Gaol in *Essex*, sequestered and plundered.

Maudlins Milkstreet, Mr. *Jones* sequestered.

Maudlins Old Fish Street, Dr. *Gryffith*, sequestered, plundered, imprisoned in *Newgate*, and when let out, forced to flye.

Michael Bassishaw. Dr. *Gyfford* sequestered.

Michael Cornhill, Dr. *Brough*, sequestered, plundered, Wife and Children turned out of doors, and his Wife dead with grief. But Mr. *Weld* his Curate, assaulted, beaten in the Church and turned out,

Michael Crooked lane ——— ———

Michael Queenhithe, Mr. *Hill* sequestered.

Michael

Michael Quern, Mr. *Launce* sequestered.

Michael Royal, Mr. *Proctor* sequestered, and forced to flye.

Michael Woodstreet ———— ————

Mildred Breadstreet, Mr. *Bradshaw* sequestered.

Mildred Poultry, Mr. *Maden* sequestered and gone beyond Sea.

Nicholas Acons, Mr. *Bennet* sequestered.

Nicholas Coleabby, Mr. *Chibbald* sequestered.

Nicholas Olaves, Dr. *Cheshire* molested, and forced to resign.

Olaves Hartstreet, Mr. *Haines* sequestered.

Olaves Jury, Mr. *Tuke* sequestered, plundered, and imprisoned.

Olaves Silver-street, Dr. *Boohe* abused, and dead with grief.

Pancrafs Soper-lane, Mr. *Eccop* sequestered, plundered, and forced to flye, his Wife and Children turned out of doors.

Peters Cheap, Mr. *Votier* sequestered, and dead wieh grief.

Peters Cornhill, Dr. *Fairfax* sequestered, plundered, imprisoned in *Ely-house*, and the Ships, his Wife and Children turned out of doors.

Peters Pauls Wharf, Mr. *Marbury* sequestered.

Peters Poor, Dr. *Holdsworth* sequestered, plundered, and imprisoned in *Ely House*, then in the *Tower*.

Stephens Colemanstreet ——————

Stephens Walbrook, D. *Howel* through vexation forced to forsake it, sequestered out of all, and fled, divers since turned out.

Swithens, Mr. *Owen* sequestered.

Thomas Apostle, Mr. *Cooper* sequestered and plundered, sent prisoner to *Leeds Castle* in *Kent*.

Trinity Patish, Mr. *Harrison* dead with grief.

————— ——— —— ———

In the 97 Parishes within the Walls, besides St. *Pauls*, outed **85.** dead 16.

————————————

Parishes without the Walls.

Andrew Holborn, Dr. *Hacket* sequestered.

Bartholomew Great, Dr. *Westfield* abused in the streets, sequestered, forced to flye, and dead.

Bartholomew Lefs ——— —— ———

Brides Parish, Mr. *Palmer* sequestered.

Bridewell Precinct, Mr. *Brown* turned out.

Botolph Aldersgate, Mr. *Booth* sequestered.

Botolph Aldgate, Mr. *Swadlin* sequestered, plundered, imprisoned at *Gresham Colledge* and *Newgate*, his Wife and Children turned out of doors.

Botolph Bishopsgate, Mr. *Rogers* sequestered.

Dunstans West, Dr. *March* sequestered, and dead in remote parts.

George Southwark, Mr. *Cook* sequestered.

Giles Cripplegate, Dr. *Fuller* sequestered, plundered, and imprisoned at *Ely House*: and *Mr. Hatton* his Curate assaulted in the Church, and imprisoned.

Olaves Southwark, Dr. *Turner* sequestered plundered, fetched up Prisoner with a Troop of Soldiers, and afterwards forced to flye.

Saviours Southwark ——— —— ——

Sepulchers Parish, *Mr. Pigot* the Lecturer turned out.

Thomas Southwark, *Mr. Spencer* sequestered and imprisoned.

Trinity Minories ——— ——— ——

————————————

In the 16. Parishes without the Walls, outed 14, and 2 dead.

In the Ten out-Parishes.

Clement Danes, Dr. *Dukeson* seque-stered, and forced to flye.

Covent Garden, Mr. *Hall* sequestered, and forced to flye.

Giles in the Fields, Dr. *Heywood* se-questered, imprisoned in the *Counter*, *Ely House*, and the ships, forced to flye, his Wife and Children turned out of doors.

James Clerkenwell ———— ———

Katherine Tower ——— —— ——

Leonard Shoreditch, Mr. *Squire* se-questered, imprisoned in *Gresham-College*, *Newgate*, and the *Kings Bench*, his Wife and Children plundered and turned out of doors.

Martins in the Fields, Dr. *Bray* se-questered, imprisoned, plundered, forced to flye, and dead in re-mote parts.

Mary Whitechappel, Dr. *Johnson* se-questered.

Magdalen Bermondsey, Dr. *Paske* se-questered.

Savoy, Dr. *Balcanqual* sequestered, plundered, forced to flye, and dead in remote parts, and Mr. *Fuller* forced to flye.

In the ten out Parishes, outed 9. dead two.

In the adjacent Towns.

The Dean and Prebends of the Abby-Church of *Westminster*, (but only Mr. *Lambert Osbaston*) sequestered.

Margarets Westminster, Dr. *Wimber-ly* sequestered.

Lambeth, Dr. *Featly* sequestered, plundered, imprisoned, and dead a prisoner.

Newington, Mr. *Heath* sequestered.

Hackney, Mr. *Moor* sequestered.

Rederif ———— —— ———

Islington, Divers turned out.

Stepney, Dr. *Stamp* sequestered, plundered, and forced to flye.

In the adjacent Towns, besides those of the Abby-Church, and *Islington*, outed 7, dead 1.

The total of the Ministers of London, *within this Bill of Mortality, besides* Pauls *and* Westminster, *turned out of their Livings* ———— —————— } 115.

Whereof Doctors in Divinity above ———— ———— 40. *most of them plundered of their Goods, their Wives and Children turned out of doors.*

Imprisoned in London, *and in the Ships and in several Gaols and Castles in the Countrey* ——— —— } 29

Fled to prevent Imprisonment ———————— 25.

Dead in remote parts and Prisons with grief ——— 22.

And at the same time about forty Churches void, having no constant Mi-nister in them.

Usque quo Domine. *Rev.* 6. 1.

30. By this sad Bill confined within the *Lines of Communication*, and some Villages adjoining, we may conjecture at the greatness of that *Mortality* which fell amongst the Regular Clergy in all parts of the Kingdom, by *Plundering*, *Sequestering*, and *Ejecting* ; or finally, by vexing them into their Graves, by so many Miseries as were inflicted on them in the Ships, or their several Prisons. In all which ways, more men were outed of their Livings by the *Presbyterians* in the space of Three years, then were deprived by the *Papists* in the Reign of Queen *Mary* ; or had been *silenced*, *suspended*, or *deprived* by all the Bishops, from the first year of Queen *Elizabeth*, to these very times. And that it might be done with some colour of Justice, they instituted a *Committee for Plundered Ministers*, under pretence of making some provision for such godly Preachers as had either suffered loss of Goods by His Majesties Souldiers, or loss of livings for adhering to the Houses of Parliament. Under which stiles they brought in a confused Rabble of their own perswasions, or such at least as were most likely to be serviceable to their ends and purposes ; some of which had no Goods, and most of them no livings at all to lose. But the truth was, they durst not trust the Pulpits to the Regular Clergy ; who if they had offended against the Laws, by the same laws they ought to have been tryed, condemned, and deprived accordingly ; that so the Patrons might present more deserving persons to the vacant Churches. But then this could not stand with the main Design : For possibly the Patrons might present such Clarks as would go on in the old way, and could not be admitted but by taking the Oaths of Supremacy and Allegiance to our Lord the King, and by subscribing to the Discipline and Doctrine of the Church of *England*, which they were then resolved to alter. Or, could they have prevailed so far with the several Patrons, as to present those very men whom they had designed unto the Profits of the Sequestered Benefices ; yet then they were to have enjoyed them for *term of Life*, and might pretend a legal Right and Title to them, which would have cut off that dependance on the Houses of Parliament, which this design did chiefly aim at. So that the best of this new Clergy were but *Tenants at Will*, and therefore must be servile and obsequious to their mighty Landlords, upon whose pleasure they depended for their present livelihood.

31. Such were the Mischiefs of this year. For remedy whereof, His Majesty most graciously published two Proclamations, one of them bearing date the 15th of *May* ; and the other on the 9th of *October*. In the first of which, His Majesty takes especial notice, *That many of the Clergy, no less eminent for their Learning then their Zeal and Piety, were either driven or forced from their habitations, or silenced, or discharged from attending on their Cures : That they suffered these oppressions for no other reasons, but because they published his legal and just Commands, or had refused to pray against Him, or to submit against their Consciences, to illegal Taxes for the continuance of the War ; or were conformable to the Book of Common Prayer, or preacht Gods Word according to the purity of it, without any mixture of Sedition ; That being for these Crimes discharged of their several Cures, others were put into their Places to sow Sedition, and seduce His Majesties Good Subjects from their due obedience, contrary to the Word of*
God,

God, and the Laws of the Land. His Majesty thereupon commandeth, *That all such courses be forborn for the time to come. That all His good Subjects for the present set forth their Tythes, and pay them to the lawful Incumbents, or their Farmers only. That the Church Wardens, Side men, and other Parish-ioners shall resist all such persons as have been or shall be intruded into any of the Cures aforesaid: but, that they should contribute their best assistance to the lawful Ministers, for the receiving and enjoying of their Glebes and Tythes. With an injunction to all Sheriffs, Mayors, and other Ministers of Justice to be aiding to them, and to resist by force of Arms all such as should endeavour to disturb them in their lawful possessions.* But this served rather for a Declaration of His Majesties Piety, then an example of His Power. For notwithstanding all this Care, his faithful Subjects of the Clergy in all parts of the Realm, were plundered, sequestered, and ejected for the Crime of Loyalty; some of them never being restored, and others most unjustly kept from their Estates till this present year *Anno*, 1660.

32. In the other Proclamation he forbids the tendring or taking of the Covenant before remembred. Which Proclamation being short, but full of substance, shall be recited in his Majesties own words, which are in these that follow. *Whereas* (saith he) *there is a Printed Paper enti-tuled, A Solemn League and Covenant for Reformation and Defence of Religion, the Honor and Happiness of the King, the Peace and Safety of the Three Kingdoms of* England, Scotland, *and* Ireland *; pretended to be ordered by the Commons in Parliament, on the* 21 *of September last, to be printed and published. Which Covenant, though it seems to make some spacious expressions of Piety and Religion, is in truth nothing else but a Traiterous and Seditious Combination against us; and against the established Religion and Laws of the Kingdom, in pursuance of a Traiterous Design and Endeavour to bring in Forrein Forces to invade this Kingdom. We do therefore straightly charge and command all Our loving Subjects, of what degree or quality soever, upon their Allegiance, that they presume not to take the said Seditious and Traiterous Covenant. And We do likewise hereby forbid and inhibit them to impose, administer, or tender the said Covenant, as they and every of them will answer the contrary at their utmost and extreamest perils.* Such was the tenour of this Proclamation of the *9th* of *October* ; which though it served for a sufficient testimony of His Majesties Prudence, yet it prevailed as little as the other did: For, as the Two Houses did extend their Quarters, and enlarge their Power; so were the Subjects forced more generally to receive this yoak, and to submit themselves to those Oaths and Covenants which they could neither take for fear of Gods and the Kings Displeasure; and dared not to refuse, for fear of losing all which was dear unto them. So that it was esteemed for a special favour, as indeed it was, for all those which came in on the *Oxford Articles*, to be exempted from the taking of this leud and accursed Covenant, by which they were to bind themselves to betray the Church, and to stand no further to the King, then as he stood for the *defence* of that *Religion* which they then allowed of, and of those *Liberties* which they had acquired by what way soever.

33. And to say truth, it was no wonder that the *Presbyterians* should impose new Oaths, when they had broken all the old ; or seize

upon the Tythes and Glebes of the Regular Clergy, when they had sequeſtered the Eſtates of the Loyal Gentry, and intercepted the Revenues of the King and Queen. And it would be no wonder neither that they ſhould ſeize on the Revenues of the King and Queen, when they were grown to ſuch a high degree of impudence, as to impeach the Queen of Treaſon, and were reſolved of having no more Kings to comptrol their Actions. They had already voted for the making of a new Great Seal, (though ſo to do was made High Treaſon by the Statute of King *Edward* the third) that they might expedite their Commiſſions with the more Authority, and add ſome countenance of Law to the preſent war : which muſt be managed in the Name of the King and Parliament, the better to abuſe the people, and add ſome Reputation to the crime of their undertakings. And being Maſters of a Seal, they thought themſelves in a capacity of acting as a Commonwealth, as a State diſtinct ; but for the preſent, making uſe of his Majeſties Name as their *State-holder*, for the ordering of their new Republick. But long he muſt not hold that neither ; though that was locked up as a Secret amongſt thoſe of the *Cabala*, till it was blurted out by *Martin*, then Knight for *Berks* : By whom it was openly declared, *That the felicity of this Nation did not conſiſt in any of the Houſe of STUART* Of which His Majeſty complained, but without reparation. And for a further evidence of their good intentions, a view is to be taken of the old *Regalia*, and none ſo fit as *Martin* to perform that Service. Who having commanded the Subdean of *Weſtminſter* to bring him to the place in which they were kept, made himſelf Maſter of the Spoil. And having forced open a great Iron Cheſt, took out the Crowns, the Robes, the Swords and Sceptre, belonging anciently to King *Edward* the Confeſſor, and uſed by all our Kings at their Inaugurations. With a ſcorn greater then his Luſts, and the reſt of his Vices, he openly declares, *That there would be no further uſe of thoſe Toys and Trifles.* And in the jollity of that humour inveſts *George Withers* (an old *Puritan Satyriſt*) in the Royal Habiliments. Who being thus Crown'd and Royally array'd (as right well became him) firſt marcht about the Room with a ſtately Garb, and afterwards with a thouſand Apiſh and Ridiculous actions, expoſed thoſe Sacred Ornaments to contempt and laughter. Had the *Abuſe* been *ſtript and whipt*, as it ſhould have been, the fooliſh Fellow poſſibly might have paſſed for a *Prophet*, though he could not be reckoned for a *Poet*.

34. But yet the miſchief ſtayed not here. Another viſit is beſtowed upon theſe *Regalia* ; not to make merry with them, but ſome mony of them. *Mildmay*, a *Puritan* in Faction, and Maſter of the Jewel Houſe by his Place and Office, conceived that Prey to belong properly to him ; and having ſold the King, muſt needs buy the Crowns. But being as falſe to his new Maſters as he was to his old, he firſt pickt out the richeſt Jewels, and then compounded for the reſt at an eaſie rate. The like ill fortune fell unto the Organs, Plate, Coaps, Hangings, Altar-Cloaths, and many other coſtly Utenſils which belonged to the Church ; all which were either broke in pieces, or ſeized upon and plundered for the uſe of the State. Amongſt the reſt there was a goodly Chalice of the pureſt Gold ; which though it could not be

less worth then 300 *l.* was sold to *Allyn* a decayed Gold smith, but then a Member of the House, at the rate of 60 *l.* The Birds being flown, the Nest is presently designed to the use of the Souldiers, who out of wantonness, and not for want of Lodging in that populous City, must be quartered there. And being quartered, they omitted none of those shameless Insolencies which had been acted by their Fellows in other Churches. For they not only brake down the Rails before the Table, and burnt them in the very place in the heats of *July* ; but wretchedly prophaned the very Table it self, by setting about it with their Tobacco and Ale before them, and not without the company of some of their zealous Lecturers to grace the Action. What else they did in imitation of the Brethren of *Exon,* in laying their filth and excrements about it also, I abhor to mention. And now I must crave leave to step into the College, the Government whereof was trken from the Dean and Prebendaries, and given to a select Committee of fifty persons, some Lords, but Members, for the most part of the Lower House; who found there a sufficient quantity of Plate, and some other good Houshold-stuff, to a very good value ; which was so Husbanded amongst them, that it was either stoln or sold, or otherwise imbezilled and inverted to the use of some private persons, who best knew how to benefit themselves by the Churches Patrimony.

35. But the main business of this year, and the three next following, was the calling, sitting, and proceedings of the new Assembly, called the *Assembly of Divines*; but made up also of so many of the Lords and Commons, as might both serve as well to keep them under, and comptroll their Actions, as to add some countenance unto them in the eye of the people. A Convocation had been appointed by the King when he called the Parliament, the Members whereof being lawfully chosen and returned, were so discountenanced and discouraged by the Votes of the Lower House, the frequent Tumults raised in *Westminster* by the Rascal Rabble, and the preparatives for a War against the King, that they retired unto their Houses, but still continued undissolved, and were in a capacity of acting as a Convocation, whensoever they should be thereunto required, and might do it with safety. But being for the most part well affected to the Church of *England,* they were not to be trusted by the Houses of Parliament, who then designed the hammering of such a *Reformation* both in Doctrine and Discipline, as might unite them in a perpetual Bond and Confederation with their *Scottish* Brethren. And that they might be furnished with such men, the Knights of every Shire must make choice of two to serve as Members for that County ; most of them *Presbyterians,* some few *Royallists,* four of the *Independent* Faction, and two or three to represent the Kirk of *Scotland.* Which ploughing with an Ox and an Ass, (as it was no other) was anciently prohibited by the Law of *Moses.* And yet these men, associated with some Members of either House, as before is said, no ways impowered or authorized by the rest of the Clergy, must take upon them all the Powers and Privileges of a Convocation ; to which they were invited by an Ordinance of the Lords and Commons, bearing date *June* the 12*th.* His Majesty makes a start at this encroachment on his Royal Prerogative, and countermands the same by His Proclamation of the

In which he takes notice, amongſt other things, That the far greateſt part of thoſe who had been nominated to the preſent Service, were men of neither *Learning or Reputation, eminently diſaffected to the Government of the Church of* England, *and ſuch as had openly preached Rebellion, by their exciting of the people to take Arms againſt him ;* and therefore were not like to be proper Inſtruments of Peace and happineſs, either unto the Church or State : For maintainance whereof, and for the preſervation of His own Authority, he inhibits them from meeting at the time appointed, declares their Acts to be illegal, and threatens them with the puniſhments which they had incurred by the laws of the Land.

36. But they go forwards howſoever, hold their firſt meeting on the firſt of *July,* and elect Dr. *Twiſſe* of *Newberry,* (a rigid *Sabbatarian,* but a profeſſed *Calvinian* in all other points) for their Prolocutor) called to this *Journey work* by the Houſes ; they were diſpenſed with for Nonreſidence upon their Livings, againſt the Laws, preferred to the beſt Benefices of the Sequeſtred Clergy, (ſome of them three or four together) and had withall four ſhillings a man for their daily wages, beſides the honour of aſſiſting in ſo great an action as the ruine of the Church, and the ſubverſion of the preſent Government of the Realm of *England.* In reference whereunto, they were to be employed from time to time, as occaſion was, *to ſtir up the people of the Counties,* for which they ſerved, *to riſe and arm* themſelves againſt the King, under colour of *their own defence,* as appears plainly by the Order of the tenth of *Auguſt.* And that they might be looked upon with the greater reverence, they maintain a conſtant intercourſe, by Letters, with their Brethren of *Scotland,* the Churches of the *Netherlands,* the *French* and *Switzers ;* but chiefly with *Geneva* it ſelf. In which they laid ſuch vile Reproaches on his Majeſty and the Church of *England ;* the one for having a deſign to bring in Popery ; the other, for a readineſs to receive the ſame ; that His Majeſty was neceſſitated to ſet out a Manifeſt in the *Latin* Tongue, for laying open the Impoſture to the Churches of all Forreign Nations. Amongſt the reſt of this Aſſembly, Dr. *Dan. Featly,* not long before made Chaplain in Ordinary to the King, muſt needs ſit for one ; whether to ſhew his Parts, or to head a Party, or out of his old love to *Calviniſm,* may beſt be gathered from ſome Speeches which he made and printed. But he was theirs in heart before, and therefore might afford them his body now, though poſſibly he may be excuſed from taking the Covenant, as the others did. An *Exhortation* whereunto was the firſt great work which was performed by theſe Maſters in *Iſrael,* after their aſſembling ; the Covenant taken by them in moſt ſolemn manner at St. *Margarets* in *Weſtminſter,* on the 25th. of *September,* the *Exhortation* voted to be publiſhed on the 9th of *February.*

37. Now to begin the bleſſed Reformation which they had in hand, the Houſes were reſolved upon exterminating all external Pomp, and comely Order, out of the Worſhip of Almighty God. And to this end, upon the humble motion of theſe Divines of the Aſſembly, and the ſollicitation of ſome zealous Lecturers, who were grown very powerful with them ; or to ingratiate themſelves with the *Scottiſh* Covenan-

ters, whose help they began to stand in need of; or finally, out of the perverseness of their own cross humours, they published an Ordinance on the 28th of *August*, *For the utter demolishing, removing, and taking away all Monuments of Superstition and Idolatry.* Under which it was ordered, *That before the last of* November *then next following, all Altars and Tables of stone* (as if any such were then erected) *should be demolished in all Churches and Chapels throughout the Kingdom. That the Communion Tables should in all such places be removed from the East end of the Chancel, unto some other part of the Church or Chapel. That all such Rails as had been placed before or about the same, should be taken away, and the ground levelled with the rest, which had been raised for the standing of any such Table, within the space of twenty years then last past. That all Tapers, Candlesticks, and Basons, which had of late been used on any of the said Tables, should also be removed and taken away; neither the same, nor any such like, to be from thenceforth used in Gods Publick Service. That all Crucifixes, Crosses, and all Images and Pictures of any one or more Persons of the Trinity, or of the Virgin* Mary, *and all other Images and Pictures of Saints, should be also demolished and defaced, whether they stood in any of the said Churches or Chapels, or in any Church-yard or other open place whatsoever, never to be erected or renewed again:* With a Proviso notwithstanding, *for preserving all Images, Pictures, and Coats of Arms, belonging to any of their Ancestors, or any of the Kings of this Realm, or any other deceased persons which were not generally considered and beheld as Saints.*

38. But yet to make sure work of it, this Ordinance was re-inforced and enlarged by another of the 9th of *May*, in the year next following; wherein, besides the particulars before recited, they descend to the taking away of all Coaps, Surplices, and other Superstitious Vestments, (as they pleased to call them) as also to the taking away of all Organs, and the Cases in which they stood, and the defacing of the same; requiring the same course to be also taken in the removing and defacing of Roods, Rood-Lofts, and Holy-water-Fonts (as if any such things had been of late erected or permitted in the Church of *England*, as indeed there were not) whereupon followed the defacing of all Glass Windows, and the demolishing of all Organs within the compass of their power; the transposing of the holy Table from the place of the Altar, into some other part of the Church or Chancel; the tearing and defacing of all Coaps and Surplices, or otherwise employing them to domestick uses; and finally the breaking down and removing of the Sacred Fonts, anciently used for the Ministration of holy Baptism; the name of *Holy-water-fonts* being extended and made use of to comprise them also: hereupon followed also the defacing and demolishing of many Crosses erected as the Monuments of Christianity, in Cities, Towns, & most of our Country Villages; none being spared which came within the compass of those enemies of the Cross of Christ. Amongst which Crosses none more eminent for Cost and Workmanship, then those of *Cheapside* in *London*, and *Abington* in the County of *Berks*; both of them famous for the excellencies of the Statu's which were placed in them; more for the richness of the trimming which was used about them. But the Divine Vengeance fell on some of the Executioners, for a terror to others; one of them being killed in pulling down the Cross of *Cheapside*; and
another

another hanged at *Stow on the Wold*, within short time after he had pulled down the first Image of the Cross in *Abington*. And because no Order had been made for the executing of this Order in His Majesties Chapels (as there was in all Cathedrall and Parish Churches) a private Warrant was obtained by *Harlow*, a Knight of *Herefordshire*, for making the said Chapels equal to all the rest, by depriving them of all such Ornaments of State and Beauty with which they had been constantly adorned in all times since the Reformation. And all this done, (or at the least pretended to be done, as the Ordinance tells us) as being pleasing unto God, and visibly conducing to the blessed Reformation so much desired; but desired only, as it seems, by those Lords and Commons who had a hand in the Design.

39. So far they went to show their hatred unto Superstition, their dislike of *Popery*: but then they must do somewhat also for expressing their great zeal to the glory of God, by some Acts of Piety. And nothing seemed more pious or more popular rather to enjoin the more strict keeping of their *Lords day Sabbath*, by some publick Ordinance. With this they had begun already on the fifth of *May*, on which it was ordered by no worse men then the Commons in Parliament, (the Lords being either not consulted, or not concurring) That His Majesty's Book for *tolerating sports on the Lord's Day*, should be forthwith burned by the hands of the common Hangman, in *Cheapside* and other usual places; and that the Sheriffs of *London* and *Middlesex* should see the same put in execution; which was done accordingly. Then which, an Act of a greater scorn, an Act of greater Insolency and disloyal impudence, was never offered to a Soveraign and Anointed Prince. So as it was no marvel if the Lords joined with them in the Ordinance of the sixth of *April*, 1644, for to expose all Books to the like disgrace which had been writ, or should be writ hereafter by any person or persons, against the Morality of the Sabbath: By which Ordinance it was also signified, *That no manner of person whatsoever, should publickly cry, shew forth, and expose to sale any Wares, Merchandises, Fruits, Herbs, or other Goods, upon that day, on pain of forfeiting the same; or travel, carry burthens, or do any act of labour on it, on pain of forfeiting Ten shillings for the said offence. That no person from thenceforth on the said day should use, exercise, keep, maintain, or be present at any wrestling, shooting, bowling, ringing of Bells for pleasure or pastime, Mask, Wake, (otherwise called Feasts) Church-Ale, Games, Dancing, Sport, or other pastimes whatsoever, under the several penalties therein contained.* And that we may perceive with what weighty cares the heads of these good men were troubled, when the whole Nation was involved in Blood and Ruine; a Clause was added for the taking down of *May poles* also; with a Command unto all Constables and Tythingmen, to see it done, under the penalty of forfeiting five shillings weekly, till the said *May-poles* (which they looked upon as an *Heathenish Vanity*) should be quite removed. Which Nail was driven so far at last, that it was made unlawful for any Taylor to carry home a new Suit of Clothes, or any Barber to trim the man that was to wear them; for any Water-man to Ferry a passenger cross the *Thames*; and finally, to any person whatsoever (though neither new trimmed, or new apparelled) to sit at his own door, or to walk the streets, or

take

take a mouthful of fresh air in the open Fields. Most Rabinical Dotages!

40. The day of publick Worship being thus new-molded, they must have new Priests also, and new Forms of Prayer, a new Confession of the Faith, new Catechisms, and new Forms of Government. Towards the first, an Ordinance comes out from the Lords and Commons in *October* following, (Advice being first had with the Assembly of Divines) by which a power was given to some chief men of the Assembly, and certain Ministers of *London*, or to any seven or more of them, to impose hands upon such persons whatsoever whom they found qualified and gifted for the holy Ministry ; a Clause being added thereunto, That every person and persons which were so ordained, should be reputed, deemed, and taken for a Minister of the Church of *England*, sufficiently authorised for any Office or Employment in it, and capable of receiving all advantages which appertained to the same. To shew the nullity and invalidity of which *Ordinations*, a learned Tractate was set out by Dr. *Bohe*, Chaplain sometimes to the Right Reverend Dr. *Houson*, Bishop of *Oxford* first, and of *Durham* afterwards. Never since answered by the *Presbyterians*, either *Scots*, or *English*. Next after, comes the *Directory*, or new Form of Worship, accompanied with an Ordinance of the Lords and Commons on the third of *January*, for authorising the said *Directory* or Form of Worship ; as also, for suppressing the publick Liturgy, repealing all the Acts of Parliament which confirmed the same, and abrogating all the ancient and established Festivals, that so *Saint Sabbath* (as sometimes they called it) might be all in all. The insufficiency of which *Directory* to the Ends proposed in the same, pronounced the weakness of the Ordinance which authorised it, and the excellency of the publick Liturgy in all the parts and offices of it, was no less learnedly evinced by D. *Hamond*, then newly made a Chaplain in Ordinary to his Sacred Majesty. Which though it might have satisfied all equal and unbyassed men, yet neither Learning nor Reason could be heard in the new Assembly ; or if it were, the voice thereof was drowned by the noise of the Ordinances.

41. For on the 23d of *Aug. An.*1945, another Ordinance comes thundering from the Lords and Commons, for the more effectual Execution of the Directory for publick Worship ; with several Clauses in the same, not only for dispersing and use thereof, but for calling in the Book of Common Prayer, under several penalties. Which coming to his Majesties knowledge, as soon as he returned to his Winter Quarters, he published his Proclamation of the 13th of *Nov.* commanding in the same the use of the Common Prayer, notwithstanding any Ordinance to the contrary from the Houses of Parliament. ' For taking notice, first, of those ' notable Benefits which had for eighty years redounded to this Nation ' by the use of the Liturgy ; He next observes, that by abolishing the said ' Book of Common Prayer, and imposing the Directory, a way would ' be left open for all Ignorant, Factious and Evil men, to broach their ' Fancies and Conceits, be they never so erroneous, to mislead people ' into Sin and Rebellion against the King, to raise Factions and Divi- ' sions in the Church ; and finally, to utter those things for their Pray- ' ers in the Congregation, to which no Conscientious can say *Amen*. And ' thereupon he gives Commandment to all Ministers in their Parish Chur- ' ches, to keep & use the said Book of Common Prayer, in all the Acts &

Offices

' Offices of Gods Publick Worship, according to the Laws made in that
' behalf ; and that the said *Directory* should in no sort be admitted, re-
' ceived, or used ; the said pretended Ordinances, or any thing contain-
' ed in them to the contrary notwithstanding.   But His Majesty sped no
better by His Proclamation, than the two Doctors did before by their
Learned Arguments.   For if He had found little or no obedience to his
Proclamations when he was strong, and in the head of a victorious and
succesful Army, He was not to expect it in a low condition, when his
Affairs were ruinated and reduced to nothing.

42. For so it was, that the *Scots* having raised an Army of Eighteen
thousand Foot, and Three thousand Horse, taking the Dragoons into
the reckoning, break into *England* in the depth of Winter, *Anno* 1643,
and marched almost as far as the Banks of the River *Tine*, without opposition.   There they received a stop by the coming of the Marquess of
Newcastle, with his Northern Army, and entertained the time with some
petit skirmishes, till the sad news of the surprise of *Selby* by Sir *Thomas
Fairfax*, compelled him to return towards *York* with all his Forces, for
the preserving of that place on which the safety of the North did depend especially.   The *Scots* march after him amain, and besiege that
City, in which they were assisted by the Forces of the Lord *Fairfax*,
and the Earl of *Manchester*, who by the Houses were commanded to attend that Service.   The issue whereof was briefly this ; that having worsted the great Army of Prince *Rupert* at *Marston Moor*, on the second of
July, *York* yielded on Composition upon that day fortnight ; the Marquess of *Newcastle*, with many Gentlemen of great Note and Quality,
shipt themselves for *France* ; and the strong Town of *Newcastle* took in
by the *Scots* on the 19th of *October* then next following.   More fortunate
was His Majesty with His *Southern* Army, though at the first he was necessitated to retire from *Oxon* at such time as the Forces under *Essex* and
Waller did appear before it.   The news whereof being brought unto
them, it was agreed that *Waller* should pursue the King, and that the
Earls Army should march Westward to reduce those Countreys.   And
here the *Mystery* of *Iniquity* began to show it self in its proper colours.
For whereas they pretended to have raised their Army for no other end,
but only to remove the King from his *Evil Councellors*, those *Evil Councellors*, as they call them, were left at *Oxon*, and the King only hun-
ted by his insolent Enemies.   But the King having totally broken *Waller* in the end of *June*, marched after *Essex* into *Devonshire*, and having
shut him up in *Cornwall*, where he had neither room for forrage, nor
hope of succours, he forced him to flye ingloriously in a Skiff or Cock-
boat, and leave his Army in a manner to the Conquerors Mercy.   But
his Horse having the good fortune to save themselves, the King gave
quarter to the Foot, reserving to Himself their Cannons, Arms, and
Ammunition, as a sign of His Victory.   And here again the War
might possibly have been ended, if the King had followed his good fortune, and marcht to *London* before the Earl of *Essex* had united his scattered Forces, and *Manchester* was returned from the Northern Service.
But setting down before *Plymouth* now, as he did before *Gloucester* the
last year, he lost the opportunity of effecting his purpose, and was fought
withal at *Newberry*, in his coming back, where neither side could boast
of obtaining the Victory.

43. But

43. But howſoever, having gained ſome reputation by his Weſtern Action, the Houſes ſeem incinable to accept His offer of entring into Treaty with Him for an Accommodation. This He had offered by His Majeſty from *Eveſham* on the 4*th* of *July*, immediately after the defeat of *Waller*; and preſſed it by another from *Taveſtock* on the 8*th* of *September*, as ſoon as he had broken the great Army of the Earl of *Eſſex* To theſe they hearkned not at firſt. But being ſenſible of the outcries of the common people, they condeſcend at laſt, appointing *Uxbridge* for the place, and the 30*th* day of *January* for the time thereof. For a preparative whereunto, and to ſatisfie the importunity and expectation of their Brethren of *Scotland*, they attaint the Archbiſhop of High Treaſon, in the Houſe of Commons, and paſs their Bill by Ordinance in the Houſe of Peers, in which no more then ſeven Lords did concur to the Sentence; but being ſentenced howſoever by the malice of the *Presbyterians* both *Scots* and *Engliſh*, he was brought to act the laſt part of his Tragedy on the 10*th* of *January*, as ſhall be told at large in another place. This could preſage no good ſucceſs to the following Treaty. For though Covenants ſometimes may be writ in blood; yet I find no ſuch way for commencing Treaties. And to ſay truth, the Kings Commiſſioners ſoon found what they were to truſt to. For having condeſcended to accompany the Commiſſioners from the Houſes of Parliament, and to be preſent at a Sermon preached by one of their Chaplains, on the 1*ſt* day of the meeting they found what little hopes they had of a good concluſion. The Preachers Name was *Love*, a *Welſh man*, and one of the moſt fiery *Presbyters* in all the Pack: In whoſe Sermon *there were many paſſages very ſcandalous to His Majeſties Perſon, and derogatory to his Honour ; ſtirring up the people againſt the Treaty, and incenſing them againſt the Kings Commiſſioners ; telling them, That they came with hearts full of Blood ; and that there was as great a diſtance betwixt the Treaty and Peace, as there was between Heaven and Hell.* Of this the *Oxon* Lords complained, but could obtain no reparation for the King or themſelves; though afterwards *Cromwell* paid the debt, and brought him to the Scaffold when he leaſt looked for it.

44. But notwithſtanding theſe preſages of no good ſucceſs, the Kings Commiſſioners begin the long wiſht for Treaty, which is reduced to theſe three Heads, *viz.* Concernments of the Church, The Power of the Militia and the War of *Ireland*. In reference to the firſt (for of the other two I ſhall take no notice) His Majeſty was pleaſed to condeſcend to theſe particulars: that is to ſay, 1. *That freedom be left to all perſons whatſoever in matters of Ceremony ; and that all the penalties of the Laws and Canons which enjoin thoſe Ceremonies be ſuſpended.* 2. *That the Biſhops ſhould exerciſe no act of Juriſdiction or Ordination, without the conſent and counſel of the Presbyters, who ſhall be choſen by the Clergy of each Dioceſs, out of the Graveſt and moſt Learned men amongſt themſelves.* 3. *That the Biſhop ſhall be conſtantly reſident in his Dioceſs, except he be required to attend His Majeſty ; and ſhall preach every Sunday in ſome Church or other, within the Dioceſs, if he be not hindered either by old age or ſickneſs.* 4. *That Ordination ſhall be publick, and in ſolemn manner ; and none to be admitted into Holy Orders, but ſuch as are well qualified and approved of by the Rural Presbyters.* 5. *That an improvement be made of all ſuch*

Vicaridges as belonged to Biſhops, Deans, and Chapters ; the ſaid improvement to be made out of Impropriations, and confirmed by Parliament. 6. That from thenceforth no man ſhould hold two Churches with Cure of Souls. And 7. That one hundred thouſand pound ſhould be forthwith raiſed out of the Lands belonging to the Biſhops and Cathedral Churches, towards the ſatisfaction of the Publick Debts. An Offer was alſo made, for regulating the Juriſdiction of Eccleſiaſtical Courts, in Cauſes Teſtamentary, Decimal, and Matrimonial ; for rectifying ſome Abuſes in the exerciſe of Excommunication ; for moderating the exceſſive Fees of the Biſhops Officers, and ordering their Viſitations to the beſt advantage of the Church ; and all this to be done by conſent of Parliament.

45. His Majeſty alſo offered them the Militia for the ſpace of three years ; which might afford them time enough to ſettle the Affairs of the Kingdom, had they been ſo pleaſed ; and to aſſociate the Houſes with Him in the War of *Ireland* ; but ſo, as not to be excluded from His Care of that People. But theſe Propoſals did not ſatisfie the *Puritan Engliſh*, much leſs the *Presbyterian Scots*, who were joined in that Treaty. They were reſolved upon the abolition of *Epiſcopacy*, both Root and Branch ; of having the Militia for Seven years abſolutely, and and afterwards to be diſpoſed of as the King and the Houſes could agree : and finally, of exerciſing ſuch an unlimited power in the War of *Ireland*, that the King ſhould neither be able to grant a Ceſſation, or to make a Peace, or to ſhow mercy unto any of that people on their due ſubmiſſion. And from the rigour of theſe terms, they were not to be drawn by the Kings Commiſſioners ; which rendred the whole Treaty fruitleſs, and fruſtrated the expectation of all Loyal Subjects, who languiſhed under the calamity of this woful War. For as the Treaty cooled, ſo the War grew hotter, managed for the moſt part by the ſame Hands, but by different Heads : Concerning which, we are to know, That not long after the beginning of this everlaſting Parliament, the *Puritan* Faction became ſub-divided into *Presbyterians* and *Independents*. And at the firſt, the *Presbyterians* carried all before them both in Camp and Council. But growing jealous at the laſt of the Earl of *Eſſex*, whoſe late miſcarriage in the Weſt was looked on as a Plot to betray his Army : they ſuffered him to be wormed out of his Commiſſion, and gave the chief Command of all to Sir *Thomas Fairfax*; with whoſe good Services and Affections they were well acquainted. To him they joined Lieutenant General *Oliver Cromwell*, who from a private Captain had obtained to be Lieutenant to the Earl of *Mancheſter* in the aſſociated Counties, as they commonly called them : and having done good Service in the Battel of *Marſton-Moor*, was thought the fitteſt man to conduct their Forces. And on the other ſide, the Earl of *Brentford* (but better known by the Name of General *Ruthuen*) who had commanded the Kings Army ſince the Fight at *Edg-hill*, was outed of his place by a Court Contrivement, and that Command conferred upon Prince *Rupert*, the Kings Siſters Son, not long before made Duke of *Cumberland*, and Earl of *Holderneſs*.

46. By theſe new Generals, the Fortune of the War, and conſequently the Fate of the Kingdom which depended on it, came to be decided. And at the firſt, the King ſeemed to have much the better by the taking

of

of *Leicester* though afterwards it turned to his disadvantage : For many of the Soldiers being loaded with the Spoil of the place, withdrew themselves for the disposing of their Booty, and came not back unto the Army till it was too late. News also came, that *Fairfax* with his Army had laid siege to *Oxon*, which moved the King to return back as far as *Daventry*, there to expect the re-assembling of his scattered Companies. Which happening as *Fairfax* had desired, he marcht hastily after him, with an intent to give him battel on the first opportunity: In which he was confirmed by two great Advantages ; first, by the seasonable coming of *Cromwell* with a fresh Body of Horse, which reach'd him not untill the Evening before the fight : and secondly, by the intercepting of some Letters sent from General *Goring*, in which His Majesty was advised to decline all occasion of Battel, till he could come up to him with his Western Forces. This hastened the Design of fighting in the adverse Party, who fall upon the Kings Army in the Fields near *Naisby*, (till that time an obscure Village) in *Northamptonshire* : on *Saturday* the 19th of *June*, the Battels joined, and at first His Majesty had the better of it, and might have had so at the last, if Prince *Rupert* having routed one Wing of the Enemies Horse, had not been so intent upon the chase of the Flying Enemy, that he left his Foot open to the other Wing. Who pressing hotly on them, put them to an absolute Rout, and made themselves Masters of his Camp, Carriage, and Canon: and amongst other things of his Majesties Cabinet : In which they found many of his Letters, most of them written to the Queen, which afterwards were published by command of the Houses, to their great dishonour. For whereas the *Athenians* on the like success had intercepted the Packet of Letters from *Philip* King of *Macedon*, their most bitter enemy, unto several Friends, they met with one amongst the rest to the Queen *Olympias* ; the rest being all broke open before the Council, that they might be advertised of the enemies purposes, the Letter to the Queen was returned untouched ; the whole Senate thinking it a shameful and dishonest act to pry into the Conjugal Secrets betwixt Man and Wife. A Modesty in which those of *Athens* stand as much commended by *Hilladius Bisantinus*, an ancient Writer, as the chief Leading men of the Houses of Parliament, are like to stand condemned for want of it, in succeeding Stories.

47. But to proceed, this miserable blow was followed by the surrendry of *Bristol*, the storming of *Bridgwater*, the surprise of *Hereford*, and at the end of *Winter*, with the loss of *Chester*. During which time the King moved up and down with a Running Army, but with such ill Fortune as most commonly attends a declining side. In which distress he comes to his old Winter-Quarters, not out of hope of bringing his Affairs to a better condition before the opening of the Spring. From *Oxon* he sends divers Messages to the Houses of Parliament, desiring that He might be suffered to return to *Westminster*, and offering for their security the whole Power of the Kingdom, the Navy, Castles, Forts, and Armies, to be enjoyed by them in such manner, and not for so long time as they had formerly desired. But finding nothing from them but neglect and scorn, His Messages despised, and His Person vilified, He made an offer of Himself to *Fairfax*, who refused also. Tired with re-

pulse upon repulse, and having lost the small remainder of His Forces near *Stow on the Wold* ; He puts himself in the beginning of *May*, into the hands of the *Scots* Commissioners, residing then at *Southwell* in the County of *Nottingham*, a Mannor House belonging to the See of *York*. For the *Scots* having mastered the Northern parts in the year 1644, spent the next year in harrasing the Countrey, even as far as *Hereford* ; which they besieged for a time, and perhaps had carried it, if they had not been called back by the Letters of some special Friends, to take care of *Scotland*, then almost reduced to the Kings obedience, by the Noble Marquess of *Montross*. On which Advertisement they depart from *Hereford*, face *Worcester*, and so marcht Northward : From whence they presently dispatch Col. *David Leslhy* with 6000 Horse, and with their Foot employed themselves in the Siege of *Newark* ; which brought down their Commissioners to *Southwell*, before remembred. From thence the King is hurried in post haste to the Town of *Newcastle*, which they looked on as their strongest Hold. And being now desirous to make even with their Masters, to receive the wages of their iniquity, and being desirous to get home in safety with that Spoil and Plunder, which they had gotten in their marching and re-marching betwixt *Tweed* and *Hereford*, they prest the King to fling up all the Towns and Castles which remained in His Power, or else they durst not promise to continue Him under their Protection.

48. This Turn seemed strange unto the King. Who had not put Himself into the Power of the *Scots*, had he not been assured before hand by the *French* Embassador, of more courteous usage ; to whom the *Scots* Commissioners had engaged themselves, not only to receive His Person, but all those also which repaired unto Him into their protection, as the King signified by His Letters to the Marquess of *Ormond*. But having got Him into their Power, they forget those Promises, and bring Him under the necessity of writing to the Marquesses of *Montross* and *Ormond* to discharge their Souldiers, and to His Governours of Towns in *England*, to give up their Garrisons. Amongst which, *Oxford* the then Regal City, was the most considerable, surrendred to Sir *Thomas Fairfax* upon *Midsommer day*. And by the Articles of that Surrendry, the Duke of *York* was put into the Power of the Houses of Parliament ; together with the Great Seal, the Signet, and the Privy-Seal, all which were most despitefully broken in the House of Peers, as formerly the *Dutch* had broke the Seals of the King of *Spain*, when they had cast off all Fidelity and Allegiance to him, and put themselves into the Form of a Commonwealth. But then to make him some amends, they give him some faint hopes of suffering him to bestow a visit on his Realm of *Scotland* (his *ancient and native Kingdom*, as he commonly called it) there to expect the bettering of his Condition in the changes of time. But the *Scots* hearing of his purpose, and having long ago cast off the yoke of subjection, voted against his coming, in a full Assembly ; so that we may affirm of him, as the Scripture doth of our Saviour Christ, viz. *He came unto his own, and his own received him not*, John c. 1.2. The like resolution was taken also by the Commissioners of that Nation, and the chief Leaders of their Army, who had contracted with the two Houses of Parliament, and for the sum of two

hundred

ʰundred thouſand pound, in ready mony, ſold and betrayed him into ᵗhe hands of his Enemies, as certainly they would have done the Lord Chriſt himſelf for half the mony, if he had *bowed down the Heavens, and came down to viſit them*. Being delivered over unto ſuch Commiſſioners as were ſent by the Houſes to receive him, he was by them conducted on the third of *Feb.* to his Houſe of *Holdenby*, not far from the good Town of *Northampton*, where he was kept ſo cloſe, that none of his Domeſtick Servants, no not ſo much as his own Chaplains were ſuffered to have any acceſs unto him. And there we leave him for the preſent ; but long he ſhall not be permitted to continue there, as ſhall be ſhewn hereafter in due place and time.

49. Such being the iſſue of the War, let us next look upon the *Presbyterians* in the acts of Peace ; in which they threatned more deſtruction to the Church, then the War it ſelf. As ſoon as they had ſetled the ſtrict keeping of the Lords day Sabbath, ſuppreſſed the puplick Liturgy, and impoſed the Directory, they gave command to their Divines of the Aſſembly, to ſet themſelves upon the making a new Confeſsion, The Nine and thirty Articles of the Church of *England*, were either thought to have too much of the ancient Fathers, or too little of *Calvin*, and therefore fit to be reviewed, or elſe laid aſide. And at the firſt their Journey men began with a Review, and fitted Fourteen of the Articles to their own conceptions ; but in the end, deſpairing of the like ſucceſs in all the reſt, they gave over that impertinent labour, and found it a more eaſie task to conceive a *new*, then to accommodate the old Confeſsion to their private Fancies. And in this new Confeſſion, they eſtabliſh the Morality of their Lords day Sabbath, declare the Pope to be the *Antichriſt, the Son of Perdition, and the Man of Sin*. And therein alſo interweave the *Calvinian* Rigours, in reference to the abſolute Decree of Predeſtination, Grace, Free will, *&c.* But knowing that they ſerved ſuch Maſters as were reſolved to part with no one Branch of their own Authority, they attribute a Power to the Civil Magiſtrate, not only of calling Synods and Church-Aſſemblies, but alſo of being preſent at them, and to provide that whatſoever is therein contracted, be done agreeably to the Mind and Will of God. But as to the matter of Church-Government, the Divine Right of their Presbyteries, the ſetting of Chriſt upon the Throne, the Parity or Imparity of Miniſters in the Church of Chriſt, not a word delivered. Their mighty Maſters were not then reſolved upon thoſe particulars ; and it was fit the Holy Ghoſt ſhould ſtay their leiſure, and not inſpire their Journey men with any other Inſtruction then what was ſent them from the Houſes.

50. But this Confeſſion, though imperfect, and performed by halves was offered in the way of an *Humble Advice to the Lords and Commons* ; that by the omnipotency of an Ordinance it might paſs for currant, and be received for the eſtabliſhed Doctrine of the Church of *England.* The like was done alſo in the tendry of their *Larger Catechiſm*, which ſeems to be nothing in a manner but the ſetting out of their *Confeſſion* in another dreſs, and putting it into the form of Queſtions and Anſwers, that ſo it might appear to be ſomewhat elſe then indeed it was. But being ſomewhat of the largeſt to be taught in Schools, and ſomewhat of the hardeſt to be learned by Children, it was brought afterwards in-

to an Epitome, commonly called *The leſſer Cetechiſme*, and by the Authors recommended to the uſe of the Church, as far more Orthodox then *Nowel*'s, more clear then that contained in the Common Prayer Book, and not inferior to the *Palatine* or *Grnevian* Forms. But in all three, they held forth ſuch a Doctrine touching Gods Decrees, that they gave occaſion of receiving the old *Blaſtian* Hereſie, in making God to be the *Author of Sin*. Which Doctrine being new publiſhed in a Pamphlet, entituled, *Comfort for Believers in their Sins and Troubles*, gave ſuch a hot Alarm to all the *Calviniſts* in the new Aſſembly, that they procured it to be burnt by the hands of the Hangman. But firſt they thought it neceſſary to prepare the way to that execution, by publiſhing in print their *deteſtation of that abominable and blaſphemous Opinion, That God hath a hand in, and is the Author of the ſinfulneſs of his people*, as the Title tells us. So that now *Calvins* Followers may ſleep ſupinely without regard to the reproaches of uncivil men, who had upbraided them with maintaining ſuch blaſphemous Doctrine. The Reverend Divines of the Aſſembly have abſolved them from it, and ſhowed their *Deteſtation* of it; and who dares charge it on them for the time to come?

51. But theſe things poſſibly were acted as they were *Calvinians*, and perhaps *Sabbatarians* alſo, and no more then ſo. And therefore we muſt next ſee what they do on the ſcore of *Presbytery*, for ſetting up whereof, they had took the Covenant, called in the *Scots*, and more inſiſted on the abolition of the Epiſcopal Function, then any other of the Propoſitions which more concern them. To this they made their way in thoſe Demands which they ſent to *Oxon*, the Ordinance for Ordination of Miniſters, and their advancing of the Directory in the fall of the Liturgy. They had alſo voted down the Calling of Biſhops, in the Houſe of Commons, on *Sept.* 8. 1642, and cauſed the paſſing of that Vote to be ſolemnized with Bells and Bonfires in the ſtreets of *London*, as if the whole City was as much concerned in it, as ſome Factious Citizens. But knowing that little was to be effected by the Propoſitions, and much leſs by their Votes, they put them both into a Bill, which paſt the Houſe of Peers on the third of *February*, ſome two days after they had tendred their Propoſals to the King at *Oxon*. And by that Bill it was deſired to be Enacted, That from the Fifth of *November*, (the day deſigned for the blowing up the Parliament by the Gun-powder Traytors) which ſhould be in the year of our Lord 1643, there ſhould be *no Archbiſhops, Biſhops, Commiſſaries. &c.* (with all their Train recited in the *Oxon* Article, Numb. 21.) *in the Church of* England : *That from thenceforth the Name, Title, and Function of Archbiſhops, Biſhops, Chancellors, &c. or likewiſe the having, uſing, or exerciſing any Juriſdiction Office, and Auth rity, by reaſon or colour of any ſuch Name, Dignity, or Function, in the Realm of* England, *ſhould utterly and for ever ceaſe.* And that the King might yield the ſooner to the Alteration, they tempt him to it with a Clauſe therein contained, for putting him into the actual poſſeſſion of all the Caſtles, Mannors, Lands, Tenements, and Hereditaments, belonging to the ſaid Archbiſhops, or Biſhops, or to any of them. And for the Lands of Deans and Chapters, the Brethren had a hope to parcel them amongſt themſelves, under the colour of encouraging and maintaining of a Preaching Miniſtry ; ſome ſorry pittance being allowed to the old Pro-

prietaries, and ſome ſhort Penſion during life to the ſeveral Biſhops.

52. Such was the tenour of the Bill ; which found no better entertainment then their Propoſitions. So that deſpairing of obtaining the Kings conſent to advance Presbytery, they reſolved to do it of themſelves, but not till they had broken the Kings Forces at the Battel of *Naisby*. For on the 19th of *Auguſt* then next following, they publiſh ' *Directions* in the name of the Lords and Commons, (after advice with ' their Divines of the Aſſembly) for the chuſing of *Ruling-Elders* in all ' Congregations, and in the Claſſical Aſſemblies, for the Cities of *London* and *Weſtminſter*, and the ſeveral Counties of the Kingdom, in or- ' der to the ſpeedy ſetling of Presbyterial Government. Amongſt ' which no ſmall care was taken for making twelve Claſſes of the Mi- ' niſters of *London* only ; and after, for dividing each particular Coun- ' ty into ſeveral *Claſſes*, with reference to the largeneſs and extent there- ' of. Which Orders and Directions were after ſeconded by the Ordi- nance of *October* the 20th ; containing certain Rules for the ſuſpenſi- on of ſcandalous and ignorant perſons from the holy Supper, and giving power to certain perſons therein named, to ſit as Judges and Tryers, as well concerning the Election, as the Integrity and Ability of all ſuch men as are elected *Elders* within any of the Twelve *Claſſes* of the Pro- vince of *London*. It is not to be thought, but that the *London Elder- ſhips* made ſufficient haſte to put themſelves into the actual poſſeſſion of their new Authority. But in the Country, moſt men were ſo cold and backward, that the Lower Houſe was fain to quicken them with ſome freſh *Reſolves* ; by which it was required on the 20th of *Feb. That choice be forthwith made of Elders, throughout the Kingdom, according to ſuch former Directions as had paſt both Houſes : and that all Claſſes and Parochial Congregations, ſhould be thereby authoriſed effectually to proceed therein.* And that the Church might be ſupplied with able Miniſters in all times ſuc- ceeding, the Power of Ordination, formerly reſtrained to certain per- ſons reſiding in and about the City of *London*, (according to the Ordi- nance of the 2d of *Octob* 1644.)is now communicated to the Miniſters of each ſeveral *Claſſes*, as men moſt like to know the wants of the Pariſh- Churches under their Authority.

53. But here it is to be obſerved, that in the ſetling of the Presbyte- rian Government in the Realm of *Eugland*, as the Presbyteries were to be ſubordinate to the Claſſical, Provincial, and National Aſſemblies of the Church, ſo were they all to be ſubordinate to the Power of the Parliament, as appears plainly by the Ordinance of the 14th of *March*, which makes it quite another thing from the *Scottiſh Presbyteries*, and other Aſſemblies of that Kirk, which held themſelves to be ſupream, and unaccountable in their actings, without reſpect unto the King, the Parliament, and the Courts of Juſtice. But the truth is, that as the *Engliſh* generally were not willing to receive that yoak : ſo neither did the Houſes really intend to impoſe it on them, though for a while to hold fair quarter with the *Scots*, they ſeemed forward in it. And this appears ſufficiently by a Declaration of the Houſe of Commons, publiſhed on the ſeventeenth of *April* 1646, in which they ſignifie, That they were not able to conſent *to the granting of an Arbitrary and unlimited Power*

and

and Jurisdiction to near Ten thousand Judicatories to be erected in the King-dom, which could not be consistent with the Fundamental Laws and Government of it, and which by necessary consequence did exclude the Parliament from ha-ving any thing to do in that Jurisdiction. On such a doubtful bottom did Presbytery stand, till the King had put himself into the Power of the *Scots,* and that the *Scots* had posted him in all haste to the Town of *Newcastle.* Which caused the Lords and Commons no less hastily to speed their Ordinance of the fifth of *June, For the present setling of the Presbyterial Government, without further delay,* as in the Title is exprest. And though it was declared in the end of that Ordinance, That it was to be in force for three years only, except the Houses should think fit to continue it longer ; yet were the *London* Ministers so intent upon them, that they resolve to live no longer in suspence, but to proceed couragiously in the execution of those several Powers which both by Votes and Ordinances were intrusted to them. And to make known to all the World what they meant to do, they published a Paper with this Title, that is to say, *Certain Considerations and Cautions agreed upon by the Ministers of* London *and* Westminster, *and within the* Lines *of* Communication, *June the 19th 1646. According to which they resolve to put the Presbyterial Government into execution, upon the Ordinances of Parliament be-fore published.*

54. In which conjuncture it was thought expedient by the Houses of Parliament, to send Commissioners to *Newcastle,* and by them to pre-sent such *Propositions* to his Sacred Majesty, as they conceived to be a-greeable to his present condition. In the second of which it was desi-red, *That according to the laudable Example of his Royal Father, of happy me-mory, he would be pleased to swear and sign the Solemn League and Covenant, and cause it to be taken by Acts of Parliament in all his Kingdoms and Estates.* And in the third it was proposed, That a Bill should pass for the utter abolishing and taking away of Archbishops, Bishops, Chancellors, Commissaries, Deans, *&c.* as they occur before in the *Oxon* Articles, Num. 21. That the Assembly of Divines, and Reformation of Religion, according to the said Covenant, should be forthwith setled and con-firmed by Act of Parliament ; and that such unity and uniformity be-tween the Churches of both Kingdoms, should in like manner be con-firmed by Act of Parliament, as by the said Covenant was required, after Advice first had with the Divines of the said Assembly. It was required also in the said Propositions, That he should utterly divest him-self of all power to protect his people, by putting the Militia into the hands of the Houses ; and that he should betray the greatest part of the Lords and Gentry which had adhered unto him in the course of the War, to a certain ruine ; some of which were to be excluded from all hope of Pardon, as to the saving of their Lives ; others to forfeit their Estates, and to lose their Liberties ; the Clergy to remain under seque-stration ; the Lawyers of both sorts to be disabled from the use of their Callings. Demands of such unreasonable and horrid nature, as would have rendred him inglorious and contemptible both at home and abroad, if they had been granted.

55. These Propositions were presented to him on the eleventh day of *July,* at *Newcastle,* by the Earls of *Pembroke* and *Suffolk,* of the House

of

of Peers; *Erle*, *Hipifly*, *Robinfon*, and *Goodwin*, from the Houfe of Commons: Of whom his Majefty demanded, whether they came impowered to treat with him or not? And when they anfwered, *That they had
no Authority fo to do*: He prefently replied, That then the Houfes might
as well *have fent their Propofitions by an honeft Trumpeter*, and fo parted
with them for the prefent.   His Majefty had fpent the greateft part of
his time fince he came to *Newcaftle*, in managing a difpute about
Church Government with Mr. *Alexander Henderfon*, the moft confiderable Champion for *Presbytery* in the Kirk of *Scotland*.   *Henderfon* was
poffeft of all advantages of Books and Helps, which might enable him
to carry on fuch a Difputation.   But His Majefty had the better caufe,
and the ftronger Arguments.   Furnifhed with which, (though deftitute
of all other Helps then what he had within himfelf) he preft his Adverfary fo hard, and gave fuch fatisfactory Anfwers unto all his Cavils,
that he remained Mafter of the Field, as may fufficiently appear by the
Printed Papers. And it was credibly reported, that *Henderfon* was fo confounded with grief and fhame, that he fell into a defperate ficknefs,
which in fine brought him to his Grave; profeffing, as fome fay, that
he dyed a Convert; and frequently extolling thofe great Abilities which
when it was too late, he had found in his Majefty.   Of the particular
paffages of this Difputation, the *Englifh* Commiffioners had received
a full Information; and therefore purpofely declined all difcourfe with
his Majefty, by which the merit of their Propofitions might be called in
queftion. All that they did, was to infift upon the craving of a pofitive
Anfwer, that fo they might return unto thofe that fent them; and fuch
an anfwer they fhall have, as will little pleafe them.

56. For though his Fortunes were brought fo low, that it was not
thought fafe for him to deny them any thing; yet he demurred upon the
granting of fuch points as neither in Honour nor in Confcience could be
yeilded to them. Amongft which, thofe Demands which concerned Religion, and the abolifhing of the ancient Government of the Church by
Archbifhops and Bifhops, may very juftly be fuppofed to be none of the
leaft.   But this delay being taken by the Houfes for a plain denial, and
wanting mony to corrupt the unfaithful *Scots*, who could not otherwife
be tempted to betray their Soveraign; they paft an Ordinance for abolifhing the Epifcopal Government, and fetling their Lands upon Truftees
for the ufe of the State.   Which Ordinance being paft on the ninth of
October, was to this effect; that is to fay, *That for the better raifings of
moneys for the juft and neceffary Debts of the Kingdom, in which the fame hath
been drawn by a War mainly promoted in favour of Archbifhops and Bifhops,
and other their Adherents and Dependents; it was ordained by the Authority
of the Lords and Commons, That the Name, Title, Stile and Dignity of Archbifhop of* Canterbury, *Archbifhop of* York, *Bifhop of* Winchefter, *and Bifhop of* Durham, *and all other Bifhops or Bifhopricks within the Kingdom,
fhould from and after the fifth of* September, 1646, *then laft paft, be wholly abolifhed or taken away; and that all perfons fhould from thenceforth be
difabled to hold that Place, Function, or Stile, within the Kingdom of*
England *and Dominion of* Wales, *or the Town of* Berwick, *or exercife
any Jurifdiction or Authority thereunto formerly belonging, by vertue of
any Letters Patents from the Crown, or any other Authority whatfoever: any*
Law

Law or Statute to the contrary notwithstanding. As for their Lands they were not to be vested now in the Kings possession, as had been formerly intended ; but to be put into the power of some Trustees which are therein named, to be disposed of to such uses, intents and purposes; as the two Houses should appoint.

57. Amongst which uses, none appeared so visible, even to vulgar eyes, as the raising of huge Sums of mony to content the *Scots*, who from a *Remedy* were looked on as the *Sickness* of the Commonwealth. The *Scots* Demands amounted to Five hundred thousand pounds of *English* mony, which they offered to make good on a just account ; but were content for quietness sake to take Two hundred thousand pounds in full satisfaction. And yet they could not have that neither, unless they would betray the King to the power of his Enemies. At first they stood on terms of Honour ; and the Lord Chancellor *Lowdon* ranted to some tune (as may be seen in divers of his Printed Speeches) concerning the indelible Character of Disgrace and Infamy which must be for ever imprinted on them, if they yielded to it. But in the end, the *Presbyterians* on both sides did so play their parts, that the sinful Contract was concluded, by which the King was to be put into the hands of such Commissioners as the two Houses should appoint to receive his Person. The *Scots* to have One hundred thousand pounds in ready mony, and the *Publick Faith* (which the Houses very prodigally pawned upon all occasions) to secure the other. According unto which Agreement his Majesty is sold by his own Subjects, and betrayed by his Servants ; by so much wiser (as they thought) then the Traytor *Judas*, by how much they had made a better Market, and raised the price of the Commodity which they were to sell. And being thus sold, he is delivered for the use of those that bought him, into the custody of the Earl of *Pembroke*, (who must be one in all their Errands) the Earl of *Denbigh*, and the Lord *Mountague* of *Boughton*, with twice as many Members of the Lower House; with whom he takes his Journey towards *Holdenby*, before remembered, on the *3d* of *Feb.* And there so closely watcht and guarded, that none of his own Servants are permitted to repair unto him. *Marshall* and *Caril*, two great sticklers in behalf of Presbytery, (but such as after warped to the *Independents*) are by the Houses nominated to attend as Chaplains. But he refused to hear them in their Prayers or Preachings, unless they would officiate by the publick Liturgy, and bind themselves unto the Rules of the Church of *England.* Which not being able to obtain, he moves the Houses by his Message of the *17th* of that month, to have two Chaplains of his own. Which most unchristianly and most barbarously they denied to grant him.

58. Having reduced him to this streight, they press him once again with their Propositions; which being the very same which was sent to *Newcastle*, could not in probability receive any other Answer. This made them keep a harder hand upon him then they did before ; presuming, that they might be able to extort those Concessions from him by the severity and solitude of his restraint, when their Perswasions were too weak, and their Arguments not strong enough to induce him to it. But great God ! How fallacious are the thoughts of men ? How wretchedly do we betray our selves to those sinful hopes which never

shall

shall be answerable to our expectation? The *Presbyterians* had battered down *Episcopacy* by the force of an *Ordinance*, outed the greatest part
of the Regular Clergy, of their Cures and Benefices; advanced their
new Form of Government by the Votes of the Houses, and got the King
into their power, to make sure work of it. But when they thought themselves secure, they were most unsafe.　For being in the height of all their
Glories and Projectments, one *Joice*, a Cornet of his Army, comes thither with a Party of Horse, removes his Guards, and takes him with
them to their Head Quarters, which were then at *Woborn*, a Town upon the North-west Road in the County of *Bedford*: Followed not long
after, by such Lords and others as were commanded by the Houses to
attend upon him.　Who not being very acceptable to the principal Officers, were within very few weeks discharged of that Service. By means
whereof the *Presbyterians* lost all those great advantages which they had
fancied to themselves, and shall be better husbanded to the use of their
Adversaries, though it succeeded worse to his Majesties person, then
possibly it might have done, if they had suffered him to remain at *Holdenby*, where the Houses fixt him.

59. This great turn happened on the fourth of *June*, *Anno* 1647. before he had remained but four moneths in the Power of the Houses.
Who having brought the War to the end desired, possest themselves
of the Kings Person, and dismissed the *Scots*, resolved upon disbanding a
great part of the Army, that they might thereby ease the people of some
part of their burthens.　But some great Officers of the Army had their
Projects and Designs a part, and did not think it consonant to common
prudence, that they should either spend their blood, or consume their
strength, in raising others to that Power, which being acquired by
themselves, might far more easily be retained, then it had been gotten.
Upon these grounds they are resolved against disbanding, stand on
their guards, and draw together towards *London*, contrary to the Will
and express Commandment of their former Masters, by whom they were
required to keep at a greater distance.　The Officers thereupon impeach some Members of the Lower House; and knowing of what great
consequence it might be unto them to get the King into their Power,
a Plot is laid to bring him into their head Quarters without noise and
trouble; which was accordingly effected as before is said,　Thus have
the *Presbyterians* of both Nations, embroiled the Kingdom first in Tumults, and afterwards in a calamitous and destructive War.　In which
the Sword was suffered to range at liberty, without destruction of Age,
Sex or Quality.　More goodly Houses plundered and burnt down to the
ground, more Churches sacrilegiously prophaned and spoiled, more
Blood poured out like Water within four years space, then had been
done in the long course of Civil Wars between *York* and *Lancaster*.
With all which Spoil and publick Ruine, they purchased nothing to
themselves but shame and infamy; as may be shown by taking a brief
view of their true condition before and after they put the State into these
Confusions.

60. And first, the *Scots* not long before their breaking out against
their King, had in the Court two Lords High Stewards, and two
Grooms of the Stool, successively one after another,　And at their taking

king up of Arms, they had a Mafter of the Horfe, a Captain of the Guard, a Keeper of the Privy Purfe, feven Grooms of eight in His Majefties Bed Chamber, and an equal number at the leaft of Gentlemen Ufhers, Quarter-waiters, Cup-bearers, Carvers, Sewers, and other Officers attending daily at the Table. I fpeak not here of thofe who had places in the Stables, or below the Stairs ; or of the Servants of thofe Lords and Gentlemen, who either lived about the Court, or had Offices in it. All which together, make up fo confiderable a number, that the Court might well be called an Academy of the *Scots* Nation ; in which fo many of all forts had their Breeding, Maintenance, and Preferment. Abroad, they had a Lieutenant of the Tower, a Fortrefs of moft confequence in all the Kingdom ; and a Mafter-Gunner of the Navy ; an Office of as great a Truft as the other : and more of thofe Monopolies, Suits, and Patents, which were conceived to be moft grievous to the Subjects, then all the *Englifh* of the Court. In the Church they had two Deanries, divers Prebendaries, and fo many Ecclefiaftical Benefices, as equalled all the Revenues of the Kirk of *Scotland*. All which they had loft, like *Æfops* Dog, catching after a fhadow. And yet by catching at that fhadow, they loft all thofe Advantages which before they had both in Court and Country ; and that not only for the prefent, but in all probability for the time to come. Such lofers were the *Scots* by this brutifh bargain ; but whether out of pure zeal to the Holy Difcipline, or their great love to filthy lucre, or the perverfnefs of their nature, or the rebellious humour of the Nation, or of all together, let them judge that can.

61. If then the *Scots* became fuch lofers by the bargain, as moft fure they did ; as fure it is that their dear Brethren in the Caufe of *Presbytery*, the *Puritans* or *Presbyterians* in the Realm of *England*, got as little by it. The *Englifh Puritans* laid their heads and hands together to embroil the Realm, out of a confidence, that having alienated the greateft part of the Tribes from the Houfe of *David*, they might advance the Golden Calves of their Presbyteries, in *Dan* and *Bethel*, and all other places whatfoever within the Land. And for the maintainance thereof, they had devoured (in conceit) all Chapter-Lands, and parcelled them amongft themfelves into *Augmentations*. But no fooner had they driven this Bargain, but a Vote paffed for felling thofe Lands towards the payment of the Debts of the Commonwealth. Nor have they lived to fee their dear Presbytery fetled, or their Lay-Elders entertained in any one Parifh of the Kingdom. For the advancement whereof, the *Scots* were firft incouraged to begin at home, and afterwards to purfue their Work by invading in *England*. Nor fared it better with thofe great *Achitophels* of the popular Party, who laboured in the raifing of a new Commonwealth, out of the Ruins of a Glorious and Ancient Monarchy. To which end they employed the *Presbyterians*, as the fitteft Inftruments for drawing the people to their fide, and preaching up the piety of their Intentions. Which Plot they had been carrying on from the firft coming of this King to the Crown of *England*, till they had got His Sacred Perfon into their poffeffion. Which made them a fit parallel to thofe Husband-men in S. *Matthews* Gofpel, (*Mat.* 21.38.) who faid *amongft themfelves, This is the Heir, come let us kill him, and let us feize on his Inheritance.*

tance. A Commonwealth which they had founded, and so modelled in their brains, that neither Sir *Thomas Moor's Utopia,* nor the Lord *Verulam's* new *Atlantis,* nor *Plato's Platform,* nor any of the old *Idea's* were equal to it. The Honours and Offices whereof they had distributed amongst themselves, and their own dependance. But having brought the King (though as it chanced by other hands) to the End they aimed, and being intent on nothing more then the dividing of that rich Prey amongst themselves, gratifying one another with huge sums of mony, and growing fat on the Revenues of the Crown, and the Lands of the Church, and guarded as they thought by invincible Armies, they were upon a sudden scattered like the dust before the wind, turned out of all, and publickly exposed to contempt and scorn. All which was done so easily, with so little noise, that the loss of that exorbitant Power did not cost so much as a broken Head, or a bloody Nose; in purchasing whereof, they had wasted so many Millions of Treasure, and more then One hundred thousand Lives.

Thus have we seen the dangerous Doctrines and Positions, the secret Plots and open Practises; the Sacrileges, Spoils and Rapines; the Tumults, Murthers, and Seditions; the horrid Treasons and Rebellions, which have been raised by the *Presbyterians* in most parts of Christendom, for the time of One hundred years and upwards. Which having seen, we shall conclude this History in the words of that Censure which by the Doctors of the *Sorbonne* was once passed on the Jesuits; that is to say, *Videtur hæc Societas in negotio fidei periculosa, pacis Ecclesiæ perturbativa, Religionis rectæ eversiva; & magis ad destructionem quam ad ædificationem.*

F I N I S.

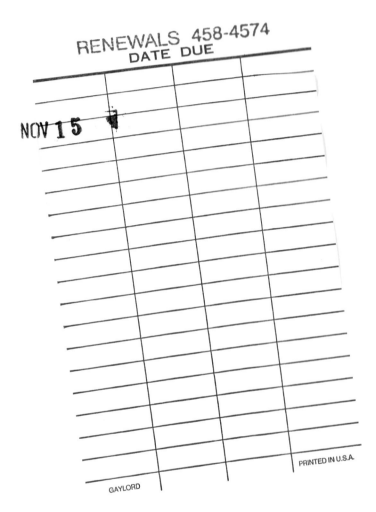

RENEWALS 458-4574
DATE DUE

NOV 15

GAYLORD

PRINTED IN U.S.A.